International Legal Theory

Essays and Engagements, 1966–2006

Nicholas Onuf's *International Legal Theory: Essays and Engagements 1966–2006* is a collection of the author's articles and book reviews from the period, including some previously unpublished material. The book records the author's efforts to address important questions in international legal theory and to engage other scholars who were also addressing these perennial, ever-challenging questions. Where does international law come from? To whom, or what, does it apply? How does international law relate to, and differ from, other legal orders? And what is law anyway?

As well as demonstrating Onuf's own constructivist contribution to the theoretical dimension of international law and international relations, each piece is preceded by a short introduction progressively charting the author's engagement with developments in and beyond the field of international law over the last 40 years.

Now retired, **Nicholas Onuf** taught at Georgetown, American and Florida International Universities and has been a visiting professor in Brazil, Japan, Sri Lanka and the US. He wrote *World of Our Making* and *The Republican Legacy in International Thought* and has co-authored or edited four other books.

International Legal Theory

Essays and engagements, 1966–2006

Nicholas Onuf

Routledge-Cavendish
Taylor & Francis Group
LONDON AND NEW YORK

Published 2008
by Routledge-Cavendish
2 Park Square, Milton Park, Abingdon, Oxon, OX14 4RN

Simultaneously published in the USA and Canada
by Routledge-Cavendish
711 Third Avenue, New York, NY 10017

Routledge-Cavendish is an imprint of the Taylor & Francis Group, an informa business

First issued in paperback 2011

Typeset in Times New Roman by
RefineCatch Limited, Bungay, Suffolk

British Library Cataloguing in Publication Data
A catalogue record for this book is available from the British Library

Library of Congress Cataloging in Publication Data
A catalog record for this title has been requested

ISBN13: 978–0–415–77590–8 (hbk)
ISBN10: 0–415–77590–6 (hbk)

ISBN13: 978-0-415-67784-4 (pbk)
ISBN10: 0-415-67784-X (pbk)

ISBN13: 978–0–203–89477–4 (ebk)
ISBN10: 0–203–89477–4 (ebk)

For Jessie, David, Julia and Nicky

Contents

Preface

As the title of this book insists, its subject is theory – theory as a set of questions and puzzles that inform a field of study, in this case the study of international law, and shape its development over an extended period. The book's subtitle is meant to suggest that I have made the development of theory my primary focus for 40 years. For this book, I have gathered my most important essays on the perennial, ever-challenging questions for international legal scholars and practitioners: Where does international law come from? To whom, or what, does it apply? How does it work? Why are its rules followed? As a system of rules, does international law constitute a legal order in its own right? How does international law relate to, and differ from, other legal orders? And, most consequentially for theory, what is law anyway?

I engage other scholars who puzzle over these same questions, not just to expose the inadequacies in their answers, but to address the inadequacies of my own. I situate these questions in the literature of international law and I go back to this literature's earliest days. I approach them from various vantage points anchored in the great philosophical traditions of the West. A political scientist by training, I deploy the conceptual resources of several disciplines. I follow the linguistic turn in social theory, reconsider how rules form and function, and assess the trajectory of modernity. I believe that cumulatively these essays offer an internally consistent set of answers no less plausible for their novelty. At the same time, they document a career given over to theory as a practice.

For a book rather austerely entitled *International Legal Theory*, the reader may find the tone disconcertingly informal, the contents unexpectedly personal. As one of the publisher's referees observed, it is somewhat unusual to see scholarly writing like this (though not at all unusual in postmodern scholarship). The author's *I* is always nearby, ready to interrupt the text, calibrate its distance from the reader, modulate its flow. This is most clearly the case in the Introduction, indicatively subtitled, "Theory as Autobiography." From the beginning, I have conceived of the project as a record of one scholar's journey as a theorist – my journey. Over the many years of this journey, not only did I find my own voice, so to speak, but I found the voice adopted by scholars in general, and international lawyers in particular, to be disingenuously neutral – has the passive voice ever neutralized or even disguised authorial presence and judgment? – and presumptuously authoritative. Paradoxically, scholars who use the first person singular and otherwise take responsibility for what they say are, in my opinion, a good deal more modest than scholars who write with Olympian detachment.

In short, the book's introductory material *needs* to be personal. The books 28 substantive chapters are far less so. They contribute to the development of theory by engaging theorists on their own terms, with every effort to avoid being tendentious or disrespectful, in the conventional language of scholarly discourse. In order to contextualize these contributions, I begin each chapter with a short (two paragraph) anecdotal preface. An attentive reader will notice a gradual turn toward a less formal style from chapter to chapter as I matured as a scholar and became more confident as a prose stylist.

If my objective is to bring readers along on one theorist's journey, the actual outcome may be somewhat disappointing, because it is not at all clear that I got anywhere in my travels. The problem here is the tendency to believe that scholarship in general, and theory in particular, is one long story of progress. We look back and we see how much progress we have made; we note with satisfaction our specific contributions to an edifying story; we look forward to a future time in which theory explains everything we need to know. In the version of this story that international lawyers identify with, theoretical developments progressively enable international law to harness the destructive energies of international relations, and eventually the world will end up resembling a liberal society where people live securely, prosperity reigns and justice is served.

This is, however, *not* the story I'm telling. To be more precise, the book's three parts tell three stories. As Part I makes clear, I adopted a conventionally progressive stance at the beginning of my career as a theorist. I thought my forays into theory would help to make the world a better place. I stand by these endeavors – they *are* good theory. If I had pulled them together in 1980, a reviewer might have said, "this book is an important (or useful, or careful, or suggestive, or modest) contribution to the development of theory, upon which, it is hoped, the author and other scholars will continue to build." Instead, I felt that if I continued writing in this vein, I would be repeating myself.

Over the last three decades, there have, of course, been all sorts of changes in the way governments manage their relations. Given the theoretical concerns I had already developed, I could have addressed these changes more or less as they took place. Yet none of my efforts would have taken international legal theory even a short step forward. As I say in the last chapter, I have read in recent years an endless stream of articles and books about sources of international law, for example, and I see nothing *theoretically* new. Instead I see familiar ideas endlessly recycled, and I see pompous, self-important and unsubstantiated claims about new theories.

In short, there is no perspective. I came to this conclusion nearly 30 years ago, when the postmodern critique of the liberal story of progress challenged my easy assumptions. Part II tells the story of this challenge and my attempts to meet it in a way that was both theoretically and personally satisfying. Converging in this part of the story are my investigations of social theory and my efforts to bring international legal theory and international relations theory together.

If this story ends inconclusively, Part III tells why. Few scholars have responded to the postmodern challenge, or even recognize it as a challenge. My large, if implicit, claim is that the lack of perspective in international legal theory is obviously connected to a big story that few students of international law trouble themselves to focus on. The modern world took centuries to become what it is, and international law is intelligible only as an integral feature of that development, with all of its blessings and pathologies.

International lawyers live in an unfolding present and find all of the nourishment they need in current events. They are too busy and too well rewarded for what they do to take an interest in the big story. It might seem to some readers that I have turned my back on the present and given them nothing to build on. To other readers, however, I believe I have opened up a perspective that would make them less complacent and pieced together a story that puts international legal theory at the center of a centuries-long struggle to understand how our social arrangements have come to be what they are and why we ever feel obligated to make them work. In other words, international legal theory is not *just* about the way governments deal with each other. It enables us to ask some of the perennial questions to which we may never have good answers. My overall objective is to put these questions, and much else, in front of readers to do with as they may.

Over time, scholars are prompted to write for many reasons and in many forms. Our work appears in such a variety of places. Often enough, we move on to a new project before applying the finishing touches to an old project or seeing it through to publication. Even if we think what we write has the coherence of many pieces cumulatively working together as a whole, no one else does. The more times passes, the less likely we are to go back and look at what we have already written, much less pull it together and put it in order.

Despite appearances, I had always thought of my work on international legal theory as a whole. When I decided to go ahead a few years ago and mold this material into a decades-spanning single volume, I also decided the pieces should nevertheless appear substantially in their original form and in the order in which I had written them (not always the order in which those that were published had appeared in print). The first step was to locate and review material for possible inclusion. Dismissing out of hand pieces that did not fit (too slight, not relevant), I saw the whole more clearly, but was still left with an unmanageably large amount of material.

Much of this material I had written before personal computers transformed the process of composing, editing, storing and retrieving documents intended for public distribution. I am grateful to my colleague Peter Craumer, who helped me master the technology I needed to render hundreds of typed and printed pages in machine-usable form. I am also indebted to Barbie Bischof, Chris Brown, Carlos Rueda and Jason Weidner for their help and encouragement. As members of the last seminar I taught before retiring in 2004, they read and discussed everything I had assembled for possible conclusion and wrote reports as if they were referees for a publisher. On their advice, I discarded some material and held onto the rest; with them in mind I wrote the volume's Introduction.

Of my colleagues at Florida International University, François Debrix and Harry Gould deserve special mention for their interest in this project, not to mention their interest in international legal theory. As former student, collaborator and office-mate, Harry helped me more in our innumerable conversations than I am sure he realizes. Soon after I had finished drafting the book's concluding chapter, Wayne Sandholtz graciously invited me to discuss it in his graduate seminar in international law at the University of California, Irvine. Over the decades, there are many others who helped me in all sorts of ways that affected the contents of this book. Some I thanked in print when the opportunity first arose.

I have deleted those acknowledgments when preparing this book for publication, just as I have deleted many unneeded footnotes and consolidated some others. For the most part I have left material unchanged, except to fix grammar, syntax and punctuation, correct a few factual errors that somehow went unnoticed, make word choices consistent from chapter to chapter, and occasionally clarify an obscure passage. Here and there a long paragraph has become two. I have deleted a few pages of material (and marked where I have done so), in effect disavowing what I had said in them, and deleted superfluous phrases and sentences here and there (not marked). Throughout the text, reformatting brought many small changes. I resisted any temptation to update older materials in the view that this is a potentially endless undertaking, and I have cross-referenced the book's chapters with a considerable number of parenthetical insertions.

I am, of course, obliged to acknowledge the many publishers who have give me permission to reprint material for which they hold the copyright. The following 10 items were published in the *American Journal of International Law* and are reproduced with copyright permission © from The American Society of International Law:

(Chapter 2) "Professor Falk on the quasi-legislative competence of the General Assembly," vol. 64, 1970, pp. 349–55;

(Chapter 4) "Further thoughts on a new source of international law: Professor D'Amato's 'Manifest Intent,' " vol. 65, 1971, pp. 774–81;

(Chapter 9) "International legal order as an idea," vol. 73, 1979, pp. 244–66;

(Chapter 11) Review: Clifford Geertz, *Negara, The Theatre State in Nineteenth-Century Bali*, vol. 76, 1982, pp. 663–6;

(Chapter 12) Review: Terry Nardin, *Law, Morality, and the Relations of States*, vol. 78, 1984, pp. 939–42;

(Chapter 15) Review: Anthony D'Amato, *Jurisprudence: A Descriptive and Normative Analysis of Law*, vol. 80, 1986, pp. 730–4;

(Chapter 16) Review: David Kennedy, *International Legal Structure*, vol. 83, 1989, pp. 630–40;

(Chapter 17) Review: Martti Koskenniemi, *From Apology to Utopia: The Structure of International Legal Argument*, vol. 84, 1990, pp. 771–5;

(Chapter 18) Review: Louis Henkin, *International Law: Politics, Values and Functions* (General Course on Public International Law), *Receuil des cours de l'Academie de droit international de la Haye*, vol. 213, 1989/I, vol. 86, July 1992, pp. 834–41;

(Chapter 20) "*Civitas Maxima*: Wolff, Vattel and the Fate of Republicanism," vol. 88, 1994, pp. 280–303.

Three items are reprinted with the permission of Cambridge University Press:

(Chapter 3) "The Principle of Nonintervention, the United Nations and the International System," *International Organization*, vol. 25, 1971, pp. 209–27;

(Chapter 8) "Law and Lawyers in International Crises," *International Organization*, Vol. 29, 1975, pp. 1035–54.

(Chapter 21) Review, Onuma Yasuaki (ed.), *A Normative Approach to War: Peace, War, and Justice in Hugo Grotius, American Political Science Review*, vol. 88, 1994, pp. 805–6.

The following is reprinted with the permission from Copyright © 1985 The President and Fellows of Harvard College and the Harvard International Law Journal.

(Chapter 14) "Do Rules Say What They Do? From Ordinary Language to International Law," *Harvard International Law Journal*, vol. 26, No. 2 (Spring 1985), pp. 385–410.

Copyright holders have kindly granted permission, when needed, to reprint the following:

(Chapter 5) "Peremptory Norms of International Law: Their Source, Function and Future," *Denver Journal of International Law and Policy*, vol. 4, 1974, pp. 187–98;

(Chapter 6) some parts of "Law-Making in the Global Community," in N. Onuf (ed.), *Law-Making in the Global Community*, Durham, NC: Carolina Academic Press, 1982, pp. 1–81;

(Chapter 7) *Reprisals: Rituals, Rules, Rationales*, Research Monograph No. 42, Center of International Studies, Princeton University, July 1974;

(Chapter 10) "International Codification: Interpreting the Last Half-Century," in R. Falk, F.V. Kratochwil and S.H. Mendlovitz (eds), *International Law: A Contemporary Perspective*, vol. 2, *Studies on a Just World Order*, Boulder: Westview, 1985, pp. 264–79;

(Chapter 19) "The Constitution of International Society," *European Journal of International Law*, vol. 5, 1994, pp. 1–19;

(Chapter 22) Review: Anthony D'Amato, *International Law and Political Reality: Collected Papers, Volume One, Journal of International Legal Studies*, vol. 1, 1995, pp. 181–90;

(Chapter 23) " 'Tainted by Contingency': Retelling the Story of International Law," in R. Falk, L.E.J. Ruiz and R.B.J. Walker (eds), *Re-Framing the International: Law, Culture, Politics*, London: Routledge, 2002, pp. 26–45;

(Chapter 24) "How to Think about 'The Golden Age of International Law'," (in Portuguese) "Uma Reflexão sobre 'A Idade de Ouro do Dereito Internacional'," *Contexto Internacional*, vol. 23, 2001, pp. 223–44;

(Chapter 26) "Normative Frameworks for Humanitarian Intervention," in A.F. Lang, Jr. (ed.), *Just Intervention*, Washington: Georgetown University Press, 2003, pp. 28–45;

(Chapter 27) "Eurocentrism and Civilization," *Journal of the History of International Law*, vol. 6, 2004, 37–41.

Many writers save an acknowledgment of family for last, not just by custom, but surely to signal how important families are to most of us. Indeed, I owe more than I can ever express to my wife Sandra Keowen, my daughter Jessie Onuf and our close-knit, far-flung family. I need not try; they know how I feel. To Jessie and her family I dedicate this book, this labor of love that began before she was born.

Introduction

Theory as autobiography

The title of this book, *International Legal Theory*, might seem to suggest a systematic exposition of international legal theory from a distinctive point of view. Or the title might suggest an integrated survey of established theoretical frameworks for the study of international law. This book is neither a systematic exposition nor integrated survey. As its subtitle, *Essays and Engagements, 1966–2006*, indicates, it is a record of my efforts, over many years, to address important problems in international legal theory and to engage other scholars who were also addressing these problems or, in some instances, putting forward systematic expositions.

As a result, the book's 28 chapters vary a great deal in objective, organization and length. Most chapters are substantially unchanged from their published form, though several were never published at all. Some are essays in a form typical of the journal literature in law and the social sciences. Many are book reviews. Two were written as systematic expositions, though not of the whole of international legal theory. Several are inquiries into the development of international law's central concepts. Not one specifies the content of international legal theory, as if this were some fixed body of knowledge awaiting systematic exposition.

Instead, topics and themes weave through the chapters. The ways in which they do so show how repeated efforts to address theoretical puzzles produce only the most tentative solutions belying any hope for the accumulation of reliable knowledge. They show how perennial philosophical questions constantly reassert themselves. They show how the *Zeitgeist* affects the way theorists choose topics and how fashionable themes rise and fall. I believe they show why anyone would spend decades sorting through topics and themes to find new purchase on the same old puzzles and questions. They show how one theorist spent the best part of his working life, what he learned about his craft, and why he thinks that theory-making is an integral feature of world-making.

It is hard to imagine anyone growing up wishing to be a theorist. Most people (at least in the US, where I was born and raised), and certainly most children, have only the vaguest idea what the term *theory* connotes. Often they use it for bald generalizations: "In theory anyone could be president of the US"; "Theoretically we can blow ourselves off the planet." Sometimes and quite properly, they use the term for abstract, highly generalized explanations: "Evolution is a theory that explains the diversity of life"; "Evolution is just a theory, not a fact." When I was a child I recall people, even my classmates, talking about Einstein's notoriously incomprehensible theories with awe in their voices. Everyone knew that Einstein was a physicist. In theory anyone who is really smart – really good at science – could be a physicist, and a really smart physicist could become a theorist, "an Einstein."

As a child with no noticeable gifts and an indifferent public education, I did not aspire to be a physicist. Oddly, perhaps, I had no aspirations at all, despite having a librarian for a mother, an engineering professor for a father, and a childhood full of what I later recognized to be intellectual stimulation and moral education. In 1959 I began my university education at Johns Hopkins (a relatively small, research-oriented university) thinking I might become a diplomat, and this only because my father insisted that I choose *something*. In my second year, I took a seminar in international politics from a still young scholar named Robert Tucker, and I read Hans Morgenthau's *Politics among Nations*. Right away and with complete certainty, I knew I wanted to be a scholar and university teacher in what was then emerging as a distinctive field of study called International Relations (IR).

The following year I took a postgraduate seminar in IR theory from George Liska, a cerebral scholar who introduced me to the work of the few other scholars who collectively were in the process of giving the field its theoretical moorings. I sensed the excitement they all must have felt as they assembled the field from diverse materials by using abstract questions to frame their concerns. Why war? What is power? How do nations ever manage to get along? I told Liska that I wanted to be an IR theorist. Given to gnomic utterances, he replied, "Theory is the hardest thing of all."

Undeterred, I took Tucker's seminar in international law the following year. Like Liska, a political realist, Tucker had studied under Hans Kelsen at the University of California and had written on the law of war, not as a lawyer but as a naval officer, before turning to the use of force in international politics. Hopkins has no law school; Tucker and Liska taught in the political science department. Tucker might not have taught international law at all if Kelsen had not asked him to prepare a second edition of Kelsen's *Principles of International Law* (1952). Tucker soon took me on as his research assistant. Already immersed in *Principles*, I also read Kelsen's *General Theory of Law and the State* (1945) cover to cover, and I delved into theoretical material by the likes of J.L. Brierly, Percy Corbett, Charles DeVisscher, Richard Falk, Wolfgang Friedmann, C.W. Jenks, Philip Jessup, Josef Kunz, Hersch Lauterpacht, Myres McDougal and his associates, Georg Schwarzenberger and Julius Stone. At the same time, I got my first taste of Grotius, Pufendorf,

Wolff, Vattel, Wheaton and Maine as luminaries in no need of their full names.

Tucker had asked me to find and read everything written in the preceding decade on the subjects and sources of international law. This I did, though ploddingly with materials in French. If there were anything in German or Russian that I should have read, I would not even have known. Tucker busied himself with a third topic, sanctions and self-help, only later turning his attention to substantive developments in the law. I realized then that the three Ss (as I have thought of them ever since) – subjects, sources and sanctions – constitute international legal theory's primary zones of theoretical inquiry. I also realized that the *ur*-problem for legal theory is the basis of obligation and that international law, as an operative system of restraints on the behavior of sovereign, self-interested nation-states, presents legal theory with compelling evidence that this problem has no easy solution.

In 1963 I went to Yale University to study IR theory with Karl Deutsch, a major figure in the field. For a variety of reasons, I soon regretted doing so. Even the seminar I took at the law school with Myres McDougal, Harold Lasswell and Oscar Schachter was unrewarding for an outsider. A year later I returned to Hopkins to continue my work with Tucker and Liska, also bolstering my interests in IR with studies in political theory and diplomatic history. I never did master a foreign language sufficiently to appreciate the richness of Continental social and legal thought. I considered myself a political scientist by training, substantively concerned with international politics, international law and international institutions, at a time when political scientists in the US had already begun to lose interest in international law and IR theory consolidated around the strong, even dogmatic assumptions of political realism. Liska was right: being a theorist is hard work. IR theory is hard enough by itself; using theory to bridge international law and politics is even harder, especially with lawyers ruling one roost and political realists the other.

I started teaching at Georgetown University in 1966 while I completed my doctoral dissertation. Working in a professional school of international affairs in Washington DC, I was surrounded by people who were utterly absorbed in policy issues. I taught large classes in international law (for which I was asked to use a casebook and from which I learned a great deal about the way lawyers in the US are trained to think) and international organization, but none in international politics. A few doctoral students shared my interest in theory. The times were anxious; the war in Vietnam dominated everyone's attention and drained everyone's emotions; to most people an interest in theory looked like escapism at the very least. To think of myself as a theorist by vocation was to confirm a deep sense of alienation – from the time and place, the world I lived in, myself.

Debates over the US intervention in Vietnam clarified contrary tendencies in my theoretical commitments. I was brought up in an environment that nourished liberal, cosmopolitan values, and yet political realists had trained me to think systematically about international relations. In general, political realists claim that wars are instruments of statecraft and thus an inescapable feature of international politics. In particular, Liska's prescient essay on *Imperial America: The International Politics of Primacy* (1967) impressed on me the consequences of concentrated power – imperatives that I would later conceptualize as a condition of rule. Consistent with realist premises, the war's supporters argued that intervention was both responsible and necessary.

Most of the war's critics responded to pervasive images of the carnage in Vietnam with horror, anger and calls for peace, but they failed to counter realist premises systematically. Progressive liberal sentiments offered little more than a familiar recipe of rules and institutions for mitigating struggles over ideology, the exercise of power and the conduct of hostilities. The New Left in the US distanced itself from an Old Left that had betrayed its own principles. Even if Marxism (or more precisely, European Marxists) could have provided the antiwar movement in the US with a coherent conception of agency, most movement activists discounted theory in any form. I see now that what I needed then was just such a conception to overcome both the contrary tendencies in political realism and liberal institutionalism and the sense of paralysis they had induced in me. Even if the term *alienation* captures my state of mind at the time, the concept of alienation, whether Marxist or psychoanalytical, was not a useful point of departure for the theorist in me.

Thus began my 40 years reading and writing theory. A vocation spanning 40 years, like the arc of one's life, seems to proceed in stages, phases, chapters, generations or, as historians are wont to say, *periods* that seem to punctuate the passage of time. Historical periods seem natural, as do many deep-seated conventions. Sometimes momentous events mark the end of one period and the beginning or another (for example, disruptive wars or the resumption of relatively peaceful relations among nations), and sometimes a convenient benchmark (turn of a decade, century or millennium). Convention favors calling the first of two periods *early* (early Marx, early Wittgenstein, the early modern period); what follows might be *late* (late Wittgenstein) or not qualified at all (Marx, the modern period). Life spans are often modeled as having three periods – young, mature, old – marking rapid growth, full vigor, and decline.

Not just for convenience I have organized the four decades of my work on international legal theory into three equally long periods, represented by this book's three parts. Life-span metaphors spring to mind: first comes youthful enthusiasm as I learn my craft (the hard years, 1966–1980); then comes maturity and mastery (the good years, 1980–1993); finally comes the gradual loss of powers, inducing repetition and embellishment as I tidy up my legacy (the long goodbye, 1993–2006). I would prefer not to characterize my life as a theorist this way, but someone reading this book might think otherwise. Instead, I see these three periods as having been marked by turning points in my theoretical interests and normative commitments, with each period taking on a life of its own (possibly to be described by life-span metaphors). Large events in the world did not trigger these significant alterations in my theoretical concerns – at least not directly. Nevertheless, each of the periods that I have marked out here reflects the shifting concerns of theorists in many fields of study, and these shifts broadly reflect the temper of the times.

The 10 chapters making up Part I explore legal theory, whether to its limits or my own. I had devoted my dissertation work to international codification – not a surprising choice for someone with progressive liberal inclinations but, as I discovered, not an altogether satisfying topic for a theorist (Chapter 10 contains what little of theoretical interest I was able to glean). Having explored international personality for Tucker, I realized that the development of European supranational institutions held greater theoretical promise. In this case, however, IR theorists, among them Deutsch, had already deployed the concept of political integration in ways that I thought left little room for legal theory. Superpower rivalry and a divided Europe, the ever-present threat of nuclear annihilation, chronic conflict between Israel and its neighbors, Vietnam: nothing from this dreary list seemed to offer a budding legal theorist an antidote to alienation, an opportunity to say something significant. (Perhaps I exaggerate; see Chapter 7.)

Decolonization and the emergence of the nonaligned movement seemed to be different. A host of new states with a host of demands presented the legal order with a challenge that was just as much a challenge to legal theory. I had learned from my early work with Tucker that the established sources of international law modulate the tempo of change in the law in ways that tend to benefit established states. To identify and promote a new source that the governments of these states might accept was just such a challenge – one that Falk had addressed in a theoretically sophisticated effort to reorient international law. Much as I admired Falk's political motivations, I thought it was important to clarify and develop the theoretical claims he had made on behalf of a new source.

In short, to advance international legal theory I sought to engage a major theorist on his own terms. Falk signaled his appreciation for both my constructive intentions and critical efforts by arranging for me to join him in a general reconsideration of global lawmaking. Among the many benefits of this experience was the opportunity to observe first-hand the way Falk and his associates in the World Order Models Project sought to revive the liberal dream of a global legal order. I had myself been fascinated by this dream from my earliest student days, attracted to the cosmopolitan versions Falk and others were developing, but also skeptical about their optimistic assessment of long-term global trends.

Just as the Project reached its zenith in the mid-1970s, the nonaligned movement seemed to lose its momentum and hopes for significant international economic reform faded rapidly. Finally, in a position to teach IR theory, I saw political realism lose its vitality to positivist science on the one hand and political economy on the other. Discussions of limits to material growth and Marxist treatments of "late capitalism" fueled my sense of foreboding, reinforced my skepticism about liberal nostrums, and disabused me of any hope that legal theory could tell us anything important about the global future. After constitutional crisis and a disastrous response to revolution in Iran, the public mood in the US was little better than my own bleak state of mind.

The turning point for me was intensely personal *and* explicitly theoretical. At a moment when feminism directly challenged male domination and masculine complacency, especially in university life, some of my feminist doctoral students challenged my ingrained sexism and complicity in the systematic exploitation of women. I realized they had a point, made most insistently by Spike Peterson (my collaborator in Chapter 13 and today a leading feminist scholar), who also introduced me to feminist theory. Situating feminist theory in recent social theory was an inevitable next step: if gender is a social construction, as I was persuaded it is, then so is everything else, no matter how natural it seems or materially manifest in human experience.

The nine chapters comprising Part II bear witness to my newfound interest in recent social theory. I was hardly alone. Indeed I was swept along in a broad movement inspired by French poststructuralists (Pierre Bourdieu, Jacques Derrida, Michel Foucault), critical theorists in the Frankfurt School (Theodor Adorno, Jürgen Habermas, Max Horkheimer) and philosophers (J.L. Austin, Richard Rorty, Ludwig Wittgenstein). This eclectic combination of influences assured considerable diversity, not to mention disagreement over a proper name for the movement: Was it poststructuralist, postpositivist, postmodernist or, most inclusively, postmodern? I began to think of myself as a late modern postpositivist. Drawn to Kant's epistemology and Anthony Giddens' work on processes of social construction, I began to call myself a constructivist. In IR theory there were a few others joining the post-movement, as did a number of legal scholars under the banner of Critical Legal Studies. The latter eventually resulted in major contributions to international legal theory from David Kennedy and Martti Koskenniemi (see Chapters 16 and 17 for my reviews).

In IR it took even longer for the movement to yield comparably systematic expositions. In 1989 there finally appeared two such books: Friedrich Kratochwil's *Rules, Norms, and Decisions: On the Conditions of Practical and Legal Reasoning in International Relations and Domestic Affairs* and my own *World of Our Making: Rules and Rule in Social Theory and International Relations*. Kratochwil and I took advantage of our backgrounds in international legal theory, drew widely on recent developments in social theory and embraced the "linguistic turn" in philosophy. Kratochwil emphasized the relation between rules and reasoned argument, while I emphasized the resemblance between rules and speech in accomplishing social ends (Chapter 14). Both of us pointed up the centrality of rules in "the social construction of reality" (to appropriate the title of a book by Peter Berger and Thomas

Luckmann that Kratochwil had brought to my attention many years before), but I also sought to develop a systematic relation between functionally differentiated categories of rules and forms of rule operating even in the allegedly anarchic world of international relations.

Devising a novel theoretical framework, applicable in principle to the totality of social relations, and presenting it in systematic form to an audience whose primary concern is international relations was exhilarating and finally exhausting. I needed to do something else. The end of the Cold War prompted many younger scholars in IR to rediscover normative phenomena, reinvent liberal institutionalist theory and call what they were doing constructivism. I confess that their smug liberalism and utter ignorance of international legal theory (and quite a bit else) irritated me. (I say more about this in Chapter 28.) Indeed, irritated by liberal triumphalism in all its forms, but struck nonetheless by the pace and effects of globalization, I found myself all the more curious about the trajectory of the modern world. The question of where we are going had always concerned me. How we got here and how that affects where we are going are additional questions that I had not given the attention they deserve. Nor, I thought, had most other theorists. Historians had much to say about these questions, but few of them are inclined, by disposition or vocation, toward theory.

As it happens, my brother, Peter Onuf, is a distinguished historian of the early American republic; not so surprisingly an historian with a distinct appreciation for theory as I practice it. In the mid-1980s we did some preliminary work for a project taking advantage of his interest in jurisdictional issues in the federal union and mine in international law. After I finished *World of Our Making*, I turned my attention to republican theory and its relevance to the federal union constituted in 1787, and we proceeded to write a book, published in 1993, situating this extraordinary experiment in what we called the Vattelian moment in international law and diplomacy. We also decided to write a second volume on the rise of the liberal world after 1815 and its impact on federal union sundered by sectional conflict and finally a bloody Civil War in 1861.

Two of the nine chapters in Part III (Chapters 24 and 27) are byproducts of this undertaking, which took far longer to complete and proved a greater challenge for us both than we had ever imagined. A major reason is the difficulty we had, along with everyone else, in explaining coherently the transition from Enlightenment republicanism to modern liberalism – from political theory to political economy – given the simultaneous arrival of positivism in law and science, and of Romantic ideas about nation-making. The standard view has rights-conscious individuals creating liberal states and thus the liberal world. In our view, sovereign states constituted a liberal world in practice, and this allowed some few states to domesticate liberalism. Several other chapters in Part III deal with the legacy of republicanism in international thought as a casualty of liberalism's long-term success. Early in my inquiries into republicanism, I recognized Aristotle's importance. His voice echoes through the modern world, sometimes muffled by the triumph of liberal individualism, but always discernible in modernity's metaphysical foundations, social arrangements, and regard for human agency and moral worth. Whenever we talk about the functions of parts and functioning wholes, whenever we ask how people work together or why societies work at all, we are speaking his language.

Historical periods do not simply follow one another. In some degree each period overlays the one that it appears to replace. In all three parts of this book, I seek to engage other theorists, often by reviewing theoretically innovative books, I hope with some sensitivity to their author's intentions. The same strategy warrants the reconsideration of earlier masterworks that the reader will also find throughout this volume. Given the forgotten circumstances in which these books were written and the long history of interpreting them to suit later circumstances, the risk of misconstruing the intentions of these masters is even greater.

Perhaps I have not done Aristotle justice; perhaps no one can today. Nevertheless, the theorist's most important task is to rework the diverse materials at hand to suit the circumstances of the moment. Historically speaking, modernity's remarkable career offers up a succession of periods, the latest of which may be ending. What next? This book ends, as it must, with this question waiting to be asked yet another time, but only to be answered by the passage of time into history.

If I were to imagine a dozen more years, a fourth quarter, in my theoretical career, the same question arises. By ending this book as I do, I imply that the most recent period in my career has also come to an end or indeed that there is nothing left for me, as a theorist, to say about international law. The closer we are to the end of a period, the harder it is to see what is happening. And there is, after all, something arbitrary, almost willful, about declaring an end to things. Inevitably I am still thinking about what is next for me as a theorist in light of what I am guessing is next for the world.

My best guess for the world's future is continued, with very rapid globalization, at least for the remaining years of my life. The largest implication of this trend is too often and much too crudely characterized as "the clash of civilizations." As a theorist, I would want to learn as much as I could about the metaphysical foundations, social arrangements and concepts of human agency in other civilizations than my own, and to do so by asking how language informs different civilizational experiences. After a decade, I might write a book along the lines of Adda Bozeman's *Politics and Culture in International History* (1960), updating a neglected masterpiece by drawing on a half century's worth of theory. Then I might follow up with something like Bozeman's *The Future of Law in a Multicultural World* (1971) – if I had the institutional resources, collegial encouragement, opportunities for engagement, the powers of mind, the energy and the will, the years.

Part I

Legal theory and its limits, 1966–1980

1 Changing international law (1966)

This essay embodies the first half of the first chapter of my doctoral dissertation, entitled *The Conscious Development of International Law*, which Robert W. Tucker supervised and I defended at Johns Hopkins University early in 1967. I wrote these pages last, not just to introduce its subject (the codification of international law – a subject then discussed a good deal more than it is today), but also to give the dissertation the heft and feel of the magisterial treatises in which I had immersed myself from the beginning of my studies in international law. Even now, after some light editing of the text, my intentions are, I think, clearly conveyed by the prose style I had adopted: this was to be the first draft of a big book – a book that I ended up never writing.

Nevertheless, the form and content of those first pages effectively introduce the subject of this volume and, even more, adumbrate some of the claims and concerns that run through my work. Two stand out:

(1) If one defines a system of law as a coercive order, the international legal system does not qualify . . . If one defines a system of law informally, however, as an option to coercive disorder, rather than formally, as a coercive order, the international legal system does qualify.
(2) Clearly, the international legal order, being as decentralized as it is in all respects, is a legal order only because it is reckoned as such by all its subjects.

Both claims identify the core problem of international legal theory. Today I find the first of these claims offering a vacuous solution, and the second a tantalizing solution. Much of the work constituting the first part of this book records my subsequent efforts to follow up on both solutions.

Public international law

Public international law, once known as the law of nations, is to be distinguished from private international law. The latter refers specifically to:

> the rules of law applied in matters involving a foreign element in municipal courts, and not [to] the rules relating to conflicts between states, unless such conflicts have been expressly submitted to a municipal tribunal for determination according to some system of municipal law.[1]

Private international law, then, is a loose system of laws drawn from various municipal legal orders, and it deals with a single aspect of the relations of nation-states, that is, the conflict of their laws.

The former term – public international law – refers not to a collection of municipal laws, but to an independent system complete with its own, exclusive sources and subjects. In keeping with its character as an inclusive system of order, it deals with all the public relations of nation-states and, by implication, of organizations of nation-states.[2] It is the *international law* of standard usage. International law is the body of norms or prescriptions, which by their legal character regulate the behavior of states in their relations with each other. These norms have a legal character because there is *prima facie* evidence that states consider them as having legal effect. Norms with legal effect impose obligations on states with regard to the conduct prescribed for by these norms.

If one defines a system of law as a coercive order, the international legal system does not qualify. Violation of a norm results in retaliatory violations by other states. Arguments that confuse retaliatory violations of law involving coercion with a coercive sanction simply to allow the international legal system to be identified truly legal are mistaken.[3] If one defines a system of law informally, however, as an option to coercive disorder, rather than formally, as a coercive order, the international legal system does qualify. Law as coercive order depends on the centralization of coercive potential with the sanctioning agent. This insures the automaticity and effectiveness of the sanction. Law as an option to disorderly coercion merely requires the channeling and confinement of coercion in prescribed ways. Since international law is highly decentralized, it is susceptible to the latter, but not the former.

The evidence that states do in fact attribute legal effect to norms takes two forms: explicit and implicit. Treaties, as agreements between states concluded in good faith, are explicit evidence of the attribution of legal effect to

1 B.A. Wortley, "The Interaction of Public and Private International Law," *Recueil des cours de L'Académie de droit international de La Haye*, vol. 85, 1954/I, p. 255.

2 Many contemporary writers favor the view that international law does more than "govern relations solely between states. It may also govern relations between two or more international organizations, between states and private persons, and between international organizations and private persons." O.T. Lissitzyn, *International Law Today and Tomorrow*, Dobbs Ferry, NY: Oceana, 1965, pp. 38–9.

3 This statement is directed against the teachings of Hans Kelsen, which have otherwise profoundly influenced the writer. See *Principles of International Law*, New York: Rinehart, 1951, p. 18.

particular norms between specified states. The customary responses of states to recurring situations – responses which by virtue of their predictability are described as conforming to law by judges of national and international courts and by eminent writers and, which having been so described, are affirmed or at least not rejected as such by states – are implicit evidence of the attribution of legal effect to norms by states in general.

Clearly, the international legal order, being as decentralized as it is in all respects, is a legal order only because it is reckoned as such by all its subjects.

The sources of international law

The source of rules of international law is the attribution by states of legal effect to norms of interstate behavior. Since this attribution cannot be known apart from the evidence that it has taken place, the source of rules of international law is indistinguishable from the evidence that states attribute legal effect to them. Thus, the sources of international law are explicit evidence of the attribution of legal effect in the form of treaties and implicit evidence of the attribution of legal effect in the form of customary practices of states considered as binding by states.

The evidence that some customary practice of states has acquired legal effect, being implicit, must be inferred from the frequency, importance, consistency, duration, generality, and acceptance of this practice. In the ideal case of perfect conformance to these criteria, legal regulation of the practice is superfluous, for there is no likelihood of deviant behavior to be regulated. Short of the ideal, the better these criteria are met, the stronger is any given rule of law, for the more likely is it to be controlling in an applicable situation. Thus, some customary rules of law are "better" than others: the imputation of legal effect and the effectiveness of the rule are directly related. States will admit to violations of a rule of law only if they intend to make amends, and they will deny the validity of a rule before admitting that a projected course of action violates it.

Although writers have frequently argued the contrary, generality of practice is almost always required. Particular (regional) customary law can result only when the kinds of relations for which customary norms have arisen are confined to the particular states or region. Otherwise, the criteria of consistency and acceptance are not met.

While implicit evidence for a rule of customary law implies generality of practice and therefore a rule with a general range of application, a rule of law created explicitly has by definition a restricted (particular) range of application. This apparent anomaly has given rise to tendencies in recent literature on sources either to deny that treaties are a source of law at all, or to assert that they are a source of law effectively superior to customary law, the latter being abrogated as between the treating parties for the situations regulated by the former. Both of these tendencies involve mistaken conceptions about the sources of international law.

The first tendency, which denies the status of being a distinctive source of international law to treaties, finds its fundamental expression in a paper by Judge Sir Gerald Fitzmaurice.[4] Fitzmaurice's arguments have gained warm approval among other British writers, including Clive Parry and R.Y. Jennings.[5]

Fitzmaurice stated his position in the following terms:

> Considered in themselves, and particularly in their inception, treaties are, formally, a source of obligation rather than a source of law. In their contractual aspect, they are no more a source of law than an ordinary private law contract: which simply creates rights and obligations. Such instruments (as also, on the international plane, a commercial treaty, for example) create obligations and rights, not law. In this connexion, the attempts which have been made to ascribe a law-making character to *all* treaties irrespective of the character of their content or the number of parties to them, by postulating that some treaties create "particular" international law and others "general", is of extremely dubious validity. There is really no such thing as "particular" international treaty law, though there are particular international treaty rights and obligations. The only "law" that enters into these is derived, not from the treaty creating them – or from any treaty – but from the principle of *pacta sunt servanda* – an antecedent general principle of law. The law is that the obligation must be carried out, but the obligation is not, in itself, law. A genuine law may of course be applicable only to certain particular subjects of the legal system, but if so it is usually as members of a class, not as individuals.[6]

Fitzmaurice's position is based on a mistaken identification of international law and municipal law. Unlike a municipal legal order, the international legal order is decentralized, and more specifically the formation of international law is a decentralized process. In international law, each source of obligation is a source of law individually, since there is no centralized source of law regulating recurring contract situations. In municipal law things work differently. Individual obligations not having a legal character can result from contracts made in accordance with pre-established legal regimes regulating particular situations or classes or events and susceptible to centralized judgment and enforcement.

4 G.G. Fitzmaurice, "Some Problems Regarding the Formal Sources of International Law," *Symbolae Verzijl*, The Hague: Martinus Nijhoff, 1958, pp. 153–76.

5 C. Parry, *The Sources and Evidences of International Law*, Manchester: Manchester University Press, 1965, pp. 28–55; R.Y. Jennings, "Recent Developments in the International Law Commission: Its Relation to the Sources of International Law," *International and Comparative Law Quarterly*, vol. 13, 1964, pp. 387–90.

6 Fitzmaurice, "Some Problems Regarding the Formal Sources of International Law," pp. 157–8; emphasis in original.

Obviously, some rules are required to govern particular, recurring situations. General principles, being abstract, are not in themselves sufficient. If there is no centralized source for these rules, then they must arise in a decentralized fashion, such as by treaty making. These treaties are then considered to have legal effect themselves. Treaties are not contracts, nor by analogy, must one turn to the superior rule *pacta sunt servanda* for the law regulating the contract situation. Unlike laws regulating contracts, *pacta sunt servanda* is not a rule that governs particular situations, but merely a rule that gives legal effect to rules that are consciously created individually to deal with these situations. A generalized formulation like *pacta sunt servanda* is superfluous as a rule of law in a municipal legal order, where there are rules that create legal regimes for various kinds of explicit agreements.

The other tendency that accords treaties a legal position effectively superior to that of law deriving from custom is characteristic of certain Continental and Soviet writers. It is put forward with lesser or greater emphasis by Paul Reuter, Charles Rousseau, Georges Scelle, and G.I. Tunkin.[7] Curiously, this position is deduced from the assertion that treaty law and customary law are equal in their legal effect. In Tunkin's words, "on the plane of the legal obligation they create, conventional and customary norms are equal as between themselves."[8] Since customary law and treaty law are equally legal, they each can alter the other depending on the order of their creation. More precisely, new rules have the effect of abrogating and replacing older rules regulating a particular, recurring situation, even when the content of the older rules is unchanged by the newer ones. It is of no consequence that the earlier rules are conventional and the new ones customary, or vice versa. As Rousseau has phrased it, "just as a treaty can abrogate or modify a custom, a custom has exactly the same abrogating or modifying effect with regard to an anterior treaty."[9] Reuter is briefer: "A treaty carries the day over custom, but custom can modify a treaty."[10]

All of these writers do not hesitate to acknowledge that customary law by its nature takes a great deal of time to emerge. Thus, it is not often that a customary rule emerges to replace a treaty rule, particularly if the treaty rule stands as evidence of state practice contrary to the emerging customary rule. Consequently, the point in this argument that captures the full interest of its proponents is that "treaties can modify or abrogate the principles and norms

7 P. Reuter, "Principes de droit international public," *Recueil des cours de L'Académie de droit international de La Haye*, vol. 103, 1961/II, pp. 484–6; C. Rousseau, "Principes de droit international public," *Recueil des cours de L'Académie de droit international de La Haye*, vol. 93, 1958/I, pp. 483–4; G. Scelle, "Report on Arbitration Procedure," UN doc. A/CN.4/18, p. 7; G.I. Tunkin, *Droit international public: Problèmes théoriques*, Paris: Pédone 1965, pp. 92–6.

8 Tunkin, *Droit international public*, p. 96. All translations my own.

9 Rousseau, "Principes de droit international public," p. 484.

10 Reuter, "Principes de droit international public," p. 484.

of general international law."[11] Scelle follows this line of thought to its logical extreme with reference to treaties that organize customary law into a code:

> The essential purpose of any codification, whether national or international, is to substitute new legal standards for pre-existing standards which it *ipso facto* abrogates, even when it formally incorporates them. The signatories to the codifying instrument are no longer bound by the former customary or conventional rule but by the rule laid down by the codification convention itself.[12]

After arriving at conclusions like Scelle's, Tunkin freely admits that, under the circumstances, treaties must be considered "as the fundamental source of international law."[13] This conclusion would seem hardly compatible with the introductory argument that customary law and treaty law are equal in their legal effect. In fact, treaty law has been elevated to a position of natural dominance, which makes its equality with customary law only formal.

This argument is faulty. It is based on the unwarranted assumption that a conventional rule created to regulate a particular, recurring situation abrogates and thus replaces the customary rule formerly regulating that situation. This is not the case, however, and it does not matter whether the treaty creates a rule identical to or different from the content of the existing customary rule.

The essence of a rule of international law is that it is considered legal by the subjects of the legal order. It is abrogated only when it is no longer considered legal. In the case of a treaty rule, it is abrogated when the parties to the treaty have agreed that it is no longer binding. Otherwise it remains in force, even if a contrary customary rule has emerged.[14] In the case of a customary rule, it is abrogated only when it has generally fallen out of use. Thus, a treaty rule does not abrogate a customary rule, because a customary rule can only be abrogated by a process similar to the one in which it was created, involving the actions of the entire community of states over a long period of time. In the instance in which the conventional rule is identical to the customary rule regulating a situation, the conventional rule is further evidence that the

11 Tunkin, *Droit international public*, p. 96.

12 Scelle, "Report on Arbitration Procedure," p. 7.

13 Tunkin, *Droit international public*, p. 92. Tunkin's version of this last part of the argument is as follows: "Once the codification of these branches of international law is achieved, and the corresponding conventions have entered into force, their norms are substituted in the relations of the contracting parties for those of customary international law." Ibid.

14 The agreement to deprive a treaty of legal effect need not be explicit, but may be registered by a uniform disregard by all parties for the provisions of the treaty. See on this point R.W. Tucker, "The Principle of Effectiveness in International Law," in G. Lipsky (ed.), *Law and Politics in the World Community: Essays on Hans Kelsen's Pure Theory and Related Problems in International Law*, Berkeley: University of California Press, 1953, p. 48.

customary rule is considered legal by states, and as a result the customary rule is reinforced, not replaced.

In the instance in which the conventional rule differs from the customary rule governing the situation, the customary rule may be weakened somewhat by the evidence of contrary practice considered as lawful, but it will not be abrogated until there is much more evidence of this character. The customary rule is, however, suspended as between the parties of the treaty, since they expressly choose to give legal effect to the treaty rule. The customary rule is only suspended because, if the treaty should be terminated, the regulation of the situation will revert to the general, still valid rule of customary law. The only exception to this generalization would occur if all or nearly all states had been parties to the terminated treaty and furthermore if there were no tendency for states to revert to practices legitimized by the customary rule that had preceded the treaty. The customary rule would then be considered as abrogated by these general expressions of its disavowal.

Thus, it is hardly ever permissible to speak of treaties as abrogating and replacing customary law. Treaties do serve as evidence of evolving custom, and they can serve as evidence of the desuetude of a customary rule. The international law of today is not becoming predominantly conventional as opposed to its former largely customary character. Instead, the rules of international law seem to be drawing their legal effect from converging and interacting sources.

It is commonly said that in addition to the two primary sources of international law, there are a number of lesser, or secondary sources. These are the judgments of courts, the opinions of writers, the general principles of law recognized by civilized nations, and the decisions of international organizations. The judgments of courts and the opinions of writers are not sources of law in themselves, but rather they are a part of the evidence of the attribution of legal effect to customary practices by states. Although the individual decisions of national courts, taken as a whole, are a better index of the attribution of legality to a rule of law by states than the decisions of international courts, it is fashionable to cite the latter first, if only because international courts "are entitled to more respect than others."[15] The grandiose

15 J.L. Brierly, *The Law of Nations*, 5th edn, Oxford: Clarendon Press, 1955, p. 65. In editing the sixth edition of Brierly's work, Waldock significantly altered this passage to read: "The decisions [of international courts] are accorded more weight than any others." J.L. Brierly, *The Law of Nations*, 6th edn by H. Waldock, Oxford: Clarendon Press, 1963, pp. 64–5. In a more persuasive discussion of the problem, Wolfgang Friedmann has put national courts in a position inferior to that of international courts because national courts tend to be "spokesmen of national interests in questions of international legal importance," instead of being "truly agents of international law." *The Changing Structure of International Law*, New York: Columbia University Press, 1964, p. 148. It is precisely this tendency of national courts to reflect the positions of their states on points of law, which makes their decisions valuable as evidence of the attribution of legal effect. At the same time it is fair to expect national courts to provide their states with prescriptive guidance, if only within limits tolerable to these states.

image of a court for the world no doubt accounts for the high value generally attached to the decisions of the International Court of Justice (ICJ) or, for that matter, any tribunal international in its composition.

The ICJ's prestige shows up in another way. Reference to the "general principles of law recognized by civilized nations" as a secondary source of international law first occurs in the statute of the ICJ's predecessor, the Permanent Court of International Justice (Article 38). Despite the fact that the members of the Advisory Committee of Jurists were unclear as to the meaning of this phrase when they devised it, despite the fact that writers have never agreed on the nature of these principles, and despite the fact that the World Court (as it is commonly known) has rarely suggested that such principles were the source of the law applied in its decisions, the contemporary literature invariably treats the general principles of law recognized by civilized nations as a legitimate source of law.

There is only one really plausible way of interpreting the reference to general principles in the Statute. In applying rules of law to specific situations, any court, including an international court, may have to interpret the rules to fit the situation: in short, it must concretize the law. Such interpretations can have an incremental effect on the law if they appear reasonable. Article 38 rather superfluously asks the World Court to be reasonable when it has to tailor a rule for a situation. Otherwise, states (civilized nations) will not recognize the altered content of the rule and it will be without general legal effect in the long run. The general principles of law are thus a limitation or guide to the Court on what states will find acceptable, so that its interpretations, though in themselves without legal effect except in the case at hand, can contribute to a change in the rule of law.[16]

The general principles of law recognized by civilized nations are not to be confused with the general principles of international law.[17] The resemblance ends with the fact that both play a role in law creation without being independent sources of law in themselves. Whenever the latter phrase is used in distinction to and not as equivalent to the more important of the rules of

> Domestic courts are an arena in which attitudes toward international law are disclosed and general impressions formed. If it becomes evident that international law is applied only when it is a convenient adjunct to foreign policy, then there is no persuasive reason for any state ever to subordinate its policy to the restraining claims of law.

R.A. Falk, *The Role of Domestic Courts in the International Legal Order*, Syracuse: Syracuse University Press, 1964, pp. 11–12.

16 M.A. Kaplan and N. DeB. Katzenbach make much the same point in their discussion of sources. *The Political Foundations of International Law*, New York: Wiley, 1961, p. 261.

17 H. Waldock, "General Course in Public International Law," *Recueil des cours de L'Académie de droit international de La Haye*, vol. 106, 1962/I, pp. 68–9, has also brought attention to this distinction. C.W. Jenks, in providing a theoretical basis for his emerging *Common Law of Mankind*, London: Stevens, 1958, pp. 120–172, has consciously sought to merge both kinds of principles.

positive law, these principles state the defining conditions of the international legal system as a decentralized order. They refer to the sovereignty and equality of states, thus defining the subjects of the law, and to the dependence of the community of states on a degree of predictability in its intercourse, thus defining the law's source of obligation. These general principles are not rules of law, but rather they are "material directives," setting limits within which any rule must fall for it to become a part of the decentralized, international legal order.[18]

Nor do the decisions of international organizations constitute an independent source of law. Insofar as states consider the decisions of international organizations as having a legal effect, it is because the treaties creating these organizations endowed with legal effect certain kinds of decisions that the organizations might make. Resolutions, especially those adopted unanimously, of organs made up of states' representatives can be tantamount to treaties, depending on their wording, but such resolutions can be considered a source of law only because they can be assimilated to treaties [an untenable view, soon abandoned]. The decisions of international organizations are an unusually fine indicator of the growth of custom and its acquisition of legal effect. Indeed, the activities of international organizations can precipitate customary practices and their identification as lawful, and they therefore become an important part of the process of law formation. These activities, however, cannot be considered a source of law independent of treaties or customs to which legal effect is attributed.

Codification

According to the *Oxford English Dictionary*, the verb *to codify* is not especially complicated in its meaning. It can mean either "to reduce (laws) to a code; to digest," or "to reduce to a general system; to systematize."[19] These two meanings are not dissimilar: they both require the same operation, that of reduction, and in both cases the purpose of this operation falls into the general category of making order from disorder. A disorderly melange of laws may be reduced (or digested or systematized) to an orderly arrangement of laws simply by the replacement of the former by the latter. The codification of law would then seem to imply four distinct steps:

(1) the existing law by virtue of its disorder must be adjudged as requiring codification;
(2) the content of the existing law must be reduced to a more orderly form;
(3) the existing law must be abrogated; and

18 P.H. Kooijmans, *The Doctrine of the Legal Equality of States: An Inquiry into the Foundations of International Law*, Leiden: Sijthoff, 1964, p. 211.
19 *Oxford English Dictionary*, vol. 1, 1961, p. 583.

(4) the content of the previously existing law, having been reduced to a more orderly form, must be promulgated as new law.

In a centralized system of municipal law, codification is conceivable in principle. Objections may be raised about the desirability of such an undertaking or about the availability of the skills it requires. Nonetheless, there is a centralized means by which a decision to codify can be made, by which the available drafting skills can be assembled, and by which the existing law can be repealed and the new law promulgated. A decentralized system of law like that of international law possesses these advantages in far lesser degree. As a result, the codification of international law is subject to confusions in theory and difficulties in practice.

In the first place, because decision-making of any kind is generally decentralized in the international legal system, a meaningful decision to undertake codification must result from a myriad of independent decisions by states to participate in such an undertaking. In the ordinary course of events this is an uncommon occurrence. In the second place, the preparation of the new law in its draft form requires more than technical skill in reformulating the content of the existing law. Not only is international law disorderly, it is in parts incomplete, or unclear, or irrelevant. Consequently, problems arise when attempts are made to reduce to order that which does not exist, or does not make sense, or does not serve any use. These problems may also occur in the case of the codification of municipal law, but presumably to a lesser degree. In the instance of international law, draftsmen must either set aside parts of the law as not permitting codification, since they are not in a fit state for reduction; or they must adapt these parts to the requirements of the drafts, their own notions of what the law should be, and what they surmise or are officially informed are the views of their own and other states on what the law should be.

In the third place, international law is exceedingly difficult to abrogate and promulgate. International law deriving from treaties can as a general rule be abrogated only with the consent of all treating parties. International law deriving from custom can be abrogated only by its general disregard over a lengthy period of time. International law deriving from custom is by definition never promulgated. International law created by treaties is law promulgated only for the parties, for which all previously applicable law is suspended, as in the case of customary law, or abrogated, as in the case of conventional law, as between themselves.

Thus, once international law is reduced to a code, it must be promulgated by treaty. Since all previously applicable law is suspended by the treaty, from the point of view of the parties the law is reduced to order. From the point of view of the legal system as a whole, however, the new law exists concurrently with all the previously applicable law not clearly abrogated, thus adding further disorder to the system, particularly if the new parts of the law contain innovations. The more numerous the parties to the treaty, the more widely the previous law is suspended or abrogated, and the better the codification has served its purpose. Thus, for the old law to be abrogated and for the new codified law to be promulgated in any meaningful degree, the treaty of codification has to be generally acceptable to large numbers of states. Since states are notoriously difficult to please, the draftsmen must handle their work with demanding care and finesse. Furthermore, draftsmen can dare to suggest only those innovations that are assured of acceptance among such a wide variety of states.

In view of these enormous difficulties, it has been argued that draftsmen can best serve a meaningful role by first distinguishing the parts of the law that are well settled from the parts that are in confusion. Since the well-settled parts of the law are in no great disorder, there is no compelling need for them to be incorporated into a treaty. Furthermore, positive reasons have been advanced against doing so. Draftsmen can easily undertake their comprehensive exposition in an accessible and convenient form, and this is all that is necessary. Such expositions would have no direct, and possibly deleterious, effect. Rather, they would be a contribution to the science of international law. They would have an intended, if indirect, legal effect, however, by being further evidence of the legality of the rules contained therein.

After having identified the chaotic parts of the law, the draftsmen can do nothing more with them, because they require the creation of new law before they are put in order. The creation of new law puts the emphasis on the process of treaty-making, which is entirely different from the process of reductive law exposition. Thus the codification of international law as an integrated process is not really feasible, as it is with municipal codification. All that is possible is reductive exposition without legal effect, coordinated with law creation having an innovative rather than reductive intent. The final product of these processes taken together merely approximates codification, but the processes themselves "are so different in purpose that a common technique is not possible."[20]

For the special province of British writers (see Chapter 10), this argument has created insurmountable terminological confusion about the word *codification*. While codification means in fact reductive law creation, codification in this argument invariably means reductive law exposition, which is distinguished from any kind of law creation – reductive or innovative. Furthermore, the argument dispenses with reductive law creation as superfluous, leaving innovative law creation, generally defined as legislation, to stand in perfect antithesis to codification. In a typical definition, "the word codification properly used means the writing down of existing law, and . . . the making of new law, either *in vacuo* or by the amendment or development of existing rules, ought to be termed legislation."[21]

20 J.L. Brierly, "The Future of Codification," *British Year Book of International Law*, vol. 12, 1931, p. 3.

21 P.J. Baker, "The Codification of International Law," *British Year Book of International Law*, vol. 5, 1924, p. 41.

The nature of international law prohibits the clear demarcation of its settled parts, suitable for exposition, and its unsettled parts, requiring innovation. The irregularities of the law are too pervasive to be isolated and dealt with in this manner. Difficult as it may prove in practice, codification as an integrated process of creating new law with reductive and innovative qualities cannot be rejected in favor of the techniques suggested by the "codification–legislation" dichotomy. The process of law creation for the purpose of introducing order into international law, no matter what proportion of reduction or innovation is required, I call the conscious development of international law or conscious law development.

The conscious development of international law is a comprehensive process. It includes the work of draftsmen that failed to be converted into law but was put forward with this purpose in mind. It also includes work put forward in the form of restatement as a complement to innovative law creation. Not only do these situations have a substantive effect on the creation of law through custom; they are an integral part of the movement, more notable for its aspirations than its successes, to give international law the form and content of a fully developed legal order. In other words, it is, properly speaking, a codification movement. Except when the term *codification* is used in such a manner to imply a general disposition instead of a specific process, it is best dispensed with altogether, since it never means for international law what it means for municipal law.

2 Professor Falk on the quasi-legislative competence of the General Assembly (1969)

In my student days at Johns Hopkins, Robert Tucker asked me to help him revise Hans Kelsen's *Principles of International Law*. While he concentrated on self-help and the use of force, I worked on the sources and subjects of international law. This experience inspired my interest in the sources of individual rules as these sources – themselves rules – relate to the development of international law as a whole. From a Kelsenian point of view, self-help has a *theoretical* significance in a decentralized legal order that sources and subjects do not: whatever the source of a rule's validity, that rule is legal only if states are prepared to make it effective, if necessary, by using force. Richard Falk's scholarship offered a sharp contrast by emphasizing the possibilities of change in a decentralized legal order in which the use of force had been invalidated and from which it could be eliminated. For Falk, an important and desirable change in the international legal order was at that time underway as new states demanded new rules to accommodate a rapidly changing world; the practical and normative importance of lawmaking underlined its theoretical significance.

Falk's substantive concerns matched my own, and his normative commitments impressed me. Furthermore, he had cogently articulated his concerns and commitments in a variety of linked essays, one of which – a comment appearing in the *American Journal of International Law* in 1966 – made very clear the need for an adequate theory of global legal change. In other words, Falk's paper provided me with an opportunity for a limited but highly visible engagement over theoretical issues with practical implications. The editors of the *Journal* published the paper with no substantive change, and I had reason to believe it was widely read and well received.

A recurring theme in the voluminous writings of Professor Richard Falk concerns the role of the UN General Assembly in the process of creating international law.[1] With a number of progressive writers in the West, he

1 R.A. Falk and S.H. Mendlovitz, "Towards a Warless World: One Legal Formula to Achieve Transition," *Yale Law Journal*, vol. 73, 1964, pp. 420–1; Falk, *The Role of Domestic Courts in*

perceives an increase in the legal significance being attributed to General Assembly resolutions and deduces a quasi-legislative competence for the General Assembly.[2] Yet he also recognizes the tendency to carry this logic to the appealing but untenable conclusion that emanations of the General Assembly can be, in themselves, formally binding rules of law. Thus, in a thoughtful essay appearing as an editorial comment in the *American Journal of International Law*, he formulates a jurisprudential basis for "attributing quasi-legislative force to resolutions of the General Assembly [as] a middle position between the formally difficult affirmation of true legislative status and a formalistic denial of law-creating role and impact."[3]

The heart of Falk's middle position is to be found in his argument that the General Assembly produces norms that functionally operate as law, even though they are not formally binding. By this he means that states respond to the prescriptive assertions of the General Assembly as if they were binding on them; in short, states comply with them. If inquiry is directed toward the functional operation of General Assembly resolutions as law, then the relevant questions to ask are empirical, having to do with the distribution, duration, and continuity of compliance. It might be observed that these questions have always been asked about the practices of states from which customary rules of law are to be inferred. The process of inferring law from evidence of law-abidingness is a general one; what varies is the material source (manner of formulation) of the putative norm against which behavior is measured. On examination, then, the determination of the functional operation of any norm as law means, in more conventional language, the gathering of evidence sufficient to indicate the existence of a rule of customary international law.

the International Legal Order, Syracuse: Syracuse University Press, 1964, pp. 170–2; "The Adequacy of Contemporary Theories of International Law: Gaps in Legal Thinking," *Virginia Law Review*, vol. 50, 1964, p. 246; "The Legitimacy of Legislative Intervention by the United Nations," in R.J. Stanger (ed.), *Essays on Intervention*, Columbus: Ohio State University Press, 1964, pp. 51–2; "The Shimoda Case: A Legal Appraisal of the Atomic Attacks upon Hiroshima and Nagasaki," *American Journal of International Law*, vol. 59, 1965, pp. 792–3; "The New States and the International Legal Order," *Recueil des cours de L'Académie de droit international de La Haye*, vol. 118, 1968/II, pp. 41–3; "On the Quasi-Legislative Competence of the General Assembly," *American Journal of International Law*, vol. 60, 1966, pp. 782–91; "On Regulating International Propaganda: A Plea for Moderate Aims," *Law and Contemporary Problems*, vol. 31, 1966, pp. 634–5; "New Approaches to the Study of International Law," *American Journal of International Law*, vol. 61, 1967, pp. 486–7; "The South-West Africa Cases: An Appraisal," *International Organization*, vol. 21, 1967, p. 22–3.

2 Like-minded writers include O.J. Lissitzyn, *International Law Today and Tomorrow*, Dobbs Ferry, NY: Oceana,1965, pp. 35–7; C. Parry, *The Sources and Evidences of International Law*, Manchester: Manchester University Press, 1965, pp. 21–3; Edward McWhinney, *International Law and World Revolution* (Leiden: Sijthoff, 1967, pp. 49–51, 80.

3 Falk, "On the Quasi-Legislative Competence of the General Assembly," p. 782.

Falk, however, does not accept the implication that his concern for the legislative impact of General Assembly resolutions is wholly empirical – an instance of the scholar's midwifery in the birth of customary law. Rather, he turns to the realm of theory by asserting that "[t]he nature of legal obligation underlies any inquiry into the status of General Assembly resolutions." He rejects the traditional positivist position that consent on the part of states is the basis of their obligation because it does not account for the recent growth of interdependence and participation as salient aspects of community at the world level. Instead, "there is a discernible trend from consent to consensus as the basis of international legal obligations."[4]

Always an elusive concept, consensus means, at minimum, generalized community *agreement*.[5] How generalized is an open question, with answers ranging from effective unanimity to the proportion required by the characteristic voting rules of the community's apparatus for expressing its will.[6] Falk himself seems to prefer agreement voiced in the General Assembly by two-thirds of the Members (the General Assembly's voting rule on substantive issues), not excluding a great Power or an entire major group.[7]

Two observations are in order here. First, the traditional doctrine of consent should not be taken too literally. As De Visscher has shown, consent presumed on the part of all states really consists of a stable, definite core of consent supplied by major states, actively invoking and applying norms, and a transient, ill-defined penumbra of acquiescence supplied by states less powerful and involved.[8] There is no polling of community members as to their consent; rather, a generalized, hardly uniform community agreement, or consensus, is manifested. While not denying the real changes in the international system, it is misleading to argue a concomitant change in the basis of obligation. Second, if Falk's formula for consensus is fulfilled, the likelihood of virtually all states agreeing is assured, and the high incidence of unanimity

4 Ibid., pp. 784, 785.

5 L. Lipsitz, "Consensus: The Study of Consensus," *International Encyclopedia of the Social Sciences*, vol. 3, 1968, pp. 266–7; J.W. Prothro and C.M. Grigg, "Fundamental Principles of Democracy: Bases of Agreement and Disagreement," *Journal of Politics*, vol. 22, 1960, p. 276.

6 As Prothro and Grigg, "Fundamental Principles of Democracy," p. 276 n.1, observe, particularly for small groups without formal voting, consensus means unanimity, while for larger groups, "some students of collective behavior employ a functional definition of consensus, taking it to mean that amount of agreement in a group necessary for the group to act." The amount of agreement necessary to act is routinely determined by community rules.

7 Falk, "On Regulating International Propaganda," pp. 634–5. Falk does make consensus a matter of degree: the strongest consensus approximates unanimity, while weaker consensuses, presumably reduced in legislative impact, tolerate nonparticipation or dissidence, even on the part of a great Power. Falk, "On the Quasi-Legislative Competence of the General Assembly," pp. 787–8.

8 C. De Visscher, *Theory and Reality in Public International Law*, rev. edn trans. by P.E. Corbett, Princeton: Princeton University Press, 1968, pp. 153–63.

in the adoption of General Assembly resolutions is not an accident but a reflection of the fact that what two-thirds of the community's members, including the great Powers and major groups, agree on, virtually all states have no difficulty agreeing on.[9] Actually, the mobilization of the community through the General Assembly assures a fuller participation in law-relevant decision-making than ever before, so that the tendency is in a sense away from consensus, with its acquiescent and irrelevant periphery, to the uniform, active granting of consent, subject to confirmation in practice, through unanimous voting.

In short, Falk establishes a basis of obligation for quasi-legislative resolutions, which is merely a refined version of the basis of obligation typically posited by positivists for customary international law. This would seem then to be further evidence that the phenomenon of resolutions functionally operating as law "is but a special case of the more pervasive processes by which the formation and decay of legal standards have always taken place in international society," as Falk readily admits.[10] Yet one detects a certain ambivalence in Falk on this point. Why is he so concerned to contrast consensus, expressing "the will of the international community," with consent, expressing "a sovereignty-centered conception of obligation"?[11] And why does he raise the question of the basis of obligation at all, if his purpose is simply to establish the place of General Assembly resolutions in the quasi-legislative process of customary law formation?

The answer to these questions may well be in Falk's normative disposition, very much present in the following remark: "If international society is to function effectively, it requires a limited legislative authority, at minimum, to translate an overriding consensus among states into rules of order and norms of obligation despite the opposition of one or more sovereign states."[12] Falk is altogether unsure that the process of customary law formation, even when it involves General Assembly resolutions, is adequate to the needs of the international order of the day. Something more is required, a more responsive technique of law-creation, more directly involving the international community as a whole.

Without so much as saying so, Falk is trying to establish the resolutions of the General Assembly as an *independent* source of international law, with consensus as its own, distinctive basis of obligation. Not satisfied with the present status of General Assembly resolutions as an adjunct to the sovereignty-dominated process of customary law creation, Falk is advocating, in

9 For a statistical picture and some analysis of the high incidence of unanimity in the adoption of General Assembly resolutions, see C.S. Manno, "Majority Decisions and Minority Responses in the UN General Assembly," *Journal of Conflict Resolution*, vol. 10, 1966, pp. 3–7.

10 Falk, "On the Quasi-Legislative Competence of the General Assembly," p. 791.

11 Ibid., p. 785.

12 Ibid.

keeping with his "transition to world order" orientation manifested elsewhere, the status of true legislation for the international community's expressions of will.[13]

Obviously, Falk's advocacy is incompatible with his claim to a middle position in dealing with the question of the legal significance of General Assembly resolutions. His position is a combination of analysis with a conservative thrust – General Assembly resolutions can be dealt with in the traditional terms of customary law formation – and advocacy with a radical thrust. The outcome is unsettling, for one feels that Falk really cannot have it both ways. If, on the one hand, Falk were to confine himself to the indicated analysis, his discussion of the basis of obligation is superfluous and, more than that, misleading, since he exaggerates the difference between consent and consensus in customary law formation. If one ignores the discussion of the basis of obligation, one is left with an analysis that adds nothing to the more thorough studies of Rosalyn Higgins, O.Y. Asamoah, and others.[14] On the other hand, if Falk were to follow through explicitly on his position that General Assembly resolutions should be a *sui generis* source of international law, then his analysis of the present status of these resolutions in terms of their functional operation as law undermines the assumption behind his advocacy that the process of customary law formation is inadequate to the needs of an interdependent international community possessing a coherent will of its own.

Rather, the analysis should be replaced with a detailed consideration of the requirements for formal bindingness – something not present in Falk's discussion of the basis of obligation. As Schachter has recently demonstrated, the test for the existence of obligation always reduces itself to two desiderata: legitimacy and effectiveness.[15] Falk's discussions of the composition of consensus, the concreteness of resolutions, contextual factors, and so on, all attest to his concern for the problem of effectiveness.[16] Virtually ignored, however, is anything having to do with legitimacy. In the analysis of General Assembly resolutions in the process of customary law formation, the question of

13 For the transition to world order orientation, see Falk and Mendlovitz, "Towards a Warless World," pp. 399–406. For a spirited defense of advocacy on the part of international legal scholars, see Falk, "New Approaches to the Study of International Law," pp. 477–84.

14 R. Higgins, *The Development of International Law through the Political Organs of the United Nations*, New York: Oxford University Press, 1963; O.Y. Asamoah, *The Legal Significance of the Declarations of the General Assembly of the United Nations*, The Hague: Nijhoff, 1966; and works cited in both.

15 O. Schachter, "Towards a Theory of International Obligation," *Virginia Journal of International Law*, vol. 8, 1968, p. 311. See also H. Kelsen, *Principles of International Law*, rev. edn by R.W. Tucker, New York: Holt, Rinehart, Winston, 1966, pp. 560–2.

16 Falk, "On the Quasi-Legislative Competence of the General Assembly," p. 786. On the criteria for assessing the effectiveness of General Assembly resolutions, see also G.R. Lande, "The Effect of Resolutions of the United Nations General Assembly," *World Politics*, vol. 19, 1966, pp. 83–105.

legitimacy, unlike effectiveness, need not have been raised, because Falk could assume that, at least insofar as Western statesmen and scholars are concerned, custom is unquestionably a legitimate source of international law.[17] The difficulty is in ascertaining the existence of such law, not in defending its legitimacy. But in regarding General Assembly resolutions as at least potentially a source of law in themselves, Falk should have dealt with the question of legitimacy in terms similar to these. Is there, or is there likely to be, a real and enduring consensus of the international community endowing consensuses of the community on other matters with legal effect once they have been duly formalized by the General Assembly? In other words, is there a willingness on the part of the international community to legitimate the legislative competence of the General Assembly?

The requisite endowment of legitimacy might come in the form of a multilateral treaty or Charter amendment. It might come in the form of foreign office statements and speeches by major officials of virtually all states proclaiming or acknowledging General Assembly legislative competence. It could come in the form of a General Assembly resolution or resolutions, unanimously accepted and subsequently undisputed, specifically providing for the legal effect of future resolutions meeting various requirements. But most likely it would come in the form of generalized community acceptance of the claim advanced by various community members that a goodly number of resolutions meeting certain conditions are in fact binding on all members.

More specifically, if overwhelmingly adopted resolutions are subsequently widely referred and responded to as binding in themselves, and if these references and responses are not disputed or, better, are acknowledged in later resolutions, legitimacy can be inferred from consensus without formal expression of consent. In other words, the legitimacy of a new source of law must be provided for in a rule of law arising from an already legitimate source. If legitimacy is established through express consent, the legitimating instrument is a conventional rule of law; if it is established through an inferred consensus, the legitimating instrument is a customary rule. The former case is exemplified by article 38 of the World Court Statute in reference to the general principles of law recognized by civilized nations, the latter by the customary rule, codified in article 38, *pacta sunt servanda*.

At the moment, generalized community agreement on the inherent legal significance of any particular resolution, much less all resolutions meeting certain requirements, does not exist.[18] This is amply illustrated in the debates

17 The Soviet conception of custom as a legitimate source of law now seems quite close to the Western conception, although the conditions for establishing the bindingness of specific rules are more stringent. See G.I. Tunkin, "Co-Existence and International Law," *Recueil des cours de L'Académie de droit international de La Haye*, vol. 95, 1958/III, pp. 9–21.

18 A small number of resolutions – notably, the Universal Declaration of Human Rights (General Assembly Res. 217 [III], December 10, 1948), and the Declaration on the Granting of Independence to Colonial Countries and Peoples (General Assembly Res.1514 [XV],

of both the Sixth Committee and the Special Committee on the Principles of International Law concerning Friendly Relations and Co-operation among States on the present legal position of the General Assembly's Declaration on the Inadmissibility of Intervention in the Domestic Affairs of States and the Protection of their Independence and Sovereignty.[19] Even though the Declaration was adopted by a vote of 109–0–1, Western states have steadfastly refused to accept the imputation of full legal significance to it by non-Western states. Increasingly defensive, aware that its historic primacy in the making of international law is endangered, the West will almost certainly reject other such efforts in the future, thereby displaying the unwillingness of a major group to grant the General Assembly a real legislative competence. There is no world consensus without the West, and Falk must concern himself with this obstacle and the means for dissipating it, if he is to play the role he so obviously desires of helping the world community gain a law-giving voice through the General Assembly.

December 14, 1960) – have received widespread acceptance, but not, at least initially, as law. This acceptance is evidence of the coming into existence of customary law, which is identical to the resolutions, so that latter-day affirmations of legality refer not to the resolutions themselves but to the corresponding customary rules.

19 General Assembly Res. 2131 (XX), Dec. 21, 1965. For an examination of the debates on the legal significance of the Declaration, see Chapter 3, below.

3 The principle of nonintervention, the United Nations, and the international system (1970)

Then a colleague at Georgetown University, William V. O'Brien invited me to contribute a paper to the fourth volume of the *Yearbook of World Polity*, which he edited. Since yearbooks often attend to current events, and given my interest in the development of international law, I decided to write about the UN's ongoing debates on the meaning and status of nonintervention as a legal principle. As I combed several years of UN documents and worked up a detailed account of these deliberations and the political dynamics they revealed, financial exigency ended publication of the *Yearbook*. In the meantime, I had been following the work of my contemporaries in the field of International Relations, many of whom were preoccupied with the "international system" and its properties. Several of them had assumed editorial control of the scholarly journal *International Organization*, making it an appropriate place to ask what the principle of nonintervention could tell us about changes in the system. With this in mind, I reviewed claims about the relevance of international law and institutions to trends in the international system, drastically shortened my treatment of what was even then going on in UN debates, and suggested that principles matter to states' leaders because they tell them – and us – what the system is like and where it is going.

Talk of systems leads inevitably to consideration of functions that must be fulfilled for systems to do what they are supposed to. Such talk makes positivist lawyers and social scientists uncomfortable, because it shifts attention away from behavior and thus blurs the fact–value distinction so dear to positivist ontology. Nevertheless, I realized then that functional language gives international legal theory a wider reach than positivism affords, and my subsequent work has attempted to situate functionalist claims in an adequate account of agency.

In the last decade a number of scholars concerned with patterns of change in the international system have turned to international law for indications of systemic trends. They have assumed that key rules and principles of international law reflect broad characteristics of the system while controversies over and changes in their content and status reflect the rate, extent, and direction of change in the system. For example, Stanley Hoffmann in an early contribution illustrated the transition from the stable international system of the 19th century to the revolutionary system of today by reference to changes in the principle of sovereignty.[1] Morton Kaplan and Nicholas Katzenbach discussed the same transition – in their terms from a balance of power to a loose bipolar system – by reference to the principle of nonintervention.[2] Somewhat later Wolfgang Friedmann treated the principles of sovereignty and nonintervention together in light of systemic trends over the last century, while Richard Falk associated the substantive law relating to civil war with the changing position of the principle of nonintervention.[3] More systematically, an article by William Coplin ranged over several critical areas of international law in describing the evolution of the traditional international system to its present form.[4] Finally, in recent but cursory essays, Andrew Scott and Oran Young have broadened the context in which the principle of nonintervention is related to systemic trends.[5]

Authors writing prior to Scott and Young concentrated on the declining position of the principles of sovereignty and nonintervention in the face of competitive East–West intervention as a dominant feature of the postwar international system. Scott, however, speculated about the impact of the developing world on the principle of nonintervention. He saw possibilities for the principle's refurbishment and provided some general guidelines, but he was not specific about the content of a principle of nonintervention that would be relevant to the post-cold-war system. For his part, Young suggestively traced an historical alternation from classical times between inward-turning, value-scarce systems debasing the principle of nonintervention and expanding, value-rich systems honoring that principle.

In another essay Young assessed the responsiveness of recent peacekeeping doctrine to systemic developments and thereby used one aspect of international organization and a different time frame in much the same way that he used the principle of nonintervention.[6] This is only one example from a substantial literature in which phenomena like the evolution of the UN

1 S. Hoffmann, "International Systems and International Law," *World Politics*, vol. 14, 1961, pp. 205–37.

2 M.A. Kaplan and N.deB. Katzenbach, *The Political Foundations of International Law*, New York: Wiley, 1961, ch. 2.

3 W. Friedmann, *The Changing Structure of International Law*, New York: Columbia University Press, 1964, pp. 262–72; R.A. Falk, "Janus Tormented: The International Law of Internal War," in J. N. Rosenau (ed.), *International Aspects of Civil Strife*, Princeton: Princeton University Press, 1964, pp. 185–249.

4 W.D. Coplin, "International Law and Assumptions about the State System," *World Politics*, vol. 17, 1965, pp. 615–34.

5 A.M. Scott, "Nonintervention and Conditional Intervention," and O.R. Young, "Intervention and International Systems," both in *Journal of International Affairs*, vol. 22, 1968, pp. 208–16 and 177–87.

6 O.R. Young, *Trends in International Peacekeeping*, Center of International Studies, Princeton University, Research Monograph No. 22, 1966.

Charter, the changing position of UN political organs, and the shifting membership and agenda patterns in the UN are viewed as barometers of world politics. In all its aspects international organization is probably more sensitive than is international law to the texture and tempo of system change, but less revealing of secular trends. This would be so because of the relatively short and discontinuous history of international organization and because of its propensity to respond quickly and diversely to all kinds of situations and demands, either transitory or enduring.

Characteristically, the several authors referred to above reject the traditional belief that the primary function of international law, as a coercive order, is to constrain the behavior of states.[7] Instead, they are attracted to the idea that international law serves the more modest function of enhancing communication between states and consequently of channeling behavior. International law, like international organization, is thus viewed as a rather passive agent – one element of an arena – which helps shape the flow of politics.

When these scholars change their analytic perspective from the level of political process to that of system action, the functional importance that they impute to international law diminishes with the increased scale and volume of phenomena subject to analysis. Playing only a minor part in individual sets of interactions, law becomes even less significant when all such interactions are considered as an aggregate from which patterns and trends can be discerned. The analytic focus becomes one of identifying and classifying such patterns and trends and spelling out their implications for state policies. Law is not thought of as decisive, or even critical, for what is happening in, much less to, the system; rather, it is something that comes out of the system as things happen in and cumulatively to it. Relatively visible and substantially dependent on the system, international law at any point in time has the analytic function of indicating (in a broad qualitative sense) the system's state at that time. Thus, taken over time, international law becomes an indicator of systemic trends. Furthermore, insofar as statesmen and publics as well as analysts use this indicator, it serves a system function. As with process analyses, this function of law has to do with communication – but less with communication of immediate expectations than with communication of a shared understanding about the nature of the system.

When adopting a system perspective, writers have generally given scant attention to the system function of international law. The major exception is

7 See, in addition to the works cited, S. Hoffmann, "International Law and the Control of Force," and R.A. Falk, "The Relevance of Political Context to the Nature and Functioning of International Law: An Intermediate View," both in K.W. Deutsch and S. Hoffmann (eds), *The Relevance of International Law: Essays in Honor of Leo Gross*, Cambridge, MA: Schenkman, 1968, pp. 21–46 and 133–52; W.D. Coplin, *The Functions of International Law: An Introduction to the Role of International Law in the Contemporary World*, Chicago: Rand McNally, 1966; A.M. Scott, *The Functioning of the International Political System*, New York: Macmillan, 1967, ch. 14.

Coplin, and even he failed to establish the consequences for the system of its own "self-awareness." More typical is Hoffman's position. In discussing communication-related functions of international law at the level of state interaction, he boldly asserted: "International law is merely a magnifying mirror that reflects faithfully and cruelly the essence and the logic of international politics."[8] The apparent contradiction is actually a switch to the system level of analysis.

If one accepts these assumptions about the impact of international law, then it is a problem to explain why, on at least some occasions, states become more than routinely involved in the handling and disposition of what are widely regarded as legal questions. In the following sections one such instance – the effort of the UN to render a definitive formulation of the principle of nonintervention – will be investigated for the light it sheds both on systemic trends and on the reasons for its apparent importance to states. The first of these tasks is in keeping with the prevailing mode of systems analysis, while the second is directed at the discrepancy between analytic assumptions and the evidence of state behavior.

Negotiating the principle of nonintervention

The principle of nonintervention as applied to states is not directly acknowledged in the UN Charter, but it has nonetheless attracted the attention of the UN membership as one of the principles of peaceful coexistence. Publicized by Soviet jurists since the mid-1950s, the principles of peaceful coexistence purportedly isolate the order-creating elements of East–West *détente*. Although they are cast in legal language, these principles combine indeterminate proportions of description, projection, evaluation, and prescription all at a level of abstraction that makes obligation meaningless.[9] Since 1960 the UN has been the focus of the movement to translate the principles of peaceful coexistence into a legal regime. Not surprisingly, the movement was inspired by members of the Socialist bloc to exploit both the dissatisfaction of the newly emerged states with "Western" international law and their desire to play a role in creating "new" international law.[10] In

8 S. Hoffmann, "Introduction," in L. Scheinman and D. Wilkinson (eds), *International Law and Political Crisis: An Analytic Casebook*, Boston: Little, Brown, 1968, pp. xi–xix, quoting p. xvii.

9 On the history and nature of the principles of peaceful coexistence, see I. Lapenna, "The Legal Aspects and Political Significance of the Soviet Concept of Co-Existence," *International and Comparative Law Quarterly*, vol. 12, 1963, pp. 737–77, and B.A. Ramundo, *Peaceful Coexistence: International Law in the Building of Communism*, Baltimore: Johns Hopkins Press, 1967.

10 See J.N. Hazard, "The Sixth Committee and New Law," *American Journal of International Law*, vol. 57, 1963, pp. 604–5, and E. McWhinney, "The 'New' Countries and the 'New' International Law: The United Nations' Special Conference on Friendly Relations and Co-Operation among States," *American Journal of International Law*, vol. 60, 1966, pp. 1–2, 29–30.

short, the movement to give the principles of peaceful coexistence a truly legal quality is one of the more subtle Socialist-bloc initiatives in the East–West rivalry for approbation and influence in the developing world.

UN involvement with the principles of peaceful coexistence is justified under article 13(1a) of the Charter, which instructs the General Assembly to promote the progressive development of international law and its codification. Ordinarily, the International Law Commission is responsible for projects undertaken for these ends but, because of the Commission's conservative, "legalistic" approach to its duties, neither the International Law Commission nor the interested states desired to have the Commission assigned this project.[11] Instead, in 1963 the General Assembly created a new organ, the Special Committee on Principles of International Law concerning Friendly Relations and Co-operation among States, composed of 27 states and concerned exclusively with the principles of peaceful coexistence.[12]

Initially, the Special Committee's attention was to be confined to four principles:

(a) The principle that states shall refrain in their international relations from the threat or use of force against the territorial integrity or political independence of any state, or in any other manner inconsistent with the purposes of the United Nations;
(b) The principle that states shall settle their international disputes by peaceful means in such a manner that international peace and security and justice are not endangered;
(c) The duty not to intervene in matters within the domestic jurisdiction of any state, in accordance with the Charter;
(d) The principle of sovereign equality of states.

Three other principles were set aside for later attention:

(e) The duty of states to cooperate with one another in accordance with the Charter;
(f) The principle of equal rights and self-determination of peoples;
(g) The principle that states shall fulfil in good faith the obligations assumed by them in accordance with the Charter.[13]

11 General Assembly *Official Records* (17th session), Supplement No. 9, §§ 58 and 61, p. 33; and UN doc. A/5771, § 110, reprinted in General Assembly *Official Records* (18th session), Annexes, Agenda Item 71, p. 38.

12 General Assembly Resolution 1966 (XVIII), December 16, 1963.

13 The General Assembly had adopted these formulations of the seven principles during its session of the year before. See General Assembly Resolution 1815 (XVII), December 18, 1962.

The Special Committee was also to take account of "the practice of the United Nations and of states in the application of the principles established in the Charter of the United Nations" and, finally, the Committee was to report its conclusions to the General Assembly. Although Resolution 1966 states that the purpose of the report was "the progressive development and codification of the four principles so as to secure their more effective application," the function of the Special Committee became a source of contention. States argued that its mandate was unclear and questioned whether the Special Committee was simply to make a critical assessment of the present place of the four principles in international law or to make a constructive exposition of them.

When the Special Committee met in the summer of 1964, Western representatives argued the former position while representatives from the new states and the Socialist bloc adopted the latter one.[14] Unable to reach an agreement, the Special Committee was forced to leave questions on the nature of its task unanswered. It decided simply that when the Committee had completed discussion of a subject, a drafting committee would prepare without voting:

(1) a draft text formulating the points of consensus; and
(2) a list itemizing the various proposals and views on which there is no consensus but for which there is support.[15]

Giving a curious twist to the usual meaning of consensus, the Special Committee itself would vote on texts prepared in this manner by the drafting committee.

A text expressing points of consensus was adopted only for the principle of sovereign equality. After a late change in the US delegation's instructions, a text on the principle that states refrain from the threat or use of force was abandoned. During the debate over the principle of nonintervention, two lines of thought emerged. Western states argued that the Charter indirectly established the principle of nonintervention in article 2(4) by calling on states to refrain from behavior inconsistent with the right of states to political independence and territorial integrity.[16] Article 2(7), although it deals with intervention directly, applies only to the UN and implies nothing about the behavior of states. By focusing on the limits instead of the forms of intervention, the Charter avoided the intractable problem of distinguishing

14 For details see UN doc. A/5746, paras. 19–25, reprinted in General Assembly *Official Records* (20th session), Annexes, Agenda Items 90 and 94, pp. 82–3.

15 Ibid., §12, p. 81.

16 The Western argument, with varying emphases, is found in the British draft proposal and accompanying commentary and in speeches of the French and US representatives. See UN docs A/AC.119/L.8, § 205, p. 116, in ibid.; A/AC.119/SR.28, pp. 8–10; A/AC.119/SR.29, pp. 8–9; A/AC.119/SR.32, p. 12.

intervention from the legitimate and necessary efforts of states to influence the behavior of other states. In short, an exhaustive definition of intervention is impossible because the motive behind the exercise of influence is more important than the methods used. Simple statement to the effect that the principle of nonintervention generalizes the interdiction contained in article 2(4) would suffice for the Special Committee's assessment of the principle.

The other line of thought, as propounded by non-Western states, interpreted article 2(7), which prohibits intervention by the UN in matters within the domestic jurisdiction of any state, as applying *a fortiori* to member states.[17] The specific strictures of article 2(4), which prohibit only the threat or use of force by states, are less relevant to the principle of nonintervention and in no way define or circumscribe this principle. Instead, many treaties subsequent to the Charter and pronouncements of international organizations have, however unsystematically and unevenly, defined the principle of nonintervention and elaborated its content. The Special Committee would thus do best to collate and organize the known elements of the principle and present them for adoption as a coherent whole. Some proposals were in fact introduced, which attempted to do this, but their sponsors had little immediate success in reconciling the many differences in their respective enumerations.[18]

Because of the UN's financial crisis, it was more than a year before the General Assembly's Sixth (Legal) Committee reviewed the work of the Special Committee. There was general agreement that while the Special Committee's efforts were disappointing they should continue.[19] In deference to Asian–African wishes a resolution was adopted, which provided for an enlarged Special Committee to study all seven principles and to submit a comprehensive report with a view to enabling the General Assembly to adopt a declaration on the principles.[20] Although the West found both its position on the Special Committee's mandate substantially rejected and the balance

17 The non-Western argument is best illustrated by speeches of the representatives of Mexico, the Socialist Republic of Romania, and the United Arab Republic. See UN docs A/AC.119/SR.26, pp. 6–8; A/AC.119/SR.30, pp. 4–6; A/AC.119/SR.31, pp. 11–12.

18 More compatible in these proposals were prefatory definitions of intervention, all of them following article 15 of the Charter of the Organization of American States (OAS), which states:

> No State or group of States has the right to intervene directly or indirectly, for any reason whatever, in the internal or external affairs of any other State. The foregoing principle prohibits not only armed force but also any other form of interference or attempted threat against the personality of the State or against its political, economic and cultural elements.

The several proposals, or at least their parts relating to the principle of nonintervention (UN docs A/AC.119/L.6, 7, 24, and 27), are found in UN doc. A/5746, paras. 203, 204, 208, and 209, pp. 115–7.

19 The debate is summarized in UN doc. A/6165, paras. 18–21, reprinted in General Assembly *Official Records* (20th session), Annexes, Agenda Items 90 and 94, p. 147.

20 General Assembly Resolution 2103 (XX), December 20, 1965.

of membership on the Committee tipped further against it, nothing was done to alter the consensual decision-making principle, effectively the veto power of Western states, adopted by the Special Committee.

At the very time that the Sixth Committee was reviewing the Special Committee's work on the principle of nonintervention, the General Assembly's First (Political and Security) Committee was considering an agenda item entitled "The inadmissibility of intervention in the domestic affairs of States and the protection of their independence and sovereignty." Despite the obvious overlap, both the First and Sixth Committees proceeded in their respective tasks, but without reference to each other's labors.

The question of the inadmissibility of intervention was brought before the General Assembly at the initiative of the Soviet Union. According to an explanatory memorandum the Soviet initiative was prompted by the fact that certain powers were "seeking to impede the advance of history by aggressive acts and open intervention in the domestic affairs of sovereign states and peoples fighting against colonial domination, for their national liberation and for their independent sovereign existence."[21] Clearly, the Soviet Union was capitalizing on an opportunity to embarrass the US over its actions in the Dominican Republic and Vietnam. That the question was regarded as having more political than legal significance is clear from the decision to have the General Assembly's political committee and not its legal committee deal with it.

In its operative paragraph the draft declaration on the topic submitted by the Soviet Union dealt in specific terms only with the use of arms "against the just struggle of peoples for national independence and freedom." The UK and the US offered amendments that sought to counter the Soviet emphasis on armed intervention in internal struggles with a concern for indirect intervention and subversion against orderly political process. In so doing these states abandoned their preference for a generalized statement of the principle of nonintervention in favor of their own versions of the principle's content. Latin American and Asian–African states also offered draft resolutions. By associating for the first time the principle of nonintervention with a wide range of North–South issues, these drafts differed substantially, not only from the Soviet draft and the amendments proposed thereto, but also from the non-Western proposals submitted earlier to the Special Committee.[22]

Through the efforts of an informal working group, which consisted solely of representatives of Asian, African, and Latin American states, a compromise draft resolution eventually emerged sponsored by 56 states from these

21 UN Document A/5977 reprinted in General Assembly *Official Records* (20th session), Annexes, Agenda Item 207, pp. 1–2.

22 The relevant documents are reprinted ibid., pp. 2–8.

three groupings plus Yugoslavia.[23] The compromise text blended elements in roughly equal parts from Latin American and Asian-African drafts, but at the same time it required concessions on both sides. The first of the draft's eight operative paragraphs formulated the principle of nonintervention in the familiar terms of article 15 of the OAS Charter. Also conforming to a long-standing inter-American formulation were the prohibitions of paragraph 2 against interference in civil strife, complicity in subversion, and attempts to obtain advantages of any kind. The Asian-African concern for the dislocation of peoples and the denial of national identity entered halfway into the compromise draft as the third paragraph: "The use of force to deprive peoples of their national identity constitutes a violation of their inalienable rights and of the principle of non-intervention." Paragraph 4 affirmed the conviction expressed in the Latin American draft that intervention "violates the spirit and the letter of the Charter" and endangers peace and security. The sense of the fifth paragraph, which referred to the right of states to choose their own "political, economic, social, and cultural systems," had been expressed in both the Latin American and Asian-African drafts although its wording was taken directly from the latter.

Paragraph 6 affirmed the right of self-determination "to be freely exercised without any foreign pressure, and with absolute respect for human rights and fundamental freedoms." Nothing more was said in the draft about human rights, although the Latin American draft had linked them with measures taken by international organs in accordance with the Charter. Nor was anything said about apartheid and racial discrimination, much less their international effects, than the same paragraph's directive that racial discrimination be eliminated along with "colonialism in all its forms and manifestations." The Asian-African draft had devoted an entire paragraph to these activities and their relation to the principle of nonintervention.

The last two paragraphs found no precedent in either the previous Latin American or Asian-African drafts. Paragraph 7 extended the term *state* to cover states individually and in groups. Paragraph 8 ensured that none of the preceding provisions would detract from the Charter and, in particular, from chapters VI, VII, and VIII. This may have been a concession to the West, and possibly to the Socialist bloc as well, since it implied that the principle of nonintervention does not affect or circumscribe the security structures created under the umbrella of the Charter.[24]

The efforts of the Latin American and Asian-African groupings transformed the Soviet initiative from an exercise in East–West politics into a vehicle for the legitimization of positions long held by dissatisfied states in the

23 UN doc. A/C.1/L.364/Add.1. Despite its geographical position, Yugoslavia's stance on non-alignment put it in a grouping with most other Asian-African states.

24 Speaking for the US, Charles Yost emphasized the importance of this paragraph as a condition of its acceptance of the 57-power draft. General Assembly *Official Records* (20th session), First Committee, 1423rd meeting, para. 6, p. 436.

North–South confrontation.[25] Indeed, the First Committee was far more successful than the Special Committee in dramatizing the relevance of the principle of nonintervention for Latin American, Asian, and African interests. The expansive character of the draft, which went greatly beyond what had earlier been unacceptable to the Western grouping in the Special Committee, generated surprisingly little controversy. Except for a few explanations of vote the First Committee adopted the draft without debate by a vote of 100 to none, with five Western states abstaining. On December 21, 1965, the draft was adopted in plenary session by a vote of 109 to none, with only the UK abstaining, as Resolution 2131 (XX). Despite the changes it bore precisely the same title as the original Soviet draft: "Declaration on the Inadmissibility of Intervention in the Domestic Affairs of States and the Protection of Their Independence and Sovereignty."[26]

Why the First Committee succeeded in doing, without premeditation, what the Special Committee could not do and why, in particular, the Western position seems to have changed so thoroughly can be explained at least in part without reference to conscious changes in policy. Western states especially tend to draw a distinction between political and legal arenas; the former is understood in terms of parliamentary tactics and subjective interests while the latter is understood in terms of formal procedures and objective rights and duties. Because Western states viewed the First Committee's concern with intervention as essentially political, they were willing to participate in determining the principle's content, granting concessions to other interests in return for concessions to Western interests. In exchange for the dilution of the obviously anti-American emphasis of the original Soviet draft, Western states allowed intrusions of points that in a legal context would have been unacceptable. Non-Western states also found the atmosphere of the First Committee less inhibiting if only because they were permitted to dominate backroom negotiations without having to contend with a formal drafting committee or working group in which Western interests were represented. Furthermore, the fact that the principle of nonintervention was considered in isolation and not as one of several related principles permitted non-Western states to introduce North–South considerations, such as the right of self-determination, which in the Special Committee were to be taken up separately. In a political arena Western states had little reason to impede an inclusive construction of the principle

25 See I.L. Claude, Jr., *The Changing United Nations* (New York: Random House, 1967) on collective legitimization by the UN, as illustrated by decolonization.

26 In a remarkably parallel process the Declaration on the Granting of Independence to Colonial Countries and Peoples (General Assembly Resolution 1514 [XV], December 14, 1960) also had its source in a Soviet initiative, which was transformed in content, though not in title, through Asian-African efforts and was overwhelmingly adopted. See D.A. Kay, "The Politics of Decolonization; The New Nations and the United Nations Political Process," *International Organization* vol. 21, 1967, pp. 787–94, for details.

particularly since most of the inclusions had already received the imprimatur of the General Assembly.

The reconstituted Special Committee on Principles of International Law concerning Friendly Relations and Co-operation among States convened in the spring of 1966. Debate on the principle of nonintervention turned to the necessary place of Resolution 2131 in any text on that principle adopted by the Special Committee.[27] Three lines of thought were voiced. Representatives of Western states felt that the Special Committee was not bound in the scope of its work by the resolution since in fact the committee, in accordance with its mandate, was not bound by the UN Charter but was free to suggest such improvements as it deemed appropriate. These suggestions were permissible because they were without legal effect, even when they were cast as a declaration, just as Resolution 2131 was without legal effect and could be amended by the General Assembly at the suggestion of the Special Committee.

Conversely, Latin American and Asian-African representatives accepted the authoritative character of Resolution 2131 as a near-unanimous emanation of the General Assembly's will. A subsidiary organ of the General Assembly had no choice but to be governed by such an emanation, and thus the resolution was final and irrevocable insofar as the Special Committee was concerned. All that was possible in such a situation was to have the Special Committee go beyond the resolution and find additional points within the principle of nonintervention. Representatives of the Socialist bloc went one step further by arguing that continued work on the principle of nonintervention was made unnecessary by Resolution 2131. It remained for the Special Committee only to incorporate the provisions of the resolution in its own draft declaration.

After several meetings these issues were addressed squarely although at a procedural level. Chile and the United Arab Republic introduced a draft resolution that expressed the willingness of the Special Committee to abide by Resolution 2131 and directed the Special Committee's drafting committee to concern itself with "widening the area of agreement" of General Assembly Resolution 2131. Several Western states responded with amendments requiring the Special Committee to accept Resolution 2131, only as the basis for discussion, and directed the drafting committee to consider all proposals in the hope that it would reach "the widest general agreement . . . on the legal definition of non-intervention."[28]

27 The debate is summarized in UN Document A/6230, paras. 292–9, reprinted in General Assembly *Official Records* (21st session), Annexes, Agenda Item 87, pp. 67–8. See also P.-H. Houben, "Principles of International Law concerning Friendly Relations and Co-Operation among States," *American Journal of International Law*, vol. 61, 1967, pp. 703–36.

28 UN docs A/AC.125/L.17, A/AC.125/L.19, reprinted in UN doc. A/6230, paras. 284–5, p. 66.

Western amendments were easily defeated and the resolution was adopted.[29] Since it turned over responsibility for work on the principle to the drafting committee, the Special Committee went on to other matters. At the close of the session the drafting committee reported that "no agreement was reached on the additional proposals made with the aim of widening the area of agreement of General Assembly resolution 2131 (XX)," and the Special Committee took note of this in its report.[30] Although the Special Committee had succeeded in adopting a text on the principle of the peaceful settlement of international disputes and in revising the 1964 text on the principle of sovereign equality, the Sixth Committee's debate on this report centered on the principle of nonintervention and its relation to Resolution 2131.[31] The outcome was again a resolution calling for the Special Committee to prepare a draft declaration on all seven principles.[32]

During the 1967 session of the Special Committee, the drafting committee reached agreement on texts for the principle that states shall fulfill their obligations in good faith and for the duty of states to cooperate with one another. In its final two meetings, the Special Committee had before it these texts and a draft resolution sponsored by 13 states from the Latin American, Asian-African, and Socialist groupings. The draft resolution would simply have included the operative paragraphs of Resolution 2131 in the draft declaration on the principles of friendly relations, thereby disposing of the problems generated by earlier discussions of the principle of nonintervention.[33] Western representatives threatened to disavow all of the committee's work of that session if the 13-power draft were adopted by a majority vote as its sponsors had proposed. Latin American representatives retaliated by withdrawing their support for the two texts presented by the drafting committee. The Special Committee concluded its work by deciding not to vote on the draft texts, as was its usual procedure, but simply to take note of and transmit them to the General Assembly.[34]

At the heart of these events was the attempt of the three non-Western groupings to circumvent Western resistance to their joint formulation by avoiding the drafting committee in which Western states in effect exercised a veto. The resulting confrontation actually threatened the capacity of the Special Committee to function at all. In its two sessions since this crisis the Special Committee has been content to work on formulations for the principles of self-determination and the non-use of force so that only the

29 The roll-call votes are given in ibid., paras. 337–9, pp. 73–4.

30 Ibid., para. 584, p. 109. The report of the drafting committee is found in para. 353, p. 77.

31 The Sixth Committee's debate is summarized in UN doc. A/6547, paras. 52–8, reprinted in General Assembly *Official Records* (21st session), Annexes, Agenda Item 87, pp. 124–6.

32 General Assembly Resolution 2181 (XXI), December 12, 1966.

33 The draft resolution (UN doc. A/AC.125/L.54) is found in General Assembly *Official Records* (22nd session), Annexes, Agenda Item 87, p. 45.

34 Ibid., paras. 457–80, pp. 65–7.

principle of nonintervention would be left.[35] Meanwhile, the debates of the Sixth Committee continued to reflect the positions taken in the Special Committee and in the resolutions concluding debate calling for completion of work on the principle.[36]

Although the Sixth Committee is enmeshed in the same insistent politics of the Special Committee, both are nonetheless well insulated from the more volatile politics of daily international life. Thus, the invasion of the Czechoslovak Socialist Republic by several Socialist states and the subsequent enunciation of a doctrine justifying interventions of this kind have had no discernible effect in ameliorating the isolated and defensive position of the West on the principle of nonintervention.[37] Whatever had transpired on the world political scene, no such change was possible because of the irreversible spiral of commitment and counter-commitment that has made that one principle the critical test for the Special Committee.

Why states care

Even this brief review of UN involvement with the principle of nonintervention makes it clear that states have attached progressively greater importance to the political process and the possible consequences of this involvement. Indeed, the hardening of positions makes a compromise difficult for either side to accept. Obviously, it also makes it difficult for either side to give in to the other. If the deadlock is not broken, then it would probably have the effect of freezing or even terminating UN efforts to deal with the principles of friendly relations among states. Of course, the non-Western coalition could proceed without the West, but any outcome would be significantly reduced in legitimacy. The alternative would be simply to blame the West for the failure of the Special Committee, knowing that this blame could not be dismissed lightly.[38]

35 This order of priority was formalized by the Sixth Committee through a statement of its chairman. UN doc. A/7429, para. 71, reprinted in General Assembly *Official Records* (23rd session), Annexes, Agenda Item 87, p. 11.

36 General Assembly resolutions 2327 (XXII), December 18, 1967, 2463 (XXIII), December 20, 1968, and 2533 (XXIV), December 8, 1969.

37 In the 12 meetings that the Sixth Committee devoted to the principles of friendly relations among states in 1968, only once was the invasion of Czechoslovakia referred to explicitly and then only in passing by the US representative. Also in passing, the Soviet representative defended the new doctrine of legitimate Socialist intervention. See the speeches of Marvin Warner (US) and Yakov Ostrovsky (Soviet Union) in General Assembly *Official Records* (23rd session), Sixth Committee, 1091st and 1092nd meetings, pp. 10 and 7, respectively.

38 After these words were written, the deadlock in the Special Committee was resolved and a draft declaration adopted *ad referendum* (May 1, 1970). The General Assembly then adopted the draft declaration without vote as an annex to Resolution 2625 (XXV), October 24, 1970. A compromise appears to have been arranged, which involves two significant changes in the formulation of the principle of nonintervention contained in Resolution 2131. First, the legal

The unacceptability of each of these outcomes for some or all states in the Special Committee is sufficient testimony of the seriousness with which they regard the Committee's efforts. Yet, as I have suggested, both process and system analyses tend to minimize the objective importance of law and law-related emanations of the system, such as the principle of nonintervention, in causing change either in state behavior or system action. If these emanations are not very important, why then have states found themselves so much at odds over the principle of nonintervention?

Three explanations might aid us in resolving this question. Each one plausibly fits into our knowledge of the circumstances and each contributes at least something to an overall explanation. The first explanation has to do with the dynamics of the negotiation process. However unremarkable the principle of nonintervention might have seemed to states initially, the very fact that states were unable to agree on either its content or significance could have had the effect of making it important. The more hardened positions became, the more importance had to be attached to these positions simply to justify the effort of maintaining them. Such an effort would have required the commitment of prestige, which has an importance of its own. In a related vein, positions on the principle may have come to "stand in" for larger differences and long-standing animosities as a kind of proxy. Thus, the principle of nonintervention may not be important in itself, but may instead have been a trigger for successive levels of reinforcing responses that create or borrow their own importance.

A second explanation of why UN work on the principle of nonintervention is of such concern to states could stem from a belief on their part that this work actually has concrete consequences that are themselves important. It would be a mistake to assume that new concrete obligations of any note would be created or, for that matter, have already been created by Resolution 2131. Even without addressing the issue of whether General Assembly resolutions can have legal effect in themselves (see Chapter 2), it is arguable that virtually all of the provisions of Resolution 2131 are already part of the law in the form of long-standing customary rules and UN Charter requirements or that they are in the process of becoming prohibited through specification in a multitude of General Assembly resolutions that are widely thought to be a source of new customary rules.

Nor should we assume that states are mistakenly persuaded that new obligations are forthcoming. Rather, it would seem that states are concerned with

character of the principle of nonintervention is expressly affirmed and, second, reference to the principle of self-determination is deleted. The first change obviously reflects the position of non-Western states on the status of the principle of nonintervention, while the second reflects the Western position on its content. Yet, neither change is really substantive in nature since the legal character of the seven principles of friendly relations has always been stipulated (as in the Special Committee's full title) and since the draft declaration also formulates the principle of self-determination and provides that all seven principles are interrelated.

the expression of obligation, whether new or existing, as an instrument of policy. Thus, the work of the UN in this area may be viewed as a context in which the invocation and application of norms is likely to have a constraining effect on behavior. While such norms may not constrain simply by existing or by being brought into existence, statesmen may view their constant reiteration, with all the authority that can be mustered, as doing so. In the instance at hand, seemingly abstract discussions of the content and status of the principle of nonintervention may really be thinly veiled assertions and denials of specific issue-related obligations, which are associated with the idea of intervention more by opportunity than logic and are indeed contended over in a host of forms and contexts, many of them not legal at all.

A third explanation of the importance ascribed to UN efforts to formulate the principle of nonintervention relates to the system function of international law mentioned above and is clarified by distinguishing general principles from substantive rules of international law. General principles of international law individually state aspects of the international system and collectively define its nature. They are only broadly empirical because they tell us what kind of behavior is consistent with the system as defined, but not how much contrary behavior the system can absorb. They are normative only to the degree that they assume the value of maintaining the system's present form. In short, because the principle of nonintervention, as one of these general principles, really refers to the level of intervention consistent with the system, this principle can say nothing concrete about the precise amount, distribution, form, or purpose of any particular state's behavior toward other states.

What general principles do, then, is convey symbolically to all states, and only incidentally to analysts, critical information about the style and scope of relations in the international system. If states are embroiled in a controversy over one such principle, then this could reflect an awareness on their part that symbols and myths are somehow related to the overarching pattern of events in the ongoing system.[39]

Since the general principles of international law state the defining characteristics of the international system, important changes in the system are registered by changes in the manner in which general principles are related to each other and to the substantive rules that constitute the body of international law. Changes sufficiently important to transform the system itself are registered by the disappearance of existing general principles and the

39 This discussion owes much to Coplin's work on the system function of international law. What Coplin has not done, however, is to differentiate between general principles and substantive rules and then identify the former especially with the communication of "assumptions about the state system." See also M. Barkun, *Law without Sanctions: Order in Primitive Societies and the World Community*, New Haven: Yale University Press, 1968, ch. 8, for a discussion of law in all societies, international included, as a "set of interrelated symbols" (p. 151).

emergence of new ones. Historically, the principle of nonintervention has been closely related to, and indeed has been viewed as a corollary of, the principle of sovereignty. Predictably, the Western position in discussions at the UN has been rooted in an attempt to maintain this relationship. Relating nonintervention to sovereignty produces a laissez faire view of the international system: as long as the ability of any number of them to survive is not impaired, all states are equally free to do whatever they please to affect the behavior of other states. The emphasis is on freedom to act instead of freedom from the acts of others. This of course favors the interests of the larger, well-established states, and today many of these are Western.[40]

Much of the action on the principle of nonintervention in the General Assembly has revolved around efforts of non-Western groupings to relate nonintervention to self-determination.[41] These efforts reflect a belief that the level of intervention, or behavior affecting other states' behavior, usually permissible among states, is unacceptable when the states affected are the new and weak states. Until these states have had time to make their positions firm, they are to be protected from the kind of international relations typical of the system. Protecting new states from the usual pressures of other states is clearly analogous to protecting workers and other "small" people through social legislation. As such the principle of nonintervention circumscribes the freedom of all to act by asserting for some freedom from the acts of others. It symbolizes a change in the system because less than viable actors are given an opportunity to consolidate their statehood. The system is not transformed, however, because the traditional laissez faire pattern of behavior is maintained among states that have become or have always been viable.

There have also been a few rather tentative efforts to subsume under the principle of nonintervention a responsibility on the part of individual states not to impede activities sanctioned by the world community through the UN and directed toward the elimination of social and economic problems wherever they occur and, beyond this minimum in the case of states able to afford it, to give material aid in support of these activities. It seems likely that the hardening of positions regarding the place of Resolution 2131 in the Special Committee's work has had the effect of postponing a non-Western thrust in

40 This paragraph and the ones following bear a debt to B.V.A. Röling's suggestive thesis that "sociological change in the community of nations and in the accompanying function and content of the law is comparable to the change on the national level." *International Law in an Expanding World*, Amsterdam: Djambatan (1960), p. 56. Röling developed his thesis, pp. 56–65, in terms of what he called the law of liberty, protective law, and the law of welfare.

41 The term *self-determination* here refers not just to the simple act of decolonization, but more generally to the protection of developing states from neo- and postcolonial influences. For a detailed discussion of the term as used in this sense, with particular reference to UN practice, see V. Van Dyke, "Self-Determination and Minority Rights," *International Studies Quarterly*, vol. 13, 1969, pp. 223–53.

this direction.[42] In time, however, we can expect more serious efforts to begin, and to the extent that they succeed the principle of nonintervention will be associated with a new principle or principles based on cooperation and redistribution at the expense of autonomy and maximized self-interest. This is a way of saying that the principle of sovereignty is not simply rearranged in its relationship with other principles but is in the process of being replaced altogether. New principles of cooperation and redistribution find analogy in the welfare orientation of the modern post-capitalist state.

The appearance of principles defining a world system of welfare redistribution would not imply the immediate disappearance of the traditional laissez faire state system. Rather, there seems to be emerging a period in which logically inconsistent permissive, protective, and redistributive principles coexist as symbolic indicators of an empirical condition. Together they define a mixed, evolving system in which different patterns of behavior prevail at different levels, different times, and in different arenas.[43]

If, indeed, states care deeply about the authoritative formulation of the principle of nonintervention because of its symbolic position in a changing system, we could further ask whether states – since they consist of people – need the psychic support of favorable symbols or myths, particularly as a means of easing the transition from one social reality to another, or whether they feel that the manipulation of symbols and myths is a key to promoting or impeding such a transition. The former belief is surely reflected in the perpetuation of the Commonwealth idea by the UK; the latter is reflected in the Gaullist concept of France's grandeur.

It would seem to follow from the premises of system perspective that symbolic manipulation cannot have decisive effect. In this view the future of the system is determined by a whole range of factors beyond the control of any grouping of states. Only marginally, for small gains and momentary advantage, can the patterns of change be managed. Thus, the attempt by the West to conserve the old system will prove futile, but it can serve to establish positions from which selective and orderly retreat is possible. For the West to retreat rather than risk collapse of negotiations on the principle of nonintervention would mean that the retention of the traditional symbols, though placed in new relationships, would be the most significant feature of the

42 Indicatively, when the Special Committee decided in 1966 to widen the scope of Resolution 2131, but failed to agree on additional points doing so, five Asian-African states proposed as one such addition that "aid and assistance given to peoples under any form of colonial domination" cannot be considered intervention. UN doc. A/AC.125/L.12/Rev.1 and Corr.1, in UN doc. A/6230, para. 278, p. 65.

43 A.A. Fatouros has delineated (and also given due credit to Röling) the emergence of the "two new international legal principles" discussed here, but he has interpreted them in a substantive rather than symbolic sense. "Participation of the New States in the International Legal Order of the Future," in C.E. Black and R.A. Falk (eds), *The Future of the International Legal Order*, vol. 1, Princeton: Princeton University Press, 1969, pp. 364–8, quoting p. 364.

newly formulated principle, not the least for the sense of continuity it would provide in a time of fundamental change. Alternatively, for the West to be unyielding now would mean facing a stronger and more radical challenge in the near future.

In this light it might be noted that at least in regard to the principles of friendly relations among states, the Socialist bloc has already learned to make the best of systemic trends over which it has had little control. Bringing these principles to the UN, the states of the Socialist bloc found that Asian, African, and Latin American states dominated subsequent action. Yet, they took advantage of this development by assuming a subordinate position in a grand coalition of non-Western states and thereby forced Western states to stand alone in the North–South struggle over these principles.[44]

On the other hand, if analytic assumptions were revised to allow system symbols to be conceived of as causal foci rather than trend indicators, then a radically different policy recommendation suggests itself: the West should continue its tenacious fight to retain traditional symbols intact, for the long-run, cumulative impact of the outcome will have a profound bearing on the future course of the system.

It is not the purpose here to resolve the question of what role symbols play in system action, but merely to raise it. There is reason to believe that states are sensitive to this question, even without being conscious of it. Otherwise, we would have to presume that their deep concern with the principle of nonintervention has depended wholly on the escalatory dynamics of a given political process or on the policy use of assertions of obligation. Insofar as all three reasons play some part in explaining what has happened in this one case, they raise questions about the adequacy of recent process and system analyses of law and organization in international relations.

44 B.M. Russett, *Trends in World Politics*, New York: Macmillan, pp. 69 and 83, found this a characteristic maneuver of the Socialist bloc in the case of self-determination issues. Curiously, he identified these issues, along with cold-war issues, as having an East–West dimension in contrast to the North–South dimension of economic development issues. For Russett, the two dimensions are defined by reference not to the substance or source of issues facing the General Assembly but to the voting patterns they elicit. Thus, the commitment to, and leadership for, General Assembly action on self-determination (and the principles of friendly relations) comes from the South, not East; the dominant voting pattern pits a tactically created coalition of South and East against the West. For the conventional view that self-determination is a North–South issue, see Claude, *The Changing United Nations*, pp. 54–6.

4 Further thoughts on a new source of international law: Professor D'Amato's "Manifest Intent" (1971)

My first opportunity to engage in the discussion of an important theoretical matter in a highly visible forum took the form of responding to Richard Falk's position on the quasi-legislative competence of the General Assembly. Since I believed that the progressive development of international law – to borrow a phrase from the UN Charter – depended on conceptual clarity, the challenge had been to respond cogently and yet constructively. I felt that I had risen to the occasion and looked forward to doing so again. I did not have long to wait. When the *American Journal of International Law* published Anthony D'Amato's comment on the relevance of the 1969 World Court Judgment in the *North Sea Continental Shelf Cases* to the conceptualization of customary law, I saw that the Court's Judgment and D'Amato's comment could shed light on the possible emergence of an entirely *new* source of international law – a turn of phrase I had used only once and in passing in my earlier comment. Here, the challenge was bringing Falk's and D'Amato's concerns together to show that something new and important really was in the works.

Whether I met the challenge is another matter. The *Journal*'s editors published the piece substantially unchanged. Any claim of novelty is a rhetorical ploy designed to attract attention. The failure of this essay to prompt a response of any kind suggests two possibilities: (1) Drawing fine distinctions and assessing implications struck others as an unduly scholastic exercise best met with silence; (2) Identifying a trend in complex developments struck others as premature and unduly speculative – just the sort of wishful thinking best met with silence. Enduring silence supports the second possibility without precluding the first.

In a recent number of this *Journal* (Chapter 2 above), I examined Professor Richard Falk's position on the quasi-legislative competence of the UN General Assembly, which turned out to be an amalgam of two rather contradictory positions.[1] On the one hand, Falk was disposed to view some General

1 "On the Quasi-Legislative Competence of the General Assembly," *American Journal of International Law*, vol. 60, 1966, pp. 782–91. For a more recent, quite elaborate presentation

Assembly resolutions "as evidence of a general practice accepted as law," to use the familiar language of the Statute of the International Court of Justice referring to international custom (article 38, para. 1b). Yet, on the other hand, Falk simultaneously propounded a position that went far beyond the terms of article 38 and most writings on the subject by positing the existence of a new source of international law to explain the apparent legal effect of certain General Assembly resolutions. Beyond illustrating the confusion in Professor Falk's work on this important and increasingly discussed topic, the point of my comment was to show that the radical position, however appealing, was subject to one overriding difficulty. That difficulty was the absence of a legally expressed consensus of the world community on the existence of this new source of international law, a consensus of this overarching nature being requisite if any new source were to be brought into being. It is a matter of some irony that the problem is one of consensus, in view of Falk's argument that consensuses on specific issues give rise to new rules of law. There are two conceptually and empirically distinct levels of consensus that have to be taken into account.

In a subsequent number of the journal in which Falk's and my essays appeared, Professor Anthony D'Amato, dealing with the seemingly unrelated question of the generation of customary international law through treaties,[2] has actually, if inadvertently, cast additional light on the possibility of a new source of law. In this essay, I summarize D'Amato's principal arguments and then relate them to Falk's views and my own, with an eye to drawing some more general conclusions.

D'Amato has isolated from the recent judgment of the International Court of Justice in the *North Sea Continental Shelf Cases* certain identifying characteristics of treaty provisions, which "generate customary law," or, in the Court's language, have "a fundamentally norm-creating character such as could be regarded as forming the basis for a general rule of law."[3] First, such norms are ascertainable by virtue of what we might call structural characteristics of the treaty containing them. Specifically, the provisions in question must be so cast as to be generalizable, and there must be signs of their being set apart from non-generalizable provisions of the same treaty. Second, the identification of such norms does not depend on their meeting the traditional tests for determining the existence of a customary rule of law. Therefore, the number of parties to the treaty is irrelevant, as is the treaty's duration or

of this position, see R.A. Falk, "An Argument to Expand the Traditional Sources of International Law – With Special Reference to the Facts of the South West Africa Cases," in Falk, *The Status of Law in International Society*, Princeton: Princeton University Press, 1970, pp. 126–73.

2 A. D'Amato, "Manifest Intent and the Generation by Treaty of Customary Rules of International Law," *American Journal of International Law*, vol. 64, 1970, pp. 892–902.

3 Quoted ibid., p. 895. The Court's judgment is reprinted in *American Journal of International Law*, vol. 63, 1969, pp. 591–631; *International Legal Materials*, vol. 8, 1969, pp. 340–85.

the extent of subsequent state practice.[4] While it is not absolutely clear whether scholarly or juridical acknowledgment is required, the answer would seem to be no; the Court's acknowledgment that such norms might exist is important only in assisting theoretical appreciation of the phenomenon of general norms actually being generated through treaties.

Obviously, no little confusion arises when D'Amato and the Court itself describe general norms arising from treaty provisions as "customary."[5] If the traditional requirements for the existence of customary law are irrelevant – and D'Amato faulted the Court for raising them as "make-weight arguments"[6] – then such law simply cannot be customary. If, however, the word *customary* is used synonymously with the word *general* because historically the only general rules we had were customary, then the usage is misleading, albeit understandable. In theory, there is no a priori reason to suppose that all general norms are or must be customary in character, and to suppose this as an actuality obscures the very real difference between general norms created through treaty provisions and customary law as traditionally understood.

If general norm-creating treaty provisions are not customary, what are they? Wolfgang Friedmann has suggested that they might be general principles of law.[7] These are not general principles recognized by civilized nations, but "general principles of customary international law," which in turn are indistinguishable from ordinary rules of customary law.[8] Friedmann then imputed to the Court the view that the general norms on the continental shelf reflected in articles 1 to 3 of the 1958 Geneva Convention on the Continental Shelf are actually rapidly precipitated or "instant" custom.[9] This would mean that, in the Court's view, the traditional requirements for the existence of customary law are not at all irrelevant; on the contrary, they have been met with exceptional speed and uniformity. And if Friedmann is right in his interpretation of the judgment, then D'Amato's arguments, and the implications drawn from them here, are simply wrong. I will return to this problem at a later point.

4 D'Amato, "Manifest Intent and the Generation by Treaty of Customary Rules of International Law," pp. 895–9.

5 Judgment, *North Sea Continental Shelf Cases*, paras. 71, 74.

6 D'Amato, "Manifest Intent and the Generation by Treaty of Customary Rules of International Law," p. 898.

7 W. Friedmann, "The North Sea Continental Shelf Cases – A Critique," *American Journal of International Law*, vol. 64, 1970, p. 231.

8 Ibid. But see pp. 231 n. 6 and 234 n. 12, in which Friedmann seems to regard custom and general principles as distinct if not easily distinguished sources of law.

9 Ibid., pp. 232–3. See also the careful analysis of R.R. Baxter, "Treaties and Custom," *Recueil des cours de L'Académie de droit international de La Haye*, vol. 129, 1970/I, pp. 57–69. In his dissenting opinion, Judge ad hoc Sørensen expressly adopted the argument of rapidly emerging custom, while candidly admitting that "the word 'custom' with its traditional time connotation, may not be an adequate expression for the purpose of describing this particular source of international law." *International Legal Materials*, p. 427.

As they are usually understood, general principles of law recognized by civilized nations might still be seen as figuring, at least implicitly, in the Court's judgment. In particular, the Court dealt with the equidistance principle articulated in article 6 of the Continental Shelf Convention in terms of equity, naturalness, and reasonableness. Yet the Court was obliged to think in just these terms because it had specifically rejected article 6, and the equidistance principle, as a general norm, in contradistinction to articles 1–3 of the same convention.[10] The Court must be seen, then, as invoking general principles not as a source of law, but as an alternative to law.[11]

If general norm-creating treaty provisions are neither customary law nor general principles, however these two categories are construed, the question remains: What are they? The most appropriate answer is that they are akin to those resolutions of the General Assembly which manifestly are intended to have legal effect in themselves. Falk has noted the importance of language in assessing the legal impact of General Assembly resolutions.[12] Operationally, a concern for language means verifying the presence of two structural characteristics that all general norm-creating resolutions must possess. The first is generality of language (obviously making such resolutions generalizable) and the second a declaratory format (differentiating them from other resolutions).[13] That these characteristics parallel those that D'Amato ascribes to general norm-creating treaty provisions goes almost without saying.

Additionally, Falk established certain contextual characteristics, that is, characteristics relating to their adoption and subsequent reception, which these resolutions must equally possess. They must be adopted overwhelmingly, or at least by a two-thirds majority with all major powers and groups represented. And there must be some pattern of support subsequent to their adoption. This need not be the systematic and enduring practice required for the formation of customary law. Rather, the combination of frequent, favorable citation in forums such as the General Assembly and infrequent contrary practice would probably suffice. Resolutions meeting these conditions express a consensus of the world community on specific issues which, to Falk's mind, is a source of obligation and thus of law.[14]

10 Judgment, *North Sea Continental Shelf Cases*, paras. 60–73.

11 This was Friedmann's opinion also, although the Court attempted to create a contrary impression. "The North Sea Continental Shelf Cases," pp. 234–6.

12 Falk, "On the Quasi-Legislative Competence of the General Assembly," pp. 785–6.

13 Conventionally, writers have accounted for the existence of these characteristics by assuming that the General Assembly was merely restating existing law. See, for example, J. Castaneda, *Legal Effects of United Nations Resolutions*, trans. by A. Amoia, New York: Columbia University Press, 1969, pp. 168–71. While this position eliminates the need to attribute legal effect to resolutions directly, it ignores the fact that the content of many of these resolutions is deliberately innovative and could not possibly have acquired legal effect through the operation of custom.

14 Falk, "On the Quasi-Legislative Competence of the General Assembly," pp. 787–90, 784–5.

While Falk tried to relax the traditional requirements of customary law formation to embrace these consensuses,[15] he need not have bothered to do so. All norms emanating from a given source of law display a set of common characteristics not displayed by norms arising from any other source. If the legal effect of General Assembly resolutions can arise only from the operation of custom, then it is necessary to relax the requirements of customary law formation or, at best, only one or two of these resolutions will have the necessary characteristics to qualify. If, on the other hand, a new source of law is responsible for the legal effect of certain General Assembly resolutions, then the stringent, consent-oriented characteristics of customary law are simply irrelevant (unless one wishes to demonstrate that there also exist customary rules of identical content). Furthermore, the invocation of customary law requirements impedes the scholar's task of verifying characteristics whose presence is required by a new, consensus-oriented source of law.

Unlike Falk, D'Amato was not concerned with the problem of consensus.[16] Yet the problem should not be ignored in the case of general norm-creating treaty provisions and can actually usefully be dealt with in Falk's terms. The forum for expression of community consensuses is not the General Assembly, but rather ad hoc international conferences called for the purpose of concluding multilateral treaties. Such conferences frequently involve dozens of states representing all segments of the community and have rules of decision comparable to those of the General Assembly. For decisions of conferences to generate law, they must have both the structural characteristics already discussed and, we can easily see, the additional contextual characteristics of participation of all major powers and groups in their adoption and of subsequent favorable reception in the community.

When the "conditions of requisite formality and consensus" are met either for General Assembly resolutions or treaty provisions (actually, conference decisions that become treaty provisions), we can rightfully say that one of two general requirements for a legal obligation to exist, namely, its effectiveness, have been met.[17] This leaves, however, the requirement of legitimacy, through which a putative norm is related to the legal order as a whole. Neither Falk nor D'Amato touched on this matter at all.

The matter can be resolved, as indicated above, by asking if there is an overarching consensus of the world community that community consensuses on substantive issues displaying specified characteristics can have legal effect in themselves. Were an overarching consensus of this kind given a fully legal expression through an existing source of law, this would be a grant

15 Falk was quite explicit about doing this in "An Argument to Expand the Traditional Sources of International Law," pp. 153–61.

16 D'Amato has treated the problem of consensus elsewhere: "On Consensus," *Canadian Yearbook of International Law*, vol. 8, 1970, pp. 104–22.

17 Quoting R.A. Falk, "The New States and the International Legal Order," *Recueil des cours de L'Académie de droit international de La Haye*, vol. 118, 1966/II, p. 42.

of legitimacy, not for a given community action, but for a class of community actions that can thus be said to constitute a source of law.

My argument in the case of General Assembly resolutions (Chapter 2 above) was that there is no such overarching community consensus because of the position adopted by Western states in the General Assembly. In the case of what are claimed to be general norm-creating treaty provisions, however, the answer is not so clearly negative. This is because the authoritative voice of the International Court of Justice, speaking, as it were, for the international community, seems to have affirmed the legitimacy of these general norms created outside the conventional sources of international law. And this is another way of saying that the World Court is helping to legitimate a new source of law. This new source is seen in specific relation to general norm-creating treaty provisions, but it has been argued here that the latter are part of a generic class of community actions, which also include certain General Assembly resolutions. Thus, the legitimating impact of the Court's judgment may be imputed to the class of actions as a whole, obviously including the specified General Assembly resolutions. If this were done, the problem that this writer raised in connection with Falk's work would be substantially solved – the consensus of the world community granting legal effect to consensuses on substantive issues bearing certain attributes may actually have been articulated by the International Court of Justice.

This is not to say that the Court has created a new source of international law. Nor is it to say that a community consensus, as reflected by the Court in a given judgment, has created a new source all by itself. What I am saying is that a community consensus to the effect that there should be a new source can create that new source if it is legally expressed. While the Court cannot give legal expression to a consensus of this kind, it can voice that consensus so persuasively and authoritatively that a truly legal expression is rapidly forthcoming through the operation of an existing source of law.

It is well known that the immediate affirmation of a landmark decision of the International Court of Justice can yield a new rule in a short period of time. One such rule of law is the straight baseline method of delimiting the point from which the territorial sea is measured, as propounded by the Court in its 1951 Judgment in the *Anglo-Norwegian Fisheries Case*.[18] There is no difference at all between this process as it relates to the generation of specific rules and the generation of a new source of international law, since the vehicle for a new source is a specific rule stating the nature and requirements of the new source in question.

It is not a foregone conclusion that a judgment of the Court, even when it deals with an unsettled area of the law, will have a decisive impact on the development of specific rules. It may happen that the Court's conclusions are significantly out of step with community preferences. If the Court has not

18 Reprinted in *American Journal of International Law*, vol. 46, 1952, p. 348–70.

stepped too far ahead, then it should be able to lead the community through the cogency and reasonableness of its arguments, so that a consensus is formed around the Court's judgment rather than simply reflected in it. In the instance of the *North Sea Continental Shelf Cases*, we might ask whether a split Court (11–6), in which only six judges are directly associated with the judgment, can ever crystallize a community-wide consensus. Without answering the question in principle, it should be noted that none of the separate concurring or dissenting opinions openly questioned the radical implications of the judgment. On the contrary, the dissenting opinions of Judges Vladimir Koretsky and Manfred Lachs reinforced the radical position.[19] Furthermore, in view of the conservative tendencies of Western states in matters of international law, it is significant that three of the six judges associated with the judgment itself are from Western states.

In the *North Sea Continental Shelf Cases*, a more serious problem for the Court as consensus builder is the highly ambiguous character of crucial passages of the judgment. We saw above how much at variance D'Amato's radical interpretation is with Friedmann's more conventional one. Possibly the Court itself was unclear on the doctrinal subtleties of its judgment and so inadvertently gave support to both arguments, however contradictory, in successive sentences. A careful reading of the text is not persuasive one way or the other.[20] Friedmann does seem to be right in saying that the Court addressed the matter of sources "almost casually."[21] This alone weakens the authority and persuasiveness of the Court's judgment and lessens the credibility of the radical doctrine that D'Amato adduces from that judgment.

19 *International Legal Materials*, pp. 400–3 (Koretsky) and pp. 419–21 (Lachs). Both held that article 6 of the Continental Shelf Convention was part of general international law. In so arguing, Lachs abjured use of the word *custom*, while Koretsky said the following (p. 400):

> One may ask whether these principles are or have become an institution of international law either as general principles developed in relation to the continental shelf, or as an embodiment of international custom. There are sufficient grounds for considering them to qualify in both these ways, but I am inclined to consider them as principles of general international law, seeing that established doctrine lays much stress on the time factor as a criterion of whether a given principle belongs to customary international law: by and large, customary international law turns its face to the past while general international law keeps abreast of the times, conveying a sense of today and the near future by absorbing the basic progressive principles of international law as soon as they are developed.

Friedmann, "The North Sea Continental Shelf Cases," p. 234 n. 12, completely missed the point of these remarks of Koretsky's by taking them to affirm general principles of law recognized by civilized nations as a source of law.

20 See especially paras. 71–7. Actually, only the one sentence from para. 71 quoted by D'Amato (and above) is unambiguous in its language. It alone hardly gives credibility to D'Amato's claim that "the Court for the first time gave explicit, and indeed overwhelming, substantiation of the thesis that provisions in treaties can generate customary law, that they can be of a 'norm-creating character.' " "Manifest Intent and the Generation by Treaty of Customary Rules of International Law," pp. 894–5.

21 Friedmann, "The North Sea Continental Shelf Cases," p. 232. For a contrary view, see Baxter, "Treaties and Custom," p. 33.

All of this means that the judgment can only be viewed as the first small step toward the legitimation of a new source of law. The next step is a willingness on the part of legal scholars, and then state spokesmen, to accept D'Amato's interpretation and its implications, thus endowing the judgment of the Court with a retroactive clarity and force. If there is a willingness to applaud the Court's judgment while interpreting it in a radical sense, then eventually we may have an identifiable community consensus, expressed through an existing source of law (custom as precipitated by a landmark decision of the International Court of Justice) that all other consensuses of a certain character create general norms.

Any meaningful follow-up to the Court's first tentative step in this direction is itself dependent on clearing up the present web of terminological confusion. Only then will there be a common perception of the issue as one even warranting a major response from the scholarly community. With this in mind, it is worth suggesting that an incipient new source of law deserves a name of its own, hopefully breaking the spell that custom seems to have on writers. The traditional, commonsense meaning of *custom* has increasingly been stretched and distorted, first by the idea of its rapid, almost instantaneous creation and now by the idea of its creation through intentioned behavior. In order to accommodate these aberrations in the original concept, "a general theory of how customary law comes into being" becomes in fact a partial theory of law-creation in general, the consistency, clarity, and economy of which as a theory is severely jeopardized by an unnecessary attachment to the concept of custom.[22]

If the new source, whether incipient or only imagined, deserves a distinctive name, D'Amato's notion of manifest intent seems to express the most distinctive feature of this source. If the new source is manifest intent, the law to which it gives rise also deserves a name, and one that refers as well to the other distinctive feature of this law – its origins in an organized community forum. Hence, we might call it "manifest community law."

Beyond this preliminary operation of acknowledging the distinctive character of a new kind of law with distinctive labels, an appropriate second operation might well be to inventory those rules that would constitute this new kind of law. Conceivably, some rules have been around a long time without their distinctiveness ever having been recognized. Examples might be the *règlement* on diplomatic ranks contained in the Protocol of the Congress of Vienna (1815), the Declaration of Paris (1856), or, less plausibly, the Geneva Protocol (1925).[23] Even Chapter XI of the UN Charter might be

22 Quoting D'Amato, "Manifest Intent and the Generation by Treaty of Customary Rules of International Law," p. 901.

23 Although General Assembly Resolution 2603A (XXIV), December 16, 1969 (*American Journal of International Law*, vol. 64, 1970, p. 393), affirmed that "the Geneva Protocol embodies generally recognized rules of international law," with no specific mention of their customary

viewed this way, as might many of the formal emanations of the Inter-American system, the latter being understood as manifest regional community law. D'Amato suggested that some provisions of the other three 1958 Geneva Conventions on the Law of the Sea might qualify,[24] as would some provisions of many other UN sponsored multilateral conventions. And, of course, most of those resolutions of the General Assembly entitled "declarations" would also qualify.[25]

The procedure for determining the rules of manifest community law is simply the application of D'Amato's and Falk's checklists of characteristics. In practice, intent is not likely to be so manifest as D'Amato assumed. Nor, as Falk wisely insisted, is the use of "mechanical requirements" always adequate for determining the existence of a consensus.[26] Yet none of the tasks for ascertaining the existence of manifest community law is likely to be as subjective as the ones associated with the identification of customary law. In the latter instance, the intervention of the scholar has been so characteristic that "the teachings of the most highly qualified publicists" have been institutionalized as a subsidiary source of law.

Once we get beyond the speculative stage and can point to a body of rules that could reasonably be manifest community law, we can legitimately begin to think that such law exists. After all, in the history of international law, only when concrete rules of customary law began to be identified, was it clear that international law was a reality and not just a metaphysical postulate.

character, the Geneva Protocol nonetheless fails the test of manifest intent. Widespread reservations stipulating reciprocity as a condition for the Protocol's operation effectively deny a generalizing intent. For details on these reservations, see R.R. Baxter and T. Buergenthal, "Legal Aspects of the Geneva Protocol of 1925," *American Journal of International Law*, vol. 64, 1970, pp. 869–70.

24 D'Amato, "Manifest Intent and the Generation by Treaty of Customary Rules of International Law," p. 898.

25 One exception would be Resolution 1653 (XVI), November 28, 1961, declaring against the use of nuclear weapons. Neither the US nor the Soviet Union voted in favor of this resolution.

26 Falk, "On the Quasi-Legislative Competence of the General Assembly," p. 788.

5 Peremptory norms of international law: their source, function and future (1973, with Richard K. Birney)

Some few rules of international law are said to have an importance markedly exceeding that of other rules and formal properties marking their importance. Such rules, which are generally referred to as peremptory norms or *jus cogens*, only exist if there is a generally accepted *category* to which they could be assigned. Yet to say that there are different categories of international legal rules – *kinds* of international law – is a tendentious claim given the prevailing theoretical disposition to regard international law as differentiated by the source and scope of its rules, but not their weight or rank. Furthermore, we might plausibly guess that significant political differences lie behind theoretical disagreements on this issue. The 1960s had seen a good deal of theoretical discussion, largely because the UN's International Law Commission, in providing for the possibility of peremptory norms, built the category into the framework for a multilateral treaty on the law of treaties.

Having considered peremptory norms as a theoretical issue with my graduate students, one of them joined me in writing a paper relating such norms to the functionally defined categories of international law that I had already developed in earlier work (Chapters 3 and 4 above). There was nothing even remotely like this in the literature. While we had no single piece of work from such scholars as Richard Falk and Anthony D'Amato to engage and build upon, I conceived of the project as complementing my comments in the *American Journal of International Law*. After the *Journal*'s editors rejected the paper as dense and inaccessible, I expanded the discussions of functions and submitted the paper elsewhere. Occasional citations suggest that a few legal scholars may have understood the argument.

Peremptory norms of international law (*jus cogens*) have been the subject of much recent interest.[1] In light of their extensive and quite unprecedented

1 V. Paul called it "one of the most discussed and controversial questions in the theory of international law today." "The Legal Consequences of Conflict between a Treaty and an Imperative Norm of General International Law (*jus cogens*): Critical Appreciation of Article 61 of the Draft Articles on the Law of Treaties Prepared by the International Law Commission," *Österreichische Zeitschrift für offentliches Recht*, vol. 22, 1971, p. 19.

treatment by the International Law Commission and the Vienna Conference on the Law of Treaties, it may be surprising that attention has not been greater.[2] At the same time, inquiry into the relationship between peremptory norms and the sources and functions of international law has been virtually nonexistent.[3] This is indeed surprising, given the recent substantial interest in these areas as part of a larger "theoretical explosion" in international legal studies.[4]

In the following pages, we propose to examine the conceptual ramifications of the simple question: What is the source of peremptory norms? Further, we propose to use this conceptual examination to shed some light on certain profound, but only dimly perceived, trends that are currently at work in the international legal order. We do not intend to undertake a systematic examination of purported peremptory norms. Instead, our interest is focused on peremptory norms as a *category* of norms with an identifiable source and a distinctive function to perform in the international legal order of today's world.

Precisely why the source and function of peremptory norms have gained so little attention is a matter that deserves consideration. The idea that some norms are "higher" than other norms in the international legal order has enjoyed a considerable revival in recent decades. Many writers believe that peremptory norms are the concrete form taken by higher law.[5] As a matter of definition, peremptory norms are those that cannot be changed except by norms of a comparable status. All other norms can be changed by subsequent treaty or customary practice. The difference is such as to encourage the inference that peremptory norms have their origin in a higher natural order and that our knowledge of them is received directly. The law-making procedures of the community would simply be one available means for articulating and formalizing norms whose existence is independent of and antecedent to the perception of their existence.

Given the inherent nature of peremptory norms, their status would not be affected by imperfect adherence to established law-making procedures while

2 For an exhaustive set of citations on the relevant deliberations of the International Law Commission and the Vienna Conference, see S. Rosenne, *The Law of Treaties: A Legislative History of the Vienna Convention* (1970), pp. 290–3. Paul's research uncovered approximately a dozen articles on the subject during the last decade. "The Legal Consequences of Conflict between a Treaty and an Imperative Norm of General International Law (*jus cogens*)," pp. 22–3 nn.13–15.

3 The principal exception seems to be M. Virally, "Reflexions sur le '*jus cogens*,' " *Annuaire Français de droit international*, vol. 12, 1966, pp. 19–29.

4 A.A. D'Amato, *The Concept of Custom in International Law*, Ithaca: Cornell University Press, 1971, p. xii.

5 A good example is A. Verdross, "Jus Dispositivum and Jus Cogens in International Law," *American Journal of International Law*, vol. 60, 1966, p. 55.

they are being articulated. Their emanation from such forums as the UN General Assembly does not circumvent existing sources of international law or suggest the emergence of a new source. It merely indicates that the General Assembly is one likely place for the collective awareness of such norms to be concretized. Even if there is significant resistance in some quarters to the particular formulation adopted by the community as a whole, such that the emergence of an ordinary rule of law would be prevented, we would assume that either the formulation itself is defective or the capacity of some participants in the legal order to see the higher quality of such norms is blocked by narrow prejudice. The peremptory norm is not actually prevented from existing because of that resistance. This line of reasoning would see any concern for the formal source of peremptory norms as falsely conceived in its reference to the sources of ordinary positive norms, and any concern for their material source as properly a matter of metaphysical rather than legal inquiry.

As in most metaphysical matters, it is impossible to prove that peremptory norms are not the substance of higher law. The inclination to view them in this manner is understandable in light of recent history and certainly helps to explain the fascination that the concept of peremptory norms holds for some scholars. Conversely, it is no easier to demonstrate that peremptory norms are superior because they are part of the natural order. However, even in the strictly positivist view, there is nothing in the logic of law or the structure of legal orders to prevent some norms from being given a superior status. On the contrary, this is one frequent configuration in a structurally differentiated legal order. Differentiation is an inevitable accompaniment to social complexity. It means that norms are divided into groups that are distinguishable in terms of some attribute, such as source, scope, conditions of bindingness and validity or, most notably, function. Structures differentiated by function promote, but by no means guarantee, improved performance of functions.

Although the identification of peremptory norms of international law as a distinctive category indicates a differentiated legal order, one is not forced to conclude on this basis alone that peremptory norms are superior to ordinary rules. Actually, their differentiated, putatively superior status is not demonstrable by reference to level of compliance or other empirical criteria. Their status must be inferred from the stipulation that peremptory norms are not subject to derogation by ordinary norms. This could be a way of classifying peremptory norms as superior to other norms, but it could also mean that peremptory norms are simply unrelated to other norms. In fact, their status and substance are in no way dependent on changes in the substance of ordinary rules because they are doing something in the legal order upon which ordinary rules have little bearing.

On inspection, then, what appears to be a hierarchically arranged legal order could be something quite different, that is, a legal order in which different kinds of law seem to be of differing importance because of the functions they perform. Although individual peremptory norms seem to have a *content* intrinsically more important than ordinary rules, it may actually be that they perform a *function* more vital to the workings of the legal order than do the overriding number of individual norms not designated as peremptory. If peremptory norms have nothing to do with ordinary rules in terms of their operation and yet seem to be superior because of their function, this is not to say that either kind is more legal in character than the other. Both kinds of norms are equally legal because they arise from a legally designated source of international law and are stated as law, no matter what function they perform in the legal order.

Norms in the international legal order can be arranged in different categories to serve different purposes if nation-states, as the major participants in the order, choose to have it that way. Peremptory norms are one category intended to be set apart from the bulk of norms making up the legal order. Furthermore, since nation-states can and do decide what the law shall be, the creation of peremptory norms is subject to the same rules of lawmaking as any valid norm. Finally, the process of acquiring legal status is identical to the process of acquiring a peremptory nature. The two processes may take place independently, as in cases where long-standing norms become peremptory at a later date, but they operate in the same way. This means simply that they operate in conformity with the requirements of one of the several modes in which the international community creates its norms. In short, peremptory norms, whether in becoming norms or in becoming peremptory or both, must be considered in terms of the sources of international law.

For our purposes the most salient feature of peremptory norms is their *general* nature. Thus, the Vienna Convention on the Law of Treaties as well as the literature treats peremptory norms as general in character. In the language of article 53 of the Vienna Convention:

> A treaty is void if, at the time of its conclusion, it conflicts with a peremptory norm of general international law. For the purposes of the present Convention, a peremptory norm of international law is a norm accepted and recognized by the community of States as a whole as a norm from which no derogation is permitted and which can be modified only by a subsequent norm of general international law having the same character.[6]

One of the stock assertions of international law texts is that general international law has its source in custom, whereas conventions yield particular international law, that is, law whose binding effect is restricted to the parties. Of course, a convention with a great many parties may well be regarded as

6 Convention on the Law of Treaties, May 22, 1969, conveniently found in *American Journal of International Law*, vol. 63, 1969, pp 875–903.

expressing rules of general international law, but what has happened is that the terms of the convention are coextensive with customary law. Such law may have already existed, with the convention merely a declaratory expression of it, or it may have arisen in response to wide adherence to the convention and a community-wide appreciation of its salience in the relations of all states.[7]

It should also be noted that the source identified in article 38 of the Statute of the International Court of Justice as "general principles of law recognized by civilized nations" would by definition yield rules of general international law. Without entering into the perennial doctrinal disputes over general principles as a source of international law, we might observe that there are very few specific norms actually attributable to this source and those few seem generally to be procedural guidelines for international tribunals. As such, it is unlikely that they would be viewed as having a peremptory character. Insofar as norms relating to the substance of interstate relations may be identified with general principles of law, the operative source is likely to be custom, doubtless structured by community responsiveness to the relevant general principles. Certainly in the instance of peremptory norms customary factors will have been brought to bear in their formation.

One might conclude, then, that peremptory norms are necessarily customary in character. The fact that those actual norms commonly asserted to be peremptory typically find their definitive formulation in the provisions of such conventions as the UN Charter does not mean that those provisions are themselves peremptory. It means only that there exist identical customary norms that are peremptory. The moment at which such norms come into existence or acquire full cogency is not something that can be determined by reference either to the convention or the manner of its conclusion. Thus, when we are told that "a new norm of the character of *jus cogens* may appear in the form of a treaty or custom,"[8] we would be inclined to regard this as a convenient shorthand description of a more subtle process in which the terms of a convention can codify norms that have already acquired a peremptory nature or are in the process of doing so. The process of codification, by focusing community attention on the importance of the norms in question, may be empirically related to the process of acquiring cogency, but the two are analytically separable.

The principal difficulty with this position arises in connection with the concluding words of article 53: "a peremptory norm . . . can be modified only

7 The relation of conventions to customary law formation is thoroughly presented in R.R. Baxter, "Treaties and Custom," *Recueil des cours de L'Académie de droit international de La Haye*, vol. 129, 1970/I, pp. 31–104, and D'Amato, *The Concept of Custom in International Law*, pp. 103–66.

8 Paul, "The Legal Consequences of Conflict between a Treaty and an Imperative Norm of General International Law (*jus cogens*)," p. 42

by a subsequent norm having the same character." This entirely reasonable proposition indicates that peremptory norms are subject to alteration only through the emergence of new norms with the same overriding character but a different content.[9] Yet in the instance of norms that emerge by way of custom, such a development is hardly conceivable. In order for any established peremptory norm ever to be changed through subsequent contrary practice, there would have to be a full display of cogency in what is only a nascent, just discernible normative pattern. Without manifest cogency, legal effect would be denied as a matter of course. If, nonetheless, the normative pattern persisted and gathered cogency over time, it would have to be admitted that the prior norm was not peremptory after all but merely mistaken as such. As one writer put it: "to change a valid norm of *jus cogens* by means of a custom seems to be impossible in most cases, as any act, contrary to *jus cogens*, would be incompatible with it and unlawfull [sic]."[10]

On the few occasions in which anyone has addressed this problem, the proffered solution is simple enough. The International Law Commission, in its commentary on the draft articles on the law of treaties, noted that "a modification of a rule of *jus cogens* would today most probably be effected through a general multilateral treaty."[11] Similarly, Vladimir Paul observed that changing a peremptory norm "seems to be possible only by a subsequent treaty."[12] This is, however, a bogus solution, since conventions do not create peremptory norms in their own right. If we accept the usual understanding of the term *general international law*, this conclusion is inescapable.

This line of reasoning, with its logically unacceptable outcome, should cause us to re-examine the initial premise that custom alone can yield norms of general international law. There has in fact been a minor flurry of discussion on this very issue, revolving around the apparent fact that at least some provisions of some multilateral conventions become general norms very rapidly, even "instantaneously," or indeed may be general norms from the

9 S.A. Riesenfeld, would disagree.

> Certainly a peremptory norm might be subject to replacement by a non-peremptory norm. The rule accomplishing this change in status would itself be non-peremptory. The essential question is, how widespread the international acceptance of such a *capitis diminutio* would have to be.

"*Jus Dispositivum* and *Jus Cogens* in International Law: In Light of the Recent Decision of the German Supreme Constitutional Court," *American Journal of International Law*, vol. 60, 1966, p. 514.

10 Paul, "The Legal Consequences of Conflict between a Treaty and an Imperative Norm of General International Law (*jus cogens*)," p. 43.

11 Report of the International Law Commission on the Second Part of its Seventeenth Session, January 3–28, 1966, and on its Eighteenth Session, May 4–July 19, 1966, reprinted in *American Journal of International Law*, vol. 61, 1967, p. 411.

12 Paul, "The Legal Consequences of Conflict between a Treaty and an Imperative Norm of General International Law (*jus cogens*)," p. 42.

outset.[13] Calling such norms customary, as is usually done, distorts the concept of custom almost beyond recognition. Alternatively, one of the present writers has argued (in Chapter 4 above) the conceptual utility of viewing these norms as products of a new and distinctive source of international law.

The putative new source is identified with certain outcomes of community-wide forums like the General Assembly and ad hoc international conferences called to conclude multilateral conventions. When these outcomes – whether resolutions or convention provisions – are set apart from other outcomes of the same forum by being formal in language, distinctively labeled or not susceptible to reservation, and when they are overwhelmingly supported, they reflect an intent of the participants to create direct and immediate obligations for all members of the community. At a more abstract level, we are suggesting that an increasingly complex and institutionalized international system has, or will soon have, both the need and the means for a more nearly legislative form of law-making than presently exists.

Two things prevent this new source from becoming a reality: (1) the resistance displayed by Western statesmen, who see it as a threat to their historic control over international law; and (2) its concomitant lack of expression in a legal vehicle, which would establish its formal validity.[14] Western acquiescence would surely result in rapid validation of the new source through expression in a rule arising from an existing source. Continued resistance of the West makes validation highly unlikely in the short run, since the embodiment of a new source in general law implies a supportive consensus that includes all major groups of states. Nonetheless, pressure for legal expression can build up gradually, with the point being conceded piecemeal by states unwilling to accept it outright. This has always been the way customary law emerges in situations of mixed or inconsistent practice and, barring a major change of heart in the West, must be the specific method by which a rule providing for the formal validity of a new source will arise. It should be emphasized, however, that it is a process involving a lengthy, if indeterminate, passage of time.

There are scattered signs of the first tentative movement toward legal

13 Much of this discussion is occasioned by the 1969 judgment and other opinions of the International Court of Justice in the *North Sea Continental Shelf Cases*, reprinted in *International Legal Materials*, vol. 8, 1969, pp. 340–433. In addition to the several opinions in that case, see Baxter,"Treaties and Custom," pp. 57–74; D'Amato, *The Concept of Custom in International Law*, pp. 103–12; D'Amato, "Manifest Intent and the Generation by Treaty of Customary Rules of International Law," *American Journal of International Law*, vol. 64, 1970, pp. 892–902.

14 Chapter 2 examines this claim more fully. See L.F.E. Goldie, "The North Sea Continental Shelf Cases – A Ray of Hope for the International Court?" *New York Law Journal*, vol. 16, 1970, p. 344, for a critique of the concern for formal validity, as displayed in this essay, and a brilliant characterization of processes that exceed in density and self-consciousness the processes whereby practice consolidates into customary law. To Goldie, they yield a law different enough from anything we have had until now to be called "international common law." This of course is the law whose source is described here in briefer, more general terms.

expression of such a new source. Simply in their perception of it, certain publicists are contributing to that movement. More importantly, at the public level the International Court of Justice in its 1969 Judgment on the *North Sea Continental Shelf Cases* gave some support, however ambiguous, to the idea.[15] Some of the dissenting opinions in those cases did so less ambiguously. Further, the formulation of article 53 of the Vienna Convention on the Law of Treaties can be adduced to support the notion that a new source of general norms is emerging. The important thing here is that a large number of states, including many Western states, have joined in an authoritative statement whose terms can be seen to imply the operation of a new source in what is admittedly a restricted context. That context is of course the production of peremptory norms. While the source of peremptory norms where none existed previously is not delimited in this fashion, it seems quite likely that they too will arise from this new source.

More specifically, either new peremptory norms are generated or existing norms are made peremptory. In either case, that process is conveniently described as a source of international law. Note that the term *source* refers not simply to the named thing, like custom or customs, but to a dynamic, if structured, process of law coming into being through the agency of whatever that thing happens to be. In the instance at hand, the process is novel and not well delineated. To the extent that it exists, it is a new source, one that manifestly involves an intent of the community, as expressed in a community-wide forum, to create general norms directly.

The concept of peremptory norms originated in the thinking of Western publicists. Their faith in Western culture and institutions shaken by the convulsions of recent decades, these individuals were prompted by a desire to strengthen the international legal order as a vehicle for justice and order. Yet the concept was embodied in the Vienna Convention at the insistence of Asian, African, and Latin American states for altogether different purposes – purposes that looked to the future rather than the past. Specifically, these states saw the concept of peremptory norms as both an immediate symbol and eventual instrumentality for restructuring the international legal order.[16]

15 *International Legal Materials*, vol. 8, 1969, pp. 373–7, and see Chapter 4 above.

16 As early as 1963, comments in the General Assembly's Sixth Committee on the International Law Commission's draft articles on peremptory norms reveal the affirmative orientation of Asian, African and Latin American states toward the concept. UN doc. A/CN.4/175 (1963), pp. 267–79. Socialist states also displayed a favorable though more particularized view of the concept. They also saw peremptory norms as reinforcing the fundamental position of the principles of peaceful coexistence in the international legal order, because the content of peremptory norms could be ascertained by reference to such principles, known in the context of the UN as the principles of friendly relations. In general, Western states were much less enthusiastic about the whole idea of peremptory norms. They tended to view the ILC's formulation as not legally operationalized, on the grounds that there was neither a definitive

It would be instructive at this point to view peremptory norms as a subset of "general principles" of international law, which is something they would seem to be almost as a matter of definition. Non-Western states have demonstrated an active concern for establishing the importance and defining the content of these general principles. (For elaboration, see Chapter 3 above.) The latter task has proven exceedingly difficult and where successful has been undertaken at a level of considerable generality. Inasmuch as general principles are inefficient for identifying individual instances of deviant behavior, we might conclude that their function is not specifically constraint-oriented. The major alternative is that they perform a symbolic function. Concretely, this could mean that such principles stand as generally understood and accepted characterizations of the abiding concerns of the international community. Apparently, general principles perform a service comparable to myth in any culture. A substantial change in the thematic content of such symbols signals the emergence of new concerns in the community, including particularly the concerns of its newer, more restless members.

The ability to shape the content of prevailing symbols is usually an important psychological value in its own right. Beyond that, the expectations of members of the community are continuously being conditioned by these symbols. Ultimately, control over symbols yields a cumulatively significant element of control over behavior. The value in having such control is material as well as psychological.

All this helps to explain why the general principles of international law have engaged so much interest among non-Western states in the forum of the General Assembly. Equally, it helps to explain why peremptory norms, as the paramount category of norms with a symbolic thrust, have been so important to those same states. Thus far the relative lack of concern for the content of peremptory norms indicates that their existence as a category, however devoid of content, is itself a substantial change in the structure of the international legal order. Furthermore, non-Western states see themselves as eventually being able to specify the content of peremptory norms along lines of their choice.

These observations lead to a second general factor in explaining why non-Western states have become so concerned about peremptory norms. These states are deeply resentful of the grip that Western states have on the content of existing international law through their control over its traditional sources. Manipulation of symbols will eventually expedite a change in the content of specific norms, but non-Western states would like to hurry that process. The existence of a new source, having the attributes discussed in these pages,

list of peremptory norms nor the means for determining when a treaty was in conflict with such norms. See also the comments of I.M. Sinclair, a member of the British delegation to the Vienna Conference, to the same effect. "Vienna Conference on the Law of Treaties," *International and Comparative Law Quarterly*, vol. 19, 1970, p. 66.

would be indispensable for this purpose. The process of renovating the legal order is further hastened if, instead of changing the content of myriad existing norms one by one through such a new source, attention were focused on a smaller number of norms, which are designated as peremptory and thus central to the emerging legal order. The consequence would be to enormously amplify the amount of change actually undertaken. Effectively, the designation of some few new norms as peremptory obviates the need to change everything at once to accomplish great change. It recognizes that some norms, especially those called peremptory, are constitutive of the legal order, while the rest are merely declaratory of the effect of the legal order in stipulated circumstances.

Conceived this way, generally stated peremptory norms are simultaneously the decisive symbols of the international legal order and its constitutive propositions. Moreover, these two roles are powerfully and reciprocally reinforcing. If this is an accurate representation of the situation, then the struggle over peremptory norms first as a category, and then as items whose content is to be elaborated, and the emergence of a new source of international law are related developments that are integral to the future of the international legal order.

With so much ultimately at stake, it is hard to believe that the participants in the Vienna Conference never really thought about the implications of the way they worded article 53. Obviously, they could have been careless or simply absorbed in other concerns. At least on the surface, it does seem to be true that the matter was never faced; one Western spokesman raised a series of unanswered questions about the source and nature of peremptory norms, only to be completely ignored in subsequent debate.[17] Yet statesmen are generally careful not to acquire unwanted obligations by being absent-minded. Alternatively, there may have been a tacit agreement not to raise these issues, knowing full well what their implications were, because doing so would merely expose sensitivities unnecessarily. The desired result may possibly have been to obscure the intent of article 53.

In contrast to the generation of norms through the new source in question,

17 The Swiss delegate asked:

> First, how did a new peremptory norm of international law emerge? Secondly, was a peremptory norm engendered by custom, by a treaty, or by both? Thirdly, to become a peremptory norm, did a rule have to be accepted by all States of the international community, or only by a majority of those States, and, in the latter case, by what majority? Fourthly, must a new peremptory norm contain an express declaration concerning its peremptory character, or did that character follow from the content of the new norm? Fifthly, was a peremptory norm valid only for the parties to a treaty or for all States?

UN Conference on the Law of Treaties, 22nd Plenary Meeting, UN doc. A/CONF.39/11/Add. 1 (1969).

where intent is decisive, custom as a source is ultimately dependent on behavior, to which intent is contributory along with many other factors. Obviously, where intent is clear, its impact is heightened. Although no such clarity of intent surrounds the drafting of article 53, the very act of drafting it in such a way as to imply the existence of a new source is indicative behavior. It promotes, however modestly, the emergence of a customary rule expressing that new source. Much more in the way of germane behavior is required, particularly if the new source is not to be restricted to the narrow domain of peremptory norms. Some of that behavior may even come in the form of responses to article 53 as a significant expression of a new source, regardless of whether that was even the intention.

6 Law-making in the global community: a working paper (1974)

For a number of years, Cyril Black and Richard Falk had directed a major project at Princeton University's Center of International Studies on the future of the international legal order. The project resulted in four volumes of studies, much cited in these pages, and the idea of pursuing a follow-up project on lawmaking in the global community. After a preliminary meeting to which Falk graciously invited me, I came to the Center as visiting research fellow to lead the project. In residence for several months in 1973 and again in 1974, I organized two conferences and invited a number of scholars who might contribute to a volume that I would edit on global lawmaking. My working paper for the second conference is reprinted here with some material omitted and some editing of text too obviously in draft form.

I devoted the first half of the paper to sources as an outmoded way of thinking about global lawmaking. The second half develops my view, already evident in Chapters 3 and 5 above, that there are two different kinds of law performing quite different functions in ordering the relations of states. It then demonstrates that making these two kinds of law involves readily distinguishable activities on the part of lawyer-bureaucrats on the one hand, and state leaders, judges and scholars on the other. For several years, the volume remained unfinished as I awaited draft chapters, sought a publisher and dealt with some unusual obstacles in bringing the volume out. During that time I periodically revised and expanded the working paper. When finally published in 1982, the paper was several times longer and much broader in scope. Black and Falk eventually concluded that having me write a monograph would have served the project better than an edited volume.

Law-making and legal thought

Many studies of jurisprudence and legal philosophy have something to say about lawmaking. Characteristically, these studies introduce the venerable notion that there are *sources* of law. Particular sources are presented one by one, until all that goes by the name of law is accounted for. Then perhaps it is asked how sources come to be what they are. The problem of the source of sources is not without interest. Indeed, it embodies the one great problem at the heart of all jurisprudential studies, for it "reflects the dualistic character of law as a metaphysical union of reality and validity."[1] Because it is part of our jurisprudential heritage, talk of sources cannot be ignored. Nor should it be dwelt upon. For we must eventually abandon sources thinking to find out anything more than we already know about lawmaking itself.

Lest I seem too harsh about the classical jurisprudential orientation toward lawmaking, I will put to service – as indeed I already have – an unusually intelligent treatment of the sources problem, that of Alf Ross. I begin by having Ross summarize the conventional view of legal sources:

> Positive law (the law of the land) is the sum and substance of norms that have come into existence in a historical process which by virtue of certain external, observable characteristics qualify the norm as valid law.
>
> The doctrine of the sources of law is the doctrine of these external characteristics. A source of law – e.g. statutes – denotes such an external characteristic – the form of legislation – which as a general form guarantees the content of norms expressed herein as law. The concept "legal source" thus denotes a certain general form, which is the epistemological basis for the knowledge that the normative content given therein is law.
>
> A plurality of legal sources is assumed, standing in the relation of principal and subsidiary to each other.[2]

Ross immediately identifies the "problem" implied in this characterization:

> If law is an *a priori* validity, the source of knowledge can only be pure reason and nothing else. And if the law is an empirical fact, the source of legal knowledge can only be experience and nothing else. The fact is that, just because the law is neither conceived (exclusively) in one way or in the other way, but as a *validity revealing itself in reality through empirical acts*, a peculiar problem will arise. Which, it may be asked, are the empirical acts that have a specific power of creating validity? What distinguishes them in general from others, and on what does this power depend? It is these questions that form the nucleus of the traditional theory of the legal sources. It is, it might be said, the problem as to how *validity invades* reality or, conversely, how reality can *form part* of validity, so that certain texts, generated empirically, have validity, while others have not.[3]

1 A. Ross, *Towards a Realistic Jurisprudence: A Criticism of the Dualism in Law*, trans. by A. I. Fausbøll, Copenhagen: Munksgaard, 1946, p. 127.

2 Ibid., pp. 125–6.

3 Ibid., pp. 127–8. Emphasis in original.

I submit that this problem is, in its own right, insoluble. In my commentary on the sources problem in international legal scholarship, I offer numerous opinions, both critical and (I hope) constructive, but I do so only to clarify the problem and not to solve it. This is Ross's view as well. When he concludes that "the antimonies of the doctrine of sources will be dissolved if the law is considered a phenomenon," he has in effect discarded the sources problem in favor of the more manageable lawmaking problem.[4]

Ross does this in a way that is schematically useful. He employs a dialectical format of dissolution and reconstruction to accommodate the dualistic heritage of jurisprudence, but in the process he makes only occasional contact with the empirical bedrock of actual lawmaking. Much the same format underpins the thematic development of this essay. The sources of international law, and with it the problem of the sources, are described, reconstructed, dissolved, and finally supplanted with an empirical assessment of global lawmaking. Each step involves a correlative and for the most part explicit description, reconstruction, and dissolution of prevailing ideas about international law.

The classical conceptualization of lawmaking

Traditional sources: custom, courts and writers; treaties

For a century now writers in international law have organized their discussion of lawmaking in terms of sources. These writers decry the "history of confusion" over the concept of *source* and criticize each other's formulations.[5] Yet they uniformly come to agreement when they itemize the actual sources of international law. There are two primary sources – custom and treaties – and two secondary sources – judicial decisions and scholarly writings. The latter pair are treated separately from custom only as a matter of convention. The 20th century has seen the addition of a new source – general principles recognized by civilized nations – which first gained expression in the famous recitation of sources found in the Statute of the International Court of Justice (World Court). Since 1919, when the Court's Statute was drafted, there has been widespread acceptance, not only of the list of sources, but of the specific language used to describe them. A signal exception is the description of custom as a source, perhaps reflecting the particularly unsettled state of doctrine in this area. For the rest, the Statute's language is sufficiently generalized that an air of acceptance hardly signifies a dissipation of the historic controversies associated with sources doctrine.

4 Ibid., p. 157.

5 For a brief but effective review of this "history," see C. Parry, *The Sources and Evidences of International Law*, Manchester: Manchester University Press, 1965, pp. 1–6, quoting P.E. Corbett on p. 2.

Still, law is a matter of language, and we would be well advised to have such widely received language before us. Article 38 of the Statute of the World Court reads as follows:

> 1. The Court, whose function is to decide in accordance with international law such disputes as are submitted to it, shall apply:
>   a. international conventions, whether general or particular, establishing rules expressly recognized by the consenting states;
>   b. international custom, as evidence of a general practice accepted as law;
>   c. the general principles of law recognized by civilized nations;
>   d. subject to the provisions of Article 59, judicial decisions and the teachings of the most highly qualified publicists of the various nations, as subsidiary means for the determination of rules of law.
> 2. This provision shall not prejudice the power of the Court to decide a case *aequo et bono*, if the parties agree thereto.

Only the ordering of items in article 38 is commonly ignored by writers, who generally prefer to begin their discussions with *custom*, the more basic and historically the more important of the two main sources. I do the same. Custom is invariably seen as having two components, one behavioral and quantitative, the other attitudinal and qualitative, which together reflect an uneasy marriage of legal theory's dualistic tendencies.[6]

Each component presents a significant problem for writers. In the instance of the behavioral, quantitative component, the problem is obvious: How much of the behavior of state actors, which is typically called practice, makes a custom "accepted as law"?[7] The problem must be pursued in three dimensions at once, these being temporal, spatial and distributional dimensions. A legal custom requires the passage of time almost by definition. How much time is impossible to say in the abstract, although there appears to be an inverse relationship between the amount of time and the amount of behavior required for a given pattern of behavior to become a legal custom. The greater the volume of behavior, the less time must pass. Similarly, to have legal character a custom must be widespread. But how widespread? We can only say that the more widespread a practice, the less volume as a function of time is required. The distribution of behaviors affirming and disconfirming a custom must be seen the same way. The higher the ratio of affirming to

6 For a lucid and much fuller discussion, see A.A. D'Amato, *The Concept of Custom in International Law*, Ithaca: Cornell University Press, 1971.

7 Equally obvious is the problem writers have with the wording of article 38. It is practice that is seen as evidence of custom accepted as law and not the contrary, as suggested by the Statute. I take this to be a matter of faulty drafting and nothing more. Hereinafter I denote custom accepted as law, on the evidence of general practice, as *legal custom*.

disconfirming behavior, the less volume as a function of time and space is required.

Altogether, we achieve a general proposition that the volume of practice necessary to constitute a custom as law is a function of the product of transitive values for duration, extent, and consistency of practice. The limiting cases are: *one point in time*, requiring overwhelmingly generalized and consistent practice and establishing instantaneous custom; *two actors*, requiring overwhelmingly consistent and durable practice confined to the actors and establishing special or local custom; and *unilateral acts*, requiring the indefinite passage of time free from inconsistent and contesting acts and establishing a prescriptive exception to generally valid law.[8]

The limiting cases are intrinsically interesting and even have an occasional application. But they do not solve the quantitative problem for the vast number of situations in which some practice of some duration, extent, and consistency may or may not be a legal custom. Writers rather frequently display a tendency to state arbitrary but demanding criteria for establishing the existence of legal custom in the abstract and in particular situations relax these criteria without admitting to having done so. In fact they must relax their criteria or they would find that very few rules of customary international law could be said to exist at all.

The problem with the qualitative, attitudinal component of legal custom is no less evident. Some kinds of behavior are voluminous, durable, widespread and uniform, and yet they are not regarded as binding. They are seen and always referred to as courtesies but not as law. Obviously what differentiates this kind of behavior from law-generative behavior is how the actors feel about it and their willingness to say how they feel about it. Anthony D'Amato would say that there must be *articulated* recognition that behavior has legal consequences for those consequences to take place.

The notion of articulation is a great advance over the historic but hopelessly circular notion of *opinio juris*, namely, of behavior being undertaken in "conscious accordance with law preexisting the action."[9] Nonetheless, D'Amato's position is a restrictive one, taken in light of his observation that articulation must be visible. By employing the articulation criterion we would again have to conclude that there are very few customary rules (excepting

8 As to instantaneous custom, see B. Cheng, "United Nations Resolutions on Outer Space: 'Instant' International Customary Law?" *Indian Journal of International Law*, vol. 5, 1965, pp. 23–112; as to special custom, see D'Amato, *The Concept of Custom in International Law*, ch. 8; as to unilateral acts, see E. Suy, *Les acts juridiques unilatéraux en droit international public*, Paris, Librairie générale de droit et de jurisprudence, 1962; as to whether unilateral acts can create general law, see Z. Slouka, *International Custom and the Continental Shelf: A Study in the Dynamics of Customary Rules of International Law*, The Hague: Nijhoff, 1968, and D'Amato, ch. 7.

9 D'Amato, *The Concept of Custom in International Law*, p. 66. On the circularity of *opinio juris*, see pp. 66–72; on articulation, pp. 73–87.

those coextensive with treaties – see below), particularly if articulations are to be evaluated by their volume, duration, extent, and consistency. The problem generally resembles the difficulty with the constitutive theory of recognition. How many acts of recognition, or articulation, are required for a legal condition to be constituted: one, all that are possible, or some arbitrary number in between? As an alternative to articulation as a necessary ingredient for customary law, I suggest that articulation is required to establish only that a custom is *not* law. Thus, a courtesy remains a courtesy so long as there are periodic statements by actors to the effect that they continue to see the matter as one of simple custom.

Such articulations are indeed commonplace and that is precisely how we know that courtesies are not binding. In the absence of statements disavowing legal consequences of particular customs, we may assume that when quantitative criteria, whatever they are, have been fulfilled, then law does exist in customary form. This position would seem to be consistent both with contemporary, more flexible conceptions of the nature of international law and the practice of states, which involves a good deal of unarticulated acceptance of legal consequences, as we shall see below.

A sharp distinction between behavior and articulated attitudes is hardly manifested, after all, in the concrete emanations we call practice. While I use the terms *behavior* and *practice* interchangeably in these pages, practice is the generic description of everything that state actors do, and what they do involves indeterminate proportions of verbal and nonverbal behavior, and verbal as well as nonverbal demonstrations of what they take to be the significance of that behavior. There is little value to be gained from distinguishing behavior from attitude and even less value in perpetuating the doctrinal dualism contained in the distinction. For our purposes, what counts is the *intensity* of practice as it relates inversely to volume.

The more intensely expressed an act, the fewer such acts are required for a legal custom to emerge.[10] Articulation as formalization may be the best measure of intensity. Articulation may thus be instrumental to intensity, which is what makes the practice count more heavily. Articulation in its own right is without a consistent meaning and significance, except in the special case of articulations to the effect that customary practices are without legal effect. With this in mind, we can say: the volume of practice necessary to constitute a custom as law is a function of the product of transitive values for duration, extent, consistency, and intensity of this practice.

A discussion of articulation is obviously incomplete without taking into account the place in customary law formation occupied by court decisions

10 There is some evidence that in small groups the most intensely held rules are least articulated, that articulation can invalidate such rules, and consequently a prime, if unarticulated rule states that rules are not to be articulated. See W.O. Weyrauch, "The 'Basic Law' or 'Constitution' of a Small Group," *Journal of Social Issues*, vol. 27, 1971, pp. 49–63.

and writers. As is well known, the decisions of international tribunals do not set precedents, for customary law is fundamentally different from common law. Such decisions are seen as evidence of the existence of customary law and, in the very process of providing evidence of such law, are items of practice further substantiating the evident practice. Decisions of national courts may be of comparable value to the international legal order. Indeed, if the value of such decisions is in the evidence they provide of state practice, then we must accept Richard Falk's argument that the decisions of domestic courts are more important than those of international tribunals because they more authoritatively capture the practice of *states*. In many domestic legal orders such decisions are indistinguishable from actual practice of states.[11] By the same reasoning, the arguments of litigants before an international tribunal would be more valuable than the judgment itself. Only insofar as decisions of international tribunals receive subsequent affirmation in state practice can they be classified as practice, or more properly, evident practice and not merely evidence of practice.

In order to avoid the logical implications of Falk's position, we could assume that the practice that creates custom is larger than the practice of states. I suspect that this is a common if unarticulated assumption. It contains no guidelines on the extent of relevant practice, but we can imagine informal criteria of prestige and quality at work. The higher the prestige of the tribunal and the individuals who sit on it, and the better crafted their opinions, the greater the value of such opinions as practice. Thus, by assuming that law-generating practice does not necessarily refer exclusively to what states do, it is possible to erect an especially prominent position for the decisions and minority opinions emanating from the World Court and, correlatively, to explain the great interest that so frequently attends the drafting of decisions and opinions.

Evidently the Court is a generator of practice, in a very important but nonetheless indirect sense. By means of the visibility, salience and reasonableness of its judgments, it can prompt immediate and widespread supportive behavior from states. In effect certain decisions of the Court have a near oracular impact on community opinion, catalyzing the necessary practice for the rapid emergence of a customary norm. To give an example, the Court's judgment in the *Anglo-Norwegian Fisheries Case* is frequently cited as a landmark in the emergence of a customary role affirming the use of the straight baseline method for demarcating certain territorial waters.[12] In

11 R.A. Falk, *The Role of Domestic Courts in the International Legal Order*, Syracuse: Syracuse University Press, 1964.

12 Because the Statute of the World Court holds that the Court's decisions have "no binding force except between the parties and in respect of that particular case" (article 59), the Court could not intend that its decision be generalized to all comparable situations. On the contrary, the Court felt bound to show that in the situation at hand, it had merely found evidence of practice accepted as law.

contrast is the Court's judgment in the *Nottebohm Case*. As in the *Fisheries Case*, the Court set forth a novel construction of the controlling law, but its argument is so muddled that it is little understood and, when understood, little respected.[13]

Considerations of timing, craft and what, with Max Weber, we might call charisma, are important factors in the catalytic effect. It has occurred just often enough that every decision is awaited with an air of expectation that it may be happening again. When these expectations are dashed, great criticism is voiced and the Court's prestige is eclipsed, only to be revived in anticipation of the next oracular event. Although the Court's light caseload is invariably bemoaned by its supporters, we might observe that the cycle of expectation and oracular event, whether followed by catalysis or catharsis, is immeasurably supported by the spacing of decisions allowed by a light caseload. By contrast the oracular impact of the US Supreme Court is diminished by the swamping effect of its vast number of decisions.

The seriousness with which legal scholars take the Court's decisions also helps to account for its prominence. They do so because the Court's work is highly visible and, at the same time, sufficiently modest in volume to be assimilated into scholarship. Beyond this, legal scholars, particularly in the common law world, are trained to think in terms of "cases" and as teachers they characteristically use cases to illustrate the content and application of rules of law. The influence of the Anglo-American preoccupation with cases in international law extends far beyond the influence of the common law tradition generally. There are obvious reasons for this. Since customary law is so difficult to establish, all legal scholars are impressed with the Anglo-American procedure of looking at cases: it gets results. The signal importance of Britain and the US in the development of international law has inevitably created an intense interest in case-oriented Anglo-American scholarship. Finally, the sheer volume of Anglo-American literature in international law has the effect of flooding out different perceptions of the Court's influence that might arise in other legal cultures.

The World Court's prestige is handsomely reinforced by the fact that its membership is drawn from the community of scholars and state practitioners who are generally given to emphasizing the importance of the Court's decisions. Not only do these individuals wish someday to crown their careers

> The Court is thus led to conclude that the method of straight baselines, established in the Norwegian system, was imposed by the peculiar geography of the Norwegian coast; that even before the dispute arose this method had been consolidated by a constant and sufficiently long practice, in the face of which the attitude of governments bears witness to the fact that they did not consider it to be contrary to international law.

ICJ Reports, 1951, p. 139.

13 *ICJ Reports*, 1955, pp. 5–26. Properly understood, the judgment deprives Nottebohm of any nationality at all and not, as is usually thought, of the one of two nationalities to which the Court determined he was less effectively linked.

with election to the Court, but their friends and colleagues are sitting there already. The decisions of the Court receive the attention that the work of the most senior and respected scholars would receive in any discipline.

Historically writers occupied a place very close to what I have attributed to the World Court. Writers have had a marked effect on the emergence of rules if their opinions were timely, reasonable, and well crafted. Such writers acquired the prestige to have their opinions quoted and requoted almost as if they were oracular pronouncements. Each time the oracle's name is invoked with greater deference and awe.

It is generally assumed that landmark opinions of revered writers have decisively effected the emergence of legal custom by catalyzing supportive state behavior. While this was doubtless the case in some instances, it is arguable that quite often the catalytic effect was rather more on writers than on states. The tendency for writers to seize on oracular pronouncements and reiterate them for generations can create an impression in the minds of those same writers that the rule exists simply because they are writing about it as if it exists. The relevant "practice" is largely the opinions of earlier writers, salted with the occasional instances of supportive state behavior that have come along. Instances of contrary behavior are dismissed in footnotes as irrelevant to the consensual view of scholars, if they are acknowledged at all.[14]

At least to a degree this was the history of the putative rule establishing the limit of the territorial sea at three miles. Scholars were shocked when a substantial number of states resisted codification of the three-mile limit at the Hague Codification Conference of 1930. Subsequent state practice strongly suggests that many states had never supported the prevailing scholarly view of the three-mile limit. The practices of these states could be ignored as long as scholars represented a significant element in the connective structures of the international system. With the bureaucratization of foreign policy in the 19th century, diplomat-bureaucrats replaced writers as an integrative feature of the system, very much as jurists began to replace writers as lawmaking catalysts. Legal order became progressively detached from the system, a structure unto itself, tended by writers with strong preferences for order and coherence.

Codification is virtually synonymous with the quest for a detached, almost mechanical orderliness. The promotion of codification and systematic improvement of the law was a characteristic activity of the 19th century legal order and the special province of writers. Yet codification is also highly susceptible to bureaucratization (see Chapter 10 below). One can almost guess what happened over a period of decades. Codification was first undertaken through private initiative, then by "scientific societies" and finally in coordination with public bureaucracies. At first, codification resembled

14 G. Schwarzenberger has called this process "inductive mimicry." *The Inductive Approach to International Law*, London: Stevens, 1965, pp. 47–50.

compilations of oracular pronouncements, then elaborately organized scholarly systems, and finally practice-sensitive draft treaties for state signature.

Only when the last stage was reached were scholars able to test their status as agents in lawmaking. As the 1930 Hague Conference so eloquently testified, scholars found not only that they could no longer make oracular law, but that the oracular pronouncements of earlier centuries were not nearly so much cherished by states as they were by successive generations of scholars.

In recent decades the bureaucratization of codification is nearly complete, with the role of scholars now close to nominal. Thus, scholars are superseded by the World Court in catalyzing lawmaking and superseded by public officials in codification. Only by being jurist or state bureaucrat is the scholar still able to occupy his traditional place. For the greater number of scholars who are simply private persons, they can contribute to the development of law only in a general way through their efforts to comprehend and rationalize state behavior as that behavior is played out against the backdrop of existing but frequently ignored rules of law. Such activity is important because its cumulative effect is to anchor the legal order in the international system without fully sacrificing the scholarly community's normative preferences. After a century of the legal order being detached from the system, this task is hardly trivial. But it is not one that relates directly to lawmaking.

Treaties are a good deal easier to discuss than custom, for there is only one major controversy about them as a *source* that commands our attention. While most writers simply state that properly concluded treaties are a source of law, some British writers have argued that such treaties are demonstrably a source of *obligation*, but that the source of law is a customary rule, *pacta sunt servanda*, which grants an obligatory character to properly concluded treaties.[15] In effect, a treaty is analogous to a contract in municipal law. In advanced municipal orders obligations are clearly differentiated from the law by virtue of which the discharge of certain obligations is guaranteed. In primitive orders legal obligations are undifferentiated, meaning that every rule bears a potential obligation but no obligation exists without a rule. The legal order treats every obligation individually, and not as a class, by endowing each with individual legality. The demands on a primitive order are sufficiently slight to allow individualization. The demands for *special law* through treatymaking may well be reaching an intolerable magnitude in the international legal order, but that in itself does not make a contract regime operative.[16]

15 First stated by G.G. Fitzmaurice, "Some Problems Regarding the Formal Sources of International Law," *Symbolae Verzijl*, The Hague: Nijhoff, 1958, pp. 153–76.

16 For a sense of the magnitude, see P.H. Rohn, *Institutions in Treaties: A Global Survey of Magnitudes and Trends from 1945 to 1965*, Syracuse: Maxwell Graduate School of Citizenship and Public Affairs, Syracuse University, 1970, Annex. On special law, see M. Rheinstein (ed.), *Max Weber on Law in Economy and Society*, trans by E. Shils and M. Rheinstein, New York: Simon and Schuster, 1954, pp. 140–54.

There would seem to be little substantive difference in viewing treaties as a source of law or as a source of obligation *if* what results is a legal obligation on a par with the legal obligations that result from the operation of custom. The latter of course are general, the former specific to the parties, but they are treated by states as comparable kinds of obligations. Thus it is widely agreed that a treaty obligation supersedes a prior customary obligation as between the parties. A contract in a municipal order, however, cannot supplant generally binding law, but instead must be consistent with it. Moreover, an emergent customary legal obligation supersedes a prior treaty obligation of the same content. If a treaty obligation has the same content as a customary obligation, no matter which came first, both continue to be obligations in their own right.

As D'Amato has taken pains to show, the relationship between legal custom and treaties is really an organic one. Perhaps the most visible index of a state's practice in the present day is its treaty obligations. Multilateral treaties in particular show a considerable tendency to have significantly prompted the emergence of coextensive customary norms. D'Amato is inclined to see treaties as the principal means by which states articulate their acceptance of the legal consequences of their practice. Since he regards such articulation as a necessary component of a legal custom, the effect is to make custom nearly synonymous with treaties. Since I do not attach the importance to articulation that D'Amato does, I would say that he does not go far enough. Not only is much of the vast volume of treaty law coextensive with customary law for which treaties, by virtue of their public and formal nature, are decisive practice, but there also exists a great deal of informal and unarticulated practice which is nonetheless treated as if it were law by those who are exposed to it.

New sources: general principles, declarations

Ever since its hasty and rather unreflective drafting in 1919, the source called "general principles of international law recognized by civilized nations" has been the subject of furious but inconclusive debate. I do not propose to rehearse these debates at any length, because they do not seem to have affected the conclusion drawn by many writers that, whatever we might say about their source, very few such principles can be shown to exist. Those that do exist appear to be procedural guidelines for international tribunals substantially derived from the Western legal tradition. In these recurring debates, the school of thought with which I am most sympathetic merely claims that such guidelines are all that we might reasonably expect to find as general principles of law.

The existence and utilization of procedural guidelines implies nothing about general principles as a source but does tell us a good deal about the training of jurists. Arguably, there is now something akin to a common law of international judicial procedure, created by judges and applying to them. The source of this specialized law, doubtfully international law at all, is international law in the form of article 38 and its subsequent interpretation, through which states tolerate the recourse to procedural precedents in international tribunals under the guise of general principles. Only indirectly are states subject to the judges' common law of procedure, if this is what it is, but at least there are tangible rules to show for it. Otherwise, insofar as states are directly concerned, widely held principles and doctrines in various municipal orders can serve as fertile analogies in the hands of scholars and statesmen as well as jurists, who apply them to international law situations as they see fit. Though legally intangible in themselves, such principles can contribute to the catalytic success of oracular pronouncements by enhancing their saliency to practitioners.

The alternative school of thought sees general principles of law as truly the most important source of all. Thus we find references to general principles as the "common law" or "basic foundations" of the international legal order.[17] Some writers in this school are clearly making projections or stating preferences. They think that if there were, or will ever come to be, substantive rules emanating from this source, these rules would be fundamental in character. Other writers would appear to see general principles as part of the underlying structure of the international legal order, given formal expression in the Statute of the World Court for reasons of recent history but nonetheless incidental to the matter of sources *per se*. This view is quite consistent with the position adduced above that prevalent municipal principles can give structure and thrust to landmark pronouncements in the formation of custom. Only when the substratum is called law simply by the authority of article 38 are these irreconcilable views. I see no grounds in theory or in the behavior of states for the direct attribution of international legal validity to general principles of law.

The phrase *general principles of law recognized by civilized nations* has engendered confusion as well as controversy, for the language of international law has long known the phrase *general principles of international law*. Some writers have attempted a sleight of hand by trying to assimilate the two into a unified term, *the general principles of national and international law*. Since general principles of international law are substantive in character, then there would be at least a superficial connection between general principles as a source and general principles as substantive law. But the connection is only superficial. The use of the phrase, general principles of international law, has been a casual means of denoting rules that are taken to be more notable than other rules. They are not generally seen as superior in

17 For a brief critical review of the main positions on general principles, appropriately cited, see G.I. Tunkin, " 'General Principles of Law' in International Law," in R. Marcic (ed.), *Internationale Festschrift für Alfred Verdross zum 80. Geburtstag*, München: Fink, 1971, pp. 523–32.

the obligations they create, unless they are further set apart as peremptory norms. General principles of international law are undeniably important because of the depth and extent of affirmative practice, but not different in legal quality for that reason. By the same token, they do not arise from a source of general principles that is the source of their importance as well.[18]

Informally designated as general principles because of their history and content, such rules of international law are rarely subjected to dispute over their legal status because they are rarely given sustained attention as a class for any reason. What little attention writers have granted general principles of international law stems from the possibility that some multilateral treaty provisions may create general law directly. These provisions are best understood as general principles, set apart from the rest of the treaty's obligations in style and form. As D'Amato would have it, the world community has displayed a "manifest intent" to make these provisions general law directly. None of the traditional sources describes this law-generative process: it must be described as a new source.[19]

This revolutionary doctrine is not merely a matter of casual speculation on the part of a few writers. There are ambiguous but intriguing passages in the World Court's 1969 Judgment on the *North Sea Continental Shelf Cases*, which encourage the belief that articles 1–3 of the 1958 Geneva Convention on the Continental Shelf are set apart from the rest of that document (only they could not have reservations attached to them by ratifying states) and now have the status of general law. How these provisions came to acquire general legal status is rather more difficult to say on the basis of the judgment alone. One of the minority Opinions, by the well-known Danish publicist Max Sørensen, forcefully argued the instantaneous custom explanation. But Vladimir Koretsky, a greatly respected Soviet jurist, offered an unambiguous opinion to the effect that the relevant provisions of the Continental Shelf Convention are general principles of international law, made so by the intent of the participants in the Geneva Conference.[20]

We might say that the Conference in 1958 constituted a forum of the world community. The UN General Assembly represents a comparable forum but has at its disposal a different instrumentality – resolutions as opposed to a draft treaty – with what is ordinarily a very different legal status (see Chapter 2 above). But the status of the instrumentality is unimportant, for the instrumentality is being "borrowed" by the forum for the promulgation of a rule whose legal status is already assured. Such emanations from community

18 In Chapter 5 above, I hold that peremptory norms are a variant of general principles, set apart as a whole from other rules neither in source nor status but in function.

19 A.A. D'Amato, "Manifest Intent and the Generation by Treaty of Customary Rules of International Law," *American Journal of International Law*, vol. 64, 1970, pp. 892–902. D'Amato failed to see that he was talking about a new source; I argue in Chapter 4 above that it can be nothing else.

20 *ICJ Reports*, 1969, pp. 41–4 (Judgment), 156–8 (Koretsky), 244–7 (Sørensen).

forums are set apart in style, tone and generality of language, taking the generic form of a declaration. They are unanimous or near-unanimously adopted, they are infrequent occasions, and they are patently a serious matter for the participants in the forum.

D'Amato has even suggested that some few overwhelmingly supported rules that are ordinarily taken to be customary are indeed general law emanating directly from community consensus and not custom at all.[21] There is a certain appeal to D'Amato's position, since it gives an historical dimension to what is then not a new source but only a newly recognized source. Nonetheless, it requires us to employ the image of a decentralized forum of the world community. While the passage of time may well substitute for the collective aspect of the forum, we then have a condition that is indistinguishable from customary law formation. Yet D'Amato's position is predicated on being able to distinguish between the ordinary run of customary rules and exceptional instances of consensus as a source of law.

On the face of it, declarations are general principles of international law, notable for their formality as much as their content and readily altered in content only through community decisions of comparable formality. The provisions of such declarations are simultaneously potent organizing symbols and potential constitutive propositions for a world order that may be decades in emerging. Put in these terms, we can see that there is a great deal at stake in attributing legal status directly to declarations. We can well guess that some states have far more to gain than others in the establishment of a new source giving legal consequence to the voice of community consensus. In fact, the resistance of Western states to the operation of a new source is notorious. Arrayed against the Western states are a modest number of Western scholars, I among them, and a much larger number of statesmen from the non-Western world, who have in their diversely motivated and articulated ways sought to establish that a new source can, should, or does exist.

Proponents of a new source are disunited in their perceptions of the present situation, not to mention their strategies for changing it. They are united only in their belief that significant changes in the structure and substance of the received liberal-mercantile order of the West can be significantly abetted through the validation of a new source. Only a new source of international law can permit the direct and determinative participation of all peoples in the workings of an order, which is now only nominally for all to share in.

Nevertheless, the unwillingness of Western states to accept a new source is an insurmountable obstacle to its existence in fact actually existing. Before these attitudes are likely to change, the pervasive sense of stalemate and confrontation over the future development of the international legal order must dissipate. Even in the unlikely event that Western states were to yield on this crucial point, there is a lurking suspicion that many non-Western states

21 D'Amato, *The Concept of Custom in International Law*, pp. 41–2.

would be far less innovative in concretizing these principles than they are in sending them forth as resplendent rhetoric. Stripped of the convenient shelter of Western obstinacy, many of the leaders in these states could well realize the threatening implications of the social changes contemplated on a world scale in the programmatic statements they now so heartily declare their support for.

The source of sources: can custom be the source of custom as a source?

The decisive obstacle to the emergence of declarations of general principles as a source of international law is the unwillingness of the world community to validate it as a source. The validating procedure would be accomplished by having the new source stated in legal form through the operation of an existing source. Thus, general principles of law recognized by civilized nations are validated as a source because they are stated as such in the Statute of the World Court. In that form they are a source only for the Court, but it may be considered as having generalized validity because of the emergence of customary law precipitated by the universal acceptance of article 38 and coextensive with it.

Treaties are also affirmed as a source in article 38, but this was merely declaratory of a legal condition long established in custom. Finally custom itself is affirmed as a source in article 38, and again this may be taken as declaratory, for we have long known that custom is a source of law. But what is the source of the rule validating custom as a source? It is hard to see how it can be any of the known sources: Can custom be the source of custom as a source? Can a treaty be the source of custom when treaties gain their validity as a source from a legal custom?

The logical problem is so obvious, but apparently unanswerable, that it is as much ignored in the literature on the sources of international law as it is debated in legal and social philosophy. Three general positions on the basis of legal obligation are apparent, each of them taking the form of a familiar metalegal postulate. The basis of obligation for any system of law is said to be formal agreement (social contract) or spontaneous general agreement (consensus) or the instinct or need for order (social imperative). These are not mutually exclusive possibilities, even though they tend to be posed as such. Taken together in given mixes or combinations, they may tell us in very general terms how social orders begin or are fundamentally transformed.

In recent decades, there has been remarkably little opinion, much less systematic consideration, as to the particular mix of what might be called first causes in the international legal order. This is not to suggest that we are all too sophisticated for 18th century social philosophizing; it means only that we tend to be unwitting adherents to one position or another. Perhaps Hans Kelsen has given the matter the most thought. He concluded that a social imperative ("states ought to behave as they customarily have behaved") was at the root of the international legal order (to which all domestic legal orders were formally subordinated). This was Kelsen's famous *Grundnorm*, which he took to be sociological in character and thus beyond appreciation in legal science.[22]

Kelsen's concern for formally validated hierarchies of legal orders distinguishes his work from conventional positivist thought. Positivism, by holding consent to be the decisive element for participation in the international legal order, suggests a voluntarist worldview that is unsympathetic, if formally compatible with the Kelsenian *Grundnorm*. One might think that a consent-oriented view of international law would incline writers instead toward a contractual view of the international legal order's origins. Custom could be a source only to the extent that states so consented, very much as if they had agreed to a tacit treaty.

While this position is latent in positivism, the emphasis in this school on the decentralized character of the international legal order yields a concern for what states do with respect to each other and not how the system of states came into being. The positivist doctrine of recognition provides a means of assimilating new entities into an existing system but begs more fundamental questions. Since positivists display so little interest in the tacit treaty that validates custom, we are obliged to identify it on their behalf as a social contract, or validated by a social contract, which amounts to the same thing.

Contract theories have lost favor to the idea that consensus makes the international legal order what it is. Present-day apostles of the consensus position have generally been concerned to expose the anomalies of the long prevailing positivist paradigm. By taking the battle to the positivists, the consensus school has tended to accept positivist assumptions about what the war is all about. The focus is always on whether custom as a source requires or implies literal consent or something less demanding in the formation of *particular* rules. The question not being asked is whether consent, collectively yielding a tacit treaty or social contract, or consensus, as a concretization of a Rousseauian general will, is the constitutive source of custom as a source.

This is the ultimate issue in the debate over consent and consensus, although only D'Amato has come to recognize it so far. D'Amato's first probings of the problem are intriguing but inconsistent. He has argued that the source of custom, as a secondary rule in the sense of H.L.A. Hart, may well be provided for by consensus, but he has separately argued in convincing fashion that consensus is not a "metarule" effectuating declarations as a source, "but merely a definition of what we *mean* by the expression 'international law.' "[23] If consensus is simply the latter, it is not immediately evident

22 See, for example, H. Kelsen, *Principles of International Law*, New York: Rinehart, 1952, Part V.

23 D'Amato, *The Concept of Custom in International Law*, pp. 41–4; "On Consensus," *Canadian Yearbook of International Law*, vol. 8, 1970, p. 122; his emphasis.

how it came to be the metarule creating custom as a source. I am not arguing that this is not the case. I am saying that the *mechanics* of consensus operating to this effect, which D'Amato elaborates so carefully in respect to declarations, are hardly to be taken for granted in the case of custom.

In short, how do we know that several hundred years ago mechanical requirements for the expression of a consensus of states necessary to constitute custom as a source of legally binding rules were properly fulfilled? If mechanical requirements are unnecessary because consensus is in reality nothing more than the spontaneous emanation of the general will, how do we know that kind of emanation when we see it? Consensus seems to be little different from contract, as a postulated beginning of the legal order and of custom as a source, in failing to answer any of the questions on *how* things began. We can only conclude that while there are general intellectual preferences, reducible to postulates, which orient discussion of the problem of the source of sources, there is indeed no solution currently available to us.

The reason for sources: the twin myths of sanction and source

For all the problems it causes, we might well wonder why we bother to think about the sources of law at all. The same question is as pertinent when we turn our attention from how law comes into being to how it is applied: why do we fret about the sanctions of international law so much and to so little avail? International legal scholarship has not always been cast in such terms as source and sanction. For example, an inspection of Emerich de Vattel's principal treatise, *Le droit des gens* (1758) fails to reveal the use of either term. Perhaps we should not be surprised because of Vattel's position in the secularized Enlightenment school of natural law thought. Questions of how legal order worked were dismissed with the assumption that the natural order was the source and sanction of the international legal order. Suspended from natural law doctrine and anchored only by Vattel's diplomatic experience and Enlightenment sensibilities, the substantive law he described has just the disembodied quality that early positivist thought so stridently rejected.

Late 18th century positivism, as in the hands of Johann Jakob Moser and Georg Friedrich von Martens, was dedicated to determining the existence of actual rules. This involved the systematic examination of the practice of states. In effect, the anchoring of inquiry in the solid ground of empirical reality was accomplished by severing all ties with any sort of doctrinal edifice for establishing the legal quality of certain kinds of state behavior. Positivism in the 19th century represents a dramatic departure from the crudely inductive tendencies in the school's origins. Doctrine became an important concern, indeed of far greater interest than it had been for naturalists in the preceding century. First with Jeremy Bentham, then John Austin and eventually to our century with German and English language variants on positivism, certain doctrinal considerations have received continuous and cumulative attention, albeit with only an ephemeral relation to the ongoing compilation and analysis of the positive law. We might even say that positivism has developed distinct branches of macro and microanalysis.

In positivist doctrine, law has certain definitional properties. Without these properties, what first might appear to be law simply is not law. If international law is truly law, then it too must manifest the same properties. Following in Thomas Hobbes' footsteps, Bentham and most memorably Austin, identified *sanction* as the singularly decisive property that law must possess. Austin concluded that international law in particular could not be law since no centralized enforcement procedure existed. Writing nearly a century later, Weber could say that international law was a marginal case of law, while his near-contemporary Kelsen could defend the view that international law was indeed law.

Since all three conclusions started with the same Austinian premise, we infer that an extraordinary amount of doctrinal manipulation is possible. For Austin the critical factor is the absence of centralized sanctioning procedures, for Weber external guarantee of law by an independent and professional staff is crucial, and for Kelsen existence of self-help through reprisals is sufficient for the purpose of proving that sanctions exist in the instance of international law. Despite its inconvenience and possibly its irrelevance, the notion of sanction has long since become an article of faith in positivist doctrine. Distortions in the notion are inevitable, as is disquiet over the resulting doctrinal incongruities.

Quite plausibly, the notion of source has become second only to sanction as a property of legal orders. Less discomfort arises when international law is being scrutinized because the international legal order demonstrably does possess sources of its law. Fears about the status of international law as law, raised by the sanctions problem, may thus be allayed by invoking its sources as a property of law discernibly fulfilled. Any difficulties raised by this idea are general in nature and thus do not constitute a basis for singling out international law as defective.

Sources thinking is not so much the invention of positivist thought that sanctions thinking is. Rather it is an importation from Roman law. Largely a vehicle in our own time for systematic and comparative thinking about law, Roman law does not make sources a logical requirement of law. Instead, sources form a convenient organizing tool borrowed from Roman law with such modifications as needed to give a designated legal order a classification of the particular means by which its rules are elaborated. No such classification itself makes the modes of lawmaking so classified proper or valid; there must be an independent basis for validity. Apparently the problem of the ultimate source of validity is insoluble, even in its own terms. Yet positivist thought has inextricably associated sources, as a taxonomic convenience, with the separable question of the ultimate source of validity, as if the former were somehow, implicitly, an answer to the latter.

In no way does the presence of sources answer the question of validity. At best it provides clues to the first causes of legal order, as we noted in the previous section. If the connection between source and validity cannot be taken for granted, then we cannot assume that sources are intrinsic to legal orders. Whether we can ever answer the question of validity, we can always inquire into the utility of a particular classification of sources. We can retain the Roman law classification, update it or, if the nature of the law and modes of lawmaking that we are dealing with so warrant, we can cast it aside for an alternative classificatory system.

Interestingly, sanctions thinking has received a good deal of critical scrutiny in recent times.[24] Each assault gradually erodes the inherited myth of law as sanctioned behavior and forces us to regard international law, and perhaps all law, in fundamentally different terms. Yet we persist in adhering to the twin myth of positivism – that law must be validated through a formal source as well as made effective through the availability of a sanction – even though the sources myth is less integral to the positivist view and less thoroughly articulated in positivist thought. Had sources thinking received the same buffeting as sanctions thinking, we cannot be sure that there would be anything at all left of the sources myth. With all its anomalies and difficulties, the present arrangement of sources in international law might better stand replacement than refurbishment.

Reconceptualizing law and lawmaking

Law as solution and law as artifacts: Durkheim and Weber

The way scholars look at law is largely dictated by their intellectual heritage. Most legal scholars, including most international legal scholars, have been trained as lawyers by lawyers, and the intellectual tradition in which they are steeped is drawn from jurisprudence and legal philosophy. For the greater number today, this means the Austinian tradition – a tradition that is little changed from the time of Austin. Any systematic thinking that legal scholars do about law seems destined to bear a direct or dialectical relation to Austin's thought.

There are other intellectual heritages, which many legal scholars are passingly familiar but usually uncomfortable with, even when the common object of concern is the nature of law. Anthropologists, political scientists, psychologists and sociologists have to varying degrees established subfields in their disciplines devoted to the study of law. As a crude generalization, we might

24 M. Barkun, *Law without Sanctions*, New Haven: Yale University Press, 1968; G. Gottlieb, "The Nature of International Law: Toward a Second Concept of Law," in C.E. Black and R.A. Falk (eds), *The Future of the International Legal Order*, vol. 4, Princeton: Princeton University Press, 1972; Chapter 7 below.

say that these social science subfields have more in common with each other than they have with the lawyer's intellectual heritage. The study of law in the social sciences is developing into a fully articulated alternative perspective on law. How has this come about?

Let us look quickly at the emergence of concern for law in the social sciences. Anthropology has had an abiding interest in and an important literature about law virtually from the discipline's earliest days. Thus, despite its age, Bronislaw Malinowski's *Crime and Custom in Savage Society* (1926) continues to receive the attention only accorded seminal works in any discipline. As a seminal figure, Malinowski's strong preference for systematic description based on intensive field investigation militated against the development of a disciplined set of generalizations about law. Instead, law has been viewed contextually as the ordering nexus in any given community subject to the anthropologist's scrutiny. To the extent that generalizations were employed, they were casually borrowed from legal philosophy and put to unconvincing use to explain things in the alien terms of Western legal thought, obviously for the benefit of Westerners. Thus feuding is often seen as a system of self-help to enforce the law, since Austinian law is posited as something that must exist if order is being maintained (I elaborate and illustrate this point in Chapter 7). Happily, this tendency to apply the categories of Western legal thought is less evident in the case of lawmaking, as opposed to law doing, because one such category – custom – is taken to comprehend all varieties of "primitive" lawmaking.

Political science, more than any of the other social sciences, has historically shared its perspective on law with lawyers. Many political scientists in recent decades have consciously rejected the close ties with legal thought that they felt were inhibiting the investigation of innumerable political phenomena unrelated to legal categories, legal methods, and legally defined institutions. The so-called behavioral movement contrasts such legal or, more pejoratively, "legalistic" concerns with political behavior, to be understood in terms of social behavior generally and explored inductively and where possible, quantitatively.

Political science tends in the direction of a discipline without a core of its own. Its members see politics as the adjective to some other discipline's noun: economy, society, community, personality. Failure to cast one's lot with one of the other social science disciplines for the development of fundamental notions and appropriate research strategies leaves the political scientist with the one thin concept of authority to hang everything on and a number of residual categories from legal thought that survive in political science as the traditional way of looking at authority. The upshot of the changes in political science in recent decades is that students of politics have no more to say about law in their own right than do anthropologists, though for different reasons.

Psychology represents a rather different course of events. Psychology's concern for law *per se* has always been minimal because its students see law primarily as a social instrumentality. The effect of law on behavior, especially when measured as deviance, is another matter and has received ample attention. Yet this kind of work requires very little consideration of what the law is, what kinds of law there may be, and how law comes to be. The psychologist is principally interested in how law works or fails to work but, as with anthropologists, this leads in the direction of exhaustive study of individual situations. Generalizations on how law works, irrespective of social factors, are obviously hazardous and tend to be shunned. Only insofar as psychologists enlarge their perspectives to include such factors does there emerge a place in their discipline for the study of law.

By now it is clear that the one social science discipline left to provide a unifying perspective for the analysis of law in other than Austinian terms is sociology. We have attempted to show why this is so, but before turning to sociology directly we would like to note that this was by no means an inevitable course of events. In particular, anthropology before Malinowski held definite promise of developing a sufficiently unified and generalizable perspective on law that it could have oriented the subsequent emergence of systematic social science investigation on the subject. Sir Henry Maine, after all, is a name equally familiar to anthropologists and legal scholars today. Deserted by modern, field-oriented anthropology, resisted by formal positivism, and severely damaged by its own tendency to generalize metaphorically and parochially, the so-called historical school is mostly a matter of history. Had it been otherwise, the Austinian view might be the anachronism and the gulf between legal thought and social science might not exist at all.

Sociology began in Continental Europe basically to provide a frame of reference for making sense of the stupendous and unprecedented growth of 19th century industrial society. In the hands of such towering figures as Karl Marx, Emile Durkheim, and Weber, there developed a systematic and comparative study of the advanced social economies. Economics was freed from the need to be concerned with social setting and grew in a highly technical and formal direction, while the heritage of the social-economic systematizers expanded substantively to become sociology as we now know it.

Although inevitably attenuated by the widening scope of sociology, the original link between society and economy nonetheless continues to be crucial to organizing explanations on the working of social orders. As such it represents a direct alternative to the long-standing presumption of legal–political thought that the crucial relationship for explaining the operation of social orders is between law and order. Apparently legal thought and sociology offer a choice of approaches to the problem of social order that can be captured in their characteristic terminology. Sociologists seize on the *social* as the critical factor and find it substantially dependent on economy, while legal scholars seize on *order* as critical and find it substantially dependent on law. Durkheim and Weber, for example, may be considered the fathers of the sociology of law, and their different treatments of the general problem of social order provide us with two quite different ways of looking at law without assuming in an Austinian sense that the legal nexus is the root source of social order.[25]

Durkheim's ideas about the place of law in society are an integral part of his famous early treatise, *De la division du travail social*, first published in 1893. He identified two major forms of social order: those we would call primitive, which he described in terms of "mechanical solidarity," and those we would call complex or modern, which he described in terms of "organic solidarity." Organic solidarity takes place through the division of labor. Fundamentally different types of law characterized the two kinds of solidarity. Mechanical solidarity yields, and uses, repressive law, meaning law possessing a repressive sanction in response to deviancy and describing criminal law even today. Organic solidarity yields, and uses, restitutive law, meaning law the sanction of which "consists of a simple *return in state*." Restitutive law is thus roughly analogous to civil law and, most eminently, contract law. It performs "special tasks," largely unrelated to "transcendental authority which, when offended, demands expiation."[26]

As social orders grow more complex, labor is further and further divided, and special tasks and their regulation increase as an overlayer on the formerly dominant substratum of repressive law. In an organically solidified social order, restitutive law vastly outweighs the law for which forcible sanctions are normally brought to bear, with significant institutional consequences.

> While repressive law tends to remain diffuse within society, restitutive law creates organs which are more and more specialized: consular tribunals, councils of arbitration, administrative tribunals of every sort. Even in its most general part, that which pertains to civil law, it is exercised only through particular functionaries: magistrates, lawyers, etc., who have become apt in this role because of very special training.[27]

In short, Durkheim has given us a comprehensive description of social orders as legal orders without assuming the dependence of social orders in general on a particular kind of law.

To what extent does the international legal order resemble either of the types of social order presented by Durkheim? Mechanical solidarity is notoriously absent, as are effective repressive sanctions. Laws that depend on such sanctions exist in a rhetorical but otherwise unrealized sense. Yet organic

25 The inspiration, though little of the substantive detail, for the following comparative treatment of Durkheim and Weber as the founders of the sociology of law, comes from B.C. Cartwright and R.D. Schwartz, "The Invocation of Legal Norms: An Empirical Investigation of Durkheim and Weber," *American Sociological Review*, vol. 38, 1973, pp. 340–54.

26 E. Durkheim, *The Division of Labor in Society*, trans. by G. Simpson, New York: Free Press, 1933, p. 111, emphasis in translation; p. 127.

27 Ibid., p. 113.

solidarity is a reality of contemporary international life, just as much as modern social orders are, for no other reason than that such orders are in constant and interpenetrating relations with each other. Following Durkheim, the advanced condition of the division of labor in the international social order compels the utilization of an extensive body of restitutive laws. These laws need not come from a legislative fount; they do not come exclusively from such a fount in any order. They do come from the formal agreements or treaties comparable in function to contracts in municipal orders and the myriad practices on which all functionaries and administrative organs performing innumerable specialized tasks are forced to rely in the process of generating further practice.

There is a singular resemblance between Durkheim's conceptions of social order types applied to the contemporary international legal order and Wolfgang Friedmann's notable schematization in his book, *The Changing Structure of International Law* (1964). Friedmann confirmed the rapid growth of what he called the law of cooperation in the international legal order, very much as Durkheim would have predicted. Durkheim might nonetheless have been surprised at the vigor of an organic order underlain only by the rudest kind of mechanical order, embodied for Friedmann in the law of coexistence. Although he was sensitive to abnormal forms, Durkheim's frame of reference was almost exclusively the Western European experience. As Malinowski demonstrated so brilliantly, civil law based on economic relationships is an integral and important part of many apparently primitive orders. Furthermore, with Malinowski, Durkheim simply imputed a repressive sanction to primitive orders without demonstrating its existence. The international legal order may well resemble a multitude of orders, including those of Europe, which were well developed organically long before the emergence of a coercive apparatus of any consequence.

If law and law-relevant institutions in an organically solidified order arise in response to the division of labor, it is because they solve, through available instrumentalities, the particular kinds of problems that arise for participants in a very much divided society. Standard solutions are supplied in diverse situations. Standard operating procedures are employed. Contract law, as the most characteristic form of organic law, "has for its function much less the creation of new rules than the diversification in particular of pre-established rules."[28] Since the international legal order is decentralized in its lawmaking procedures, that very diversification is simultaneously the particularization of new rules incidental to particular solutions.

The foregoing raises an issue that Durkheim himself addressed, although in the instance of the international legal order it appears in aggravated form. If law is nothing more than solutions to problems created by the division of labor, then is not each solution constructed from the particulars of

28 Ibid., p. 215.

the situation, representing nothing more than a balance of private interests? If such were the case, then each solution is a law, one that lives only for that solution. Durkheim argued that "law is, above all, a social thing and has a totally different object than the interest of its pleaders."[29] This is actually a definition of law that requires the solutions to be made by reference to some objective standard. Not all problems generated by the division of labor are dealt with by reference to law. Although law must be seen in terms of solutions, all solutions are not law. Those solutions using law as an objective standard, whether legislated, created by agreement or divined from prior solutions, are the solutions in which the social order has a direct role.

Law is the aggregate of solutions, but more especially of solutions connected to other solutions by reference to each other or common, objectively stated standards for handling problems. In the international legal order more than in centralized orders, solutions are likely to be obtained by reference to comparable solutions, the first of which was not legal, or nearly as legal as the latest, rather than by reference to objective standards. In due course standard solutions are of course objective standards. For our purposes, legality is a relative condition. Standardization is the empirical measure of relative legality. To speak of standard solutions is to employ a convention meaning only – standard enough to be called law.

Weber's work on law is perhaps even more extensive than Durkheim's; at any rate, it is more systematically presented and set apart from the rest of his sociology. Though only one part of Weber's monumental unfinished treatise *Wirtschaft und Gesellschaft* (1922), the work on law begins with a tightly related set of definitions and proceeds to a comparative and developmental systematization of legal orders and legal thought. However much my reading of Durkheim's thought was selective, the complexity and richness of Weber's contribution compels even greater selectivity. As a starting place, Weber's formal definition of law is little help. It is recognizably in the Austinian tradition but avoids Austin's necessary link between law and political authority or the state: "An order will be called law if it is externally guaranteed by the probability that coercion (physical or psychological), to bring about conformity or avenge violation, will be applied by a staff of people holding themselves specially ready for that purpose." Weber countenanced a greater variety of ordered situations as being legal than did Austin, but he doubted that international law is truly law.[30]

Weber's background in the pandectist, or Germanic ultra-positivist school, is evident in his definition of law, yet his subsequent sociology of law is not really dependent on this definition. Weber is justly famous for his interest in bureaucracy, which can be inferred even from his definition of law – sanctions

29 Ibid., p. 113.
30 Rheinstein, *Max Weber on Law in Economy and Society*, pp. 5–6, emphasis in translation.

are applied by a staff – and is a constant theme in his review of legal orders. But his concern is not simply or even primarily for that single class or group of persons called bureaucrats. Rather he is interested in any distinguishable group involved in the operation of legal orders. Weber determined that most such groups in all but the most primitive social orders are composed of lawyers, that is, persons trained in and having scarce or possibly even exclusive knowledge about how law works.

Lawyers' groups in different orders tend to be organized differently, and Weber took pains to show that the organization of lawyers and of legal thought is a complex phenomenon only generally connected with socio-economic developments. Social orders have distinctive legal systems reflecting separate developmental experiences for their specialists in legal knowledge. For Weber this turned out to be a good deal more revealing than the stipulated presence of enforcement staffs. Weber saw a social order as dependent on a legal order, but only as a standard item that all advanced orders possessed without its decisively affecting the direction of socioeconomic development. Furthermore, the existence of a legal order gave rise to the distinctive organization of legal knowledge and activity that accompanied the developing social economy without either the organization of legal knowledge or the social economy being decisively affected by or dependent on the other. This parallel development is Weber's rationale for treating the sociology of law apart from the rest of his sociology of advanced orders and is simultaneously his critique of more deterministic treatments of economy, society, and law.

What does this have to do with international law? Conceivably foreign office legal advisers and their staffs are "an organized coercive apparatus for the nonviolent exercise of legal coercion," possessing "such power that there is in fact a significant probability" that norms will be respected.[31] Whether legal advisers are indeed enforcement staffs, they are only a small part of the organization of legal knowledge and activity at the international level. Just as with municipal orders, the more dominant feature is the substantial presence of lawyers organized in a distinctive fashion. Obviously, the presence of lawyers is not a consequence of the creation of a legal order, as Weber defined it. The creation of an international legal order is only now and only possibly taking place, and it is very much the creation of lawyers or the lawyers' wish to create. In fact, lawyers have been supplied by the domestic orders where they exist in abundance.

It is one of the ironies of history that the Austinian tradition should dominate so much of 20th century legal thought and yet lawyers should persist in viewing international law as an appropriate subject for training, scholarship and career. The fact that they do means that we have on a world scale a substantial, well-organized legal community. Following Weber, it does not mean that we have an international legal order. What would appear to be the

31 Ibid., p. 14.

legal organization of the international order does not make the latter a legal order, for there are good reasons why lawyers would undertake to organize themselves as if they were the instrumentalities of an advanced legal order, even a state. Most obviously, there are psychological benefits in lawyers engaging in the collective conceit of organizing the way they do. Hence we have the World Court, made by lawyers for lawyers, legal committees of the General Assembly, and so on. Weber would not say that the way lawyers are organized is inconsequential, but he would be inclined to see it as symptomatic of developments in advanced orders and not a signification of the existence of an international legal order.

We can proceed one last step to the inevitable if heretical conclusion that what international lawyers care to describe as international law is their own invention. It builds the illusion that there is an international *legal* order and that they are in charge of it. They see their rules of law as the specific, tangible instrumentalities by which states are made a part of that order and their behavior governed by it. The alternative is to say that lawyers exist in their currently organized form at the international level at the sufferance and for the convenience of states, and that order is achieved through circumstances and processes largely unrelated to the availability of law or laws created by lawyers.

In this view law is little more than a set of artifacts. They appear to be germane to international life simply to fulfill their illusory function for lawyers. For their part, lawyers make their artifacts as realistic as possible. Like popguns for children, international laws can look deceptively like real laws without working, because there is no legal order for them to work in.

International law can nonetheless have considerable utility without being operative. It can serve as a model of what the law in an operative international legal order would or should look like, and thus may serve an educational function both for statesmen and publics. Negative educational effects are hardly unheard of, however, as when artifacts demonstrably fail to function as law in highly publicized situations or when swiftly changing circumstances make artifactual laws look irrelevant or outmoded. Such occasions, of course, give further employment to the international lawyers who are so well organized to refurbish and refine their artifacts.

I have derived from the sociologies of Durkheim and Weber two characterizations of law as different from each other as they are from Austinian law. Neither characterization excludes the other. Both characterizations fit some of what we take to be international law, and together they account for most of that law. Both kinds of law – law as standard solutions and law as lawyers' artifacts – command our attention.

Standardizing solutions: the role of practice, treating and codifying

The traditional sources of international law are conventionally understood to yield one kind of law. But if indeed there are two kinds of law, then could there not be two kinds of sources? If we remember that sources are not intrinsic to law, but merely external descriptions of how law comes into being, it may be useful to align the two kinds of law with two kinds of sources. Segregating a specific traditional source into one or the other class could be complicated or even confounded by the usual meaning of the specific source. In this event we would have reason to reconceptualize the source at that level of specificity, and in the process we might remove some of the anomalies and ambiguities that we have already noted in the traditional formulations.

Let us look first at custom as a source of law. Is it a source of law as solutions or law as artifacts? The answer is unclear and the attempt to segregate it unhelpful. If we reconceptualize custom into customary state practices, on the one hand, and reiterations of legal principles on the other, we are bringing to the surface a latent idea in the traditional idea of custom. The distinction is kept latent by assuming that reiterated principles are abstracted from state practices. This assumption is of course made necessary by the definition of legal custom as practice recognized by states as having legal consequences.

Yet the definition is essentially arbitrary, being too stringent for much customary law to exist apart from that which generalizes treaties. If we discard the definition, we can exchange the assumption of a relationship between practice and principle for an assessment of the extent to which practice and principles are actually related. Short of a systematically empirical survey, which is extraordinarily difficult to perform, our assessment must be informal and inconclusive. Nonetheless, it seems likely that the overwhelming proportion of the work of legal advisers and other bureaucrats involved in technical international problem-solving through the utilization of standard solutions is not subjected to principled restatement. There is no need to do so, it is costly to do so, and it can easily be embarrassing to do so.

Legal advisers and other bureaucrats can and consistently do act in a way that is law-minded without having to couch everything they do in terms of legal principles.[32] Law-mindedness is being attentive to standard procedures and always selecting the most formal of available solutions consistent with desired outcomes. Law-minded behavior need not draw a firm distinction between legal and illegal possibilities. It merely presumes in favor of the solution most nearly articulated as principle when other considerations are roughly equal. Many circumstances permit behavior that is consistent with principles, if they were to be articulated or invoked, but permit that behavior to be undertaken without principles being articulated or invoked. Other circumstances require some level of elaboration on how a particular solution can be said to be standard, but the argumentation never reaches the level of public visibility that is almost definitionally required for the reiteration of

32 See R. Fisher's well-known discussion of bureaucratic law-mindedness in "Bringing Law to Bear on Governments," *Harvard Law Review*, vol. 74, 1960, pp. 1130–40.

principles. Finally, in a few circumstances solutions must be sorted into the few publicly available possibilities and advanced as lawful in the fullest sense of being consistent with practice and its public articulation.

The practice of foreign office legal advisers is thus largely a matter of solutions whose standardization is for the most part subterranean. That solutions are cast in legal language is more a consequence of the lawyer's training and habits of mind than it is of his consideration of legal weight or merit *per se*. The standardization of solutions is surely expedited by the use of standard forms and terms in legal language, but this is hardly synonymous with articulation, which implies the identification of legal principles that are seen as determinative for the situation at hand (and any others like it).

For simplicity's sake, I have used the work of foreign office legal advisers to illustrate the nature of international law as standard solutions. Yet there is no clear boundary between those in governments whose activities make up international law and those whose activities do not. Any time public functionaries have recourse to a standard solution to any kind of situation with an international component, it may be said that they are using international law. Whether they recognize it to be international law, or whether we could find written confirmation anywhere of the solution's legal status, is immaterial. Most such solutions are so specialized and their standard character appreciated by so few people that there is no conceivable way that all of them could be transcribed into the public record as "the law." Even if this were possible through vastly improved record collection and utilization systems, the very fact of making at least some of these solutions public would undermine their value, for they would be seen as private bargains by any number of interests not represented in their fashioning or previous use.

There is no particular reason why we should restrict our attention to governmental activity. Major governments formally defined are surrounded by a penumbra of institutions and agents, granted varying degrees of public status, but very much a part of the network of activity centered in the government. The boundaries between government and subgovernment are harder to find the closer one looks. As soon as we countenance the relevance to international law of quasi-public governmental activity, there is little reason to hesitate about activity that is almost entirely centered in private governments like corporations, foundations and universities. All such institutions are faced with the consequences of divided labor. When these consequences are transnational – whether public, private or somewhere in between – and are treated in terms of standard solutions, then international law in Durkheim's image is the result. Currently, transnational relations are a matter of great interest to scholars, but their discussions either deal diffusely with everything transnational or concretely with a small number of transnational actors.[33] My concern here is with the whole class of transnational activities,

33 For illustration, see R.O. Keohane and J.S. Nye (eds), *Transnational Relations and World Politics*, Cambridge, MA: Harvard University Press, 1972.

which are inter-institutional solutions to problems defined in specialized terms through the division of labor in institutions.

The full range of activities so comprehended is beyond assessment, perhaps beyond imagining. Except for the fact that a small proportion of all such standard solutions have always been called law, or in conformity with law, we might not be inclined to use the term law at all. But if we use the term for some such solutions, we must use it for them all. Otherwise, we should disclose what additional attribute we use to differentiate law from non-law.

One such attribute might be that lawyers must be the ones to use solutions if they are to be called law. Another attribute is indeed public acknowledgment of standard solutions as legal. The latter is the traditional way of demarcating law from similar activity, but it is severely restrictive, as I have noted. The former is untried and undoubtedly ambiguous with respect to marginal situations in which lawyers are only occasional users. Whether all standard solutions or just those made or used by lawyers are considered law, it must be obvious that the traditional tools of legal analysis are next to useless in examining such law. Rather it is the province of organization theory, decision analysis, and even operations research, in which there is already a substantial accumulated knowledge about standard solutions and operating procedures, especially in bureaucratic settings.

Treaties are public and objective solutions to problems and are agreed to as such. We could simply conclude that this is the best boundary between standard solutions as law and not law. So restricted, there is surely enough law to occupy the attention of legal scholars. Yet there are problems with this position. What is the status of unratified treaties, agreements between public and private entities, reservations to treaties not accepted by most other parties? What is the status of subsequent interpretation, supporting documents and patterns of use? If we look not at the treaty as a solution attaining a high level of formality but at the treating process, is it so generically different from the processes by which solutions of lesser formality are arrived on? The answer to this and all the other questions is that treaties are less easily portrayed as the only law solutions than might first appear to be the case.

Treaties differ from practice in degree only, and most of the time the treating process is little different even in degree from the kinds of activity that go into less formal problem-solving.[34] It is probably fair to say that treating is more concerned with creating a new solution than applying available ones to a particular situation, but the distinction between old and new is so much manipulated from case to case that any generalization is not very useful.

34 For a similar view, see M.S. McDougal *et al.*, *The Interpretation of Agreements and World Public Order: Principles of Content and Procedure*, New Haven: Yale University Press, 1967, p. 5 n. 5.

Thus, when a particular solution is provided for a situation by treaty the parties to the solution have an interest in seeing it as a new solution. When the same solution is provided less formally, there is an interest in seeing it as well established. More often than not, any solution is a particularization of an earlier solution, so that it is specifically novel and generically familiar at one and the same time.[35]

The difficulty in identifying particular solutions as old or new is graphically illustrated in contemporary international codification. The Statute of the International Law Commission (ILC), a subsidiary organ of the General Assembly, clearly differentiates between progressive development, meaning the drafting of new solutions, and codification, meaning the reproduction of old solutions. The distinction has been utterly unworkable in practice and abandoned for some time. In the deliberations of the ILC the bureaucrat specialists who make up its membership (most are foreign office personnel presumed to function in an independent capacity) sort through the intricacies of state practice and render it in standardized form (for more on this, see Chapter 10). Increasingly they do this without reference to, or need of, the abstract and generalized statements which dominate legal treatises.

Effectively the ILC has superseded the scholar in sifting through state practice because it is in a better position to do so. Both the intricacy and immediacy of law solutions defy capturing by individual scholars and even teams of specialists systematically plumbing narrowly defined areas of such law are barely scratching its surface. Codification has become the visible surface of the vast network of activity whose full dimensions are beyond discernment. Endeavoring to standardize solutions to the chronic consequences of complexity is the present business of the ILC, just as it is with foreign office legal advisers, phalanxes of government lawyers, and private as well as public bureaucrats and managers in general. This is hardly the original intent of codification, however much it bears out Weber's prophecy that codification is integrally related to bureaucratization.

If we consider law as standard solutions, we find that we have very little access to the solutions themselves. These solutions are so many, so specialized and standard in such a relative sense that we may well decide that there is little advantage to be gained from trying to investigate them directly. Instead we are drawn to the integral process of standardizing solutions and utilizing standard solutions. We become interested in the kinds of individuals whose activity fits this description and the kinds of situations in which such activity takes place. We conclude that international law in the image of Durkheim is

35 This recalls Durkheim's view of contract law, quoted above, pp. 38–9. On "individualization" in international law, i.e., particularization, see also C. De Visscher, *Theory and Reality in Public International Law*, rev. edn trans. by P.E. Corbett, Princeton: Princeton University Press, 1968, pp. 144–63.

both a collection of things and a way of doing things and that the latter lends itself more fruitfully to inquiry. The less we talk of things and the more about ways of doing, the less we need the language of sources and the more we learn about lawmaking.

Artifacts and functionaries: the role of scholars, jurists, and the General Assembly

In its way the history of international codification is quite revealing. Codification at present is largely devoted to standardizing solutions, yet at the beginning it was an opportunity for scholars to reiterate legal principles in as formal a manner as possible. Concern for state practice was frequently subordinated to the integrity of the principles. Codification became more disciplined in time and, as we have seen, the distinction between development and codification gained currency, only to disappear again as principles became less and less relevant to the bureaucratized codificatory process.

The transformation of codification tells most of the story on the changing status of scholars in the international legal order. At least at one time scholars were significant agents for the articulation of the kind of law deriving from Weber's work. Custom consists of practice *and* reiterated principles, which have been associated together as much by definition as anything else. The role of scholars in generating practice may have been something more than nominal in the earliest days of the international system, when all roles were diffuse. As labor became divided and subdivided, the activities of legal scholars were fictionalized as integral to *the* lawmaking process, when in fact there were two such processes, not integrally related and with a place for scholars in only one of them. Even if scholars had no place to speak of in making and using standard solutions, they were paramount in publicizing general principles stated in the form of law. The best evidence of this is 19th century codification and the great treatises of that time.

Ostensibly scholars derived principles from the evidence of practice and treaties, thus making their texts the key link between standard solutions and reiterated principles as necessary components of international law. I do not mean to suggest that in those simpler days scholars were incapable of assessing practice and erecting principles consistent with it. I am skeptical that they were able to do these things often enough to justify the image that the international law depicted in their books has very much to do with the international law used by states in their daily intercourse. Yet this is the image that they have left us with.

The exponential growth of foreign affairs bureaucracies and interstate activities over the last century has altogether outstripped the capacity of scholars to stay even nominally in touch with the burgeoning body of standard solutions. Statements of principles were increasingly supported by metalegal arguments and reciprocal citation. The legal order emerging in the 19th century was perforce detached from the law patterns of the ever-more institutionalized international system. The legal order was all the scholar saw about him, for it was an order of his own making, an artifactual order.

The chronic upheaval of the 20th century has all but destroyed the credibility of the legal order invented by scholars. The world has come largely not to believe in international law even as the daily working of the world is dependent on law solutions. Scholars have been the principal casualty in the demise of their creation. Literally, of course, international legal scholars survive and their number has increased (though surely not in proportion to the growth in numbers of lawyers or intellectuals overall). Gone is the scholar's preeminent role in the articulation of a renewed legal order, in setting forth symbols systematically organized in relation to key principles yet dressed in the concrete language of law solutions. This does not mean, however, that the manufacture of legal artifacts and their assembly into a legal order are activities no longer with us. On the contrary, scholars have been superseded by public functionaries.

Among the relics of the scholar's legal order has been the principle that a truly legal order requires judicial machinery. The creation of the World Court is something of a memorial to the old order, although its activities are hardly those envisaged for it. The World Court has become the scholar's institutional equivalent. Though technically occupied with discrete situations, the Court and its audience quietly collude in treating judgments as something more than an adjunct to the processes of standardizing solutions. The Court's procedure for delivering extended judgments and minority opinions, the stature and independence of its members, and the weighty, principled style the members individually employ all contribute to the position of the Court in producing artifacts for the legal order.

To some degree this role is thrust upon the Court, and its members are unsure whether the principles they are supposed to articulate are representative of the 19th-century legal order or some dawning order whose principles are more inchoate.[36] By its nature, the World Court is severely restricted in the range and volume of its activities. Frequently it has been denied the opportunity to expound principles relating to sensitive aspects of state relations and deeply contested values. The Court's necessary reliance on the multiple fictions of being a problem-solving institution further inhibits its venturing into areas beyond the purview of the 19th-century legal order. Thus, for a variety of reasons the Court's half-willing judges are pressed into service but found wanting as formulators of artifacts.

Whatever the inadequacies of jurists, artifacts are irreversibly in the public sphere. Clearly there is a yearning for the artifacts of legal order even as there is dismay over their irrelevance. The symbolic and ultimately manipulative

36 The Court's ambivalence is graphically illustrated in its infamous judgment in the *South West Africa Case. ICJ Reports*, 1966, pp. 4–51.

importance of artifactual law is widely recognized and control over the production of artifacts is sought by statesmen with large stakes in the way the international system is ordered and, quite conceivably, with a sense of having lost control over routine problem-solving activities. Inevitably, a highly visible public forum, less constrained by considerations of decorum and legal sanctity, has become the locus of activity for making legal artifacts. The General Assembly is almost ideally suited for the purpose, in part because its outcomes can have a very formal but not strictly legal status. The decisive factor, though, is the General Assembly's view of itself as a forum of the world community, the only such body permanently constituted to deal with the full range of contemporary community concerns.

The General Assembly has, as one of its seven main standing committees, a legal committee (the Sixth Committee), which is populated by lawyers with a high annual rate of return to the Committee. And it has an agenda usually less crowded than the agendas of the other main standing committees. Under the circumstances it would be no great surprise if the Sixth Committee has carved out for itself a major role in making artifacts. In its earliest years, for example, the Sixth Committee prepared and adopted a series of draft resolutions affirming the Nuremberg Principles and the criminal status of genocide as principles of international law.[37] And in 1970 the Sixth Committee completed an intensive effort to formulate the so-called Principles of Friendly Relations and Co-operation among States (recall Chapter 3 above).

Yet the decade of the 1960s may be remembered as the golden age for the General Assembly's production and promotion of artifacts. During this time the Sixth Committee was conspicuously not a participant in these activities. What is the reason for this? One reason appears to have been the Sixth Committee's preoccupation with supervising the ILC's work. The energy and success of the ILC, combined with the fact that many of the ILC's members are veterans in the Sixth Committee, has engendered an intense, though hardly overbearing, interest in the Commission.

Another reason for the Sixth Committee's failure to engage in the making of artifacts comes from the very fact of its competence in legal matters. The General Assembly as a whole has been alive to the need for a new order, penetrating substantive domains untouched in the traditional legal order. With its concern for legal niceties, but without the substantive charge of the other main standing committees, the Sixth Committee could only be a hindrance in artifactual lawmaking. Declarations on Colonialism, Permanent Sovereignty over Natural Resources, Elimination of Racial Discrimination, Exploration and Use of Outer Space, and Non-intervention, to use prominent examples, were drafted and adopted entirely without reference to the

37 These resolutions are listed and their legal significance briefly discussed by J. Castañeda, *Legal Effects of United Nations Resolutions*, trans. by A. Amoia, New York: Columbia University Press, 1969, pp. 191–3.

Sixth Committee.[38] After the initial burst of activity in which the innovative as opposed to the legal qualities of artifacts were emphasized, a period of consolidation has set in. At least it would appear to be consolidation such as one finds in customary law formation. The content of declarations of artifacts are reiterated in subsequent resolutions. All other resolutions even vaguely related in content make reference to such declarations in their preambular paragraphs. Having declared principles, the General Assembly makes them integral to its practice.[39]

If reiteration is a case of legal custom forming, then it must be a special case, in which the relevant practice need only be rhetorical since the rules being affirmed are only artifacts. This process is no different from the activity of scholars reaffirming artifactual statements originating in landmark form with either scholars or jurists. I would prefer to avoid recourse to the language of custom altogether, because it is in the nature of an artifact that it does not actually have to be consolidated to become law, as does a custom. Once articulated at a requisite level of formality, subsequent activity, unless equally formal, does not decisively affect either the content or status of the artifact. For an artifact, having legality is simply a level of formality, generality and rhetorical acceptance that can be achieved in a variety of ways, but most easily and directly in a community forum. That we call these artifacts law is because we use lawyers to provide the appropriate language and statesmen to provide the rhetoric of acceptance. More fundamentally, it is because we have a deep-seated cultural need to arrange many of our artifacts in what we prefer to call a legal order.

The generation of artifacts by the main standing committees of the General Assembly does not in itself make a new legal order. If the old order were unchallenged, it would be a relatively simple matter to fit new artifacts into it. But we are faced instead with a situation in which numerous and possibly competing principles are promulgated as elements, or even pedestals, of a new order but are not assembled in an orderly way. Some of the subsequent reiteration has the effect of sorting out and ordering the host of new artifacts, and scholars and jurists contribute to envisioning the whole from the newly minted pieces. The Sixth Committee, however, may come to occupy the most important place of all in this process. The construction of a draft declaration on the Principles of Friendly Relations is precisely a major effort to restate and reconcile the most important of the new artifacts with each other and with the UN Charter. The result is the most formal and sustained delineation of an emerging, renovated legal order for the system of states. The artifacts

38 Respectively Resolutions 1514 (XV), December 14, 1960; 1803 (XVII), December 14, 1962; 1904 (XVIII), November 20, 1963; 1962 (XVIII), December 13, 1963; 2131 (XX), December 21, 1965.

39 For an important discussion and quantitative survey of the General Assembly's reiterative tendencies, see S.A. Bleicher, "The Legal Significance of Re-Citation of General Assembly Resolutions," *American Journal of International Law*, vol. 63, 1969, pp. 444–78.

are endowed neither with greater legality nor with greater persuasiveness for problem-solvers; they are rendered in a form which illuminates the function of artifacts in providing us with a sense of systemic order and coherence consistent with changing ideas of what is just and fair on a world scale.

In effect, I have conceptualized the emergence of artifactual law in two stages. The first is the articulation of principles and the second is their assembly in a form recognizable as legal order. The Sixth Committee has recently assumed what could become the preeminent role in the second stage, just as it is precluded from the first because of its lack of substantive competence and heritage of concern for law. As the new order becomes less new and necessary principles are already articulated, then it is likely that the highly visible role of the other main standing committees will recede. The Sixth Committee, on the other hand, virtually defines the legal community of public functionaries who will be custodians of the artifacts already existing. If the task of refining and ordering artifacts is shared at all, then it is only with a small circle of jurists and scholars, most of whom are Sixth Committee intimates. [Looking back, I can see how naïve my hopes were.]

Sources as artifacts: the source of sources reconsidered

The source of artifacts cannot be adequately described in the language of the traditional sources, any more than the source of standard solutions can be. I have reconceptualized custom into practice and reiterated principles and aligned the two components with standard solutions and artifacts, respectively. Doing this immediately suggested the connection between practice in general and treating in particular. And it suggested that the articulation of principles has progressed from scholars to jurists and finally to functionaries in the General Assembly. In a crude way it would seem that once custom is reconceptualized, the remaining sources (except the non-source, general principles of law) fall into place to give us two kinds of sources for two kinds of law. The fit is not perfect, for some treaty forums are used to enunciate artifacts just as functionaries in the General Assembly use that forum for the kind of problem-solving that relies on standard solutions.

The real point is whether very much is gained by realigning sources in this fashion. The traditional sources are artifacts made and used by many observers-scholars, jurists and statesmen because these were the artifacts that complemented a collective vision of international legal order while they corresponded at least in a general way, given the state of social knowledge at the time, to actual processes of lawmaking in the system. The vision has faded, the characteristics of lawmaking have changed, knowledge has become more specialized, and the artifacts make less sense of what we see and know. New artifacts are needed, not to make things work better, but to make them look neater. If declarations become enshrined as a source because they are articulated as such in the most formal sense possible, it does not mean that declarations will suddenly be used to produce standard solutions, for which they are not suited. It does mean that they will continue to embody artifacts, for which they are ideally suited.

Actual changes can be made in lawmaking processes, but not through the process of making artifacts. Promulgating a new source either confirms a change that has taken place or creates an illusion. If declarations are made a source, it will confirm the reality that the production of artifacts is now largely in the hands of public functionaries using world community forums, and it will create an illusion for those who wish to believe that declarations are a source of standard solutions. Promulgated or not, declarations are a source for those for whom it serves as a convenient label describing what has already come to pass with respect to the production and organization of artifacts. We could just as well use other labels, in greater or lesser harmony with what actually happens, without benefit or detriment to what happens. We could cease to speak of sources altogether, and speak only of making law solutions and making law artifacts, if we or anyone else found these particular artifacts useful. Even if they were to become law artifacts, they would not be the *source* of anything that happens.

In short, none of this affects the problem of the source of sources. Sources as artifacts have their source in the process of artifact production. But what is the vehicle by which a particular process among many possible ones gets to make the artifacts we call law? The answer to this question is no more accessible than the answer to the question – What is the source of custom as source? We would guess from the kinds of changes in lawmaking we have described, that what makes lawmaking processes what they are is the structure of international society. To say this hardly begins to provide an answer as specific as the question. The same may be said about such answers as social contract, consensus, and social imperative, and yet these are the only answers we have.

7 Reprisals: rituals, rules, rationales (1974)

Studying with Robert Tucker mandated an interest in the use of force in international relations – a subject on which he wrote extensively. Assisting him in revising Hans Kelsen's *Principles of International Law* focused my attention on the use of force short of war. In Kelsenian terms self-help makes any decentralized order properly legal by authorizing an injured party to enforce the law. Even if the language of law is available only to the observer, the act of responding to an injury with a comparable act of violence – taking a reprisal – functions as an enforcement measure. In the relations of states, all parties *talk* about law when force is used.

I wrote a paper on the way lawyers and government officials talk about reprisals for a study panel organized by the American Society of International Law. I also wrote a paper for a meeting of the American Political Science Association on the practice in many societies of exchanging comparable acts of violence in a continuing series. Even if reprisals in a series might look like failed enforcement measures, they also look like a series of moves in a contest – functionally speaking, something very different. Moreover, reprisals as self-help and as moves in a contest with two sides and limited stakes are subject to strikingly similar rules.

In residence at Princeton's Center of International Studies, I combined these papers and added material inspired by my reading of social and legal anthropology for publication in the Center's monograph series. For publication here, I have deleted one-fifth of the original text, smoothed some passages and made one substantive change. In discussing reprisals-series, I had identified two functionally complementary sorts of rules: interaction rules and institutive rules. I chose *institutive* over *constitutive* to avoid the implication of a hierarchy of rules. Below, I call them *framing* rules.

Reprisals

Reprisals are widely observed phenomena in social life. Particularly in those social orders that are conventionally described as "primitive," such as tribal orders and the international system, the patterning of low-level violence in action and reaction, "tit-for-tat" form has occasioned some commentary.[1] Nevertheless, there are only a few sustained treatments of reprisal practices, undertaken for the most part by international legal scholars and substantially devoid of conceptual interest.[2] There are scattered shorter studies and tangentially related material in several disciplines, but there is little evidence of the cross-referencing and cumulative development we normally associate with what is euphemistically called a literature. In sharp contrast with the state of knowledge about arms races or deterrence or any number of similar social phenomena, the study of reprisals lacks even preliminary attempts at conceptually aware synthesis.

The following study seeks to be reasonably comprehensive by organizing and interpreting available knowledge about reprisals in the international system (and to a lesser extent in other social orders) under four headings reflected in the title of this work. First I examine reprisals as acts of revenge having no discernible social function, and I show that reprisals do tend to take place in open-ended series. Then I consider reprisals as forms of ritual activity. In this connection I use the term *ritual* in the sense it is employed by H.L. Nieburg: "to designate the general tendency of actions to acquire a symbolic meaning which tends to have a function different from the raw act."[3] Reprisals in this sense can be understood as having an established place in the functioning of the social order.

I offer two interpretations of reprisals as ritual activity. One interpretation conforms to traditional legal ideas about reprisals by seeing individual acts of reprisal in terms of law-enforcement. The other interpretation is, as far as I know, mine alone. It sees an ongoing series of reprisals as contest-playing. I proceed to deduce the rules that define the proper use of reprisals from the requirements of the alternative rituals and compare them with what the rules seem to be as a matter of practice. Finally, I identify and evaluate the rationales that are available to states to justify reprisal-like activity in the international system. This leads me to formulate a composite rationale.

The point of departure in this framework is *not* international law in particular or primitive law in general. Yet the study as a whole is focused on ongoing reprisal exchanges in the international system, [several paragraphs

1 "Action and reaction patterns" and " 'tit-for-tat' patterns" are the labels preferred respectively by J.S. Milstein, "American and Soviet Influence, Balance of Power, and Arab-Israeli Violence," in B.M. Russett (ed.) *Peace, War, and Numbers*, Beverly Hills: Sage, 1972, pp. 145–53, and E.E. Azar, *Probe for Peace: Small State Hostilities*, Minneapolis: Burgess, 1973, pp. 68–9.

2 The standard monograph on reprisals is E.S. Colbert, *Retaliation in International Law*, New York: King's Crown, 1948. There is rather more work on reprisals undertaken in wartime against individual combatants and whole populations in occupied territories. See, for example, the major studies by B.J. Brungs, "Hostages, Prisoner Reprisals, and Collective Penalties: The Development of the International Law of War with Respect to Collective and Vicarious Punishment," PhD Dissertation, Georgetown University, Washington, 1968, and F. Kalshoven, *Belligerent Reprisals*, Leiden: Sijthoff, 1971.

3 H.L. Nieburg, "Agonistics – Rituals of Conflict," *Annals of the American Academy of Political and Social Science*, no. 392, 1970, p. 61.

deleted here] and the rules said to guide this kind of conduct. Rules are presumed to be made by states to suit a variety of needs and situations. But why do given rules have a particular content? While some situations simply call for a rule, any rule, without prefiguring its content, others seem to dictate a content falling within a limited range of possibilities. The rules associated with reprisals would appear to belong to the latter category.

Thus it is said that the proportionality rule reflects the practice of states because their acts of reprisal must be proportionate, broadly speaking, in order to perform the function of law-enforcement. Interestingly, proportionality follows equally if the function of reprisals is understood in terms of contest playing. The point is that such rules are not phenomena in their own right, set apart from and applied or not, as a matter of choice, to the ritual activity they are found in conjunction with. Instead, they can be seen as epiphenomena, distinctively associated with a particular kind of ritual activity. That such rules are called legal is as much a semantic convention as it is anything else.

Obviously not all rules are of this character. While some – perhaps most – are demonstrably phenomenal, or real (really do have a function), this has to be demonstrated. Only further studies of specific situations can establish which rules are real and which are epiphenomenal. The former are available to guide decision-makers in particular situations. The latter merely describe situations which themselves rule out decision-making choices, whatever remains being garbed in the volitional language of law.

Even in situations in which putative rules are only epiphenomenal, these situations have been created in the sense that earlier choices make them inescapable. Such structuring choices can also be cast as rules, and they are clearly phenomenal in character. Yet they tend not to be articulated in legal language or, for that matter, articulated at all. In the instance of reprisals one such rule requires that there be just two sides in the situation of ongoing reprisal-taking. A situation involving more than two sides can be chosen by the participants in the interaction, but exercising that choice makes the situation something other than one involving reprisals. Classical legal formulations with respect to reprisals pass over these rules in favor of ones that are more visible but paradoxically do not exist in the usual sense of legal rules.

If the discussion of rules will only be secondarily concerned with law, the discussion of rationales will primarily be set forth in legal terms. By linking abstract normative propositions called rules to state behavior, on the one hand, and widely shared images of order, on the other hand, rationales are integral to the process of using, and making, law. Rationales are erected and doctrine is elaborated in defense of behavior, not just because the behavior is suspect (which it may well be), but because the rules are perceived as suspect (which they may be just as well) either in content or applicability. States bother with rationales to make their behavior more tolerable to other states, not to mention their own populations, and more comprehensible to themselves when they stand back from what they are doing.

The need for some kind of rationale is forced especially by the occurrence of ritual activity, since this is behavior states tend to see as determined for them by circumstances. Even so, the selection of a particular rationale is a choice limited only by the availability of rationales. Historically states have justified their recourse to low-level coercion by reference to broadly defined legal categories, like self-defense, reprisals and intervention, which have always lent themselves to permissive construction. While the UN Charter severely limits the permissive quality of these legal categories, recourse to low-level violence continues, as does the habit of rationalizing its use in legal terms. No discussion of the use of force in the international system today can proceed without reference to the place and purpose of doctrinal rationales.

Reprisals is a term whose meaning is rarely discussed, still less disputed. A reprisal is widely understood to refer to a retaliatory act provoked by a prior act seen as unwarranted by its recipient. Most reprisals are coercive responses to coercion, for it is coercion in particular which is likely to be seen as unwarranted. Although the presence or open use of force is not technically a necessary attribute of a reprisal, forcible reprisals will be our concern here. International law provides a more refined meaning for reprisal and in so doing imparts a significance to the term that cannot be inferred from its general or material meaning. The legal sense of the term, already alluded to, will emerge more fully in the discussion of reprisals as ritual activity.

If for the moment we confine our attention to reprisals as raw acts of revenge by asking what function such acts serve in their own right, we could well begin with Lewis Coser's exposition of "safety-valve" institutions:

> An illustration of safety-valve mores which provide a sanctioned outlet for hostilities against the *original* object is supplied by the institution of the duel both in Europe and in nonliterate societies. Dueling brings potentially disruptive aggressive self-help under social control and constitutes a direct outlet for hostilities between members of the society. Socially controlled conflict "clears the air" between the participants and allows a resumption of their relationship. If one of the participants is killed, his kin and friends are assumed not to continue the hostility against his adversary: the affair is then "socially closed" and relations can resume.
>
> Socially approved, controlled and limited acts of revenge fall into the same category.[4]

The safety-valve institution can work only if two different sets of conditions are met. The first set has to do with the question of right and wrong. If the

4 L.A. Coser, *The Functions of Social Conflict*, Glencoe, IL: Free Press, 1956, p. 42; his emphasis.

safety valve is conceptualized as a duel, then we can safely assume that the parties agree, though perhaps only tacitly, that the question of right and wrong will be settled by the outcome of the duel. If, on the other hand, acts of revenge are to be understood as the safety valve, then we have a unilateral determination of right and wrong by the revenge-seeker, who furthermore can decisively set the conditions for executing his determination. Obviously the respondent in this situation will dispute the determination and will resent his adversary's unfair advantage in executing it. Thus he will assume the stance of being wronged and the advantage in rectifying his wrong in a subsequent round of vengeance. Then, of course, the tables are turned again and vengeful activity continues as long as the adversaries possess the resources to continue it.

This brings us to the second set of conditions that must be satisfied if the safety valve is to work. In a duel, the parties are normally assumed to be single individuals whose resources are limited to themselves. If one of them kills or severely wounds the other, the presumption that the winner is right is reinforced by the inability of the loser to contest that presumption. In cases of revenge, however, groups – even large groups – may be involved. Unless one such group is intimidated by the disproportionate size of the other, they both have the capability and the incentive to perpetuate exchanges of violence.

Coser indicated that limited acts of revenge are analogous to duels as safety-valve institutions, but he failed to examine the circumstances that would serve to limit revenge. Normally exchanges of violence that can be characterized, like reprisals, in terms of revenge, tend not to release tension but, on the contrary, serve to maintain it at a constant or accelerating pitch. Continuing tension between roughly comparable adversaries almost inevitably results in ongoing episodic violence. This we commonly call a feud.

Feuds are distinguished from duels by "locking in" violence instead of closing it out through the initial exchange. A violent exchange that locks in may or may not have the immediate effect of releasing tension. It does have the larger effect of creating an expectation among both participants and observers that further exchanges will take place. The interest and excitement that go into anticipating, preparing for, and participating in these subsequent exchanges are also likely to be functional for considerable units in the social order, and possibly the social order as a whole, through enhancing group cohesion.

In the international system retaliatory acts that have given rise to retaliatory acts in a potentially infinite series can be called a reprisals-series or an international feud. While reprisals have a widely acknowledged material and legal meaning, reprisals-series are a phenomenon largely untouched by analysts. The principal extant reprisals-series, involving ongoing Arab–Israeli activity, is of course subject to wide comment in both general political and technical legal terms. Yet the frame of reference is invariably one or another individual act of reprisal or the whole gamut of conflict – major and minor – in the area. The special qualities of a reprisals-series, taken as a whole, are not so much ignored as unimagined.

Rituals

An isolated act of revenge is quite possibly without functional consequence for the system in which it takes place. A feud is simply too much a part of the system to be without consequence – it must almost certainly take on a ritual dimension. Yet the standard view of reprisals as ritual acts that have a well-established function in the social order focuses on individual acts. Such isolated acts are said to function as sanctions in what is then, by definition, a legal order. As sanctions, reprisals presumably work the way duels do to answer the question of right and wrong definitively. Consequently a reprisals-series does not exist by definition. This view is held both by international legal scholars and social anthropologists, and thus it must be regarded as a characteristically Western construction of the significance of retributive acts.

Inasmuch as the function of such acts is more often deduced from a received set of beliefs about how social orders work than empirically demonstrated, we could fairly say that the belief in reprisals as sanctions may not describe ritual activity in the system so much as constitute ritual activity among its observers. Later, I suggest an alternative ritual, tentatively identified as *contest-playing*, that relates more directly to the persistence and apparent significance of reprisals than does the reprisals-as-sanctions idea.

It might be pertinent at this point to inquire briefly into the origins of the belief that reprisals operate as sanctions in a social order. If we accept the view identified with Jeremy Bentham and, in its purest form, with John Austin, that law is the sanction-bearing command of the sovereign or, more simply, that law has teeth, then we are faced in the examination of social orders with no enforcement procedures to conclude either that they are not legal orders, or that they operate as legal orders because sanctions are present, despite the absence of centralized sanctioning procedures.[5] This is to say that the existence of order can be explained in two ways. The first imputes to the members of a social order a degree of conditioning to abide by the order that coercive enforcement is unneeded. The second supposes decentralized enforcement through self-help, by the victims of delictual behavior, on behalf of the order.

In the history of 19th and 20th century legal philosophy, the dominance of positivist doctrine has guaranteed a prominent place in international legal thought for the second of these solutions. In the work of Hans Kelsen, in particular, the "essence of international law" – its truly legal nature – is

5 In the words of E.A. Hoebel, *The Law of Primitive Man: A Study in Comparative Legal Dynamics*, Cambridge, MA: Harvard University Press, 1954, p. 26, "[t]he law has teeth: teeth that can bite if need be."

dependent on the existence of coercive sanctions in the form of reprisals.[6] While Kelsen may be the extreme case, most other writers take it for granted that reprisals are the concrete form that sanctions take in the international legal order and accept the implication that this is the technique by which the legal order works.[7]

Perhaps surprisingly, there is little evidence to support this widespread belief. Quite to the contrary, the evidence suggests that there is no substantial practice among states in the international legal order that can be identified as reprisals undertaken self-consciously as sanctions.[8] There are numerous reciprocities in international behavior, formal and informal, peaceful and violent. Violent reciprocities are graced with many labels, including war, aggression and self-defense, and reprisals. In short, low-level coercion has abounded in international relations. States have frequently argued that their acts are in response to an injury suffered at the hands of another state. But it is legal scholars, and not statesmen, who have devised the fiction that redressing a material injury is the same as repairing a delict on behalf of the legal order.

The conjunction between sanctions as a property of a legal order and as an observable relationship between disapproved behavior (fictionalized as disobedience) and punishment goes back to Bentham.[9] Presumably, the observed relationship gave rise to the posited property as an inference, although even with Bentham this may have been confused.[10] Certainly with later positivist doctrine the inversion is complete, and the posited property requires the analyst to discover relationships having that character. What results is the following argument, now held as an article of faith: (1) sanctions take the form of coercive responses to disruptive acts; (2) coercion, or its threat, tends to have a deterrent effect; (3) law works chiefly through deterrence; (4) acts that take the form of sanctions are enforcing the law.

This line of reasoning confuses deterrence and enforcement. Deterrence is one possible result of using force; retaliation is another possibility. The deterrent effect may be unintended or even undesired. Only when deterrence is the specific objective of coercion as a specific technique is it possible to talk about law-enforcement. The presence of either the objective or the technique does

6 H. Kelsen, "The Essence of International Law," in K.W. Deutsch and S. Hoffmann (eds), *The Relevance of International Law*, Garden City, NY: Anchor Books, 1971, pp. 115–23.

7 Recent cases in point are D. Bowett, "Reprisals Involving Recourse to Armed Force," *American Journal of International Law*, vol. 66, 1972, pp. 2–3; R.W. Tucker, "Reprisals and Self-Defense: The Customary Law," 66 *American Journal of International Law*, vol. 66, 1972, pp. 589–90; and, in a fuller discussion, Kalshoven, *Belligerent Reprisals*, pp. 22–6.

8 This is the overwhelming impression one carries away from Colbert's *Retaliation in International Law*. An exception must be made for wartime practices.

9 J. Bentham, *An Introduction to the Principles of Morals and Legislation* (1823 edn), New York: Hafner Press, 1948, ch. xii–xv.

10 H.L.A. Hart, "Bentham, Lecture on a Master Mind," in R.S. Summers (ed.), *More Essays in Legal Philosophy: General Assessments of Legal Philosophies*, Berkeley: University of California Press, 1971, pp. 40–1.

not necessarily entail the other. Even when both are present, a relationship between them cannot be assumed; it must be empirically determined. In other words, the deterrent function may be achieved through a variety of structures, and the coercive structure may serve a variety of functions.

Logically, all acts taking the form of enforcement acts need not be enforcing the law. For centralized legal orders the logical problem disappears, because the order defines in advance which coercive acts are true sanctions, and which are spurious, by specifying agents, conditions and so on. The international legal order, being decentralized, has historically left the determination of real and spurious sanctions to the inventive mind of the scholar. With the advent of collective security responsibility was said to have shifted to the organs of the order. The attempt to centralize law-enforcement failed for reasons that are all too well known. Nevertheless, we are not quite where we were, for decentralized enforcement procedures have not been formally revived.

In comparison with legal philosophy, the situation in social anthropology is rather more complicated. The prevailing sentiment in social anthropology in its early days in the 19th century reflected Henry Maine's influence.[11] Interest was focused on the integrative effect of blood relationships and statuses. Order was seen as the result of internalized responses to ordained circumstances, which included the corporate institutions of the order. Sanctions, if the term were used at all, were called "psychological" rather than "social," meaning that they did not involve coercion. To the Western mind, such an order could be conceptualized as "primitive communism" or something similar.[12]

This idealized description of so-called primitive orders, in which formal institutions of government are not present because they are not needed, failed over time to meet the test of empirical scrutiny. Particularly for Bronislaw Malinowski, anthropology's pioneer in systematic field research, the tradition represented by Maine failed to account for more primitive orders that are both more complex and more given to coercive and otherwise disruptive behavior than predicted by the prevalent model.

Maine was a conceptualist in the grand manner of his time. Malinowski was stridently anti-conceptual. In his famous monograph, *Crime and Custom in Savage Society* (1926), Malinowski did go so far as to adopt a distinction between criminal law and civil law. As a matter of definition, he saw the former in terms of crime and punishment, delicts and sanctions. While Malinowski brilliantly described the substantive nature of crimes and punishment in a particular primitive order, he simply accepted the categories

11 See M. Gluckman, *Politics, Law and Ritual in Tribal Society*, Chicago: Aldine, 1965, pp. 1–35, for a vivid account of anthropology's early years.

12 The phrase is Durkheim's. For some useful comments, see T.O. Elias, *The Nature of African Customary Law*, Manchester: Manchester University Press, 1956, pp. 56–75.

themselves as self-evident. They were, after all, justified by a legal theory that required enforcement through sanctions to supplement the internalized tendency to obey the law. Malinowski seems to have brought this perspective to bear unexamined because it was the Austinian legacy in British intellectual life.

For Malinowski, criminal law was a good deal less important or interesting than civil law. The latter he saw in terms of reciprocal rights and duties, creating a legal order dependent on a web of economic and social relationships. The complexity of such an order, not so very different from the civil order in the most advanced contemporary states, defied hasty conceptualization but, at the same time, compelled exhaustive description on a case-by-case basis.

Malinowski's basic distinction between the criminal and the civil in primitive orders encouraged the growth of two quite separate intellectual traditions in social anthropology. On the one hand, there was the tendency to think of all social orders as sanction-bearing legal orders.[13] To the extent that social anthropology came to adopt a consistent intellectual focus, as in the hands of A.R. Radcliffe-Brown, any *system* of order required the identification of structures that had to exist to perform pre-established functions.[14] However phrased, one of these functions has always been the maintenance of order.

Structural-functionalism comes very close to making the law-as-sanction idea inevitable, for it sends the investigator searching for order-generating and maintaining structures that he knows must be out there somewhere. When he finds that retributive practices are endemic in tribal life and that they are frequently justified in other than personal terms, he automatically concludes that he has found the means by which even apparently primitive orders maintain order.[15] Consequently these practices are called sanctions, and the social order is a legal order. So as not to seem patronizing, the anthropologist reminds us that it is a primitive legal order, not because it is ineffective, but because it is decentralized.

On the other hand, Malinowski's distinction helped social anthropology develop an empirical, case-oriented and anti-conceptual tradition. Strict definitions were abjured and behavior that appeared to be related to the maintenance of order was carefully described in terms of process and context. The titles of major books, like Max Gluckman's *The Judicial Process among the Barotse in Northern Rhodesia* (1955) and Paul Bohannan's *Justice and Judgment among the Tiv* (1957) reflect the generally limited purview of this kind of work.

13 A striking example is A.R. Radcliffe-Brown, "Sanction, Social," in *Encyclopedia of the Social Sciences*, vol. 13, 1934, pp. 531–4.

14 See, for example, Radcliffe-Brown's *Structure and Function in Primitive Society: Essays and Addresses*, New York: Free Press, 1952. His essay on sanctions, just cited, is reprinted in this volume.

15 For a lengthy survey of such practices, see H. Kelsen, *Society and Nature: A Sociological Inquiry*, Chicago: University of Chicago Press, 1943.

In a quite satisfactory way each of the many studies in this tradition demonstrates the complexity and sophistication of individual tribal orders. Less satisfactory is their tendency to assume that self-help is present as an enforcement procedure without undertaking to demonstrate it empirically. A case in point is Gluckman, who saw self-help enforcement at work in the settlement of disputes "through the adjustment of rival claims."[16] Yet this kind of "ordered anarchy" does not *have* to be viewed as a self-help system, in the sense of self-help to enforce the law. Self-help may be just that – helping oneself in circumstances in which "people judge situations of dispute in terms of rights and duties, and wrongs." Enforcement has nothing to do with the workings of this permissive yet normative order, because the participants in it do not see their behavior as enforcing or otherwise being affected by a law, but instead as redressing "a balance of wrongs."

A major exception to this casual mingling of a "functional orientation" toward the operation of social orders and the formalistic dogma of law-as-sanctions is Bohannan's work.[17] Bohannan clearly differentiated three forms of self-help among the Tiv, each of them carefully established empirically. One form of self-help is indeed, as he called it, a "jural institution," for the participants in a dispute "must do their own police-work." The second form of self-help is "self-right enforcement, in which the self-help, often in the form of violence, constitutes one's protection of one's own rights, and in which no jural institution is involved." This of course is analogous to Gluckman's notion of self-help, which he falsely identified in terms of law-enforcement. Bohannan's third form of self-help is revenge. "Vengeance or reprisal is a sort of social action that does not automatically end in restitution of the breach of norm which it was meant to counter."

Bohannan's conceptualization of self-help is, to my knowledge, the most serious effort of its kind in either legal philosophy or social anthropology.[18]

16 Gluckman, *Judicial Process among the Barotse of Northern Rhodesia*, p. 263. All the quotations are from Evan-Pritchard's commentary on the Nuer, on which Gluckman was commenting in his turn. For another glaring example, see Hoebel, *The Law of Primitive Man*, including the passage quoted above.

17 "Functional orientation" is J. Stone's label. *The Province and Function of Law as Logic, Justice and Social Control*, Cambridge, MA: Harvard University Press (1950), pp. 715–8, and is not to be confused with "structural-functional," also frequently called functional analysis. For a summary statement of Bohannan's position and the quotations to follow, see *Justice and Judgment among the Tiv*, London: Oxford University Press, 1956, p. 149.

18 It was anticipated to some degree by Max Weber:

> Prior to the existence of any coercive machinery, and prior even to the regulated enforcement of norms through the sib members' duty to participate in vengeance, the function later fulfilled by the "legal" guaranty of a norm was undoubtedly performed by the general convention that the person who was admittedly "in the right" could find others who would help him against an offender.

M. Rheinstein (ed.), *Max Weber on Law in Economy and Society*, trans. by E. Shils and M. Rheinstein, New York: Simon and Schuster, 1954, p. 69.

The distinction between self-help as law-enforcement and as self-right enforcement effectively denies that self-help operates automatically on behalf of the social order. The consequences of individualized problem-solving are indeed problematic for the social order. Only when self-help supports an objective legal regime by deterring further disorder is it truly a jural institution.

The distinction between self-right enforcement and revenge is less clear. The two are not mutually exclusive categories. Although revenge might well be an attempt to right a wrong, it may not, in Bohannan's words, "automatically end" the matter. This suggests that the difference is not in function, as Bohannan implied, but in their structure. If this is so, the difference between self-right enforcement and revenge directly parallels my earlier attempt to distinguish between duels and feuds: self-right enforcement is structured to dispose of the question of right and wrong once and for all, while revenge tends to perpetuate a sense of grievance, tension, and the recurrence of violence.

A very small number of political scientists have concerned themselves with the apparent resemblance of primitive social orders and the international system. One example is Roger Masters, who argued in a much-cited 1964 essay that the self-help enforcement mechanism is a central property of both kinds of orders.

> In stateless systems, disputes cannot be referred back to an impartial government backed by a police force. The characteristic pattern of responding to criminal or civil wrongs is "self help": the individual or group which feels injured considers himself or itself legitimately responsible for punishing a crime or penalizing a tort.
>
> Consciously, retaliation is a means of maintaining the well-being of an offended group and of responding to a specific wrong. Unintentionally or unconsciously, self-help serves to preserve and unite a group which has been threatened by another, to fix responsibility for wrongs, and thus to maintain a legal order. For a specific individual who executes retaliation, the dangerous exploits required for self-help may consciously be a means of gaining glory and influence as well as a means of preserving his legal rights.[19]

According to Masters, if self-help operates to enforce a legal order, those who practice self-help need not know about it – indeed they are probably behaving in this fashion for altogether different, quite personal reasons. Actually, all that Masters can show in a general and comparative sense is that retaliatory activities are commonplace and that order seems to be maintained. The link

19 R. Masters, "World Politics as a Primitive Political System," *World Politics*, vol. 16, 1964, p. 600.

between these facts is hypothesized as a "latent function" of the system.[20] If this link is granted a priori, we would have to agree with Masters "that it would be unwise to see in retaliation and deterrence merely a means of maximizing the advantage gained by one of two or more rivals."[21] Yet if this link is not assumed, then this statement of Masters' becomes a curious twist of logic that denies the wisdom of an obvious explanation, namely, that retaliation is a legitimate means for rivals to seek advantage with respect to each other.

A more recent study by a political scientist, Michael Barkun's *Law Without Sanctions* (1968), studiously avoids law-as-sanction thinking but does so at the cost of a sustained examination of vengeful and retaliatory behavior. In fact, Barkun tended to see law mainly as symbols or manifestations of social processes. Such a perspective, however salutary as an antidote to ritualized sanction-thinking, ends up ignoring order or the lack of it as a tangible social condition. Barkun's concern for the complex of social and psychological relationships in an operative decentralized order tends to ignore what the order actually looks like.

It is rather startling to discover that political scientists, with their long-standing concern for conflict, conceptualized primitive orders as either self-help enforcement systems or complex systems of relationships that militate against conflict, and not as conflict-prone, rivalrous and relatively disorderly systems of order. Malinowski long ago emphasized the lack of order in primitive life, yet international relations scholars to this day hold the primitive order as a model by which to study the comparatively defective international system. Quite possibly the relationship between model and reality could be reversed. The international system as we generally characterize it (unless we accept the ritualized legal view) may serve as a model to tell us more about order and conflict in tribal life than anthropologists have been able to tell us.

Like the international system of order (indicatively, it is rarely called this), many tribal orders may be characterized by a relatively low level of order. As a cultural matter, its participants may simply tolerate disorder as natural or inevitable. Relative disorder may be tolerable because of the limitation that scarce resources impose on disruptive activity. Resource scarcity was, of course, an important feature of the international system until recent decades, and is understood to have been a considerable factor in keeping perpetual conflict within tolerable levels.[22]

20 On the distinction between manifest and latent functions, Masters cited M.J. Levy, *The Structure of Society*, Princeton: Princeton University Press, 1952; it is also closely identified with R.K. Merton, *Social Theory and Social Structure*, rev. edn, Glencoe, IL: Free Press, 1957. For Levy and Merton, the visibility of functions is a concern not for the system's actors, but for its observers. Many system functions go unnoticed by those involved in their performance but are readily ascertained by an outside observer who knows what to look for.

21 Masters, "World Politics as a Primitive Political System," p. 607.

22 R.E. Osgood, *Limited War: The Challenge to American Strategy*, Chicago: University of Chicago Press, 1957, pp. 45–53.

Beyond this, as Bohannan has suggested, some forms of violence may be a legitimate means of adjusting rival claims on the presumption that there is a meaningful relationship between the level of violence and the importance of the claims. The use or threat of force in claiming processes is a well-known and much studied fact of international life. Finally, some (or the same) forms of violence may satisfy a variety of personal needs for members of the social order. This is especially so when violence takes a psychologically intense but materially modest form. Be it in the name of rebellion, liberation, or reason of state, such behavior has had too large an impact on political life at all levels to have gone unattended.[23]

Students of political science and international relations have another advantage over anthropologists. To complement their greater interest in disorder, they have long possessed an appropriate analytical framework for the study of orders that neither support nor remove disorder, but merely confine it to the bounds of what is aptly if metaphorically called an arena. This framework is conventionally known as group or interest theory.[24] It presumes to describe a universe of bounded disorder models of order, just one type being the classical balance of power model. Considerable work has gone into analyzing the formal structural characteristics of these models as well as their processes of interest adjustment.[25] Yet little attention has filtered down to the place of low-level, ongoing, non-escalatory but nonetheless violent conflict in such models. Too often it is simply taken for granted that "conflict systems" are "conflict spirals."[26]

It seems that legal philosophy and social anthropology are of limited help in understanding reprisals-series because of their substantive focus on individual acts and their conceptual focus on system maintenance through law-enforcement. By comparison, political science and especially international relations are more concerned with endemic disorder and to have at their disposal an attractive conceptual framework for dealing with it, but they do no better than the others in helping us to understand ritualized and contained exchanges of violence for which there is no presumption of cessation or consummation.

If we are to look elsewhere for inspiration, we should be guided by a concern both for reprisals-series taken as a whole and for the functional

23 Recent works of interest include: T.R. Gurr, *Why Men Rebel*, Princeton: Princeton University Press, 1970, and I.K. Feierabend *et al.* (eds), *Anger, Violence and Politics: Theory and Research*, Englewood Cliffs, NJ: Prentice-Hall, 1972.

24 See O.R. Young, *Systems of Political Science*, Englewood Cliffs, NJ: Prentice-Hall, 1968, pp. 79–92, for a brief exposition.

25 The first significant systematic work in this direction is K.E. Boulding, *Conflict and Defense: A General Theory*, New York: Harper, 1962. The subsequent literature is voluminous.

26 Azar, *Probe for Peace*, pp. 66–73, drew the distinction between "conflict systems" and "conflict spirals" and then, as just one example, ignored it.

significance of ritualized behavior. Standing at the juncture of sociology, anthropology and psychology is a provocative body of literature devoted to the universal pastime of playing.[27] Play is determined to be a preeminently ritualized activity whose functionality is related not to individual acts but instead to an overall pattern of such acts. Of the several categories of play that have been identified, the one that best suits my analytical need is frequently called a *contest*.[28] What is fundamental to this kind of play is its agonistic character: it is a competition or rivalry, necessarily involving two sides (antagonists) of roughly equal strength playing in a delimited space.[29] Because there are just two sides or teams, when there are more than two individuals involved, they are utilized as players and individual activity is consolidated into team moves.

A contest is a simplified but fully realized world (to borrow from Erving Goffman's *Encounters*), an arena within an arena. As such it formalizes the interaction of the participants. Goffman's description of contest interaction is quite illuminating for our purposes:

> [W]e see that a game perspective reduces the situation to teams, each acting rationally to press a single type of interest or pay-off while accepting very special conditions for action. Each move must be selected from a small number of possibilities, these being largely determined by the previous move of the opposing team, just as each move largely determines the possibilities next open to the opponent. Each team is aware of this mutual determination and oriented to the control of it, the entire outcome for each team being dependent on how it fares in this outmaneuvering. The concept of interaction is thus transformed: instead of referring to mutual influence that might be peripheral and trivial, it now refers to a highly structured form of mutual fatefulness.[30]

We can immediately see that feuds or reprisals-series possess all the attributes

27 Major works are J. Huizinga, *Homo Ludens: A Study of the Play-Element in Culture*, London: Routledge & Kegan Paul, 1949; R. Caillois, *Man, Play, and Games*, trans. by M. Barash, New York: Free Press, 1961; E. Goffman, *Encounters: Two Studies in the Sociology of Interaction*, Indianapolis: Bobbs, Merrill, 1961.

28 Caillois, *Man, Play, and Games*, ch. ii. The terms *contest* and *game* are used almost interchangeably by most writers. I use *contest* here to avoid confusion with game theory and its formal analytic orientation.

29 Whether these attributes are logical requirements or empirical generalizations is discussed below. A typical formulation of one such attribute is Caillois' (*Man, Play, and Games*, p. 14):

> The search for equality is so obviously essential to the rivalry that it is reestablished by a handicap for players of different classes; that is, within the equality of chances originally established, a secondary equality, proportionate to the relative powers of the participants, is dealt with.

30 Goffman, *Encounters*, p. 35.

of a contest. There are two sides, be they Albanian clans or contemporary nation-states. Players are designated, be they all adult males or professional specialists in violence. Each act of reprisal is a move that immediately creates the expectation of a move on the other side. There is no predetermined end to the feud and it may proceed for decades, all the while maintaining the tension of "mutual fatefulness."

Rules

Perhaps the most interesting attribute of feuds as contests is the tendency for each of them to have a well-established set of rules. All playing is governed by rules, and the rules of contests are the most formal and explicit of all. These rules, like all "rules of the game," confine the contest and make it a wholly realized world in itself.[31] In such a world the rules are simpler, more generally sufficient, and more likely to be honored than in the larger world from which it is set apart.

Consider the situation with Albanian blood feuds, an institution that persisted into the 20th century:

> The rules of the blood feud were carefully regulated by customary law. This provided that nobody might kill surreptitiously without leaving some article to identify himself as the author of the murder. Nobody, of course, would wish to kill anonymously, since one of the main purposes of the blood feud – the public retrieving of family honour – would thereby be thwarted. After a murder was committed, within 24 hours any member of the murderer's clan might be killed in revenge "whilst the blood is boiling." [note omitted] Thereafter, the feud lay between the two households, although this restriction was never too strictly observed. As soon as other clansmen became involved, the feud between the two clans became general and any member of the one might fall victim to the vengeance taken by any member of the other. The ideal was to exact vengeance as quickly as possible; public opinion spurred the avenger.
>
> The normal rule of a blood feud would be a life for a life, with the qualification that the victim must be adult, but not enfeebled, and physically fit to carry a rifle . . . Property was never damaged in a feud, and in this sense a woman was counted as property, "a sack for carrying things." . . .

31 According to Huizinga, *Homo Ludens*, p. 11: "All play has its rules. They determine what 'holds' in the temporary world circumscribed by play. The rules of a game are absolutely binding and allow no doubt." See also Caillois, *Man, Play, and Games*, pp. 27–35, for some equally strong statements and a fascinating exposition of the "spirit of calculation and contrivance" that gives birth to rule-making.

> The blood feud might rage for years until one side lost so many men that further killing became impossible.[32]

Undoubtedly because practice is relatively limited in the contemporary international system, the body of rules for reprisals-series is less precise. The only such feud of consequence is the one between several Arab states and Israel, now better than two decades in duration. There is a considerable tendency to assume that the pertinent rules are those said to have governed that conduct of reprisals in classical international law.[33] That reprisals are clearly outlawed in the UN Charter is a problem that I deal with later. For present purposes, the important consideration is that there is one rule, whatever its technical legal status, that is widely known and accepted because it fits the needs of the contest reasonably well. This is the rule of proportionality.

Like the doctrine of reprisals-as-sanctions, the rule of proportionality received its most characteristic expression in 19th century legal philosophy. In the Benthamite tradition, punishment, which is what reprisals are for, is seen in terms of proportionality.[34] If punishment is simply to deter, a uniformly disproportionate measure of punishment may have the highest deterrent value and may well be the simplest to administer. Effectively it is the Benthamite position that deterrence would not be significantly impaired and in the long run would be cheaper, and the additional goal of reforming the delinquent might be possible, if instead the severity of the punishment were linked to the seriousness of the crime. The more serious the crime, the heavier the penalty. The proportionality rule, then, is imputed to international law because of its impeccable credentials as a social idea at a formative period in the development of international legal doctrine.

Doctrine aside, Julius Stone has observed that proportionality in acts of reprisal "may arise between the subversions by both sides of the branch of law concerned."[35] Proportionality in this sense is neither compelled by doctrine nor is it simply a random occurrence. Acceptance of proportionality is decisive for making the contest work. It inhibits rapid escalation to major conflict by establishing limits on the responses each side can anticipate from the other. The rule is sufficiently imprecise to permit an element of surprise, but it is precise enough to prevent something so surprising that it upsets the contest (assuming, of course, that the rule is followed).

32 I. Whitaker, "Tribal Structure of National Politics in Albania, 1910–1950," in I.M. Lewis (ed.), *History and Social Anthropology*, London: Tavistock, 1968, pp. 267–8. See, also, M. Hasluck, *The Unwritten Law in Albania*, Cambridge: Cambridge University Press, 1954, ch. xxii–v, for a detailed account.

33 The definitive, and probably the first, statement of these rules was given by a special arbitral panel in connection with the Naulilaa Incident. This case is presented in most international law casebooks.

34 Bentham, *An Introduction to the Principles of Morals and Legislation*, ch. xiv.

35 J. Stone, *Legal Controls on International Conflict: A Treatise on the Dynamics of Disputes- and War-Law*, New York: Rinehart, 1959, p. 355

The utility of the proportionality rule can be seen by turning to what might be considered a natural corollary rule – the rule of correspondence. This idea again seems to flow from the dominant 19th century view of effective punishment. Punishment should at least to some extent be in the kind of the criminal act. Murder was to be punished by death, acts of violence and destruction by imprisonment, and other acts by the imposition of financial penalties. Certainly feuds can incorporate a correspondence rule, as evidenced by Albanian blood feuds. Such a rule has the virtue of permitting relatively accurate measurement of the proportionality of reciprocal moves and encourages symmetry in the contest. Symmetry is aesthetically satisfying and would seem generally to be the best guarantee of stability in the contest.[36]

The flaw in the correspondence rule is in its cutting off imaginative possibilities in moves and making the contest as a whole less interesting for its participants. Furthermore, literal correspondence eliminates the indispensable element of uncertainty, however limited, in a contest.[37] A response in kind is easier to anticipate and prevent. This is undoubtedly in the interest of the initiating side but could lead to cancellation of the contest by the frustrated respondents. Consequently, in the Arab–Israeli reprisals system we note a preference for correspondence wherever practicable, but its status as a rule is perhaps more controvertible than the proportionality rule.

A particular form the correspondence rule might take is the identification of players as the only acceptable targets of violence. The idea is to protect innocents. Again, though the protection of innocents is regarded as desirable by all, the definition of a true innocent is always subject to controversy. In the end it is the concept of team or side, with its suggestion of guilt by voluntary association, which is generally used to demarcate acceptable targets. This tendency is no different from the very strong pressure in modern warfare to blur the distinction between combatant and noncombatant.

It is frequently said that there is one other rule governing the use of reprisals. This is the requirement that the offended party seek redress before undertaking an act of reprisal. At first glance this would seem to be a concretization of a more general rule of information. We saw that in Albanian blood feuds acts of violence could never be anonymous. In like fashion it would seem to be appropriate for each move in any contest to be labeled as such, so that there is no confusion about where the contest stands. Providing such information simultaneously with a move or shortly thereafter fulfills the

36 It might be argued that reciprocity, by making symmetry manifest, is itself a higher-order rule that is presupposed by the proportionality and correspondence rules. Malinowski, *Crime and Custom in Savage Society*, saw reciprocity as the basis of the civil-legal order. A.W. Gouldner has gone so far as to posit a universal norm of reciprocity, which is among other things at the basis of retributive behavior. "The Norm of Reciprocity: A Preliminary Statement," *American Sociological Review*, vol. 25, 1960, p. 172.

37 While Caillois, *Man, Play, and Games*, has emphasized the need for uncertainty in play, Goffman, *Encounters*, has emphasized the need to limit it. These are complementary views.

information need; providing such information in advance may have the destabilizing effect of allowing preventive action. Nor should we overlook the possibility that a skillfully calibrated act of violence contains all the information necessary to establish it as a contest move.[38]

Consequently, a request for amends prior to taking a reprisal is not likely to contain specific information on the form, place and timing of the promised reprisal. The information rule is likely to be operative independent of the ceremonial requirement of asking for redress. In fact, the practice in the Middle East quite clearly conforms to the information rule as it relates to reprisals that are being taken or have just been taken.

The precise content of the proportionality, correspondence and information rules is not fixed. Given the limits of the contest structure, contests can be as varied as circumstances and imagination permit, with an individual set of rules being erected for each variation. If there is a contest, as I have defined it, there must be some kind of proportionality and information rules and there will very probably be a correspondence rule. Absence of anything resembling these rules is a clear warning not to assume the existence of a contest; but the resemblance to ideals of proportionality or whatever need not be perfect.

The three rules that we have just described – proportionality, correspondence and information rules – are only part of the normative structure of reprisals contests. Together they constitute the necessary *interaction rules* for such contests, by which we mean that these rules are sufficient to the needs of a sequence of moves in a contest. But we cannot forget that a contest's dynamics presuppose certain static conditions, which are also provided for through rules. Three *framing rules* were already apparent when we introduced the notion of contest playing. The first of these is that there are two sides. The second is that the two sides are roughly equal. The third is that the contest occupies a delimited space.

Rules of this kind tend to be taken for granted. There are no classical legal formulations to embody them. We either have them or we do not, but if we do not, then there is no interaction. We are forced to consider them, however, when we are asked the question, why are there so few reprisals-series?[39]

Taking first the rule that there must be two sides – which I will call the antagonism rule – it is immediately apparent that contests can have more than two sides.[40] For example, golf tournaments have entire fields and track

38 On this point consult T.C. Schelling's vivid discussion of "the idiom of reprisal," in *Arms and Influence*, New Haven: Yale University Press, 1966, pp. 141–151.

39 I am indebted to Peter Cowhey who, by asking this question, compelled the following explication of framing rules.

40 The term *antagonism* suggests both a psychological motive for the consolidation into two sides – there must be a sense of antagonism – and the resulting structure of *us* and *them*, good guys and bad guys. Note that Niehurg's derivation of the term is clearly mistaken

and field events involve small but indeterminate numbers of participants. In some athletic competitions an individual may set himself against the clock (which may represent the past achievement of another competitor or a plausible goal).

When a contest is dependent on the use of violence for its moves, however, non-antagonistic forms are less likely. Still they are possible. To illustrate, a series of teams (or players) may undertake to wreak as much violence as each is capable against an innocent object, with the winner being the team causing the most damage. Only if the teams are both the givers and the takers of violence is an antagonistic contest nearly inevitable. In addition to the psychological pressures toward an antagonistic structure, the difficulties in "scoring" many-sided violent contests militate against their use.

Recapitulating, most contests have two sides, but they need not. Especially if they use violent moves, contests are exceedingly likely to be antagonistic. This is not a logical necessity, for we can imagine a structurally quite different form of contest in which an indeterminate number of teams or players direct their violence against a common object and compare the results. Consequently, the antagonism rule, which states that there are two sides and assumes that the antagonists are directing violence toward each other, must be honored for a reprisals-series to take place. This rule is not inevitable; it must be adopted.

Not adopting the antagonism rule means either no contest or an altogether different kind of contest – for example, one that victimizes third parties. By no contest we really mean no contest involving the use of force. An alternative to no contest at all is to adopt an antagonistic contest in which violence is replaced by some other kind of activity such as conspicuous consumption or hurling insults. Such contests tend to merge into the form in which moves are directed toward third parties. Here though the third party may benefit instead of being victimized, as when it receives competitive offers of foreign aid.

The point is that in situations that lend themselves to ritualized structuring, there are significant alternatives to the kind of contest represented by a reprisals-series. In view of the attritional consequences of initiating an antagonistic contest utilizing violent moves, the resort to an alternative form is quite understandable. Once instituted, reprisals-series may prove to be quite durable because of the nature of the interaction, but some other kind of ritualized outlet may initially be preferred under the circumstances. Thus, to the extent that potential antagonists are capable of flexibility and control in their response to each other, we have one good reason why international relations are not a riot of reprisals-series.

The second framing rule postulates rough equality between the two sides.

("Agonistics," p. 58 n. 3): " 'Antagonistic' refers to real hostility; reduced to its roots, it means 'pre-ritual conflict.' " Actually the roots are *anti*, not *ante*, and *agon*. The "antis" of course are the adversaries in an *agon* or ritualized struggle.

The reason for the equality rule does not require extended comment. If there were not something approximating equality, then the results of the contest would be a foregone conclusion. Reality is no longer suspended and replaced with structured uncertainty, and we cease to have a contest. Although neither side has an incentive to engage in a contest, this obviously does not preclude engaging in violence for reasons unrelated to the contest ritual.

Equality does not have to be perfect, and the degree to which equality is approximated is not a decisive concern. Rather equality must be *stipulated*, which means that the side that is inherently superior must accept some kind of artificial limitation on its capacity to act. Since voluntary restraint by itself tends to be unreliable, handicaps must be devised.[41] There are at least three kinds of handicaps. The first is nothing other than the proportionality rule, which proscribes the disproportionate response the superior party is capable of. The second kind of handicap comes with player designation. Even if two sides are unequal in resource potential, they may designate a comparable number of players. In the Middle East, for example, the proportion of Israelis who are selected from the general population to serve as players is much higher than with the Arabs. Third, the space delimited for the contest may be arranged in favor of the weaker side. Although sanctuaries tend not to be comparable, there is a strong interest in honoring them, as studies of limited war situations have shown.[42]

Manipulating playing space for handicapping purposes brings us directly to a consideration of the third framing rule. Contests have to take place in a designated space, provided through what we might call a perimeter rule, because an unbounded contest becomes too unpredictable and loses its distinctive quality as a world set apart. The perimeter rule does not establish what the perimeter is, of course: only that there must be a perimeter, which can be directly negotiated or tacitly agreed on by using focal points. For most reprisals-series, the operation of the antagonism rule, which assumes that violence is exchanged between the sides and is not externally directed, suggests the correlative operation of a perimeter rule: the perimeter of the contest encloses the territory belonging to the two sides. As with all rules, the content of this particular rule is contingent; many variations are possible, including boundaries that give some of this territory the character of a sanctuary and boundaries that allow personally directed violence to be carried out in territorial jurisdictions with which the affected persons have no affiliation. To illustrate the latter situation, Arab and Israeli agents regularly exchange personal violence in the territory of European states.

Boundaries that are not coextensive with the territorial frontiers of the two sides are less salient, less easy to agree and stay bound to, than those that are.

41 Recall Callois, *Man, Play, and Games*, p. 14, quoted above.

42 See, for example, T.C. Schelling, *The Strategy of Influence*, Cambridge, MA: Harvard University Press, 1960, and *Arms and Influence*.

Third parties are more likely to be inadvertently involved. Consequently, the perimeter rule, and with it the contest, tends to degenerate into randomly directed terror. This seems to be what has been happening in the Middle East reprisals-series, in which the perimeter has rapidly expanded and may no longer exist. To many observers the result is that the reprisals-series is losing its contest-like structure, as we would describe it, and the interaction rules are increasingly being flouted. The tendency toward random terror may continue to be personally functional for some participants, but it is unlikely in the long run that the degenerate contest, deprived of its ritualistic structure, can serve any larger function for what were once its sides.

Like the antagonism rule, the equality and perimeter rules are matters of choice. Very great differences in capability strain the compensatory prospects of handicapping.[43] Even if handicapping were convenient for such situations of disparity, the incentives for engaging in contest playing are lessened. For the weaker side there is always the threat of the rules breaking down, and for the stronger a lack of challenge or status playing with a significantly lesser adversary. The absence of at least an order of magnitude parity between potential antagonists provides us with another reason why some reprisals-series do not get started or, as in the case of Vietnam, why ongoing violent exchanges do not manifest the normative structure of reprisals-series. In like fashion, the absence of the defined boundaries required by the perimeter rule helps to prevent violent exchanges from settling into the pattern of reprisals-series. The availability of quick, cheap and poorly monitored transportation has put all such perimeters under enormous pressure and, again, creates another good reason why there are so few reprisals-series.

In summary, the three framing rules must be operative for a reprisals-series to take place. Without them the interaction rules are irrelevant. The framing rules are not natural or inevitable. Particularly in the present day they rarely represent attractive choices for potential antagonists. All of this means that we are unlikely to see the emergence of many more reprisals-series in international relations. Even the one we do have, in the Middle East, shows signs of deteriorating because of the stress that circumstances have put on its framing rules. It should be borne in mind, however, that once a contest has been established, it has a strong tendency to continue for substantial periods of time. In effect, the framing and interaction rules lock together to reinforce each other, keep the contest going, and insure that its social function is performed. Stated as a paradox, reprisals-series are a rare but persistent phenomenon at the international level.

It is quite obvious by now that the rules governing reprisals contests in the international system are few in number and crude in nature. This spare

43 Vietnam is a notable case in point, as B.M. Russett has neatly demonstrated in "Vietnam and Restraints on Aerial Warfare," *Ventures*, vol. 9, 1969, pp. 55–61.

normative framework is compensated for in a way that is characteristic for contests. There is an umpire. Group theory conceives of government as the arena-maker and umpire for the political process. All sorts of contests and parlor games that people devise for their amusement provide for third parties committed to neither side. The impartial third party is supposed to assess facts and interpret rules as they apply to factual situations. In the best of possible worlds, umpires have enough independence and authority to have their determinations accepted and not be dragged into the contest.

In the instance of the international system the umpire for reprisals-series is the Security Council.[44] Though frequently criticized for its bias and notably lacking in enforcement capability, the Security Council has been active in evaluating reprisals activity in the Middle East for some time and has acquired a certain degree of credibility in performing this task. The Security Council is not asked to evaluate the legality of reprisals under the UN Charter, nor is it interested in doing so. For all intents and purposes, the Security Council has accepted the legitimacy of reprisals by failing to condemn them when they conform to the contest's interaction rules, which, as we have seen, are very little different from the classical rules relating to the use of reprisals.

The Security Council, then, is performing what amounts to a judicial function in evaluating rival claims in a reprisals-series as to the appropriateness of specific acts of reprisal. Frank Popper has suggested that certain kinds of internal wars can have a constructive effect on the political development of states. He mentioned reprisals specifically.[45] The same argument seems applicable to the international system, in which the existence of a long-standing reprisals-series has provided an otherwise underemployed but highly visible institution with a significant responsibility. That responsibility in effect promotes the development of a system structure to cope with a function previously performed in a diffuse way in the system.

The case for the Security Council's emergent judicial competence can easily be exaggerated. Reprisals-series are reasonably easy to judge because they do have rules – perhaps crude but very much in evidence. Yet to be limited to refereeing reprisals-series is at best parochial and at worst trivial, if only because our one extant international feud generates a paltry caseload. To assume judicial responsibility for a broader range of low-level coercive activities is to abandon firm and familiar ground for a normative and even more

44 The Security Council's role is documented R.A. Falk, "The Beirut Raid and the International Law of Retaliation," *American Journal of International Law*, vol. 63, 1969, pp. 414–43; Bowett, "Reprisals Involving Recourse to Armed Force." Particularly helpful is Bowett's tabular presentation (pp. 33–6) of some 20 reprisals-like incidents involving Israel from 1953 to 1970, all but two of which were brought before and acted on by the Security Council, with Israel more often condemned than not.

45 F.J. Popper, "Internal War as a Stimulant of Political Development," *Comparative Political Studies*, vol. 3, 1971, pp. 420–1.

a political quagmire. The price to be paid for a premature claim to wider competence might well be impotence. Following Popper's argument to its logical conclusion, one is almost bound to argue that an increase in the number and distribution of reprisals-series would best serve the Security Council's developmental thrust toward a significant judicial role in the world community.

Rationales

Even a cursory reading of the UN Charter leaves little doubt that reprisals involving the use of force are no longer permitted – in principle. It has recently been affirmed by the UN General Assembly in its Declaration on Principles of International Law concerning Friendly Relations and Co-operation among States (Resolution 2625 [XXV], October 24, 1970 [Annex]). The result of an arduous drafting process, this resolution unequivocally maintains that "States have a duty to refrain from acts of reprisal involving the use of force."

Yet we have already noted the fact that the Security Council is developing a body of practice, which fails to condemn reprisals simply for the fact that they are reprisals. Instead, reprisals are evaluated individually for their consistency with a widely understood and accepted set of requirements – widely understood and accepted because they are basically the requirements of the traditional law governing the recourse to reprisals. Whatever the formal status of the traditional law, a coherent and abiding practice of the Security Council can hardly be said to have no legal significance as a matter of course. Thus we have an apparent contradiction, since in substance and in legal significance, the Charter and practice are radically at odds. The fact that the Charter also requires the Security Council to "act in accordance with the Purposes and Principles of the United Nations" (Article 24[2]) gives this knotty problem another twist.

For the most part, neither the Security Council nor states individually seem to be interested in the problem or even aware of its existence. This does not mean we are faced with nothing more than a minor academic curiosity. For even as the problem goes unnoticed, both statesmen and scholars are busy rationalizing the kind of behavior that creates the problem in the first place. The consequence is that the problem identified here gets a good deal of attention without ever being addressed directly.

Logically, there are four solutions to the apparent contradiction between the Charter and practice. The first would hold that the Security Council's practice does not affect the legal relevance of the Charter. Conversely, the second would deny the legal relevance of Charter prescriptions in light of practice. The third solution would hold that the Charter and practice are legally compatible, while the fourth would hold that the Charter and practice yield different kinds of law pertaining to reprisals. There is of course a fifth solution to be had by combining the first and second; it would hold that neither the Charter nor practice is legally relevant and thus the problem raised here is fundamentally illusory.

Turning first to the proposition that Security Council practice has no bearing on the legal status of reprisals under the Charter, at least three concrete lines of argument are possible. One would ascribe to the Charter – or at least its provisions relating to the use of force – a peremptory character, from which no derogation is permitted. Of considerable interest in this regard is the recent affirmation of *jus cogens* in the Vienna Convention on the Law of Treaties. While the treaty itself does not specifically stipulate the peremptory character of the Charter, the International Law Commission's commentary on the preparatory draft articles used the Charter's provisions on the use of force as possible examples of peremptory norms.[46]

Jus cogens is usually thought of in connection with treaties that might otherwise be lawfully concluded. Yet to be consistent with the idea of *jus cogens*, a body of practice would have to be viewed the same way that a treaty is: namely, that it cannot change peremptory norms unless the norms emerging from this practice are themselves peremptory. (The implications of this proposition are examined in Chapter 5 above.) In a related vein, it may be said that the Charter is not just a treaty but, at least in some of its provisions, a constitutive instrument for the world community.[47] As such it would not be susceptible to alteration through the ordinary, decentralized law-making procedures of the community, but would normally require formal amendment as provided for in the Charter.

Peremptory and constitutive conceptions of the Charter share the presumption that some norms are more intensely held than others and that norms can only be replaced by norms of at least comparable intensity. Furthermore, higher intensity is most easily recognized in the degree of formality in the procedures through which norms gain expression.[48] Thus norms coming out of informal law-making procedures must achieve a level of intensity such that they become recognizable as supplanting norms of greater formality, if indeed they are to do so. While this is at least a possibility in principle, it is hardly conceivable in practice.

In the instance at hand, it is a major step from the position that Security Council practice is legally relevant to the position that it conveys a community

46 Article 53, Vienna Convention on the Law of Treaties, May 23, 1969, in *International Legal Materials*, vol. 8, 1969, pp. 698–9; Reports of the International Law Commission on the Second Part of Its Seventeenth Session, January 3–28, 1966 and on Its Eighteenth Session, May 14–July 19, 1967, in *American Journal of International Law*, vol. 61, 1967, p. 410.

47 A. Ross, *The Constitution of the United Nations: Analysis of Structure and Function*, New York: Rinehart, 1950, pp. 30–40; R.A. Falk, *The Status of Law in International Society*, Princeton: Princeton University Press, 1970, pp. 214–28; Chapter 19 below.

48 M.S. McDougal *et al.*, "The World Constitutive Process of Authoritative Decision," in C.E. Black and R.A. Falk (eds), *The Future of the International Legal Order*, vol. 1, 1969, p. 99.

preference of such unmistakable intensity that it modifies the use of force provisions of the Charter. The easier course is to challenge the conception of international legal order that makes it necessary to take this step at all. The strongest challenge is conventional doctrine, which says in effect that material considerations like intensity of support and formality of expression may well affect the substance of a norm as it comes into being but not its subsequent legal status. The Charter is just a treaty then, for there is nothing in the legal order that can make it be more than a treaty. That some of its provisions are unusually worded for a treaty simply makes it an unusual treaty.

A second line of argument on the legal irrelevance of Security Council practice is drawn from the suggestive work of Inis L. Claude, Jr., on what he calls "collective legitimation." Claude focuses on the role of the General Assembly in making collective normative judgments without reference to international law. Indeed, according to Claude, "the legitimacy of international law is widely challenged," and so collective legitimation, as an alternative to international law, has emerged "as essentially a political function, sought for political reasons, exercised by political organs through the operation of a political process, and productive of political results."[49]

Although it is doubtful that the participants in the judgments of either the General Assembly or the Security Council draw such a sharp distinction between legality and legitimacy with any regularity, some of them may do so occasionally. Yet, whatever the perceptions of their makers may be, it would be arbitrary for the analyst to deny the legal impact of these judgments. International law is not some collection of rules so designated through formal and inalterable procedures; it is whatever norms (and rationalizing statements) the international community has clearly legitimated. Nor does collective legitimation represent "a political revolt against international law," as Claude would have it.[50] Rather, it should be seen as a revolt against Western control over the traditional sources and thus the substance of international law, and not against the legal order itself.

The third line of argument, which takes Security Council practice to be legally irrelevant, has consistently been used by Israel in the Security Council. Instead of asserting in practice that such a practice can have no legal impact, it makes a case against this particular body of practice on the grounds of consistent bias.[51] Whether or not the Security Council is in fact biased against Israel and its reprisals policy, it might be asked if bias in itself can diminish

49 I.L. Claude, Jr., "Collective Legitimation as a Political Function of the United Nations," *International Organization*, vol. 20, 1966, p. 371.

50 Ibid., p. 377.

51 The Israeli position is reviewed in Bowett, "Reprisals Involving Recourse to Armed Force," pp. 22–3. See, also, Y.Z. Bluhm, "The Beirut Raid and the International Double Standard: A Reply to Professor Richard A. Falk," *American Journal of International Law*, vol. 64, 1970, pp. 98–105.

the legal consequences of the Security Council's practice. Certainly legal consequences flow from bodies of state practice fulfilling certain conditions, yet no one seriously doubts the fact that states engaging in such practices are biased. That some states are more engaged in and have a greater effect on the international relations that yield such bodies of practice accounts for the fact that specific rules of international law favor some states over others. Unless we say that the Security Council must put abstract justice before political reality for its judgments to be authoritative, bias will be a fact of life in that organ as it is in the rest of international relations.

We move now to the proposition which is the converse of the one just examined. It asserts that it is not the Security Council's practice but indeed the Charter itself that is without legal relevance in situations involving forcible reprisals. This might be argued by reference to the principle of effectiveness, for whatever states have said about the use of force today, their practice has been in mocking disregard of the Charter. Contrary practice on such a scale has rendered the Charter invalid, leaving a vacuum that the Security Council's practice is beginning to fill through the process of customary law formation. Indeed, this process is accelerated by the authoritative nature of the Security Council and the clear need for some kind of normative regulation of the use of force.

In an essay graphically entitled, "Who Killed Article 2(4)?" Thomas Franck has recently argued that the Charter's central provision relating to the use of force has in fact been invalidated through what we may infer was its ineffectiveness.[52] Franck pictured Article 2(4) as having been "eroded beyond recognition" because of the disparity between the injunction against using force and "the perceived national interests of States, especially the super-Powers."[53] We are left with little doubt as to who killed Article 2(4), but Franck neglected to tell us how the murder was accomplished. Certainly it is the burden of his position that widespread contrary practice can invalidate any norm and that this is precisely what has happened with Article 2(4).

Although Franck may have taken the process of invalidation through ineffectiveness for granted, he has been rather more concerned with the corollary process whereby the invalidating practice simultaneously generates new norms. With Edward Weisband, Franck has written extensively on the pronounced symmetry of superpower transgressions of Article 2(4) to maintain

52 T.M. Franck, "Who Killed Article 2(4)?" *American Journal of International Law*, vol. 64, 1970, pp. 809–37.

53 Ibid., p. 835. J.H.W. Verzijl, *International Law in Historical Perspective*, vol. 1, Leiden: Sijthoff, 1968, has made much the same argument about Article 2(7): "[T]he commandment of the Charter that there shall be abstention from intervention in the domestic jurisdiction of Member States is increasingly losing its authority as a legal injunction and degenerating into a plaything of opportunist international policy." (p. 238)

spheres of influence.[54] In particular they have emphasized the reciprocal expectations that both flow from and reinforce this pattern of practice, which they labeled the "two ghetto system." Quite clearly, they have come to regard this system as having a normative character, but they are less clear on its precise legal status. By combining Franck's position on the demise of Article 2(4) and the Franck–Weisband position on superpower practices, we may conclude on their behalf that new law has emerged to fill the vacuum created by the invalidation of Article 2(4).[55] While Franck and Weisband have not done so themselves, their position is easily translated to the circumstances of Security Council practice in connection with reprisals.

The application of the principle of effectiveness to treaty provisions is not without difficulty. A far greater volume and consistency of practice is required for a treaty to be superseded than for this to happen to a customary rule. Since a treaty acquires its binding effect through an express and intentional agreement of the parties, contrary practice must be simply overwhelming to establish a commensurate explicitness and intentionality. Such a practice would obviously have to include high rhetoric as well as concrete verbal and nonverbal behavior, for the former conveys the intent that is so critical for invalidating a treaty.[56] At least in their rhetoric, states have not signaled their desire to invalidate Article 2(4), however small its effect on their behavior. Indeed, their constant reaffirmation of the use of force provisions of the Charter is surely conclusive.

There is a more subtle way of arguing the legal irrelevance of the Charter. Instead of holding that Article 2(4) has been invalidated because of its ineffectiveness, one might say that Security Council practice represents a kind of prescriptive exception to a generally valid rule. Thus the Charter would remain valid for all but a given class of situations, articulated in Security Council practice. In fact, a prescriptive exception to an established rule need not require the invalidation of that rule even for a narrow range of situations. Rather, the situations at hand may be novel ones, not known or anticipated at the time the established rule emerged and usually brought on by technological change.

To use a well-known example, it has been argued that despite appearances the practices of submarine warfare during the World Wars did not violate the existing law governing the conduct of naval hostilities, because the circumstances surrounding the use of submarines were unanticipated when that law was established. The practices in question may then be construed to have

54 There are several articles, but see T.M. Franck and E. Weisband, *Word Politics: Verbal Strategy among the Superpowers*, New York: Oxford University Press, 1971, for a comprehensive statement.

55 While Franck and Weisband used some language to this effect (ibid., p. 129), they generally preferred to talk about "systemic behavior" rather than rules or law.

56 Franck and Weisband have themselves made a convincing case for the importance of "levels of intentionality in verbal behavior." Ibid., pp. 122–6.

taken place in the interstices of the law, gaining legal effect without first having to do away with existing rules.[57] Had there been no practice, there might be no reason to doubt that the old rules applied to novel circumstances that did indeed have much in common with the situations to which the old rules referred.

As we have noted, the practice of the Security Council on reprisals deals almost entirely with the Arab–Israeli conflict. This conflict may be thought of as a novel situation, though in a political rather than a technological sense. One could even argue that the very novelty of the conflict compels Security Council treatment that ignores the Charter. Thus the Charter is not so much ineffective as inappropriate for dealing with the situation, and a constructive addition to the Charter's provisions on the use of force is being devised to meet the needs of the situation through consensual validation.

The main difficulty with this argument relates to the intention of the framers of the Charter when they set out their rules on the use of force. They clearly intended the Charter to be a comprehensive system proscribing forcible measures, as a matter of principle, in any conceivable situation.[58] If the ongoing situation in the Middle East cannot be viewed as unanticipated under the Charter, then the formation of a prescriptive exception to the general requirements of Article 2(4) must meet the more stringent criteria for invalidation through ineffectiveness.

There is an alternative argument that nonetheless focuses on the special circumstances of the Middle East situation. It is implicit in the fact that the participants in that situation are and have long been belligerents. Since belligerency refers to a state of war that is not possible under the Charter, we can infer that the belligerents, by the fact of their belligerency and with UN support, have created a prescriptive exception to the Charter's use of force provisions.[59] Here though it is not the situation that warrants exceptional treatment but the parties to it whose exceptional behavior yields a localized or special custom of permissive content.

Anthony D'Amato has demonstrated that an exception-creating special custom can exist only as a matter of literal consent among the states subject to the exception.[60] This gives the prescriptive exception the objective if not the

57 On the doctrine of novel circumstances in relation to submarine warfare, see R.W. Tucker, *The Law of War and Neutrality at Sea*, Washington: US Government Printing Office, 1955, pp. 67–70. For a recent general affirmation of the doctrine, see Verzijl, *International Law in Historical Perspective*, pp. 70–4.

58 R.B. Russell's minute discussion of the Charter's preparation amply confirms that inclusiveness was intended. *A History of the United Nations Charter: The Role of the United States, 1940–1945*, 1958, pp. 205–302.

59 On belligerency in the Middle East, see A. Lall, *The UN and the Middle East Crisis, 1967*, New York: Columbia University Press, 1968, ch. 3. On its legality, see Q. Wright, "The Middle East Problem," *American Journal of International Law*, vol. 64, 1970, pp. 270–81.

60 A.A. D'Amato, *The Concept of Custom in International Law*, Ithaca: Cornell University Press, 1971, ch. 8.

formal character of a treaty derogating from more generally binding law. Even if we could safely assume that Israel in particular has actually consented to the prescriptive exception that is incipient both in its own and in its neighbors' behavior, we run afoul of Article 103 of the Charter. "In the event of a conflict between the obligations of the Members of the United Nations under the present Charter and their obligations under any other international agreement, their obligations under the present Charter shall prevail."

The third solution to the dilemma posed by the Charter and Security Council practice on reprisals is the proposition that the Charter and practice are in fact compatible, appearances notwithstanding. There would seem to be three ways in which this proposition might be argued.

The first argument would be one that concerned itself with the interpretation of Article 2(4), prohibiting the use of force, and Article 51, permitting the use of force in the instance of self-defense. Not surprisingly, there is a substantial literature on whether these provisions can be interpreted to permit anticipatory self-defense.[61] Of less concern has been the question of interpreting self-defense so as to include reprisals, but Robert Tucker has now filled this gap. Tucker stated his position with great economy: "Forcible measures of reprisal may be forbidden by the Charter, but the functional equivalent of such measures may nevertheless be permitted in the form of self-defense."[62]

Everything hinges on the assumption of functional equivalence, the function performed in common being self-help. Tucker's analysis shows that there are marked similarities in the structure of self-defense and reprisals when both are properly taken. Both require the commission of a prior act necessitating a response and both require proportionality in the response. This is all that Tucker needed to conclude that self-defense and reprisals are interchangeable means for states to enforce the law on their own behalf.

Quite plausibly self-defense is a means of self-help, more especially the kind of self-help discussed earlier as self-right enforcement. The structural attributes of legitimately exercised self-defense, as Tucker identified them, are entirely suitable for the purpose. The other half of Tucker's assumption is less defensible. Like his positivist predecessors, Tucker is persuaded that reprisals are a form of self-help, because that is how the legal order is defined to work. We saw above that reprisals in series could be understood in altogether different functional terms and yet still display the same structural features that one would expect to find with self-help.

The resemblance between self-defense and reprisals can be seen as strictly

61 See R.W. Tucker, "Legal Constraints on Coercion," in A. Wolfers *et al.*, *The United States in a Disarmed World*, Baltimore: Johns Hopkins Press, 1966, for a survey of positions in this debate.

62 Tucker, "Reprisals and Self-Defense," p. 586.

fortuitous. While Tucker might well have been right about isolated acts of reprisal, an inspection of the Middle East reprisals-series discloses certain weaknesses in his position. In the first place, Tucker chose to minimize the difference in magnitude between typical acts of self-defense and typical acts of reprisal. Self-defense usually involves substantial levels of coercion, as Tucker himself has noted in reference to the debates on anticipatory self-defense.[63] The right that self-defense is often claimed on behalf of is the very right to exist.

Secondly, Tucker minimized the fact that states are inclined to regard self-defense and reprisals as separate and narrowly defined enterprises. State practice confirms both the difference in gross dimensions of the two kinds of acts and a restrictive definition of self-defense. Thus while Israel has long since given up arguing that its low-level reprisals activity is a matter of self-defense, its claim of anticipatory self-defense in a major conflict situation like that of 1967 was unsympathetically received in the UN.[64] It would seem that Tucker preferred to overlook the evident dissimilarities between self-defense and reprisals because this kind of evidence tends to undermine the self-help model he started with. The same evidence nicely supports the alternative, contest-playing model developed in these pages.

The work of Myres McDougal and his associates provides us with an alternative to Tucker's argument. Of interest here is the notion of complementary norms. "The world community's prescriptions about coercion, like other world prescriptions, march and must march in pairs of complementary opposites. An absolute interdiction of all coercion is scarcely conceivable, or if conceivable is hardly within the limits of the achievable."[65] The Charter simultaneously prohibits the use of force in Article 2(4) and permits it in Article 51. This is not a matter of equivalents but rather of equally valid alternatives.

The legality of a particular act of coercion is determined not by reference to the Charter, which can be selectively drawn upon to justify virtually any form of international behavior, but by reference to the "basic community policy" of advancing a world public order of human dignity. This is best done by authoritative decision-making bodies like the Security Council through "the most comprehensive test of all law, reasonableness in particular context."[66] While McDougal's analysis is most directly concerned with the modalities of major coercion, conventionally called aggression and self-defense, he and his collaborator did make passing reference to the "ordinary

63 Tucker, "Legal Constraints on Coercion," pp. 141–3.

64 On Israel's position on low-level reprisals and self-defense, see Bowett, "Reprisals Involving Recourse to Armed Force," p. 10. For a review of General Assembly debates on Israel's claim of anticipatory self-defense, see Lall, *The UN and the Middle East Crisis, 1967*, chs. 8–10.

65 M.S. McDougal and F.S. Feliciano, *Law and Minimum World Public Order*, New Haven: Yale University Press, 1961, p. 127.

66 Ibid., p. 227.

reciprocities and retaliations against . . . tortious conduct of another state," which they seemed to consider permissible if there were a reasonable relationship between the level of coercion and the values to be conserved.[67]

In this view, the Charter does not tell us what is lawful; it merely structures the claims and counterclaims as to lawful behavior. The actual determination of legality in the case of particular reprisal acts resides with the Security Council and any other actors in the international community that care to offer an opinion conforming to McDougal's judgmental criteria. Of course all this dismisses the notorious relativity of conceptions of public order and human dignity, not to mention differing images of reasonableness and contextual specifics. As McDougal's critics have repeatedly pointed out, the likely consequence of his scheme is the identification of law with those policies that are subjectively most agreeable and objectively most successful.[68]

Insofar as there is a consensus among statesmen and scholars that given reprisals policies benefit the needs of the community at large and consequently a willingness to ascribe normative value to them, McDougal has given us a rather elaborate method for ascertaining the emergence of customary law. Since what the Charter says is of no direct importance in this process, the result is reminiscent of the position that only the Security Council's practice is legally relevant. If, as is more likely, such a consensus does not exist, then McDougal's approach effectively denormativizes international relations – a result that suggests the fifth solution posed above to the apparent discrepancy between the Charter and Security Council practice, namely, that there really are no rules governing the use of force among states [three paragraphs deleted].

The next proposition to be examined maintains that the law of the Charter and the law emerging from Security Council practice are really different kinds of law, which may thus coexist despite having contrary content. Again, there would seem to be three concrete ways in which this proposition could be argued. Richard Falk has recently employed the first of them.

Falk characterized the law of the Charter as a formally conclusive "first order of legal inquiry." But, "[i]n view of the inadequacy of Charter doctrines," Falk argued the relevance of a more permissive second order of legal inquiry in the use of force, "so as to retain criteria of reasonableness in a situation that threatens at many points to deteriorate into intense and limitless forms of conflict."[69] This second order of legality is exemplified by the customary law of reprisals, which was technically superseded by the Charter.

67 Ibid., pp. 130, 218, 227.

68 See most recently O.R. Young, "International Law and Social Science: The Contributions of Myres S. McDougal," *American Journal of International Law*, vol. 66, 1972, pp. 70–6, and McDougal's reply in the same issue, "International Law and Social Science: A Mild Plea in Avoidance," pp. 77–81.

69 Falk, "The Beirut Raid and the International Law of Retaliation," p. 430 n. 39.

There is even a third order of legal inquiry, having to do with the specifics of a particular reprisal situation.

Falk called this "a method of successive legal approximations."[70] It is really an attempt to establish a tenable middle ground between the poles of legal formalism and the more rabid version of political realism by instituting a controlled relativity for international law. The control mechanism is a decreasingly stringent series of requirements by which law can be said to apply to a given situation. The first step is the requirement of conforming to the stated law. If this is too demanding on states in view of the situation, the next requirement is that of reasonableness-in-context with an eye to restraint. The third step, though not easily generalized, seems to require minimized disruption and maximized clarity of intention, even after other constraints are cast off.[71]

The normative impact of third step is questionable. As with McDougal, the range of interpretations of reasonableness and contextual relevance is close to infinite unless there is some external basis for agreement. In the case of reprisals, what Falk ascertained to be reasonable in the situation at hand is indistinguishable from the requirements of the pre-Charter customary law on reprisals reasonably adapted to that situation. It is a matter of curiosity, however, that Falk failed to see this himself.

Falk's novel legal method has the effect of reviving the traditional law. Had there been no such law, his determination of an appropriate normative standard for reprisals in today's Middle East conflict would not have the *prima facie* credibility that it does possess. In short, Falk's legal method worked out in this instance because of its hardly accidental congruence with already available guidelines and continuing practices. It is not guaranteed to work out in instances in which the legal and international communities are not preconditioned in their perception of what is reasonable and thus permissible by the existence of technically defunct customary rules.

A second argument for different kinds of law relating to the use of force has been suggested by Evelyn Colbert in her classic monograph on reprisals and has been systematically treated by Richard Lillich in the context of humanitarian intervention. Colbert asked, in 1948 necessarily rhetorically:

> whether a reprisal, ostensibly undertaken for no other purpose than to secure justice which would otherwise be denied, is a use of force

70 Ibid.

71 Ibid., p. 442 n. 73. Falk has since used much the same method and more clearly acknowledged the reason for doing so in a discussion of aggression. He substituted the term "constraints" for "legal inquiry" in describing the three orders of normative control and he established a different and more tangible content to the third order constraint on aggression, namely, that provisional measures (as under Article 40) be instituted as quickly as possible in a conflict receiving second order "indulgence." R.A. Falk, "Quincy Wright: On Legal Tests of Aggressive War," *American Journal of International Law*, vol. 66, 1972, pp. 565–71.

> "inconsistent with the purposes of the United Nations," or not "in the common interest." It might indeed be argued in certain cases that the reprisal in question not only served to rectify the wrong done to the retaliating power but also served to advance the purposes of the United Nations.[72]

There are three assumptions built into this argument. The first is that the UN, despite its elaborate provisions, may not be able to fulfill its purposes. The second is that these purposes ought to be fulfilled anyway. The third is that member states may act on behalf of the organization in seeing that these provisions are fulfilled, even if this means ignoring or distorting the provisions of the Charter that would limit the capacity of states to act so that the organization might do so.

Writing 20 years later, Lillich no longer had to assume that the organization might be incapable of fulfilling many of its purposes; this is demonstrably the case.[73] At the same time, some of these purposes, such as "promoting and encouraging respect for human rights," had taken on real substance and meaning during that time and therefore can be seen as a good deal more imperative in character. Finally, it is no longer just a fanciful idea that states might act on behalf of the organization in fulfilling its purposes – this is only the next logical step beyond the doctrine of institutional effectiveness, which holds that the UN ought to have the powers necessary for the performance of its functions, even if these powers are not specifically granted in the Charter.[74] Since there are limits to the expansion of the organization's powers, it would seem to follow that by accepting reasonable restraints and subsequent collective review, states could take over responsibility for realizing Charter objectives.

The thrust of this kind of argument is to emphasize the difference between the law embodying "fundamental values" and "blackletter" law. The former is embodied in Article 1 of the Charter, the latter in Article 2 and many other specific provisions.[75] Article 1 is thus superior to Article 2. When the requirements of the former happen to conflict with the latter, as they may in practice if not in principle, then the former must take precedence. This of course comes very close to saying that the ends justify the means.

72 Colbert, *Retaliation in International Law*, pp. 203–4.

73 R.B. Lillich, "Forcible Self-Help by States to Protect Human Rights," *Iowa Law Review*, vol. 53, 1967, pp. 325–51. Lillich expanded on his position in subsequent essays and restated it most recently at a conference devoted to the subject. "Conference Proceedings, Part II: The Present," in Lillich (ed.), *Humanitarian Intervention and the United Nations*, Charlottesville: University Press of Virginia, 1973, p. 61.

74 On the doctrine of institutional effectiveness, see L. Gross, "Expenses of the United Nations for Peacekeeping Operations: The Advisory Opinion of the International Court of Justice," *International Organization*, vol. 17, 1963, pp. 26–35.

75 Lillich, "Forcible Self-Help by States to Protect Human Rights," p. 344.

Lillich sought to blunt the criticism that such a position engenders by proposing some concrete criteria of restraint "by which international validity of a state's resort to forcible self-help should be judged."[76] While particularization lends itself to controversy, there may be something approaching a consensus in support of the underlying premise that the community has an important stake in human rights and the concomitant presumption that action on behalf of the community may be tolerable when guided by community standards and supervision.[77] Reprisals, however, are rarely undertaken on behalf of the community, the fiction of self-help notwithstanding. Nor can we see the restraints on acts of reprisal as purposeful responses to the likelihood and legitimacy of community supervision. Such restraints are born of the reprisals dynamic itself and are not derived from the ends to be served. Without a tangible link between community purposes and concrete restraints, the rationale for permitting forcible action for reasons of self-help is severely weakened.

The third argument for different kinds of law is a general one, which can be applied to controls on the use of force just as much as the rest of international law. In its general form William Coplin and Barkun have expounded it.[78] Its application to the problem of force is not fully developed, although I used it in an attempt to understand the UN's work on the principle of nonintervention (Chapter 3, above). In this argument, international law is viewed as performing two major functions in the international system. The first of these is the one conventionally attributed to all law, namely, that it functions as "a system of coercive norms," or a "system of restraint."[79] Since this is the dominant image of all law, including international law, Coplin has rightly observed that wide skepticism about the efficacy of international law should be no surprise.

The second, less understood function of international law is that of "an institutional device for communicating to the policy-makers of various states a consensus on the nature of the international system."[80] In practice, the same norm can be different kinds of law depending on the function it serves. Indeed, a rule may be different kinds of law at the same time, since its functions may be served simultaneously. It would be surprising, however, if there were no structural differentiation at all in the performance of these functions. In the international legal order, at least, there does seem to be some

76 Ibid., p. 345.

77 See T.J. Farer, "Humanitarian Intervention: The View from Charlottesville," in Lillich, *Humanitarian Intervention*, pp. 163–4. But *cf.* I. Brownlie's essay in the same volume, "Thoughts on Kind-Hearted Gunmen."

78 W.D. Coplin, "International Law and Assumptions about the State System," *World Politics*, vol. 17, 1965, pp. 615–34; Barkun, *Law without Sanctions*, New Haven: Yale University Press, 1968.

79 Coplin, "International Law and Assumptions about the State System," pp. 615, 616.

80 Ibid., p. 617.

differentiation, though hardly resulting in one-to-one structural-functional correspondences.

The symbolic function in international law can be identified primarily with general principles of international law (not to be confused with general principles of law recognized by civilized nations). The principles of sovereignty, nonintervention and self-determination are well-known examples of general principles of international law. Actually, what we know in UN parlance as the principles of friendly relations are a comprehensive, if not exhaustive list of these principles. One of the seven principles of friendly relations reiterates Article 2(4) of the Charter.

General principles are cast at a level of abstraction that precludes any real normative guidance from them in concrete situations. Such guidance must come from the network of ordinary rules, which refer to some facet of state behavior also focused on by a general principle. The latter are really consensual statements about essential features of the international system in a given era. The importance of the UN's work on friendly relations lies not so much in its attempt to elaborate the content of general principles, but rather in using such an elaboration to give currency to new general principles and new relationships among traditional and more recent and controversial general principles. The symbolic significance of this activity is testified to by the seriousness with which non-Western states have regarded it. At stake is recognition by the international community of the transformation of traditional international relations to those of a new era in which the non-Western world plays a decisive role.

Thus the UN's position on reprisals should not be seen as a deliberate attempt to concretize the abstract notions of the Charter. Instead it is a secondary result of an effort to use detailed, interlocking statements of general principles to usher in a new era of the international system. Inasmuch as the Charter, at least in its articulation of purposes and principles, is symbolic rather than restraint-oriented in character, it follows that the traditional law, which also refers to the subject matter of those principles and purposes, remains intact. This would obviously include the traditional law of reprisals, which is what the Security Council has in effect been applying through its practice.

However persuasive this argument may ultimately prove in conceptual terms, there is a practical problem with it. Its unconventional nature means that it is either unknown or suspect to policy-makers. While whether policy-makers realize that rules on the use of force are doubly functional, they will still regard clear statements of general principles like Article 2(4) as substantive rules of law whenever it suits them. This in turn makes it difficult for scholars who are presumably sensitive to state practice to sustain what is an unusual doctrinal stance.

There is a final proposition to be reviewed here, one that dismisses rather than solves the dilemma posed by the Charter and Security Council practice. It is implicit in realist contempt for international law and organization. Stanley Hoffmann has made it explicitly.

The argument is a simple one. The entire Charter system for the control of force – Chapter VII as well as Article 2(4) – is unworkable in practice and inadequate in concept. The Charter system is predicated on the "clearcut case"; yet "the prevalence of marginal situations" is our contemporary reality. Furthermore, although these situations "do not fall squarely under the prohibition of the 'new' international law of the Charter, they should come under the rules of the 'old' international law." But "those rules have been widely disregarded because they are grossly inadequate." Simply stated, the international law of the Charter is "premature," the traditional law "obsolete."[81] Neither law is germane to the marginal, small-scale use of force that is handsomely illustrated by contemporary reprisals activity.

Concise and complete, Hoffmann's argument cannot help but be appealing. Its weakness is not so much what it says, however, as in what it fails to say. To the extent that substantial segments of international relations involving the use of force resist control or apparent mitigation, his argument is hard to deny. His examples of subversion and indirect aggression are well taken.[82] Yet it does not account for those few areas of behavior like reprisals activity, which show signs of being regularized, rule-oriented and susceptible to community review, whatever doctrinal incongruities may result.

My purpose has been to illustrate the range of doctrinal rationales for reprisals-like behavior by using the logical problem of Charter decree and contrary Security Council practice as a kind of prism. In effect, rationales are refracted through the prism into several sets of "solutions." All of these solutions are beset with difficulties. Many fail in doctrinal, logical or empirical terms. Others fail because they have received little consensual acceptance. Finally, some fail because they are inadequate to what I believe are the normative needs of a just and more orderly world. All of them fail for one further reason. They attempt to comprehend a complex and persistent phenomenon by applying just one legally relevant set of considerations. This is reminiscent of the common but much excoriated device of using a single factor to explain complex social phenomena.

An adequate rationale would have to deal with several factors simultaneously: (1) reprisals-series are highly ritualized; (2) the nature of the ritual is reflected in a body of rules which only incidentally happen to be embodied in classical legal formulations; (3) the Security Council characteristically

81 S. Hoffmann, "International Law and the Control of Force," in Deutsch and Hoffmann, *The Relevance of International Law*, pp. 28, 34.

82 Ibid., p. 28. The example of intervention is less persuasive. Tacit superpower constraints on intervention beyond established spheres of influence appear to operate rather well. Hoffmann himself was encouraged by the existence of such "observed restraints," as opposed to "legal norms," although the former can be viewed as operative law (pp. 41–2).

avoids condemning reprisals-series that stay within the rules; (4) reprisals as a form of self-help are outlawed by the Charter in passages that are clearly set apart in tone and substance from the rest of that document; (5) the international legal community insists on maintaining a comprehensive prohibition on reprisals-like behavior.

These factors summarize the empirical considerations that must be taken into account in developing a rationale. They also imply two overarching normative considerations that must be acknowledged directly. We speak of world order, yet we are willing to rationalize the continuing recourse to coercive instrumentalities in a disorderly world. Although hardly desirable in the abstract, such coercion is notoriously resistant to efforts to stifle or suppress it – so much so that a major review organ of the world community condones it when it exhibits non-escalatory, rule-bound behavior. We may even be consoled by such positive effects of reprisals-series as tension release for antagonists and strengthening of the review organ. More importantly, justice would not necessarily be served by suppressing reprisals-series in pursuit of a better order.

In primitive orders generally, justice, by whatever conception, is obtained through self-right enforcement. The consequent disorder and inequities are still to be preferred to a more orderly order in which the larger questions of justice remain unsettled. In these circumstances the assertion of parochial rights, like the right to feud, is difficult to prevent without damaging the principal means for obtaining justice of any kind. To have self-right enforcement at all means that reprisals will be claimed as just and proper coercion, as indeed will anticipatory self-defense, humanitarian intervention and the protection of nationals, and the promotion of transnational principles like democracy and socialism. Given a world order perspective, it is easy to lose sight of the importance of self-right enforcement when its decidedly unattractive side effects are so much in evidence. If there is little choice but to accept these effects, then the task at hand is to advance plausible rationales to limit their least desirable features.

No one could hope to produce a new, unifying rationale of sufficient scope and power to accommodate all of these considerations. Failing a rationale on a higher order, I am obliged to settle for something fashioned from the wealth of available material. As befits a piecemeal creation, this rationale I will present in two parts, which I then piece together.

In the first place I accept the argument that the UN Charter is really two legal instruments at once. One part, set apart as Chapter I, is a constitutive instrument for the world community. It is a symbolic apparatus setting forth what we might call the architectural premises of world order. These principles, as principles, have always been characterized by a high level of intensity, cogency and formality. The proscription on the use of force is one of them and as such is no different from statements of institutional purpose. The attempt to identify the former as black letter law and the latter as law of fundamental values is artificial and unconvincing since at the same time it obscures the very real difference between the principles and purposes of the Charter on the one hand and the rest of that black letter document on the other. The emergence of different principles can only come about through proceedings equal in formality to those surrounding the emergence of the principles we have now. They cannot be superseded simply through widespread, sporadic but normatively structured practices with a contrary thrust.

This view of the Charter accommodates the almost reverential treatment that statesmen accord to Chapter I. It accommodates what would otherwise be inexplicable anomalies in the Charter.[83] It accommodates my own normative preferences of the writer. What it fails to do, however, is provide any place whatsoever for the use of force that characterizes moves in a reprisals contest. Not all uses of force are precluded, for Article 51 is unaffected by the status of Chapter I. An inclusive conception of self-defense, as the only formally authorized vehicle for self-right enforcement, would be consistent with our world order perspective and a constitutive interpretation of Article 2(4), and would nonetheless permit reprisals-like behavior. Although we might agree with this conception in principle, states simply do not, as I indicated earlier.

At most, the continuing right of self-right enforcement helps to provide a permissive setting for taking reprisals but hardly a sufficient reason for doing so. For the latter we must look again at a reprisals-series as a distinctive phenomenon. What makes it distinctive is the strictly patterned, rule-bound behavior of its antagonists. It is immediately recognizable. It possesses an intensity and cogency that cannot be denied internally or thwarted externally. It unfolds of itself, little affected by the weaker patterns of behavior and expectations that surround it. It seems almost to have a life of its own.

This tight, very nearly imperative pattern of behavior defines a set of norms that both permit and confine a reprisals-series. They override more generally applicable norms of a contrary content. In effect the norms of a reprisals-series enjoy a localized cogency or peremptory character excepting the series from concrete prohibitions on the use of force that might otherwise obtain. The antagonists accept the exceptional nature of these norms, willingly or unwillingly, because they cannot escape their part in the unfolding of the contest.

To claim that the normative structure of a reprisal-series has a localized intensity and cogency is not to suggest that its norms have the requisite formality to displace constitutive principles of the Charter. There is no need for them to do so. The Charter principles are general principles, abstract in

83 I have in mind Article 2(6), which seeks to extend the Charter's principles to non-members, and Article 103, which invalidates agreements among members subsequent to and conflicting with the Charter. Both are pronounced departures from the law of treaties and create a strong presumption that the Charter is something quite different from the treaties governed by that law.

form and symbolic in function. The norms defining a reprisals contest are not just restraining rules but indeed behavioral derivatives, the restraint being inherent in behavior that is nonetheless inherently violent. Though differing in content, they can coexist with generalizing statements, which are formally enunciated and intensely held, because these statements carry presumptive weight only as the norm – the measure of normal – for the legal order.

8 Law and lawyers in international crises (1975)

In 1967 the American Society of International Law sponsored a Study Panel on "the role of international law in governmental decision-making for war-peace crises." Chaired by Roger Fisher, the Study Panel embarked on an ambitious research program resulting in the publication of three case studies in 1974: Robert R. Bowie, *Suez 1956*; Abram Chayes, *The Cuban Missile Crisis*; Thomas Ehrlich, *Cyprus 1958–1967*. Another case study on the Congo crisis 1960–1964, and Fisher's slim summary volume, *Points of Choice*, were not published until 1978. In the meantime, the editors of *International Organization* had asked me to write an essay reviewing the first three case studies.

International crises were then the subject of a burgeoning literature in the positivist mode of social science: theories are to be formulated in such a way as to yield propositions subject to systematic empirical testing. The volumes under review gave no attention at all to this literature. Instead they focused on the role of law, explicitly understood as the ways in which governments put legal rules to use and implicitly understood as the function those rules perform in maintaining a decentralized order. Reliance on a term so loosely conceived gave me an opportunity to develop my thoughts on the functions of law. Whether positivist or naturalist, legal theory holds that law is of a single kind; functionalists generally adhere to this view. In Chapter 6 I derived two kinds of international law from the sociologies of Max Weber and Emile Durkheim. In this essay, I proceeded inductively by gleaning evidence from the case studies and proposed four types of rules. (*Types* are empirically discerned, *kinds* are conceptually defined.) For publication here, I have eliminated an inadequate treatment of *role* contained in a long footnote, and I have substituted *use* or *function* for *role* in several places.

Under review here are three case studies in the "international crises and the role of law" series.[1] All three follow the general procedure of grafting an informal functional orientation toward international law onto a brief

1 R.R. Bowie, *Suez 1956*; A. Chayes, *The Cuban Missile Crisis*; T. Ehrlich, *Cyprus 1958–1967*; all New York: Oxford University Press, 1974.

political-diplomatic history of certain major events in recent history.[2] Unfortunately, none of them undertakes even a casual definition of crisis. The morphology of crises is completely ignored, despite significant scholarly developments in this direction.[3] With or without the assistance of pertinent social science scholarship, the organizing and systematizing effects of having adopted a common conceptual orientation toward crises are sorely missed.

The authors do share a common view of international law as an instrument of policy, thus aligning themselves with progressive scholarship in the field. The role of law is interpreted rather consistently to mean the uses to which law as an instrumentality are put by governments, such that governments' behavior is other than it would likely have been without such recourse to law. The specific effects on governments of resorting to legal forms for policy purposes are seen as the functions of laws, for which each author has a roughly comparable checklist.[4] Comparative assessment of the role of law is invited on the assumption that the crisis situations in which law is being used need not be comparable. This assumption is so suspect as to make any generalizing across cases an exceedingly hazardous enterprise. Nonetheless, I will advance some tentative statements of my own about the nature and role, or *function*, of law but refrain from suggesting (with one exception) that these roles are restricted to crisis situations or even affected by such situations in specifiable ways.[5] The higher level of generality trades specious substantive specificity for at least a modicum of analytic utility.

2 S. Hoffmann's "International Systems and International Law" is surely the most succinct and presently influential example of functional analysis in international law, especially in the US and among political scientists. Hoffmann's essay appeared in *World Politics*, vol. 14, 1961, pp. 205–37 – a special issue devoted to "The International System: Theoretical Essays." In this same issue, C.A. McClelland's "The Acute International Crisis," pp. 182–204, proved as seminal for the study of crises as Hoffmann's essay did for functional analyses of international law. The subject of crises has subsequently been more actively studied and now engages the attention of a major community of scholars. The influence of functional analyses of international law is pervasive but far more passive.

3 This is not to suggest that the study of crises has cleared up major conceptual difficulties or developed a consensual view. See C.F. Hermann (ed.), *International Crises: Insights from Behavioral Research*, New York: Free Press, 1972.

4 Bowie, *Suez 1956*, pp. 114–5; Ehrlich, *Cyprus 1958–1967*, pp. 120–3; H. Linde, "Comment," in Ehrlich, pp. 143–5; Chayes, *The Cuban Missile Crisis*, in chapter headings and throughout.

5 Scholars concerned with crisis have tended to use the term to denote situations of grave peril or threat, sharply defined in temporal terms. The term has been stretched in popular usage to include chronically distressed situations. I am forced to adopt the latter conception, and consequently forfeit any analytic assistance from scholarship utilizing the former conception, because of the three "crises" under consideration. The Cuban crisis easily fits the narrow conception and is much studied as such. The Suez crisis might be construed either as one rather drawn-out crisis or a string of closely related crises. But there is no way the ongoing situation in Cyprus from 1958 to 1967 can intelligibly be referred to as a crisis in the narrow sense.

In short, the three books in question have a sufficiently comparable if largely implicit analytic orientation toward the function of law that some comparative assessment is possible. They provide utterly no basis for assessing crises of various types or the relationship between types of legal activity and types of crises. Before undertaking the limited and highly generalized comparative assessment that is possible, I proceed to a brief examination of each book in its own right.

All three books are standardized in certain superficial respects. They each have slightly more than a hundred pages of text, plus appendices of documents where available and appropriate, and comments from other panel participants. Each author is a professor, a lawyer, and was, at an earlier time, a public servant. As noted, each book is a political-diplomatic history larded with observations about the nature of international law and its place in public life.

Bowie's study of Suez and Ehrlich's of Cyprus are little rewarding, I suspect, even for students. The diplomatic-political histories are necessarily superficial and the analysis so obviously derivative that a serious student would see them immediately as exercises: formal, predictable, and ultimately trivial. Bowie's volume is further marred by a subtle cultural insensitivity, which is manifested in the tendency to label Western governments as governments and non-Western governments as personifications of their leaders. At one point Bowie seems almost startled that Nasser appears to have benefited from astute legal advice, as if it were unlikely that he bothered with advisers. Ehrlich, on the other hand, errs in the direction of treating all participants so abstractly that his narrative is a history of states and not of diplomats and their chiefs.

In marked contrast is Chayes' study of the Cuban missile crisis. The book is alive with personalities whose governmental positions are fully articulated. Chayes expressly acknowledges the influence of Graham Allison's major analytical work on the same crisis, *Essence of Decision* (1968), and of course the memoirs and intimate accounts of the decision process are far greater in number than for either Suez or Cyprus. Furthermore, Chayes was actually in the midst of it, and his personal presence is felt throughout the narrative. Perhaps most important of all, he deals with a more limited situation than the other two. His is a single event, transpiring in a matter of days and from the point of view, and workings, of just one government.

None of the foregoing is intended to explain away my belief that Chayes' is a better, richer book than its companion volumes. The reading is fascinating, as is much of the missile crisis literature, for its immediacy. At the same time Chayes has used the passage of years to gain perspective on the subject. While Chayes' volume may be enhanced, as the others are not, by reference to a comprehensive analytic orientation like Allison's, Chayes as observer, by habit of mind, seems inevitably to impose order and meaning on the complex interplay of persons, roles, settings, and events that he experienced as a participant.

In particular, I find Chayes' extended passages on law as justification altogether brilliant, perhaps because they converge on some aspects of my own recent attempt to examine the nature of rationales involving legal doctrines on the use of force (Chapter 7 above). The justificatory use of law is somehow lost between the categories of law as constraint and law as communication.[6] These now standardized categories, though varied in nomenclature and subdivided for purposes of specification, fail to capture the extent to which law serves to categorize available modalities of behavior, as Myres McDougal is wont to tell us, and, in so doing, to objectivize the attitudinal and intellectual structures that involved individuals inevitably bring to service in dealing with choices they find they must make. It is this latter quality of law that Chayes so tellingly coaxes out of his discussion of the reasons for having recourse to the Organization of American States once the pertinent officials had decided on a quarantine. Though less thoroughly inductive than Percy Corbett's pathbreaking examination of justification as "the primary purpose of the appeal to law," Chayes' exposition nonetheless eludes the usual functional dichotomy and even McDougal's vastly more complicated system of categories.[7]

For all his insight, Chayes provides us in the end with another checklist of law functions, novel only for the emphatic addition of justification of policy as a use of law. How do we know that other additions are not required? Is there a more systematic way of organizing the functions performed by international law?

One way to proceed is with the identification of systemic structures and correlative manifest bodies of patterned behavior, the latter being bodies of law or legal regimes. Thus, the classic distinction between the law of peace and the law of war reflects different systemic realities. Within the law of peace, the law of state responsibility, to give a further example, articulates the sub-regime of patterned behavior in the system of resource-exporting vs. capital-exporting states. The well-known efforts of Stanley Hoffman and Wolfgang Friedmann to characterize the international system and correlative legal regimes, respectively, in terms of the law of political framework, of reciprocity and of community, and the law of coexistence, of universal cooperation and of regional cooperation, are more contemporary examples

6 See W.D. Coplin, "International Law and Assumptions about the State System," *World Politics*, vol. 17, 1965, pp. 615–34, for the twofold functional categorization of law as a communications device and law as means of coercive restraint.

7 P.E. Corbett, *Law in Diplomacy*, Princeton: Princeton University Press, 1959, p. 275. As an early member of the functional school, Corbett relies on his own largely implicit dichotomy of law as a constraint on diplomatic conduct and law as an adjunct to conduct. McDougal's framework is available in unadorned form in "Some Basic Theoretical Concepts about International Law: A Policy-Oriented Framework of Inquiry," *Journal of Conflict Resolution*, vol. 4, 1960, pp. 337–54. Some would argue that justification of policy is integral to McDougal's conception of law and thus informs all of his categories.

of the same orientation.[8] Note that the substance or use of particular norms is generally unspecified, for the specifics could only be inferred from structures that are themselves too specific or submerged in the sea of state behavior to be readily identified. On the contrary, by recourse to the so-called sources of international law, the content of rules can be far more readily appreciated in a direct, inductive sense.

If the relevant system structures are general in character, the function of legal regimes is comparably general, though implicit; namely, to support the survival of the system as it is generally configured. Whatever epistemological weaknesses arise from this classic structural-functional conception, not the least of which is its self-evidently tautological nature, for our purposes it fails to provide a way of getting from the general case of the legal regime to the specific uses that international law may serve in relatively concrete, specifiable situations.

If we start with general statements about the nature of international law and deductive statements of the requisite specificity fail us, possibly it is because we are making our general statements about a number of phenomena that go under one name but are in fact little related, except in appearance. In short, we may have to disaggregate the concept of international law before we can say anything more about the uses to which specific rules are put. What international law does is dependent on what international law is. By reference to the efforts of numerous contemporary scholars to grapple with the ambiguities in the concept of international law, we can devise a checklist, not of functions, but of separable phenomena, which for various reasons have been lumped together as international law.

I believe there is no logical way to be sure that our checklist of law-types is exhaustive, although we can be more confident about approaching that end by employing two kinds of checks. First we can infer from the different kinds of law the uses that rules of each type have and then match this list against available checklists, or a composite checklist, of the functions claimed for international law. The better they match the more assured we are of the comprehensive character of all such lists; if they do not match, we can formulate a new list of ways in which international law seems to work which is at least *prima facie* more credible than its predecessors.

Second, we can order the law-types we have garnered from the literature on a continuum constructed from some crucial set of attributes of all such law-types to see if there are any obvious gaps in the ordering. As will soon become evident, the law-types to be set out here do fall out rather neatly on a continuum. The pertinent attribute of this continuum is the size of the arena in which particular law-types operate; the end points of the continuum are the minds of involved individuals and the system as a whole.

8 Hoffmann, "International Systems and International Law"; W. Friedmann, *The Changing Structure of International Law*, New York: Columbia University Press, 1964, ch. 6.

If we start with the smallest arena – the minds of individuals involved in making significant public choices – the first problem is the identification of individuals whose activities may be seen as the stuff of law, to paraphrase Karl Llewellyn. Obviously many involved individuals are at least peripherally aware of law. The three volumes under review provide cumulative evidence that practically everyone important enough to be mentioned by name knew that the use of force involved significant legal considerations, that international institutions were "there" and had to be taken into account, and that treaty obligations could not be dismissed lightly.

For the highest ranking public officials, this would appear to be the full extent of their awareness of the substantive requirements of international law. A professional background in law is not likely in itself to mean a more detailed awareness of the law, substantively speaking, except insofar as it inclines such senior officials to solicit information on particular questions from advisers who are legal specialists. Thus the law established a frame of reference for these individuals. Because this framework tends to be congruent with the moral disposition of most such officials, its importance can easily be underestimated.

For individuals whose role is to advise and assist the most senior public servants, the possession of a more complex orientation toward international law depends on the more specialized kind of training that is usually associated with the study and practice of law. Lawyers share a set of attitudes about the nature and uses of law, whatever the substantive nature of the problems to be dealt with and their specific responsibilities with respect to these problems. Lawyers most characteristically have in common a tendency to evaluate problems in separable and thus more manageable pieces for each of which there is a more or less standardized, publicly defensible, solution. What lawyers do as a consequence of this shared attitude is produce memoranda, copies of documents and anything else that breaks down a given present problem in terms of past solutions.[9]

Whether the activities of lawyers come before or after the problem is dealt with has no bearing on the nature of the advice. If it happens to be afterwards the lawyer's role is seen as justificatory, even if he did not know that his efforts would be utilized simply to justify choices made on other grounds entirely. The subordinate official who is a lawyer proceeds as if his effort would make a difference whenever his advice is sought. For the most part lawyers carry out routine activities in which their advice is decisive precisely because it immediately and conclusively puts to rest situations that would become problems only if left unattended. The artifacts of such routine problem-preempting

9 For a much fuller development of these themes, see Chapter 6, above. The sources of inspiration for my work in this area include Karl Llewellyn's claim that what public officials do about disputes is the law itself, and Max Weber's and Emile Durkheim's masterworks in the sociology of law.

are much of what lawyers turn to when a larger problem engages the attention of superiors who then require advice.

A relatively small coterie of politicians, usually lawyers or lawyer-assisted, manufactures artifacts without reference to specific problems needing solution. They do so in the belief that they are providing class solutions in advance of or in response to the need of their employment, and in the process they provide themselves with something important to do. This activity is called legislation. At the international level it is largely in the hands of the UN's lawyer-politicians.[10] The artifacts they produce, usually in the forms of declarations and multilateral treaties, are little effective as class solutions to what have come to be called crises.

At numerous points, Chayes deals with the role of lawyers and their artifacts, even employing the latter term. The moral stances of lawyers in high places, exemplified by Robert Kennedy and Dean Acheson, become powerful illustrations of lawyerly thinking, as opposed to thinking about law. For Kennedy the broad injunctions of law relative to the use of force gave substance and meaning to a deeply felt moral sensibility. For Acheson the lawyer's mind could cut through the mystification inherent in legal invocation. Accustomed to the role of manipulating through legal mystification, Acheson displayed no hesitation about dispensing with mystification when the need arose. Chayes quotes Acheson as implying that only lawyers know when law is needed and thus, by further implication, when it is not. Bowie leads us toward a similar conclusion, again without saying so, by showing how senior French and British officials underestimated legal considerations to their disadvantage.

While Bowie does not identify the background of his French and British principals, it happens that for the most part they were not lawyers. By contrast Chayes emphasizes the presence of legal training among the American principals in the Cuban missile crisis, and he attaches some importance to the fact that four of 14 regular participants in the "Executive Committee" which advised the President throughout the crisis were lawyers, as were two other occasional participants. To Chayes this is an "extraordinary concentration" (p. 13), although Donald Matthews in his classic monograph, *The Social Background of Political Decision-Makers* (1954), called lawyers "the high priests of American politics," inasmuch as "a large majority of America's top-level public officials" have been lawyers (p. 30). If anything, lawyers were underrepresented in the select group that handled the missile crisis.

Does the picture differ if we include all of the individuals identified by name in all three case studies? As an illustrative enterprise, to which no

10 Note that it is the general character of the activity and not stipulated qualities of the results – for example, being binding or promulgated in set manner – which warrants description as legislation. To focus on artifactual specifics is to be embroiled in the interminable controversy as to whether there is any such thing as international legislation properly speaking.

scientific ambition should be attached, I collected names of all individuals who took some part in the three narratives under consideration, excluding only the names of commentators and historical figures mentioned for purposes of background (for example Hitler). Bowie has 45 names that qualify under these requirements, Chayes 44 and Ehrlich 37 names. Six names appeared twice, one (Harold Macmillan) three times, and biographical data on three others were not procured. Thus there were 115 individuals on whose professional background I found relevant information. Of these 36 were lawyers by training and profession, at least at some time in their careers. An additional nine attended law faculties and probably had some law training.[11] If Chayes thinks that four out of 14 (28.6 percent) is an extraordinary concentration, then what do we make of 32 percent across the board, for all three studies?

It will be pointed out immediately that the studies in question are, after all, devoted to the role of law and would therefore be skewed in favor of the participation of lawyers. To deal with this bias, I separated the 115 names into two groups. The first consists of chiefs and deputy chiefs of states, prime ministers and their deputies, senior ministers, senior party leaders, and secretaries-general of international organizations, and the second consists of all others. The first group would arguably be roughly the same whether studies were directed toward the role of law or not. In the instance of the three studies under review the first group included 61 individuals (slightly more than half of the total), of whom 15 were lawyers, seven others had some background in law, and 39 had no legal background.

That very nearly a quarter of the highest public officials involved in these three situations were lawyers surely suggests the presence of lawyerly ways of thinking in world politics. It also suggests that President Kennedy's Executive Committee was a remarkable concentration only when measured against the proportion of lawyers in the population at large. It is actually remarkably consistent with the density of lawyers in the level of policy personnel immediately above or at the same level as the Executive Committee's members, depending on their respective ranks.

At least in the US, lawyers are drawn to public life. The above figures merely confirm what we have long taken for granted. Rather more interesting is the apparent concentration of lawyers in all states whose policy makers figured in these studies. It is conventionally assumed that the importance of lawyers in American public life is idiosyncratic. The only comparable concentration of professional personnel in public life worldwide is drawn from the military, or so the belief goes. Although the presence of military minds in

11 Biographical data was drawn from various international and national *Who's Who's*. Information on educational background is often quite scanty and difficult to interpret. More adequate biographies are either unavailable or excessively time-consuming to locate. The problem is compounded by the degree to which legal and social studies are integrated in the curricula of European universities.

high places is unevenly distributed for reasons of history and culture, it is hardly an idiosyncratic phenomenon such as we associate with the presence of lawyers.

To provide at least a crude check on this loose collection of beliefs, I identified the number of lawyers and military careerists in the highest echelon of public life (the 61 names collected above) who were (1) North American, (2) North European, and (3) Mediterranean. A pattern is readily discernible. Of the 16 North Americans, six are lawyers, one a career military man. Of the 21 North Europeans, only three are lawyers, two others have some law background, and three are military professionals. Of 21 Mediterraneans, six are lawyers, with five others having some law, and seven are military in background. Obviously lawyers are more prominent in the US and Canada than in Northern Europe, but not appreciably more than in the Mediterranean. Military careerists are roughly as important as lawyers outside of North America. Northern Europe has the largest number of officials who are public servants or politicians throughout their career.

Given the nature of the data, apparent differences may not be real. Even greater differences may be buried by placing, say, Britain and France together in one category. Nonetheless, if we assume the differences are along the lines indicated, additional considerations present themselves. First, military men are quite respectful toward law and law-supplied institutions. Their habits conduce to law-abidingness.[12] Military men may differ from lawyers on specifics relating to the use of force, but both sets of professionals can have quite similar doctrinal orientations toward the general problem of force. The presence of lawyers and military men alike suggests the likelihood of a greater attentiveness to legal considerations as part of their instrumental view of doctrinal mystifications.

Reading Bowie's book especially, one senses that the British and French were ill-served in terms of legal advice, not because they do not have excellent sources of such advice, but because they were unaccustomed to the idea that it might be useful to have. By contrast, Nasser, a military man, seems to have made effective use of his legal advisers, as Bowie notes. We should not see this as any more out of character than the strong tendency of developing world rhetoric, like the rhetoric of American politicians, to be couched in the language of law. Legalism is hardly an American trait alone, nor is it somehow the antithesis of militarism.

Second, it is occasionally suggested that US State Department personnel are prone to reject legalism and accept realism in its stead. Such officials are said to have a permissive, flexible and "tough-minded" view of the possibilities of force. Without the likes of George Kennan and Hans Morgenthau

12 See J. Ellis and R. Moore, *School for Soldiers: West Point and the Profession of Arms*, New York: Oxford University Press, 1974, on the step-by-step, by-the-book problem-solving habits inculcated in cadets of the US Military Academy.

to lead them, it is unlikely that British civil servants and their superiors are given to quite the same intellectual fashions. Perhaps in the British case circumstances are a sufficient explanation for the slighting of law in Suez; perhaps the lesser importance of lawyers does make a difference. In the biographies of other Europeans, however, it is striking to observe how many of the leaders of the decades of the 1950s and 1960s had earlier been resistance fighters and provincial activists. Quite possibly the salient professional socialization for many of these high officials lies in irregular, often illegal, but always honorable, conduct during the years of disruption in Europe. We would expect from them a more casual attitude toward legal strictures and doctrinal niceties.

For all the suspicions about lawyers and generals in public life, their presence is probably a blessing. Politicians unhampered by legal and military doctrinalists seem to find it too easy to do the rash, unreflective or readily available thing. All of this is little more than guessing. Although spurred by the derivative data presented above, such guesses doubtless find their source in the reviewer's prejudices. The collection of data on senior public officials on a country-by-country basis, and the formulation and testing of relevant hypotheses, are not impossible tasks, however, and represent a possible direction for further research.[13]

Of the 54 individuals not counted in the highest echelon of public figures, virtually all occupied the next lower echelon of political deputies and career civil servants. Twenty are lawyers (37 percent) and two others had legal training. Obviously legal advice was abundantly available to senior officials. Yet only the Chayes study directs attention to this law-laden stratum. Ehrlich makes occasional references to what legal advisers might have advised; Bowie, as noted, briefly touches on the quality of legal advice. Neither gives a concrete reality to the advisors. It is first a matter of numbers. In the Bowie and Ehrlich books nearly two-thirds of the individuals named are top echelon officials, while in Chayes' book better than two-thirds are in the second tier. But secondly, it is a matter of artifacts. Chayes produces or reconstructs the memoranda bearing legal advice. Bowie and Ehrlich obviously did not have access to comparable documents. They do not so much as indicate whether such documents exist.

Once we get beyond the thin veil of generalizations about legal attitudes on the part of a few dozen leaders, no amount of political historical narrative is likely to generate further understanding of the way law is brought up from below, sometimes even sucked up, and brought to bear in times of crisis, unless it deals with the kinds of materials that Chayes uses. Perhaps a lesson

13 For a pioneering effort along these lines, see G. Modelski, "The World's Foreign Ministers: A Political Elite," *Journal of Conflict Resolution*, vol. 14, 1970, pp. 135–76. In 1965, 46 percent of the world's foreign ministers (at least the 97 for whom Modelski had biographical information) were lawyers (Table 6, p. 147, and p. 149). This probably includes those who had some legal training but were not law professionals.

can be learned from professional historians and their indefatigable pursuit of personal reminiscences, private correspondence, file copies of in-house documents and all the other unpublished artifacts to be found amid bureaucratic litter. If artifactual evidence about the workings of law on minds is not available, then we should consider whether some other orientation toward the role of law might prove more rewarding.

A second major type of law would identify law with deliberative behavior. Whenever statesmen engage in deliberations for the purpose of adjusting rival claims, any decision reconciling such claims or settling them in determinative fashion has the status of law. Readers will immediately recognize the stamp of the New Haven school of international legal scholarship in this conception, and will probably respond with the perennial objection that it fails to distinguish adequately between law and power. While it could be argued that blurring the distinction between law and power is precisely the value of this way of thinking, it would be better to say that power is offered as an abstraction, the concrete, organizing consequences of which are in the form of law, money, status, property, and so on.

If law is but a manifestation of power in adjusting conflicting interests, its importance lies in forcing the articulation of private, particular interests in publicly acceptable form. Public interests, by virtue of their abiding and generally appreciated character, prominently figure in the modalities for settling more transient and self-interested claims. Such public forms become the currency through which claims can be measured and into which they can be converted for the purposes of deciding on the distribution of claimed values. The currency metaphor suggests that law so conceived is both a means of measuring the intensity with which values are claimed and a medium for transferring or exchanging values of differing intensity.[14] Decisions adjusting rival claims are thus no more than records of bargains struck, including those many bargains of simple, reciprocal exchange which are so predictable as to be recognized everywhere as rules of law.

Furthermore, the currency metaphor grants law the integrity we associate with a working medium of exchange. The metaphor probably also contains an assumption that law-users seek to maximize their values short of discrediting

14 The more frequent association is between power and money. The limitations and implications of identifying power as analogous to money is superbly treated by D.A. Baldwin, "Money and Power," *Journal of Politics*, vol. 33, 1971, pp. 578–614. Baldwin aptly suggests that power is not suitable as a medium of exchange because it is impossible to measure conveniently. If we follow Baldwin and take political power as analogous to purchasing power, then it would seem that law as a formalization of power has at least crude and limited commensurability. Economic transactions are not just either directly bartered or facilitated through the medium of money. There is a continuum from direct exchange to the instantly recognizable, perfectly measurable and infinitely exchangeable medium (approximated by gold). Law would seem to fall near the barter end of the continuum, as befits a relatively primitive social order.

the medium of exchange and other attributes of the marketplace in which the currency of law is used. Thus the product of individual efforts to maximize is presumed to be in equilibrium. Law is not the only currency nor legal order the only marketplace in the international context. Any one such marketplace is likely to impinge on what might otherwise be an equilibrium situation in any other. We can easily guess that the marketplace in which law serves as currency is one of those most subject to impingement.

The three books under review provide little evidence of law operating as a medium of exchange, principally because they are little concerned with deliberative behavior. In crisis-ridden situations interests surely conflict, but are more likely hardened than compromised through expression in public forums. The importance of law as a communications device is undoubtedly greater in situations characterized by a deliberative format, such as arms control negotiations. If communicating differences is undertaken for the purpose of doing something about those differences, the virtues of an available medium of exchange are easily recognized. If differences are communicated as emblems of intransigence, then crises exist because statesmen have an interest in crises and law communicates the felt-rightness of one's intransigently defined interests. The role of law in crises slides from communication to justification.

The impression conveyed by the three studies is that critical claims resist definition in all but the crudest legal terms. Hence crisis outcomes are similarly crude, and few warrant being labeled law. If law is a medium of exchange, then the law relative to crises suffers from a chronic liquidity problem. Attempts to cope with this problem by augmenting the supply of crisis-generated norms with negotiated regimes, like the recent one defining aggression, are simply insufficient to the need. One also suspects that speeding up the supply of norms through such means, without a commensurate growth in shared values, has effects akin to those experienced through inflation.

These are preliminary ideas. They need further development before the system of adjusting rival claims can be made sense of as a not entirely primitive market economy constantly subjected to the intrusions and distortions represented by crisis situations. A more limited concern with deliberative behavior in the crisis context is just as apparently limited in value.

Once we have dealt with law as what lawyers do and law as deliberative behavior, we come to a third law-type: law as guidance criteria. I am indebted to Richard Falk for this phrase, which he uses in reference to the place of law in decision-making. For Falk, such criteria may express rules of law, the requirements of reasonableness and restraint, or possibly even contextually specified advice offered by informed bystanders. Presumably, anything decision-makers use for guidance is law, but resort to express rules is to be preferred to the resort to reasonableness, which in turn is preferable to advice on specifics. In concrete situations decision-makers employ all three categories of guidance, without clearly attempting to distinguish them from one another.

In this conception rules form the lesser part of law, while the larger part is the discretion exercised in fitting rules to circumstances. Discretion is hardly exercised in a void, inasmuch as value preferences and social policies inform all guidance criteria, whatever form they take. Equally important is the structure of the situation facing a decision-maker. He knows who his adversaries are and what the stakes are, and he can assess probable outcomes of different courses of action (whether correctly is not the question). The criteria guiding his choice must therefore be tied to the situation at hand. Specific rules tend to be specifically suited to some other situation, so that recourse is to the more abstract and consequently more permissive criteria of being reasonable, expecting reciprocity, and acting with due proportion in relation to the situation.

The books under review offer some illustrations of guidance criteria at work. Bowie notes for example that the Egyptian government terminated the 99-year concessionary arrangements for the Suez Canal 11 years in advance of their expiry. It did so in defiance of specific legal requirements on grounds that were self-evidently reasonable. The passage of so many years alone warranted a modest acceleration of an inevitable outcome – it is a 99-year lease that is intrinsically unreasonable.

Ehrlich's material shows how reciprocal expectations can dominate the unfolding of a crisis. The tightly interdependent structure of Greek and Turkish responses to the situation in Cyprus suggests that Greeks and Turks were watching each other at least as closely as they were watching the situation. Decisions to act or, more often, not to act seemed to be guided by this reciprocal awareness. Yet in 1964 the Turkish government waged a bombing attack against Greek Cypriot forces engaged in reducing the principal remaining Turkish Cypriot enclave after earlier hostilities had subsided on the strife-ridden island. This apparent violation of the pattern of reciprocal restraint between Greece and Turkey merely illustrates a change in the situation. As Ehrlich tells us, "some military action by Turkey seems to have been almost inevitable if the continued threat of force was to remain plausible" (p. 86).

Integral to the pattern of Greco-Turkish responses was the recurring threat of force by Turkey, which was necessitated by the superior position of Greek Cypriots on the island. Failure to use force in due course could only weaken the credibility of Turkish responses and undermine the reciprocal structure of Greek and Turkish behavior. The fact that Turkey was willing to violate specific and well-known norms and invite condemnation by the Security Council must be placed against the fact that the Turkish Cypriot situation stopped deteriorating and the pattern of Greco-Turkish interaction resumed. The importance of guidance criteria, not to mention their relativity, is all the better seen in a situation in which relevant substantive rules failed to affect behavior.

Chayes also provides us with examples of guidance criteria at work and, not surprisingly, displays a degree of analytic awareness in doing so. He describes at some length the problem for American officials in the missile crisis of deciding on a response that was proportionate to the threat. Settling on a quarantine as the only concretely articulated decision point between the extremes of immediate air attack on Cuba and full capitulation to the Soviet *demarche* had practically nothing to do with substantive rules, but it fitted geopolitical circumstances on the one hand and the value premises of the American principals on the other. In short, the quarantine was a "focal point," in Thomas Schelling's justly famous formulation, if not for the adversaries then for the bureaucratic chiefs surrounding the President.[15]

Chayes relies directly on Schelling in discussing the well-publicized possibility that the US tacitly agreed to remove missiles from Turkey in exchange for the Soviet removal of missiles from Cuba.[16] Not only is this a plausible interpretation of events, it is a convincing demonstration that the determination of a focal point comes from fitting a guidance criterion – in this case, reciprocity – to the circumstances of a given situation. Reciprocity meant specifically a symbolically but not materially significant equivalence between Soviet and American behaviors.

The role of law as guidance criteria is to channel behavior. To this day Schelling's classic treatment of bargaining strategies provides the basic text on this law-type. A more systematic presentation of guidance criteria and their channeling effects in typical situations has yet to be undertaken, though hardly for the reason of being too difficult to imagine doing. Rather it is the wide sway of the single case study format, with its individualizing effect, which seems to have inhibited progress in this direction.

The last type of international law to suggest itself on a continuum from the minds of individuals to the structure of the system must of course be systemically conceived. "Rules of the game" is a label often used informally in the study of international relations (but less often in international law) to describe the underlying structure of the international system as it permits or impedes certain kinds of activity. Morton Kaplan used similar but somewhat more formal language to the same effect.[17] Such rules are system determined. To the extent they do not determine behavior, the fact of their being thwarted or ignored may imperil the system itself. The rule derived from the operation of the balance of power, as a particular system structure, that major entities shall not be eliminated from the system, can be violated only at the price of endangering the balance of power system. Another example, stated permissively, is a putative rule tolerating superpower intervention in spheres of

15 T.C. Schelling, *The Strategy of Conflict*, Cambridge, MA: Harvard University Press, 1960, chs. 3–4.

16 E.C. Hoyt in his "Comment" appended to Ehrlich, *Cyprus 1958–1967*, also expressly utilized Schelling's notions as they relate to legal doctrines serving as "salient points at which compromise can be reached" (p. 136).

17 M.A. Kaplan, *System and Process in International Politics*, New York: Wiley, 1957.

influence. The same rule can also be construed as forbidding the intervention of either superpower in the other's sphere of influence because of the risk of system failure.

Other rules of the game come from discrete subsystemic structures and processes. Elsewhere I have attempted to state some rules of reprisals-contests, that is, the recurring, highly structured pattern of reprisals-taking such as we find in the Middle East.[18] The proportionality rule, for example, is conventionally understood as having been customary law, but it can also be understood as an epiphenomenon of the contest dynamic. One cannot speak of the source of such rules, for they are not so much made as entailed. Although behavior described (not prescribed) by rules of the game and contest rules may seem inevitable or imperative to those undertaking it, others see it as both volitional and unacceptable.

Although they are not identified as such, rules of the game occasionally figured in the crisis situations under consideration. In the 1956 Suez crisis, for example, it seems clear that British and French officials thought that a rule of the game compelled the US to take an adversary position vis-à-vis the Soviet Union. The symmetrical bipolar structure of the international system combined with Soviet support of Egypt would thus force the US into supporting its allies no matter what reservations American officials might have. The British and French received a rude awakening, of course, but not simply because they misperceived structural realities. More plausibly the rule of superpower symmetry was then still valid but at the same time mediated by numerous intervening variables in the situation, which had the effect of delimiting the rule's domain of operation.

All three authors comment on the inevitable recourse to international forums such as the UN during crises. As Chayes emphasized, "international organizations are a recognized feature of the setting of decision" (p. 105). Once this is said, however, we are left with the realization that international organizations represent a quite differently configured feature in each crisis situation. The behavioral effects of decision-makers knowing that international organizations need to be taken into account do not yield to generalization across situations. International organizations are best seen as mediating between structural realities and decisional possibilities in such a way as to help define the domains within which rules of the game operate.

Rules of the game are not written down as such. Yet high officials pride themselves on being able to "read" the rules in any given circumstance. Thus we are talking about what goes on in their minds. This brings our continuum of law-types full circle, so to speak. Law as rules of the game and law as what

18 See Chapter 7, above. The same kind of rules may have been operating in the pattern of adversary interaction over Cyprus, as described above in connection with guidance criteria. The resort to guidance criteria and the appearance of rules for geographically and historically confined "games" may be different phases of a single process or possibly even different aspects of the same or related phenomena at work.

well-placed lawyers think about are apparently related. A structural reality must somehow become translated for operational purposes into a broadly but nonetheless formally (legally) stated proposition about desirable conduct in projected circumstances. In the process of translation the relationship between systemic imperative and state of mind is susceptible to attenuation and distortion. Nonetheless, there is a connection.

Whether we convert a continuum to a circle hardly matters. The important thing is its organizing properties. A continuum obviously has more than four points on it; by definition it has any number of points. The only limitation is in our ability to distinguish points clearly. The four points on the particular continuum utilized here seem to me to be well spaced and clearly identified, moving from individual attitudes and bureaucratic behavior, to deliberative behavior, onto strategic behavior, and ending with systemically compelled behavior. In effect, we have four categories, herein labeled *law-types*, into which international law, as a conceptual conglomerate, is disaggregated. The four law-types are identified as (1) what lawyers do, (2) the adjustment of rival claims, (3) guidance criteria, and (4) rules of the game. Characteristic activities are identified with these law-types: (1) the production of artifacts, especially to justify behavior and demonstrate the indispensability of lawyers; (2) the communication of intentions, capabilities, expectations, and outcomes; (3) the channeling of behavior with the consequence of making it less surprising; and (4) the constraining of behavior which if attempted would prove futile, even disastrous.

I have advanced the proposition that these activities point to the several ways that governments use international law to achieve their ends. More abstractly they constitute an exhaustive list of the functions of international law, or at least a list has a more credible claim to exhausting the functions of law than have previous lists, including those found in the volumes under review. Certainly none of these lists identifies a function not enumerated here. Finally I have culled through these volumes for some unsystematic and generally impressionistic evidence that these categories are useful in organizing narrative material on roles attributed to international law in crisis situations. Some elements of my organizational scheme are to be found scattered in Chayes' book, though generally in latent form, and it is this book too, which provides the most digestible material for this enterprise.

It may seem that I think the three volumes taken together have little value on their own terms. I do find them analytically unadventurous, even when one in particular is executed with unusual grace and intelligence. Their tone collectively suggests that their basic premises and conclusions met with the approval of the study panel that sponsored them. They can fairly be said to represent what more traditional British scholars see as the American school of international law, represented by Myres McDougal and his associates at Yale, Richard Falk of Princeton, the late Wolfgang Friedmann, Louis Henkin and others at Columbia, and Roger Fisher and Stanley Hoffmann of

Harvard. The institutional identification of these figures is itself enough to make the general perspective they share seem like an establishment view in the eyes of younger American scholars. It is nonetheless an innovative, even radical, departure in terms of scholarship outside the US. Were these studies less impeccably sponsored, or less self-assured in their conception of law, or more wide-ranging in their use of social science credentials on conflict and crisis, or more daring in their conceptual development, they would all the more likely be dismissed by that larger audience.

9 International legal order as an idea (1978)

Political scientists teaching international law have long bemoaned the lack of appropriate instructional materials. Yet rarely have they sought to remedy the situation by writing a general text that did justice to the full reach of the substantive law *and* to political context in which international law operates as a whole. Instead of taking up the challenge individually, several of us decided to write the book we desired together. To launch this brave plan, we divided up the subject to accord with our interests, organized a panel for the 1976 meeting of the International Studies Association and presented draft chapters. When we realized how much additional work would be required to meet our own high standards, the project languished and finally expired.

My contribution to this venture was to render the main issues of international legal theory plausible to political scientists. To do so I argued that international legal theory and political theory share a concern for the relation of order to authority. My review of the relevant history of political ideas now seems to me rather superficial, indeed superseded by several of the later essays in this book, and I have deleted it. I have also abbreviated an exposition of Hans Kelsen's and Myres McDougal's conceptions of order in the absence of a central authority. Remaining is my treatment of Richard Falk's "intermediate view" focused on functional needs and institutional developments since the Peace of Westphalia. As it became clear that the book project was moribund, I folded in material I had earlier drafted on the UN's institutional evolution. This I have kept, along with some additional consideration of the concept of order the editors of the *American Journal of International Law* had asked for. The material appearing here is somewhat more than half of the essay as originally published.

The problem of international order

International law, its masters tell us, is "the vanishing point of jurisprudence;"[1] so must be international politics, and all of international relations, for

1 Written by T.E. Holland, a turn-of-the-century master, the quoted words preface a major essay by contemporary masters M.S. McDougal *et al.*, "Theories About International Law: Prologue to a Configurative Jurisprudence," *Virginia Journal of International Law*, vol. 8, 1968, p. 188.

political theory. The recurrent and directing theme in political theory is the problem of order – how it is provided, maintained, altered, and so on.[2] Order resides in orderly relations, that is, patterned and predictable relations, among people, but is abstracted from those relations as any arrangement of norms and institutions that distributes values among people.[3] Among peoples, political theorists favor the alternative premise that anarchy, not order, reigns.[4] By not existing, international order needs no explaining. Evidence to the contrary can be explained away as anomalous or ephemeral, and therefore not of theoretical interest. From this follows the dominance of concern for conflict and disorder and the paucity of theory in the study of international politics.[5]

International legal order is doubly ignored because its existence is inexplicable in the languages of both law and order. Political theory ignores the problem of international order by denying it empirical credibility. Legal theory is less cavalier. International law exists, most theorists agree, but efforts to explain how it works fail the test of credibility. To reformulate the proposition, political theory banishes the problem of international order, while legal theory vanishes in the face of international law; both remain absent in the instance of something called *international legal order*. Thus, we should not be surprised that the use of this phrase is so limited in theoretical discussions, despite the fact that it has the good and solid ring of two intellectual traditions behind it.

Indeed, as far as I can tell, only two major figures in international legal scholarship – Hans Kelsen and Richard Falk – have troubled to use these words in other than casual terms and to develop theoretically significant meanings for them. We can turn to their respective forays into this no-man's-land, however, only after giving further consideration to the dilemma posed for theory by the possibility that order, understood in terms of law, rather more than anarchy can prevail in those human relations, like international relations, not constrained by higher, more highly organized relations. Said

2 See, in particular, S. Wolin, *Politics and Vision: Continuity and Innovation in Western Political Thought*, Boston: Little, Brown, 1960, pp. 8–11. The following discussion is as such influenced by this book.

3 The often ambiguous meanings attached to the word *order* in many disciplines are surveyed in P.G. Kuntz (ed.), *The Concept of Order*, Seattle: University of Washington Press, 1968. No definition can claim consensual acceptance.

4 "Whereas men within each state are subject to a common government, sovereign states in their mutual relations are not. This anarchy it is possible to regard as the central fact of international life and the starting-point of theorizing about." These are the opening words of H. Bull, "Society and Anarchy in International Relations," in H. Butterfield and M. Wight, (eds), *Diplomatic Investigations: Essays in the Theory of International Politics*, Cambridge, MA: Harvard University Press, 1968, p. 35.

5 M. Wight, "Why Is There No International Theory?" in Butterfield and Wight, *Diplomatic Investigations*, pp. 17–34.

otherwise, how can order exist in the absence of authority? [Here I have deleted several pages on the "authority–order dilemma" in the history of Western political and legal thought, which led to a brief discussion of Kelsen's treatment of the dilemma, also deleted.]

The analogy between international and primitive order centered on self-help tells us too little about either by obscuring the great differences between them. Kelsen's proof that the international order is truly legal is so logically stated that most of his readers come away impressed by it, but unconvinced. Kelsen treats us to two magnificent illusions. One we see when he orders all law under one validating norm; the other, when he effectuates rules through self-help. What is left after the tricks? The one important thing is the idea that the order is an order because states have consented to it and made it work as such – as an order without authority behind it. Kelsen formulated this insight in his own cogent way by stating that "legal order, as a whole, must be by and large effective in order to be valid," and that this principle is itself a rule of international law.[6] States must live by the rule that the legal order has to work like an order, or there is no order. Presumably, they consent to this rule because they have no tolerable alternative. In short, we can say for Kelsen (who would not say it for himself) that the need for order, acknowledged in the form of a rule, makes for order.

As the other major writer to use the term *international legal order* meaningfully, Richard Falk is by his own admission indebted to Kelsen. His other, even greater debt is to Myres McDougal and his associates at Yale Law School, whose many works focus on "world public order." This choice of words is noteworthy: at once it suggests something novel and something familiar. *Public* is a term referring to the realm of politics without directly invoking the presence of authority.[7] Its use permits McDougal to write about international law without having to call it that. Thus, McDougal avoids two failings of the positivist position: the dilemma posed by the not so obvious legal status of international law and the tendency to see international law as more than a body of rules, that is, as an order simply because it seems to be legal in character. This important corrective of McDougal's is more than offset by his disinterest in how a public order without the support of authority might happen to be orderly. [Deleted here is a long paragraph on McDougal's treatment of the order–authority dilemma. I realize now that I had misconstrued the formula *authoritative and controlling decisions*, reading it as a political scientist would, but a lawyer would not.]

[Instead] McDougal and his associates invoke the idea of a world community. In this instance the community is a collection of like-minded individuals who make policy for states and who understand the need for order to conduct international relations, to protect other communities consequential

6 H. Kelsen, *Principles of International Law*, New York: Rinehart, 1952, p. 414.
7 Similarly on *public*, see Wolin, *Politics and Vision*, pp. 9–10.

to the business of states, and, most diffusely, to advance universal values.[8] This community of statesmen promotes order so that members can do their jobs for states, even though these jobs may be to further disorder for state ends.

Where does the community get its decisive role? Who authorizes its members to manufacture an orderly environment within which to conduct relations? It would take an order in the first place to set up or permit the evolution of such a community. McDougal and his associates imply precisely this by distinguishing between constitutive and public order processes of decision.[9] The former create the circumstances under which the latter occur. Reference to constitutive decisions is McDougal's last and most direct attempt to explain the presence of order at a level transcending states. Constitutive decisions cumulatively represent an order among states – a legal order – made and consented to by states collectively through their duly authorized agents.

McDougal has taken us full circle by positing a constitutive order to explain public order. The route is so circuitous that we barely realize we are back, not just to legal order, but specifically to Kelsen's order constituted by states for themselves and in the form of law to help make it work as an order without authority. McDougal differs from Kelsen by not reducing the constitution of the order to a single, logically prior norm. Instead, the constitution is substantive, ongoing, and empirically accessible. The emphasis on these qualities is entirely salutary. It is also McDougal's great legacy to Falk. The formal, logical qualities of the order and its constitution are McDougal's least concern. His greatest concern, of course, is the context in which the order resides. Contextual specifics march through McDougal's pages in veritable regiments, mustered to delight the mind's eye. Yet the intellectual order McDougal so forcefully imposes on the context serves to obscure the underlying legal order, which becomes evident when the contextual specifics are stripped away.

Falk's joint endowment from Kelsen and McDougal is an awareness that the international legal order is an order that lacks the support of enforcement mechanisms but is constituted to work as an order nonetheless. Falk clearly differentiates between vertical and horizontal systems of order and finds the international legal order just as clearly an instance of the latter.[10] He wisely avoids a frontal assault on the question – How can the order be what it is?

8 M.S. McDougal and H.D. Lasswell, "The Identification and Appraisal of Diverse Systems of Public Order," in McDougal *et al.*, *Studies in World Public Order*, New Haven: Yale University Press, 1960, pp.10–12, 15–16.

9 M.S. McDougal *et al.*, "The World Constitutive Process of Decision," in C.E. Black and R.A. Falk (eds), *The Future of the International Legal Order*, vol. 1, Princeton: Princeton University Press, 1969, p. 73.

10 This was Falk's first intellectual task. "International Jurisdiction: Horizontal and Vertical Conceptions of Legal Order," *Temple Law Quarterly*, vol. 32, 1959, pp. 295–320. See also G. Gottlieb, "The Nature of International Law: Toward a Second Concept of Law," in Black and Falk, *The Future of the International Legal Order*, vol. 4, 1972, pp. 331–9.

– by asking instead: How did the international legal order, as a historical reality, come to pass?

His answer is disarmingly simple and genuinely persuasive: It was constituted by ranking statesmen in the setting of peace deliberations at the end of the Thirty Years War. The historic international legal order is indeed the Westphalian system of order. It is strictly horizontal in character, being deprived of hierarchical structures of authority. Falk borrows McDougal's nomenclature by insisting that this system of order involves authority relations, but this is a confusing and unnecessary formulation since it departs from the usual sense of authority as involving the reality of control as well as expectations about the propriety of control. Bearing this in mind, Falk is quite to the point in saying that "the international legal order is a socio-historical product of convergent perspectives on formal authority and actual behavior."[11]

If states created an order in Westphalia, then it is important to realize that they understand it as a whole thing, an order to be effectuated as such. This is the reconciliation of Kelsen and McDougal: the order is treated by its makers and benefactors as historical reality and formal entity at one and the same time. Falk also points out, as its makers and users surely know, that the order was designed to provide a bare minimum of order, that controlled disorder is a reasonable expectation, and that the order itself grew continuously, even exponentially and as a result of disorder. While the body of law and institutions expanded enormously, and with it the domain of order, the means for securing and supporting that order grew only modestly. After nearly three centuries, the order was still fundamentally horizontal in structure.

Falk believes that the members of the Westphalian order, sensitized to its limitations and problems after two world wars, reconstituted it in 1945 through the UN Charter. The Charter stitches into the fabric of the received order some new material, especially on the subject of what and how much the UN can do as an organization. Though small in number, these added strands are remarkable for their elasticity. To pursue the metaphor, they give the fabric rewoven at San Francisco a shape wholly different from the flat, horizontal order fashioned centuries before. Indeed the new order, as Falk sees it, has functional pockets capable of vertical as well as horizontal expansion in response to propitious circumstances and the passage of time.

11 R.A. Falk, "The Interplay of Westphalia and Charter Conceptions of the International Legal Order," in Black and Falk, *The Future of the International Legal Order*, vol. 1, p. 34. "Actual behavior" means generally behavior that does not reflect a stable pattern of control. Stable patterns that do emerge, like major powers' spheres of influence, are not matched by perceptions that they are appropriate. Falk perhaps underestimates the extent of Anglo-American control matched with doctrinal dominance during international law's so-called golden age of stability and acceptance. See, also, R.A. Falk, "A New Paradigm for International Legal Studies: Prospects and Proposals," *Yale Law Journal*, vol. 84, 1975, pp. 975–92.

The new order is basically organized like the old one, because the absence of authority necessitates this. The new departs from the old, however, by incorporating in the Charter a small supply of broadly stated provisions (Chapter I) that lend the weight of constitutional validity (a claim further developed in Chapter 19, below) to changes in the order, especially those expanding the ordering capabilities of the UN and its organs, to which states have overwhelmingly consented. In due course the order would have responded to these changes anyway, but the pace is so much quickened that a transformation of the order is at least conceivable.

Falk is not by sleight of hand dismissing the role of states in effectuating an order only latent in the Charter. He is really only showing how the Charter makes it easier for states to consent to its emergence. He is misleading, perhaps, in dramatizing the difference between old and new by contrasting the consent needed to make and maintain the Westphalian order with the formation of consensus in the Charter order. Consensus requires virtual unanimity, as far as Falk is concerned, so the contrast with consent is less substantive than symbolic. Consensus takes on special meaning because the Charter, as Falk interprets it, endows such expressions of collective will with an immediate constitutive impact not possible in the traditional order as it was once constituted.

The difference between consent and consensus is also procedural. States usually consent to quite specific things, and a general legal obligation with respect to classes of such things can be inferred only with the greatest of care. Consensus is something states express all at once and in general enough terms for the extent of obligation to be immediately evident to all. Voting in the UN plenary organ, the General Assembly, for the most part means less than the variety of acts affirmed by tradition as acts of consent to law in the Westphalian order. Yet, there are occasions when the votes are on statements of principle. Typically, they are unanimously adopted, referred to as expressions of consensus, and constantly reiterated and reaffirmed. They are not taken lightly in UN circles and many writers, including Falk himself, attach exceptional significance to them.

Chapter I of the Charter, which states the principles and purposes of the organization, is also cast in a generalized form that is set apart from the concrete terms of the rest of the Charter. As Falk observes, Chapter I is a study in ambivalence, being in part a recapitulation of the Westphalian order and the limits that order places on institutional arrangements and in part a schematic statement of something altogether different – the new order not operationalized in later chapters. When the principles elaborated by the General Assembly are placed next to Chapter I, the effect of the former becomes obvious. They flesh out the bare bones of the new order anticipated in the Charter. Chapter I stands out from the rest of the Charter because it was intended to; similarly, the elaborating principles, for the most part embodied in declarations, stand out from the bulk of General Assembly resolutions. By their nature these statements are generalized in language and universal in scope. Such attributes would seem to characterize the constitutive elements of a legal order. In a sense, then, the General Assembly has become the center stage for the constitutional congress that was begun in San Francisco.

Predictably, the impetus for the continuing effort to reconstitute the world's legal order comes from its newer, relatively deprived members. Conversely, resistance has come from the Western states, which exercise the greatest control over the day-to-day reality of the present order. The principles constituting the new order emphasize over and over again the changing relationship of sovereignty to the responsibility of all members for each other's welfare and the requirement for them all to tolerate the concern of the legal order's institutions with the administration of that welfare. (See Chapter 3, above, on the way new principles and old are related to convey the impression that a new order is in the making.)

The principles of the new order clearly imply an eventual redistribution of authority to make it all work. It is possible that such a level of consensus on these principles obtains that they operate automatically, but this is unlikely. The only alternative is that the order is endowed with sufficient authority to permit it to be effective in the face of dissidence. Falk intimates that the technique for solving the order–authority dilemma, made all the more evident by the drastic increase in the things to be done in the name of the order, is built into the new order itself. The promulgation of the order gradually conditions its members to accepting the consequences of its operation, which includes the eventual redistribution of authority as well as substantive benefits. By being there the new order becomes a way of thinking and then a way of doing things.

The organization of the international legal order

Falk's emphasis on the functional possibilities contained in Chapter I does not change the fact that most of the Charter's provisions are devoted specifically and unambiguously to institutional forms. These forms and their counterparts in similarly constituted organizations of varying regional and functional scope are the primary features of the international legal order's current organization. While Falk may seem to construe the "black-letter" Charter as a facade for the real Charter within, waiting to come into its own, this is a misleading impression that he might have corrected had he organized in one place his many observations on the organization of the legal order since 1945.[12]

12 Consistent with Falk's view of the Charter in terms of its functional possibilities is his functionalist view of international law *per se*. R.A. Falk, "The Relevance of Political Context to the Nature and Functioning of International Law: An Intermediate View," in Falk, *The Status of Law in International Society*, Princeton: Princeton University Press, 1970, p. 41. No single work fully develops Falk's view of the functional possibilities built into the Charter order, although coming closest is "The United Nations: Constitutional and Behavioral Tendencies," in R.A. Falk, *A Global Approach to National Policy*, Cambridge, MA: Harvard University Press, 1975, pp. 169–96.

At worst, Falk is guilty of suggesting that the drafting of Chapter I by the Charter's framers was clever, almost conspirational, when quite plausibly their functional formulations are ambiguous and overly general, not because of a shared vision of the future like Falk's, but because of insoluble differences on preferred principles and purposes. Whether a new order was ingeniously secreted in the old or the old ambiguously reinvented is much less to the point than the trend of events after 1945. Falk is clearly right in depicting the trend as taking the direction of more elaborate organization and institutional innovation, within broadly constituted limits, to cope with the burgeoning demand for order and the meager allocation of authority.

Falk accounts for organizational developments by offering the maxim that form follows function.[13] However true this may be at a very general level and over great periods of time, it obscures a problem raised by the Charter's brief history. Would not the Charter's fixed forms get in the way of the pursuit of functional possibilities? Even if we ignore the likelihood of a lack of consensus among states on the virtue of great changes and the inevitability of organizational inertia, the problem remains in the very fact that the organization was set up to do the kinds of things done in greater or lesser degree in the Westphalian order. Just as clearly, the organization was not set up to do those things contemplated in or made possible by Chapter I. Competing orders may be chartered but not equally charted.

Because he ignores the problem as stated, nowhere does Falk offer a solution to it more specific than that contained in the formula that form follows function. Apparently, specific forms are infinitely adaptable because they are secondary to functions, which are open-ended by design. Such a view dismisses textual considerations beloved not just by lawyers but also by statesmen not so insightful, or visionary, as Falk. They, in turn, are likely to dismiss Falk as a dabbler, even a meddler, and a dreamer, unpracticed in the gritty details of daily diplomacy.

The problem of an order with fluid functions and fixed forms also disappears if we go to the other extreme and discern in the Charter not functional implications divorced from institutional specifics, as Falk does, but, instead, specific realizations of generic forms comparable to the organs that exercise the authority of governments. Comparable functions are obviously not performed but are said to be latent in the arrangements. The view of the Charter as a pre- or proto-government is taken for granted in most legal treatments of international institutions. The Charter's framers gave the Security Council the form of an executive organ, the General Assembly a legislative organ, and the World Court a judicial organ.[14] Depending on the willingness of the

13 Falk, "The Interplay of Westphalia and Charter Conceptions of the International Legal Order," p. 61.

14 See, typically, D.W. Bowett, *The Law of International Institutions*, 3rd edn, London: Stevens, 1975. Commonly, the General Assembly is said to be a deliberative body, "not invested with legislative powers," because its resolutions are not binding. It is nonetheless assumed that the

membership, the organization could grow into responsibilities prefigured by its institutional arrangements. It is as if the Charter were a full-scale model of governmental authority waiting for mankind to grow up to it.

Exactly the same model underlies the presumably radical measures favored by proponents of world government. Restless over mankind's perennial immaturity, advocates of world government simply take the proto-government of the Charter and make it real by giving it authority. While they would tinker with institutional forms, they remain committed to the basic format already half a century old.[15]

If institutionalists avoid Falk's tendency to make too little of the Charter's institutional forms, they err just as much by making too much of them. More accurately, they make these forms into something historically and analytically they are not – conventional organs of government. Were they this, they would divide up governmental tasks into functional stages. There is a legislative stage, in which a specified kind of organ makes the law for all the social order's concerns; an executive stage, in which a specified organ applies the law; and a judicial stage, in which a specified organ evaluates the law and its application. This arrangement is perhaps the most efficient way of dealing with the tasks of governance when the authority exists to do so.

The Charter did not provide a legislative organ, or a prototype thereof, or an executive or, the World Court's name notwithstanding, even a judicial organ, simply because the need did not exist then, nor will it in the foreseeable future. In fact, the Charter itself is little more than an ensemble of 19th-century instrumentalities cobbled together to deal with the diverse failings of the Westphalian order. Thus, a full-membership conference organ was devised to promote discussion and action on a range of concerns salient to most states, but critical to very few. Other organs were more specifically allocated responsibility for such matters as control of conflicts, administration, cooperative endeavors, legally definable controversies, and some dependent peoples. While anything but precise in their delimitation of responsibilities, these several institutional arrangements divide up things to be done into substantive areas.

With some overlap, each organ is responsible for whatever is to be done by the organization as a whole in that area. The extent to which any organ has the authority to get things done effectively varies from one to the next and

General Assembly is modeled after a legislative organ in all respects save that of being able to make law directly. Such deviations from typical forms are accounted for by the "rudimentary character" of the organization. A discussion in these terms, and the source of the quoted words, is L. Oppenheim, *International Law*, 8th edn by H. Lauterpacht, vol. 1, New York: McKay, 1955, pp. 423–4.

15 On the practicality of revising the Charter to achieve world government or drafting a new treaty for world government nonetheless supplementing "existing machinery of the United Nations," see G. Clark and L.B. Sohn, *World Peace Through World Law*, 3rd edn, Cambridge, MA: Harvard University Press, 1966, Introduction, which justifies the latter expedient, earlier editions having preferred the former.

generally stands at a low level in comparison to that held by the organs we associate with governments. This is in keeping with the requirements of the Westphalian order, which presupposes the surrender of authority by participating units only to the bare minimum needed for a very modest servicing of the system.

The principle of organizing governance by substantive areas is fundamentally different from that of organizing it by functional stages. The literature of comparative government and politics seems generally inattentive to the difference, as does that of liberal political theory, even though the latter has sanctified the functional stages principle as the doctrine of the separation of powers.[16] Nevertheless, a significant increase in the international legal order's ordering capabilities, implying as it does a comparable increase of authority available to international institutions, clearly demands a change in the ordering principle employed. Forms would not simply extend their functional range, or expanded functions alter the forms available for their performance. Rather, a given form would broaden its substantive range while a given function would begin to be consolidated in one of the several organs in which it was previously found. These changes would be interactive and more or less simultaneous, yielding a transformation of the constituted order. The result would approximate the institutionalists' mistaken sense of what already exists; functionalists like Falk would be more sensitive to the fact that something quite profound was happening.

More than anyone else, Falk has been the one to alert us to behavioral and constitutional changes already under way and to provoke interest in their ultimate significance. He has identified an emerging quasi-legislative competence of the General Assembly and a quasi-judicial competence of the Security Council. An emergent executive competence of the Secretary-General is, of course, something many writers have commented on. Taken with the obviously decrepit condition of the World Court, these developments, however hesitant, point to the possibility of a transformation from the institutions of a horizontal order, dividing labors into substantive areas, to a vertical order organized by functional stages.

The pattern of changes, as they have become visible over three decades, is full of surprises. Only the General Assembly fits the institutionalists' preconceptions about the Charter as a proto-government. The rise of the Secretary-General was barely anticipated and the decline of the World Court not at all. Nothing is more surprising than the Security Council in the place thought to belong to the Court. No one, not even Falk, has gone from disparate

16 This is most egregiously the case with G.A. Almond and G.B. Powell, Jr., *Comparative Politics: A Developmental Approach*, Boston: Little, Brown, 1966. This influential book expressly links its functional theory with liberal political theory's concern over the separation of powers.

constitutional developments to the general interpretation offered here. Its virtue is that it solves the puzzle of diverse changes by construing them as elements of a single, sweeping transformation caused by a change in ordering principles. Its weakness is what it leaves unexplained: whether transformation is ineluctable.

The unanswered question is whether and at what pace this transformation from horizontal to vertical order through constitutional adaptation, apparently just begun, will actually take place. If in some autonomous fashion states have shifted some authority to the legal order, then it follows rather nicely that the institutional arrangements of the Charter are gradually being reoriented to resemble the conventional branches of centralized governments. This is not, however, a strictly necessary relationship. The reorientation could be taking place in advance of the transfer of authority.

Does a bird fly because it grew wings or grow wings because birds fly? The international legal order may be getting the wings it will need before it is actually permitted to fly. The fact that wings are not needed yet does not mean that having them is pointless. On the contrary, the existence of appropriate organs bolstered by statements of principle signifies that the new order is in place. The only hope for solving the order–authority problem at the global level resides in conditioning states by the presence of a fully articulated order to accept the consequences of its operation. If tangible benefits to states are one consequence, a gradual shift of authority to the institutions of the order is another.

As this learning experience takes place, it is likely to be manifested in a growing tendency of states to accept a truly legislative status for the General Assembly and other plenary organs when they are engaged in the production of principles. At the same time, there could be a broadening of the Security Council's activities in the evaluation of behavior in nonconflictual situations. As these activities begin to be routinized, they too will gain in acceptance and formality, as we would expect of judicial activity. Finally, beginning more slowly, there could be a renewed growth of executive competence – which emerged after 1945 and has since faded – probably focused in the office of the Secretary-General, as the new order is brought to bear on states. In short, as the new order consolidates its authority, that authority will be predictably distributed among organs developed for the purpose. Their emergence as full-fledged organs of government is likely to be sequenced, with the legislative stage coming first, then the judicial, and finally the executive stage.

Quite clearly, this very general model unduly tidies up what is really a congeries of overlapping developments. The process of consolidating the instrumentalities of the new order is sure to be problematic. It may not take place at all. It may even have unanticipated negative consequences, such as promoting cynicism over the gap between principles and reality, which in turn may cause a rollback of gains to that time or even a deterioration of ordering capabilities in the current legal order.

In the interim, authority is "decomposed."[17] It has ceased to be an exclusive property of the subordinate orders, but it has yet to become a general property of the larger order. Well before truly governmental organs emerge, pockets of authority will be found in loosely linked institutions of limited substantive scope, as they are even now.[18] The global order represented by the UN is equipped to deal with this melange of semiautonomous entities chiefly as a holding company deals with the numerous operating enterprises it subsumes. Holding companies are really entrepots for the accumulation and transfer of assets insufficiently available to operating units individually. In the business world the most obvious asset is capital; in the global order the important assets are legitimacy, experience and expertise, and established relationships among participants. Such assets may reveal the emergence of a specialized elite community that operates the intricate global order, and they also contribute to the acceptance by states of their diminished control over certain realms of activity.

While acceptance of control is a decisive element in making authority out of control, it does not follow that states accept the general proposition that the UN should have the material assets of a holding company because this implies the recomposition of authority at the global level. The grant of authority to substantively limited regional or global institutions is paid for with the guarantee of perpetual autonomy for such institutions implicit in their separate charters, staffs, and budgets. Hence, we have the likelihood of an enduring condition of decomposed, differentiated authority, more or less made to be that way indefinitely. The development at the highest level of organs with the capacity to perform governmental tasks may thus be super-

17 To say that authority is divisible would be a more conventional formulation, but it improperly suggests that authority must be located in territory (sovereignty); and if it is not to be found in the larger unit of territory, then it resides in the divided units. Thus, authority can never disappear, no matter how often territory is divided. The formulation used here parallels E. Haas, "Turbulent Fields and the Theory of Regional Integration," *International Organization*, vol. 30, 1976, pp. 206–8, although he refers to the decomposition (and recomposition) of issues and concomitant "asymmetrical overlap" in institutional vehicles of authority.

18 An example of a pocket of authority is the International Civil Aviation Organization, as revealed in T. Buergenthal, *Law-Making in the International Civil Aviation Organization*, Syracuse: Syracuse University Press, 1969, pp. 57–122. ICAO's promulgation and implementation of "technical legislation" are enhanced by the fact that it has no formal authority to bind states with its International Standards. Acceptance of these standards comes rather from the elaborately technical and comprehensive character of the standards themselves. States that ignore them imperil their effective participation in international civil aviation, not to mention the joint stake of collaborating national and international personnel and the bureaucratic advantages accruing to the former in persuading their states to comply. The effectiveness and formality of ICAO's authority thus appear to be inversely related qualities, making the locus of authority all the more difficult to assess in the traditional terms of political and legal theory. Buergenthal refers to executive and legislative activity in ICAO in a way that further supports the conclusion that authority, though incompletely formalized, is securely fixed at the operational level.

imposed on a ragged authority pattern resistant to the consolidation needed to get on with global governance. There is some question, therefore, whether the more salient learning experience is associated with the possibilities of global governance or with the needs of the global holding company and its operating subsidiaries.

The UN bears the potential of becoming the central public reality of a future time. It needs, in addition to the right circumstances, a good deal of time to get there. The spontaneous emergence of higher levels of social organization seems generally to be a slow and unpredictable affair. Furthermore, the process resists management. Viewing the Charter either as an inventory of functional possibilities or as a template for global government underestimates the difficulty of turning the current international legal order into a world order supported by authority. Both views interpret the current order's history and organization permissively, so that only the attitudes and behavior of states impede a global solution to the order–authority dilemma. I find this unhistorical and excessively rationalistic.

For all the emphasis on constitutions, functionalists and institutionalists alike show their positivist origins by sharing a belief in the strictly voluntary nature of the order. If states can make the order, they can reorganize it, instantly if they choose, to solve the problems currently built into it. I would argue that the constitution of the international legal order combines functional generalities and institutional specifics in a rich blend that conserves an abundance of historical experience and projects it into the consciousness of statesmen in an especially palpable, "living" form. Statesmen cannot help but find this inhibiting, even intimidating. They are likely to be deterred from breaking sharply with the past simply by fiat, except in the unlikely event they are willing to reject the past's relevance entirely. Falk sees the fiat of states in consensus, institutionalists in Charter revision. Either way it is assumed that those who speak for states can seize on something already there and make it the focus of the solution all have agreed is needed. In a cluttered functional and institutional landscape, making a new order out of the old is probably as hard as abandoning the old and consenting in advance to something altogether revolutionary in principle.

Such changes as we have seen are not by the active choice of states. They have happened to states, as they see it. If there is a trend, states have not directed it; many resent or resist it. If events follow a timetable, no one has a copy. If the international legal order has somehow been turned into a potential vehicle for authority, virtually no one knows it. Given the obstacles – the weight of history, the perplexities of a living constitution, the stresses of modernization and complexities of modernity, the crushing awareness of time running out – will the order be transformed? Not Falk, not I, not many other students of the situation are willing to predict it.

If I may conclude on an anticlimactic note, there remains a small problem of nomenclature. A transformed global order would be indisputably legal. But can we properly call the current international order legal? I believe the answer to this question is yes for two reasons. First, the order is a constituted one. It is customary in Western political theory and practice to call constitutions endowing states with authority legal documents, even though, logically speaking, such constitutions cannot gain their legal status from the states created by them. Presumably, constitutions are organic or fundamental law supported by the authority of a people, a community, or some more mystical entity. Consequently, the international legal order is legal in precisely the same sense that any properly constituted order is, whether or not the constitution creates a system of law supported by authority to guarantee its principles and carry out its purposes.

Second, I think the international legal order is truly legal because its guardians are lawyers. In any social order the place of law depends on the existence of a class of trained professionals devoted to something they call law. What they call law is law for that social order. International law is law, and the international order legal, because international lawyers and statesmen influenced by lawyers, their language, and their categories insist on viewing certain categories of orderly behavior and stated expectations about the persistence of that behavior as law.[19] Were there no lawyers, the international order might be no less orderly, but it might not be called a legal order, any more than the impressively orderly, stable, and articulated relations of Ming China and its tributaries are called a legal order. Even if the Ming order could be said to have been constituted as an order, it was not constituted in legal forms and categories. When the constitution of an order is articulated by its makers and users in the language of law, it indisputably becomes a legal order.

19 This is admittedly an unconventional position, despite a pedigree that includes Max Weber. I attempt an elucidation and defense in Chapter 6.

10 International codification: interpreting the last half-century (1980)

Between 1981 and 1985, Richard Falk and Saul Mendlovitz oversaw the publication of five large volumes of material, most of it previously published, under the general title, *Studies on a Just World Order.* For each volume they recruited additional editorial assistance; for the volume devoted to international law, Friedrich Kratochwil joined Falk and Mendlovitz as editors. A close friend, Fritz Kratochwil knew of my interest in international codification. In planning the volume, he asked whether I could recommend a paper on this subject or prepare such a paper myself. Since I had published no part of my doctoral dissertation (the first pages of which constitute Chapter 1, above), I decided to adapt a significant part of the third chapter for the purpose and then add some new material at the end.

I undertook this project in 1980, exactly half a century after the Hague Codification Conference had convened with disappointing results (hence this chapter's title). I offered a novel interpretation of international codification in the years following the Conference, with a focus on the International Law Commission (the UN body responsible for codification); on request I prepared a somewhat shorter version in 1981. The book finally appeared in 1985, after the paper had been shortened again, this time by one-fifth and not by me. I was distressed, most of all because I thought the excisions left the text ragged to the point of incoherence. This chapter reproduces the second draft with minor changes. For readers wishing to update the material presented here or assess my interpretation against another quarter century of experience with international codification, the International Law Commission has an excellent website. On quick inspection, I would say that the interpretation offered here readily passes the test of time.

The origins of most movements in social thought and public behavior defy certain dating. So it is with the movement to fashion international law in code form. The idea finds philosophical acceptance with Immanuel Kant and Jeremy Bentham. As a movement, it is fueled by the success of the Napoleonic Code and the rise of multilateral treaties – "international legislation" – which promised to supplant custom as international law's primary source. With arbitration and free trade, it becomes an inseparable part of the liberal peace movement of the 19th century. International codification gains practical significance with the emergence during that time of international institutions and enters the realm of public sponsorship with the Hague Peace Conferences of 1899 and 1907.[1]

In its time the League of Nations assumed responsibility for international codification. A Committee of Experts on the Progressive Codification of International Law began work in 1925 by identifying, in consultation with member states, bodies of customary law sufficiently ripe for consolidation in code form. Three topics were settled on – nationality, territorial waters and state responsibility – preparations undertaken and the assistance of states solicited, all for the purpose of convening an international conference. The Hague Codification Conference of 1930 drew representatives from 48 states, nine of them, including the US, not members of the League. The Conference was universally judged a failure, mitigated perhaps by modest concurrence on some aspects of nationality, but marked by severe cleavage on the principle of state responsibility for injury to aliens and their property and unanticipated disagreement on the actual limit of territorial seas.

In 1931 the League of Nations adopted procedures for any future efforts to transform international law.[2] The new procedures thoroughly integrated governments into the process of selecting and preparing topics while relying on committees of experts to advance draft conventions, which states could judge as potential permanent obligations. By placing initiative in the hands of states, the League effectively codified its members' understandable disenchantment with international codification. The dispirited movement to do something about the state of international law was saved from complete dormancy only by continuing, if largely unrewarded, efforts within the Inter-American System to establish the content of a distinctively American international law and secure acceptance from the US of the principle of nonintervention.[3]

The UN Charter provides for the General Assembly to encourage "the progressive development of international law and its codification," in article 13(1)(a). During its second session the General Assembly created a subsidiary body called the International Law Commission (ILC) to assist in this duty.[4]

1 On the history of the international codification movement, see "Historical Survey of the Development of International Law and its Codification by International Conferences," UN doc. A/AC.10/5, reprinted in *American Journal of International Law*, vol. 41, supp., 1947, pp. 29–111, and D.P. Dhokalia, *The Codification of Public International Law*, Manchester: Manchester University Press, 1970, pp. 3–133.

2 Reprinted as Appendix 11 in "Historical Survey of the Development of International Law and its Codification by International Conferences," pp. 110–11.

3 "Outline of the Codification of International Law in the Inter-American System," UN doc. A/AC.10/8, reprinted in *American Journal of International Law*, vol. 41, supp., 1947, pp. 116–38; Dhokalia, *The Codification of Public International Law*, pp. 133–40.

4 Resolution 174 (II), November 21,1947; ILC Statute annexed thereto.

The Commission consists of 25 members (initially 15, later 21 and 25, and 34 since 1981), each from a different state, but not formally representing those states. Members are elected for five-year terms, with seats carefully distributed among the world's regions and legal cultures. The Commission meets for 12 weeks each Spring in Geneva, and its work is debated each Fall by the General Assembly's Sixth (Legal) Committee.[5]

Unimpeded by the great changes and controversies affecting its parent – the General Assembly, and many of its specialized siblings in the UN family – the ILC has an enviable series of accomplishments to its credit. After some early distractions, it prepared detailed drafts that were to become the 1958 Geneva Conventions on the Law of the Sea, the 1961 Vienna Convention on Diplomatic Relations, the 1963 Vienna Convention on Consular Relations, and the 1969 Vienna Convention on the Law of Treaties.[6] Remarkably, half a century has seen the international codification movement come from a condition of virtual self-destruction to one in which success seems almost to have been inevitable.

Success has inspired a substantial though, under the circumstances, unremarkable number of scholarly studies of international codification and the ILC. Most of them are careful assessments of the Commission's organization and activities. They view the ILC as the natural culmination of a progressive movement, which had been abruptly but only temporarily thwarted by the failure of the 1930 conference. Errors of the League experiment were obvious and lessons were learned, as any analysis of the ILC Statute made evident. Experienced and sensible men, gathered by the General Assembly as the Committee on the Progressive Development of International Law and Its Codification, commonly known as the Committee of Seventeen, put the movement back on course when they drafted the Statute.[7]

Implicit in these interpretations of the last half-century of international codification is a curious combination of assumptions. The first is that the codification movement, despite the high ideals, diverse schemes and projects, infrequent triumphs and, finally, grave disappointment over the preceding century, possessed a coherence and momentum of its own. The second is that the individuals who brought the movement to a full and mature expression in the form of the ILC Statute could make right choices for the movement's

5 For detailed treatments of the ILC's Statute, working methods and institutional relations, see H.W. Briggs, *The International Law Commission*, Ithaca: Cornell University Press, 1965; Dhokalia, *The Codification of Public International Law*, pp. 147–350; B.G. Ramcharan, *The International Law Commission: Its Approach to the Codification and Progressive Development of International Law*, The Hague: Nijhoff, 1977.

6 Conveniently assembled, along with the ILC's Statute, in UN Office of Public Information, *The Work of the International Law Commission*, rev. edn, New York, 1972, Annexes.

7 See preeminently H. Lauterpacht, "Codification and Development of International Law," *American Journal of International Law*, vol. 49, 1955, pp. 16–43. Also, see the important general works on the ILC cited above.

realization, unimpeded by conflicting interpretations of what it stood for. That the ILC was successful apparently attests to the judgment of this particular aggregation of individuals.

A third and correlative assumption is that such disagreements as were found in the Committee of Seventeen were reflections of the larger political context of East–West confrontation. Because the codification movement is presumed to be an autonomous and overriding force, political considerations could not subvert the Committee's consensual wisdom or the integrity of its work. Positions taken by representatives of the US and UK on the one hand and representatives of the Soviet Union on the other, competed for recognition in the Statute. Nevertheless, the Anglo-American position prevailed on most points, honoring, we are left to conclude, its own internal logic, the meaning of the codification movement and liberal legal values.[8]

A challenge to these assumptions permits a different interpretation of international codification since 1930. The codification movement need not be viewed as coherent in content and compelling in consequence as most writers assume it is. More plausibly several intellectual traditions competed for primacy throughout the movement's checkered history. There follows in this essay a brief characterization of three such traditions – Continental, British and American (not to be confused with a tradition often styled *American* by its Latin American members) – which dominate the codification movement after 1930. I then consider the appearance of these positions in deliberations of the Committee of Seventeen as preferred strategies for meeting the requirements of article 13(1)(a). The drafting of the ILC Statute is indeed the codification movement in microcosm. It bridges the League era to our own, not as lessons learned, but as beliefs projected into the possibilities of an especially propitious historical juncture. The Statute itself is a scorecard on the consequences for each tradition of their confrontation in the Committee.

Explication of the Statute's major provisions also serves as a platform from which to observe the subsequent trajectory of the ILC. Simply stated, the two intellectual traditions with Procrustean tendencies canceled each other out in the Committee of Seventeen, allowing the remaining, pragmatically inclined tradition identified with American writers to shape the Statute's contents. What results we will find to be procedurally permissive and organizationally pliable enough to allow the ILC to take advantage of opportunities long heralded but never tapped by the codification movement in its previous incarnations. At the same time the Statute prefigures a significant change in the character of international codification made possible by the fact that the

8 The US representative on the Committee, Philip Jessup, subsequently affirmed this view, even though an examination of his and other positions held in the Committee, such as is undertaken below, provides no support for it. Review, "*International Law, Being the Collected Papers of Hersch Lauterpacht, Q.C., LL.D., F.B.A.* Systematically Arranged and Edited by E. Lauterpacht, Q.C.," *American Journal of International Law*, vol. 65, 1971, p. 217.

ILC's place is secure and its work admired. This development is integrally related to the widely observed phenomenon of global bureaucratization, but is nevertheless unanticipated in the intellectual traditions guiding the codification movement and even today virtually unrecognized. It is the subject of the concluding section of this essay.

Before proceeding with the interpretation just outlined, some terminological clarifications would seem to be in order (and see Chapter 1 for a complementary exposition). We speak generally of the codification of international law and use that phrase to describe the ILC's business. Yet the UN Charter and the Commission's Statute both refer to the progressive development of international law and its codification. *International codification* obviously has two meanings.

Its more general meaning relates to a collection of activities – retrieving and writing down existing law in an orderly fashion and, where necessary, reconciling inconsistencies and filling gaps, all for the purpose of reducing that law to a simpler, more accessible form. Consistent with this general meaning, codification can also involve a more radical reduction of many laws to a few underlying principles applicable to a variety of situations previously regulated individually, or the revision of existing rules, for the purpose of rationalizing the law.[9] The second, more restricted meaning of codification differentiates it from development, the latter corresponding to activities other than restatement encompassed by the term codification in its larger meaning. If codification is merely restatement, then it need not require official sanction or assistance and final disposition has no effect at all on the legal status of restated rules.

The early years of the codification movement found the term construed in this second sense, as private individuals compiled ever-more comprehensive codes. Presumably the result of such prodigious labors was to endow a great code with intrinsic authority by virtue of its monumental scope and the eminence of its progenitors. Vitiating this objective, however, was recognition that states were unlikely to accept the authority of a great code in any active or immediate manner. Therefore, a code's authors rarely hesitated to suggest improvements in the positive law on normative or esthetic grounds, with predictable consequences for the code's public value.

A restatement, however, may supplant the melange of rules it restates if procedures exist for it to do so. This is typically the case in the history of municipal codification, in which drafting the restatement is undertaken by instruction of appropriate public officials with the expectation that the results will take a legislated form and thus acquire extrinsic authority. Some early proponents of international codification even saw privately initiated

9 See also H.W.A. Thirlway, *International Customary Law and Codification: An Examination of the Continuing Role of Custom in the Present Period of Codification of International Law*, Leiden: Sijthoff, 1972, pp. 12–13, on definitions and distinctions.

restatements as a means of prompting the emergence of a global legislative technique, despite the fact that municipal experience with codification is closely associated with a strengthening executive.[10] In the absence of global legislative machinery, the technique for supplanting existing law with restated law lies with opening multilateral conventions for ratification. This is, of course, the same technique for promulgating new law, so that reductive or innovative intentions are equally vulnerable to the indifference or hostility of at least some states. The process of making new law is bound to be arduous, and often unsuccessful, in a decentralized order.

Codification can therefore mean: (1) restatement, (2) restatement become law, (3) restatement combined with innovative elements become law, and (4) restatement combined with innovative elements not intended to become law or prevented from becoming law. For our purposes, considering codification a term of general import, we call restatement alone reductive law exposition and restatement become law reductive law creation. Deliberately introduced innovations in the law, when they stand alone, stand apart from codification by any conception. While innovative elements may be introduced into either kind of reductive texts, innovative exposition fails to result in any direct development of the law. Reductive and innovative creation together, in whatever proportion, might be called the conscious development of international law. *International codification* then refers residually to the movement to do something about international law, whether by its conscious development or only its exposition, or both, to impose order on the law and improve it while, or by, doing so.

None of the foregoing is meant to suggest that international law is static unless consciously developed. The conclusion of innumerable treaties, many of them multilateral, is of course conscious activity, but not undertaken to develop law as such. As with the operation of custom, the spontaneous development of law is a cumulative consequence. Spontaneous development is pervasive and accelerating at the expense of order in the law and mastery over the legal order, and therefore provides the international codification movement with its most compelling rationale.

It should be evident that the terminology adopted here is not consistent with the UN Charter and ILC Statute. The phrase *the progressive development of international law and its codification* is synonymous with *codification* in its more general meaning. As defined in article 15 of the Statute, codification is "the more precise formulation and systematization of rules of international law where there has already been extensive state practice, precedent and doctrine." Clearly this is restatement, but not clear from this article is the final form of the text. Article 15 defines progressive development as "the preparation of draft conventions on subjects which have not yet been sufficiently developed in the practice of states." Here we find final form specified to

10 M. Rheinstein (ed.), *Max Weber on Law in Economy and Society*, trans. by E. Shils and M. Rheinstein, New York: Simon and Schuster, 1954, pp. 256–83.

exclude innovative law exposition. While the clear thrust of these words is in the direction of innovative law creation, which should not be confused with conscious development or codification generally, reference to areas of law insufficiently developed opens the possibility of texts combining innovation and reduction.

We would be mistaken to attach great significance to the wording of the Charter, to which the Statute's definitions are necessarily tied. The drafting history of article 13(1)(a) strongly suggests that the language found there is an artifact of diplomatic interaction and not the result of careful drafting.[11] The working nomenclature in draft materials before Dumbarton Oaks and during San Francisco referred to the *development and revision of international law*. The alternative formula, *progressive development and codification*, was chosen in the end to sound somewhat less radical in spirit. The emphasis throughout had been on upgrading the law rather than merely digesting it. The records of the San Francisco Conference convey an optimistic sense of future possibilities as wide as the international codification movement's multifarious traditions and influences. Specification of terms and requisite activities, in terms of these historic forces or otherwise, was not a task for the statesmen assembled in San Francisco, but instead one assigned to the General Assembly and discharged by the Committee of Seventeen.

Perspectives on codification

Legal scholarship often contrasts, perhaps unduly, Anglo-American and Continental schools of law.[12] Their stance toward codification, respectively being hostility and attachment, presumably marks their differences.[13] We should not be misled by the fact that the first great advocate of codification was an Englishman, Bentham, and the first great critic of the idea on grounds of law's organic character a German, Friedrich Karl von Savigny. It is specifically the organic relation of the common law system of justice to the growth of law which is widely believed to prevent codification in any other sense than reductive exposition unless lawmaking techniques are greatly altered. The choice is to substitute legislation for the common law or let the latter develop, as it will. Enduring support for codification in Continental legal thought derives from its longstanding positivist tendencies reaching their ascendancy in the half century prior to the World Wars. This predilection is strengthened by recognition that codification on Napoleon's grand scale contributed to political modernization in a number of countries.

This simple view is not so much wrong as unrefined. If the peculiar character

11 S. Rosenne, "The International Law Commission 1949–1959," *British Year Book of International Law*, vol. 41, 1960, pp. 109–10.

12 H. Lauterpacht, "The So-Called Anglo-American and Continental Schools of Thought in International Law," *British Year Book of International Law*, vol. 12, 1931, p. 31.

13 See, illustratively, R. Pound, *Jurisprudence*, vol. 3, St. Paul: West, 1959, pp. 673–7, 705–38.

or "genius" of the common law inhibits its codification, that inhibition is far greater for British than American lawyers. The US has a long and varied experience with municipal codification enabled by the federal principle and consequent multiplicity of jurisdictions within which to codify. Britain has no such experience. Nor is there an Anglo-American view of the nature of international law.[14] American scholarship tends to place considerations of process and context over the content of rules. It is the heritage of pragmatism and legal realism. British writers are rather more concerned with the quality and integrity of rules, and this is in keeping with their tradition of pride in judicial craft.

The British, far more than writers from the US, perceive international law, so much of it customary in origin, as analogous to common law. The absence of effective legislative procedures makes international law, if anything, more resistant even than common law to conscious development. Furthermore, success, if it is possible, brings with it the danger of freezing the law in place. By contrast, the American view finds little that is analogous between municipal and international contexts and legal processes, and thus accepts the limited opportunities to improve international law uniquely presented by its notorious substantive and institutional underdevelopment. The League's ill-fated experience with conscious law development reinforced already well-established Anglo-American differences. While Americans believed in remedying organizational deficiencies manifest in that experience, for the British, long-suspected conceptual flaws in the whole idea of international codification stood confirmed.

For their part, Continental writers brought to the international codification movement before 1930, a mood of optimism and a simple conception of method. They generally felt that international law could be consciously developed in a relatively simple two-step sequence: officially sanctioned, expert preparation of a rationalized law followed by its adoption in multilateral form by international conference. Obviously they were impressed (and deceived) by successes in just these terms registered by the Hague Conferences of 1899 and 1907, and the attendant illusion shared by writers in all schools that multilateral conventions were analogous to legislation. The product of such legislation would be a great code promulgated in regular segments without the passage of exceptional periods of time. For Continental writers, the main problem was to determine which areas of international law were best suited for treatment and order them in a long-term program of work.[15]

Undue optimism on the extent to which large segments of international law were indeed suitable for treatment lay at the heart of the Hague Codification

14 R. Higgins, "Diverging Anglo-American Attitudes to International Law: Introductory Statement," *Georgia Journal of International and Comparative Law*, vol. 2. supp. 2, 1972, pp. 1–4.

15 The classic exposition of the Continental position, still a monument to scholarship, is C. De Visscher, "La codification du droit international," *Recueil des cours de L'Académie de droit international de La Haye*, vol. 6, 1925/I, pp. 329–452.

Conference's overreaching agenda and proportionately dramatic failure. Recalling the positivist premise that international law is the product of states' wills, the simplicity of the League's codification machinery coupled to an ambitious program reveals a certain naivete about the *willingness* of states to alter their obligations in either content or form. Expert preparations for the Hague Conference were undoubtedly adequate on a purely technical plane.[16] Attention to the felt need of states, including at a minimum a need to assimilate the implications of all that they were being asked to accept, was not. Organizational innocence contributed to unwarranted optimism, inherent in the positivist view that states can make or change law at will. Continental writers learned from The Hague a lesson repeated throughout the decade: realism must temper positivist sentiments. The law's maturity proved a necessary but not a sufficient condition for its conscious development.[17]

We might note that the format of experts and conferences evolved independently as the pattern of conscious law development in the Inter-American System. Even more than in Europe, the tradition of a great code embodying overarching principles of a reconstituted law animated Latin American proponents of the codification movement.[18] Regional differences aside, Latin American, American and Continental ideas bore more in common with each other than did any of them with the British position. Latin Americans were perhaps most concerned with developing principles, Continentals with laying out bodies of positive law, and Americans with organizing all such activities. Of them all, Americans were least interested in doctrinal considerations but, for all that, were no closer to their common law brethren, to whom we now turn.

Among the early and more lucid expositions of the British position is a much-cited article by P.J. [Noel-]Baker, which begins by differentiating between codification and legislation "in accordance with the best British opinion."[19] Differences in meaning pointed to differences in purpose and technique.

16 C. De Visscher, "Stages in the Codification of International Law," in W. Friedmann *et al.* (eds), *Transnational Law in a Changing Society: Essays in Honor of Philip C. Jessup*, New York: Columbia University Press, 1972, p. 18.

17 Read in this light De Visscher's latter-day reflections on international codification. Ibid., pp. 17–33, and *Theory and Reality in Public International Law*, rev. edn trans. by P.E. Corbett, Princeton: Princeton University Press, 1968, pp. 145–53.

18 Over a period of decades the prolific Chilean jurist, Alejandro Alvarez, consistently placed an architectural emphasis on principles. See, for example, *La codification du droit international: ses tendances, ses bases*, Paris: Pédone, 1912; *Le droit international nouveau dans ses rapports avec la vie actuelle des peuples*, Paris: Pédone, 1959.

19 P.J. Baker, "The Codification of International Law," *British Year Book of International Law*, vol. 5, 1924, p. 41. The British position can be traced back much earlier, for example, to British proposals leading to the program of the 1908–1909 London Naval Conference. "Historical Survey of the Development of International Law and its Codification by International Conferences," p. 44.

The purpose of codification is of course to improve not the substance but the form of the law, to make its rules easier to understand and apply, not to alter the rules themselves. It is to improve the form of the law by getting rid of apparent ambiguities or conflicts, by bringing customary law and statutory law together into one coherent and consistent whole, and thus to clarify the obligations of the subjects of the law without adding to or diminishing those obligations.

> The method of codification is likewise quite different from that of legislation in that it is necessarily a work for professional lawyers alone. It can only be carried through by the intensive study by commissions of lawyers of existing rules, statutes, custom, practice, decisions of courts, etc. On the basis of such studies the lawyers reduce their conclusions to writing for the acceptance of the law-making authority in substitution for existing law.[20]

Finally, Baker found a difference in the results of codification and legislation. The results of codification were negligible because "an adequate legal basis of existing rules" upon which to build a code simply did not exist. Legislation was more promising because it did not rely on existing rules.[21]

A few years later, in restating the British view, J.L. Brierly returned to the relationship between techniques and results.

> The materials of the international codifier do not consist of known and accepted rules, and before he can even begin the process of clarifying and systematizing them, he finds himself confronted by another and more difficult task, that of securing agreement on the substance of the rules themselves . . . The legislative element in the attempt to codify any part of international law is not merely incidental and subordinate; it outweighs the codifying element to such an extent that it becomes misleading to describe the process as one of codification at all.[22]

In 1946 Sir Cecil Hurst read a paper before the Grotius Society re-examining the British view, especially with regard to techniques and results. Hurst's primary argument concerned the effect of convention-making conferences on attempts at codification.

20 Baker, "The Codification of International Law," pp. 43–4.

21 Ibid., p. 52. Baker was never clear on whether he conceived of codification as reductive law exposition or creation. While the work of codification was to be converted into conventions, this was evidently different from the "quasi-legislative process of general conventions" because no new obligations were involved. Ibid., p. 64.

22 J.L. Brierly, "The Future of Codification," *British Year Book of International Law*, vol. 12, 1931, pp. 2–3.

> The two processes, that of scientific determination of the law and that of achieving the adoption for rendering the law so defined and determined binding on States get mixed up together. No matter how well the preparatory work for the conference in the way of scientific investigation and determination of existing law is done, the moment the Government Delegates assemble and decide to conclude a Convention to render the rules so defined binding on States, their efforts are directed to laying down the law as it ought to be and not as it is. This is precisely what happened at the Codification Conference of 1930.[23]

By means of a strict construction of the codification–legislation dichotomy as regards technique, Hurst's immensely influential paper refocused the British view on results.

In the Baker–Brierly interpretation, the nature of international law made codification impractical. In Hurst's interpretation, however, corruption of technique had confounded previous attempts at codification. International codification was nonetheless practical so long as the results of a scientific determination of law stood as such. Hence Hurst recommended the creation of national study groups working in coordination with "some central scientific organisation" to deal solely with codification.[24]

Hurst's reinterpretation of the feasibility of codification made an immediate impact on British thinking. The so-called McNair Report to the 1947 Conference of the International Law Association followed the traditional British view with respect to meanings, purposes and techniques, and explicitly seconded Hurst's proposed program.[25] Similarly, in an essay published in the same year, R.Y. Jennings, after citing Hurst, affirmed the value of multilateral conventions to develop new law, but argued that "where the aim is merely to declare or consolidate . . . a suitable vehicle may be found in the scientific restatement conceived as an authoritative, written evidence of existing customary law."[26] Even Brierly relaxed his earlier view that codification was a pointless undertaking because of the nature of international law and adopted Hurst's position on scientific restatement.[27]

Perhaps the most notable articulation of the American position is Elihu Root's. Root established the need for international codification, which he

23 C. Hurst, "A Plea for the Codification of International Law along New Lines," *Transactions of the Grotius Society*, vol. 32, 1946, p. 147.

24 Ibid., p. 153.

25 "Report of the Committee on the Development and Formulation of International Law," A.D. McNair, Rapporteur, *International Law Association, Report of Forty-Second Conference, Prague 1947*, p. 83. Membership of this committee was dominated by Britons, including Brierly, Lauterpacht, Colombos and McNair.

26 R.Y. Jennings, "The Progressive Development of International Law and Its Codification," *British Year Book of International Law*, vol. 24, 1947, p. 310.

27 J.L. Brierly, "The Codification of International Law," *Michigan Law Review* vol. 47, 1948, p. 6.

understood as conscious law development, by pointing out the differences between international and municipal law.

> It is curious that codification should be especially necessary in a system of law which is based on custom more exclusively even than municipal law; but that is necessarily so in the case of the law of nations, because there are no legislatures to make the law and there are no judicial decisions to establish by precedent what the law is.[28]

In this context, not only was the necessity of codification clearly established, but also its function indicated. "To codify international law is primarily to set in motion and promote the law-making process itself in the community of nations in which institutional forms appropriate for the carrying on of such a process have become so vague, indistinct, uncertain, and irregular that they could hardly be said to exist at all."[29]

If the point of codification is to set lawmaking in motion, then the British distinction between codification and legislation was patently irrelevant. Indeed, both reductive and innovative law creation have a place in conscious law development.

> The codifier's task is to find out what the rules really are; to put them in due relations with each other under appropriate heads in accordance with some systematic scheme of arrangement; to bring order out of confusion; to furnish a methodical statement of the result of his researches which may make the law plain to the people who live under it and may relieve countless lawyers from going through the same wearisome process of inquiry in each separate case. When the work is complete, if it is acceptable, the legislative power of the state puts its stamp of approval upon it and resolves any doubts or uncertainties by its acceptance of the codifier's conclusions. It may indeed be that the research of the codifier and the clearer view presented by a systematic arrangement will have revealed inadequacies of expression, incongruities, and omissions in the existing law, but, as to these, the suggestions of the codifier for the defects discovered will be accepted or rejected by a simple fiat of the legislative body which enacts the code.[30]

For Root, reduction and innovation were inextricable elements in a greater

28 E. Root, "Should International Law Be Codified? And If So, Should It Be Done through Governmental Agencies or by Private Scientific Societies?" *Proceedings of the American Society of International Law*, vol. 9, 1915, p. 163.

29 E. Root, "The Function of Private Codification of International Law," *American Journal of International Law*, vol. 5, 1911, p. 579. See, also, Root, "The Codification of International Law," *American Journal of International Law*, vol. 19, 1925, p. 681.

30 E. Root, "The Function of Private Codification of International Law," pp. 578–9.

process, that of guiding the development of international law. This is the point on which British and American views were diametrically opposed. Because the British did not wish to see the law consciously shaped, they maintained a sharp distinction between reduction by exposition and innovation by law creation, thereby severely limiting the possibility of direct influence by either of these isolated processes on the development of the law. Because an American like Root did wish to see the development of the law consciously shaped, he drew attention to law creation combining reductive and innovative elements in such proportion as best satisfied this ambition.

Root recognized that the "codifier's task" was an undertaking too abstract in nature to be of immediate value to governments.[31] Consequently, this work could not be left in the hands of governments, which had neither time nor interest to pursue it properly. Instead, preparations for the conscious development of international law had to come from other sources, where interest was deep and sustained. At the same time, approval of governments was essential if such efforts were to mean anything. After private initiative had resulted in necessary preparations, governments could signify their approval by assenting to international conventions embodying draft texts.

Other American writers spelled these themes out in greater detail. For example, James Garner, claiming to speak for "most Americans who favor codification," called for a piecemeal approach, thereby introducing the question of ripeness. His emphasis, though, was on a "practical mode of procedure" by which to develop selected topics. He observed that:

> intelligent codification requires a large amount of careful preliminary work which should be done by a select and relatively small number of jurists and technical experts. This preparatory work cannot be safely left to unwieldy conferences composed mainly of diplomats and statesmen.

Garner noted "much sentiment in favor of the view that drafting experts should not be appointees or representatives of particular governments," but appeared to view the matter pragmatically. Only his judgment that results must take a legislative form required strong, unreserved language.[32]

After the failure of the Hague Codification Conference, American writers discussed that disheartening experience at length.[33] Predictably the question of whether given topics lend themselves to treatment surged into the foreground of attention, bringing American and Continental perspectives closer together. In the background were reflections on the time and expertise needed

31 Ibid., p. 581.

32 J.W. Garner, "Some Observations on the Codification of International Law," *American Journal of International Law*, vol. 19, 1925, pp. 330–3.

33 See papers by American delegates to the Conference appearing in *American Journal of International Law*, vol. 24, 1930.

for adequate preparation and the precise role of governments. Only one American writer in the 1930s punctured the generally practical tone of such discourse by expressing disillusionment with what he called "the progressive codification of international law by treaty enactment."[34]

Drafting the Statute of the International Law Commission

To assist the General Assembly in acting on article 13(1)(a), the Secretariat prepared in 1947 a policy memorandum on "Methods for Encouraging the Progressive Development of International Law and Its Eventual Codification."[35] This report, which was adopted by the Committee of Seventeen as one of its bases of discussion, followed Hurst's argument for codification by means of restatement. Whereas the convention method was described as having "many drawbacks when it is considered as a method for securing general agreement on general rules and principles of international law," restatements were:

> a useful step in promoting international agreement with regard to the formulation of certain rules of international law which may lead to their eventual codification in an international convention. . . . If such restatements, possessing no governmental authority, were to be drawn up by a committee of jurists functioning under the imprimatur of the United Nations, they might serve as a useful guide to statesmen and judges.[36]

The striking resemblance of this argument to Hurst's is no accident. The chief of the Secretariat division responsible for it, Yuen-li Liang, was an acknowledged advocate of Hurst's position.[37]

The Committee of Seventeen was exposed to the British view from a more direct source. The British member of the Committee, J.L. Brierly, commanded a position of influence as rapporteur. He took a leading role in the Committee's deliberations, hewing close to the British position, which he summarized in the following terms:

> (a) Codification is a scientific and not a political task.
> (b) The method for drawing up international conventions, as employed

34 P.M. Brown, "The Codification of International Law," *American Journal of International Law*, vol. 29, 1935, p. 36.

35 UN doc. A/AC.10/7, reprinted in *American Journal of International Law*, vol. 41, Supp., 1947, pp. 111–47.

36 Ibid., pp. 115–116.

37 Y. Liang, "The Progressive Development of International Law and Its Codification under the United Nations," *Proceedings of the American Society of International Law*, vol. 41, 1947, pp. 44–5.

by the League of Nations, is appropriate for international legislation but not for codification.

(c) A small committee of personal experts would be required.

(d) The result of the work of these experts would be binding on no one, neither on the governments of Members of the United Nations nor on any tribunal. The authority of the work done by this small committee of experts would be based solely on its intrinsic merits.

(e) This, however, would not exclude the possibility of giving at a later date a higher authority to the work . . ., but it would be preferable to leave this question open for the time being.[38]

Brierly and the British view were challenged point by point by the Soviet representative, Vladimir Koretsky. Soviet doctrine was an unrestrained version of the historic Continental approach, which followed from Soviet insistence, especially at that time, on treaties as the only valid source of international obligations. Koretsky attacked the idea of a small body of experts

> The task of progressive development of international law and its codification is entrusted by Article 13(a) [sic] of the Charter to the General Assembly itself. If this task should be entrusted to a Committee of Experts, this would seem to be imitative of the old custom of isolating those who have to determine the will of the people. In my opinion there is no need for an Olympic oracle endowed with greater powers than governments themselves have.[39]

Finally, on the question of results, Koretsky argued that "rules resulting from the work of codification must . . . become generally obligating rules, but this can only be achieved by the method of concluding multilateral conventions."[40]

Because their positions were consistent, thorough and irreconcilable, Brierly and Koretsky were the focus of much debate in the Committee of Seventeen. Nevertheless, a compromise was reached and eventually embodied in the ILC Statute. The question of meanings was settled in favor of the British view. The fortuitous wording of article 13 of the Charter served as a starting point in the construction of the dichotomy of definitions found in article 15 of the ILC Statute.

The logical implications of the dichotomy were substantially ignored, however, because the Committee chose in favor of techniques not completely

38 UN doc. A/AC.10/SR.2, p. 5. Since UN speeches are rendered into the third person past tense in summary records, Brierly's speech is here rendered back into the present tense in order to duplicate its original form. The next three quotations have also been changed. It must be remembered, however, that these documents are not verbatim records.

39 UN doc. A/AC.10/SR.4

40 UN doc. A/AC.10/32, p. 2. See also UN doc. A/AC.10/SR.4. add. 1, p. 3.

alien to the Soviet view. Contrary to Soviet preferences, a separate commission of experts was created; but it was twice the size preferred by the British, it was obliged to consult governments and, most importantly, the question of the independence of its members was left in abeyance. This hybrid of techniques implied nothing certain about the form of results. Provision was made for both possibilities – scientific restatement and multilateral convention-making – with the choice to reside with the Commission itself. In short, the standoff between British and Soviet doctrine enabled a pragmatic solution, which was indeed an American solution.

The American view offered no middle ground on the question of meanings. Consequently, the Charter formulation sustaining the British view was adopted, but at the price of irrelevance to the Commission's activities. While it is true that the ILC Statute designates separate procedures for codification and progressive development, the substantive differences between them disappear on inspection and in the Commission's subsequent practice. It was the American view which prevailed in matters of technique. As the US representative, Philip Jessup proposed to the Committee of Seventeen that a commission of experts should provisionally be established for three years. Its members should be "persons of outstanding competence in the field of international law," to be selected either by governments or by a procedure similar to that by which judges are elected to the International Court of Justice (ICJ).[41]

Although Jessup felt that codification and progressive development deserved separate procedures for their realization, these dual procedures, envisaged by stages, would be substantially interchangeable. In both instances the commission would initiate work, enlist cooperation from other expert groups and prepare a draft text to be submitted to governments for comments and then revised for transmittal "to the General Assembly for action thereon either by resolution of the General Assembly; by the adoption of a convention to be submitted to governments for ratification; or by simple authorization of publication of the report."[42] The commission could thus draw on a modest repertory of techniques.

A joint proposal offered to the Committee of Seventeen by the US and China made a few changes in Jessup's original suggestions.[43] A full-time commission of nine was anticipated, with members on three-year terms. The parallel procedures for conscious law development were modified at the point at which work would be initiated. In the case of progressive development, governments or other bodies might ask the commission to begin a project, or the commission might undertake to do so on its own initiative, with General Assembly approval. In cases of codification, either the General Assembly or

41 UN doc. A/AC.10/14, p. 1.
42 Ibid., p. 3.
43 UN doc. A/AC.10/33.

the Commission could select work. The joint proposal served the Committee of Seventeen as a basis of discussion on questions of organization, filling the vacuum created by the stalemate of competing doctrines. It is clearly recognizable in the ILC Statute and accounts for that instrument's greatest virtue, which is its capacity to accommodate a working institution's evolving self-conception.

The dual procedures for the progressive development of international law and its codification, finally presented in articles 16 through 23 of the ILC Statute, share an American pedigree, but broader parentage, in the procedure for conscious law development adopted by the League in 1931.[44] All three procedures utilize an autonomous body of legal experts, which must be kept closely informed of the views of states on the topics under consideration. In the case of the League procedure, once a state initiates and the Assembly approves an activity, a committee of experts "will make necessary enquiries." In the case of progressive development in the UN design, once activity has been initiated on a topic, a questionnaire is circulated for the ILC soliciting relevant information from states. Finally, in the case of codification, once activity has been initiated, states are requested to provide the Commission with relevant information.

In every instance that the expert body completes a draft on the basis of information so received, the process of securing the comments of states repeats, although in the League procedure, approval of the Assembly comes first. All three procedures then provide for revision of the preliminary draft on the basis of these comments and for the submission of the final draft to the Assembly or General Assembly. The League procedure anticipated that a draft would finally be sent to an international conference to serve as a working text for a multilateral convention. This is also one of the procedures envisioned in both UN procedures and is the ordinary course of events in the ILC's experience.

The need to reconcile scholarly detachment with governmental participation in conscious law development dictates a particular sequence of activities, which are twice stated in the ILC Statute for reason of formal completeness. There are, however, two major differences in the Commission's procedures for progressive development and codification, and they occur at the beginning and end of these procedures. In the instance of progressive development, initiation of work lies with the General Assembly, or with states or other agencies upon

44 The League's procedure in turn shows much in common with the standardized procedure for preparing general conventions also adopted by the League in 1931 and the International Labor Organization's 1926 guidelines for preparing conventions. Both sets of generalized procedures sought to establish a sequence of roles and responsibilities for states and international institutions involved in convention-making. Both are reprinted in "Historical Survey of the Development of International Law and its Codification by International Conferences," pp. 97–8, 100–1.

approval of the General Assembly. While their interests are directly affected by what topics *are* selected, states are infrequently motivated to do the selecting. A role for the General Assembly follows almost inevitably. In the instance of codification, legal criteria for selecting topics acquire proportionately greater weight. Consequently, initiating the reductive procedure is a function of the ILC, with priorities to be determined by the General Assembly.

The differences in the two procedures is a good deal clearer at the point of initiation than at their termination. This is the problem of the proper form for the results of conscious law development. With respect to work undertaken in the name of progressive development, the ILC is instructed to transmit its final draft to the General Assembly with recommendations on the final disposition of the text. Nothing is stipulated about the nature of these recommendations.

With respect to the final draft of codificatory texts, however, article 23 outlines four kinds of accompanying recommendations the ILC may make to the General Assembly:

(a) To take no action, the report having already been published;
(b) To take note of or adopt the report by resolution;
(c) To recommend the draft to Members with a view to the conclusion of a convention;
(d) To convoke a conference to conclude a convention.

Two of these possibilities definitely provide for the reduction of law by exposition (restatements) and two provide for reductive law creation (conventions).

It has been suggested in the Commission itself that there is no reason why the four possible types of recommendations prescribed for the disposition of codificatory drafts are not equally suitable for drafts directed toward the conscious development of international law.[45] This position is not sound; the wording of article 15 – "the expression 'progressive development of international law' is used for convenience as meaning the preparation of a draft convention" – utterly defeats it. Recommendations providing alternatively from the restatement and the convention form do not appear in the procedure simply because the notion of restatement lacks meaning in the context of innovative law creation. Without the approval of states there is no law creation.

To assume that an innovative draft will not secure approval effectively concedes that the subject of the draft defies conscious shaping. If this is the case, it ought to have been discovered during the drafting process, when the views of governments had been solicited. The Commission's early attempt to codify arbitral procedures supports this conclusion. Because of substantial innovation in its draft, about which states were demonstrably

45 Briggs, *The International Law Commission*, p. 276–7; Briggs himself supported this view.

unenthusiastic, the Commission settled for a set of *Model Rules of Arbitral Procedure*, that is, an innovative text in expository form.[46] The ILC deliberately chose an irregular form for its work because its members knew that progressive development was impossible, codification pointless, and the proper form for each, irrelevant.

Experts and bureaucrats

The ILC is generally referred to as an independent body of legal experts. Article 2 of the Statute supports this view by providing that members "shall be persons of recognized competence in international law." Article 8 also presents confirming evidence: "At the election the electors shall bear in mind that the persons to be elected to the Commission should individually possess the qualifications required and that in the Commission as a whole representation of the main forms of civilization and of the principal legal systems of the world should be assured." Observe that while the Statute is amply concerned with the expertise of the Commission's members, there is no explicit reference to independent status. It must be inferred. For example, Herbert Briggs stated that:

> the requirement of Article 8 that representation of the main forms of civilization and of the principal legal systems of the world shall be assured in the Commission as a whole is a clear indication of the General Assembly's decision that members of the International Law Commission, like ICJ judges, shall not be regarded as representatives of States.[47]

In like manner Shabtai Rosenne remarked that "as in the case of members of the Court, and by the combined effects of articles 2, 8, and 9 of the Statute, the members of the Commission sit in their individual capacity, and not as representatives of their governments."[48]

Reference to the independent character of ICJ judges and to the analogous procedures for establishing the competence of the Court's judges and the ILC's members is nevertheless insufficient to establish the independence of the latter. While article 8 of the Commission's Statute is substantively identical to article 9 of the Court's Statute, the latter does nothing to insure the independence of judges. Article 2 of the Court's Statute provides that "the Court shall be composed of a body of *independent* judges, . . . who possess the qualifications required in their respective countries for appointment to

46 The Commission's *Model Rules* are set forth in "Report of the International Law Commission Covering the Work of Its Tenth Session, April 28–July 4, 1958," reprinted in *American Journal of International Law*, vol. 53, 1959, pp. 239–48.

47 Briggs, *The International Law Commission*, p. 63. Also see pp. 31–2.

48 Rosenne, "The International Law Commission 1949–1959," p. 123. Article 9 provides for the General Assembly's election of ILC members.

the highest judicial offices, or are jurisconsults of recognized competence in international law" (emphasis supplied). Mark the difference between this article and its parallel, article 2 of the Commission Statute.

Reference to the discussions of the Committee of Seventeen yields even less evidence for the independence of ILC members.[49] As we saw above, the Committee's leading voice for independent legal experts was Brierly's. His emphasis on codification as scientific restatement of existing law virtually demanded independence. So as to put their integrity and independence beyond question, the experts of a codificatory agency should be "lawyers of international repute, selected purely on their individual capacities and in no sense representatives of their governments."[50] For complete consistency Brierly ought to have argued that two separate agencies were required to carry out the distinctive functions of codification and progressive development. While reductive exposition depends on independent legal expertise for its success, innovative law creation necessarily involves dependence on governments. Brierly's failure to acknowledge the full organization implications of the codification–legislation dichotomy he espoused follows from the Hurstian emphasis on codification at the expense of legislation. The Committee of Seventeen was unanimous in proposing a single commission.[51]

In stark contrast were Koretsky's declarations that conscious law development must be placed in the hands of governmental representatives. As we saw, Koretsky argued that the creation of multilateral conventions, which in the Soviet view were the exclusive means by which law developed, inevitably required the explicit representation of states' interests for their success. Obviously the views of Brierly and Koretsky on the status of ILC members were irreconcilable. Neither could prevail. Instead the issue was sidestepped. In his initial exposition of the American position, Jessup simply ignored the question of independence. All the US desired was that "the Commission of experts should be composed of persons of outstanding competence in the field of international law." Selection of experts "directly by governments" was perfectly acceptable as long as their competence was assured.[52] American pragmatism prevailed.

The actual procedure for selecting members of the Commission was also designed to evade meaningful commitment in the Statute on the question of

49 Even Briggs, *The International Law Commission*, p. 31, admitted this to be true.

> The documents of the Committee of Seventeen do not record any formal vote on whether the proposed International Law Commission should be composed of individual experts or representatives of governments, but the rejection of the latter conclusion is implicit in the provisions of the Statute of the International Law Commission which deal with election to the Commission and its composition.

50 UN doc. A/AC.10/16, p. 3.

51 UN doc. A/AC.10/40, p. 1.

52 UN doc. A/AC.10/14, p. 2

their independence. Article 3 prescribes that "members of the Commission shall be elected by the General Assembly from the list of candidates nominated by the Governments of States Members of the United Nations." Other articles go on to outline the conditions under which nominations are made. According to Rosenne, the ILC's election procedure is a debased version of the procedure for electing judges to the ICJ. As such, it "represents the abandonment of objective scientific criteria as the primary consideration in the choice of individual members of the Commission and the application of more pronounced political criteria – the General Assembly being itself an exclusively political body."[53] In short, the ILC procedure does not assure the independence of the Commission's members in the manner it is assured for the Court's judges. Undoubtedly the best hope for independence in either instance is the integrity of competent personnel, on the assumption that independence and competence are correlative qualities of mind. No instrument can guarantee such qualities.

A tendency toward independent legal experts was apparent in the original ILC membership. The first election in 1948 produced a number of members, Brierly being a notable example, who were scholars not then serving in governmental posts. Others, Koretsky among them, held foreign ministry positions. In the Commission's second session Koretsky objected to the presence of Shuhsi Hsu because he did not represent the Chinese legal system. Although Koretsky's contention would seem to have been based on article 8 of the Statute, it was ruled out of order by the chairman, Manley O. Hudson, who happened to be an American. After pointing out that the application of article 8 was not the Commission's concern but the General Assembly's in electing members, Hudson proceeded to argue that members "do not represent states or governments; instead, they serve in a personal capacity as persons of 'recognized competence in International Law' (Article 2 of the Statute)."[54] While this construction of the Statute is unwarranted, the Commission supported it by a vote of 10 to 1.

Procedural challenges like Koretsky's are no longer heard and, if they were, would not be put to a vote, as Koretsky's was. Consensus has long prevailed as the Commission's characteristic mode of arriving at decision. From the beginning the ILC has displayed an informal, collegial spirit in its meetings. Place cards and favored forms of address are personal. Members never refer to each other as "the representative of ____," and only rarely to "my government," as is typically the case in UN organs. Sessions are held in Geneva because New York is said to be a more political and therefore distracting place.

53 Rosenne, "The International Law Commission 1949–1959," p. 122. See, also, Dhokalia, *The Codification of Public International Law*, pp. 172–3.

54 Briggs, *The International Law Commission*, p. 78. The incident is described ibid., pp. 78–80.

If early sessions established a climate of independence in the Commission, the professional affiliation of members has shifted over three decades. Members with scholarly careers and no concurrent governmental duties have markedly declined in number. New states, as they become better represented on the ILC, send proportionally fewer scholars, if only because they have fewer to draw on.[55] But this explains only part of the decline. The US, for example, has available to it an abundance of scholarly resources. Yet its last two members have also been government officials during their terms of service. This is now the norm for the Commission.

Many members, including the current (1980) member from the US, *also* hold university posts as renowned scholars. This condition, fully expressing the possibilities contained in the Statute, could be held up as an ideal and not the contradiction in terms (government official *v.* independent scholar) it appears to be. Members see themselves as independent and uninstructed because, practically speaking, no one else from their own governments is competent to issue instructions. In fact, many members are the self-same officials who would write instructions if there were any.

Members who work in governments are a significant asset to the Commission. They are likely to serve their governments in the General Assembly's Sixth Committee, which passes on the Commission's work, and in the international conferences called to render ILC drafts in a form suitable for ratification. Given their investment in the Commission's work, it is reasonable to expect that members will take considerable pains to see that all goes well. Clearly, ILC members are part of a tight community of foreign ministry legal personnel who dominate the intricate world of global lawmaking.

An organizational, or what I have called the American, approach to international codification works as well as it does precisely because this community administers it at every stage. Indeed, the Statute contributes to the community's informal organization and functioning. The consequent blurring of formal role designations is not to be confused with the well-known phenomenon of politicization in the UN System. The presence of governmental personnel does not automatically mean an intrusion of politics in presumably technical activities. Arguably it lessens the chance that the Commission will be seen as politically irresponsible and an easy target for politicization in the rawest sense.

Long before the ILC was born, at a time when "international legislation" was an organizing metaphor, Max Weber observed that codification (of course referring to municipal experience) marks the bureaucratic rationalization of legal orders. As foreign ministries bureaucratize, their need for a rationalized and professionally administered body of law increases at least proportionally, if not exponentially. The conscious development of

55 L.T. Lee, "The International Law Commission Reexamined," *American Journal of International Law*, vol. 59, 1965, p. 549.

international law by lawyer-bureaucrats succeeds upon the earlier phase of scholars and statesmen occupying distinct roles in a less mature legal order (also see Chapter 6, above). International codification is paradoxically ever-more technical as it is removed from the domain of those whose political disinterest is presumably guaranteed by their private status. The paradox disappears with recognition that conscious law development is becoming a closed system of activity, which governments alone can foster and they alone need to have undertaken. Politics and private concerns are equally irrelevant.

Changes in the nature of conscious law development are so profound as to be indistinct in the foreshortened perspective of the present. Yet they were at least dimly perceived as the Commission used the 20th and then the 25th anniversary of its founding to reflect on the future of its work.[56] This period, between 1968 and 1973, was marked by concern that the ILC would soon exhaust its original program of work, which had consisted of 14 items considered sufficiently ripe to invite attention.[57] The Commission has been asked on occasion to consider a few additional items, some of which proved to be exceptionally ill-suited for ILC attention.[58]

Having worked through the several items most readily developed and being rewarded with a series of successes capped by the 1969 Vienna Convention on the Law of Treaties, the ILC was forced to adopt a more leisurely approach to its remaining agenda of less ripe items. Work on these remaining items stretches on interminably – B.G. Ramcharan estimated in 1977 that a topic

56 See, notably, the Commission's review of its program of work on the occasion of its 25th anniversary, as reported to the General Assembly in UN doc. A/9010, paras. 134–169, reprinted in 2 *Year Book of the International Law Commission*, vol. 2, 1973, pp. 225–30.

> Compared to the wide possibilities that seemed to be within reach in the late 1940's, a different situation presents itself at the opening of a new era in the Commission's existence. The new trends in the development of international law which manifested themselves at an early date have in the meantime generated a mass of authoritative statements of a legal nature. There is no reason to assume that this process will slow down in the years to come, nor that the present specialization in law-making functions will diminish (p. 229).

57 The list of 14 items was drawn from a comprehensive list of 30 items which, if completely exhausted, would yield a great code, by its then anonymous author's reckoning. "Survey of International Law in Relation to the Work of Codification of the International Law Commission," UN doc. A/CN.4/1, reprinted in E. Lauterpacht (ed.), *International Law, Being the Collected Papers of Hersch Lauterpacht*, vol. 1, Cambridge: Cambridge University Press, 1970, p. 445.

58 Only in the early years did the General Assembly burden the ILC with such inappropriate topics as formulating the Nuremberg Principles, considering the creation of an international criminal court and preparing a Draft Code of Offences against the Peace and Security of Mankind. These the Commission dispatched quickly, typically using an expository format for necessarily innovative formulations. By contrast, latter-day additions have been specialized extrapolations of regimes like Diplomatic Relations and Treaties earlier reductively conventionalized through ILC initiative. Such progeny require protracted treatment, article for article even more than their parents, as ripe topics, did.

takes six to eight years to reach final draft form.[59] For all the memoranda and debates on future activities, the Commission no longer needs a program of work in a formal sense. Its present rate of progress means that the original program and occasional additions will suffice for at least another decade and perhaps as long again as the ILC has already existed.

The prospect of diminishing output as the Commission grapples with its current agenda – in 1980, state responsibility, state succession, treaties between states and international organizations or between two or more international organizations, the law of nonnavigational uses of international watercourses, jurisdictional immunities of states and their property, and the status of diplomatic couriers and the diplomatic bag – does not imply that political considerations stymie agreement, although some of these topics are historically controversial. Ample precedent exists for leaving the points of controversy aside for development in a different, more political forum. The slow pace of ILC work stems from technical intricacies demanding inordinate attention, which indeed no other body is competent to provide. Comfortable with its craft, the Commission whittles away at each topic with full appreciation that each is a permanent feature of daily bureaucratic life. Any progress, at whatever stage of formality, contributes to and draws from the bureaucratic milieu of which the ILC's members partake. Law develops dynamically in relation to what the Commission does, not by reference to conclusive texts ultimately acceptable to states as formal obligations. To borrow a metaphor, the Commission is a medium of development in which its deliberations as much as its determinations are the message.

Seen in this light, recent discussions about the Commission's inadequacies seem misplaced.[60] Concern for the fact that the ILC takes so long in its work mistakenly assumes that only the products of such labors matter. Concern that states choose not to ratify such products when they duly reach final form also mistakes the relation of medium to message.[61] The consequences of unremitting participation by government officials in extended, detailed discussions of successive drafts compel gradual ingestion of their contents. Belief that the drafting process could be expedited and the ratification problem solved if the Commission undertook restatements not only exhumes the distinction between codification and progressive development but misapprehends the value of their respective textual forms.[62]

Restatements are cheapened by the very fact that they are easier to draft

59 Ramcharan, *The International Law Commission*, p. 40.

60 See especially ibid., pp. 64–85, 202–10, which also presents views expressed in the ILC's debates over its program of work.

61 A concern also expressed by De Visscher, "Stages in the Codification of International Law," p. 33.

62 The Commission itself rejected this possibility. UN doc A/9010, para. 169, in *Year Book of the International Law Commission*, vol. 2, 1973, p. 260.

because governments do not anticipate their adoption as formal instruments. Potential draft conventions, even if they fail to get beyond the drafting stage, require governments to participate in their formulation with complete attention to the diverse implications of possible adoption. Suggestions that the Commission meet for longer sessions or become a full-time body appear to make sense from a bureaucratic point of view, but overlook the role of ILC members in a larger network of lawyer-bureaucrats populating foreign ministries and the UN. These roles would have to be shorn in order to boost the rate at which work is produced. The dilemma of meeting competing demands of the world's foreign affairs bureaucracies cannot be so easily solved.

The ILC can do no more than it does now and still be suited to its mission. That its work pace is fixed and the needs of a burgeoning bureaucratic world suggest a course of institutional proliferation. This means the creation of substantively fractionated iterations of the Commission.[63] It is the fashion to criticize bureaucracies for mindless expansion and differentiation. Circumstances here as elsewhere leave little choice if all the work for which only the ILC is suitable shall be taken up adequately, effectively and promptly, to use a familiar phrase.

The fact that criticisms of the ILC are easy to refute may obscure a deeper problem, one that is perhaps more conspicuous in the constitutional order of a modern state like the US. Described as pluralism and defended as the free play of interest groups, the political process as it has evolved in the US permits legislative enactment of only the vaguest guidelines for public policy. Pluralism depends on bureaucracy for its administration.[64] The rise of bureaucratic regulation is indeed a progressive substitution of individual rulings covering specific situations for rules that are general in form but specific enough in content to cover those same situations. While legislative enactments may purport to direct behavior of subjects of the legal order, they are actually working instructions to bureaucrats. Rulings proliferate into an unruly mass, undercutting comparability and accountability presumably guaranteed by the rule of law. In effect, administrative order, enabled by permissive legislation, replaces legal order. The presence of lawyers and the persistence of legal forms mask the character of the change.

The international legal order lacks the constitutional and legislative paraphernalia of advanced pluralist orders, but nevertheless displays the same tendency for rules of general or generalizing import to fall before rule-like formulae concocted to suit bureaucratic need and circumstance. The latter seem less like rules when we find that their origin, subject and consequence

63 Regional iterations – the Inter-American Juridical Committee, the Asian-African Legal Consultative Committee and the European Committee for Legal Cooperation – help to meet current needs only in limited degree because these needs are characteristically extraregional. See Ramcharan, *The International Law Commission*, pp. 177–201, for a review of these institutions and their activities.

64 The argument here follows T.J. Lowi, *The End of Liberalism: The Second Republic of the United States*, 2nd edn, New York, Norton, 1979, pp. 92–126.

merge. They are nothing more than factual summaries of deals struck and problems solved, codified for future reference. Here codification has a minimalist meaning, more akin to the place of articulation in converting customary practices into law than to the conscious development of law.

If law is forthcoming, it must be seen as a byproduct of administrative routinization and then only insofar as this kind of activity acquires predictive value. The ILC appears to be identifying rules as law when indeed it is ruling on fact summaries. These activities can be reconciled if factual conditions and relations hold still long enough for rulings to cumulate as rules. If instead, the Commission finds facts constantly changing and cannot fix them in place for long, then its ceaseless quest for law serves the ordering of administrative practices at the expense, but in the name, of legal order.

The Commission's bureaucratically defined activities stand at the core of contemporary international codification. Other activities, being peripheral and episodic, also fit into the codification movement's complex evolution. More than a decade of arduous discussions under UN auspices produced in 1982 a multilateral convention on the law of the sea. Why this cycle of preparation and conference negotiation was conducted outside of existing codificatory machinery casts light on the ILC's drift toward bureaucratic rationalism. Politically sensitive oceans issues not settled at codificatory conferences in 1930, 1958, and 1960, compounded and intensified thereafter. For the Commission to have returned to these issues would have condemned it to unending travails, insurmountable obstacles and certain politicization.

That same fate was happily avoided when the UN also devised an alternative ad hoc mechanism to prepare what were to become the Principles of Friendly Relations and Cooperation among States. As an articulation and reorientation of principles found mostly in Chapter I of the UN Charter, work on this subject revived the long-standing Latin American dream, taken up by the international community's newer and less privileged members everywhere, of restructuring the international legal order. A necessary preliminary to the current push for a new international economic order and preeminently a matter of high politics, the conscious (re)development of principles proceeded in political arenas unhampered by considerations of the ILC's special history and place. Other such reversions to the codification movement's earlier preoccupations are bound to crop up occasionally. They are important in fostering a larger public awareness that there should be more to law than can be discerned in the successively more detailed drafts of industrious and obscure lawyer-bureaucrats, however useful administratively these never finished codes might prove to be.

Part II

Social theory and the linguistic turn, 1980–1993

11 Review: *Negara: The Theater State in Nineteenth-Century Bali*, by Clifford Geertz, 1980 (1982)

For many years I read the social anthropological literature on "primitive orders" and "primitive law." No doubt a Romantic interest in all things exotic motivated me, but so did a desire for conceptual leverage in approaching the core questions of international legal theory: Does international law have properties making it truly a species of law, or is its name simply an artifact of inadequate theorizing or time-honored practice? How does the system of relations among states work – *function* – as an order? The value of anthropology in freeing these questions from the encumbrance of positivist legal theory should be obvious to anyone reading Part I. As readers may also have discerned, I was increasingly troubled by anthropology's failure to reach beyond the always fuzzy and evidently teleological language of function.

At that time some anthropologists were expressing the same concern and situating it in what would soon become a general critique of the positivist assumptions of modern social science. Among them Clifford Geertz secured an unusual degree of attention, including mine, with his extraordinary book, *The Interpretation of Cultures: Selected Essays* (1973). When I read Geertz's *Negara: The Theater State in Nineteenth-Century Bali*, I realized that a review for an audience of international legal scholars would afford me an opportunity to summarize some of my thoughts about the kinds and functions of legal rules. After some hesitation, the editors of the *American Journal of International Law* accepted my proposal to undertake a review. In writing it, I could not help but notice the parallel between Bali and the international system as ceremonially inclined, status-ordered societies. The importance of status and the requirements of honor would become a large concern in my subsequent turn to social theory. Published substantially as drafted and here unchanged, this short piece remains a favorite of mine.

What can we of the international legal community possibly learn from classical Bali? One answer comes easily. Bali, a remote and exotic place, must have exhibited a primitive order, somehow, suggestively, comparable to the international legal order. Geertz's *Negara* invites such comparison without substantiating the analogy as framed: neither order is primitive in the usual sense of the word.

It is, of course, one of the frequent, apparently contagious assertions of international theory, obtaining the status of irreducible wisdom, that the law among nations is a species of primitive law. Primitive legal orders have long histories of autonomy, few subjects (whose demands on the order are furthermore modest and well defined), high levels of regard for rules, and low levels of institutionalization. All these family features get summed up as decentralization – synoptic statement, master concept, all-purpose explanation, incantation. The deficiency of this view is that decentralization is made possible, but not demanded, by an order's autonomy and small size. Beyond this, orders may vary considerably in complexity and formality without appreciably shedding their decentralized character.

In other words, centralization is a particular kind of institutionalization that makes a legal order a "modern" one possessing modalities for making and enforcing rules *in their appearance* external to, and poised above, the subjects of the order. Legal orders may take other forms of institutionalization, acquiring an intricacy and formality quite unlike that of the primitive model, but equally unlike the modern one. Such orders may develop as they do because they are not as isolated or as penetrated, as small or as big, as narrow or as broad in scope as available models posit. International law would seem to be one of these intermediate orders, neither fish nor fowl by the usual reckoning, and thus inadequately understood by the usual comparative procedure, that is, comparing it with primitive orders on the one hand, and modern orders on the other.

These remarks are intended to suggest that international law theory needs a new model for the purposes of comparison. Such a model cannot be just of itself or of its earlier states of development, if the comparison is to have any independent meaning, but must be adduced from the experiences of other legal orders, which, from the vantage point of existing models, appear equally intractable. Judging from Geertz's *Negara*, the decentralized state system and complex legal order of 19th-century Bali may be an exceptional candidate for model building. Geertz, already renowned for anthropological studies of Bali, emphasizes the ceremonial dimensions of political order on the island at a time when it was organized into seven principal kingdoms, each with less than 100,000 residents.

Ancient ties of blood among rulers counted only for rank. Dutch control was nominal and outside influences inconsequential. Deftly using abundant ethnographic materials, Geertz depicts the incessant politics of ruling class culture, the organization of rice growing, trade, religious practice, and public ceremony. Everywhere we find extensive demonstrations of power and position, fractious and often violent behavior nonetheless rule-bound to an extraordinary degree – conflict almost always arising from alleged violations of rules and incompatible interpretations of obligation – *and* a remarkably stable order, indeed, one that structurally and institutionally has been unchanged for centuries despite, or because of, the extremely fluid quality of the island's politics.

Stability of the system and political flux are occasioned by a "myth of the exemplary," a peculiar transcendence of sovereignty as centralized control in the idea that rule exemplifies a "supernatural order, 'the timeless Indic world of the gods' upon which men should, in strict proportion to their status, seek to pattern their lives" (p. 13). Politics is jockeying over status and success is being confirmed in one's status by having to do nothing. Manifest control is thus *inversely* related to position, for exercising power derogates from the presumption that one's status makes such an activity unnecessary. If we make allowances for the exaggerated quality of these features of Balinese political life, we can easily see their correspondence with features of international life today: Status depends on having power but not using it; politics uses up capabilities and requires much ceremonial display without changing anything very much; actors with high status identify themselves as exemplars of some mythic order of their own making and find themselves accordingly inhibited in what they can do; perennial conflict coexists with, indeed, reinforces, rule-oriented behavior, while the superfluity of rules and their connection to status and exemplary considerations present numerous opportunities for conflict. Bali as a model points up signal features of our own global order, which is exactly what a model should do. These very features are obscured to us otherwise, because we are conditioned to look for other things by other models.

Geertz means to correct some of the undue emphasis in Western political theory on coercive control as the defining quality of the state – "[i]mpressed with command, we see little else" – by restoring "our sense of the ordering force of display, regard and drama" (p. 121). What he seeks to do for the theory of the state is *a fortiori* appropriate to the system of states and becomes an even more telling critique of international theory because, like Bali after all, centralization of coercive potential is not even an ostensible condition of the order. And what Geertz's reconstruction of 19th-century Bali shows us about the international order generally, it does more specifically for its legal properties.

Law as we understand it was hardly the exclusive source of the complex order of Bali but was certainly one of its more visible elements, whether in treaty or customary form. Consider treaties:

> written treaties contracted among various of the major powers of the island. These treaties were hardly the most crucial element in that complex of symbols which maintained at least the vision and promise of overall order, if not very much of its substance. Nor were the treaties so terribly binding as documents, as directed toward such politically central issues as to provide a structural backbone for a genuine "international" polity. They were as purely ceremonial, in their juridical way, as were politesse, gift exchange, and cosmopolitan worship (p. 41).

Now contrast this with the role of customary law at the less exalted level of rice cultivation, and of daily life in general.

> Here, rather as with the treaties between states already discussed, the main framework for . . . case-by-case adjustment was a very highly developed, almost obsessively specific collection of customary practices – established precedents which, though there was no superordinate political body to enforce them, had nonetheless the force of law, if only because they provided a dictionary of legitimate, agreed-upon grievances. . . . The number of these "customary laws" was extremely great, and their content varied widely from place to place. . . . The Balinese seem rarely to have been faced with a situation without an applicable "law," or at least some sort of rule from which they could plausibly draw an analogy (p. 83).

We ought not to be misled by easy linguistic parallels. The correspondence between treaty law and customary law in the Balinese and international orders, respectively, is not exact. By examining the differences, we lay bare two generic kinds of law worked into these intricately institutionalized, ceremonially inclined, but substantially decentralized orders. The first kind, represented in Bali by treaties and in the international order by some of the grander multilateral treaties, General Assembly declarations, agreements like the Helsinki Final Act, judgments of the World Court, and conceivably some unilateral actions labeled doctrines, seem to reflect symbolic, but deeply normative concerns. They look like rules, but they cannot be enforced. The point is precisely that they are not supposed to work as enforceable rules, only as reinforcements of the order in its general proportions. As such, they are an indispensable but almost uniformly overlooked adjunct to high politics – they are lawyerly artifacts revealing the ceremonial arrangements within which high politics takes on meaning for its celebrants.

The other kind of law is customary on Bali. In the international order it consists of customary rules, most treaties, codificatory texts, international administrative regulations, and the lion's share of the material written by or passing through the hands of lawyers in foreign ministries and, of course, many other government ministries with specialized foreign affairs to discharge. What all these rules have in common is that they are almost invisible to outsiders.

Their complexity and specificity defy the kind of general statement that the conventional model of law from John Austin on requires. These rules are formalized operating procedures found wherever bureaucracies function. Enforcement is neither possible nor needed. They serve as a dictionary, to use Geertz's apt word, too great ever to be assembled in one place, for the daily life of the contemporary order.

Geertz's book, for all its intrinsic value, may have an additional worth, which even its author could not have anticipated. It grants us who gaze perhaps too steadfastly at the international legal order an undeniable exotic model of law and order, which may nonetheless be closer to global reality than any of the models we currently use, to frame our vision and organize our thoughts.

12 Review: *Law, Morality, and the Relations of States*, by Terry Nardin, 1983 (1984)

As book review editor for the *American Journal of International Law*, Leo Gross asked me to review a new book by Terry Nardin, a political scientist by training and a contemporary of mine. Obviously important, the book "blurred genres" (a turn of phrase I took from Clifford Geertz) in a highly original and carefully worked out fashion. For all that, I found the book's conceptual apparatus deeply flawed. I took great care in drafting a highly critical, and highly compressed, review, a copy of which I sent to Professor Nardin as a courtesy. For his part, Nardin sent me a thoughtful response, which we both sent to Professor Gross. I have always thought that Gross decided not to publish Nardin's letter, but Nardin, remembering the situation differently, tells me now that he declined Gross's invitation to respond publicly. In any event, the *Journal* published the review, substantially as drafted and here virtually unchanged. Nardin's letter follows my review. When I asked him if I might include the letter here, he remarked that it could use some polishing but decided it was more important for readers not to wonder if anything had been changed that would affect the exchange between us.

Rereading this material and thumbing through the book (which I have consulted many times over the years), I still think the latter is seriously flawed, from the beginning, in treating two kinds of human association as categorically different. I also think my critical remarks made undue demands on readers in the interest of brevity. Had I only read and reviewed the book this year, I would say quite a bit about Nardin's conception of *purpose* and *practice* (and thus about the abuses of Aristotle), and less about *rule* and *authority* (and thus about Nardin's misplaced reliance on Michael Oakeshott).

Once upon a time, political philosophy and international legal studies were but one. In our time, international legal scholars attend very little to political philosophy, political philosophers even less to international law. Professor Nardin is one of a small contingent of younger scholars in the US whose interests in international law coexist with a predilection for "blurred genres" of discourse. The book under review is undoubtedly the most substantial effort yet by a member of this intrepid band to permeate the sclerotic tissues separating political philosophy and international law, the former contributing decisively to Nardin's style of discourse, the latter providing familiar but intractable puzzles for philosophical inspection: Is there an international society? What is the specific character of international law? How are international law and morality related? The book's methodical approach and substantive concerns are well captured in these lines from the preface:

> I want to defend the view that the practices of international law and international morality constitute indispensable foundations of all durable international association. To the extent that the relations of states achieve a significant degree of permanence, rising above the level of mere episodes in the separate histories of isolated political communities, they must be understood as taking place on the basis of common, authoritative practices and rules. And this, I shall argue, means that they must be understood as occurring within a world of legal and moral ideas (p. ix).

Nardin's pace is always this leisurely. Each puzzle is turned every which way before the philosopher's gaze. Antecedent ideas are exhumed, illustrations offered, implications pursued. The journey is not an aimless one, however; an introductory chapter discloses the destination and details a map. Thereafter, the path is as well marked as it is circuitous. In the crucial first chapter, Nardin outlines two modes of human association, which he adapts to the circumstances of international relations, one understood by reference to shared purposes of participants, the other by reference to the minimum constraints on conduct necessary to allow participants to pursue "different and possibly incompatible purposes" (p. 9).

Nardin's inspiration for this scheme is Michael Oakeshott's elegant and influential book, *On Human Conduct* (1975), which, Nardin tells us, "was the catalyst that transformed my reflections on the law of nations into an argument by confirming a pattern that I vaguely discerned, but could not articulate, in the materials with which I was working" (p. xi). For Oakeshott, the operative categories are enterprise association and civil association, deriving respectively from the medieval concepts of *universitas* and *societas*, the latter constituting the foundation of the modern European state, the former infiltrating the state with a welfarist ideology and administrative burden it is ill-equipped to handle. Needless to say, Oakeshott has been widely interpreted as a powerful critic of 20th-century political propensities, continuing a tradition of British thought whose liberal contractarian premises, left behind by history, increasingly invite conservative dispositions. While Nardin does not entirely accept Oakeshott's affection for the pre-welfarist state as a minimal social contract, he does express fear over the burden communitarian demands place on the original minimal structure of international society (pp. 267–71). Whether Nardin escapes the reactionary implications of his dependence on Oakeshott's scheme, as he would seem to wish, is unclear.

Nardin renames the two modes of association purposive and practical. The term *practical* may pose some difficulty for students of international law, for whom practices contribute to and give evidence of the existence of authoritative rules. Nardin fixes on practices that are authoritative. They are the rules of association without which social intercourse of any sort is impossible. Two related problems arise here. One of them Nardin attempts, though unconvincingly, to dispatch (pp. 311–16). The other is less than fully acknowledged and the more devastating. The first problem has to do with the suggestion that the purpose of practical association is categorically different from that of purposive association. Is not agreement to pursue different purposes a common purpose, the possibility of deviance from which indeed requires that agreement be authoritative? Even if we observe some real difference in the aims of the two types of association, what makes them operative is the same in both instances. This, of course, is authority.

Following Oakeshott, Nardin relies on what Richard Flathman has called a formal-procedural definition of authority, in which authority is said to inhere in rules and offices. This stands in contrast to a substantive-purposive definition, which emphasizes the claims to rule, capabilities of rulers and the reception of rulers' claims by the ruled.[1] The latter definition Nardin misrepresents as stipulating a consensus of shared values, which he correctly determines need not, and does not, characterize all human associations. More properly, it should be seen as the coordinative conditions of rule – the exercise and acknowledgment of rule, however instrumental, through the agency of rules. For Nardin's purposes, the difficulty with a formal-procedural definition is that it never decisively answers the question – Why are only some rules authoritative? To avoid tautology (some rules are authoritative because certain practices are authoritative) or regress (they gain authority from rules that gain authority from rules that . . .), one must answer either with a natural law argument Nardin does not – and surely would not wish to – make,[2] or a definition of authority that allows for purposes that cannot be categorically restricted, such as to establishment of minimal association.

The second problem can be seen in Nardin's approach to authority. A formal-procedural definition would seem to view rules as empty of content. They create offices but not policies. To the extent that civil association is formed of authoritative practices, they would thus secure a common interest, which is to allow participants to follow policies of their own devising, without being prejudged in any way by the rules themselves. Flathman finds in Oakeshott just this judgment: "Oakeshott insists that rulers as such are not managers, arbitrators, patrons of interests, or persons of substantive wants, and that ruling is indifferent to the objectives of individuals or groups."[3] Evidently, a substantive-purposive definition of authority would fit the

1 R. Flathman, *The Practice of Political Authority: Authority and the Authoritative*, Chicago: University of Chicago Press, 1980.

2 As evidenced by his discussion of Myres S. McDougal, pp. 198–210. Oakeshott forthrightly rejects any such argument. *On Human Conduct*, Oxford: Clarendon, 1975, p. 174.

3 Flathman, *The Practice of Political Authority*, p. 43, footnote deleted.

situation of rules in a purposive association, in which instance the rulers reflect the modalities of interest and influence operative in that association at that moment. How plausible is this division of rules into two sorts: those stipulating minimal conditions for independent endeavor but otherwise having no impact on such endeavor, and those determining common endeavors and distribution of consequences? Not very.

I would concede that rules of minimal association may, by virtue of their purpose, be less overtly interest-laden than other rules. But all such rules have content, which simply cannot be neutral in its effect on individual endeavors. Nor is there any reason to think that such rules do not massively and systematically benefit some over others. Inasmuch as the content of rules cannot be neutral, it seems altogether likely that the distribution of consequences will favor those who managed, through whatever artifice – including the appropriation of authority or its definition as neutral – to determine that content.

It is commonplace, after all, to observe that a guarantee of right to property, which in Oakeshott's intellectual tradition (though not by Oakeshott himself) is typically defended as a minimal requirement of association, has anything but trivial consequences for the distribution of privilege. Furthermore, the mountain of evidence that rules, however styled, are never neutral, has inspired those very claims of a substantive character on states and now increasingly international society to redress this situation. If the burden of such communitarian policies is becoming materially insupportable, then is the proper solution to condemn them as a threat to morally insupportable rules? Or is the better way to acknowledge the injustice of those rules? Perhaps lawyers cannot afford the luxury. But can philosophers afford not to?

This is too harsh a verdict on Nardin's consistently intelligent efforts. His shortcomings are nevertheless intellectual and not moral in origin. When he treats the two modes of association as analytical constructs, which is the effect of much of his text, they facilitate an engrossing discussion of international legal history and theory. Only when he hypostatizes his categories does he create intellectual difficulties that are also morally problematic. Nardin dismisses Flathman's careful dissection of Oakeshott's position as a discussion "of certain alleged difficulties" (p. 8 n.5). The difficulties are real and, given Nardin's intellectual capacities, philosophical disposition and years of thought on the subject, such a dismissal is both uncharacteristically complaisant and gravely disappointing.

June 30, 1984

Dear Nick:

Thank you for sending me an advance copy of your review; it was a most considerate gesture. I'd like to respond to the two major criticisms you make of the argument of the book, both of which seem to me to rest on a misunderstanding of that argument and of the tradition within which it is rooted.

The first criticism has two parts. The first is that there is no significant difference between the ideas of practical and purposive association because to respect the constraints of a practice is in effect to pursue a purpose. Thus, toleration of differences or respect for rights can be regarded as an end or goal of practical association. On this please look once again at pages 12 and 13 of the book where, anticipating this objection, I attempted right at the outset to meet it. My argument there turns on the old distinction between two categorially distinct kinds of end or good – what Alasdair MacIntyre, attempting in his own way to revive Aristotle's version of the distinction, refers to in *After Virtue* [1981] as "internal" and "external" goods. External goods like wealth or fame can be pursued in a variety of ways none of which are intrinsically linked to the good itself: there are lots of ways to get rich or to become famous. Internal goods, in contrast, are those that are immanent in a particular practice, for example, being good at raquetball, violin solos, or Arabic calligraphy. In other words, there are kinds of excellence or virtuosity which can be pursued only in relation to a particular practice. So you can only get good at raquetball by playing it and the quality of your playing is judged in relation to the rules and standards that define both the game and the kinds of excellence peculiar to it.

Oakeshott's suggestion, which I find quite illuminating, is that the ideas of morality and of the rule of law invoke a mode of human association that is more like a game or an artistic tradition than it is like a club or partnership. Not only do the former have "purposes" in a sense quite unlike that in which organizations like the latter may be said to have a purpose, but the kinds of authority that "make them operative" are likewise distinguishable, as I argue on pages 10 and 11.

This brings me to the second part of your first criticism, which attacks the conception of authority that I have argued is central to practical association: what Flathman calls the "formal-procedural" conception. Your argument is complicated and I don't understand all of it, but the key point seems to be that such a definition, by itself, is unable to explain why some rules are authoritative and others are not. One must be careful here to be clear by what one means by "authoritative." In particular, it is important to distinguish the authority of a rule within some particular system of rules, that is, its "validity," and the moral or other authority that might be claimed for the system itself. The existence of a system obviously depends on practice – people have got to be living to some degree according to the rules, and (as [H.L.A.] Hart emphasizes) it is particularly important that in a legal system legislators and judges respect the constitutional procedures that provide the foundation of the system. You can't ask whether the fundamental procedures are authoritative in the sense of "valid within the system." The question doesn't make sense, because the procedures are the source of that validity. Hence they are neither valid nor invalid. The only sense in which they can be said to be "authoritative," then, is that they are part of the actual practice of the members, especially public officials, of a society. The existence of ordinary rules, in short, is a matter of authority understood as validity within the system; the existence of the basic procedures "a matter of fact" (*The Concept of Law [1961]*, p 107).

To answer your question, then, some rules are authoritative because they are valid parts of existing systems of practice. The question whether they are authoritative in some other sense – for example, divinely ordained or morally defensible – is of course a wholly separate matter (as I argue at the end of Chapter 8). But this is just what your criticism denies, for by saying that a satisfactory account of the authority of international law would have to invoke either natural law or shared purposes, you are in effect saying that questions about legal authority and obligation cannot be divorced from questions of morality and of the proper aims of law. This may be so, but you do not offer any argument for it. Nor do you discuss the many arguments I make against this view, such as that it confuses the authority of legal rules with their desirability.

All this has to do with your first criticism. The second is that I'm wrong to claim that the rules of practical association are neutral between different purposes, in the sense that they do not effectively favor some endeavors more than others. This is just a mistake. Neither Oakeshott nor I make any such claim. When Oakeshott says that "ruling is indifferent to the objectives of individuals or groups" (to use the words you quote from Flathman), what he means is not that everyone benefits equally, which would be absurd, but that the ruler (that is, the ideal ruler, not his corrupt worldly counterpart) must administer the rules impartially. Of course any rule will benefit some more than others: the rules of track certainly do favor the faster runners, and our criminal law does not favor the endeavors of murderers, whom we might choose to reward rather than punish. And where rules are made, those with power do often make the rules to favor purposes dear to themselves. That's why in criticizing the claims made for a new international economic order I wrote the following:

> To some extent these charges and claims are well founded, for to some extent it is accurate to characterize the institutions of the society of states as enterprises for the promotion of the interests of the rich and powerful. It is therefore understandable and reasonable that the disadvantaged should wish to use these institutions for their own purposes. Nor is it surprising or unreasonable that in these circumstances they should adopt an instrumentalist approach to the question of obligation. The attractions of instrumentalism grow when expressions like "civility" and "the rule of law" are invoked hypocritically to justify the pursuit of self-serving policies. Insofar as international institutions are indeed enterprises for the pursuit of

> particular purposes, judgments of their desirability and of the authority of their rules will appropriately depend upon instrumentalist considerations (pp. 268–9).

If your two main criticisms rest on misunderstandings (for which of course the author may be to blame), then there is not much support for your charge that the book is an uncritical apology for reaction.

Sincerely,

Terry Nardin

cc: Leo Gross [Book review editor, *American Journal of International Law*]

13 Custom and discourse (1984, with V. Spike Peterson)

Throughout the 1970s I assumed that advances in theory depended on the methods and thus the assumptions of science – methods and assumptions applicable to the natural *and* social worlds. Early in the 1980s, my dismay over the prospects of international legal theory coincided with doubts about the positivist worldview of modern science. I read widely in critical, poststructural and feminist theory – none of it *theory* in positivist terms – and in the philosophies of science and language. Prompting me in this transformative experience were some of my doctoral students, foremost among them Spike Peterson, now a leading feminist theorist. In 1983, she and I wrote a paper on the kinds of rules constituting the international human rights regimes. As we say below, it was "cast in the conventional, objectivist language of the problem and requirements of social order," with the effect of making rules stand alone. By contrast, postpositivists emphasize discourse, as we say, "to penetrate through the figurative renderings of language, as it constitutes our reality and rules our actions, to the people whose discourse does indeed make things."

In this spirit we wrote a second paper linking discourse to my work then underway on rules (Chapter 14, below). We felt that a critique of the positivist concept of custom and a review of the postpositivist literature on meaning, intersubjectivity and discourse (which Peterson drafted) were necessary preliminaries for such an ambitious undertaking. We presented the paper at a professional meeting and submitted a revised version to the *International Studies Quarterly*. It was rejected for lack of an "integrating theme"; this we took to be an insuperable defect. What I see now is less a defect than a tension between Peterson's interest in intersubjectivity and mine in language philosophy. I have deleted some material and edited what remains for clarity and consistency.

Customs are everywhere. Custom calls attention to itself most particularly in social settings we see as lacking centralized institutions for the maintenance of order. In these settings we seek a different explanation for order. This custom offers, at least as a beginning. Particular customs cohere sufficiently to perform necessary ordering functions. However well this model fits social settings that are simple, remote, "primitive," it manifestly does not work for the multicentric and incomparably more complex setting of international relations.

The problem as we see it comes from making custom (not to mention order and perhaps most other concepts we ask too much of) into a thing. By the usual canons of understanding, it is indeed a thing: custom exemplifies the process by which anything acquires the properties of something. We do not disagree with this view so such as deny its sufficiency. In this we follow Ferdinand Tönnies: "Custom cannot be imagined without people who want what custom wants. Who are these people?"[1] Custom is produced by people who say, however indirectly, what they want. To find out who *they* are, what they want, and why making what they say into things gets them what they want is our objective.

These are matters of discourse. What we can find out about discourse depends on our discursive choices. The discursive strategy we defend and deploy here is one whose choice was dictated by our need, not to observe things, for which positivist methods are appropriate, but to penetrate through the figurative renderings of language, as it constitutes our reality and rules our actions, to the people whose discourse does indeed make things. Discourse is a term whose current fashion in postpositivist discourse, and value to us, derives from its dismantling of the persistent dualism in social theory which fosters, among many oppositions, that of thoughts and things. To avoid faked positivist finality, we do not define discourse so much as to allow its sense, and its relevance for international relations, to emerge from our enterprise. Of this Michel Foucault has provided a better description than we could devise ourselves:

> What, in short, we wish to do is to dispense with "things". To "depresentify" them. To conjure up their rich, heavy, immediate plenitude, which we usually regard as the primitive law of a discourse that has become divorced from it through error, oblivion, illusion, ignorance or the inertia of beliefs and traditions, or even the perhaps unconscious desire not to see and not to speak. To substitute for the enigmatic treasure of "things" anterior to discourse, the regular formation of objects that emerge only in discourse. To define these *objects* without reference to the *ground*, the *foundation of things*, but by relating them to the body of rules that enable them to form as objects of a discourse and thus constitute the conditions of their historical appearance. To write a history of discursive objects that does not plunge them into the common depth of a primal soil, but deploys the nexus of regularities that govern their dispersions.[2]

1 F. Tönnies, *Custom: An Essay on Social Codes*, trans. by A.F. Borenstein, Chicago: Regnery, 1971.

2 M. Foucault, *The Archeology of Knowledge*, trans. by A. M. Sheridan Smith, New York: Pantheon, 1972, pp. 47–8.

The customary conception of custom

Custom is a concept long employed by legal scholars and anthropologists, its core meaning well settled: a matter of custom, apparently, subject to definition by evocation disputed mostly in its relation to, or standing, as law.[3] The latter's meaning, of course, is not a settled matter. Contested definitions dominate jurisprudence and legal anthropology.

All writers take custom to be a matter of repetitive and routinized behavior. It is the social correlative of habit. Compare Sir John Davies' words, written in 1612, with a contemporary statement:

> For a Custom taketh beginning and groweth to perfection in this manner: when a reasonable act once done is found to be good and beneficiall to the people, and agreeable to their nature and disposition, then do they use it and practise it again and again; and so by often iteration and multiplication of the act it becometh a *Custoume*; and by being continued without interruption time out of mind, it obtaineth the force of a *Law*.[4]

> In a very basic sense, a custom is an observed regularity in conduct, the more or less spontaneous product of events that generates expectations about future conduct, thereby providing in today's thought a link between the past and the future. It constitutes a regular, routine response to what are judged to be similar circumstances. In addition, it goes without saying that custom does not constitute an iron yoke.[5]

Custom emerges gradually. The contours of consistent behavior harden, making consistency a virtue, first expected, then prescribed, and finally obligated. Max Weber summarized the process, with its successive steps of externalization, as follows:

3 So well-settled that the *Encyclopedia of the Social Sciences*, New York: Macmillan, 1930, devoted nine pages to *custom* and *customary law*, the *International Encyclopedia of the Social Sciences*, New York: Macmillan, 1968, none. In his article on "Custom" in the former, E. Sapir observed: "Custom is a common sense concept. . . . It is not as purely denotative and objective a term as culture and has a slightly affective quality" (vol. 4, p. 658).

4 Quoted in J.G.A. Pocock, *The Ancient Constitution and the Feudal Law: A Study of English Historical Thought in the Seventeenth Century*, Cambridge: Cambridge University Press, 1957, p. 33; emphasis in original.

5 W.L. Gould and M. Barkun, *International Law and the Social Sciences*, Princeton: Princeton University Press, 1970, p. 180. It was not always self-evident that custom is no "iron yoke." B. Malinowski observed some decades ago:

> The savage – so runs today's verdict of competent anthropologists – has a deep reverence for tradition and custom, an automatic submission to their biddings. He obeys them "slavishly", "unwillingly", "spontaneously", through mental inertia combined with the fear of public opinion or supernatural punishment, or again through a pervading group-sentiment if not group instinct.

Crime and Custom in Savage Society, New York: Harcourt, Brace, 1926, from which these words are taken (pp. 9–10), permanently upset this verdict.

> The psychological "set" which arises with the habituation of an action causes conduct which in the beginning constitutes plain habit later to be experienced as binding; then, with the awareness of the diffusion of such conduct among a plurality of individuals it comes to be incorporated as "consensus" into people's semi- or wholly conscious "expectations" as to the meaningfully corresponding conduct of others. Finally these "consensual understandings" acquire the guaranty of coercive enforcement by which they are distinguished from mere "conventions."[6]

Weber found this description incomplete: it fails to explain "how anything could ever change in this inert mass of canonized custom." For most writers, however, what is problematic in this process is the point at which custom is, if only figuratively, canonized, that is, endowed with *opinio juris sive necessitatis* – a sense that what custom requires is required as a matter of law.[7] This would seem to be the only definitional concern for theorists of international custom.[8]

Not considered a problem is the early part of the process in which a particular course of practice becomes established. It has been suggested that Thomas Schelling's influential discussion of games of coordination and, much earlier, David Hume's famous depiction of the emergence of conventions provide a sufficient explanation for the particular paths that customs take.[9] Nor does there seem to be a problem establishing the point at which practices acquire normativity, that is, take on a prescriptive character, which is the central feature of any rule. Indeed, it is often assumed that they are normative as a function of their being identifiable as custom.[10] The Historical School of the 19th century, which prompted and in degrees influenced much of the early writing on custom, even supposed that particular customs embodied the spirit of the community, normatively understood. Thus normativity prefigured custom, which is given necessary substantive expression through practice.[11]

6 M. Rheinstein (ed.), *Max Weber on Law in Economy and Society*, trans by E. Shils and M. Rheinstein, New York: Simon and Schuster, 1954, p. 67.

7 This concept and its explication are apparently attributable to F. Gény, *Méthode d'interprétation et sources en droit privé positif*, Paris: Chevalier-Marescq, 1899. A.A. D'Amato, *The Concept of Custom in International Law*, Ithaca: Cornell University Press, 1971, pp. 47–9.

8 D'Amato, *The Concept of Custom in International Law*, pp. 47–102; G.I. Tunkin, *Theory of International Law*, trans. by W.E. Butler, Cambridge, MA: Harvard University Press, 1974, pp. 113–33; K.V. Raman, "Toward a General Theory of International Customary Law," in W.M. Reisman and B.H. Weston (eds), *Toward World Order and Human Dignity: Essays in Honor of Myres S. McDougal*, New York: Free Press, 1976, pp. 366–73.

9 T.C. Schelling, *The Strategy of Conflict*, Cambridge, MA: Harvard University Press, 1960, pp. 83–118; F.V. Kratochwil, *The Humean Perspective in International Relations*, Occasional Paper No. 9, World Order Studies Program, Center of International Studies, Princeton University, 1981, pp. 15–23.

10 Tönnies, *Custom*, p. 30.

11 Geoffrey Sawer, *Law in Society*, Oxford: Clarendon Press, 1965, pp. 171–81.

There is a pattern in all this. Scholars universally accept the psychological model that Weber outlined so effectively, as it pertains to the emergence of rules, but not laws. Human beings make rules unconsciously and inadvertently. The implications of their doing so dawn on their consciousness ever so slowly. Most customs stay in this shadowy zone forever, obeyed but not acknowledged, capable of being stated publicly, as rules must, but not typically public except in the pattern of behavior they elicit.[12] Advanced cultures solve the problem of custom's stasis, and relieve scholars of their irritation over custom's objective indeterminacy, by substituting formal, deliberative lawmaking. Rules of law are public because they are made that way. In this model, dominant even before John Austin's classic formulation of it in the 19th century, custom gives way to legislation as the expression of sovereign or popular will. The state prevails, in politics, as law. Rule is the rule of law.

Custom acknowledged as *law*, suspended uneasily between the poles of custom as such and legislation as law, is only briefly the ruling form of rule in most cultures.[13] The instability of customary law is compelled, and revealed, by its major features, as recounted in the best recent discussion in anthropology. Rules of customary law are generally unwritten and local in ken. They are general in form but concrete in application, so that their use does not make them more specific: "the law returns, as it were, from its brief excursion into detail and reverts to its normal condition of generality."[14] This last property of customary law is the most baffling. By definition, laws are publicly stated rules; otherwise, no public could respond to them as obligatory by virtue of knowing them to be law. Yet the application of customary law cannot be considered public, or particular applications would have the effect of changing the general rule's content, if only to make it more specific.

Refined neither by writing nor use, heavily dependent on immediate contextual realities, customary law is often seen to represent, not the totality of a community and its traditions, but the particular interests of those "who monopolize the *knowledge* of the laws," to use Henry Sumner Maine's memorable words. "The law thus known exclusively to a privileged minority, whether a caste, an aristocracy, a priestly tribe or a sacerdotal college, is true unwritten law." For the "juristical oligarchy" to write down the rules it

12 On the properties of rules, including that they be capable of public statement, see N.G. Onuf and V.S. Peterson, "Human Rights from an International Regimes Perspective," *Journal of International Affairs*, vol. 37, 1984, pp. 329–30.

13 *Cf.* H.L.A. Hart, *The Concept of Law*, Oxford: Clarendon Press, 1961, pp. 89–96.

14 I. Hamnett, *Chieftanship and Legitimacy: An Anthropological Study of Executive Law in Lesotho*, London: Routledge & Kegan Paul, 1975, p. 11; also, see, J.L. Comaroff and S. Roberts, *Rules and Processes: The Cultural Logic of Dispute in an African Context*, Chicago: University of Chicago Press, 1981, pp. 70–84, 231–40; C. Geertz, *Local Knowledge: Further Essays in Interpretive Anthropology*, New York: Basic Books, 1983, pp. 207–14.

chooses from the possibilities offered by custom would be to risk losing control over the law and thus the social situation.[15]

Set down in codes, customary law becomes public and signifies the emergence of imperial or state bureaucracies with public responsibilities: "the substitution of 'reglementation' for 'privilege.' "[16] By contrast, common law, based on precedents – judgments tending to be written down and collated – is subject to increasing substantive specificity through use, and public in character. Law made by judges is more likely to deny immoderate privilege to the custodians of the rules, not only because it is a matter of public record and constrained by precedent, but also because of the practice of keeping judicial officers from simultaneously holding other public office.

The rise of writing permits the supersession of customary law by legislation or judges' law, or its conversion into codes. Any one of these alternatives requires the formation of a professional class of specialists (lawyers) to assist public bodies with the technical demands associated with written law. This class may also seek a monopoly over legal knowledge, but at least in principle their adjunct status – as counselors and advocates – inhibits the privatization of rule, which exclusive knowledge of customary law enables.

Some writers have remarked that rules rather like customary law can persist in the era of written law and the state. Given "the degree of autonomy of organizations and arenas outside of government," and recognition that autonomous entities and activities are nonetheless rule-informed, custom is a source of "reglementation."[17] Such rules are tantamount to law in their effect (being routinely accepted) but not their form (not being publicly stated). They negotiate the distance between participants' suffuse, largely unspoken appreciation of a particular social situation, which means the norms informing it, and their public practices, whose extreme differentiation defies the consistency apparently required of rules. Rules like these can never be public and consistent at the same time; law-like character must be projected onto the "dialectical" relation between rules too diffuse to take a definite public form and publicly defended practices lacking a distinctive normative pattern.[18] Thus they mediate personal and institutional realities in complex societies.

Such a view comports with Paul Bohannan's definition of law as an instance of the "double institutionalization" of rules:

> All social institutions are marked by "customs" and these "customs" exhibit most of the stigmata cited by any definition of law. But there is

15 H.S. Maine, *Ancient Law*, London: J. M. Dent, 1931, p. 10; emphasis in original.

16 Rheinstein, *Max Weber on Law and Society*, p. 266; see, further, pp. 256–83; R.M. Unger, *Law in Modern Society: Toward a Criticism of Social Theory*, New York: Free Press, 1976, pp. 47–133.

17 S.F. Moore, *Law as Process: An Anthropological Approach*, London: Routledge & Kegan Paul, 1978, p. 21.

18 Comaroff and Roberts, *Rules and Processes*, pp. 245–8.

> one salient difference. Whereas custom continues to inhere in, and only in, those institutions which it governs (and which in turn govern it), law is specifically recreated, by agents of society, in a narrower and recognizable context – that is, in the context of the institutions that are legal in character and, to some degree at least, discrete from all others.[19]

Customary rules, institutionalized once and less visible than laws, may well be the abiding and defining feature of social landscapes which the looming edifice of the state blocks, like so much else that matters, from view.

Only the peculiar landscape of relations among states appears to have a formally acknowledged place for customary rules, though convention here also holds that they be called law. These rules are extrapolated from the activities of state agents and made fully public only as a second order matter by legal professionals who are adjunct to the executive realm – legal advisers, scholars, judges in their lengthy, scholarly opinions. All of these individuals are acting as double functionaries (*dedoublement functionnel*).[20] They are creating rules for the closed realm of relations among states, and for a global institution, styled the legal order, transcending and apprehending states.

This already anomalous situation is further complicated by the admixture of judicial decisions that are public but, not being expressly precedential, closer to custom than to common law, and formally agreed on written rules, not easily kept private, known as treaties. While treaty rules presume to prescribe only for those accepting their terms publicly (making them non-customary and legal in a limited domain), they also contribute to the larger, diffuse domain of customary rules.[21] That a network of legal professionals advise executive officers, decide cases and draft treaties as if these were customary activities of a legal order has the cumulative effect of making customary rules public and more law-like. Not so easily decided is whether the pressures against private rules on a global scale fully mitigates the tendency, long ago observed by Maine, toward oligarchical control by such rule custodians.

Beyond positivism

The literature on custom in anthropology and jurisprudence takes us no further than this. We believe that identifying those who have control through

19 P. Bohannan, "The Differing Realms of Law," in Bohannan (ed.), *Law and Warfare: Studies in the Anthropology of Conflict*, Garden City, NY: Natural History Press, 1967, p. 45.

20 This is a well-known concept offered by Georges Scelle and extended by Myres S. McDougal. For critical discussion see T. Nardin, *Law, Morality and the Relations of States*, Princeton: Princeton University Press, 1983, pp. 162 n. 14, 206–7. One might say that this is a temporally collapsed and incomplete version of Bohannan's "double institutionalization."

21 R.R. Baxter, "Treaties and Custom," *Recueil des cours de L'Académie de droit international de La Haye*, vol. 129, 1970/I, pp. 57–74; D'Amato, *The Concept of Custom in International Law*, pp. 103–66.

rules to be the crucial consideration. Even when the "folk in power" are chiefs, presidents or any others whose powers are duly established in custom or law, the task of detailing their "folkways," through which their power is indeed effectuated, is difficult enough.[22] But many social settings are not ones in which relations among the folk in power are readily discerned and the implications of their ways easily explored. We propose that recent scholarship in allied disciplines, which finds people's discursive activities symptomatic of their position and power, can help us examine some of the riddles of custom now exposed. The utility of such an orientation, appropriately introduced in this section, begins with its acceptance of a rule-orientation toward all social reality. If custom rules through discourse, rules make custom, and discourse, possible.

This shift in perspective permits us to transcend the limits of positivism – a subject of much recent debate in the literature – and warrants an explication. Calls for reconstruction indicate that the paramountcy of social theory emulating the natural science model is no longer assured.[23] A series of challenges to the standard model has eroded its standing, while amplifying consideration of issues posed all along by alternative orientations. Although numerous debates over specifics rage on, implications for social science inquiry demand new premises. The most fundamental of these is the centrality of intersubjective meaning, mediated through and constituted by language, for understanding human action and consequently for the social or, as the French prefer, human sciences. Phenomenology, modern language philosophy, hermeneutics and critical theory of the Frankfurt School share rejection of a naturalistic version of the social sciences. Since elaborations of these richly diverse approaches are available elsewhere, our remarks are no more than suggestive portrayals.

What we take as the important contribution of phenomenology is its focus on the significance of intersubjective meaning in any understanding of social action. Self-interpretation, the unique feature of human behavior, cannot be ignored or treated as a nuisance to be overcome by ever greater methodological sophistication. Rather, as the distinctive feature of human sciences, reflexivity implies an epistemological break, the need for logical forms of explanation different from those of natural sciences' bounded domains.

Any response to Georg Simmel's query, "How is society possible?" must

22 The phrase is Hamnett's. *Chieftanship and Legitimacy*, p. 114.

23 A. Giddens, *New Rules of Sociological Method*, New York: Basic Books, 1976; R.J. Bernstein, *The Restructuring of Social and Political Theory*, Philadelphia: University of Pennsylvania Press, 1978; Giddens, *Central Problems in Social Theory: Action, Structure, and Contradiction in Social Analysis*, Berkeley: University of California Press, 1979; Giddens, *Profiles and Critiques in Social Theory*, Berkeley: University of California Press, 1982; M.B. Hesse, *Revolutions and Reconstructions in the Philosophy of Science*, Bloomington: Indiana University Press, 1980; M.J. Shapiro, *Language and Political Understanding: The Politics of Discursive Practices*, New Haven: Yale University Press, 1981.

inevitably address the production and reproduction of the social system – a "duality of structure" that Anthony Giddens characterizes as "the reflexive monitoring of action [as] both draw[ing] upon and reconstitut[ing] the institutional organization of society."[24] Such a response posits knowledgeable self-monitoring agents constituted by and through their own action, reconstituting the society. Human self-monitoring or reflexivity refers to the intentionality or purposiveness of human behavior consistent with the actor's understanding of social reality.[25] But the very meaning action has for an actor cannot be identified in isolation from shared, that is, intersubjective meaning:

> "[U]nderstanding" is not merely a method for making sense of what others do, nor does it require an emphatic [empathetic?] grasp of their consciousness in some mysterious or obscure fashion: *it is the very ontological condition of human life in society as such.* This is the central insight of Wittgenstein and certain versions of existentialist phenomenology: self-understanding is connected integrally to the understanding of others.[26]

The shared background knowledge and social practices conferring meaningfulness on individual acts have been variously characterized: *Lebenswelt* (Edmund Husserl), ground plan (Martin Heidegger), or common-sense reality of everyday life (Peter Berger and Thomas Luckmann). The unifying feature is the taken-for-grantedness of shared assumptions and practices, the immediacy of our everyday reference system which endows meaning and accountability to actions. Much of the *Lebenswelt* is of course acquired through primary socialization. "At all times, in all societies with cultures, every new generation has been taught and is taught how to conceive of things."[27] But the process never stops: in making sense of our lived experiences we continually choose among "interpretive schemes which are themselves essentially social and intersubjective."[28]

Understanding the operative *Lebenswelt* then is clearly central to social inquiry. Yet positivism insists on taking the background practices of social

24 Giddens, *Central Problems in Social Theory*, p. 55.

25 Intentionality refers not to mental events as "causes but as criteria for determining what rules should be involved to account for what has been done." Shapiro, *Language and Political Understanding*, p. 110. See his ch. 4 for important clarifications of this and other problematic terms: meaning, interpretation, action, and constitution. On meaning, see below and also Giddens, *New Rules of Sociological Method*, pp. 86–91; C. Taylor, "Interpretation and the Science of Man," in F.A. Dallmayr and T.A. McCarthy (eds), *Understanding and Social Inquiry*, Notre Dame, IN: University of Notre Dame Press, 1977, pp. 107–12; Hesse, *Revolutions and Reconstructions in the Philosophy of Science* (1980), pp. 112–13.

26 Giddens, *New Rules of Sociological Method*, p. 19; emphasis in original.

27 K.H. Wolff, "Phemomenology and Sociology," in T. Bottomore and R. Nisbet (eds), *A History of Sociological Analysis*, New York: Basic Books, 1978, p. 500.

28 Bernstein, *The Restructuring of Social and Political Theory*, p. 145.

reality for granted, thereby minimizing any chance of comprehending the transformative nature of social reality, the duality of structure which is "its ontological condition." Natural science is successful precisely because these background practices can be taken for granted and ignored.[29] Social science eliminates its very subject matter by doing so.

Phenomenology is most frequently criticized for the potential solipsism of its focus on subjectivity. This almost ritual denunciation is warranted most of all in Husserl's case. Relegating understanding to the private sphere of "intuition" misrepresents the necessarily intersubjective, therefore public and accessible aspect of meaningfulness. While recognizing as well the limitations of the phenomenological approach, we commend its attention to the centrality of intersubjective meanings as being "constitutive of the social matrix in which individuals find themselves and act."[30]

> Intentionality, in the phenomenological sense, is not thus to be treated as an expression of an ineffable inner world of private mental experiences, but as *necessarily* drawing upon the communicative categories of languages. . . . Understanding what one does is only made possible by understanding, that is, being able to describe what others do, and vice versa. It is a semantic matter, rather than a matter of empathy; and reflexivity, as the distinctive property of the human species, is intimately and integrally dependent on the social character of language.[31]

Here phenomenology converges with the revolution in analytic philosophy precipitated by frustrated efforts to provide logical positivism with a value neutral linguistic framework. Ludwig Wittgenstein took the first crucial step from a "picture theory" of words as representations to identifying words with their use, language with activity. To make sense, statements must be considered in context. In exploring language use, Wittgenstein concluded that knowing a "language game" is like knowing how to play chess: once the system of rules is mastered, an unlimited number of moves is available. The rules are like grammar. Underlying such language genes and all linguistic practices are what Wittgenstein calls "forms of life."[32]

Peter Winch took Wittgenstein's brief remarks on rule-governed language games and forms of life and applied them systematically to social action.[33]

29 H.L. Dreyfus, "Holism and Hermeneutics," *Review of Metaphysics*, vol. 34, 1980, p. 16.

30 C. Taylor, "Interpretation and the Sciences of Man," in Dallmayr and McCarthy, *Understanding and Social Inquiry*, p. 119.

31 Giddens, *New Rules of Sociological Method*, p. 20; emphasis in original.

32 L. Wittgenstein, *Philosophical Investigations*, 3rd edn trans. by G.E.M. Anscombe, New York: Macmillan, 1968, paras. 226, 338. On the impossibility of language or rules as the invention of an isolated individual act, see para. 202.

33 P. Winch, *The Idea of a Social Science and Its Relation to Philosophy*, London: Routledge & Kegan Paul, 1958.

Only by applying intersubjective criteria of consistency – that is, on the basis of rules, which presupposes a social setting – can we achieve access to what constitutes meaningful behavior. If meaningful behavior is that which is social and thus rule-governed, then the object of social inquiry must be investigation of rules and activities oriented to them. But these rules are not simply the causal relations sought in the natural sciences. The intersubjective reality of the social world is not comprised of "brute data" amenable to causal analysis but, as the preceding reveals, ever-changing language, social practices and institutions cohering in forms of life, or, following Giddens, frames of meaning. As is readily apparent, frames of meaning are similar to the phenomenologically derived conceptions of *Lebenswelt*, ground plan and paradigm.

We arrive then at an identification of frames of meaning as internally consistent, "rule-governed" linguistic and social practices endowing meaningfulness to individual actions. These in turn reconstitute the frame of meaning in an ongoing, dialectical process. This rendition of social reality – and therefore what's appropriate to the study of it – we believe represents significant advances over the received model. At the same time it fails in some literally critical ways.

While phenomenology and language philosophy after Wittgenstein have enriched our vision of the nature of social inquiry, they leave certain perennial problems unresolved – and raise some new ones. If the rules of frame of meaning do not resemble causal relations, how are we to analyze them? If frames of meaning represent internally consistent, coherent universes, how do we mediate between them? How are particular interpretive schemes selected? Which are retained? How do we incorporate changes in frames of meaning? What capabilities and competences are significant? How are asymmetries of personal and institutional power acknowledged?

The sense that recent language philosophy no less than phenomenology brings us this far – and leaves us here – is well taken. The analysis of ordinary language favored by British philosophers clarifies the way language, as used by individuals, performs actions the social character of which is taken for granted. Emphasis on the internal consistency of given forms of life, as in Winch's case, effectively denies the inevitable tension and potential inherent in contact between forms of life. Lacking historical perspective and unable to deal with change, language philosophy offers no insight into the question of power or how different interpretive schemes are selected and retained. Positing discrete frames of meaning or forms of life makes the problem of mediation or evaluation between them insuperable.

But the problem is misstated: "we must substitute as a *starting point*, that *all paradigms* (read 'language-games', etc.) *are mediated by others*."[34] Or, even more accurately, there is *no* "starting point." To proceed from here requires taking the implications of intersubjective meaning seriously: acknowledging

34 Giddens, *New Rules of Sociological Method*, p. 144; his emphasis.

the universality of an interpretive approach, which not only permits but necessitates the incorporation of change and "translation" between frames of meaning. It incorporates change in a process occurring over time because "the dialectical confrontation of what is one's own with what is foreign leads, for the most part imperceptibly, to revisions. Translation [interpretation] is the medium in which these revisions take place, and language [intersubjective understanding] is continuously developed further." Translation between frames of meaning occurs as the background knowledgeability of agents permits us to bridge "disturbances of communication, respond to new situations, assimilate what is foreign and find a common language for diverging tongues."[35]

The rules for translating frames of meaning are not to be analyzed as parallel to grammar (which is still "precise and unequivocal") but as subject to the duality of structure that permits a reconstitution of the rules as context. Wittgenstein's and Winch's rules, envisaged as grammar, assume conformity as unproblematic. In practice, the exercise of judgment and diverging interpretations of rules reflect a dialectical, negotiated process.

> Only dialogue-free [formal] languages have a complete order. Ordinary languages are incomplete and provide no guarantee of the absence of ambiguity. . . . Whoever starts from the normal case of conversation – and not from the model of a [formal] language – immediately grasps the open structure of ordinary language.[36]

If all frames of meaning are mediated by others, presumably the choice of interpretive schemes and their differential retention will reflect prior context and current options. Results will be explicable *ex post facto* but, as with all open systems, not predictable. The conversation metaphor captures this: "always open-ended, contingent, loaded with alternative directions and possibilities. Here is the locus of human agency, capacity and possibility."[37]

We have yet to address the question of power. To do so requires us to emphasize again the contextual nature of social reality. "Resources are drawn upon by actors in the production of interaction, but are constituted as structures of domination. Resources are the media whereby power is employed in the routine course of social action; but they are at the same time structural elements of social systems, reconstituted in social interaction. Social systems are constituted as regularized practices, practices reproduced across time and space."[38]

35 J. Habermas, "A Review of Gadamer's *Truth and Method*," in Dallmayr and.McCarthy, *Understanding and Social Inquiry*, p. 339.

36 Ibid., p. 341.

37 A. Dawe, "Theories of Social Action," in Bottomore and Nisbet, *A History of Sociological Analysis*, p. 411.

38 Giddens, *Profiles and Critiques in Social Theory*, pp. 38–9.

Viewing language as social practice presupposes that holding up the "linguistic mirror" can reveal power relations as reflected in language use. British language philosophers limited their attention to the semantic dimension of "use," avoiding the pragmatic, interest-laden dimension: how speakers use language to "achieve their individual purposes."[39] To look at these pragmatic relationships we turn explicitly to discourse – spoken or written linguistic usage.

Paul Ricoeur has identified four traits differentiating discourse from language: (1) discourse is realized temporally and in a present (language is outside of time); (2) discourse refers back to its speaker (language lacks a subject); (3) discourse is always about something (the symbolic function of language is actualized); (4) in discourse messages are exchanged, an addressee is assumed (language is only the condition for communication).[40] All discourse is ultimately figurative, even if the figurative origins of apparently literal statements are lost to memory. We owe the rediscovery of rhetoric – figurative language – and its connection to discourse as language in use chiefly to contemporary French scholars.

Foucault has, perhaps more than anyone else, probed the significance of discursive practices. In several books analyzing the discursive practices of various disciplines, Foucault concluded that the apparent unity of a discipline is illusory. Named things do not confer obvious boundaries on a discipline. Thus a static definition of *health*, for example, is not a unifying concept in medical discourse. What counts as health and how and by whom it is maintained vary within a framework of social, economic and political relationships.

"Embedded in everyday discourse are affirmations of a system of authority, that is, acceptance of various allocations of control as legitimate."[41] Questioning the implicit mode of authority in all discourse – uncovering who is privileged – reveals social control processes normally hidden.[42] By enshrining privilege discourse must also reveal it, as when we choose to reflect on the customs of our speech. Custom is discursive evidence of privilege in the implicit mode.

39 Shapiro, *Language and Political Understanding*, pp. 60–1, 29–30.

40 P. Ricoeur, "The Model of the Text: Meaningful Action Considered as a Text," in Dallmayr and McCarthy, *Understanding and Social Inquiry*, p. 317.

41 Shapiro, *Language and Political Understanding*, p. 63.

42 Language as social control has been considered from a variety of perspectives: C.W. Mills, "Language, Logic and Culture," *American Sociological Review*, vol. 4. 1939, p. 677; T.B. Strong, " 'Hold on to Your Brains,' An Essay in Meta-Theory," in P. Green and S. Levinson (eds), *Power and Community: Dissenting Essays in Political Science*, New York: Pantheon, 1969, pp. 335–8; P. Bourdieu, *Outline of a Theory of Practice*, trans. by R. Nice, Cambridge: Cambridge University Press, 1977, pp. 27, 169–70; Habermas, "A Review of Gadamer's *Truth and Method*," p. 360.

Discourse on rules, rules of discourse

The preceding discussion has clear implications for any discourse about rules whose indeterminate origin secures for them the label *customary*. There are no "pristine" rules, which are rules that define the social situation *ab initio*.[43] All rules are the product of a social situation itself defined by rules. This social situation is one specifically constituted by such rules and the discourse they bring about. Thus rules and discourse must be seen as interactive, separable only analytically. To speak about rules *in vacuo*, as is the custom, captures only part of our ruled social reality, and, arguably, just the epiphenomenal part. To address discourse about rules without identifying the rules engendering that discourse might also be an incomplete account of the ruled reality of the social situation, but at least it is a refreshing alternative to the usual preoccupation with rules *per se*. And it very well may be closer to the heart of that ruled reality, to resort to a metaphor that conveys a sense of the rules-discourse relationship as a circulatory system. A fully adequate account of rule-informed social reality would see rules, though accorded independent status in most discourse, as focal points in certain characteristic types of discourse – discourse that we believe revolves around activities fundamental to intersubjectively meaningful human arrangements, or, to put the matter rather more conventionally, objectively necessary for social order.

In our earlier work together, which was cast in the conventional, objectivist language of the problem and requirements of social order, we identified three fundamental types of rule-generating activities. "Rules provide guidance respectively [as] to what things (including people) are called and how they are related; to who owns or has use of things; and to whose will or wishes prevail."[44] The distinctive kinds of rules produced by these activities we then chose to call *norms, rights* and *commands*, and now prefer to call *instruction-rules*, *commitment-rules* and *directive-rules*. (See Chapter 14, below, on the source and significance of these terms.) The first designates position through naming, the second allocates ownership or use, the third conveys imperative wishes. In this work we identify the characteristic discursive activities accompanying these objective activities and correlative rule categories.

This endeavor allows the identification of rules *as if* they were independent of the discourse in which they are situated, but does not require or even recommend doing so except provisionally. To speak of a directive-rule, for example, in such a way as to suggest that it gives rise to discourse (or, as is more often said, behavior) is to mislead unduly. Of course it does and, of course, discourse gives rise to the rule. But, more subtly, the directive-rule is a

43 The term *pristine* is flavored by M.H. Fried's concept of long-vanished pristine states. *The Evolution of Political Society: An Essay in Political Anthropology*, New York: Random House, 1967, pp. 231–5. While such societies may have fixed historical origins, they are necessarily the product of a ruled social setting that can never be pristine.

44 Onuf and Peterson, "Human Rights from an International Regimes Perspective," p. 330.

rule of this kind only to the extent that its discursive context makes its status as a directive-rule plausible. A directive-rule is directive in kind only insofar as its audiences respond to it in the discursive mode properly belonging to that kind of rule.

Discursive activities associated with naming and instruction-rules we have elected to call the realm of significations, those associated with possession and commitment-rules, we call the realm of implications, and those with control and issuing directives, justifications. Turning to significations first, we mean by this term all those activities in which something, real or imagined, tangibly specific or ineffably abstract, is said to stand for some other thing, more, less or equally real or specific. A vast range of human discourse is given to signification, by no means all of it having an abiding impact on rules and social arrangements.

Thus at one extreme is the deliberately induced free association of psychology – here the idea is to break the prison of received, ruled significations. Much significatory activity occupies a middle ground of plausible and recurrent associations and differentiations that people invent and reinvent unselfconsciously. Some of these significations become embedded in daily discourse, and people learn them by exposure rather than reinvent them. Such significations would seem to be taking the "path" leading to customary rules (to use a metaphor so often applied to the processes described above). And the accumulated weight of significatory activities would seem to be the constitutive element in all intersubjective meaning. In this sense, as is so often asserted about custom, there is no known or knowable source of a particular complex of embedded associations and differentiations – say, signifying kin statuses – and commentators signify it as representing the community's will or reflecting its accumulated wisdom or experience. Notice that such a chain of associations undercuts the possibility of seeing the particular, embedded complex of significations (customary rule) as privileging some members of or some activities in the community over others.

At the other extreme of significatory activities are those associations and differentiations accorded weight or seen as of the moment from their first utterance. This of course comes from the status of the person making such a signification, which gives it significance, or from circumstances surrounding its initial statement. In either instance (they are usually conjoined), ensconced significations "center" newly formed ones. In other words, custom will have institutionalized a privileged position for some person or persons, acting under certain circumstances, to make momentous significations, which then short-circuit the usual path to ruleness. This, we saw above, gives rise to the customary distinction between custom and customary law, the latter having a particular origin which therefore can be seen as privileging those originating it. Our position should now be clear: all customs so-called are customary rules having a distinct origin, which reflects a privileging move in the original signification. Furthermore, the embedding of that signification through repetition no less and no differently than a formal centering enunciation, continues to reflect a privileging effect. Otherwise the signification itself would change through the discursive activities surrounding it over time. Such changes would also reflect a privileging effect, which however is no longer the same one originally operating.

The more firmly established the rule, by whatever means, the more certainly it effectuates the differentiation of privileges by altering the very fabric of intersubjective meaning. Having the privilege to make and alter symbols is the deepest, most pervasive, yet least acknowledged form and means of domination human beings have available for use over other human beings. That the history of particular symbols is lost and the advantages they bring not immediately traceable to particular interests only adds to their value in fostering social arrangements that work to benefit some over others. Social order may seem to arise out of the needs of the whole community; the choice of words intends to signify as much. Social arrangements are arranged; this we intend our choice of words to signify.

Turning next to discursive activities associated with having and using and the assertion of rights – discourse about the implications of having or using things others claim to have need of or right to – we notice immediately that the range of this discourse is narrower than its discourse over significations. But, relatively speaking, a much larger share of this discourse is germane to the constitution of social arrangements. Drawing implications and challenging those drawn by others are sufficiently self-conscious activities that it is easier to trace the genealogies of particular assertions and counter-assertions and, more importantly, to establish the pattern of privilege that accords with a history of adjusting and disposing of competing claims to having or using the same or similar things. The locus of choice between claims in such situations – institutionalized as dispute settlement – is also relatively easy to find, as is the effect on privilege of having the privilege of choosing between others' claims.

Although the proximate source of particular rights – acknowledged claims – is discernible, the choice conferring rightness on a particular claim tends to be seen as determined: the third party chooser "finds" the right answer to the problem as presented. Particular rights established in practice or precedent are derived from (implied by) some principle (signification) invoked by or imposed on those making choices, such as that a particular set of choices about who has rights to what reflects, for example, the natural harmony of things. Particular rights may in this conception be the product of choice bespeaking a pattern of privilege, but they are warranted, like customs whose origins are lost in time, by some larger, fictionalized social reality not captured by particular interests.

This particular rationalization of the privileging property of rules, some version of which may nevertheless be necessary to have working social arrangements, is sufficiently obvious to have come to attention some time ago in jurisprudence. The primacy of rules and social reasoning by reference to implications in Anglo-American life particularly makes most of us especially sensitive to claims made on behalf of particular interests and at the same time for the good of the order. Here the order is not just passive and disinterested, but indeed the template through which a fair distribution of rights can be, and, though imperfectly but progressively is, extruded.

That some of us acknowledge this proposed congruence of the particular and the general, and some of us do not, spells out the basic terms of such ideological conflict in the world today. Again, our position is clear: the pattern of choices among competing claims should be understood as privileging some choices, and thus some people, over others. Those who are so privileged define the pattern of choices as just and necessary not only or even principally in the discourse over implications, but in the discourse on significations. They can participate in the latter to advantage because of the advantages already accrued in the discourse over implications.

The last realm of discursive activities we turn to is associated with making it possible for people to get their way as against others by issuing directive-rules. We call this the realm of justifications because such endeavors – giving oneself or some designate the means to act or prevent others from acting – are normally accompanied by justifications, that is, grounds offered in the instance of issuing or responding to a directive. When, as is usually the case, force is involved or implied, its use or availability is also held out as warranted. The range of justifications, like significations, runs from the impromptu (I'm doing this for your, or my or everybody's good) to the institutionalized (Exercising the power invested in this office by God, history or the people, . . .). Impromptu justifications tend not to have a permanent effect on social arrangements. When they become patterned, just as with significations and implications, they "grow," like custom, into privileged institutions, which in turn tend to be cloaked in the mantle of justifications depending on the association of individual privileges and the good of the order.

Thus we explain the asymmetry in justificatory discourse. Those issuing directive-rules tend to find their justifications go unchallenged, while those directed find their justifications for not doing as directed unconvincing and ineffectual. The result is a second order rule – quite possibly a customary rule arising from the pattern of directive-rules and responses to them – authorizing the director to issue directive-rules of that sort. The consequence of this situation is that the justifications of those issuing directives and those receiving them are usually complementary in their effects, but asymmetrical in their individual potency. It is a commonplace, however, that the individual efficacy of the director's justifications for acting can be overwhelmed if the *collective* response is to deny validity to that justification. It is for this reason that governments fall and revolutions occur.

The consequences for privilege of a particular pattern of justifications are perhaps the easiest of all discursive activities to diagnose. Normally, those whose position enables them to issue directives, which others find difficult to justify not giving force to, find their position allows them to bestow great privilege on themselves, their favorites and their benefactors. Because of the obvious connection between their power and their and others' privilege, they are vulnerable, as we have seen, to a rising tide of disgust justifying their removal. Only when they disguise their privileged position by manipulating symbols and altering rights does it become difficult to identify the exploitive possibilities in their dominant position.

The point of constitutional government and the separation of powers is precisely to prevent those with the advantages of justification from redefining significations and implications to their additional advantage. Thus we can see institutionalization of discursive realms of significations, implications and justifications in the legislative, judicial and executive branches, respectively. Fears about the potential for undue dominance by some over others in one such discursive realm requires that the powers of each be publicly specified. That these three realms may be substantially congruent in those whom they privilege is the larger danger, and the constitutional response has been the doctrine of the separation of powers.

International relations discourse

Does the identification and delimitation of discursive realms help with some of the ambiguities and inadequacies in the customary analysis of customary rules that we earlier uncovered? Of course we think so, and we propose to show how by looking briefly at the body of rules informing contemporary international relations and conventionally described as customary international law. We have already observed that these rules are once institutionalized, to recur to Bohannan's language, which means that they define the social arrangements constituting the reality of international relations without having been "specifically recreated by agents of society, . . . in the context of institutions that are legal in character and, to some degree at least, discrete from all others." Customary rules *seem* to be doubly institutionalized, and thus law properly called, because lawyers and legal scholars, often with official roles, busy themselves rendering these rules in an ordered, written form that resembles law (see Chapter 6, above).

Such activities "recreate" rules, without – custom decrees against the evidence – markedly changing their content. Nor does this make them legal directive-rules, because – we are forever told – no agents are authorized to issue such rules. Hence the anomalous character of international law: custom that has left the realm of the customary, law that is not legal. The paradox is compounded by treaties that do seem to create law in their own right, for they are not analogous to contracts, but their constitutive authority derives from a customary rule of (non)law.

We can make some sense of this paradox, if not dispel it, by returning a last time to our earlier work. There we proposed that rules of *all* three categories can be institutionalized in legal form. Yet because of their differences in kind, they will not all result in laws as formalized directives-rules.

> Rules that function by naming and positioning may be called *principles* when they take a legal form. The formal statement of principles gives them weight and thus importance in the rule set. Knowing that some [instruction-rules] are weightier than others simplifies the task of responding to the requirements of an ever larger rule set. Rules that function by allocating function or use [that is, commitment-rules] give rise to formal acknowledgment of the pattern of allocation in the form of *regulations*, that is, rights are regularized in legal form. This simplifies the task of pressing particular claims. Rules that function by the imposition of will are more likely to be seen as disinterested when expressed formally and abstractly as *laws*. They permit respondents the illusion that instead of having to obey arbitrary [directive-rules], they follow laws because everyone does. A system of laws simplifies learning and lessens the costs of enforcement by equating compliance with law in general.[45]

Evidently the social arrangements of international relations deny the possibility of laws, as defined, but not of principles and regulations, which indeed are abundantly available. Treaties embody and convey regulations and, in their preambular and hortatory language, also articulate principles. There are other vehicles for principled statement, including summit manifestoes, World Court judgments and resolutions of plenary international bodies.

What always needs remembering is that those persons who are duly authorized to formalize instruction-rules into principles and rights into regulations are almost invariably executive agents acting for institutionalized power-laden interests (usually states, generally styled actors). These same agents are the principal authors of customary rules as byproducts of goal-oriented activities in environments of mixed cooperation and conflict. Knowing that other such agents are endeavoring to secure or retain advantages for institutionalized interests they represent, and that the possibility of succeeding by arbitrary command is remote at best, executive agents realize they cannot operate in paradigmatic fashion by issuing rules (much less by promulgating laws) that would enable them to fulfill their objectives. Instead they must take actions which they justify as at least not inconsistent with existing rules and which they know may contribute to a rule authorizing them to act – depending on the response of other actors.

All actors are thus faced with a situation in which they can issue directive-rules that are authorized as such within the institutions they act on behalf of, with the consequence of marshaling resources for the actualizing of a stated objective, *but* which are not directives for other such agents and the institutions they represent. Those others may nevertheless respond as if such directives are appropriate by acknowledging the justifications proffered and issuing supporting or similar directives with comparable justifications. (An

45 Onuf and Peterson, "Human Rights from an International Regimes Perspective," p. 332; emphases in original, footnotes and parenthetical material deleted.

example of this reasonably rare phenomenon is the 1945 Truman Proclamation extending adjacent state jurisdiction to the continental shelf.) Or unilateral directives as rule-candidates and accompanying justifications may be greeted as inappropriate and rebutted. Most likely is a confused pattern of acceptance, rejection, qualification and indifference, which leaves the content and status of any putative rule uncertain.

What we see instead is an aura of justifications such as would normally accompany the response to a directive-rule, but no clearly identifiable rule. To help with this confusing situation, executive agents use lawyers to tell them what rules coming out of past activities might apply in particular situations, how various actions will be regarded, and what justifications work best. *Dedoublement fonctionnel* is better understood in this light. Aided by their legal advisers, executive agents issue directive-rules and accompanying justifications to those for whom they are agents. These highly limited rules simultaneously qualify as rule-candidates affecting all agents depending on their reception. This in turn is largely a matter of discourse over justifications. Directive-rules with the best chance of success as rule-candidates in the larger setting are those that accommodate the interests of others and are couched in the language of community interests.

Note that justifications for unilateral action tend to work best (generate least resistance and thereby lower costs of achieving objectives) when they are cast as momentous significations. Persuading others that one's rule-candidate is warranted because it embodies an important principle is to switch the terms of discourse from what is justified by reference to what a rule says to discourse about what acceptance of the rule would signify. Thus rule announcing agents conflate proto-legislative and proto-executive functions – the deeper meaning of *dedoublement fonctionnel* – in activities that cloak would-be directives in favorable significations. The clearest illustration of this move is undoubtedly the interventions of the United States in the Dominican Republic in 1965 and the Soviet Union in Czechoslovakia in 1968. Justification was "upgraded" to signification by associating intervention respectively with the need to protect democracy and socialism.

Continuing discursive resistance to this pair of self-serving moves to the realm of significations does not defeat the rule enabling discretionary superpower intervention because of the exceptional capabilities of the two actors issuing it within their spheres of influence. Yet these actors have not been able to disguise the rule's privileging impact. Progressive writers tend to treat *dedoublement fonctionnel* as an indispensable mechanism for securing community interests in an institutionally multicentric social arrangement. We would point out that it also is a means of endowing privileged interests with community respectability. Indeed, to say one is to say the other.

Executive agents and their legal advisers are not the only participants in the significatory realm of international relations discourse. Writers and public speakers of all species contribute to the normative climate within which executive activities are justified. A current illustration is the debate over the nuclear weapons build-up. All these suffuse activities generate instructions through what may be broadly described as custom. Certain forums, such as the UN General Assembly, the 1982 Convention on the Law of the Sea (UNCLOS III) and the World Court in its elaborate opinions, locate nodes of heightened significatory discourse, which we may associate with the production of principles.

The General Assembly expressly views itself as the voice of the world community. Its resolutions – especially those designated declarations – deliberately seek to alter and ramify the symbolic structure of community discourse. Indisputably its products are principles. Much the same can be said for those international conferences charged with interpreting the meaning of General Assembly principles like the seas as common heritage and space for peaceful uses. When such conferences move as directed from the significatory realm to the formulation of community-warranted regulations, which (as a matter of double institutionalization) spell out the allocation of rights, their progress is arduously slow. Not only do no *particular* rules derive from significations (they cannot), but particular interests and their privileging are directly at stake in formalizing rights into regulations. When conflicts over privilege block agreement on doubly institutionalized rules (laws) – something rarely even attempted – justifications for obstructive acts may well revert to the level of significations: Witness excuses offered by the US for rejecting UNCLOS III because of its supranational provisions.[46]

The World Court's ostensible function is dispute settlement. For reasons all too well known, it receives precious few disputes, but it has turned this unpromising situation to its advantage by using those occasions for judgment – which is properly the realm of implications – to make important statements about significations. (See Chapter 6, above.) To identify the chains of associations and differentiations which signify meaning in international relations in order to evaluate the implications parties to a dispute draw as to their respective rights suggests that judgment is not just a matter of "finding" the right answer but indeed of finding the right context in which to formulate the questions – Whose rights and who's right?

We are reminded of the peculiar quality of customary rules that their general form is unaffected by their specific application and, furthermore, that the connection between the general rule and the specific application is radically indeterminate. The World Court's activities fill this picture out. Specific applications, any one of which is defensible in its own narrow terms (specifying which among possible implications will be approved), are not just disconnected from the realm of significations in the sense that the former cannot be derived from the latter. The contained activity of drawing implications may proceed in the container significations provide, or they may be used to reshape the container. The presumed causal relation of implication

46 J.L. Malone, "Who Needs the Sea Treaty?" *Foreign Policy*, No. 54. 1984, pp. 44–6.

and signification is reversed. Implications can be chosen deliberately to affect received significations, even though the usual trick is to rationalize such choices as required by signification if properly interpreted (meaning: if recast by reference to an allegedly necessary derivation).

Executive agents tend to disguise their propensity to issue directive-rules, not just in the language of signification, as we have seen, but in the language of implication, as when they make claims and counterclaims based on conceptions of what they have right to. They go to the World Court too infrequently for the Court very often to turn the matter about by translating its assessment of rival claims into new sets of significations. But other forums locate discourse over implications, including the Security Council. (See Chapters 7 and 9, above.) In this instance an organ with executive powers it cannot fulfill hears debates on who is entitled to what, which is a proto-judicial function, conducted by executive officers who are using this forum to play out their quest for directives they can issue and others will acknowledge. The forum may occasionally respond to justifications disguised as implications by asserting an important signification. The Security Council's legendary Resolution 242 is an example.

Obviously customary rules of all sorts, and discursive activities mixed and matched to rules present a dismayingly complex picture of the social arrangements called international relations. These arrangements are reasonably clear only from the point of view of the most abstract significations (states are sovereign) and the most specifically focused acts of authorized agents. Everything in-between appears to be massively confused. While confirming the complexity of the arrangements, our explication suggests that confusion is not so much a feature of the situation as a failure to assess it fully from a rules-discourse perspective. It further proposes that such confusion arises from the propensity of those operating these arrangements to disguise their rule-oriented activities (perhaps not consciously) by switching or merging the kinds of discourse characteristically associated with such activities.

Finally, we believe that this rampant confusion making is not incidental. It serves not just the interests of particular participants to confuse other participants as to what they are doing; it serves all such participants to confuse everyone else not participating about what is going on. They are assigning privileges for and among themselves and those to whom they are personally, professionally and institutionally indebted. They profit from operating social arrangements that have fixed routines for naming, allocating and controlling, which they manipulate to protect themselves from discovery. Only the vicissitudes of rule need frighten them.

14 Do rules say what they do? From ordinary language to international law (1985)

While the postpositivist movement had affected me in many ways, my interest in rules was restored, even strengthened, by following Ludwig Wittgenstein into the "linguistic turn" (a turn of phrase Richard Rorty popularized). I soon discovered J.L. Austin's *How To Do Things with Words* (1962) and speech act theory. While many postpositivist scholars focused on discourse and the power of persuasive speech (as Spike Peterson and I had in Chapter 13, above), I saw that Austin's claims about what we *do* when we speak – what we intend our utterances to accomplish – corresponded to my sense of what we *make* and *use* rules for.

When the editors of the *Harvard International Law Journal* asked me to contribute to a special issue on new directions in theory, I took the opportunity to revisit two closely related questions that had long attracted my interest: are there different kinds of rules, including legal rules, and, if so, what makes them different (see, for example, Chapters 6 and 7 above)? The answer, I knew, was unavoidably connected to the social functions of normative phenomena, however troublesome the available conceptual language. When we do what we do with words and rules, *function* is what observers see. If speech acts have social and thus normative effects, different kinds of speech acts should parallel different kinds of rules in their functional implications. I identified three categories of speech acts that seemed fundamental to me, and derived corresponding categories of rules. I thought then that I had worked out an important set of functional relations linking agents and society; I still do. The article is difficult; its impact was minimal. Revised as a key chapter in my book *World of Our Making* (1989), it garnered more attention; here I have edited some passages to make "things" clearer.

Most of us inhabit a positivist world. More particularly, we are likely to make use of a legal positivist worldview in the spirit of the great utilitarians Jeremy Bentham, James Mill, and John Austin. The utilitarian tradition takes positive law to have a consistent and immediately identifiable linguistic form, that of a command or imperative statement.[1] For utilitarian positivism, rules

1 J. Bentham, *An Introduction to the Principles of Morals and Legislation*, 1823 edn, New York: Hafner Press, 1948, pp. 330–6.

always say what they do: they require behavior indicated in the content of an imperative statement. Such rules transparently convey the wishes of those who issue them.

However, not all imperative statements are rules of law, or even rules of any sort. "Bring me a glass of milk" is an imperative statement, perhaps honored as a rule, but certainly only on a case-by-case basis. Austin identified several species of command and restricted his attention to those having general applicability.[2] Only these raise the important question of whether there exists a standing obligation to honor them independent of utilitarian calculations in each instance. The general position of utilitarian positivists is that there is such an obligation for at least some rules and, to the extent that obligation is positive and real, those rules are legal.

In international law, few rules meet the positivist threshold of legality – or so Austin thought. Despite this, there is a sense that the international order is legal. What is needed is a better philosophical ground to justify this view. After discussing some of the problems associated with past efforts to provide such a foundation, I will argue that the legality of the international order can be anchored in contemporary philosophy of language. Specifically, I will use speech act theory to establish a scheme for the classification of rules, and then use this scheme to show that the international order is a legal order.

Legal positivism

Legal positivism contains two basic flaws. The first arises from asking what the basis for a specifically legal obligation is. The usual answer goes beyond the rule and what it says, to what is interchangeably called the legal order or the legal system. The legal positivists take the existence of the legal order to explain both the obligation attaching to that rule and the propensity for utilitarian calculators to honor it. This order has two defining properties: the competence to issue legal rules and the capacity to secure compliance with them. Inasmuch as I may well have the capacity to ensure that you will bring me a glass of milk if I demand it, the distinctive property of a legal order cannot be the ability to secure compliance. It must be the competence to issue rules.

Here the problem arises. If an order is legal, it must be so because the rules constituting it are legal. Yet such rules can only be legal if a prior legal order produces them. The result is an infinite regress unless we postulate a primary

2 But he improperly concluded that all such commands issue from a determinate lawgiver or sovereign. See J. Austin, *Lectures on Jurisprudence; or, the Philosophy of Positive Law*, 5th edn, London: Murray, 1885, pp. 88–9, and *The Province of Jurisprudence Determined, and The Uses of the Study of Jurisprudence*, 1832, 1863 edns, ed. by H.L.A. Hart, London: Weidenfeld and Nicolson, 1954, p. 133. See, also, Hart's reconstruction of Austin's position in *The Concept of Law*, Oxford: Clarendon, 1961, pp. 18–76.

agreement or learning process in a state of nature. Alternatively we may argue that ultimately the legal character of the rule comes from the fact that it is obeyed; compliance precedes and causes obligation. But this substitutes circularity for regress: that rules work makes them law, that rules are legal makes them work. This closed circle limits law to a hard core of rules without providing criteria for determining what that core is. This circle of positivist reasoning substitutes for any real theory of rule and compliance.

The second problem with legal positivism stems from the fact that the pursuit of legal facts and the postulations of legal theory are apparently unrelated in legal craft. Modern science is also positivist. Strictly separating "objective" facts from "subjective" values, scientific positivism advocates a unified, methodical approach to the facts of the world and explicit theorizing as mutually supportive activities (see, further, Chapter 28, below). Influenced by scientific positivism, legal positivists assume that specifications of the theory, by explaining what rules in stipulated settings are legal, exhaustively define the theory's relation to the fact of rule compliance. Legal positivists overlook what that theory does before it is put to such specific use. It determines whether a given setting is properly a legal one, which in turn limits inquiry to a particular set of rules. Counted out are rules that seem to be law, but are not obeyed. Also excluded are rules that cannot be traced to any such legal authority but are obeyed.

Most legal positivists deal with this second problem by ignoring it, which they can afford to do so long as they stick to the hard core of law as they see it. Scholars of international law, where there is not even the same minimal agreement over a hard core, cannot avail themselves of the luxury of ignorance without making critical mistakes. But to solve the problem and spare their theory means a return to the regressive reasoning of searching for a recognizable authorizing voice. The alternative is to change the theory.

Legal positivism has encountered this suggestion before. Sociological jurisprudence and legal realism can be interpreted as efforts to broaden the theoretical domain of positive law without abandoning the notion that law can be treated as a distinctive phenomenon. Both show, in their formulation and development, the considerable influence of scientific positivism's claim to portray objective reality. But legal positivists have resisted these efforts. They fear that saving legal positivism from circularity or regress will strip it of anything distinctively legal.

International legal theory of the last three decades has been especially marked by the sway of scientific positivism in the social sciences. Scholars, disproportionately from the US, have borrowed freely from the models and techniques of sociology, anthropology, and political science in hopes of finding an explanation for the order in decentralized social arrangements such as international relations. By definition, the standard positivist model of law as the sovereign's sanction-bearing command is unacceptable. Little better is the working premise that a hard core of international law exists.

At the extreme, those drawing on the social sciences have been content to establish regularities in international behavior and explain them by reference to "psychological pressures."[3] Obligation disappears as an inconvenient concept or is transmuted into "shared expectations" and "community policies."[4] A less extreme view finds different types of rules performing different functions for their users and, in a logical leap, for the "system" as a surviving, ordered entity.[5] Inasmuch as all rules are seen as taking the same general form, independent of their function, recourse to particular rules tells nothing about their particular functions. It seems that rules do not say what they do. Only the observer can say, and observers have no agreed method for sorting out the functional or systemic meaning of what they see.

Functionalists are inclined to retain the positivist notion of law as command by seeing its function as that of coercion, and then to group all other functional possibilities for law into a single, loosely defined category: the communication function.[6] Thus the standard functional model is a legal system with two types of rules: rules either control behavior or communicate intentions and perceptions. Rules in the latter category are at the edge of law, but they, like coercive laws, serve functions imperative for the system's survival.

These communicative rules may only be imperative for the system and they may seem indeterminate as to the obligation they impose on individuals. Such indeterminacy may even spill over into the hard core of rules imperative for participants. This is because a legal system is unlikely to fail simply because any given participant ignores a command and coercive instrumentalities are not available. Indeed, in the international arena, enforcement is often an illusion, though perhaps a necessary one.

A high point for such scientific positivism in international legal theory came in 1974 when Gidon Gottlieb used these two functional categories of rules to construct two separate models for legal systems.[7] Gottlieb restored coercive rules to their historical position as the focus of a traditional model of law and developed a second model of law built on the notion that rules can have a communicative function. The *acceptance model*, as he called the latter,

3 Quoting F. Kratochwil's critical assessment. "Thrasymmachus Revisited: On the Relevance of Norms for International Relations," *Journal of International Affairs*, vol. 37, 1984, p. 350.

4 See M.S. McDougal and W.M. Reisman (eds), *International Law Essays: A Supplement to International Law in Contemporary Perspective*, Mineola, NY: Foundation Press, 1981.

5 R.A. Falk, "The Relevance of Political Context to the Nature and Functioning of International Law: An Intermediate View," in K. Deutsch and S. Hoffmann (eds), *The Relevance of International Law*, Garden City, NY: Doubleday, 1968, pp. 177–202.

6 W.D. Coplin, "International Law and Assumptions about the State System," *World Politics*, vol. 17, 1965, pp. 615–34.

7 G. Gottlieb, "The Nature of International Law: Toward a Second Concept of Law," in R.A. Falk and C.E. Black (eds), *The Future of the International Legal Order*, vol. 4, Princeton: Princeton University Press, 1974, pp. 362–74.

is not just a characterization of the functions of some rules (especially those of doubtful legality). It is also a characterization of the function of *all* legal rules: to secure acceptance of their content.

By comparison, policies may also be designed to secure acceptance, but they achieve this goal by suggesting the likelihood of coercion. Unlike the unalloyed coercion of policy, acceptance-based rules require a "willingness to limit one's discretion" and so imply a principled content.[8] Legal rules, then, become those policies that are both principled enough to secure willing acceptance and specific enough to provide guidance. In this view, rules do not have to say what they do. Their specific, principled content communicates plausible expectations that they will be complied with.

For Gottlieb, neither hierarchical command nor legal obligation causes compliance. Instead, it comes from "the resolve to make principled and consistent decisions wherever possible" – a disposition that depends on "procedures of reasoning" and the "logic of choice," and not the prospect of enforcement or even the presumption of lawfulness. Yet Gottlieb's model also has limitations. Legal reasoning is only possible when rules provide "a 'marked degree' of firmness of guidance," in turn requiring "specificity of language." Gottlieb fails to say how specific the rules need to be. Indeed, he makes a virtue of not being able to do so: "Here again there looms a vast undemarcated terrain between the legal and the political – but the more specific the guidance in a system becomes, the more specific the norms, the policy goals and their application, the more 'legal' this system becomes."[9]

Gottlieb's much-cited essay helps make functional categories intelligible in the language of law. His effort to replace a command model with an acceptance model also gives a theoretical warrant to the notion that "soft" rules can be law, even if these rules cannot be shown to have become legal through a specific validating or "legalizing" process. In both the functionalist view and Gottlieb's reformulation, legal indeterminacy is a characteristic of the system. This indeterminacy permeates those situations where rules are always relevant but rarely determinative.

Given the extraordinary growth of international agreements and practices of uncertain legal standing, especially in international economic relations, lawyers have happily embraced the notion of soft law.[10] Yet legal positivists have responded with sharp hostility by arguing that legal indeterminacy

8 Ibid., p. 369.

9 Ibid., pp. 371–6. "Logic of choice" is also the title of Gottlieb's book presenting more systematically his deeper theory. *The Logic of Choice: An Inquiry into the Logic of Judicial Argument*, New York: Macmillan, 1968.

10 See, for example, D. Carreau *et al., Droit international économique*, Paris: Librairie générale de droit et de jurisprudence, 1977; Ignaz Seidl-Hohenvelden, "International Economic 'Soft Law,' " *Recueil des cours de L'Académie de droit international de La Haye*, vol. 163, 1979/II, pp. 165–246.

cannot be reconciled with their theory of obligation.[11] Needless to say, Gottlieb had intended this very conclusion, which represented the culmination of scientific positivist reasoning about international law. The result has been a stalemate. Legal positivists insist in theory on a narrow conception of law and its function, but slip into a broader notion in the practice of law. For their part, scientific positivists insist in theory on a broader view of the rules that matter, but fail to explain which rules really matter for the order.

Indeterminacy

The vogue for scientific positivism in international legal studies has clearly passed in the last few years, and not necessarily for the inadequacies just noted or indeed because functionalist arguments make strict scientific positivists uneasy. Throughout the social sciences, the scientific positivist project has faltered for lack of definite progress in answering a host of difficult questions. Meanwhile, doubts about its philosophical premises have come to the fore.[12] In a curiously parallel development, the re-emergence of naturalist ideas in the form of rights thinking has had much of the same effect on legal positivism – an effect scientific positivism was never able to achieve.[13]

Even a cursory search of the current literature leaves the impression that international legal theory is without direction in its perennial task of offering grounds for knowing when rules are legal and when they are not. The current impasse has its cause in the failure of scientific positivism to provide itself with an adequate philosophical grounding. If some alternative is to be devised today, in the backwash of positivism, it must deliberately honor postpositivist premises. The alternative I wish to suggest is drawn from modern philosophy, especially the philosophy of language.

Twentieth-century philosophy of language was revolutionized by the work of Ludwig Wittgenstein. In his early work, Wittgenstein endorsed the then prevailing view that language represents reality; words have meaning as representative of simple objects, and sentences, built on words, represent relationships between objects.[14] In his later writings, Wittgenstein rejected this

11 M. Bothe, "Legal and Non-Legal Norms – A Meaningful Distinction in International Relations," *Netherlands Year Book of International Law*, vol. 11, 1980, pp. 65–95; P. Weil, "Towards Relative Normativity in International Law?" *American Journal of International Law*, vol. 77, 1983, pp. 413–42.

12 R.J. Bernstein, *The Restructuring of Social and Political Theory*, Philadelphia: University of Pennsylvania Press, 1978; M.J. Shapiro, *Language and Political Understanding: The Politics of Discursive Practices*, New Haven: Yale University Press, 1981.

13 R. Dworkin, *Taking Rights Seriously*, Cambridge, MA: Harvard University Press, 1977; J. Feinberg, *Rights, Justice and the Bounds of Liberty: Essays in Social Philosophy*, Princeton: Princeton University Press, 1980.

14 L. Wittgenstein, *Tractatus Logico-Philosophicus*, trans. by D.F. Pears and B.F. McGuinness, London: Routledge & Kegan Paul, 1961.

position by arguing that the meaning of sentences depends on *rules*. This basis for language also forms the basis for thinking; one's ideas are identified *with* language, not as *preceding* language. The rules of language and thought are themselves derived from customary usage. The result is that sentences cannot say what they mean or what they do. Only rules and usage can do this; rules alone effectively constitute meaning.[15]

Philosophy of language thus oriented has increasingly abandoned scientific positivism's most cherished assumptions about the relationship between concepts and reality. Of particular interest, because of the way it bears on the question we ask about rules and obligations, is the analysis of ordinary language, and within it the theory of speech acts. By turning in this essay to the theory of speech acts for the grounding I see wanting in earlier efforts, I propose to renew discussion of the central problem of how rules work as law. And this means addressing a question all positivists ask implicitly yet never answer correctly: Do rules say what they do?

At least two scholars, David Kennedy and Friedrich Kratochwil, have undertaken critical recapitulations of the legal and scientific positivists' approaches to the central problem of characterizing law. Both have challenged positivist premises in hopes of solving the problem; both have offered significant alternatives for the hard case of international law. For their devastating exposure of positivist limitations and for their focus on discourse instead of rules, they have appropriately earned the label *postpositivist*. In reviewing these alternatives here, I will first show that for all their power and imagination, they substitute new problems for old ones. Second, I will argue that these new problems come from an undisclosed and insupportable reliance on a particular sense of what constitutes the domain of law.

Kennedy's seminal work is his 1980 essay, "Theses about International Legal Discourse."[16] His approach, however, is so complex that it is often inaccessible. I take Kennedy to make the following argument if only because his larger abstractions would make no sense without it: rules as such are determinate, just as legal positivism insists. What is indeterminate is their use which, following legal realism, depends on their relevance to particular adversarial situations. Given the extreme likelihood that several rules are relevant to a particular situation and their differential value to adversaries in determining desired outcomes, nothing in law determines which rule is decisive or, for that matter, desirable.

The discourse of lawyers engaged in these adversarial proceedings does tell us which two rules will be set in opposition. One will be chosen. Even if the

15 L. Wittgenstein, *Philosophical Investigations*, 3rd edn, trans. by G.E.M. Anscombe, New York: Macmillan, 1968.

16 D. Kennedy, "Theses about International Legal Discourse," *German Year Book of International Law*, vol. 23, 1980, pp. 353–91.

legal process is indeterminate in outcome, discourse reveals the polar structure of competing, determinate rules. But more than this, discourse is the agency through which rules are opposed because it relates each such pairing to the axial principles of sovereignty and cooperation. It is this axis of principles that gives the international legal order its distinctive character.

Kennedy appears to have performed a difficult feat. He assumes an account of legal processes that is indeterminate in outcome, and uses it to explain the structural stability of the system of rules. But his accomplishment is supported by two illusions. The first is that the structure of the system is ordered around a single, axial opposition.[17] A number of opposed, very general principles structure international legal discourse, and not all of them derive from the opposition of sovereignty and cooperation. Declaratory versus constitutive theories of recognition, arguments over whether *opinio juris* is required for legal custom, textual versus contextual grounds for interpreting treaties are examples of doctrinal polarities evidently having nothing to do with sovereignty and cooperation. The existence of such oppositions has more to do with worldview or professional training than with national or social ideologies and interests. This belies the argument that only one major polarity structures the legal process.

Kennedy's second illusion is that the legal arena is exclusively adversarial:

> As states come together in society, we imagine them pursuing private goals with a self-serving rationalism. The model of conflict resolution which will be required then, will be based upon competition. Law can gain a foothold in such a world if conflict can be transferred from the realm of action to the realm of discourse.

Such discourse must invoke principles embodying "subjective rightness" as well as self-serving propositions, that is, "sovereign statements." If the process is successful, it results in "principled decision-making."[18]

Does principled decision-making and the discourse producing it occur in other settings? This question is left unaddressed; Kennedy's conflict resolution model precludes it. Outcomes successfully blending policies and principles in particular adversarial settings have probative value in subsequent, similar settings. But this is not a property unique to these outcomes and settings. Thinking so is an error that reinforces the belief that the adversarial setting is the true locus of legal discourse.

Kennedy's conclusions are comfortable enough for someone trained in the common law tradition, but they assume rather than demonstrate that the adversarial setting is the only locus of legal activity in any advanced society or in international relations. Two others are at least as important

17 Ibid., pp. 361–72.
18 Ibid., pp. 386–7.

for ordering international relations. One is the swirl of activity surrounding the articulation of principles by major international plenary organs – the source of some of the softest law decried by legal positivists. The other is the codification of procedures and the production of administrative regulations. This bundle of activities is so dominant in the low-profile functional domain of international relations that its quantitative preponderance is hardly noticed.

Kennedy acknowledges legal indeterminacy in two senses. If rules are external to behavior, they are indeterminate in application. If they are grounded in behavior, they merge with that behavior.[19] Thus legal and scientific positivism are both condemned to indeterminacy in their respective logics. By moving to discourse, Kennedy feels he can avoid these polar perils of positivist scholarship because he is no longer talking about rules. "To me, then, international law discourse is a conversation without content."[20] The problem with Kennedy is that he arbitrarily delimits what counts as legal discourse. This limitation leads to an artificial construction of both process and structure, such that these two analytical levels can be shown to have a determinate relation. Indeed they may, but it is not the simple one that Kennedy posits. So he exchanges the old problem of obligation and indeterminacy for a new one: how is legal discourse bounded?

The problem of legal indeterminacy also figures prominently in Friedrich Kratochwil's "Is International Law 'Proper' Law?"[21] Building on Gottlieb's 1974 landmark reconstruction of the problem, Kratochwil tries to identify a "demarcation criterion." For Kratochwil, legal rules differ from those that are not legal in their specificity, especially with respect to the instrumental guidance they provide and their principled character. Their specificity, especially as to means, distinguishes them from general moral considerations (which focus on the ends to be achieved), while their principled character (which they share with moral judgment) distinguishes them from policies.

Whether or not behavior qualifies as law is determined by two tests. As if this were not difficult enough to assimilate into the legal positivist demand for a single, clear criterion, each test is a matter of degree. The emphasis is "not institutions, but *modes of decision-making* that are based on the degree and scope of guidance accepted in reasoning with rules."[22] Kratochwil does not insist that individual rules are indeterminate, but the absence of institutional requirements of specificity blurs the threshold of legality. He also affirms the indeterminacy both Gottlieb and Kennedy have in mind by emphasizing choice and reasoning in the use of rules. Finally, he builds ambiguity, if not indeterminacy, into the system of rules by using dimensions

19 Ibid., p. 383.
20 Ibid., p. 376.
21 F.V. Kratochwil, "Is International Law 'Proper' Law?" *Archiv für Rechts- und Sozialphilosophie*, vol. 69, 1983, pp. 13–46.
22 Ibid., p. 38; emphasis in original.

for demarcating legal rules that he regards as overlapping rather than mutually exclusive.

Not only does the notion of principled policy verge on a contradiction, the point of specificity in rules is to enable their use as guides without additional, reflective activity. That is, anyone who has recourse to a highly specific rule is likely to presume that the very fact of its specificity indicates that someone else has already, in the act of making the rule so specific, reflected on its relation to the principles affected by the rule. The whole point of rules, after all, is to provide ready, and one has to hope, good answers to complex questions. Even if use of a specific rule requires acknowledgment of it being principled, we also have to acknowledge that some specific rules, like tyrants' demands, are unprincipled and not legal. Does Kratochwil's set of rules qualifying as law include all specific rules except those that are *prima facie* unprincipled, or does he mean all principles subjected to specification for particular situations? How would we know if these are the same? It is in this sense that his system view is indeterminate.

This matter is important because it seems that Kratochwil wants to find something that rules have in common in order to qualify as law, but he does not want to locate this common quality either in the rules as such or in the system they constitute. Instead, he finds the common element in the use of law for persuasion.

> In this view, law is a particular form of argument and . . . legal reasoning exhibits features that are fundamentally "rhetorical" in character. . . . Rhetoric is concerned with the problem of praxis, i.e. the necessity of choice in situations in which no logically compelling solution is possible.[23]

Thus legality is a quality bestowed on rules through rhetoric, or practical reasoning, applied to particular situations by people professionally trained in drawing analogies, invoking precedents, justifying claims, and weighing alternatives. That persuasion works is what we mean when we say that the law works.

Kratochwil goes on to observe that rhetoric depends on the audience. Although the model audience is the one charged with hearing the pleas of adversaries, another is identified and a third is intimated. Identified as an audience are those charged with the evaluation of persuasion at the "technical level," that is, bureaucrats.[24] He is inclined to minimize their relevance for law but not their importance for a stable order. Only intimated to exist as an audience is the aware public which hears the rhetoric of persuasion on matters of high principle.

23 Ibid., p. 40.
24 Ibid., p. 44.

As does Kennedy, Kratochwil settles too easily on adversarial arenas as paradigmatic for the use of legal rules. Then he equates the style of persuasion particular to this arena with defining conditions for the legality of rules. Other arenas where rules appear are eliminated from consideration, and rules used in those arenas do not qualify as legal rules. Nevertheless, Kratochwil's shift in emphasis to discourse and his explication of practical reasoning for public purposes as the distinctive feature of law make a notable extension of Gottlieb's 1974 work.

Kratochwil also extends the flaws in Gottlieb's initiatives. Principles and rules of high specificity are treated as analytically separable, then conflated in order to create a uniformly operative model of law. Such a model ignores the diverse characteristics of rules ranging from principles to procedures. These rules look like and work as law, even though convention holds that they are not law. At least scientific positivists like Gottlieb acknowledge them. Kratochwil's very effort to improve on Gottlieb requires that he not acknowledge them as law. Nor does Kennedy for similar reasons.

Although these postpositivists have put rules in a larger and necessary perspective, they wrongly and unnecessarily discount discourse about principles and procedures, failing to see it as truly legal. The consistent shortcomings of these independent efforts persuade me that a rules conception of law must center even the postpositivist emphasis on legal discourse. This does not mean reversion to the standing theory of obligation or to an untrammeled behavioral perspective. Legal and scientific positivism, no less than Kennedy and Kratochwil, have failed to develop an adequate conception of rules.[25]

Social rules

In the Austinian tradition, a *rule* is defined as a special case of command. Many scientific positivists equate rules with regularities of conduct (again, see Chapter 28, below). The search for something in-between has centered on properties of rules as a class of statements or as statements yielding a particular class of effects. Philosophers engaged in this search direct attention to one crucial property: rules assist their users in drawing inferences. Wittgenstein called rules "signposts." Gilbert Ryle called them "inference-tickets."[26] This emphasis on guidance and inference broadens the Austinian imperative to include that which is permitted as well as that which is required or forbidden.[27] Among rules, certain types have the additional properties of being

25 Kratochwil's recent unpublished work [later published as *Rules, Norms and Decisions: On the Conditions of Practical and Legal Reasoning in International Relations and Domestic Affairs*, Cambridge: Cambridge University Press, 1989] considers these issues and elaborates a rules conception complementary to his position on legal rhetoric.

26 See Gottlieb, *The Logic of Choice*, pp. 33–42.

27 Ibid., p. 39; M. Black, *Models and Metaphors: Studies in Language and Philosophy*, Ithaca: Cornell University Press, 1962, p. 108.

capable of public statement and performance.[28] These types include, for example, moral rules and instructions.

The difference between rules like these and rules of logic, laws of nature, and statistical regularities is that the former have authors and histories, the latter do not.[29] The first sort of rules are made rules by their authors: they are social. It would seem, however, that the social origin of certain rules is established and then quickly forgotten. The brunt of attention shifts to the rule once it is authored. For example, in the Austinian view, the author's wish or will is contained in the rule's content and conveyed in the imperative form of the statement, so nothing further need be said about the author. In Austin's theory there can be only one function for a rule; it conveys an imperative. But what of the broader view of rules? When rules can perform several functions it may be considerably more difficult to know what the rule is about and what our relation to it is just from the rule alone.

Inference from syntax is not enough. Recourse to the context of a rule's use may help resolve some ambiguities, but introduces others. Context tends to invade a rule's content, even as it aids in clarifying the rule's function, and the rule begins to lose its distinctive position in offering guidance. Carried too far in the search for what a rule "really" says, recourse to context supports either the radically objectivist position of some scientific positivists that rules are nothing more than regularities of conduct or a radically subjectivist position that there are rules of unique content for everything that happens. Both of these extreme outcomes deny social character to rules.

In any case, neither legal nor scientific positivists have successfully used context in functional interpretation. The former do not acknowledge the need to do so, while the latter have not been convincing in their sense of what context to consider. Concerned with the uses to which rules are put, Kennedy and Kratochwil run the same risks and avoid them only by implicitly accepting received ideas about the forums in which rules must be used in order to be taken seriously enough to be called law. This leaves other rules in the conceptual murk. Kennedy's and Kratochwil's philosophical disposition to treat rules by reference to inferences and thus audiences, rather than intentions and thus authors, imposes a use orientation on them. While they have charted a course between legal positivism's vacuous equation of rules and regularities, they have solved the problems of neither concept. Nor can these problems be solved until rules are understood as being fixed, as a matter of their author's intention, both in *content* and in *function*.

In the modern philosophy of language, the theory of speech acts has systematically related speakers' intentions to the ordered possibilities of linguistic

28 More typically, but less accurately, rules are said to be "standing," as in Hart's "standing orders." *The Concept of Law*, p. 23.

29 Black, *Models and Metaphors*, pp. 109–10.

activity. The audience correctly infers the speakers' intentions by noting the *illocutionary* force as well as the propositional content of utterances. Illocutionary force is the part of speech constituting an action that fixes the "communicative function of the content uttered."[30] Invoking this property of language ruptures the long prevailing representational view of language, in which positivism is grounded, and substitutes Wittgensteinian premises. This theory was developed by J.L. Austin and other philosophers, notably John Searle. Searle may have best described the central thesis of speech act theory: "Speaking a language is engaging in a (highly complex) rule-governed form of behavior."[31]

Only one social philosopher, Jürgen Habermas, has attempted a systematic examination of speech act theory from a social point of view. My effort will depart from Habermas' according to our divergent objectives. While I hope to ground social rules in ordinary language, he seeks a theory of uncoerced communicative competence.[32]

Habermas has provided a helpful summary of the general scheme of speech act theory:

> Through *locutionary acts* the speaker expresses states of affairs; he says something. Through *illocutionary acts* the speaker performs an action in saying something. The illocutionary role establishes the mode of the sentence . . . employed as a statement, promise, command, avowal, or the like. Under standard conditions, the mode is expressed by means of a performative verb in the first person present; the action meaning can be seen particularly in the fact that "hereby" can be added to the illocutionary component of the speech act: "I hereby promise you (command you, confess to you) that p [propositional content – state of affairs]. Finally, through *perlocutionary acts* the speaker produces an effect upon the hearer. By carrying out a speech act he brings about something in the world. Thus the three acts that Austin distinguishes can be characterized in the following catchphrases: to say *something*, to act *in* saying something, to bring about something *through* acting in saying something.[33]

By following rules of sentence formation any speaker makes it possible for any hearer to know what that speaker intends. Rules for establishing illocutionary force, by enabling a sentence to take form, produce sentences that are

30 J. Habermas, *Communication and the Evolution of Society*, trans. by T. McCarthy, Boston: Beacon, 1979, p. 34. Also see pp. 59–65.

31 J.R. Searle, *Speech Acts: An Essay in the Philosophy of Language*, Cambridge: Cambridge University Press, 1969, p. 12.

32 J. Habermas, *The Theory of Communicative Action*, vol. 1, *Reason and the Rationalization of Society*, Boston: Beacon, 1984.

33 Ibid., pp. 288–9; emphasis in original.

themselves in the form of rules. These sentences require or permit an inference about the speaker's intentions. Sentences not containing an illocutionary component do not require or permit such an inference. Although all rules have an illocutionary component, it is not true that all sentences endowed with illocutionary force are rules. At best they are rule-candidates.

Whether such rule-candidates become rules depends on their reception. If the hearer understands the intentions of the speaker, and so indicates with an affirmative, then s/he:

> accepts a speech act offer and grounds an agreement; this agreement concerns the *content of the utterance*, on the one hand, and on the other hand, *certain guarantees immanent to speech acts* and *certain obligations relevant to the sequel of interaction*.

Habermas considers this "a weak normative bond."[34] Though weak, it is nevertheless decisive in giving speech acts with an illocutionary component the function as well as the form of a rule.

Such weak normativity explains how instructions can be rules. If I hereby state that *X* counts as *Y*, and you accept this statement as operative between us without qualification, then that statement rules our intersubjective situation apropos the relation of *X* to *Y*. We can always agree to change an *instruction-rule*; others can join in the agreement; it may become generally accepted. If the last of these happens, we speak of a convention emerging. Conventions are no less normatively weak than the original agreement, but their normativity is wider because more speakers and hearers are involved.

Conventions once established begin to substitute for new sets of agreements. Eventually I feel no obligation to seek your agreement; I merely invoke the convention. In this way conventions become institutionalized and then acquire additional normativity and generate expectations not dependent on fresh agreement. Institutionalized conventions are not more *rule-like* for being normatively stronger. They have merely become more visible and harder to ignore.

Rules thus institutionalized normally lack specific, attached sanctions. Certain consequences follow from disregarding them: others are confused or disappointed; coordination breaks down; unanticipated interactions take place. To the extent that instruction-rules arise in the first instance to minimize these effects, incentives exist to honor those rules.

Institutionalization allows for the mobilization of social pressure to reinforce a sense of obligation or willingness to comply with such rules, but reaches its target only because of prior normativization accomplished through illocutionary agreements and their conventionalization. So understood, institutionalization makes instruction-rules societal as opposed to merely social.

34 Ibid., pp. 296, 304; emphasis in original. Also, see Habermas, *Communication and the Evolution of Society*, pp. 62–3.

A special case of instruction-rules has *X* count as *Y*, where *Y* is a value. Such moral rules, that is, *principles*, are always instruction-rules of this sort. Institutionalization expedites the assignment of value to and through instruction-rules, which helps to explain their strengthened normativity. Nonetheless, their ruleness, on which any normativity hinges, begins in speech. As Stanley Fish has commented, "[t]he moral of this is chastening, even disturbing: institutions are no more than the (temporary) effects of speech-act agreements, and they are, therefore, as fragile as the decision, always capable of being revoked, to abide by them."[35] I would add to this observation that institutionalization and valuation serve to inhibit casual revocation.[36]

For convenience this analysis has considered just one kind of rule: the instruction-rule. Perhaps the simplest case, it is not usually the model one. Rules serving as directives (you may do *X*) are usually taken as the model case because they are *prima facie* regulative. Some writers even deny that instructions and conventions are rules.[37] Others, like Habermas, do not see them as regulative despite their normativity.[38] The above discussion, however, shows their regulative character by the fact that they are intrinsically, albeit weakly, normative. It also shows how their normativity is augmented for regulative purposes. As for other kinds of rules, these would plausibly correspond to categorical differences among speech acts. This, however, turns out to be not quite the case.

Among attempts to categorize speech acts, John Searle's classifications have been the most influential.[39] Searle's scheme offers five categories: *assertives* (also widely called *constatives*), *directives, commissives, expressives*, and *declarations*. Assertives are speech acts stating a belief, coupled to the speaker's wish or intention that the hearer accept this belief. The verbs which represent assertive speech acts include: state, affirm, report, characterize, attribute, insist, dissent. Obviously, instruction-rules uniformly issue from assertives. As a second group, directives present the hearer with a speaker's intention as to some act the speaker would like to have performed. Typical directive verbs are: ask, demand, command, forbid, permit, caution. Their relation to imperative rules – they might better be called *directive-rules* – is self-evident.

The third group – commissives – reveals the speaker's intention of being committed to a stated course of action: to promise and offer are usual

35 S. Fish, *Is There a Text in This Class?: The Authority of Interpretive Communities*, Cambridge, MA: Harvard University Press, 1980, p. 213.

36 And see ibid., pp. 318–21.

37 K. Bach and R.M. Harnish, *Linguistic Communication and Speech Acts*, Cambridge, MA: MIT Press, pp. 108–10, 120–7.

38 Habermas, *Communication and the Evolution of Society*, pp. 54–5; *The Theory of Communicative Action*, pp. 303–5.

39 J.R. Searle, *Expression and Meaning: Studies in the Theory of Speech Acts*, Cambridge: Cambridge University Press, 1979, pp. 1–29.

examples. Commitments once acknowledged are regulative and rules embodying commitments certainly exist. Thus the statement, "I am committed to going to church every week," can take the form, "I make it a rule to go to church every week." Yet none of the commonly construed rule categories seems to have a place for *commitment-rules*. To the extent that anyone acknowledges them, they are lumped together with directive-rules.

Searle's remaining categories of speech acts differ from the first three. Expressives serve to convey an emotion or attitude toward a state of affairs; examples are apologies and congratulations. They are not rule-candidates because their reception is sufficient for the speaker's point of view to fulfill his or her intentions in having made the statement. If I say, "I hereby apologize to you," and you accept, nothing further need transpire between us for the reason of my having apologized.

Declarations would appear not even to require acceptance to have completely performed the speaker's intentions. To say, "I hereby declare that you are fired," does not require acknowledgment to be successful, at least as Searle sees it. Declarations are thus regulative in a more immediate sense than other speech acts. Actually, as the illustration shows, the effectiveness of a declaration requires more information than the declaration itself provides. Can the speaker fire the hearer because s/he has the authority to do so? If so, rules exist stating such; it is these rules that give the speech act its regulative effect. In short, declarations achieve illocutionary force and performative efficiency by parasitic association with institutionalized rules. Declarations are therefore not a generic type of speech act. If firing someone is directive, then declaring war is assertive, and bidding at an auction commissive. Declarative forms exist for all three generic kinds of rules.

Hence, all rules are either assertives of the form, "I state that *X* counts as *Y*," or directives of the form, "I state that *X* person (should, must, may, etc.) do *Y*," or commissives of the form, "I state that I (can, will, should, etc.) do *Y*." Directives and commissives appear to differ only in respect of the perlocutionary subject: the person intended to act. Thus there is a rationale for lumping them together. Habermas, for example, sees them as functionally identical. He thinks both directives and commissives regulate, making them different from assertives, which he sees as having only a cognitive function.[40] I think this is incorrect. On the contrary, the distinctive feature of assertives is that they make cognition intersubjective. The consequence of this must be regulative. It hardly makes sense to speak of cognition in any other terms. On this reasoning, all speech acts should be lumped together because of their shared regulative function. But this is plainly at odds with everyone's sense that instructions and directives, at least, are generically different from each other.

40 Habermas, *Communication and the Evolution of Society*, p. 58; *The Theory of Communicative Action*, p. 329. Habermas posits three "worlds" of meaning for human beings: objective, social, and subjective. *The Theory of Communicative Action*, pp. 233–42. He suggests alignment of statement types with these different worlds, p. 444 n. 84.

Obviously instruction-rules relate back to assertives, and directive-rules to directive speech acts. But what exactly is the link between commitment-rules to commissive speech acts? Here the language of rights and duties is suggestive. To state a duty – it is my duty to go to church every week – is a way of making a promise – to go to church every week. On the other hand, a right is a way of restating a promise made by someone else. Thus a right to go to church is a restatement of somebody having promised me that I can go to church. My promises confer duties on me that are simultaneously rights others claim I have conferred on them. The same holds for others' promises as they affect me.[41] Public commitments always distribute consequences this way. When rules can be formulated in these terms, they find their character in commissive speech act; they are commitment-rules.

Statements describable as *claims* can have assertive, directive or commissive meaning, depending on context. To say, "this money is mine," is an assertive declaration when founded on a legal claim. The same phrase when backed by my authority, such as "because I am King," is a declaration of a directive nature. Note that both the assertives and directives conveyed by the word *claim* depend on the existence of a prior commissive giving me a right to the money. The core of my claim, whatever form it takes, is that I was promised money. I may even have made the promise to myself, thereby committing myself to getting the money.

The contingent character of the promise in this instance is an invitation for strategic interaction. It deliberately manipulates perlocutionary possibilities to shift the direction of illocutionary forces from the speaker to the hearer – you will end up being conmmitted to (at least something of) what has been promised, even if I have only promised it to myself. The hearer normally responds with a counterclaim. The process of interacting over these claims is a particularly fertile one for new rules in the form of agreed outcomes.[42]

Such rules would stem from paired commissives – we both promise *X*. If there are joint declarations of a commissive nature, we might call the result a contract.[43] Under highly institutionalized circumstances, in which known legal rules are invoked in support of claims, we have the adversarial setting and reasoned argument Kennedy and Kratochwil find emblematic of the legal situation. But note that claims of other sorts are no less appropriate for legal consideration.

41 The association of promising and rights goes back at least to John Locke. J. Tully, *A Discourse on Property: John Locke and His Adversaries*, Cambridge: Cambridge University Press, 1980, pp. 48–50.

42 On strategic interaction as source of obligation in utilitarian accounts, see Kratochwil, "Is International Law 'Proper' Law?" pp. 17–21, and "The Force of Prescriptions," *International Organization*, vol. 38, 1984, pp. 691–7.

43 M. Hancher, "The Classification of Cooperative Illocutionary Acts," *Language in Society*, vol. 8, 1979, pp. 1–14, pursues a similar line of reasoning, but sees contracts and other cooperative speech acts as hybrids of the generic type, rather than declarations.

I suggest that no legally relevant use of the term *claim* falls outside the categories offered by speech act theory, and all uses fit one or another category or compound categories in complex systems of use. Behind all such uses stands an original, initiating speech act, which is a commissive. Comparably, assertives and directives initiate the making of rules. No other speech acts can. In other words, with instruction-rules, directive-rules, and commitment-rules, we have an inclusive classification scheme for all social rules.

A question remains. Do the above categories truly represent fundamental units of linguistic activity? Searle and Habermas proceed from the view that a speech act can be characterized as a *fit* between words, conveying the speaker's intention, and the world. The different types of speech acts can be understood as different kinds of fit between words and world, although the two authors disagree on what kind of fit is manifested by the different types of speech acts.[44]

As an alternative, I would suggest the following framework. First, commissives as a class fit words to the world. To commit oneself is to project a desired state of affairs and bring it to bear on oneself. Second, assertives fit the world without being fit to it; they do not endeavor to change the existing arrangement. Finally, directives, unlike assertives, do make the world fit the words because directives initiate actions that will change the world.

It must be added, however, that world and words are not used in these cases to represent completely distinct realms. *World* is a convenient metaphor for propositional content, world consists of words. With this understanding, *fit* refers to the relation between sets of words, not words and *reality*. The speech act is part of the whole world of propositions. The issue, then, is the fit between a finite set of words (a speech act) and all words (all propositions).

When so understood, the three rule-making categories of speech acts exhaust the logical possibilities for relating a part to a whole. The directionless fit of assertives is always recognizable as a metaphorical construction. If the fit is world-to-words, we could also say part of a state of affairs can change the whole – you are a part of a state of affairs and I direct you to change it and yourself through your actions. This relation of part to whole is a metonymical construction. Finally, a state of affairs as a whole can have an impact on parts: I commit myself, a part, to the creation of a desired state of affairs; I want my actions to be part of what it becomes. This is a synecdochal construction.

Metaphor, metonymy and synecdoche are three basic figures of speech in rhetoric. They exhaust the possible relations of parts to wholes: whole-to-whole, which is the same as part-to-part, part-to-whole, and whole-to-part. The whole they are grounded in is, in the end, a world constituted in speech. Thus they support a view of language which, as ongoing ruled activity, makes

44 See Searle, *Expression and Meaning*, pp. 14–20; Habermas, *The Theory of Communicative Action*, pp. 323–6.

the world meaningful and meaningfully makes the world. And through speech acts language does so in particular ways.

Metaphor is indeed representational but metonymy is reductive and synecdoche is integrative.[45] Metaphor as representation requires assertion. Metonymy accomplishes reduction by direction. Synecdoche yields integration by commission. Representation, reduction and integration are the social functions of language or, more simply, the functions of discourse. The connection between rules and discourse is fundamental and indissoluble. It confirms both the importance and the limitations of Kennedy's and Kratochwil's turn to discourse.

Speech acts, rules, and international law

Almost a quarter-century ago, H.L.A. Hart observed, "A full, detailed taxonomy of the varieties of laws comprised in a modern, legal system, free from prejudice that all must be reducible to a single simple type, still remains to be accomplished."[46] Although scholarship in the intervening years supports the view that there are such varied types of law, jurisprudence has become mired in controversies inspired by Ronald Dworkin's attack on positivism. The attack would seem to mark a re-emergence of naturalism and, with it, the polarization of naturalists and positivists.[47] International legal scholarship has yet to suffer this fate, and its scientific positivism has produced at least one simple typology. We have seen how Gottlieb converts that twofold typology of law into alternative models of law – a move that simultaneously strengthens the claim that there are varieties of law and weakens the credibility of any extant scheme for typing them. Thus those who follow Gottlieb's lead, as Kennedy and Kratochwil do, and look to discourse instead of rules for guidance flounder because they have not found anything functionally distinctive in what they construe as specifically legal discourse.

This scheme for aligning rules with types of speech acts attempts to stake out fresh ground for a taxonomy of laws by discovering a finite set of mutually exclusive ways in which rules themselves say what they do. In moving from rules to laws in this scheme, two things need be done. The first is to show that a functional orientation supports the three categories of rules derived from ordinary language, instead of the simpler pair of types preferred by functionally inclined international legal scholars. The second is to show that types of laws are but special cases of rule categories, and to show what is special about such cases. Doing this will make possible a demonstration that the necessary categories of laws apply to international law. If our three

45 H. White, *Metahistory*, Baltimore: Johns Hopkins University Press, 1973, pp. 31–8.

46 Hart, *The Concept of Law*, p. 32; emphasis in original.

47 Although it remains unclear what kind of naturalist or how free from utilitarianism Dworkin is. See M. Cohen (ed.), *Ronald Dworkin and Contemporary Jurisprudence*, Totowa, NJ: Rowman & Allanheld, 1984.

categories occur frequently as international law, we are justified in calling the international order legal.

In categorizing laws, I draw on work I have already undertaken with Spike Peterson.[48] Our reading of functionalist literature, both classic and current, suggests that there are three broad categories of activity that are fundamental to making the human condition a social one. These socially constitutive activities are: (1) naming and relating, (2), enabling and disabling, and (3) having and using. We also take the Wittgensteinian position that these activities have social meaning if and because they are rule-governed. Therefore, we identify three exclusive and logically necessary rule categories: those for (1) designated position, (2) exercising control, and (3) allocating possession or use. Originally, we had chosen to call the first sort *norms*, the second *commands*, and the third *rights*. It should be clear that I now prefer to call them instruction-rules, directive-rules and commitment-rules.

Hart is certainly correct to reject the term *command* as too narrowly confined in the Austinian tradition to giving orders. Broadening it to include rules that enable and disable may invite misunderstanding. Nevertheless, such rules are *directive*. Sanctions as understood in legal positivism may be positive as well as negative. Rules that empower (make able) are likely to prompt from recipients a claim to be due those powers, like any benefit, as a matter of right. (Also see Chapter 19 for a complementary discussion of the way rule categories are related.) Transforming a power created by directive into a self-conferred right to rule is of course a characteristic move by those with such powers. Altogether, these changes in labels acknowledge correspondence between rules functionally understood and their properties as speech acts. As speech acts, rules say what they do, that is, what their social functions are.

Peterson and I hold that all social arrangements constituted by rules in all three categories, whatever their mix, are subject to formalization and that all rule-related practices are subject to institutionalization. All would agree that when directive-rules reach a certain threshold of formalization and institutionalization, such as enactment and impartial enforcement, then they are law. Legal positivists have no place for rules that are not directives and do not acknowledge their legal character. We propose that the same formalization and enactment criteria hold for rules of the other two categories. When instruction-rules and commitment-rules are sufficiently formalized and associated practices sufficiently institutionalized, they too become legal.

This threshold is neither arbitrary nor indeterminate. Enough formalization and institutionalization must take place that such rules can perform a definite function of their own. Principles do not have to be moral rules, though they tend to be. Nor are they simply instruction-rules. Their distinctive

48 N.G. Onuf and V.S. Peterson, "Human Rights from an International Regimes Perspective," *Journal of International Affairs*. vol. 37, 1984, pp. 330–3; see Chapter 13, above.

feature is that they have the weight to help users of instructions rank and choose among large numbers of sometimes incompatible instructions. Principles perform this function without necessitating the presence or operation of sanctions. They may be enacted as law, but this would seem to be no more than a formality, for it does not change the way they function (unless, of course, this is the formality that turns instructions into principles).

The specific function of formalized commitment-rules, or *entitlements*, is to constitute legal personality and regulate the relations of persons thus constituted. Thus it is an ensemble of rights and duties that call for functional assessment. Such ensembles normally include interpreting and expediting instructions. Yet they need neither these aids nor legal enactment to serve their distinctive function of forming complex patterns of rights and duties into the discrete subjects of the legal order.

Directives that become law may be the most interesting case of all. They are normally called law simply because they are formally enacted and subject to enforcement. While legal positivism does not regard these properties as matters of degree, we saw earlier why this view is difficult to sustain. But if we ask what special function laws perform once a requisite degree of formalization and institutionalization is achieved, we have a definite answer. Formalization and institutionalization shift the burden of making directives work from author to audiences. No longer are specific persons directed to undertake certain acts with specified consequences for not doing so. Instead, an abstract statement produces hypothetical responses.

If someone (I might be the one) does not accept a given law, then anyone (including me) can predict in advance the likely consequences, because they are intended to be the same for everyone. Evident indifference to individual considerations deters generally, with a qualitative increase in the efficiency of directive-rules. Acceptance of principles asserting equality before and blindness of the law assists laws in their specific function and supports the legal order when this function is not well performed because of defects in conception or execution of particular laws. Of course, when the gap between principles and performance becomes too great, the order is imperiled, notwithstanding the formalities of authorship and the availability of institutionalized enforcement.

A functional interpretation of *specifically* legal rules solves the problem of how such formalization and institutionalization are required before rules are legal. That functionally determined threshold is also linguistically accessible. Those rules that are legal in function take the form of declarative speech acts, that is, they are successful or performatively sufficient, without depending on the hearers' assent to implicate hearers in their normativity. Most such speech acts assume the characteristic of declarations because they conform to perlocutionary requirements stipulated by speech acts of the same character. Said otherwise, the speech act, "I declare war," acquires its performative sufficiency from the fact that other declarations (such as found in a constitution) specify as one of their perlocutionary effects that I may do so. Regress takes us to rules that are declarations because they are created with that specific intention in mind – they are created as rules with the specific perlocutionary effect of authorizing persons to perform certain speech acts which will then be declarations on performance. To say that rules of this sort are created means that they are successful as speech acts because assent is either formally accorded prior to the statement as declarations (for example, a vote or a signature) or can be inferred from circumstances (custom).

The familiar distinction between developed domestic orders and the international order can now be easily rendered in these terms. Domestic orders typically depend on declarations whose performative sufficiency is a specific perlocutionary effect of yet other such declarations. The international order consists of many rules lacking formality and therefore always subject to revisions in their normative strength depending on the reception accorded each use. Those rules that are sufficiently formalized to be specifically legal in function (some principles, many regulations) are performatively sufficient not because they refer to other declarations (though some regulations may), but mostly because they are made performatively sufficient as a direct consequence of their creation. They are self-referential, in the sense that they refer back only to their own authorship for their standing. This explains the difference between rules based on precedent and custom, contracts, and treaties.

As domestic orders develop, they do away with self-referential declarations. In this connection, however, principles present a special case. Self-referential assertive declarations do exist in highly developed orders, but they are not easily assimilated into the usual positivist conception of law.[49] But law they are, whatever damage this does to the positivist conception of the proper legal order.

Readers may observe a parallel in this discussion to Hart's famous distinction between primary and secondary rules.[50] In Hart's language, self-referential declarations are secondary rules recognizing the legal character of primary rules – the bulk of rules specifying conduct. If the order is without secondary rules, then, according to Hart, it is not genuinely legal, and primary rules are necessarily self-referential declarations. I might not want to call an order *constitutional* if most or all of its rules are self-referential. All the same, those rules are legal if they are performatively sufficient, that is, if invoking them is a successfully performed speech act independent of the hearers' reception. And if the rules in an order are legal, how can the order not be legal?

Whether the international order is a legal one is a different matter. Hart's

49 As Dworkin demonstrates. *Taking Rights Seriously*, pp. 44–5.

50 Hart, *The Concept of Justice*, pp. 77–120. Regress indeed implies the possibility of tertiary rules. See Kratochwil, "Is International Law 'Proper' Law?" pp. 25–7, on the problem Hart's distinction creates for students of international law.

willingness to call it legal on grounds of similarity to constitutional orders is understandable, given the conceptual autonomy he grants the legal order, but it is not persuasive for most positivists.[51] More relevant is whether the international order has enough rules that are properly legal for it to qualify as legal. Inasmuch as no criterion exists for knowing the proportion of legal rules in a legal order, much less types of legal rules, no counting exercise can do the job either.

The best we can hope is to establish a pervasive presence of "the law," by which is usually meant legal rules. Kennedy and Kratochwil agree that the law is a matter of discourse. It is true that discourse about law is what makes legal rules pervasive. Peterson and I have attempted to show that each basic rule type generates a distinctive type of discourse (Chapter 13, above). Instruction-rules prompt discourse on significations: talk about the meaning specific rules have in the ensemble of instructions already constituting social meaning. Conferring-rules give rise to discourse on implications: talk about the effects of particular claims to need or to have a right to things on the ensemble of conferrals already distributing the consequences of social activity. Finally, directive-rules are the source of discourse on justifications: talk about the reasons for advancing, accepting, or rejecting given directives in the existing social context.

Nothing prevents the real world of discourse from mixing these three categories of rules constantly. Because authoring rules tangibly bears on the arrangement of power and privilege in any order, rule authors have a stake in mixing up discourse types. For them the ideal is an order that appears not to be authored at all. Thus correspondence between rules and discourse may be difficult to trace. Directives will be cloaked in metaphors and instructions cast analytically.

The point, however, is that discourse is no less pervasive than rules and often easier to locate on the map of social arrangements. If legal rules are specific in function, with correlative formalization and institutional development to permit performance of such functions, then there ought to be a corresponding specificity in the discourse surrounding legal rules. This is probably what Kennedy and Kratochwil assume. Yet the function of such discourse would not seem to change, as it does for rules that have become legal – the discursive response to formal principles and informal instruction-rules, for example, is equally concerned with their significance for constituted meaning. The specificity of legal discourse depends on its institutional sources.

Kennedy and Kratochwil unconsciously reach the same conclusion. Consequently, they too readily equate specifically legal functions with one obvious arena – that of umpires who decide contesting interpretations of formalized rights. Even more obvious is the discourse of legally empowered agents of the

51 Hart, *The Concept of Law*, pp. 208–31.

state, which legal positivists identify with the hard core of the law. A third, more variably institutionalized arena comes readily to mind – that of the public guardians of principles.

All these are institutionally specified agents whose discourse in the instance of performing their duties is characteristically legal. In the international order, such agents may be easier to identify than most rules. One might start with legally trained professionals, since they hold the bulk of functionally specific, law-related roles in that order. While their discourse is much in evidence, it cannot lead, for reasons already noted, to particular rules to be counted. Instead, we must be satisfied in looking for patterns in their discourse such that we have some assurance that legal rules are indeed what discourse is about.

Insofar as legal professionals, publicly and formally, talk about principles in settings like the UN General Assembly, we ought to consider these principles as properly legal. Although controversy abounds on the legal standing of the General Assembly's declaratory resolutions, this is based on the argument that directives alone are capable of being legal. The unending discussion, meticulous drafting, and relentless publication of international codes substantiating the rights and duties of states as subjects of the legal order are manifestly a legal matter, whether the results are embodied in treaties, resolutions, domestic regulations or repertories of practice and procedure, because technically competent legal professionals are indispensable to the undertaking of these activities (here, see Chapter 10, above). This would appear to be an especially substantial complex of legal rules and legal discourse, only partially grasped by asking whether conventional sources of law have produced these rules.

Definitely identifying formal directive-rules in the international order – laws from a positivist point of view – is more difficult. The international environment is generally adversarial. Government leaders author numerous directives in hopes that their counterparts from other governments will accept them. They cast blame, issue threats, offer inducements. They also frequently veil their directives in the language of promises and claims, using legal advisers to do so. Actual court proceedings are infrequent, but much of the traffic in competing directives is channeled into settings that are adversarial, if only constructively. While this may often be a manipulation of metaphors to increase the chances of particular directives being accepted, the very fact that they are legalized in this fashion contributes to the likelihood of future performative sufficiency, in which case they have indeed become the law of uncertain, even clandestine authorship. The preoccupation with custom as a source of international law is recognition that by some mysterious process *practice* yields *laws*. The alchemy of custom in international law can now be seen as the displacement of directive-rule candidates into a setting that is classically legal, so that legal discourse about those speech acts expedites their acceptance as precedent to be noted in acknowledging matters of principle, claiming rights, and justifying conduct.

Nothing shows the confusion in legal positivism, at least in its Anglo-American utilitarian versions, more than the divorce of directives from justificatory discourse and their displacement into the discursive world of commissives.[52] This is the real origin of the sense that law is confined to adversarial settings. Law can be a sovereign decree and judgment call deciding competing claims in a constitutional order, if the constitution so authorizes. But decrees and judgment calls are generically different types of rules, made into law by different worlds of discourse. Not to separate these types analytically in a nonconstitutional legal order is to deny directives the property of being directives *and* lawful. They are seen as either non-lawful but directive (with cost to understanding how the order can be a legal one), or lawful but not directive, because of the commissively rooted discourse about them (with cost to understanding how they actually come to be legal). That they are not separate empirically is conversely just the reason that directives so readily get to be legal in the absence of constitutionally authorized techniques for making them so.

This functional scheme of characterizing legal rules through different speech acts allows us to separate the legal force of rules in different categories. In the international milieu, many instruction-rules take on the definite legal character of principles in large bodies of instruction-rules. Arguably, many customary rules are properly legal directive-rules. Finally, a large body of commitment-rules are embodied in treaties and codified regulations. I conclude from this that the international order, although lacking a constitutional template for the extrusion of legal rules, is very much a legal order.

52 This is not limited to international settings. Hart, for example, senses both this confusion and the way out of it when he observes that it "is the operation of a *promise* which in many ways is a far better model than that of coercive orders for understanding many, though not all, features of law." *The Concept of Law*, p. 42; his emphasis.

15 Review: *Jurisprudence: A Descriptive and Normative Analysis of Law*, by Anthony D'Amato, 1984 (1986)

The *American Journal of International Law* reflects the disposition of common lawyers to adopt a sharp distinction between theory and practice, and to emphasize the practice of law. Given my training in political science, and my conviction that writing theory is a practice in its own right, the *Journal* might seem an unlikely venue for my work. Nevertheless, to its credit, the *Journal* has often published international legal theory, including some of my early efforts (Chapters 2 and 4). As book review editor in the 1980s, Detlev Vagts asked me to review Antony D'Amato's collected essays on jurisprudence. While D'Amato is an international lawyer (who moves effortlessly between theory and practice), the *Journal* does not review general legal theory very often. Thus the mere fact of the review is an acknowledgment of D'Amato's enormous contributions to the way we think about international law.

D'Amato's basic theoretical commitments are hardly obvious. In teasing them out, I identified four theoretical frameworks to which he offered qualified support: naturalism, positivism, legal realism, and finally a position less familiar to legal scholars that I called constructivism. No one framework meets the practical needs that drive D'Amato's interest in theory. In contrast, I had been seeking a theoretical framework addressing society in all its manifestations, and I had concluded that constructivism did the job. In simplest terms, all of us use social rules to make a world for each other and ourselves; as social constructions, rules make us what we are. In this review, I offered a very brief, very preliminary expression of a position that I developed much more fully in *World of Our Making* (1989). While constructivism in various forms would become an important force in international relations theory, it has had only a modest impact on international lawyers.

For all his work in international law, Anthony D'Amato's real vocation is jurisprudence. He finds room for the perennial questions in whatever he writes: what is law, how does it work (especially in the problematic instance of international relations) and what is law's relation to morality? On occasion, D'Amato has addressed these questions directly and systematically, most notably in two essays originally appearing in the *Yale Law Journal* and *Stanford Law Review* and now bracketing 10 other essays to make up the book at hand. All but one appeared in law reviews between 1970 and 1980. The one exception is a book chapter completed in the middle of the decade but not published until 1982. Three essays concern themselves with international law. Others focus on matters as diverse as cybernetics, "computerized justice" and the death of Socrates (Chapters 4, 5, 8). Hypothetical cases and thought experiments abound. D'Amato's breadth of reading and capacity to recognize jurisprudential questions in all realms of human experience are remarkable. Equally remarkable are the thematic coherence of work so topically diverse and the clarity of its expression.

The first essay, which is the longest and easily the most important, takes as its frame of reference the perspective of a puzzled person, whom D'Amato calls *K*. The reader is immediately reminded of the puzzled protagonist in Franz Kafka's chilling novel, *The Castle*, also called K. D'Amato's brief introduction refers to "statutes, rules, codes, and regulations that are Kafkaesque in their prolixity" (p. 1). Does D'Amato hold a Kafkaesque view of law and society as a bureaucratic nightmare, overwhelming all reason in its relentless devotion to Weberian rationality? Not at all. He immediately equips his *K* with a lawyerly habit of mind, which helps in predicting what officials will do.

Here, D'Amato departs most strikingly from Kafka's vision: officials are consistent ("Consistency is a price officials pay for power," p. 7) and thus predictable. Kafka's officials are predictable only in their unpredictability. If there is reason to their behavior, never is it evident to the baffled K. What D'Amato's consistent officials have are reasons for their conduct which, if not immediately transparent, are intelligible to the lawyerly mind. Lawyers make their living by "reading" official minds and selling their readings (Chapter 3). Officials in their turn use lawyers' readings to make sense of their jobs (Chapter 12). Officials and lawyers share the same conceptual world, which is, for that reason, a reasonable one, at least to them. D'Amato does not actually state this constructivist interpretation of official consistency, but it is implied in having the lawyer serve as the puzzled person's guide to the conceptual world that lawyers share with officials.

Thus, it is unreasonable only to the uninitiated that official conduct may not correspond to rules on the books. Such a rule may reliably serve "as a shorthand description of probable official behavior" (p. 8). It may not, in which case *K* is not at a loss, for consistent official behavior is still the norm and a shorthand description always available. Then, are observable consistencies in behavior always rules? D'Amato does not say. That he does not is important, because it would have been easy enough for him to have done so. The result would have been a broadened version of the legal realist position that law is what judges say it is, which is itself a variation of the positivist doctrine that law is what legislators decree. D'Amato's officials may thus be judges, legislators and the full panoply of executive personnel whose conduct matters to private persons like *K*. If D'Amato all but affirms a comprehensive rendition of legal realism to explain what law is and how it actually works, he nevertheless will not call himself a legal realist. Indeed, the essay was originally, quite tellingly, entitled "The Limits of Legal Realism."

D'Amato's curious relation to legal realism can be explained. Legal realism is an attempt to adapt positivism to the circumstances of law in use. D'Amato obviously approves of this expedient, but fears the consequence. Legal realism undercuts the formal integrity of positivism and, driven to its logical conclusion, abandons limits. Official behavior need not be consistent or reasonable (at least to the observer) for it to be a rule in official minds. If rules are whatever officials make them, then Kafka lurks in legal realism.

For D'Amato the alternative is naturalism. It is the large, but not always the clear, intent of his work to graft legal realism onto a naturalist stance. Doing so spares *K* and everyone else the consequences of giving up the positivist view of law as a system of promulgated rules. One can still talk about rules in relation to official behavior without suggesting that the rules are nothing more than what officials say and do. Put differently, naturalism provides a substantive basis for attributing reason and consistency to officials. At the same time, it is not necessary to expect that conduct to be consistent with a formal rule set, which is realistically unwarranted.

A legal realism grounded in naturalist doctrine is not altogether original with D'Amato. One may see it in Ronald Dworkin and possibly John Rawls. While D'Amato sharply criticizes the latter for ambiguities in his antiutilitarian theory of justice (Chapter 9), he reveals a qualified affinity for the former, whom he describes as either demonstrating the deficiencies of or providing a supplement to positivism (pp. 94, 114 n.18, 146 n.29), and being either insistent or uneasy as a positivist (pp. 57 n. 9, 282). Why the ambivalence? If challenging H.L.A. Hart does not make Dworkin a naturalist from D'Amato's point of view, how can earlier challenges to Hart make Lon Fuller "the leading representative of the natural law school" (p. 191)? D'Amato cannot seem to decide whether not being a positivist makes one a naturalist.

In his novel effort to treat law in cybernetic terms (Chapter 4), D'Amato defines positivism in the narrowest possible sense – legislators make law, judges use it – and defines as naturalist any model of law complex enough to include judicial and executive/administrative "subsystems" in the legal (i.e. lawmaking) system (p. 141). Naturalist is equated with "non-positivist" (p. 139), and Dworkin no less than Fuller qualifies as such. D'Amato is at his weakest in stipulating this weak form of naturalism. Few positivists (Hart included: pp. 132–6) hold to such a circumscribed definition of positivism. Least of all do legal realists. Doctrine in the last century has tended to assign naturalism the narrowest possible definition and describe as positivist all models that are not naturalist. Thus, legal realism is positivist in the broad sense that law is made by people, usually officials, to suit human purposes.

D'Amato also insists that "law does not exist for itself but rather as a means toward the attainment of human ends" (p. 212). Who disagrees? Perhaps some analytic philosophers are discomforted by teleology in social theory, but as a working matter most social scientists share with legal scholars a functionalist view of society. Yet, virtually all of them would find D'Amato's express equation of teleologist and naturalist (ibid.) eccentric and unhelpful. D'Amato seems to believe that by showing that practically everyone is a functionalist, he has established a second, stronger form of naturalism. The emphasis is no longer on the complexity of the legal system. Instead, it is on the teleology inherent in the prevailing idea of a social system.

D'Amato takes his teacher Lon Fuller as exemplar of a purposive view of law and society: principles and norms are " 'in the air,' so to speak" (p. 156, citing Fuller).[1] Moral considerations obviously always affect those who participate in a legal system. The larger and more numerous the categories of participants (D'Amato's weak form of naturalism), the more considerations there are in the air – moral and otherwise. It is striking but not surprising that consensus operating under such conditions of diversity results in community standards, whether expressed as principles and norms, or in laws. The metaphor "in the air" deceives, for the social world is not so lacking in structure.

D'Amato's stronger form of naturalism may describe the way law counters social entropy but does not explain it (cf. pp. 140–1). As suggested earlier, he flirts with an explanation by positing official consistency. Officials are not alone in behaving consistently. We all tend to do so, and we all expect consistency from others. What makes this expectation realistic is a shared, stable frame of reference transmitted through and constructed from human practices. Each of us constructs a social world resembling that of everyone else exposed to the same structuring elements. No two individuals' social worlds are identical, but what they have in common allows for generalized articulation – as through principles, norms and laws – in their common support. Conversely, human purposes and moral concerns – as reflected in principles, norms and laws – are themselves social constructions, any number of which are capable of satisfying the material conditions of human life. Thus, they are bound to differ for individuals whose social worlds do not connect.

D'Amato finally rejects a constructivist explanation of social consistency for the very reason it is fashionable in social theory. Constructivism separates consistency from content in social conduct. D'Amato's fear of relativism elicits yet a stronger form of naturalism, in which content is assured. This is of course the naturalist tradition paradigmatically represented by St. Thomas Aquinas. Natural law so conceived depends on "the essential substantive fact that human purpose is everywhere pretty much the same," and can be formulated as "two great substantive principles: the goal of survival of the human species, and justice to individuals" (p. 214). D'Amato requires nothing further of natural law to satisfy his need for limits. Social contexts constantly change, and so do specific norms that nevertheless honor these principles. In a fascinating illustration of rights reasoning to achieve "right reason,"

1 L. Fuller, "Human Interaction and Law," *American Journal of Jurisprudence*, vol. 14, 1969, pp. 1–36.

D'Amato interprets species survival in the instance of underpopulation as proscribing abortion and in the instance of overpopulation as fostering it (pp. 215–17).

The skeptical reader may wonder whether any two substantive principles can do everything that D'Amato, for all his interpretive ingenuity, wants them to. The phrase "justice to individuals" benefits from its vagueness. D'Amato may well see it as procedurally directed – just conduct entails honesty, good faith, equal treatment in equal circumstances and proportionality of response – while species survival is truly substantive and thus primary when its requirements conflict with the procedural requirements of justice. Were he to insist on both principles as equally substantive, conflicts between them would be inevitable. Collective rights are implied by the principle of species survival and rights against collectivities by the principle of justice to individuals. In the absence of a "natural" interpretive principle, clever reasoning abets rampant relativism. If the second principle actually has priority because, in its procedural guise, it provides definitive interpretive guidance, then we need to be shown how this can be so.

D'Amato has developed his strong, "substantive" version of natural law and addressed the difficulties in Fuller's weaker teleological version in an important essay regrettably not reproduced in this volume.[2] Even there the problems just noted remain to vex the reader. Yet we do get a better sense of D'Amato's naturalism and, in passing, some unexpected light on D'Amato's otherwise obscure decision to divide the book into two unequal parts – the first given to descriptive analysis of the law, and the second to normative analysis. "Fuller did understand that 'natural law' indicates a *process* of legal interpretation that fuses the normative with the descriptive or empirical analysis of law."[3] For Fuller the "normative" is to be found in "shared purposes"; for D'Amato, in substantive principles.

Even if Fuller's position verges on relativism, the one aspect of it that D'Amato wants to keep is the process in which the normative and descriptive are fused. In Fuller's case, the interpreter's world view necessarily incorporates both elements and the process of fusing them is automatic. In D'Amato's case, nothing in the interpretive process prevents recourse to the wrong substantive principle. Process is not enough. D'Amato still needs an interpretive principle. If we look at D'Amato's interpretive efforts, we find no such principle, but we do find a proxy. Together with a description of consistent practices, D'Amato examines the pedigree of a putative rule just as a positivist would. The clearest illustration is to be found in his recent major essay on the international status of human rights, which ought to have been published in

2 A. D'Amato, "Lon Fuller and Substantive Natural Law," *American Journal of Jurisprudence*, vol. 26, 1981, p. 202–18.

3 Ibid., p. 214; his emphasis.

this collection even at the cost of dropping some of the older, slighter essays (e. g., Chapters 9, 10).[4]

What is D'Amato, then: reluctant realist, uncertain constructivist, confused naturalist, practicing positivist? That we cannot tell suggests that he does not know. It also suggests that contemporary jurisprudence in the US has become so eclectic that nobody knows anymore. There is no reason to regret this condition so long as we try not to lie with labels and admit to our uncertainty. D'Amato, though, has difficulty in accepting this conclusion. Chronic uncertainty is the existential plight of our time. It suggests that we may be no more than "machines acting out what could be an absurd drama" (p. 219). This is D'Amato's deepest fear. It lends Kafkaesque resonance to the first sentence in the book: "The United States today is a dictatorship of law" (p. 1). D'Amato's determined efforts to unmask this absurd situation, in which law out of control is in control, confirms instead that even the best jurisprudential minds cannot make complete sense of the world we have constructed.

4 A. D'Amato, "The Concept of Human Rights in International Law," *Columbia Law Review*, vol. 82, 1982, pp. 1110–59; see pp. 1127–47.

16 Review: *International Legal Structure*, by David Kennedy, 1987 (1988)

After many delays, the edited volume I had begun work on in 1973 (see Chapter 6, above) called *Law-Making in the Global Community* appeared in 1982. The following year, the *Harvard International Law Journal* published a long, critical review – critical in the ordinary sense of the term and critical as an exercise in "critical theory." The reviewer, Joshua Floum, acknowledged the influence of the Critical Legal Studies movement and more specifically of David Kennedy on his thinking. In 1980, Kennedy had arrived on the international legal scene, as I say below, with a manifesto in his hand and revolution in his heart, the manifesto being an essay in the *German Year Book of International Law* and the object of revolution being the grand edifice of modernity. For several years, I had myself explored the various streams in the postmodern movement and had adopted some but not all of the many claims made on its behalf (Chapters 13, 14); I was anxious to read and respond to the published version of Kennedy's book-length manuscript, upon which Floum had based his review. When *International Legal Structures* appeared in 1987, Detlev Vagts, a colleague of Kennedy's and book review editor for the *American Journal of International Law*, honored my request to review it.

Undeniably important, the book presents the reader with many difficulties. Both to make the book's complicated argument as clear as I could and to convey the full flavor of Kennedy's prose, I wrote a long review, at least by the *Journal*'s standards, and laced it with a good many quotations. Vagts cut a few sentences toward the end but otherwise left my prose intact. While I have no idea what Kennedy's reaction may have been, I believe the review was widely appreciated in its time and is still valuable.

David Kennedy has undertaken a remarkable project – nothing less than a reconsideration of the development of international legal doctrine over several centuries. The book under review is the most substantial contribution to the project as yet, but it lacks, perhaps surprisingly, a prospectus for the larger undertaking. Instead, its successive chapters repeat the organizational logic found in most systematic casebooks and treatises (or so Kennedy avers, p. 8). The book thus creates the firm, but misleading, impression that it stands, like most systematic works, sufficient unto itself. Only by reading it with some of Kennedy's journal articles can we appreciate his larger intentions.

What are those intentions? Clearly, Kennedy knows that in reconsidering the developmental course of doctrine, he is propounding doctrine. More than this, he wishes to launch a new era in the development of doctrine. One clue to Kennedy's intentions can be found in his essay, "Primitive Legal Scholarship." Here, Kennedy blocks out three eras in the history of doctrine: the primitive (before 1648), the traditional (1648–1900) and the modern (1900–1980).[1] Why does the modern era end in 1980? What succeeds it? At least in this sketch, Kennedy does not say, except indirectly, through his characterization of the three past eras.

Because the subject is doctrine, Kennedy confines himself to texts. Texts always have subjects. In Kennedy's judgement, texts constituting international legal doctrine have just one subject upon which they endlessly play. This is the relation of that doctrine to authority. Primitive texts posit authority in nature or justice and derive appropriate doctrine. In contrast, "[t]raditional texts argue more about the appropriateness of various authorities and their proper interpretation."[2] Doctrines are derived from a particular interpretation, which is nonetheless put forth as an internally coherent conceptual system. Modern texts doubt all interpretive claims to generality. Instead, they seek refuge in the ever-more complex technical and procedural manifestations of authority.

Texts have authors as well as subjects. In primitive texts, authors present themselves as mere messengers who speak to the truth of independent authority. In traditional texts, authors validate the authorities through their interpretations. In the modern era, authority and authorship simultaneously recede from view, for "the modern scholar typically exempts himself from his text."[3] Elsewhere, in addressing "late-modern" texts, Kennedy finds the "construction of a disembodied vantage point from which a centrist politics seems inevitable."[4] Centrist politics are the "politics of centrist management" demanded by the proceduralization of authority in the state and the move to international institutions.[5]

What now can we say about the era after 1980, Kennedy's own? Obviously, it must depart from, or self-consciously repudiate, the hallmarks of modernity. If modern authors disappear from their texts, it is because they want readers to think of those texts as transparent media. Thus, he argues, "[m]odern

1 D. Kennedy, "Primitive Legal Scholarship," *Harvard International Law Journal*, vol. 27, 1986, pp. 1–13.
2 Ibid., p. 6.
3 Ibid.
4 D. Kennedy, "The Turn to Interpretation," *Southern California Law Review*, vol. 58, 1985, pp. 255–6.
5 Ibid., p. 265. *Cf.* D. Kennedy, "The Move to Institutions," *Cardozo Law Review*, vol. 8, 1987, pp. 841–988.

theory builds space for complacency in an expansive humility."[6] After modernity, against this complacency, must come acknowledgment that texts are decisive. Modern texts work on behalf of proceduralized authority by employing the rhetorical strategy of self-effacement. Against this strategy must come a rhetoric of challenge and exposure.

The problem for a rhetoric against modernity is to find its proper voice. The voice of rectitude is primitive – too passionate for a modern, knowing world. The scornful voice is self-defeating, the voice of revolutionary abandonment unconvincing, the nostalgic voice meretricious, the Aquarian voice naive. The late modern voice of accommodation to criticism is escapist. Kennedy's own voice is unsure; his reticence lacks the "self-assurance" he finds in modernity's "theoretical structure of false humility."[7]

Kennedy's sensitivity to rhetoric effectively denies him a proper voice with which to confront modernity and launch a new era. Instead, he occupies a vantage point after modernity from which to look back on past eras. This is his stance in *International Legal Structure.* His long view permits him to see the structure of each era. More specifically, because these are eras in the development of doctrine, his focus is "upon the relationships among doctrines and arguments and upon their recurring rhetorical structure" (p. 7). "Structure" does not refer to some meta-textual, orienting feature of social reality, as the term usually connotes. Kennedy's interest is not "the relationship between international legal materials and their political and interpretive milieu" (ibid.). Nor is it "the meaning and distinctiveness of public international law doctrine" (ibid.). If rhetorical structure is all that counts, then we may be forgiven the inference that it alone grants law and society their meaning and distinctiveness. For Kennedy to say as much would be a greater challenge to modernity's smug conceits than he ever permits himself.

Kennedy's "Primitive Legal Scholarship" provides an overview of the project. The book begins abruptly, warning of "the difficulties and eccentricities" of his approach (p. 8). Oriented by Kennedy's overview, we realize that Chapter 1, "The Sources of International Law," is an examination of the traditional era, in which doctrine about sources remains firmly grounded. Chapter 2 is devoted to "The Procedures of International Law," and is an examination of modernity. Chapter 3 covers "The Substance of International Law." In keeping with Kennedy's retrospective stance, this is an assessment of modernity's impact on tradition. Unwritten is a last chapter proclaiming a new era. Instead, a brief conclusion deflects attention from such a possibility by arguing that the cross-referencing of doctrines on sources, processes and substance "constitute[s] public international law as a single rhetorical fabric" (p. 293). So much for a rhetoric turned against modernity.

Rhetoric is Kennedy's problem. He tries to avoid it by professing only to

6 Kennedy, "The Turn to Interpretation," p. 257.
7 Ibid.

read exemplary cases and materials and trace their rhetorical strategies (p. 7). The message is that reading and tracing are uncontentious activities and the author an innocent facilitator. This, of course, is the typical modern rhetorical strategy of absenting oneself from the text. Yet Kennedy is not a modern and cannot stay away; his ever-changing voice mimics the voices typically heard in each of his doctrinal eras.

This is an adroit move. Predictably, it is acknowledged, not in the book, but as a "methodological disclaimer" in "Primitive Legal Scholarship," and then only in reference to the first era. There, he claims, "[t]his essay, then, is neither a history of the development of legal doctrines nor a social history. It attempts to explain the work of the primitives as extensively and as sympathetically as possible within the four corners of their own lexicon."[8]

International Legal Structure's chapter on sources presents itself first in the same authoritative tones we hear in traditional treatments of sources. Short declarative sentences populate the text, virtually every one supported by one or more footnotes citing authoritative texts in several languages. Mimicry turns to parody, as footnotes consume three-quarters of the first 20 pages.

The next section of this chapter switches rhetorical modes because the subject shifts from "doctrinal boundaries and hierarchies" to "a quite well worked out argumentative practice about the authority or 'binding nature' of various legal instruments" (p. 29). Kennedy himself becomes argumentative. First, he introduces a controlling metaphorical opposition:

> Sources rhetoric provides two rhetorical or persuasive styles which we might call "hard" and "soft." A hard argument will seek to ground compliance in the "consent" of the state to be bound. A "soft" argument relies upon some extraconsensual notion of the good or the just (p. 29).

The opposition would seem to be the familiar one of positivist versus naturalist interpretations of the source of law's authority, which indeed dominates traditional doctrine. Why, then, use terms like "hard" and "soft," which have their own connotative force? – "hard" is sharp, clean, tough; "soft" is spongy, ragged, sentimental. They permit Kennedy to proceed "in a somewhat stylized fashion" (pp. 29–30). The result is a series of ever-more intricate substitutions and inversions, which follow the pattern of arguments generally. When confronted, every hard position reveals itself to be soft, just as every soft position reveals hardness. Therefore, "[b]ecause neither set of arguments can be convincing by itself and neither can trap the other, argument within this structure could go on endlessly without resolution" (p. 31) – as does Kennedy.

Endless argument is wearying. Kennedy shifts to a more comfortable rhetorical posture in the next three sections. He identifies a series of doctrinal

8 Kennedy, "Primitive Legal Scholarship," p. 13; footnote deleted.

puzzles – unilateral declarations, *rebus sic stantibus*, custom – and styles each one a "case." Appropriately enough, Kennedy's voice becomes that of a law school instructor. In mildly detached language, he presents the arguments in each case by referring to exemplary cases, skillfully teasing out hard and soft elements, and finally proposing a reconciliation of elements to show how rhetorical structure manages "what otherwise seems a tense relationship between an absolute sovereign autonomy to consent and a systemic pattern of legal obligation" (p. 80). Each case comes to the same conclusion: "It seems that if the 'hard' can lie down with the 'soft' in sources argument, sovereigns will be able to remain autonomous within a binding normative order" (p. 32).

After Kennedy runs through the argument several times, we are inclined to concede him the day. As a scholar, he is ingenious; as a teacher, thorough. Some may resist the simplification brought on by stylized argument. For example, this reviewer suspects that the argument over unilateral declarations is not a matter of positivism and naturalism, but instead of continental and common law traditions. In the former, law, and with it obligation, arises from authoritative assertion. In the latter, obligation, and with it law, arises from mutuality of commitment. The first is unilateral in form, the second bilateral. Kennedy himself intimates this opposition, and then stretches the infinitely elastic metaphor of hard and soft to envelop it (p. 54).

Kennedy uses the concluding section of the first chapter to recapitulate. He says of sources doctrine that it "searches abstractly," that it "constantly combines that which it cannot differentiate and emphasizes that which it can express only by hyperbolic exclusion" (p. 107). Just so. And so it is with Kennedy's rhetorical style. Like the doctrine he engages, he, too, searches abstractly, with a rhetoric of repetition, "endlessly embracing and managing a set of ephemeral rhetorical differences" (ibid.).

Chapter 2 begins with the assertion that "[d]iscourse about international legal process dominates the field of international law" (p. 109; for Kennedy, "doctrine" and "discourse" are interchangeable). A footnote refers us to "traditional" teaching materials dated to 1980. Recall, however, that doctrine's traditional era gave way to the modern in 1900. Evidently, these materials confront us with a paradox. Although they are organized traditionally (as indeed is Kennedy's book), they necessarily respond to the consuming circumstances of modernity.

Dominance notwithstanding, "process doctrines exist uneasily between discourse about the sources of international law on the one hand and its substance on the other" (p. 110). In other words, traditional discourse is mostly about rules, which are related to authority through a proper, authorizing source. Yet the proceduralization of authority calls for a discourse that cannot be about rules so understood. If rules in their fixity and generality anchor tradition, the continuous formulation of complex, transitory procedures fuels modernity.

Procedural talk must either make rules out of procedure, in which instance it is no longer modern, or escape into the space between rules, for which procedures are wanting. Modernity always searches for the unsaid; tradition always takes what modernity says into its system of rules. Ever restless, modernity always finds tradition just behind it. Although tradition fell to modernity around 1900, it has fallen forward, almost reaching the present.

Kennedy tells us nothing of this. Instead, he runs through the same rhetorical moves he has introduced in Chapter 1. Roughly one page of text and seven of footnotes mimic tradition, but only to tell us what process discourse is not (pp. 109–16). Kennedy then turns to his argument:

> Process discourse considers two broad issues. Doctrines of "participation" abstractly delimit the actors whose interests and nature will be constitutive of international law and whose substantive behavior will be controlled by international law. Doctrines of what might loosely be called "jurisdiction" abstractly delimit the avenues of legitimate interchange out of which authoritative norms grow and the spheres of activity which will be governed by substantive international law (p. 117, two footnotes deleted).

Participation, we find, relates to the traditional substantive domain of the subjects of international law. Jurisdiction's concern with "avenues of legitimate interchange" and "spheres of activities" suggests a relation to the traditional substantive domain of territorial jurisdiction. Were process doctrines about such matters, however, they would be about authoritative rules, not the proceduralization of authority, and thus they would be traditional, not modern. Consequently, process doctrine must occupy a ruleless space produced by the procedural fragmentation of authority, and it must do so in terms that are "abstract" and "independent of the content of norms" (p. 120). Specificity opens the door to sources and substance, to rules, to tradition.

It seems that if process doctrine is to be about anything, it must be about itself. This it manages by opposing its two elements – participation doctrine and jurisdiction doctrine. Such an opposition is not arbitrary, for it repeats the juxtaposition of hard and soft elements found in sources doctrine. Thus, "[d]octrine about how participants interact, which is independent of substance, promises to remain open-ended, and protect the independence of sovereigns." Doctrine such as this calls to, and works for, the positivist tradition (p. 121). However, "[d]octrine about who participates, if independent of the authority and interests of sovereigns, promises to remain determinative while protecting the integrity of the international legal system" (ibid.). Here, doctrine meets the naturalist tradition.

On behalf of modernity, Kennedy finesses the problem of participation and jurisdiction as substantive domains by construing them as topics worthy of an argument – topics like recognition (a matter of participation) and sovereign immunity (a matter of jurisdiction). Absent rules, all such topics disclose the same argumentative structure in which hard and soft positions are opposed, transformed and collapsed. Kennedy is now able to adopt the argumentative rhetorical style that he favors. Only this time he replaces "hard" and "soft" with a new metaphorical opposition:

> [P]rocess doctrine works by deploying a distinction between what might be thought of as a "subjective" and an "objective" approach to the delimitation of sovereign authority (footnote deleted). . . . An objective approach to participation defines the entities in terms of the way they are treated or act in the system. A subjective approach relies upon their self-definition or true "essence" (p. 121).

This is a regrettable choice of terms. In ordinary language, "subjective" and "objective" refer to a disposition or attitude some agent possesses with respect to some state of affairs. Kennedy uses the terms to describe properties of some state of affairs in a way to suggest the dominance of one over the other. He confuses matters further by linking subjectivity to "true 'essence,' " which inappropriately signals a transcendentalist stance. We might forgive Kennedy these awkward choices if they conveyed important information. They do not. Subjective characterizations of participation turn out to support the position of sovereigns as subjects and thus fit a positivist interpretation of authority. Objective characterizations support the integrity of obligations over which sovereigns have no immediate control and thus fit a naturalist interpretation.

Having substituted one unsuitable metaphorical construction for another, Kennedy has "subjective" and "objective" approaches "argue" with each other; predictably, they collapse into each other. He then takes recognition, sovereign immunity and state responsibility as illustrative "cases." Patiently explicating the rhetorical structure of each, he relaxes his style from the argumentative to the professorial.

The first two cases offer no surprises; we suspect Kennedy of belaboring the obvious. The third sustains greater interest because it reaches beyond "process discourse as a self-contained set of rhetorical maneuvers and projections" to its "brother discourses" (p. 173). Kennedy finds that in the instance of state responsibility, "process discourse achieves its comprehensivity in an elaborate movement of self-effacement" (ibid.). Inasmuch as self-effacement is modernity's preferred rhetorical style, we might expect the same of Kennedy the mimic. To his credit, however, Kennedy's voice is firm without being unduly argumentative or didactic. We feel his engagement with modernity, his resistance to its disappearing act.

The discussion begins with a semantic difficulty because Kennedy associates "procedural" and "objective," "substantive" and "subjective" (p. 174). Yet we know from his general argument that substance and procedure are respectively associated with tradition and modernity, the first having a rhetorical structure opposing "hard" and "soft," and the second a structure opposing "subjective" and "objective." This difficulty is compounded when

Kennedy separates "the procedural rules of responsibility" from "substantive norms" (p. 175 n.119). The former are "neutral, threshold rules." The latter are "determining rules imposing systemic values and decisions" (ibid.). This distinction is untenable. Rules by definition establish thresholds (their function) and bear values (their propositional content).

We might better say that proceduralization inevitably produces procedures that, as rules, defeat the strategy of self-effacement that proceduralization manifests. In other words, modernity inevitably loses to tradition the space it wrests for itself from tradition. Kennedy offers a complementary proposition: "Process doctrine has devoured all of law – doctrine of substance having been fully projected into it. Here the dispassionate voice of modern doctrinal discourse is created as substance disappears from law's core" (p. 180 n. 125). Evidently, modernity is not content to fill the spaces in traditional systems of rules. Rather, modernity makes space for itself by breaking up these systems and isolating their rules. Surrounded by unrelated procedures, long-established rules must atrophy. To use Kennedy's metaphor, procedural talk devours rules, only to be devoured by the rules such talk engenders. Modernity's distinguishing feature is not the self-effacement of doctrine, but its inability to defend itself from effacement by tradition.

Kennedy's conclusion to Chapter 2 briefly reverts to the theme of the dominance of process, acknowledging that "its mastery is a strange one" (p. 188). Chapter 3 resumes discussion of substance, but shifts the focus from its consumption by modernity to its capacity to generate "a legal regime more complex than its terms – partly through its relationship to the regimes of processes and sources and partly through its own imagination" (p. 193, footnote deleted). This extraordinary assertion is followed by a two-page footnote that tells us nothing about the power of imagination but almost all that Kennedy has to say, in a traditional voice, about substantive doctrine (ibid., n. 1).

To illuminate the generative power of substantive discourse, Kennedy identifies yet a third, less obviously metaphorical, opposition. Authority and autonomy are juxtaposed with community and cooperation. The former is "primarily associated" with the law of war, the latter with the law of peace (p. 199). Nevertheless, the "broad doctrinal categories" of war and peace "seem somewhat porous. Each contains within it both elements of the other and doctrines separating it from the other" (ibid.). These doctrinal categories are subject to a common fate – the invasion of procedure. More precisely, it "is the transformation of the substantive opposition between autonomy and community into procedures" (ibid.).

"Sovereign autonomy," Kennedy writes, "initially seems instantiated by procedures of jurisdictional allocation or boundary drawing, procedures which might be thought of as architectural. Sovereign community, on the other hand, is known as procedures of international intervention, institutionalization or regulation" (pp. 199–200). The invocation of autonomy and community as the controlling opposition, with architecture and regulation their procedural counterparts, is a great improvement over the metaphorical oppositions of earlier chapters. (And it brings to mind Kennedy's claim, discussed in Chapter 14, that international law is a system of rules ordered by the binary of sovereignty and cooperation.) We find Kennedy easier to follow as he penetrates the circumstances under which substance disappears into procedure, and procedure into substance. It also helps that he confines his discussion of peace to one "case," the United Nations Convention on the Law of the Sea.[9]

We note first that, like state responsibility, the law of the sea has been subject to that most traditional of doctrinal activities, codification and progressive development. The point of codification is to disclose fully a system of rules, while the point of progressive development is to fill gaps in it with additional rules. Nevertheless, codification and progressive development have inevitably succumbed to modernity. Discussion of the proper content of the system of rules points to the inadequacy of the system as such and fosters an ever-more procedurally oriented discussion of alternatives. In short, the taken-for-granted architecture of tradition comes into question as the examination of substance poses regulatory dilemmas.

As Kennedy correctly notes, these dilemmas are projected into institutions (p. 200). Endless discussion of never-completed drafts often follows. The sheer importance of oceans of questions has prohibited this outcome. Forced to closure, the law of the sea discussions required the drafting of a traditional instrument, a multilateral treaty embodying a system of rules, without denying modernity its proceduralizing voice. In a brilliant dissection of the treaty, Kennedy peels back its "dry language and committee locution" (p. 201) to show that the Preamble promises to fulfill "substantive hopes which have been deferred by sources and process" (p. 202). This promise is never kept. "Instead the lengthy Convention submerges its voice, referring through both its organization and content simultaneously forward to process and back to its sources or purposive origin in the Preamble" (ibid.).

Process here refers to both institutions and procedures, established in the treaty to deal with what its text does not provide but tradition requires: a closed set of rules. The text retains traditional architecture while it staves off tradition's insatiable propensity to absorb the products of modernity. By institutionalizing process within the treaty's traditional architecture, modernity can hold on to the space it has pried away from tradition.

Kennedy's examination of the law of force proceeds differently. A third discursive element, beyond tradition and modernity, complicates the tale: "Scholars seem to speak a very Hobbesian dialect in which law . . . ebbs and flows as order against chaos" (p. 246). Not just scholars, but states' leaders and the institutions they create, all respond to "force as fear" (section title, ibid.).

Kennedy holds that the primitive response to Hobbesian fear shifts the

9 Reprinted in *International Legal Materials*, vol. 21, 1982, pp. 1261–329.

terms of discourse from order to justice – "texts confidently distinguished between just and unjust wars" (p. 255, footnote deleted). Tradition tries a different strategy. It takes law as "the product or reflection of force" (ibid.). In both instances, "force as fear" is countered by "force as fact" (section title, p. 253). Modernity cannot be satisfied with either of these responses. Its solution is simultaneously to outlaw war and to regulate it.

The modern, procedural response to force is architectural in the first instance. This is quite unlike the modern response to the law of peace, in which traditional architecture orients procedural discussion. Thus, the move to institutions is the central feature of modern discourse on force. Through architecture, "law establishes itself as a sphere of meaning by excluding meaningless force" (p. 263, Kennedy's emphasis). Yet meaning is never self-evident, and the "struggle for an exclusion of force" is "recast as a struggle about meaning, interpretation and application rather than about authority" (p. 265). Substantive consequences are deferred, with "indeterminate yet distracting discourse" the result (p. 273).

Such an outcome is no different from the regulatory thrust of modern discourse on the law of peace. Indeed, Kennedy finds that an architecturally oriented law of force "completes, substantiates and reinforces the regimes of source, peace and process" (p. 282). Kennedy concludes his discussion of the law of war by returning to the Hobbesian rhetoric of fear.

> Recognizing that the laws of force repeat, return us to and reinforce the regimes of process and peace – are part of a single discursive system whose referent is itself rather than some external world of politics and facts – renders it more difficult to analyze these discourses as part of a struggle between law or civilization and the evils of power politics and anarchy" (p. 283).

This sentence is itself a rhetorical wonder. We are fitfully propelled along an inordinately long and winding participial phrase by a series of words beginning with the letter *r*. With the eighth, render, we perch at the top of modernity's self-made mountain of ephemeral distinctions and endless deferrals. Then we find ourselves flung down that mountain with the help of such instantly accessible but emotionally laden terms as *civilization* and *evils*.

Kennedy's rhetorical strategy insures the reader's relief at coming to the end of the sentence and, with it, to the possibility of anarchy. There is a point to "[t]he invocation of this Hobbesian 'other' " (p. 283). Kennedy uses it to take us to the edge of modernity, beyond which lies a wordless fear, "a Hobbesian imagination" (p. 286). If Kennedy takes us as far as modernity goes in his discussion of force, his conclusion takes us no further. Instead, we are reminded that "the pattern of repetitions, associations and references seems suited to a practice of interminable discourse" (p. 294). Kennedy shows all the signs of engaging in the elusive discourse of modernity no less interminably. His book does not end; it merely stops.

A proper conclusion to Kennedy's book would have to address the era after modernity, which he dates from 1980. Not at all coincidentally, 1980 is the date of Kennedy's "Theses on International Legal Discourse," the very title of which signals Kennedy's arrival on the international legal scene with a manifesto in his hand and revolution in his heart. Kennedy's manifesto also signals his abiding concern: "To me, then, international law discourse is a conversation without content – a ritualized exchange which avoids confronting the very questions it purports to address."[10] Yet this early work cannot provide a satisfying conclusion to Kennedy's great project of mapping the long development of international legal discourse.

There are two reasons. First, Kennedy had yet to discriminate previous eras. All that came before him was traditional. Second, and far more importantly, his "style of legal analysis" proved to be insufficiently innovative for a new era. That style consisted of an updated legal realism emphasizing "the indeterminacy of legal argument," matched to a structuralist concern for deep patterns of contradiction and transformation.[11] Kennedy's affiliation with the Critical Legal Studies Movement also suggests an interest in the critical theory of Frankfurt Marxism.

A few years later, Kennedy published a long and extremely sophisticated essay, entitled "Critical Legal Theory, Structuralism and Contemporary Legal Scholarship," and dedicated to exposing the limitations of structuralism and critical theory, as used in legal scholarship. Their shared failing is an inability to escape modernity. Only poststructuralism warrants description as "post-modern." His characterization of authors "[v]ariously labeled 'post-structuralist' or 'post-modern' " is apt: they all reject "any stable origin, standpoint, agency or totalizer in their work."[12]

Kennedy holds that his reading of critical theory and structuralism is "typically post-structuralist."[13] Yet his book has not fully broken with modernity. Much of the language of structuralism remains, as the title suggests. Nowhere in the book does Kennedy name his "style of legal analysis" or the influences on him (although the advertisement in the April 1988 number of this journal [*American Journal of International Law*] does so for him: "The critical stance and rhetorical method developed in this work show the influence of French structuralism and poststructuralism, German critical theory and the North American 'critical legal studies' school"). Nevertheless, a post-structuralist sensibility permeates it.

Kennedy's description of postmodern work in general fits his own later work in particular:

10 D. Kennedy, "Theses on International Legal Discourse," *German Year Book on International Law*, vol. 23, 1980, p. 376.
11 Ibid., p. 355 and n. 4.
12 "Critical Legal Theory, Structuralism and Contemporary Legal Scholarship," *New England Law Review*, vol. 21, 1985–1986, p. 276; footnote deleted.
13 Ibid., p. 280.

> [F]or all their diversity, post-modern works share a great deal stylistically. Their texts are elaborate imitations and reconstructions of other works. . . . As they recount the work of other texts they continually weave and unweave alternatives present and absent in the texts under scrutiny. Moreover, their accounts often seem quite playful."[14]

The fit is not perfect. Kennedy's rhetorical voice is not playful. He is simply too serious to be fully postmodern.

Kennedy has much to be serious about. Unlike so many of the texts post-structuralists play with, international legal discourse is about issues of the utmost seriousness – peace and justice on a global scale. Herein lies the material for Kennedy to write a fitting conclusion to his project. How can one be a playful postmodern in a deadly serious world? What is a properly postmodern response to Hobbesian fear?

Kennedy sees the dilemma precisely when he speaks of irony in post-structuralism: "It is an irony which stings. . . . The same playful tone which seems critical and affirmative can seem apolitical, disengaged and nihilistic."[15] To be playful in the circumstances that Kennedy addresses is to risk an ironic detachment, negative and ultimately conservative. Play is no less plausible a response than self-effacement to modernity's proceduralizing hegemony, and it has the mildly subversive consequences of self-awareness to recommend it. If modernity's other face is power politics and anarchy, as Kennedy seems to believe, then play is frivolous and detachment worse. Feigned indifference to the Hobbesian void tacitly capitulates to Hobbes's alternative, whether it is the unconstrained authority of the primitive Leviathan, the traditional sovereign or the modern maw of procedure.

Kennedy knows no postmodern voice in which to speak of such grave matters. Perhaps there is none that suits his deep seriousness. Even so, Kennedy has much to teach us about the way we speak of international law. If he does find a voice that avoids frivolity or capitulation, international legal scholarship will have begun a new era. If not, modernity will continue its relentless chase into the future, consuming all in its path, with tradition hard behind.

14 Ibid., pp. 286–7.
15 Ibid., p. 287.

17 Review: *From Apology to Utopia: The Structure of International Legal Argument*, by Martti Koskenniemi, 1989 (1989)

While I had known about David Kennedy's *International Legal Structures* (reviewed in Chapter 16) years in advance of its publication, I had never heard of Martti Koskenniemi until Detlev Vagts invited me to review *From Apology to Utopia* for the *American Journal of International Law*. In writing this book, Koskenniemi drew extensively on Kennedy's "unorthodox work," calling it "the most important contribution to international legal scholarship by a contemporary lawyer" (p. vi). Yet Koskenniemi was clearly not just the master's protege or *From Apology to Utopia* merely an apprentice's study. Nearly twice the length of Kennedy's book and formidably learned, Koskenniemi's book turns out to be a good deal more accessible than Kennedy's, I think for two reasons. First, it has a measured and consistent rhetorical style suggesting that Koskenniemi did not share Kennedy's postmodern preoccupation with authorial voice. Second, the relatively simple structure of Koskenniemi's argument works better as an argument about structure than Kennedy's involuted structure of oppositions and transpositions does. All of Kennedy's binaries resolve into aspects of tradition and modernity, which do not have a fixed relation to each other. For Koskenniemi, apology and utopia are the fixed, contrary tendencies of liberalism as well as legal argument. Not only does the liberal tradition give the modern world its overarching structure; it gives Koskenniemi a far better basis for critique than the ever-receding horizon of modernity does for Kennedy.

The *Journal* published my review substantially as I wrote it and as it appears here. Not surprisingly, it seems to have elicited less comment than my review of Kennedy's book. Nevertheless, acclaim for *From Apology to Utopia* has mounted ever since. Looking back, I would say that it is, to quote Koskenniemi again, "the most important contribution to international legal scholarship by a contemporary lawyer."

Recently, there has been a surge of interest in the theory of international law; less about rules and what counts as law, than about doctrine and the way lawyers argue. With this book, Martti Koskenniemi, of the Finnish Foreign Ministry, joins Anthony Carty, David Kennedy and Friedrich Kratochwil as leaders of this movement, at least in the English-language scholarship.[1] Koskenniemi is a particular admirer of Kennedy (pp. vi, xxi n. 7), whose work provides Koskenniemi's central theme: international legal arguments serve either as apologies for the primacy of states' interests or as utopian claims on behalf of common interests or the world community. More generally, Koskenniemi's methodological and ideological stance resembles Kennedy's. Nevertheless, Koskenniemi's prodigious research and relentless analytic disposition take him well beyond Kennedy's published efforts.

Koskenniemi begins with the argument that, in the course of professionalization, "post-enlightenment lawyers" separated social, political and moral theory from technical international legal doctrine (p. xiii). By leaving theory to others, modern lawyers accept irrelevance – to avoid controversy. "But doctrine constantly reproduces problems which seem capable of resolution only if one takes a theoretical position" (p. xv). Because theory cannot be discussed in a "specifically juristic way" (ibid.), technical competence offers no help and the lawyer's very identity is imperiled.

Koskenniemi thinks that controversy is inevitable because the assumptions constituting arguments are irrevocably normative. His objective is to have lawyers overcome their irrelevance by opening themselves to social theory as moral discourse. The method he proposes for realizing this objective is "regressive analysis" (p. xvii), a working backwards from particular legal arguments to their underlying oppositional structure, and finally to the point that their conceptual differentiation collapses and competing arguments appropriate each other's content. Regressive analysis penetrates to the "deep-structure" of international legal discourse. Such language acknowledges Koskenniemi's debt to structuralism, and especially structural linguistics (p. xix).

Regrettably, Koskenniemi also calls his method "deconstructive" (p. xvii). The term owes its currency to French philosopher and critic Jacques Derrida. As Koskenniemi admits, Derrida had considerably more than methodology in mind. For Derrida, deconstruction reveals the deep structures of Western metaphysics to be groundless. Foundational claims notwithstanding, all such structures secure their identity by differentiation from yet other structures, which, for the same reason, are themselves no less contingent. The methodological result can only be infinite regress or circularity; the philosophical result (many would say), an unbounded relativism leading at best to clever wordplay, or at worst to utter nihilism.

Evidently, Koskenniemi believes that deconstruction as a method can

1 See prominently A. Carty, *The Decay of International Law? A Reappraisal of the Limits of Legal Imagination in International Affairs*, Manchester: Manchester University Press, 1986; D. Kennedy, *International Legal Structures*, Baden-Baden: Nomos, 1987; F.V. Kratochwil, *Rules, Norms and Decisions: On the Conditions of Practical and Legal Reasoning in International Relations and Domestic Affairs*, Cambridge: Cambridge University Press, 1989.

be detached from the philosophical project for which Derrida devised it. Koskenniemi concedes that his "kind of deconstruction," no less than Derrida's, "may be taken to imply that ultimately all discourse will disperse into an unending play of conceptual oppositions in which there is ultimately no basis to prefer conflicting ideas *vis-à-vis* each other" (p. 479, footnote deleted). Koskenniemi cannot accept this implication because his project is to find the deepest structure of international legal argument, not to repudiate the constitutive assumptions that make such argument possible.

Koskenniemi created this problem for himself by needlessly invoking deconstruction. For many scholars, doing so amounts to a declaration of allegiance to, or at least affinity for, post-structuralism. What does such a declaration gain Koskenniemi? Post-structuralism is after all a critical response to structuralism, and Koskenniemi is simply mistaken to claim that they share a "hostility to thinking of human experience as something produced by an 'essence' or 'nature' residing outside experience itself" (p. xvii n. 1). Structuralists like Claude Levi-Strauss and Noam Chomsky postulate innate properties of mind that organize diverse human experiences into universal patterns. If Koskenniemi wishes to distance himself from the postulation of essences while taking advantage of a structuralist method, calling that method deconstructive takes him closer to radical relativism than he wishes.

Koskenniemi serves himself better when he associates his enterprise with Michel Foucault's archaeologies of knowledge (p. xviii n. 2). While Foucault is conventionally called a poststructuralist, his method is not Derrida's. It is critical in its effort to expose regimes of truth as systems of power (paraphrasing Koskenniemi's quotation of Foucault, p. xx n. 6). This is also the purpose of critique in the Frankfurt School's critical theory and the Critical Legal Studies movement. Koskenniemi claims that the very search for a "hidden code," as he calls the deepest structure of international legal argument, "bears a critical potential" (p. xxii, his emphasis, footnote deleted). Throughout the book, Koskenniemi speaks of his undertaking as critical. A regressive analysis lends itself to critical purposes because it, like Foucault's, is a method of exposure.

The point of exposing ourselves to the implications of our taken-for-granted practices, and their supposed objectivity, is to offer guidance in making something better of the world (usually; Foucault seems to have been ambivalent on this). In Koskenniemi's words, "criticism of objectivism neither entails anarchy nor cynical nihilism as a necessary consequence. The critical project implies both an institutional and a normative ideal" (p. 487). The institutional ideal is open, uncoerced discussion of alternatives, a community given to unending conversation about important issues. Behind this is the normative ideal of "authentic commitment," an "ethic of responsibility" (p. 488).

For scholars to construe their often disputatious reactions to each other's contributions to knowledge as an ongoing conversation is a flattering self-characterization. It is no wonder they responded so warmly when philosopher

Richard Rorty proposed it. However well it suits the academy, lawyers cannot afford the luxury of protracted discussion. The point of law is to close off discussion by providing reliable guidelines for behavior, immediate answers to questions and serviceable solutions to problems. Koskenniemi would have lawyers complement their technical competence with the conversational skills of theoretical scholars, without considering the possibility that the latter might detract from the former.

The connection between the institutional ideal of open conversation and the normative ideal of authentic commitment is Jürgen Habermas's belief that only in a perfectly open conversation – an ideal speech situation, he would say – could we know our real interests and their proper relation to the interests of others. Only in such a situation is agreement possible. This is a Kantian position. If Kant taught an ethic of responsibility in which we should try to see beyond ourselves, he also acknowledged our inability to do so perfectly in a contingent world. Moral certainty and complete agreement are impossible; personal qualities of commitment and integrity must guide us.

From this position, Koskenniemi draws prescriptive consequences for the international lawyer. "Rather than be normative in the whole (and be vulnerable to the objections of apologism-utopianism) he should be normative in the small" (p. 496). The lawyer should "isolate the issues which are significant in conflict, assess them with an impartial mind and offer a solution which seems best to fulfil the demands of the critical programme" (pp. 496–7). There are difficulties with these recommendations. First, the injunction to think small controverts Koskenniemi's stated goal of having lawyers overcome their technical preoccupations by becoming theoretically aware. Theories are always statements about relations in general. In the absence of a larger picture, such as theory provides, how does one know what issues are significant? How does one recognize impartiality?

Second, Koskenniemi devotes fewer than ten of his hundreds of pages to the critical program. Following Roberto Unger, he distinguishes between routines and "the institutional and imaginative constraints within which routines work and which routine helps to reproduce" (p. 491). To participate in routine concerns invites apologism; to dwell on the removal of constraints is utopian. The critical lawyer maintains an interest in transforming contexts without forgetting that contexts cannot be divorced from the routines embedded in them. The means for doing this is practical reason. "Engaging in practical reasoning the lawyer engages himself in what is a transforming routine par excellence" (p. 497). Lawyers may respond, "Practical reasoning is what I do. I am a decent, reflective person. How come my daily routine isn't transformative? Why does Koskenniemi spend five hundred pages picking on me?"

Perhaps the last of the queries is unfair to Koskenniemi. Despite his stated intention of broadening the intellectual and moral horizons of technical international lawyers, his critical concerns are more inclusive. The problem is not that legal technicians have no theoretical context within which to couch their daily routines. Liberalism or, more precisely, "the liberal theory of politics," provides just such a context, but as a given, not subject to examination, criticism or transformation.

To set up his argument about the oppositional structure of legal argument, Koskenniemi identifies concreteness and normativity as conflicting requirements of law and then associates these requirements with incompatible assumptions anchoring the liberal theory of politics. Law must reflect "the concrete wills and interests of individuals," yet the "normative order" binds these individuals against their wishes (p. 6). The result is a division of labor between those who make, and those who apply, the law. Clearly, this is a positivist theory of law, arguably a liberal theory of law and government, but hardly a general characterization of liberalism's political tenets. Koskenniemi's conclusion that the division of legal labors cannot be maintained consistently is, at least in technical terms, neither news to lawyers nor a sufficient reason to doubt that "any meaningful distinction between international law, politics and morality can be made" (p. 8).

After this unconvincing beginning, Koskenniemi adopts a larger and more telling conception of liberalism in order to characterize the historic relation between liberal thought and international legal doctrine.

> The fundamental problem of the liberal vision is how to cope with what seem like mutually opposing demands for individual freedom and social order. The liberal attempt to tackle with this conflict is by means of reconciliation, or paradox: to preserve freedom, order must be created to restrict it (p. 52, footnote deleted).

The liberal balancing act never succeeds for long. Liberals slip into apologies for either individual preferences or states' interests, depending on the actors, or utopian dreams of harmony. When either side challenges the other, both attempt to regain their balance by adding the other's argument to its own, with theoretical incoherence and prescriptive inconsistency the inevitable outcome.

The two long chapters on doctrine persuasively substantiate Koskenniemi's claim that internal contradictions in liberal theory and practice explain the progressive irrelevance of international legal doctrine. These chapters submit a remarkable array of doctrinal materials to unblinking scrutiny. Koskenniemi's conclusion is irresistible. At the bottom of all discussion is the problem of justice: justice is either purely subjective or necessarily imposed. Either alternative threatens the edifice of modern doctrine and the liberal theory behind it.

Here, Koskenniemi could profitably have proceeded with a more extensive rendition of his program, perhaps suggesting a theoretical alternative to liberalism specifically tailored to the international lawyer's technical competence and argumentative needs. Instead, he applies his critical capacities to a series of overlapping doctrinal foci – sovereignty, sources, custom and world order. We read the same story over and over again, its raw material recycled, its argument unvarying, its rhetorical rhythms too familiar, its conclusion foretold. At first awesome, Koskenniemi's extraordinary breadth of reading and analytic skill finally become tiresome.

By the end, we feel that Koskenniemi is himself wearing out. In considering arguments about world order, his voice takes on a querulous edge. The term "totalitarianism" appears without warning, to characterize first "the structures of economic domination of the present international system" (p. 432), and then the utopian position that community should prevail over autonomous units (pp. 433 and 448). Why the apologetic position of "unfettered egoism" (p. 448) is any less totalitarian in implication is hard to say; Hannah Arendt's diagnosis of the possibility of evil in the banal performance of routines suggests that it is. After Jeane Kirkpatrick's successful, if controversial, appropriation of the term "totalitarianism" for ideological purposes much at odds with Koskenniemi's, why he would want to use it at all is another question. Yet the term occurs a last time in Koskenniemi's only substantive claim on behalf of his critical program. Practical reason, aiming for authentic commitment, "positively *excludes imperialism and totalitarianism*" (p. 497, his emphasis). *Positively*?

18 Review: *International Law: Politics, Values and Function*, by Louis Henkin, 1989[1] (1991)

As book review editor of the *American Journal of International Law*, Detlev Vagts invited me to review the several volumes of the collected lectures delivered to The Hague Academy of International Law in 1989. These lectures included a variety of courses on specialized topics and Louis Henkin's general course on public international law. The general course is an annual event acknowledging the field's giants and giving them an opportunity to put forward their mature views on the nature, reach and future of international law. An opportunity to review Henkin's general course of lectures was both a great honor and a grave responsibility. I had come to know Henkin in 1981–1982 while I was a visiting professor in Columbia University's Department of Political Science. A distinguished professor in the Law School and at the time, one of the *Journal*'s editors-in-chief, Henkin had approved my peculiar proposal to review a book on Bali (Chapter 11) and had involved me in a bibliographical project on human rights. Much as I wanted to affirm Henkin's general course as an important contribution to theory, I found myself unable to do so. In my cover letter to Vagts, I voiced a concern for "the review's tone." While I hoped to convey an appreciation of what Henkin had accomplished in the general course, I was disappointed by its conceptual limitations. Even if there is a large "movement in the law from 'conceptualism' to 'functionalism'," as Henkin claimed, making clear how law functions remains as a conceptual task – one that Henkin gave too little attention to, here or elsewhere in his work.

The *Journal* published the review substantially as submitted. I heard nothing from Henkin or indeed anyone else. Here I have deleted the several paragraphs devoted to the topical lectures in the reviewed volumes.

"Where have all the treatises gone?" Thomas Franck asked this intriguing question to begin his 1987 review of Oscar Schachter's General Course

1 General Course on Public International Law, *Recueil des cours de l'Academie de Droit International de La Haye*, vol. 216, 1989/IV. Subsequently published as *International Law: Politics and Values*, Dordrecht: Nijhoff, 1995.

in Public International Law delivered to The Hague Academy in 1982.[2] Franck's answer to this question was a lament: he blamed changes in scholarly vocation and jurisprudential fashion, especially in the US, where he claimed "legal nihilism" now prevails. Yet surely there is more to it than this, as Franck himself hinted. International law is "increasingly the subject of restatements, codifications, treaties and resolutions of international organizations," all of which means that "the treatise writer can no longer be as visible or as influential as formerly."[3] We need not impugn scholarly motives to see what has happened. Treatises have been superseded.

Treatises are no longer the most efficient or reliable vehicle for the compilation and dissemination of the positive law. Either they are redundant because restatements, treaties and the like, already propound the positive law, rule by rule, authoritatively and systematically; or they are subject to charges of bias, selectivity and error stemming from the personal and material limitations of solo scholarship. Symptomatically, treatises have been replaced by the products of lengthy, well-supported collaborations and successively revised, widely distributed drafts. The sheer volume of positive international law militates against its recapitulation in a single treatise.

Consider that Hersch Lauterpacht's last edition of Oppenheim's legendary treatise fairly covered the law of peace in a thousand pages.[4] In the several decades since, positive law has swelled many times over, necessitating a treatise as many times longer to be comparable. For pedagogical purposes, too, treatises have been superseded – in this instance – by textbooks and casebooks that make no claim to cover the positive law exhaustively. Given Franck's lament, we can appreciate his surprise that Schachter had indeed written a treatise for his General Course, and had done so in fewer than 400 pages. Obviously, Schachter did not undertake a comprehensive compilation of the positive law. Instead, he distilled "the normative essence of international law."[5] We may wonder that Schachter's General Course qualifies as a treatise in view of its "many areas of incomplete research and overgeneral conclusion," as Alfred Rubin wondered in his companion review.[6]

Nevertheless, Franck had a point. Schachter's General Course presents a doctrinally supported framework for ordering and assessing the bulk of positive international law. Such a framework is necessary to, but not sufficient for, a treatise worthy of the name. Properly understood, a treatise requires not only a comprehensive, internally consistent and explicitly articulated

2 T.M. Franck, "Review Essay: The Case of the Vanishing Treatises," *American Journal of International Law*, vol. 81, 1987, p. 763.

3 Ibid., pp. 765, 764.

4 L. Oppenheim, *International Law*, vol. 1, 8th edn by H. Lauterpacht, New York: McKay, 1955.

5 Franck, "Review Essay," p. 766.

6 A.P. Rubin, Review, "*Recueil des Cours de L'Académie de Droit International de La Haye, 1982*," *American Journal of International Law*, vol. 81, 1987, p. 774.

framework, like Schachter's, but also a comprehensive accounting of the positive law. If these conditions are to be met at all, the General Course seems an unlikely place; 15 lectures represent a severe limitation, however skilled the lecturer. Yet Louis Henkin (Columbia University) has arguably done just this in the General Course on Public International Law for 1989 (vol. 216), entitled *International Law: Politics, Values and Functions*.

Under the circumstances, the more difficult task is to set forth fully the positive law: "Law is in the details" (p. 169). Henkin could not possibly have done this, despite his remarkable talent for concise and accessible exposition. Nor did he claim to: "A general course cannot aspire to be a complete course covering all international law" (p. 19). Nevertheless, few general courses have the substantive breadth of Henkin's; none fosters in this reviewer quite the same impression of completeness.

Contributing to this impression – indeed, to an impression of surpassing mastery over the positive law – is the looming presence in the General Course of the *Restatement (Third) of the Foreign Relations Law of the United States* (1987). Prepared by four scholars over eight years, with many other scholars in the US and abroad serving in an advisory capacity, the *Restatement* is just the kind of document that Franck found pushing the treatise aside. As Chief Reporter, Henkin quite properly defends his "repeated citations" to the *Restatement* as recourse "to a careful contemporary articulation by an authoritative body" (ibid.). (A quick count found 148 of these citations.) For Henkin's purpose, the *Restatement* is an annex to his General Course. Conversely, the latter serves as an annotated index to the former. Any sense that the General Course glides over the positive law is more than offset by the comforting thought that everything is to be found in the *Restatement*, where Henkin put it.

As we would expect from a scholar of Henkin's distinction, doctrine has a role in the General Course, though not the usual role. Most general courses, including Schachter's, begin with an extended, more or less complete discussion of doctrine, and then move on to a presentation of the positive law. These discussions of doctrine typically consist of three closely related activities: (1) clarification of concepts, (2) engagement in normative controversy, and (3) construction or adoption of a jurisprudential system, or theory of law, which builds a framework for the subsequent presentation of the standing law.

Henkin's approach is different. His lectures build on three "themes" already announced in the subtitle of the General Course.

> The first addresses law as politics, and international law as the law of a political system of separate States. A second theme explores the changes in the values and purposes of the international political system. The third perceives a movement in the law from "conceptualism" to "functionalism", from logical deduction from abstract principles to pragmatic attention to practical needs (ibid.).

Each theme dominates several lectures, forming the treatise's first three parts. A fourth, much shorter part turns to the future of international law.

Each part begins with a few pages of conceptual clarification. The historical development of normative controversy is not discussed; nor is there a general review of major jurisprudential systems. Instead, Henkin moves on quickly to the positive law. Since Part I is devoted to international law and the interstate system, the state gets its conceptual due (pp. 23–9) and then becomes the point of reference for a concise discussion of law relating to recognition, nonstate entities and nationality (pp. 30–44). Indicatively, Henkin devotes one chapter (22 pages) to lawmaking, which is preeminently a subject of conceptual interest and normative controversy, as compared to Schachter's four chapters (74 pages). Parts II and III and most of the 15 chapters (or lectures) show the same pattern: frame the subject at hand in a few conceptual strokes and get on with the positive law. Obviously, a great deal hinges on the success of the brief conceptual interludes.

Overall, Henkin's conceptual efforts are disappointing. The first begins with the claim that "law is politics" (p. 22, citing his own *How Nations Behave* [2nd edn, 1979]). This claim is almost immediately qualified: "the distinction between law and politics is only a part-truth" (ibid.). That distinction resides in the normativity of law, upon which Henkin sees little need to comment. The identity of law and politics is a complementary truth in need of demonstration: "Law is made by political actors (not by lawyers), through political procedures, for political ends. The law that emerges is the result of political forces; the influences on State behavior are also determined by political forces" (ibid.). Repeated use of the term *political* makes Henkin's demonstration rhetorically effective; but, on descriptive and analytic grounds, it leaves much to be desired. In Henkin's system, there is evidently nothing distinctive to or about politics. It is "a web with few seams" (p. 65), as impenetrable as it is pervasive. Such an undiscriminating view of politics necessarily puts law at a disadvantage – its autonomy is questionable, its presence debatable, its efficacy forever in doubt.

As an empirical matter, law is frequently, perhaps typically, made by lawyers or with their active and indispensable assistance. That these lawyers have more than law on their minds goes without saying; conversely, all others involved have law on their minds, along with much else. If "political forces" dominate the concrete activities of both making and using law, "normative forces" infiltrate all those concrete activities conventionally thought of as political. At a uselessly high level of abstraction, political and normative "forces" work against a clear boundary between politics and law. At a much more concrete level, political and legal activities affect each other in a host of ways that reveal themselves in the details. Lawyers are specialists in such details, but not the only ones.

Granting Henkin's failure to clarify the conceptual nexus of law and politics, does it matter? After all, the failure is hardly his alone. Henkin's several references to "soft law" suggest that it does matter. At a metaphorical level, the term "soft" works so well that additional clarification seems almost superfluous (the French honor the power of its imagery by leaving it untranslated).[7] Henkin's first reference to soft law is clear enough. Difficulties in specifying customary rules of international law arise from "the soft, indeterminate character of custom and the uncertainties of the process from which it results" (p. 49). A second reference (p. 81) finds "soft law" (his quotation marks) deliberately produced – "concessions on the substantive law were made" – during drafting of a major multilateral treaty. By implication, soft law is a separate category of rules not defined by reference to the incidents of rule formation.

What distinguishes this category? A definition of sorts comes later, when Henkin suggests that perhaps environmental law is soft law, "establishing vague guidelines, not normative standards" (p. 124). Is "vague" the same as "general" or "lacking in detail"? Are not all guidelines normative by definition? Is normativity a property of law exclusively? If soft law fails the test of normativity, can it be law at all?

In reference to the Helsinki Final Act, Henkin shifts metaphors to speak of "non-binding agreements (*sans portée juridique*) that live and work in the 'twilight zone' of the law" (p. 225).[8] He then notes parenthetically: "Of course, there are different kinds and degrees of non-binding agreements, with different significance and different lessons" (ibid.). As a conceptual matter, Henkin seems to have substituted bindingness for normativity as law's defining property, while his "of course" effectively dismisses another hard question: Is legality a matter of degree? As a practical matter, "of course" substitutes for a detailed discussion of differences in kind, degree and significance.

Henkin's skimpy conceptual treatment of law in relation to politics encourages an indifference to the very details constituting that relationship in daily life. It also undermines the credibility of his occasional forays into normative controversy regarding the status of particular rules. In the absence of a ready-made jurisprudential system to fill the conceptual void, Henkin's opinions lack a contextually supplied authority. The status of the UN Charter's Article 2(4) provides an especially revealing illustration, because Henkin's noteworthy participation in relevant normative controversy, rather than the General Course, provides a context for what seems to be an unduly Olympian pronouncement: "We do well, then, to reject all 'benign' exceptions

7 H. Thierry, "L'evolution du droit international public," *Recueil des cours de l'Academie de Droit International de La Haye*, vol. 222, 1990/III, pp. 70–1.

8 Henkin here quotes Oscar Schachter, "The Twilight Existence of Nonbinding International Agreements," *American Journal of International Law*, vol. 71, 1977, p. 296. Schachter's General Course in Public International Law, "International Law in Theory and Practice," *Recueil des cours de l'Academie de Droit International de La Haye*, vol. 178, 1982/V, pp. 123–32, lucidly discusses "political texts" like the Helsinki Final Act as "nonlegal instruments" which nonetheless have "legal significance," without mention of either soft law or twilight existence.

to Article 2(4)" (p. 162).[9] To deny the possibility of exceptions is to deny the relevance of material details and moral distinctions. For persuasion we have only Henkin's personal authority and conviction. We need more.

If Henkin's intransigent position on admissible uses of force is to be persuasive, he must provide conceptual details. Is immunity from exception a general property of international law? Or is Article 2(4) spared exception because it is a special case – because it is law in the blackest possible letters or because it is a "vague guideline," because of its cogency or its elasticity, because of its pedigree or its importance? If, indeed, "the system, and States generally, have recognized the paramount importance of the Charter norms" (p. 162), we may well conclude that Henkin gives importance precedence over pedigree in deciding legality. Given the importance of human rights (to Henkin, states' leaders, the world at large), the Helsinki Final Act would then be law no different in kind from Article 2(4) – binding in principle, valuable for the same lessons. Henkin is unlikely to support this inference, but he has granted no opportunity to defeat or even examine it.

Henkin acknowledges differences in kind, or categories, not just of "non-binding agreements" but of "general, unwritten, non-treaty law" (p. 51). There are four categories: " 'constitutional' law, 'basic' law, established customary law, and contemporary customary law" (ibid.). Constitutional law consists of "assumptions and conceptions of axiomatic 'constitutional' character" – "the concepts of State and Government," state equality, autonomy and territorial integrity, *pacta sunt servanda*, nationality, "perhaps also established norms of diplomatic intercourse" (ibid.). These assumptions take the operational form of principles; they neither derive from practice nor depend on consent; they make the system of states what it is. Obviously, it is meaningless to ask whether these principles are binding or admit of exception: tautologically, they are binding in principle. Yet they do change. People change their assumptions about the most basic features of their social realities, sometimes abruptly, often imperceptibly; and principles accordingly shift in content and relation.

Only from the point of view of customary law formation does this process seem mysterious. This happens to be Henkin's point of view, because his discussion of constitutional principles takes place in the midst of a lecture on lawmaking. For the same reason, Henkin assumes that such principles are unwritten. Better said, they are constantly reiterated in written form – Henkin's discussion provides just one instance – but no one articulation is

9 High points in Henkin's participation in the controversy over Article 2(4) are his article, "The Reports of the Death of Article 2(4) Are Greatly Exaggerated," *American Journal of International Law*, vol. 65, 1971, pp. 544–8, and his essay, "The Use of Force: Law and U.S. Policy," in L. Henkin *et al.* (eds), *Right v. Might: International Law and the Use of Force*, New York: Council on Foreign Relations Press, 1989, pp. 37–69. As for Henkin's Olympian tone, *cf.* A. D'Amato's Book Review of *Right v. Might* in *American Journal of International Law*, vol. 85, 1991, p. 201.

definitive. Because principles are never fixed by the form they take, changes in them tend to escape notice.

Henkin himself illustrates the dynamics of change. On the one hand, he dutifully reports the existence of principles attesting to or deriving from state sovereignty and even insists on their timelessness. On the other hand, he passionately defends "an 'extreme' view, that the concept of sovereignty, and its corollary sovereign immunity, are anachronistic, serve no good purposes, and should be abandoned" (p. 327). The very act of saying this makes it less extreme; perhaps one day it will be written everywhere, as more and more people change their assumptions.

By the same token, Article 2 of the Charter reaffirms the principle of state sovereignty and relates to that principle an injunction on the use of force. That Article 2 is part of a written agreement has no formal effect on the principles there embodied; what does matter is the ongoing process of affirmation, qualification or repudiation as it affects people's assumptions. In this process, Henkin's hostility toward the principle of sovereign equality expressed in Article 2(1) matters as much as it does because of his stature and experience, the forum, and the cogency of his views. So does his rejection of interpretations of Article 2(4) permitting benign, limited uses of force against bad sovereigns. We need not mind the contradiction implicit in these two positions, for rarely are people's assumptions consistent, especially when they sense the world changing around them. More to the point, the world is changing through them.

Henkin's second category of general, unwritten law – "basic law" – contains "principles of law common to every developed legal system, probably assumed to be 'natural' law, perhaps deemed to be inherent in the 'science' of law or in the very idea of law" (p. 52). Henkin offers examples – property, tort and contract – that correspond to Roman concepts of *dominium, delictum* and *obligatio* (note, p. 132). By limiting the ways we can imagine human relations to be ordered, these concepts function just as constitutional principles do. Together, Henkin's principles of constitutional and basic law make the international system analogous to the legal systems of western states; they have done so from the beginning. For lawyers, the terrain is always familiar.

In this circumstance, it is difficult to see why Henkin formed a separate category for basic law. While international law knows specific rules protecting property, for example, the importance of property is its contribution to the idea of the state as a territorial entity. Henkin suggests that rules relating to the conduct of diplomacy may belong to the category of constitutional law. Yet specific rules in both categories undoubtedly belong elsewhere. What property shares with sovereignty is a general, abstract form suiting principles performing a constitutive function. Specific, binding rules perform this function in far lesser degree, and a regulative function in commensurately greater degree.

Two of Henkin's categories are distinguishable only in content. They are indistinguishable in form and function, and there seems to be little advantage in keeping them apart. The two remaining categories, established customary law and contemporary customary law, seem to share a non-treaty form and a primarily regulative function. According to Henkin, they differ in the circumstances of their formation. Established customary law is "not created but results," which means that it is "not a product of the will of States, but a 'systemic creation' reflecting the 'consent' of the international system, and not the consent of individual States" (p. 57). In contrast, contemporary customary law often results from "a particular initiative" (p. 58) and is quickly seen to be binding. This is "purposeful activity" (ibid.) undertaken increasingly by large blocs of states in conspicuous public forums like the General Assembly. "Whereas law was made by treaty but grew by custom, now there is a tendency to treat custom as a means, alternative to treaty-making, for deliberate legislation" (ibid.).

For Henkin, this "is a radical innovation, and indeed reflects a radical conception" (ibid.). Certainly states' leaders have become more aware of the legal implications of their practices, thanks partly to international legal scholarship. Institutional developments have dramatically enhanced their ability to engage collectively in legally significant practices. Nevertheless, the conceptual implications of these changes are easy to overestimate. All custom, old and new, stems from particular initiatives, few of which mandate legal significance in themselves.

Instead, legality accrues from the congruence of initiatives and responses – indeed, of all relevant activities, whatever their motivation. The speed with which this happens can reflect the wishes of participants in the process, because these wishes affect the timing and content of relevant activities, just as material conditions, social tendencies and institutional settings do. Established custom seems to have "grown" because the passage of time separates us from the complex, purposeful activities giving rise to it. Contemporary custom seems deliberately willed precisely because we are so close to events that we know what motivates them.

Henkin finds this last category "functionally satisfactory if not conceptually pure" (p. 59). Its conceptual impurity is greater than Henkin thought, because some of this new law is constitutive, not regulative in function. Principles announced in General Assembly resolutions – not to mention summit texts, World Court judgments, multilateral treaties and lecture courses at The Hague – contribute to the ongoing constitution of the world as a public place. Reiteration of these principles may create the appearance of emergent custom, but their protean form signals their constitutive character and sets them apart from customary rules performing a regulative function. New rules rapidly formed to deal with novel situations are "functionally satisfactory" on regulative grounds and formally indistinguishable from customary rules. Principles articulated for the needs of a changing world are "functionally satisfactory" because they fit a different category altogether – one forged from Henkin's artificially separated categories of constitutional and basic law.

By introducing categories of law, Henkin takes an important step in clarifying law's relation to politics. He makes it clear that the international system has a constitution. He could have been clearer on the form and content of this constitution, although we may conclude that it is substantially embodied in generally stated principles to which legal significance is commonly attached. Henkin fails to take the next step, to conclude that, by constituting the conditions of public life among as well as within states, law affects politics perhaps even more – more deeply and less visibly – than politics affects law.

In Part II of Henkin's General Course, the conceptual problem is to clarify law's relation to values. Despite a tendency to personify the international system unduly by granting it purposes and values of its own (most scholars would confine themselves to participants' values and the system's functions), Henkin handles the way law registers values more effectively than he relates law to politics. Values are revealed most clearly in the system's constitutive principles. Part II continues to separate "constitutional axioms" (pp. 130–2) from "basic legal norms" (pp. 132–5), only to combine them in characterizing the international system as "essentially a 'liberal' system" (p. 135).

Liberalism insists on the autonomy of a system's constituent units and minimal governance. While a number of states "have seen a movement from 'liberal' to 'progressive' to 'welfare' principles," Henkin finds little in the way of "analogous developments in the international system" (pp. 135, 137). New law pressing states to cooperate in a variety of functional areas is "a radical departure," but not one derogating from the international system's liberal character (p. 138). This is because the new law of cooperation is "not for the benefit of 'the community' but of individual States" (p. 138).

Here, Henkin has surely misread developments within states, which adopt welfarist programs, not for "the community," but for members differentiated by need. Welfare principles coexist with liberal principles already coexisting with republican principles. Liberal republics become social democracies, and cosmopolitan elites eventually begin to project welfare principles globally. Logical consistency or even a strict ordering among principles is beside the point. Henkin's exposition of the positive law with respect to uses of force, economic relations and human rights, the bulk of Part II, amply supports this conclusion.

With minimal conceptual preparation, Part III offers a "case study" (p. 277) that follows the *Restatement* closely in documenting developments in the law of jurisdiction. The effect of recent developments is to challenge traditional categories:

> I suggest that realities have refined the traditional categories, made them less rigid, less conclusive; that greater attention to the interests served and the values furthered by limiting a State's authority to exercise jurisdiction would provide guidance towards a more reasonable jurisprudence (p. 281).

If recent developments have undermined traditional categories, their refinement is a conceptual task to which Henkin, through the *Restatement* and these lectures, has contributed significantly. The conceptual task is both practical and normative. A "more reasonable jurisprudence" does not automatically follow from rendering "realities" more sensitively. Any jurisprudence depends on normative claims, often implicit, that are supported, and sometimes disguised, through conceptual elaboration. The system of normative claims and conceptual refinements renders circumstances intelligible, at least to those who find the system reasonable.

Henkin's conceptual refinements follow the *Restatement* by sorting any state's exercise of jurisdiction into three categories: jurisdiction to prescribe law, to uphold such law through a state's courts, and to enforce that law through a state's police agencies. He argues against the old categories of jurisdiction exercised by reference to territory and nationality as too rigid (p. 291). By implication, the new categories are more reasonable because less rigid. Yet this position is hardly intelligible, much less acceptable, to anyone believing that territorial sovereignty provides a clear (to Henkin, rigid) normative criterion by which to evaluate jurisdictional claims.

What, then, makes Henkin's alternative more reasonable? That it reflects and supports the separation of powers as a constitutive principle within states assures its appeal, at least to an American audience. That legislative and judicial branches of many states now often engage in what amount to their own foreign relations assures the utility of Henkin's alternative. Indeed, the world is too complex for either set of categories to suffice. Both are needed in practice and neither can claim priority in principle.

Henkin acknowledges as much by turning to another principle – the principle of reasonableness (pp. 293–8), which benefits from an eponymous credibility and offers unbounded flexibility. The result is a set of necessarily vague guidelines for the exercise of jurisdiction to prescribe (pp. 296–7, quoting the *Restatement*). Of itself, reasonableness is not a principle. Its invocation disguises the presence of a principle, a normative criterion by which to decide what is reasonable, which Henkin intimated at the start of his lectures. There, it may be recalled, he announced three themes. Third is a movement from "abstract principles" to "practical needs." Only later does he drop the pretense of a neutral stance toward this movement. In defense of a functional theory of state immunity, he argues that "practical needs, not abstract principles" should be determinative, even if "conceptual rigour, jurisprudential purity, and simplicity of application" are lost (p. 323).

To speak as Henkin does of "practical needs" is to affirm a principle that, like welfare principles in general, calls for categories based on differences in need. As a principle, it is no less abstract than liberal principles basing autonomy on territorial differentiation. The principle of practical needs demands conceptual refinement (long since granted liberal principles), at cost to the purity of a jurisprudence based solely on liberal principles. Henkin's functionally oriented jurisprudence is better suited to this task than he may have thought when he titled Part III of his General Course "From Concept to Function." "From Territorial to Functional Concepts" better describes the task now just begun with Henkin's help.

Part IV briefly reviews the three themes organizing earlier parts. The world has changed "substantially" over the last half century (p. 332) but not, in Henkin's judgement, fundamentally. Nor is it likely to in the decades ahead: "There is no reason to expect change in the basic assumptions of Statehood and of a State system, no prospect of significant attenuation of State values of autonomy and independence of States and of the impermeability of their territory and society" (ibid.). On the evidence of Part III – the shifting constellation of principles underlying jurisdiction, not to mention the conceptual innovations and jurisprudential turmoil to which Henkin has contributed – a more tentative formulation of future trends may be in order. Even if the international system "shows no sign of moving to community" (p. 347), it does show many unsettling signs of movement. Not least among them are calls for community that threaten many states, and perhaps the system itself, with dissolution.

19 The constitution of international society (1993)

When Bruno Simma asked me to consider submitting an article for possible publication in the *European Journal of International Law*, a relatively new journal that he edited, I realized that this was an important opportunity to accomplish two objectives at the same time. One was to make my work on social construction, much of it developed with international relations as a reference point, available to international legal scholars. Indeed, I hoped that a European audience would be more receptive to the theoretical framework I had labeled constructivist than an audience consisting chiefly of lawyers from my own country. A second objective was to finalize an ongoing effort to develop an already comprehensive framework more fully, first by examining the relation between constitution as a process and constitution as a condition, and then by accounting for change in the constitution of any society. While some scholars were beginning to speak of constitutive processes, perhaps rather too casually, they neglected to specify the structural properties of constitutions (as opposed to discourse, including legal discourse) – a neglect that legal theory could help to remedy. By definition process is a matter of change. Yet change can only register as changes in the state of the discernible structures constituting a society; these structures are institutionalized as layers of functionally differentiated rules, and not as discursive oppositions and transformations.

To this day I am not entirely sure that conceptualizing rules in layered sets is the best way to relate the two senses of constitution. Yet my treatment follows directly from my defense of rules in any process-oriented discussion of society. The paper appeared in the *Journal* as submitted. Somewhat reorganized it appeared again as a chapter in my 1998 book, *The Republican Legacy in International Thought*.

It is hardly novel to speak of the constitution of international society. The League (or *Société*) of Nations had the Covenant as its constitutive instrument. Nevertheless, the term *international society* has a decidedly rhetorical flavor, often used interchangeably with terms like *international community* and *family of nations*. For some time, scholars have favored *order*, as in *international legal order* (see Chapter 9, above). In the field of International Relations, most scholars in the US posit a Hobbesian state of anarchy among states, while many in Britain and its Commonwealth have sought to redeem the idea of an international society by references to Grotius and Vattel.[1] Recent developments in theory present an opportunity to reconsider what might be meant by speaking of international society and suggesting that it has a constitution. Philip Allott has recently done just this in the context of proposing "a universal theory of human society."[2] Allott's work and the pages to follow share some of the same sources of inspiration. They differ, however, in one decisive respect. Allott claimed that a society – any society, including international society – "*is not a thing but a process*."[3] I claim that any society, including international society, is a thing *and* a process.

Scholarship is also a thing and a process, a series of texts and, in a familiar simile, a conversation enacted through texts. The conversation is public. Participants imagine an audience and load their texts with interlocutors formed by reference, conscious or not, to other texts. Conversations within texts spur the production of further texts, the texts themselves becoming turns in a conversation. All such conversations exhibit identifiable structures – affirmation or negation by repetition, argument by point and counterpoint, demonstration followed by confirmation or qualification, expansion through illustration, development through clarification – typically compounded in complex patterns. Through these conversations causes are promoted, allies secured, empires built, egos gratified, scores settled, reputations made and, most of us would like to think, knowledge advanced.

The audience imagined for this essay is the small but growing band of scholars who find international legal theory intriguing, along with the few theorists of international relations whose sympathies are Grotian, Vattelian or (as in my own case) Kantian. Formed from many other texts, the essay's interlocutors include a number of its intended auditors, some of those theorists of international relations with Hobbesian inclinations, and great figures (for example, Durkheim, Kelsen) from other broadly configured, long-lasting and much admired conversations. The conversational legacy of many other figures join Grotius, Hobbes, Vattel and especially Kant as a formless and, for the most part, nameless presence.

The essay repeats a number of propositions drawn from other texts and denies some others. These propositions are organized around four themes – theory, constitution, rules, society – each naming a section of the essay, which proceeds through argument, demonstration and illustration. Yet the essay's structure most of all reflects an emphasis on clarification – of constitution in

1 Notably, H. Bull, *The Anarchical Society: A Study of Order in World Politics*, New York: Columbia University Press, 1977, who managed to sow considerable confusion by conflating (as in the title of his book) all three terms – anarchy, society and order.

2 P. Allott, *Eunomia: A New Order for a New World*, Oxford: Oxford University Press, 1990, quoting p. xxiii.

3 Ibid., p. 39, his emphasis.

relation to rules, of rules in relation to society, of society in relation to constitution – for the purpose of developing a minimal account of international society. In four further sections the essay then returns to each theme to develop an account of international society's constitution and thus a fuller account of international society itself. The point of this structure is to send the essay and its audience spiraling ahead, just in the way we tend to think the advancement of knowledge should proceed. As subsequent texts continue the spiral, the process of scholarship cumulatively bears on a much larger process – the constitution of international society – of which, at any moment, it is only a modest part.

Theory

In recent years the study of international law has seen a remarkable florescence of theoretical scholarship, much of it critical in temper.[4] The most striking subject of the new scholarship is doctrine. Traditionally, theorists talked about what people say in the name of law. Within each theoretical tradition there developed "a meta-language *about* law, as distinct from the technical language *of* law."[5] Now, theorists talk about the way we talk about law. Critical of all theoretical traditions, they develop a metalanguage *about* theory on the premise that we are talking about the way we talk when we think we are talking about, and acting in, the world.

Much the same may be said of the study of international relations. Lacking the centuries-long pedigree of international legal scholarship, this field has seen a great deal of theoretical discussion, mostly divisive, over the several decades of its history.[6] Recently, however, much of this discussion has turned sharply critical. On the premise that theories about the world are not what they claim, "meta-theory" has made an entrance.[7] Some of the new, critically oriented work in international law and international relations effectively sabotages the conventional separation of these two fields of study as

4 B. Simma, "Editorial," *European Journal of International Law*, vol. 3, 1992, p. 215. Landmarks include A. Carty, *The Decay of International Law? A Reappraisal of the Limits of Legal Imagination in International Affairs*, Manchester: Manchester University Press, 1986; D. Kennedy, *International Legal Structures*, Baden-Baden: Nomos, 1987; and M. Koskenniemi, *From Apology to Utopia: The Structure of International Legal Argument*, Helsinki: Finnish Lawyers' Publishing, 1989.

5 M.S. McDougal *et al.*, "Theories about International Law: Prologue to a Configurative Jurisprudence," in McDougal and W.M. Reisman (eds), *International Law Essays: A Supplement to International Law in Contemporary Perspective*, Mineola, NY: Foundation, 1981, p. 53.

6 K.J. Holsti, *The Dividing Discipline: Hegemony and Diversity in International Theory*, Boston: Allen & Unwin, 1985; Y.H. Ferguson and R.W. Mansbach, *The Elusive Quest: Theory and International Politics*, Columbia: University of South Carolina Press, 1988.

7 A.E. Wendt, "Bridging the Theory-Meta-Theory Gap in International Relations," *Review of International Studies*, vol. 17, 1990, pp. 383–92.

substantially unrelated theoretical domains.[8] We should expect no less from recent challenges to received traditions.

International law and international relations are hardly alone in the turn to theory. It is tempting to blame, or credit, academic fashions: theory is yet another novelty; rampant empiricism and naive scientism have finally run their course. Yet something more is needed to account for a movement so pronounced in so many fields of study.[9] The *world* as (we think) we know it must somehow be implicated.

This world is neither the natural world as such nor the sum of every single person's experience. Instead, it is the *modern* world, the world of *our* experience, the world we moderns have made for ourselves. Wherever the turn to theory, and especially the quest for meta-theory, there we find talk of modernity in crisis. Two camps are discernible. One is late modern. It takes the Enlightenment project of universal reason, individual moral autonomy, representative political institutions, technical rationalization and material progress as flawed, egregiously perhaps, but not beyond the possibility of reconstruction. The other camp is postmodern. It takes the Enlightenment project as misconceived, terminally flawed, unworthy of redemption and perhaps already ended.

At this juncture I wish to affirm my late-modern allegiances. I believe that the Enlightenment project can only be salvaged by its reconstruction from the ground up. Such an undertaking requires a reconsideration of modernity's putative grounding while defending the possibility of grounds. These claims are ontological in the first instance, and thus they are self-consciously meta-theoretical. Elsewhere I call my project *constructivism* to indicate my belief that individuals and society continuously constitute each other through the medium of rules, and that rules depend on the performative power of language.[10] So conceived, constructivism complements the Enlightenment belief in the power of language to instantiate reason and qualifies the belief in the power of language to represent the world as it is.

8 F.V. Kratochwil, *Rules, Norms and Decisions: On the Conditions of Practical and Legal Reasoning in International Relations and Domestic Affairs*, Cambridge: Cambridge University Press, 1989; N.G. Onuf, *World of Our Making: Rules and Rule in Social Theory and International Relations*, Columbia: University of South Carolina Press, 1989; Allott, *Eunomia*.

9 In English language scholarship, this movement appeared in many fields of study well before its arrival in international law and international relations. See, illustratively, H. White, *Metahistory: The Historical Imagination in Nineteenth Century Europe*, Baltimore: Johns Hopkins University Press, 1973; R.J. Bernstein, *The Restructuring of Social and Political Theory*, Philadelphia: University of Pennsylvania Press, 1978; Q. Skinner (ed.), *The Return of Grand Theory in the Social Sciences*, Cambridge: Cambridge University Press, 1985; D.W. Fiske and R.A Shweder (eds), *Metatheory in Social Science: Pluralisms and Subjectivities*, Chicago: University of Chicago Press, 1986.

10 Onuf, *World of Our Making*, ch. 1.

Rules

Whether late modern or postmodern, involved in the development of a metalanguage for theorizing or not, critical theorists in international law and international relations tend to view social reality, like critique, as a process. Yet the preference for process over structure, like criticism of modernity, is hardly new. The great antinomies of order and change, classicism and romanticism, positivism and historicism, have always structured the manifold processes that constitute the modern world as we know it. Modern international legal theory exemplifies this large structure.

Consider, for example, the critique that Myres McDougal and his associates performed with respect to "the vast legacy of past theories about international law," which they organized into six "frames." First is the "non-law" frame. Its theorists associate law with certain "structures" not to be found in international relations. Process prevails. The next frame holds the opposite. Natural law theorists sever law from "social process," but in this case structure prevails. Next is the historical frame, which understands "the relation of law to process," but fails to see this relation as a two-way street. Instead, process prevails. Thereupon follows the analytical frame, or positivism, so much favored by contemporary international lawyers. Analytical theorists disregard "the relation of social process and authoritative decision" as a matter of "conscious choice." The structure of "fixed rules" dominates their attention.[11]

The last two frames are "distinctly modern creations," as indeed positivism is – "products of the 19th and 20th centuries." They are the "sociologistic" frame, and "limited factor analysis" associated with empirical social science. Sociologically oriented theorists focus on "why and how the 'law' comes about" but neglect "the ends and consequences of that process." Limited factor analyses disaggregate "world social process" into combinations of variables.[12]

Switching back and forth from structure and process, rules and context, McDougal and associates could tell their story of international legal theory in distinctly modern terms. First presented, and quickly repudiated, is a theoretical orientation that denies the "social reality" of the modern world.[13] The story then presents a chronology of modernity by starting with naturalism, moving on to historicism, followed by analytical positivism and concluding with the contributions of social thought and several social science disciplines.

Of course this story is simplified and, in the process, liberties are taken with chronology. Although the non-law position comes first, it has a place near the

11 McDougal *et al.*, "Theories about International Law," quoting pp. 60, 61, 74, 91, 93.
12 Ibid., quoting pp. 106, 107, 121.
13 Ibid., p. 64.

end of the story. This century's excesses of violence and inhumanity raise unmistakably modern doubts about the efficacy of international law. Early positivism is a response to naturalism, not the historical school. Only gradually, with the emergence of coherent doctrines about the subjects, sanctions and sources of international law, did positivist preoccupation with structure supersede an initial concern for the modalities of state practice.[14] Nevertheless, the story is familiar and satisfying because it sees international legal theory, not just as an alternation between the preference for structure and the preference for process, but as a spiral of increasingly refined positions and thus of advancing knowledge. (For addtional discussion, see Chapter 23, below.) By telling the story, McDougal and associates set the stage for their own contribution to theory.

This they call "configurative jurisprudence." It is emphatically oriented to process and context, as are the two frames preceding it. It differs from them by being inclusive and systematic and therefore seeks to supplant them in confronting analytical positivism and its preoccupation with rules. Such an ambition enables the rest of us in the modern fold to tell an even simpler story. On the one hand we find Kelsen and the analytical tradition; on the other McDougal and configurative jurisprudence. The one ignores social process, the other ignore rules as things constituting society as a thing. In the collision of these irreconcilable points of view are the makings of more sophisticated positions, reconceiving structure and process so as to account for the critiques on both sides without repeating the errors of each.[15] Knowledge advances as modernity ineluctably spirals ahead.

It is stories like these that postmodern theory challenges. It does so first by pointing out that the story is just that – a story – and second by mocking the story's happy ending. Instead of an advancing spiral, the postmodern critique sees an argument without end. The repetition of positions only seems to be about structure and process. Apologists for existing rules face reformers who would commandeer the legal process. Planners of a new world of better rules face defenders of the way the world already works. The story is about itself and thus its tellers. It is not about the march of reason; it is about the fears and fantasies of those who profess to reason.

Postmodern theory goes further. There are only stories and they are only about themselves and their tellers. Stories about international legal theory, like most legal and political talk in the modern world, relate to a single, controlling argument. Behind the contradictions and disguises is "the liberal doctrine of politics." Modernity is but a running argument over the practical

14 N.G. Onuf, "Global Law-Making and Legal Thought," in Onuf (ed.), *Lawmaking in the Global Community*, Durham, NC: Carolina Academic Press, 1982, pp. 6–8. These pages postdate the material printed in Chapter 6, above.

15 R.A. Falk, *The Status of Law in International Society*, Princeton: Princeton University Press, 1970, pp. 41–9; Chapter 9, above.

implications of liberal ideas. Are the "formally neutral and objectively ascertainable rules" implied by the rule of law even possible? Are freedom and order "compatible notions"?[16]

Where modern theory finds rules, postmodern theory puts texts. Social process is discourse by various means. Yet texts contain rules, and rules contain texts. Discourse depends on the rules that discourse produces. Rules and the choices they afford connect arguments over liberal premises to people's practical concerns. Postmodern scholars err in equating what scholars do as scholars with what everyone does all of the time. People can and do argue. They must deal with rules.

Dealing with rules prompts people to talk about reasons for following them and involves them in the many arguments to which rules relate. Nevertheless, all such talk must in the first instance refer to rules *as if* they exist apart from the reasons and arguments they elicit. By virtue of such talk, rules do exist – not just as inferences, but as things, however protean or transitory. No differently the people doing the talk also exist as agents who (according to the rules) are in a position to make choices afforded by rules. Through rules people constitute the multiple structures of society, and societies constitute people as agents.

Constitution

The co-constitution of people and societies is a continuous process. Rules are central to this process because they define agents in terms of structures, and structures in terms of agents, but never definitively. As rules change in number, kind, relation and content, they constantly redefine agents and structures, always in terms of each other. As Anthony Giddens noted in his systematic formulation of the position taken here, "all rules are inherently transformational."[17] In other words, all rules perform a constitutive function all the time. The usual view has rules performing a regulative function. Indisputably they do. "All social rules have both constitutive and regulative (sanctioning) aspects to them."[18]

So conceived, rules make constitution a comprehensive process yielding constitution as a general condition. Society is coextensive with its constitution. Yet most societies have constitutions in a more limited sense: they have a set of rules that give their societies identities and direction. These rules are commonly held to differ fundamentally from other rules. More abstractly, but incorrectly, rules are said to be either constitutive or regulative.[19]

16 Kostenniemi, *From Apology to Utopia*, pp. 52–73, quoting pp. 52, 53.

17 A. Giddens, *The Constitution of Society: Outline of the Theory of Structuration*, Berkeley: University of California Press, 1984, p. 17.

18 A. Giddens, *Central Problems in Social Theory: Action, Structure and Contradiction in Social Analysis*, Berkeley: University of California Press, 1979, p. 66.

19 For a critique of the way philosophers have handled matters, see Onuf, *World of Our Making*, pp. 51–2.

Even if all rules are always constitutive and regulative, some degree of functional specialization among rules is not only possible but likely. A few rules are disproportionately weighty in constitutive effect. This conclusion also holds when process, not rules, is the point of reference. Thus McDougal and associates comprehensively describe a "world constitutive process" regulating "public order" decisions. The latter are "specialized to the shaping and sharing" of community values. "These distinctions, between constitutive and other decisions, are matters of relative emphasis, not exclusion"; each performs the others' function "in varying degrees."[20]

Ever since Durkheim, sociologists tend to link societal development to the degree of functional differentiation. By implication any society lacking an identifiable constitution is so rudimentary or arrested in its development that it hardly warrants description as a society. Most scholars in the field of international relations hold this view. The "international system" lacks functional differentiation, not to mention a constitution. Instead of an international society, there is anarchy – a collection of autonomous, self-interested actors whose relations are shaped only by the distribution of their material capabilities. In this system rules reflect incidental accommodations to, and positional implications of, a more or less fixed distributive pattern.[21] Thus understood, rules are the ontological debris of international relations.

I reject every element in this view. In constructivist terms, the international system must be a society insofar as it is constituted by the deeds of many individuals, themselves constituted as agents. This process of constitution depends on rules, without which deeds have no social meaning, and some of these rules form what can only be called a constitution.

Society

At least in the US, the great majority of scholars in the field of international relations assiduously avoid any mention of international society in the interest of "realism." Anyone who does not, courts dismissal as a naive exponent of ideas decades, even centuries out of date – as Wilsonian idealist, Lockean liberal or Grotian legalist. Since the mid-1970s, however, many scholars have concerned themselves with "international regimes." Mistakenly thinking this was a new idea (international lawyers had long employed it) and faced with unavoidable evidence that rules abound in international relations, they seized an opportunity to reconsider matters long out of fashion.

Almost immediately there emerged what can only be called a movement,

20 M.S. McDougal *et al.*, "The World Constitutive Process of Authoritative Decision," in McDougal and Reisman, *International Law Essays*, pp. 191–201, quoting p. 192.

21 See, preeminently, K.N. Waltz, *Theory of International Politics*, Reading, MA: Addison-Wesley, 1979.

herein "the regimes movement." In 1982, the movement's principals published a collection of essays clearly intended to legitimize the movement and stabilize its terms of reference.[22] Unsurprisingly, the group's working definition of international regimes, as presented by Stephen Krasner, has now become standard: "Regimes can be defined as sets of implicit or explicit principles, norms, rules, and decision-making procedures around which actors' expectations converge in a given area of international relations."[23]

Krasner's definition assumes that any rule set corresponds to "a given area of international relations." To simplify and generalize this definition, principles, norms and the like "give" any area of social (not just international) relations what observers may take to be its objectively "given" character.[24] States are regimes. The principle of sovereignty gives the state as a large, internally differentiated ensemble of social relations its evidently sharp boundaries. Differentiation within regimes yields subregimes, each with an observable "area" of operation and degree of autonomy. Formal nesting of regimes has long been recognized.[25]

Societies are congeries of regimes. The same may be said of international relations. Obviously, regimes stand in complex relation to each other, those relations themselves constituting regimes. Society is thus a general and inclusive term for that regime, giving any observer a frame of reference. International society is nothing more than an inclusive regime, within which are nested all international regimes, themselves constituted from the relations of states and other well-bounded regimes.

Rules, again

As defined, regimes resemble grab bags, stuffed with this and that. Krasner's terse definitions of principles, norms and the rest fail to identify what a regime's constituent elements might have in common or to differentiate them systematically. As for what they have in common, Friedrich Kratochwil has noted that principles, norms and rules all possess "prescriptive force," as indeed do decision-making procedures.[26] They all take the form of prescriptive statements. As for their differences, Krasner presented his list of any regime's contents in what appeared to be descending order of generality. Kratochwil justly remarked that the differentiating criterion of generality-specificity,

22 S.D. Krasner (ed.), "International Regimes," special issue of *International Organization*, vol. 36, 1982, pp. 185–510.

23 S.D. Krasner, "Structural Causes and Regime Consequences: Regimes as Intervening Variables," *International Organization* vol. 36, 1982, p. 186.

24 See, also, Onuf, *World of Our Making*, pp. 144–5.

25 H. Kelsen, *General Theory of Law and the State*, trans. by A. Wedberg, Cambridge, MA: Harvard University Press, 1945, pp. 363–88.

26 Kratochwil, *Rules, Norms, and Decisions*, p. 57. They "are employed not to reflect the world but to apply *pressure* to it"; his emphasis.

taken by itself, points "to a certain conceptual impoverishment."[27] A second such criterion – the degree to which prescriptive statements are explicit – is acknowledged in Krasner's basic definition, but never elaborated.

I would reformulate the second criterion as degree of formality,[28] and I suggest that prescriptive statements enjoying some considerable degree of formality and institutional support are *legal*.[29] Principles and procedures are capable of being legal no less than rules – they *are* rules respectively of great generality and specificity. Norms of any durability and importance are subject to acknowledgment and support such as to make them law, specifically customary law. Furthermore, legal discourse tends to use the terms "norms" and "rules" interchangeably.[30] As prescriptive statements, principles, norms and procedures all take the linguistic form of a rule, as that term is conventionally defined by philosophers.[31]

Rules describe some class of actions and indicate whether these actions constitute warranted conduct on the part of those to whom these rules are addressed.[32] They are "prescriptive generalizations."[33] Within the broad reach of this definition, rules may be differentiated by reference to what they *are*: rules are statements of greater or lesser generality and formality, law or not, as suggested above. Or rules may be differentiated by reference to what they *do*: as statements indicating what kind of conduct is warranted, rules tell people what to do and, simply and succinctly, how to do it. This is because rules always and necessarily derive from performative speech – utterances through which people accomplish social ends directly. The primary unit of performative speech is a speech act. Like rules, speech acts convey propositional content (what to do) and indicate to some hearer an appropriate response to whatever the speaker proposes (how to do it).

27 Ibid. Krasner separated principles and norms from rules and procedures by holding the former to be "basic" to a regime's identity. Here the property of generality is related to functional specialization, yielding change of regime versus change in regime as separate categories. "Structural Causes and Regime Consequences," pp. 187–8.

28 Kratochwil has also adopted such a criterion while retaining explicitness as a criterion in its own right. His example is of the Helsinki Final Act as an explicit, but informal, agreement that I would characterize as relatively highly, but not fully, formalized. F. Kratochwil, "Contract and Regimes: Do Issue Specificity and Variations of Formality Matter?" in V. Rittberger (ed.), *Regime Theory and International Relations*, Oxford: Clarendon, 1993, pp. 84–92. By full formality, I mean scrupulous adherence to prescribed forms.

29 See, further, Onuf, *World of Our Making*, pp. 136–44.

30 See ibid., pp. 129–30, for fuller discussion.

31 Ibid., pp. 78–81.

32 This definition is adapted from M. Black, *Models and Metaphors: Studies in Language and Philosophy*, Ithaca: Cornell University Press, 1962, p. 208. The following pages draw liberally from Onuf, *World of Our Making*, ch. 2 (substantially reproducing Chapter 13, above), and ch. 4.

33 F. Schauer, *Playing by the Rules: A Philosophical Examination of Rule-Based Decision-Making in Law and Life*, Oxford: Clarendon, 1991, pp. 25–7. For Giddens, rules are "generalizable procedures." *The Constitution of Society*, p. 21.

Such acts take the generic form, I hereby [verb such as declare, demand, promise] that [propositional content]. Because people respond to these acts with their own performances, not always spoken, the pattern of speech acts and related performances constitute those practices that make the material conditions and artifacts of human experience intelligible. In so doing, the pattern of speech acts endows practices with normativity, giving rise to rules, which, in synopsizing that pattern, fix preferences and expectations and shape the future against the past.

Speech acts fall into three, and only three, mutually exclusive categories for such constitutive purposes. They are assertive speech acts (I state that . . .), directive (I request that . . .), and commissive (I promise that . . .). Deriving from them are categories of rules, also three in number, and fully independent of each other. I call them instruction-rules, directive-rules, and commitment-rules.

As the term suggests, instruction-rules inform their audience of states of affairs and the likely consequences of disregarding that information. The instruction-rule, "Wash before meals," is a useful example. The context of this instruction is immediately evident. Not washing is a bad practice because it may result in illness or social offense. When instruction-rules are general, formally stated, and, more likely than not, connected to people's larger ethical concerns, we recognize them as principles. The Victorian adage, "Cleanliness is next to Godliness," is one such principle, which may well result in the ruled practice of washing "religiously" before meals. At the other extreme of specificity and informality, the instruction-rule, "Wash before meals," may be one of innumerable instructions constituting the code of comportment by which most adults in the modern world conduct themselves.

When a parent says to a child, "Dinner's on; wash your hands," there are two speech acts to which the child responds. One asserts a state of affairs. The second is directive. The child knows that when certain conditions operate, such a directive requires a particular response, with specific, known consequences likely to follow any response. Complying with the request usually results in a pat on the head, peace in the household, dessert. Choosing not to comply risks a reprimand, a negative response to the child's next request, a meal delayed while hands are washed. The parent's directive invokes a known rule, the model of which is the familiar one of criminal law backed, as Durkheim noted, by "repressive" or negative sanctions.[34] Current scholarship would add positive sanctions, or inducements, to the equation without changing its character. Anyone encountering the linguistic formulation, "wash before meals," knows with considerable assurance whether a rule, or even a law, is at stake, or merely a speech act formulated for that one occasion, and whether that rule, legal or not, is an instruction or a directive.

34 E. Durkheim, *The Division of Labor in Society* (1893), trans. by G. Simpson, New York: Free Press, 1964, p. 69.

Commitment-rules may not be so easily recognized in every instance. They derive from mutual promising and are often left implicit. When promises are broken, however, the rule is evidenced by calls for restitution, or "the return of things as they were. . . ."[35] For Durkheim, all "juridical rules," except for penal law, fall into this category: "civil law, commercial law, administrative law and constitutional law."[36] While not all of the rules in these large bodies of law are commitment-rules, certainly the most characteristic of them are.

The model situation involving commitment-rules is a contract, including of course any putative social contract, in which rights and duties are assigned. Rights and duties formalize the implications of ruled promising, sometimes to the extent that rights are held to be inalienable or inherent. By definition rights and duties are formally symmetrical – one's right is equally and necessarily another's duty. The rule itself is contained in this formal, reciprocal relation, which, as an empirical matter, rarely distributes consequences symmetrically. Rights may entitle their holders to receive particular benefits. Alternatively, rights may empower their holders to act in particular ways with respect to designated others.[37] The latter then have the duty not to interfere with the exercise of such powers.

Commitment-rules granting powers constitute agents who act in support of rules directing other people to act in specified ways. This is a general pattern. Principles are more likely to meet with principled conduct when they are backed by directives, whether a barrage of directive speech acts exhorting and admonishing regime participants, or a tidy set of formal, general directive-rules in turn supported by empowered agents. In their turn, agents find support for their powers in detailed instruction-rules. We can also see how directive-rules specifying penalties for empowered agents' failure to observe these instruction-rules would support the latter, and how an appeals process to protect such agents' rights would use commitment-rules in support of such directive-rules, and how an appeals tribunal would have recourse to instruction-rules in support of its activities. Rules of different categories support each other in potentially endless layers.

Each layer varies in the number of rules it contains, their formality and generality, and the extent of institutional support for them. As a very general matter, rules become more numerous and more specific in propositional content as we descend through the layers in any regime. The pattern of formality and institutional support from layer to layer resists generalization. In a caste society, for example, principles defining caste membership have the formality

35 Ibid.

36 Ibid. Civil law should not be taken to exclude common law in this context. The conventional distinction between civil law and common law refers to the source of their legality (formal statement) – legislation and authoritative precedent respectively – and not their source in performative speech. Indeed, commitment-rules comprise the bulk of the common law.

37 H.L.A. Hart, *The Concept of Law*, Oxford: Clarendon, 1961, pp. 27–33; Joseph Raz, *Practical Reason and Norms*, 2nd ed., Princeton: Princeton University Press, 1990, pp. 97–106.

of sacred texts but little or no support from formal directive- or commitment-rules. Instead, an unruly mass of speech acts, many of them directive and commissive, links these principles to a fourth layer of detailed instruction-rules. Alternatively, principles may be so taken for granted that their presence and content must be inferred from the rules regime participants collectively commit themselves to when they formally constituted that regime or the rules some awesome, perhaps mythic figure has ordered them to obey.

Regimes must have at least some general rules of considerable formality, be they cherished principles, commandments from on high or formal agreements. Were this not so, it would be difficult to distinguish a given regime against a horizon of rules belonging to other regimes. In other words, legal rules grant any regime, and not just the state, the coherence presupposed by the term "regime."

Constitution, again

Few, if any, regimes consist exclusively of legal rules. Informal rules and related practices spring up in the margins of any rule set, no matter how assiduously the appropriate agents promulgate new legal rules. Few regimes have no rules deserving to be called legal; almost all regimes are legal regimes in greater or lesser degree. If a regime has at least some legal rules, it must also have rules specifying conditions under which legal rules come into being. These rules need not be legal rules themselves, in which instance they give rise to customary law or, in H.L.A. Hart's words, "a régime of primary rules."[38] When the rules responsible for the legal status of primary rules are also legal rules, Hart labeled them "secondary."

The simplest secondary rule is a "rule of recognition": "a rule for the conclusive identification of the primary rules of obligation." Other secondary rules are "rules of change." "The simplest form of such a rule is that which empowers an individual or body of persons to introduce new primary rules . . . and to eliminate old rules."[39] Hart observed that written constitutions place legal limitations on those empowered to enact or rescind primary rules.[40] Constitution in the most limited sense of the term evidently refers to those legal rules conferring and limiting powers to make legal rules within a given regime. In the usual, still limited sense of the term, a constitution also includes legal rules conferring and limiting powers to execute and adjudicate legal rules.[41]

Note that rules of change depend on a logically anterior rule, or set of rules, for their "conclusive identification," which must of course be a rule or

38 Hart, *Concept of Law*, pp. 89–96.
39 Ibid., pp. 92, 93.
40 Ibid., pp. 67–9.
41 Kelsen, *General Theory of Law and the State*, pp. 258–9.

rules of recognition. Hart effectively conceded the existence of such rules in his analysis of sovereignty.[42] These are "rules defining what members of the society must do to function as an electorate" or otherwise act to empower agents. When people follow such rules, they act "as a sovereign," and the rules themselves "are *constitutive* of the sovereign" (Hart's emphasis).

More precisely these rules empower the people to act on their sovereignty, which in turn depends on a rule, however informal, recognizing the people as sovereign. Rules of recognition answer the question, on whose behalf, and at whose sufferance, do those who make (apply, adjudicate) legal rules exercise their powers? If rules conferring and limiting such powers belong in any regime's constitution, so must the rules recognizing the legality, indeed the constitutionality, of empowering rules.

Constitutions consist of Hart's secondary rules: rules of recognition and rules of change. Rules of recognition are instruction-rules, often nesting a regime within the constitution specifically enabling the formation of rules of change. By following instructions, agents are able to recognize which other rules are legal and which are not. The agents in question may be any and all members of a society. Or they may be members of an encapsulated regime with rules that confer on its limited membership a monopoly of relevant skills.

Rules of change are always commitment-rules. They empower agents to issue and provide support for formal directive-rules themselves supporting a society's principles, or top layer of instruction-rules. Those principles need not be articulated formally, although some of them are likely to appear in the written document – or "material constitution," as Kelsen called it[43] – which collects the top layer of commitment-rules. Any constitution limits the conduct of empowered agents by specifying their duties. A written constitution may also contain commitment-rules limiting these agents by specifying rights held by some or all members of society.

Obviously the constitution as a written document – Kelsen's material constitution – may contain rules beyond those minimally necessary to the "formal constitution."[44] Thus it may contain general directive-rules, commandments to which all members of the society are subject, for example, specifying religious beliefs. Yet societies formally adopting constitutions frequently, even characteristically, forego the inclusion of many directive-rules. Instead they entrust specified agents with responsibility for issuing directive-rules, or law, as needed. To prevent those agents from issuing laws that would circumvent the limits imposed on their powers, constitutional rules are widely held to be higher or more fundamental than law in the usual sense. In James Madison's justly famous formulation, a constitution is "established by

42 Hart, *Concept of Law*, pp. 70–6. Quotations to follow are from pp. 74, 75.
43 Kelsen, *General Theory of Law and the State*, pp. 124–5.
44 Ibid.

the people and unalterable by the government," as against "a law established by the government and alterable by the government."[45]

Madison's frame of reference was the British Constitution. Its rules always subject to alteration by Parliament, the contents of that constitution necessarily remain in doubt. A model constitution, a constitution beyond all doubt, includes all rules unalterable by other legal rules and no other rules. The constitution's rules must be formally articulated so to make their status apparent, even if they are not included in a particular document materially identified as the constitution.

As a rule, the model constitution will contain rules of recognition – rules validating the constitution as such and perhaps additional rules providing for its change, the latter accompanied by rules empowering agents to undertake such change. The model constitution may well contain other principles, but few if any directive-rules. The bulk of its rules are commitment-rules specifying conditions of agency relevant to rules in the next layers of the rule set. These commitment-rules may themselves be accompanied by constitutionally specified instruction-rules.

Society, again

Societies are congeries of regimes and regimes themselves, normally distinguishable from some more inclusive regime, or society, by reference to rules notable for their formality and support. Every regime must have a rule of recognition, however informal, stipulating conditions of agency. Because regimes do not exist in a social vacuum, they are always linked to other regimes that have their own rules of recognition. Rules linking regimes also constitute regimes, consisting minimally of rules of recognition coordinating the relations of agents for the regimes nesting within it. Any statement locating sovereignty is, or proposes, a rule of recognition. As such, it defines the conditions of agency, and thus the disposition of sovereignty, for *that* regime.

International society is marked by the presence of many rules conventionally described as legal. These rules constitute a broad, historic regime well known to us as international law. This regime does not coincide exactly with international society, to which must be added other regimes identifiable to the observer despite their informality – regimes constituted by "rules of the game" instead of legal rules. Nevertheless, the international legal regime dominates the congeries of regimes constituting international society because its rules provide the chief agents in that society with their standing as such, and the scope and formality of these rules provide agents and observers alike with an unavoidable frame of reference.

The international legal regime consists of a few principles, the first being

45 *The Federalist No. 53*, in J.E. Cooke (ed.), *The Federalist*, Middletown, CT: Wesleyan University Press, 1961, pp. 360–1.

the principle of sovereignty, which formally restricts the regime's membership to states. The regime exhibits no directive-rules of any formality and generality. Instead, there are a large number of formal commitment-rules specifying the rights and duties of states. A distinctive feature of this regime is its stringent limitation of agency. Governments are the designated agents of states; at least in principle, governments collectively monopolize agency in the regime.[46]

Secondary agents hold powers by delegation. Treaties are the primary device for the empowerment of secondary agents, most notably by creating international organizations. Proliferating multilateral treaties, some creating organizations of near-universal membership, are perhaps the most arresting feature of contemporary international society. Again, consisting substantially of instruction- and commitment-rules, these treaties increase the identity and coherence of the society's many subregimes – the very regimes to which members of the regimes movement have devoted their full attention.

International society has no constitution announcing itself as such. Nevertheless, one might see the rudiments of a material constitution in the most important of multilateral treaties, the UN Charter.[47] In language strikingly reminiscent of the US Constitution, the Preamble of the Charter begins: "*We the peoples of the United Nations*." Whether this is an empty flourish or sign of a rule recognizing the sovereignty of many peoples, Article 2(1) offers another rule of recognition without clarifying its relation to the prior rule, if indeed there is one. "The Organization is based on the principle of the sovereign equality of all its Members." Article 2(7) spells out the necessary inference that the organization is to refrain from intervening in its members' domestic affairs, while Article 2(6) extends the Charter's reach to states that are not UN members. Sovereignty notwithstanding, the organization is to ensure that such states act in accordance with principles adumbrated in Article 2, including most notably Article 2(4)'s stricture against the threat or use of force.

Most of Article 2's provisions are cast in a general directive form and in the passive voice. Much discussion of Article 2(4) assumes that it is a directive-rule, and that repeated violation may have resulted in the rule's revocation and perhaps even its replacement with rules specifying conditions under

46 See, further, my "Intervention for Common Good," in G.M. Lyons and M. Mastanduno (eds), *Beyond Westphalia? National Sovereignty and International Intervention*, Baltimore: Johns Hopkins University Press, 1995, pp. 43–58.

47 A. Ross, *The Constitution of the United Nations: Analysis of Structure and Function*, Copenhagen: Munksgaard, 1950, pp. 30–40; Falk, *The Status of Law in International Society*, pp. 217–28. Indeed, Article 103 would seem to make the Charter a treaty above treaties. By stipulating that obligations under the Charter "shall prevail" over members' obligations "under any other international agreement," Article 103 departs from the longstanding rule that when the terms of two treaties conflict, the later treaty shall prevail over the earlier for parties to both.

which the use of force is permitted. Yet, Article 2 is a recitation of principles. If taken at its word, then its regulative failures are much less important than its constitutive intent, amply reconfirmed in principle.

Complementing Article 2's list of principles is Article 1's list of the UN's purposes. All but one are exceedingly general. They call for international peace and security, friendly relations among states, cooperation in economic, social, cultural and humanitarian matters, and a central role for the organization in the attainment of these ends. The Charter's remaining provisions empower the UN's organs to act on these goals, but only within narrow limits. Insofar as the organization may be said to possess some measure of implied powers to fulfill its purposes, Article 2(1) and its corollary, Article 2(7), are commensurately attenuated as rules of recognition.

If the Charter contains a material constitution, its provisions are to be found in Chapter I (Articles 1 and 2). There is much support for the view that Article 2(4) is *jus cogens* – a peremptory rule of law, which may only be superseded by another such peremptory rule. If Article 2(4) is peremptory, it is hard to see why all of Chapter I is not as well. The parallel between claims on behalf of *jus cogens* and Madison's claim that constitutional law is unalterable by law issued under the constitution further supports the view that Chapter I stands apart from the rest of the Charter – and the rest of international law.[48] That Chapter I approximates a model constitution strengthens the case for its status as a material constitution.

International society has always had a formal constitution. As a rule of recognition, the principle of state sovereignty took a clearly modern form at least from the time of Vattel. Even the topical format of great treatises, substantially fixed by Wolff and Vattel, functions as a rule recognizing the division of international law into a number of regimes, which later treaties codified, extended and supplemented. Rules of change appeared in the 19th century in the form of sources doctrine. Now embodied in Article 38 of the Statute of the World Court, they may qualify as an integral part of international society's material constitution. Whether these rules are subject to change through the several processes they specify for legal change in general is an open question (here see Chapter 2, above). A definite answer in the negative would suit the requirements of a model constitution and substantiate the claim that international society has a material constitution of its own.

48 While international lawyers frequently refer to "constitutional" rules – H. Mosler, "The International Society as a Legal Community," *Recueil des cours de l'Académie de Droit International*, vol. 140, 1974/IV, pp. 31–2; L. Henkin, "International Law: Politics, Values and Functions: General Course on Public International Law," *Recueil des cours de l'Académie de Droit International*, vol. 216, 1989/IV, pp. 60–6, are prominent examples – they have not (to my knowledge) distinguished such rules as *jus cogens*. As Mosler intimated (p. 35), this may be because the concept of *jus cogens* has developed in the narrow context of formal agreements. See also Chapter 5, above; G. Danilenko, "International *Jus Cogens*: Issues of Law-Making," *European Journal of International Law*, vol. 2, 1991, pp. 48–57.

International society law has long known rules of recognition explicitly identified as such. The foremost of these rules requires recognition of states by other states for membership in the international legal regime. Scholars have wondered whether recognition is a declaratory or a constitutive act: declaratory insofar as recognition acknowledges that the material conditions of statehood have been met; constitutive insofar as statehood depends on acknowledgment and not just material conditions.[49]

In constructivist terms, any rule of recognition, as an instruction-rule, declares some state of affairs to be regulative and, in so doing, constitutes that state of affairs as declared. Recognition of, and by, states, operationalizes sovereignty on both sides. With every member of the regime deciding independently on membership in the regime, all acts of recognition are sovereign acts with regulative consequences. Yet no one act of recognition suffices for constitutive purposes, for the performance of such an act would effectively shift agency from the aggregate of governments to one in particular.

One might think that the principle of self-determination, affirmed in Article 1(2) of the Charter, has superseded recognition as the controlling rule for the constitution of states, in the process, shifting agency entirely to the determining "self." Yet society always participates in constitution, and not just by warranting self-determination in principle. In the instance of international society, admission to the UN concludes the process of self-determination with a singular, constitutively sufficient act of recognition.[50] Without the normative and material benefits attending UN membership, some of these states might not survive in their current territorial configurations.[51] In effect, membership in the UN confers and sustains membership in international society. Once again, the Charter functions as if Chapter I were international society's material constitution.

Theory, again

Recent events attest to extraordinary changes in international society. The speed and extent of these changes surprised almost everyone, including theorists, who always have change as their subject. Some theories seek to explain why change takes place. They work backwards from a given pattern of change to its cause. That cause must also involve an identifiable pattern of change, with its own cause, and so on, in a potentially infinite regress. Other theories seek to explain how change takes place. They posit some cause and

49 H. Lauterpacht, *Recognition in International Law*, Cambridge: Cambridge University Press, 1947, pp. 38–58.

50 On "collective recognition of State through the United Nations" and its "implications for the debate between constitutivists and declaratorists," see J. Dugard, *Recognition and the United Nations*, Cambridge: Grotius, 1987, pp. 78–80.

51 R.H. Jackson, *Quasi-States: Sovereignty, International Relations and the Third World*, Cambridge: Cambridge University Press, 1990.

examine its ever-more proximate effects. To suppose that any theory can work in both directions at once – to explain how and why simultaneously – invites an unmanageable expansion in the terms of explanation and defeats the theory's purpose.

To view constitution as a process makes change the subject without making theory the objective. As presented in these pages, constructivism is not a theory. Its terms are deliberately inclusive, and it acknowledges change – change as a pervasive and inevitable feature of social construction – in the very definition of those terms. Many, perhaps most deeds are responses to rules. Rules are regulative because agents usually choose to follow them, and continuity and stability rather than change is the result. Those same rules are constitutive because they do provide agents with choices. Every time agents choose to follow a rule, they *change* it – they strengthen the rule – by making it more likely that they and others will follow the rule in the future. Every time agents choose not to follow a rule, they change the rule by weakening it, and in so doing they may well contribute to the constitution of some new rule.

Paradoxically, the constructivist emphasis on rules seems conservative – a ruled environment resists change on any scale – even as constructivism insists, quite radically, that every act in response to a rule entails a change in that rule, in the environment of rules and in the agent as a product of that environment. Constructivism is not a theory of change because it explains change indiscriminately. By definition, everything social changes – everything social. Constructivism does offer a general description of the sites of change. Every rule is an occasion for choice, every choice an incidence of change.

An inquiry into *the* constitution of any society usefully calls on the tradition of analytical positivism, represented here by Kelsen and Hart, to offer a more specific description of the more important sites of change. Some rules are functionally specialized as rules of recognition and change. When linked in a discrete structure, or constitution, these rules, I suggested earlier, give societies their identity and direction. They do so by regulating processes through which other rules are known and changed.

By focusing on these processes, constructivism offers a means for classifying the kinds of change for which theorizing is in order. Obviously the general process of constitution yields *cumulative change*, measured in a given society's changing stock of rules. Within the general pattern of cumulative change, some agents are empowered to change existing rules and make new ones. In modern societies the process of *legal change* is chiefly associated with legislation. In the instance of international society, the process has sometimes been called "peaceful change" and multilateral treaty-making "international legislation."[52] Legal change is nothing more than the normal operation of Hart's secondary rules.

52 F.S. Dunn, *Peaceful Change: A Study of International Procedures*, New York: Council on Foreign Relations, 1937. On legislation as a distinctively modern vocation, see Onuf, "Global Law-Making and Legal Thought," pp. 74–80. Again, these pages postdate material in Chapter 6.

More substantial than peaceful change is the process of *constitutional change*, both affecting secondary rules and effected through them. Material constitutions frequently include rules for their amendment; otherwise exceptional rules must be devised for the occasion. By contrast *revolutionary change* depends on self-empowered agents. They dispose of the old constitution and introduce a new set of secondary rules reflecting a new distribution of powers in the society.

Most substantial of all is *transformative change*, which alters the way regimes, or societies, are nested. These changes are not always as immediate and obvious as revolutionary change, but their consequences are epochal. Consider the emergence of an international society of substantially sovereign states, each of which drastically transformed the many regimes within its territory. Though a process of cumulative change over two centuries, the result is modernity itself. Whether modernity is subject to a comparable transformation in our own time remains to be seen.

Part III

Theory, history and modernity, 1993–2006

20 *Civitas Maxima*: Wolff, Vattel and the fate of republicanism (1993)

Early in the 1980s my brother Peter Onuf and I started talking about a collaborative project. Trained as an historian, Peter had published a groundbreaking book on the origins of the US as a federal republic. His interests in jurisdictional issues and mine in international law suggested an inquiry into a neglected subject – the place of the federal republic in the rapidly changing world of the late 18th and early 19th centuries – that would combine our respective interests to advantage. Initially we focused the federal union as a liberalizing force in the post-Napoleonic world, even more so than Britain, and saw this reflected in the development of international law. As Peter worked on the period immediately following the ratification of the Constitution and I considered the relative importance of liberal and republican ideas on the founding and then steeped myself in republican thought, we decided on a two-stage project. The first stage would cast Emmerich de Vattel as an exemplary figure for a world thrown into crisis, whether in spite or because of the republican values defining it; the second stage would make Henry Wheaton an exemplary figure in a world that emerged from crisis in a liberal form recognizable today.

Well before we published the first of two planned volumes in 1993, I realized that standard treatments of international legal history had utterly disregarded republicanism in international thought. To remedy this oversight, I carefully constructed a paper around Vattel's celebrated repudiation of Christian Wolff's claims on behalf of a *civitas maxima*, which many writers had misconstrued as an early exercise in liberal utopianism. The *American Journal of International Law* published the paper substantially unchanged. A good deal of the material also appears in *The Republican Legacy in International Thought*.

For more than two decades, historians of the US have energetically debated the relative importance of liberalism and republicanism in the 1770s and 1780s.[1]

1 See P.S. Onuf, "Reflections on the Founding: Constitutional Historiography in Bicentennial Perspective," *William and Mary Quarterly*, 3rd Series, vol. 46, 1989, pp. 350–6; D.T. Rodgers, "Republicanism: The Career of a Concept," *Journal of American History*, vol. 79, 1992, pp. 12–19, for useful summaries.

Was the late 18th century a time of progress, and events culminating in the ratification of the Constitution a triumph for individual rights and liberal society, as convention held? Or was it a time of decay, and the events of the founding a renewal of citizen virtue in defense of the common good?[2] Political theorists and constitutional scholars joined the debate, extending it beyond the founding and noting its relevance to our own time.[3] Everyone agreed that liberalism eventually prevailed, more or less completely, for better or for worse. Just when it did so, and why, were questions always asked but never satisfactorily answered as the debate ran its course.

"The concept of republicanism was one of the success stories of the 1980s."[4] Yet contemporary students of international law and relations have ignored this story. Much less has it inspired us to examine 18th century republicanism and consider the implications of its fate for our own scholarship. Another time of great changes – our own – commands our attention and directs us to the future, not to the past.

Furthermore, students of international law and relations, for all our differences, necessarily believe that the term "international" defines for us a distinctive set of concerns, a unique center of gravity. In fields where the concept of republicanism matters, scholars find it matters for, or within, the state considered apart from other states. For students of international law and relations, no state stands apart from other states. If the concept of republicanism has no bearing on the relations of states, its career is no concern of ours.

The state's conceptual and practical importance implies a boundary between two substantially autonomous orders of law, politics and discourse – the domestic and international spheres. Few scholars disavow the boundary

2 Master statement of the conventional view is L. Hartz, *The Liberal Tradition in America: An Interpretation of American Political Thought since the Revolution*, New York: Harcourt, Brace, 1955. For the republican view, see B. Bailyn, *The Ideological Origins of the American Revolution*, Cambridge, MA: Harvard University Press, 1967; G.S. Wood, *The Creation of the American Republic, 1776–1787*, Chapel Hill: University of North Carolina Press, 1969; J.G.A. Pocock, *The Machiavellian Moment: Florentine Political Thought and the Atlantic Republican Tradition*, Princeton: Princeton University Press, 1975. For liberal responses, see J. Appleby, *Capitalism and a New Social Order: the Republican Vision of the 1790s*, New York: New York University Press, 1984; J.P. Diggins, *The Lost Soul of American Politics: Virtue, Self-interest and the Foundations of Liberalism*, New York: Basic Books, 1984; J. Appleby, *Liberalism and Republicanism in the Historical Imagination*, Cambridge, MA: Harvard University Press, 1992.

3 As to political theory, see M. Lienesch, *New Order of the Ages: Time, the Constitution, and the Making of Modern American Political Thought*, Princeton: Princeton University Press, 1988; T.L. Pangle, *The Spirit of Modern Republicanism: the Moral Vision of the American Founders and the Philosophy of Locke*, Chicago: University of Chicago Press, 1988; T. Ball and J.G.A. Pocock (eds), *Conceptual Change and the Constitution*, Lawrence: University Press of Kansas, 1988. For the debate among constitutional legal scholars, see R.H. Fallon, Jr., "What Is Republicanism, and Is It Worth Reviving?" *Harvard Law Review*, vol. 102, 1989, pp. 1695–1735, and material there cited.

4 Rodgers, "Republicanism," p. 11.

between the two spheres. If they differ on the degree to which the boundary is permeable, its presence is regulative. Yet the state – "the impersonal state" we now take for granted – dates only from the 18th century. Before states there were republics. Before anyone found the distinction between domestic and international spheres compelling, there was a law of nature and of nations.

The passage from republicanism to liberalism presupposes a regulated environment, the domestic sphere, provided by the state. Once equipped with republican institutions, states sheltered liberal societies. The problem is this: the passage from republicanism is also a passage to states as we now know them. Liberalism and the impersonal state both resulted from a complex process of social and conceptual change, not under the aegis of the state (which had yet to come into its own), but under the aegis of republicanism. On this view, republicanism was an inclusive order of law, politics and discourse, a sphere unlike either of its exclusionary successors – the domestic and international spheres we now take for granted – but indispensable to their entwined success.

Two and a half centuries ago, republican thought found its most systematic expression in the great treatises on natural law. Great changes in the logic of the law, in its form and method, represent a shift in the balance of properties characterizing Enlightenment republicanism. Recent accounts of republicanism minimally refer to the law of nature and the relations of nations. Instead, they follow J.G.A. Pocock's lead in tracing the "civic ideal of personality" from Aristotle through Polybius, Machiavelli, James Harrington and English opposition politics to the founders.[5] In Pocock's influential interpretation, Niccolò Machiavelli provided later republicanism with its key themes: a preoccupation with time, contingency and human character. These are the concerns of warriors, revolutionaries, citizens, all of whom came to inhabit the domestic sphere. For students of the natural law tradition, republicanism descending from Aristotle through Cicero to Hugo Grotius and on to the 18th century suggests a preoccupation with space, universality and human association – the concerns of an enlightened public for whom philosophers mattered.

At the beginning of the 18th century, the republicanism of the latter sort dominated European intellectual life. At mid-century, Enlightenment republicanism enfolded virtue and nature within a cosmopolitan sensibility. By the end of the century, republicanism had lost all coherence; states had emerged with republican pedigrees. Soon after, republicanism vanished in the great tide of liberalism and positivism. It is at mid-century that we can expect to find the best evidence of great changes within republicanism, especially if we look away from the cosmopolitanism of such diverse figures as Montesquieu, Voltaire, David Hume and Benjamin Franklin, and toward the

5 Pocock, *The Machiavellian Moment*, p. 505.

great expositors of natural law, among whom Christian Wolff and Emmerich de Vattel were preeminent.

Almost exactly at mid-century, Wolff postulated a *civitas maxima* as the foundation of the law of nations. Within a very few years, Vattel, who was Wolff's admiring follower, unequivocally rejected the idea. Uncounted writers have remarked on this episode, but none have related it to the fate of republicanism.[6] To understand what was at stake, we need to do what writers – at

6 See: D.H.L. von Ompteda, *Litteratur des gesammten, sowohl natürlichen als positiven Völkerrechts*, Regensberg: Montags, 1785, as reported by O. Nippold, "Introduction," trans. by F.J. Hemelt, in C. Wolff, *Jus gentium methodo scientifica pertractatum*, vol. 2, trans. by J.H. Drake, Oxford: Clarendon, 1934, pp. xli–ii; [J.P.] Chambrier d'Oleires, "Note" to 1838 edn, in [E.de] Vattel, *Le droit des gens ou principes de la loi naturelle appliqués à la conduite et aux affaires des nations et des souverains*, vol. 1, ed. by M.P. Pradier-Fodéré, Paris: Guillaumin, 1863, pp. 59–63; H. Wheaton, *History of the Law of Nations in Europe and America: From the Earliest Times to the Treaty of Washington, 1842*, New York: Gould, Banks, 1845, pp. 178–9, 185–6, repeated in H. Wheaton, *Elements of International Law*, 8th edn ed. by R.H. Dana, Jr. (1866), Oxford: Clarendon, 1936; C. von Kaltenborn und Strachau, *Kritik des Völkerrechts nach dem jetzigen Standpunkte der Wissenschaft*, Leipzig: Mayer, 1847, also reported in Nippold, "Introduction," p. xliv; A. Mallarmé, "Emer de Vattel," in A. Pillet (ed.), *Les fondateurs du droit international*, Paris: Giard and Briére, 1904, pp. 589–92; L. Oppenheim, *International Law: a Treatise*, vol. 1, London: Longmans, Green, 1905, p. 86; ibid., 8th edn ed. by H. Lauterpacht, New York: McKay, 1955, p. 98; C. Phillipson, "Emmerich de Vattel," in J. MacDonell and E. Manson (eds), *Great Jurists of the World*, Boston: Little, Brown, 1914, p. 493; A. Lapradelle, "Introduction," in E. de Vattel, *The Law of Nations or the Principles of Natural Law Applied to the Conduct and the Affairs of Nations and of Sovereigns*, vol. 3, trans. by C.G. Fenwick, Washington: Carnegie Institution, 1916, p. xxv; O. Nippold, "Introduction" (written 1917), pp. xi–xv; E.D. Dickinson, *The Equality of States in International Law*, Cambridge: Harvard University Press, 1920, p. 97; J. Kosters, "Les fondements de droit des gens: Contribution à la théorie générale du droit des gens," *Bibliotheca Visseriana*, vol. 4, 1925, p. 73; P.E. Corbett, *Law and Society in the Relations of States*, New York: Harcourt, Brace, 1951, p. 30; A. Nussbaum, *A Concise History of the Law of Nations*, rev. edn, New York: Macmillan, 1954, pp. 153–4, 158; T. Ruyssen, *Les sources doctrinale de l'internationalisme*, vol. 2, Presses universitaires de France, 1958, pp. 504–11; C. DeVisscher, *Theory and Reality in Public International Law*, rev. edn trans. by P.E. Corbett, Princeton: Princeton University Press, 1968, p. 20; P.P. Remec, *The Position of the Individual in International Law According to Grotius and Vattel*, The Hague: Nijhoff, 1960, pp. 144, 190–1; F.H. Hinsley, *Power and the Pursuit of Peace: Theory and Practice in the History of Relations Between States*, Cambridge: Cambridge University Press, 1963, p. 167, and *Sovereignty*, New York: Basic Books, 1966, pp. 192–4; E.B.F. Midgley, *The Natural Law Tradition and the Theory of International Relations*, New York: Barnes & Noble, 1975, pp. 180–5; F.S. Ruddy, *International Law in the Enlightenment* (1975), pp. 70–1, 101; Manfred Lachs, *The Teacher in International Law (Teachings and Teaching)*, The Hague: Nijhoff, 1982, pp. 58–9; A. Linklater, *Men and Citizens in the Theory of International Relations*, New York: St. Martin's, 1982, pp. 94, 213–4 n. 16; J. Stone, *Visions of World Order: Between State Power and Human Justice*, Baltimore: Johns Hopkins University Press, 1984, p. 86; M. Koskenniemi, *From Apology to Utopia: the Structure of International Legal Argument*, Helsinki: Finnish Lawyers' Publishing, 1989, pp. 90–1; M. Wight, *International Theory: The Three Traditions*, ed. by G. Wight and B. Porter, New York: Holmes & Meier, 1992, p. 41. Drawn mostly from English language materials, this chronologically arranged list is illustrative, not exhaustive.

least those whose work is readily available – have never done. We need to read what Wolff said as carefully and sympathetically as Vattel himself surely did. To the extent possible, we need to put ourselves in a world separated from our own by two and a half centuries. I propose to undertake such a reading in this essay.

The first part of the essay is devoted to what Wolff actually wrote. His claims on behalf of a *civitas maxima* are to be found in his great work on the law of nations, *Jus gentium methodo scientifica pertractatum*, first published in 1749,[7] and in much briefer form in *Institutiones juris naturae et gentium*, published the following year.[8] The second part attempts to clarify what Wolff meant by subjecting the key terms – *civitas* and *maxima* – to a particularly close scrutiny. The third part turns to Vattel's repudiation of a *civitas maxima* in his famous treatise, *Le droit des gens ou principes de la loi naturelle* (1758) and concludes with a discussion of Vattel's alternative view of Europe as "*une espèce de République*."[9]

Wolff and Vattel both viewed the world – the European world, its public life, its law and diplomacy – in republican terms. Yet, as republicans, they could hardly have been more different. Wolff saw the European world in terms informed by Roman law and medieval experience. Wolff's naturalism has Aristotelian antecedents conspicuously present in the work of Aquinas, Grotius and G.W. Leibniz. In this tradition of thought, nature exhibits an order and purposiveness, a plan, to which the faculty of reason gives humanity privileged access. Natural law is our rendition of nature's plan as it pertains to human association.

Reason tells us that we are social by nature, that we form different associations for different purposes, but that all our associations are ordered, as if by plan, from the least or smallest to the greatest. Reason also tells us that all of nature is so ordered, from lowest to highest, in a necessarily perfect if sometimes inscrutable design. Wolff was the last systematic thinker to give this teleological vision unqualified support. Immanuel Kant's great project to wrest this vision from supporters like Wolff in order to save it from Enlightenment skeptics like Hume came too late.

7 C. Wolff, *Jus gentium methodo scientifica pertractatum*, photo-reproduced in M. Thomann (ed.), *Christian Wolff gesammelte Werke, Abt.* 2, vol. 25, Hildesheim: Olm, 1972. Hereinafter, I refer to the photo-reproduced 1764 edition for the Latin text of Wolff's treatise (*Jus gentium methodo scientifica pertractatum*, vol. 1, 1934), because it was used for Drake's English translation (*Jus gentium methodo scientifica pertractatum*, vol. 2) and is more widely available in the US and Britain than the photo-reproduction of the 1749 edition just cited. Rather than giving page references to the Latin and English texts, I use the paragraph numbers common to both.

8 C. Wolff, *Institutiones juris naturae et gentium*, photo-reproduced in Thomann, *Christian Wolff gesammelte Werke, Abt.* 2, vol. 26, Hildesheim: Olm, 1969, para. 1090, pp. 680–2.

9 [E.] de Vattel, *Le Droit des gen ou principes de la loi naturelle appliqués à la conduite et aux affaires des nations et des souverains* (1758), quoting III, iii, para. 47, photo-reproduced in two vols, Washington: Carnegie Institution, 1916, vol. 2, p. 251. Hereinafter, I use this edition in preference to the 1863 edition cited above for the French text.

Vattel's republicanism is closer to the way of thinking Pocock identified with Machiavelli. Unlike Machiavelli, however, Vattel was an avowed naturalist, following in a tradition conventionally said to have originated with Grotius, but decisively affected by Thomas Hobbes' austere view of the human condition. Behind this radical naturalism was, in James Tully's words, "a concept of nature as a non-purposive realm of atoms on which God imposes, by an act of will, an extrinsic order of efficient causes or regularities. The task of philosophers of natural law was henceforth to bring natural law into line with this scientific concept of nature and human nature."[10]

Not all philosophers saw this as their task: Wolff sought to bring science into line with purposive nature. Others did. More precisely, some philosophers like John Locke and Samuel Pufendorf sought to restore sociality to the human condition without reverting to an "Aristotelian and Thomistic conception of nature ordered by intrinsic teleological dispositions."[11] Such a position softened the Hobbesian emphasis on self-regarding individuals and made it palatable. It also made old-fashioned, unscientific Aristotelianism expendable; it even made natural law expendable. Some 18th century republicans could write the way Machiavelli did a century before Grotius – guided not by nature's decrees but by history's. Others, including Vattel, clung to the language of naturalism but left it with no use but the support of individual rights in a liberal society. They denied law its source in nature; it remained for their successors to find the sources of all laws in human experience.

For all the talk of nature and its law, Vattel made history – Europe's recent history – his guide. European had become "a sort of republic" because of states and statecraft, and because of commerce, civil society and constitutional development. Wolff's republic had always been what it was and would always be. The differences between Wolff and Vattel mark a world of change. That their differences crystallize around Wolff's *civitas maxima* helps to explain the sense that so many writers have had of the episode's importance.

What Wolff wrote

I begin by quoting or paraphrasing relevant passages from the 1764 edition of Wolff's treatise, translated by Joseph Drake as *The Law of Nations According to the Scientific Method*, and consisting of more than one thousand numbered paragraphs, all but a handful with commentary. As Vattel aptly remarked, "it is written after the method and scientific form of treatises on geometry," and is difficult to use as a consequence.[12] Twenty-six paragraphs,

10 J. Tully, "Editor's Introduction," in S. Pufendorf, *On the Duty of Man and Citizen*, trans. by M. Silverstone, Cambridge: Cambridge University Press, 1991, p. xvii.

11 Ibid. in reference specifically to Pufendorf.

12 Vattel, *The Law of Nations*, Preface, p. 8a.

twenty-five with commentaries, constitute the *Prolegomena*, which embody Wolff's general position and state his claims with respect to a *civitas maxima*. When needed to clarify Wolff's intent or lend coherence, I provide commentary of my own.

Paragraph 1 defines the law of nations, though unhelpfully. "By the Law of Nations we understand the science of that law which peoples or nations use in their relations with each other and of the obligations corresponding thereto." Neither "law" nor "obligation" are subject to later definition or clarification. Furthermore, the identification of law with "the science of that law" is muddled, even if the term "science" is taken in the 18th century sense as a logical arrangement ordained by nature. Unless the content of the law is fully determined, like geometry, by the logic of nature, then science cannot suffice to understand that law. Wolff knew better than to make any such claim. Indeed, we may look on Wolff's *Prolegomena* as an imaginative, even heroic attempt to reconcile his scientific view of law as geometry with his recognition that law is an indeterminate, human undertaking.

Paragraph 2 defines nation as "a multitude of men united into a state [*in civitatem consociatorum*]." Nations are to be regarded as "individual free persons, living in a state of nature." As free persons, they act as they will, yet the state of nature is the geometer's nature. Thus paragraph 3 holds that "the law of nations is nothing except the law of nature applied to nations." Just as science appears in its most conclusive form, the commentary to this paragraph issues a caution. "But far be it from you to think that therefore there is no need of our discussing in detail the law of nations. For the principles of the law of nature are one thing, but the application of them to nations another, and this produces a certain diversity in that which is inferred."

The next three paragraphs turn away from the possibility of diverse inferences. They posit a necessary, or natural, law of nations. According to paragraph 4, the necessary law "binds nations in conscience" and, according to paragraphs 5 and 6, is "absolutely immutable," as is the obligation to follow it. Wolff then left the subject of the necessary law of nations, alluding to it briefly in paragraph 22 and surprising infrequently in his substantive exposition.

Paragraph 7 declares that "[n]ature herself has established society [*societatem*] among all nations and binds them to preserve it. For nature herself has established society among men and binds them to preserve it." Apparently the establishment of society is unrelated to the formation of nations alluded to in paragraph 2. While the dual existence of "natural society" (a phrase first used in the next paragraph) and freely formed nations substantiates the paradox of immutable law and diverse inferences, it fails to prepare us adequately for the rest of paragraph 7. "Therefore, since this obligation [to preserve society], as coming from the law of nature, is necessary and immutable, it cannot be changed for the reason that nations have united into a state [again, *in civitatem*]." As the commentary to paragraph 7 makes clear, Wolff was concerned to show that because the formation of nations does not imperil "that great society" established by nature, then it cannot be imperiled when nations unite.

Paragraph 8 presumes that the purpose of natural society "is to give mutual assistance in perfecting itself and its condition" and extends the presumption of mutual assistance, as well as a concern for "the common good," to the society among nations. Did Wolff mean *societas* or *civitas*? The text clearly states the former, the title of the paragraph no less clearly indicates the latter. The commentary suggests that *civitas* "preserves" *societas* by "combining powers" – of people thereby forming nations, and of nations thus formed – for the promotion of the common good. People cannot do without each other. Nations only seem to be able to do so. Wolff insisted that any nation could always "improve its condition" with the aid of others.

Wolff's text has us shuttling between *societas* and *civitas*, the former natural and the latter discretionary. In so doing, it fails to convince us that people once organized into nations will see through the appearance of self-sufficiency and acknowledge the benefits of mutual aid. Thus it fails to demonstrate that nations must come together for any purpose. Unsupported though this conclusion may be, paragraph 9 states it baldly. "All nations are understood to have come together into a state, whose separate members are separate nations, or individual states."

The rest of paragraph 9 continues the shuttle between *societas* and *civitas*, sowing further confusion along the way. Nevertheless, Wolff did make another claim in this paragraph that warrants our attention. "[S]o what can be said except that nations also have combined into society as if by agreement?" Here Wolff had *civitas* in mind, as the commentary to paragraph 9 clearly shows. There we find reference to "the quasi-agreement, by which that supreme state [*civitas illa maxima*] is understood to have been formed between states."

If the commentary to paragraph 9 alludes to the *civitas* among nations as *maxima*, the commentary to the next paragraph tells why. "The size of a state is determined by the number of its citizens. Therefore, a greater state cannot be conceived of than the one whose members are all nations in general, inasmuch as they together include the whole human race." We are also told that "the concept of a supreme state" was not unknown to Grotius, who could have derived it from the voluntary, as opposed to the necessary, law of nations. On expository grounds, Wolff ought to have introduced the Grotian opposition between voluntary and necessary law in paragraph 7. Obviously he presumed that his audience was well acquainted with the two categories. Nevertheless, it is only the latter that presents Wolff with a "scientific" problem, which paragraph 7 and subsequent paragraphs attempt to solve.

Paragraph 11 resumes the shuttle between *societas* and *civitas* – "since the supreme state is a certain sort of state, consequently a society" – to argue that the *civitas maxima* has "the right . . . of promulgating laws." Paragraph 15 confirms that this right confers at least a degree of sovereignty understood as the power to rule. "Some sovereignty [*imperium*] over individual nations belongs to nations as a whole." The commentary admits that sovereignty so conceived will "seem paradoxical to some," meaning those "who do not have a clear notion of the supreme state, nor recognize the benefit which nature provides, when she established a certain civil society [*civitatem quandam societatem*]." Now, quite adventitiously, *societas* and *civitas* are one.

Paragraph 19 argues that the *civitas maxima* is popularly ruled. "This is because sovereignty rests with the whole, which in the present instance is the entire human race divided up into peoples or nations." Paragraph 20 observes that while "in a democratic state [*in statu populari*] it is necessary that individuals assemble in a definite place and declare their will as to what ought to be done," "the nations scattered throughout the whole world cannot assemble together." Consequently, "the will of all nations" is that "which they agree upon, if following the leadership of nature, they use right reason."

Paragraph 21 goes another, perhaps surprising step. Every nation has a leader – "*superior*" – with power to rule. Analogously, "he can be considered the ruler of the supreme state [*Rector civitatis maximae*] who, following the leadership of nature, defines by the right use of reason what nations ought to consider as law among themselves, although it does not conform in all respects to the natural law of nations, nor altogether differ from it." The concluding phrase alludes to the paradoxical relation of immutable natural law to a law of nations with its own peculiar content.

The commentary to this article begins by defending the use of fictions. It states that "all moral persons," including the *civitas maxima*, "have something fictitious in them." A "fictitious ruler of the supreme state" must be assumed so that the *civitas maxima* can adapt natural law, "as far as human conditions allow," to its purposes – purposes which, we may recall, have to do with mutual assistance and the common good. *Societas* and *civitas* now stand decisively severed, with the *Rector fictus* mediating between them.

Paragraph 22 finally makes clear that the point of the preceding discussion is to provide a scientific basis for the voluntary law of nations. Though deriving from the necessary law of nations, the voluntary law "is considered to have been laid down" by the fictitious ruler of the *civitas maxima*, "and so to have proceeded from the will of nations."[13] The paradox of a mutable yet natural law of nations is resolved: nature's leadership requires human assistance in matters relating to human wishes and intentions – matters which bring human beings together in the first place. By contrast, the necessary or natural law of nations, like society, proceeds directly from nature without such intercession.

The remaining paragraphs of the *Prolegomena* attend to law arising from agreements or custom. This law differs from the voluntary law of nations,

13 Somewhat confusingly, paragraph 22 and its commentary also hold that the voluntary law of nations derives "from the concept of the supreme state," the commentary adding, "so that it is not necessary to rely by blind impulse on the deeds and customs and decisions of the more civilized nations." Wolff had earlier (commentary, paras. 10 and 15) castigated Grotius and everyone else for failing to derive the voluntary law of nations from such a notion.

which is universal, by being particular to the nations accepting it expressly or tacitly. Whether universal or particular, all such law has its origins in the will of nations, which warrants for it the label "positive law of nations." Nevertheless, Wolff's professed concern is not the positive law in general, but only that law which is universal and thus, like geometry, available to science.

What Wolff meant

Wolff's invocation of a *civitas maxima* and his explication of its relation to the voluntary law of nations raises a number of questions, most of which are brought to the fore by the translation of key terms. The first question is whether *supreme state* is an appropriate translation of *civitas maxima*. Few writers seem to have thought so.[14] Yet few agree on any possible alternative.

Among the many translations of *civitas maxima*, we find *civitas* rendered as *city, civil society, society, republic, commonwealth, community, brotherhood, polity*, and *empire*.[15] Drake's translation of *civitas* as *state* also has support.[16] Several of these choices are misleading, including the last.

The Latin *civitas* corresponds to the Greek *polis*. Aristotle defined the *polis* as "a species of association," a voluntary partnership, which people form for their common good. Because the common good exceeds any other good for which people associate, the *polis* is "the final and perfect association," positioned above all others.[17] Like *polis*, the term *civitas* has served throughout much of Western history, and certainly in Wolff's time, to describe the primary units within which people self-consciously organize themselves to deal with their important concerns.

14 One is Midgley, *The Natural Law Tradition and the Theory of International Relations*, p. 180.

15 *City*: A. Rivier, *Principes du droit des gens*, vol. 1, Paris: Rousseau, 1896, p. 9; L. Olive, "Wolff," in Pillet, *Les fondateurs de droit international*, p. 459. *Civil society*: Corbett, Ruyssen, Ruddy, as cited above. *Society*: Chambrier d'Oleires; *Wheaton, History of the Law of Nations*; Nippold (*Staatengesellschaft*); Ruddy (again). *Republic*: Vattel, *Le Droit des gens*, p. xvii; Ompteda, Wheaton, *History of the Law of Nations* (again); Mallarmé; Phillipson. *Commonwealth*: Wheaton, *History of the Law of Nations* (yet again); *Community*: Kaltenborn (*Völkerrechtsgemeïnschaft*), Kosters. *Brotherhood*: Phillipson (again). *Polity*: Stone. *Empire*: Thomann, "Introduction," pp. xxxvii–viii.

16 J.-L. Klüber, *Droit des gens moderne de l'Europe*, ed. by M.A. Ott, Paris: Guillaumin, 1861, p. 18; Oppenheim, both eds cited; Hersch Lauterpacht," The Nature of International Law and General Jurisprudence" (1932), in E. Lauterpacht (ed.), *International Law, Being the Collected Papers of Hersch Lauterpacht*, vol. 2, part 1, Cambridge: Cambridge University Press, 1975, p. 17; W. Schiffer, *The Legal Community of Mankind: A Critical Analysis of the Modern Concept of World Organization*, New York: Columbia University Press, 1954, p. 73; C.W. Jenks, *The Common Law of Mankind*, London: Stevens, 1958, p. 68; Thomann (again), pp. xxvi–viii.

17 Aristotle, *Politics*, trans. by B. Jowett, I, i–ii (1252a1–6, 1252b27–32), in Jonathan Barnes (ed.), *The Complete Works of Aristotle*, vol. 2, Princeton: Princeton University Press, pp. 1986–7.

So understood, the city is "a body of many and diverse associations," "a unity of citizens," and a "representational or fictional person." These formulations belong to Johannes Althusius' *Politica methodice digesta*, written at the beginning of the 17th century.[18] They could just as well be Wolff's, but they would hardly occur to an English speaker. For the latter, *civil society* may seem to express the generic sense of the term *civitas*. In *De cive* (1642), Hobbes took *city* and *civil society* as interchangeable renditions of *civitas*.[19] In the *Second Treatise* (1689), Locke also used *civil society*, in his case interchangeably with *political society*, as a generic term.[20] Yet the term *society* produces a difficulty of its own.

As we have just seen, Wolff generally, though not entirely consistently, separated *societas* and *civitas*, associating one with nature and necessity and the other with human discretion and endeavor. For Locke, "the state of nature" corresponds to "society" as Wolff understood it. When people quit the state of nature, Locke had them "enter into society to make one People, one Body Politick under one Supreme Government." On such occasions, "there and there only is a *Political, or Civil Society*."[21] Whether one follows Wolff in separating *civitas* and *societas* or Locke in uniting them as "civil society," the latter term is likely to confuse contemporary students of politics, especially comparative politics, who are accustomed to distinguishing between state and civil society. Clearly the term *civitas* antedates any such distinction and, when broadly taken, effectively obliterates it.[22]

There are also grounds for translating *civitas* as *republic*. Often we find the latter term reserved exclusively for the Roman Republic. Yet, from the time of Rome, the Latin *respublica* (or *republica*) has had the generic sense we find in Cicero's *De re publica*.[23] While Classical texts separate political association and its purposes (*polis, civitas*) from the possible forms that political association might take (*politeia, status*), the term *republic* saw duty on both sides of the divide, and it continued to do so after the medieval turn to Aristotle. Thus, Bartolus of Sassoferrato, the great 14th century civil lawyer, insisted that the term *respublica* is applicable not just to Rome, but to any self-governing

18 J. Althusius, *Politica*, 3rd edn (1614), abridged, trans. by F.S. Carney, Boston: Beacon Press, 1964, pp. 35–7.

19 "*Unio* autem sic facta, appellatur *civitas*, sive *societas civilis*, atque etiam *persona civilis*." T. Hobbes, *De cive*, The Latin Version, ed. by H. Warrender, V, ix, Oxford: Clarendon, 1983, p. 134; emphasis in original. The same passage in the first English edition (1651) reads: "Now *union* thus made is called a *City*, or *civill society*, and also a *civill Person*." *De Cive*, The English Version, ed. by H. Warrender, Oxford: Clarendon, 1983, p. 89. On Hobbes' likely participation in this translation, see "Editor's Introduction," pp. 4–8.

20 J. Locke, *Two Treatises on Government*, ed. by P. Laslett, Cambridge: Cambridge University Press, 1988, 2nd Treatise, para. 89, p. 325.

21 Ibid., paragraph 6, at 270–1; emphasis in original. See also paras. 89, 95, pp. 325, 330–1.

22 L. Strauss, *The City and Man*, Chicago: Rand McNally, 1964, p. 30.

23 Cicero, "The Republic," I, xxxv, para. 49, in *De re publica, de legibus*, trans. by C. W. Keyes, London: Heineman, 1928, p. 76.

civitas in the Empire.[24] Machiavelli divorced the term *republic* from the larger sense of *civitas/respublica* and used it instead for a particular form of rule. *Stato* stands in for the generic *republic* even though the Latin equivalent, *status*, had always previously referred specifically to the form of rule.[25]

With Jean Bodin, *respublica* regained its generic meaning: "A republic is a lawful government of many households and what is theirs in common, with sovereign power."[26] Althusius expressly rejected Machiavelli's position. "Many writers distinguish between the realm (*regnum*) and a commonwealth (*respublica*), relating the former to a monarchical king and the latter to polyarchical optimates. But in my judgement this distinction is not a good one." Althusius was taking aim at Bodin as well. "For ownership of a realm belongs to the people, and administration of it to the king."[27]

Evidently Bodin and Althusius agreed on *republic* as a basic term of reference and disagreed on the properties of sovereignty. Bodin equated sovereignty (*majestas*) with absolute power.[28] For Althusius, *majestas*, the ability to inspire awe, attaches incidentally, and not exclusively, to the ruler. Power to establish conditions of rule (*potestas imperiandi*) resides with the people and can be withdrawn when the ruler fails to provide for the common good.[29] The idea of popular sovereignty has a long history in radical religious thought.[30] "Popular Sovereignty of the Republican sort," embracing Classical concerns for natural law and the common good, is an idea fully realized by Althusius – a Calvinist and Aristotelian – and clearly present in Wolff's *Prolegomena*.[31]

In English there is a close association, semantically and normatively, between *common good* and *commonwealth*, the latter referring to any political

24 C.N.S. Woolf, *Bartolus of Sassoferrato: His Position in the History of Medieval Political Thought*, Cambridge: Cambridge University Press, 1913, pp. 115–8; Q. Skinner, *The Foundations of Modern Political Thought*, vol. 1, Cambridge: Cambridge University Press, 1978, pp. 8–12.

25 Consider the opening words of *The Prince*: "All states [*Tutti gli stati*], all dominions that have held and do hold empire over men have been and are either republics or principalities." N. Machiavelli, *The Prince*, trans. by H.C. Mansfield, Jr., Chicago: University of Chicago Press, 1985, p. 61; *Il Principe*, ed. by B. Craxi, Milano: Mondadori, 1986, p. 11.

26 See J. Bodin, *The Six Bookes of a Commonweale* (1576), trans. by R. Knolles (1606), ed. by K. McRae, Cambridge, MA: Harvard University Press, 1962. Appendix B provides both the French and Latin terminology Bodin used for key concepts. "Republic" is defined on p. A74, forms of rule on p. A76.

27 Althusius, *Politica*, p. 61.

28 Bodin, *The Six Bookes of a Commonweale*, A75.

29 Althusius, *Politica*, pp. 64–9. Also, see O. Gierke, *The Development of Political Theory*, trans. by B. Freyd, New York: Norton, 1939, pp. 154–63.

30 Gierke, *The Development of Political Theory*, pp. 143–54; Gierke, *Political Theories of the Middle Age*, trans. F.W. Maitland, Cambridge: Cambridge University Press, 1938, pp. 37–61; Skinner, *The Foundations of Modern Political Thought*, vol. 2, pp. 332–48; B. Tierney, *Religion, Law, and the Growth of Constitutional Thought 1150–1650*, Cambridge: Cambridge University Press, 1982, pp. 54–79.

31 Quoting Gierke, *Political Theories of the Middle Age*, p. 38.

arrangement for the common good. English usage also associates *commonwealth* with *civitas*, but not, at least necessarily, with popular sovereignty. Thus, the English translation of Bodin's great work tells us, with credit to Aristotle, that a city is "a multitude of citizens, having all things needful to them to live well and happily withall: making no difference between a Commonweale and a citie."[32] In the same vein, Hobbes' *Leviathan* (1651) offers *commonwealth* in translation of *civitas*: "the multitude, so united in one Person is called a COMMON-WEALTH, in latine CIVITAS."[33] Locke employed a strikingly similar formulation.[34] If the term *commonwealth* now seems "slightly mandarin," as Quentin Skinner observed in using it to translate *respublica*, its virtue lies in its "normative overtones (suggestive of the common good), which have substantially withered away in the increasingly individualist atmosphere in which our political arrangements have come to be discussed."[35] One might note how decisively Hobbes' and Locke's thought, but not the basic terms they used, contributed to this change.

Concern for the common good suggests that the term *community*, which shares a common Latin root with *common*, might serve just as well in translation of *civitas*. Here the problem is the opposition between society and community, famously and permanently codified by Ferdinand Tönnies in the 19th century. Although both are seen as equally inclusive, the latter is said to be grounded in affect and solidarity. Nothing in Wolff's use of the term *civitas* anticipates this opposition. Either choice – *society* or *community* – leaves something out from his point of view. Even less satisfactory is *brotherhood*, which favors affect and solidarity over reason and individuality even more emphatically than "community" does.

Yet another possible translation of the term *civitas* is the term Julius Stone favored: *polity*. It is difficult to know whether this term is a transliteration of *politeia* or a neologism derived from "politics" and synonymous with "body politic." We find it in the title of Richard Hooker's *Of the Lawes of Ecclesiasticall Politie* (1593), although the text prefers "politic society" and "body politic."[36] Locke occasionally spoke of polities in the *Second*

32 Bodin, *The Six Bookes of a Commonweale*, p. 50.

33 T. Hobbes, *Leviathan*, ed. by C.B. Macpherson, Baltimore: Penguin, 1968, II, xvii, p. 227. *Cf.* p. 81 (Hobbes' Introduction): "For by Art is created that great LEVIATHAN called a COMMON-WEALTH, or STATE (in latine CIVITAS) which is but an Artificiall Man."

34 Locke, *Two Treatises*, 2nd Treatise, X, paragraph 133, p. 355. Locke clearly equated commonwealth with political or civil society. Ibid., VII, para. 89, p. 325. So did James Harrington: "A commonwealth is but a civil society of men." J. Harrington, *The Commonwealth of Oceana* (1656), in J.G.A. Pocock (ed.), *The Political Works of James Harrington*, Cambridge: Cambridge University Press, 1977, p. 172.

35 Skinner, *The Foundations of Modern Political Thought*, vol. 1, p. xxiii.

36 R. Hooker, *Of the Laws of Ecclesiastical Polity: Preface, Book I, Book VIII*, ed. by A.S. McGrade, Cambridge: Cambridge University Press, 1989. For "politic society," see I, ix, para. 1, and I, xv, paras. 2–3, pp. 87, 118; for "body politic," VIII, iii, para. 2, and VIII, viii, para. 9, pp. 144, 217. Book VIII was not published until 1648.

Treatise.[37] He spoke more often, and more abstractly, of the body politic, as did Hobbes. More recent usage would seem to combine in the term *polity* both *polis* as body politic and *politeia* as the body politic's apparatus of rule. Insofar as this is so, the term is more inclusive than *civitas* was in the 17th century. Lacking the normative weight and historical resonance of terms like *republic* and *commonwealth, polity* conveys too little, and too much, as a translation of *civitas*.

If *polity* lacks resonance, nothing of the sort can be said about the use of the term *state* to translate *civitas*. In this case, the resonance is all wrong, as a brief review of the term's conceptual history readily shows. Classical Latin texts use *status* to denote a condition or state of affairs. Applied to matters of politics, the affairs of the *civitas*, it refers to the contrivances of rule. As we saw, Machiavelli broke with tradition by using the vernacular version of *status* generically. "*Lo stato*" appears alone, and not in reference to a form of rule, too many times in *The Prince* for it not to have been a self-conscious choice.[38]

J.H. Hexter and Harvey Mansfield have argued that Machiavelli meant *lo stato* to convey an exploitive sense. As Hexter concluded, "*lo stato* is not a matrix of values, a body politic; it is an instrument of exploitation, the instrument the prince uses to get what he wants."[39] What is missing therefore is the distinctively modern sense of the impersonal state, one freed from an Aristotelian preoccupation with the relation between the forms and beneficiaries of rule. This conclusion is Mansfield's.[40] In his interpretation, and Skinner's as well, the republican tradition lacked any conception of the impersonal state. Machiavelli started the conceptual shift toward impersonal rule. Hobbes consolidated it, and by the time of Jean-Jacques Rousseau the process was complete.[41] Marking the ascendancy of the impersonal state, we may presume, is the term *state*, which came to displace *civitas, republic* and *commonwealth* as a generic term.

Both Skinner and Mansfield made Hobbes the central figure in the 250-year turn from ancient political ideas to modern ones. Retrospectively, we know that Hobbes was decisive for this turn. Yet the impact of his work was less than immediate, especially if we use the term *state* as a measure. Hobbes himself characteristically used *civitas* or *commonwealth* for generic purposes.

37 See, for example, VIII, paras. 112, 116. Locke, *Two Treatises*, 2nd Treatise, pp. 344–5.

38 J.H. Hexter, *The Vision of Politics on the Eve of the Reformation: More, Machiavelli, Seysell*, New York: Basic Books, 1973, pp. 150–72; Harvey C. Mansfield, Jr., "On the Impersonality of the Modern State: A Comment on Machiavelli's Use of *Stato*," *American Political Science Review*, vol. 77, 1983, p. 856; Skinner, *The Foundations of Modern Political Thought*, vol. 2, pp. 353–4.

39 Hexter, *The Vision of Politics on the Eve of the Reformation*, pp. 171, 192. Nor does *The Prince* employ generic alternatives to *lo stato*. This is in marked contrast to *The Discourses*, which of course reflects Machiavelli's republican concerns for the body politic. p. 170.

40 Mansfield, "On the Impersonality of the Modern State," pp. 855–6.

41 Ibid.; Skinner, *The Foundations of Modern Political Thought*, vol. 1, pp. ix–x; vol. 2, pp. 349–58.

In the *Second Treatise* Locke used the term *state* very rarely and never generically. Locke's contemporary, Pufendorf, consistently used *civitas* generically in his great work, *De jure naturae et gentium*.[42]

Like Pufendorf, Wolff wrote his systematic treatises in Latin; he was among the last to do so. Impersonally conceived, the state is a vernacular development, proceeding from Machiavelli to Rousseau and beyond. Wolff *could* have had the impersonal state in mind when he used the term *civitas*. Matters of statecraft find a place in Wolff's treatise, as we would expect from someone whose benefactor was Frederick the Great.[43] For example, several paragraphs are devoted to the power and wealth of nations, with paragraph 70 stating that nations ought to strive for power. This talk does not go very far, however: paragraph 72 condemns making unjust war to increase power.

Wolff's remarks on power follow a discussion of the duties of a nation and, because the nation has formed itself into a *civitas*, its form of government (*status*) and finally its head (*rector civitatis*). Paragraph 35 states that "[e]very nation ought to perfect itself and its form of government." This formula is repeated a number of times. It is extended to the *rector*, and it entails a duty of self-knowledge as well as a duty to seek fame, which is praise for displaying moral and intellectual virtue in the quest for perfection. Wolff's preoccupation with the quality of rule is an Aristotelian theme far more forcefully expressed than anything he had to say about power. It suggests that rule can be deeply personal without being partisan.

Such are my reasons for not accepting *state* in translation of *civitas*, at least for Wolff and not just in reference to *civitas maxima*. Wolff could just as well have used *respublica* instead of *civitas* to convey the conceptual and historical associations he had in mind. Any English translations using the terms *city, republic* or *commonwealth* would honor these associations, once the generic sense of any of these terms is duly established. Among them I prefer *republic* to remind us of Wolff's place in the history of republican thought.

The term *maxima* offers fewer difficulties. Among the various translations we frequently find *great, general, universal*, and *world*.[44] We also find the sense

42 S. Pufendorf, *De jure naturae et gentium libri octo* (1688 ed), vol. 1, Oxford: Clarendon, 1934, VII, pp. 646–771 *passim*.

43 Nippold, "Introduction," pp. xxi–ii. As Crown Prince, Frederick admired Wolff, commending his work to Voltaire (1694–1778), and ardently criticized Machiavelli. As King, however, he is remembered for his statecraft as much as for his "Enlightened" views. On Frederick, Wolff and Voltaire, see P. Sonnino, "Introduction," in Frederick of Prussia, *The Refutation of Machiavelli's* Prince *or Anti-Machiavel* (1740), trans. by Sonnino, Athens: Ohio University Press, 1981, p. 13.

44 *Great*: Vattel; Wheaton, *History of the Law of Nations*; Mallarmé; Rivier; Olive: all cited above. Ruyssen used the superlative. *General*: Ompteda; Chambrier d'Oleires, Wheaton, *History of the Law of Nations* (again). *Universal*: Wheaton, *History of the Law of Nations* (yet again); Kosters; Thomann. *World*: Oppenheim, both eds cited; Schiffer, Jenks; Stone. Klüber used "universal" and "world" together; Ruddy's translation is "world-wide."

of the term expressed in the prefix *super-* (as in "super-civil society" and "super-state").[45] Drake's choice of *supreme* for *maxima* is not favored.

The reason for this is not hard to find. There is a direct Latin equivalent to supreme – *supremus*, which is a variant of *summus* and thus a general superlative. We find it frequently attached to words like *potestas*. *Maximus* is also a superlative, specifically of *magnus*, meaning *greatest* or *largest*. Wolff clearly had physical scale in mind when he spoke of the *civitas maxima*. Thus the commentary to paragraph 10 refers to the size of this republic ["*magnitudo civitatis*"] and concludes than there can be none greater ["*major*"] because it includes all nations and thus the whole of humanity.

Additional support for thinking of the *civitas maxima* as the largest possible republic comes from Bartolus, one of Wolff's most important predecessors. In his tract, *De regimine civitates*, Bartolus identified three grades or classes of cities and nations. First is *magna*, second *major*, and third *maxima*, respectively being *primo, secundo* and *tertio gradu magnitudinis*.[46] The first grade refers to self-contained cities, the second refers in effect to nations, and the third to the Empire. In this order, the three grades also mark the evolution of Classical Rome, which suggested to Bartolus that political arrangements on the smallest scale are best ruled popularly, those in the mid-range as aristocracies and the largest by a single person.

What then of Wolff's *civitas maxima*, which, we know, was to have been subject to popular rule? Wolff's republican commitments included popular sovereignty. Nevertheless, practical considerations require a *rector*, always referred to in the singular. Wolff had it both ways: the step beyond known terrestrial empires is the republic of all nations. This necessitates a fourth grade in Bartolus' incomplete system. It makes that system a cycle, which is completed by returning rule to the people in principle, even as it acknowledges that for practical purposes any political arrangement on a large scale requires an individual head.

We need not conclude that Wolff self-consciously extended Bartolus' system to understand the importance of the way of thinking that lies behind it. Aristotle anticipated this way of thinking by arranging purposeful associations in ascending levels. The *polis* spans a number of villages, and the village a number of households.[47] After Bartolus, many writers conceived of associations in an ascending order of size – necessarily of size because each is a formal union of associations in the rank beneath. Higher means wider or

45 Remec, Wight, as cited above.

46 Woolf, *Bartolus of Sassoferrato*, pp. 174–82; R.W. Carlyle and A.J. Carlyle, *A History of Mediaeval Political Theory in the West*, vol. 6, New York: Barnes & Noble, 1950, which quotes Bartolus' Latin on pp. 78–79 n. 2; M. Wight, *Systems of States*, Leicester: Leicester University Press, 1977, pp. 136–7, which misleadingly refers to "classes of states."

47 Aristotle, *Politics*, I, ii (1252b10–30), p. 1987.

broader, and *vice versa*.[48] Bodin developed an elegant version of this conception, with family and college (the one natural and the other civil) occupying the lowest rank, *corpus* (in the English version, corporation) the next, and *universitas* (deleted from the English version) the rank after that. Finally comes the republic, which, though it depends on support from its constituent parts, stands apart by being sovereign.[49] Despite Bodin's attachment to "the theory of corporations" originating in Roman law, his view of sovereignty necessarily empties that theory of content, leaving a framework of little interest to those favoring Bodin's position on sovereignty.[50]

Althusius was more faithful to the theory of corporations. Indeed, he enhanced its significance by denying any intrinsic difference among associations such as sovereignty might confer. The *Politica* begins by defining politics as "the art of associating (*consociandi*) men for the purpose of establishing, cultivating and conserving social life among them."[51] Althusius then identified five species of associations in an ascending series: family, college, city (*civitas*), province (missing from the first edition of 1603) and republic (recall Althusius' unwillingness to distinguish between realm and republic).[52] Recall also that Althusius was willing to ascribe a significant degree of *majestas* to associations of the highest level, the "*universalis publica consociatio*," but that *potestas* is conceptually indivisible and only provisionally extended to the republic.[53] Finally, we should recall Althusius' observation that the city is a fictional person. So indeed are all corporate entities in this line of thought.

Writing at the turn of the 17th century, Leibniz reformulated Althusius'

48 Gierke, *Political Theories of the Middle Age*, p. 96, and *Development of Political Theory*, p. 259; see O. Gierke, *Natural Law and the Theory of Society 1500 to 1800* (1913), trans. by E. Barker, Boston: Beacon, 1957, p. 35, for "higher and wider communities" and "progressively higher and progressively broader social formations." In this context, *superior* is the equivalent of *major*, and Drake's construction of *maxima* as *supreme* has at least some justification.

49 See Bodin, *The Six Bookes of a Commonweale*, III, vii, p. 361, and ed. note, p. 128; Gierke, *Natural Law and the Theory of Society*, pp. 64–7.

50 Gierke's interpretation is similar. *Natural Law and the Theory of Society*, pp. 64, 67. On the theory of corporations, Gierke's work is indispensable. Also see E.H. Kantorowicz, *The King's Two Bodies: A Study in Mediaeval Political Thought*, Princeton: Princeton University Press, 1957, pp. 291–313; J.P. Canning, "The Corporation in the Political Thought of the Italian Jurists of the Thirteenth and Fourteenth Centuries," *History of Political Thought*, vol. 1, 1980, pp. 9–31, and "Law, Sovereignty and Corporation Theory, 1300–1450," in J.H. Burns (ed.), *The Cambridge History of Medieval Political Thought c. 350–c. 1450*, Cambridge: Cambridge University Press, 1988, pp. 454–76; Tierney, *Religion, Law and the Growth of Constitutional Thought*, pp. 19–28; H.J. Berman, *Law and Revolution: The Formation of the Western Legal Tradition*, Cambridge, MA: Harvard University Press, 1983, pp. 215–21; A. Black, *Guilds and Civil Society in European Political Thought from the Twelfth Century to the Present*, London: Methuen, 1984, pp. 76–95.

51 Althusius, *Politica*, p. 12.

52 Ibid., pp. 22–3.

53 Quoting Gierke, *Natural Law and the Theory of Society*, p. 7.

system by identifying an ascending series of "natural societies."[54] The first is between man and wife, the second between parents and children, the third between masters and servants. The fourth is the household and the fifth is civil [*bürgerliche*] society. The last of these is further divided. "If it is small, it is called a city; a province is a society of different cities, and a kingdom or large dominium is a society of different provinces – all to attain happiness." Finally "the Church of God" is the sixth natural society. "Its purpose is eternal happiness."[55] Happiness is central to Leibniz's thought, surely to be understood in an Aristotelian sense as "the energy and practice of goodness, to a degree of perfection, and in a mode which is absolute and not relative."[56] In another of Leibniz's texts we learn that happiness is the source of natural law; in the one at hand, we find that "[t]he most perfect society is that whose purpose is the most general and supreme happiness."[57]

Leibniz was a towering figure when Wolff began his career. The two were acquainted; Leibniz was responsible for Wolff's first major academic appointment.[58] While Wolff rejected the view that he was a mere Leibnizian on philosophical matters, convention has it otherwise.[59] Like Leibniz, Wolff identified happiness with human purpose.[60] In doing so, he almost certainly accepted, with Leibniz and most Western intellectuals of the 18th century, "the great chain of being" as a comprehensive ontological premise.[61]

In this great chain, all things find their place in a series of ascending levels according to the purpose for which they exist. Above the level of individual

54 In a brief text, "On Natural Law," written in German (n. d.). P. Riley (ed.), *The Political Writings of Leibniz*, Cambridge: Cambridge University Press, 1972, p. 77. A Latin heading reads "*Divisio Societam*"; the German text has "*Gemeinschaft*." According to Leibniz, "[a] natural society is one which is demanded by nature [*so die Natur haben will*]."

55 Ibid., p. 79. As Riley observed, "Leibniz's fifth and sixth degrees of natural society are grafted onto Aristotelian distinctions and appear to be derived from Johannes Althusius." p. 79 n. 1.

56 Aristotle, *Politics*, VII, xiii (1332a9–11), p. 2113. See, generally, Aristotle's *Nicomachean Ethics*, which Aristotle said this passage reprises.

57 "*Codex iuris gentium (Praefatio)*" (1693), in Riley, *Political Writings of Leibniz*, p. 171; "On Natural Law," p. 77.

58 Nippold, "Introduction," pp. xiv–xv.

59 See, for example, E. Barker, "Translator's Introduction," in Gierke, *Natural Law and the Theory of Society*, p. xliii; A.O. Lovejoy, *The Great Chain of Being: The History of an Idea*, Cambridge, MA: Harvard University Press, 1936, pp. 175–6; J. Stone, *The Province and Function of Law: Law as Logic, Justice, and Social Control*, Cambridge, MA: Harvard University Press, 1950, p. 232 n. 49. According to E. Cassirer, *The Philosophy of the Enlightenment*, trans. by F.C.A. Koellin and J.P. Pettegrove, Princeton: Princeton University Press, 1951, p. 34, "Wolff's logic and methodology differ from those of Leibniz in that they attempt to reduce the variety of their deductions to as simple and uniform an arrangement as possible."

60 "[I]ndividuals bind themselves to the whole because they wish to promote the common good, consequently the happiness of their nation." Wolff, *Jus gentium*, para. 135. Inferred is a duty to promote the happiness of oneself and others, which paragraph 162 finds applicable to nations as well.

61 Lovejoy, *Great Chain of Being*. On Leibniz: pp. 144–82; on 18th century thought: pp. 183–287.

human beings and below that of the angels are levels of human association, identified as such in the theory of corporations. At the higher levels are associations dedicated to securing the common good. Associations differing in size and form of rule – for example, Leibniz's cities, provinces and kingdoms – may even perform this function for the same people. In theory, all such associations are sorted into levels graded by size; in practice, associations at different levels tend toward functional specialization, especially as they affect the same people.

If Wolff saw the *civitas*, and thus the *civitas maxima*, in the context of an ascending series of associations, each of them a corporate person, he seems not to have said so directly in his work on the law of nations. Yet there are reasons to think of Wolff, like Bartolus, Althusius and Leibniz before him, as a corporation theorist in the republican mold. One reason is Wolff's use of the verb "*consociare*," for which there is no exact English equivalent. "To associate" is close, "to form a corporate group" even closer. Althusius made *consociandi* central to his politics; Wolff made it central to his definition of the *civitas* (paragraph 2, as quoted above, and paragraph 9).

Another reason for thinking of Wolff as a corporation theorist is his recourse to fictions. The ascription of personality to groups is a central feature of the Roman legal heritage. We saw the importance of fictional persons for Althusius. Leibniz affirmed that natural societies are civil persons, but Otto Gierke thought he did so without conviction.[62] Hobbes granted personality to civil society, but only as a formality.[63] In Locke's *Second Treatise* the individual is famously "*Proprietor of his own Person*;" there are no civil persons.[64] Liberal individualist theories of society, unlike the theory of corporations, see groups as mechanically constituted by individuals; Hobbes' "Artificiall Man" takes the place of the already shadowy *persona ficta*.[65]

By contrast Wolff gave a broad and compelling defense for the use of fictions. "Fictions are advantageously applied in every kind of science, for the purpose of eliciting truths as well as proving them" (paragraph 21, commentary). His example is astronomy, for which the geometer's repertory of curves, angles and perfect figures is especially germane. Wolff specifically claimed that "all moral persons" have a fictitious element.[66] This generalization includes the *civitas maxima*, but not as an unusual instance.

To summarize: the *civitas maxima* is composed of nations that retain their identity as *civitates*. Only by locating the *civitas maxima* at the apex of an

62 Gierke, *Natural Law and the Theory of Society*, pp. 137, 332–3 n. 253.
63 Ibid., p. 136; Hobbes, *De Cive*, English Version, p. 89.
64 Locke, *Two Treatises*, 2nd Treatise, V, para. 44, p. 298; emphasis in original.
65 Gierke, *Natural Law and the Theory of Society*, pp. 135–7. "Shadowy" is his description in reference to Leibniz.
66 Ibid. *Personae morales* clearly differ from "*personae singularis*" (paragraph 2) by being corporate in character. Equally clearly, the terms "civil person" and "moral person" are interchangeable.

ascending series of associations prescribed by the theory of corporations can we make sense of this proposition. The contemporary idea of an impersonal world-state connecting directly with individuals is irrelevant and, for Wolff, inconceivable. The ancient and imperishable ideal of a world of friendship and respect transcending politics is at best an inspiration but, for Wolff, no model. Wolff's model is the *respublica composita*.[67] Even though the US constituted itself in 1787 as a "compound republic" (James Madison's description[68]), empirical instances are not the point. Nor is Pufendorf's well-known demonstration, 60 years before Wolff, that such instances are irregular.[69] In the theory of corporations the *respublic composita* is a necessary category if there is to be any association above the *civitas*.

Enter Vattel

In the Preface to *Le droit des gens ou principes de la loi naturelle*, Vattel acknowledged a close connection between his work and Wolff's. Vattel was a man of letters and an occasional diplomat, not a systematic philosopher in Wolff's manner. Nevertheless, as a young man, he had published a lengthy defense of Leibniz's philosophical system.[70] He also had followed Wolff's monumental effort to develop a complete system of natural law, encompassing eight volumes, which Wolff promised to conclude with a full-scale application to the law of nations.[71] Vattel had "impatiently waited" for the latter, but on its appearance he was dismayed to find it "almost useless to persons," like himself, "whose chief desire and interest is a knowledge of the true principles of the Law of Nations."[72] In several attempts to prepare a digest, Vattel found himself stymied by Wolff's scientific pretensions. They produced "a very dry work and one incomplete in many respects." Frequent references to Wolff's earlier work substituted for exposition and made it impossible "to separate this treatise from the whole system" so as "to make it accessible to cultured people in a more attractive form."

67 Gierke, *Natural Law and the Theory of Society*, pp. 76, 167–8; P. Onuf and N. Onuf, *Federal Union, Modern World: The Law of Nations in an Age of Revolutions, 1776–1814*, Madison, WI: Madison House, 1993, pp. 53–69.

68 *The Federalist No. 51*, in J.E. Cooke (ed.), *The Federalist*, Middletown, CT: Wesleyan University Press, 1961, p. 351.

69 Pufendorf, *De Jure naturae*, vol. 2, trans. by C.H. Oldfather and W.A. Oldfather, VII, v, paras. 12–15, pp. 1037–43.

70 E. de Vattel, *Défense du systeme Leibnitien contre les objections et les imputations de M. de Crousaz, contenues dans l'examen de l'essai L'Homme de Pope*, Leiden: Luzac, 1741.

71 Christian Wolff, *Jus naturae* (1740–1748), in Thomann, *Christian Wolff gesammelte Werke, Abt.* 2, vols 17–24, 1968–1972. They total 6,590 pages and 9,230 numbered paragraphs. A few years later, Vattel published a commentary on selected paragraphs from these eight volumes. E. de Vattel, *Questions de droit natural, et observations sur le traité du droit de la nature de M. Le Baron de Wolf*, Berne: Societé typographique, 1762.

72 Vattel, *Law of Nations*, Preface, pp. 7a–8a. Other quotations in this paragraph are from p. 8a.

Vattel solved these problems by writing his own treatise, taking from Wolff's work what he "found most valuable, especially his definitions and general principles."[73] In plan and content, the two works are strikingly similar.[74] Vattel's definition of the law of nations follows Wolff's closely, and this despite his difficulties with Wolff's commitment to science: "The *Law of Nations* is *the science of the rights which exist between Nations or States, and of the obligations corresponding to these rights*.[75] Vattel openly disagreed with Wolff on just two substantive issues.[76] One difference Vattel succeeded in obscuring.

Wolff never described nations as sovereign in the context of their mutual relations. In quoting Wolff, Vattel noted that nation "here means a sovereign State, an independent political society," and later in the same quotation rendered "*Gentes*" "Nations or sovereign States."[77] Though unacknowledged, this difference points to another, which Vattel took considerable pains to discuss. This, of course, is Vattel's unequivocal repudiation of a *civitas maxima* as a foundation for the voluntary law of nations.

Vattel described the *civitas maxima* as "the idea of a sort of great republic," in which the voluntary law acts as civil law.[78] This failed to satisfy Vattel:

> I find the fiction of such a republic neither reasonable nor well enough founded to deduce therefrom the rules of a Law of Nations at once universal in character, and necessarily accepted by sovereign States. I recognize no other natural society among Nations than that which nature has set up among men in general.

Of course Wolff had affirmed the existence of a natural society among nations, separate from, but easily confused with, a *civitas maxima* also, in Vattel's words, "set up by nature herself." The simple explanation for Vattel's rejection of a *civitas maxima* is its redundancy. Why would nature set up two systems of law when one would suffice?

73 Ibid., Preface, p. 8a.

74 Ruddy, *International Law in the Enlightenment*, p. 69.

75 Vattel, *Law of Nations*, Introduction, para. 3, at 3; emphasis in translation. *Cf.* Wolff, *Jus Gentium*, para. 1, quoted above.

76 One was Wolff's position with respect to patrimonial kingdoms, the second Wolff's position with respect to the use of poisoned weapons in time of war. Vattel, *Law of Nations*, Preface, pp. 8a–9a.

77 Ibid., Preface, p. 7a, note k; Vattel, *Le droit des gens*, vol. 1, Preface, p. xiv: "*Nations, ou les États Souverains, étant des Persones morales*," as compared to Wolff, *Jus gentium*, Praefatio: "Gentes sint personae morales." Wolff understood sovereignty in a civil context. See *Jus gentium*, para. 103. Even that measure of sovereignty belonging to "nations as a whole," that is, to the *civitas maxima*, "has a certain resemblance to civil sovereignty." para. 15 and Commentary.

78 Vattel, *Law of Nations*, Preface, p. 9a. Ibid. for quotations in this and the following paragraph.

Vattel went further. He stipulated that civil society in general ("*Civitas*") requires an "authority capable of giving commands, prescribing laws, and compelling those who refuse to obey." Wolff demanded nothing of the sort for a *civitas*; to do so makes it indistinguishable from the state which, like sovereignty, Wolff did not understand in any modern sense. Vattel drew just this conclusion. "Such an idea is not to be thought of as between Nations. Each independent State claims to be, and actually is, independent of all others."

Vattel bolstered his position by arguing from conditions in a state of nature. While nature does not actually obligate people to form civil societies, they have compelling reasons for doing so.

> But it is not clear that there is . . . the same necessity for a civil society among Nations as among individuals. It can not be said, therefore, that nature recommends it to an equal degree, far less that it prescribes it.[79]

Wolff held that people must form *civitates* for a common good not achievable in a state of nature.

> Just as one man alone is not sufficient unto himself, but needs the aid of another, . . . so also one nation alone is not sufficient for itself, but needs the aid of the other, that thereby the common good may be promoted by their combined powers.[80]

Slightly different judgments about the state of nature give way to fully opposed conceptions of the state of nations.

For Vattel, people are not obligated to unite in civil societies because they are free by nature. The same is true of nations: "each Nation should be left to the peaceable enjoyment of that liberty which belongs to it by nature."[81] Complementing this "general law" is another, to which Vattel gave pride of place: "each Nation should contribute as far as it can to the happiness and advancement of other Nations."[82] In view of Vattel's judgement that forming civil societies is a discretionary activity, compelling perhaps for individuals, but less so for nations, it is something of a surprise that the first general law of nations requires mutual aid. Of course he formulated this law as a contingent

79 Vattel, *Law of Nations*, Preface, p. 9a. Also, see II, i, para. 3, p. 114.

80 Wolff, *Jus gentium*, paragraph 8 Commentary. Wolff acknowledged that "although a nation can be thought of which is spread over a vast expanse, and does not *seem* to need the aid of other nations," it nevertheless can and ought to aid them, and be aided by them. Ibid., emphasis added.

81 Vattel, *Law of Nations*, Introduction, para. 15, p. 6.

82 Ibid., Introduction, paragraph 13. Again, "we may boldly lay down this general principle: Each State owes to every other State all that it owes to itself, as far as the other is in actual need of its help and such help can be given without the State neglecting its duties towards itself." II, i, para. 3, p. 114.

obligation. The duty of assistance to other nations extends only "as far as" a nation's liberty and well-being permits. Nevertheless, its importance to Vattel suggests a deference to Wolff and republican concern for the common good somewhat at odds with his conception of natural society.[83]

Vattel offered a final argument against the *civitas maxima* as foundation for the voluntary law of nations.

> Mr. Wolff says that in the intercourse of this [*i. e.*, the natural] society of Nations, the natural law is not always to be followed in all its strictness; changes must be made which can only be deduced from his idea of a sort of great republic of the Nations whose laws, dictated by right reason and founded upon necessity, will determine what changes will be made in the natural and necessary Law of Nations, just as the civil laws of the State determine with respect to individuals the changes to be made in the natural law.[84]

Wolff's *civitas maxima* includes a *rector*. In paragraph 21 of the *Prolegomena*, as quoted above, the leader in a *civitas* has power to rule, but not the *rector* of a *civitas maxima*. Instead, the *rector* "defines by the right use of reason what nations ought to consider as law among themselves." As an authoritative figure, the *rector* is responsible for formulating a voluntary law suitable to the needs of nations and yet generally consistent with necessary natural law. No such figure exists in nature, though authoritative commentators like Wolff constitute the *rector*'s corporate equivalent.

Vattel thought this additional step in determining the content of the voluntary law was not just unnecessary, but inappropriate. Instead, all changes in natural law required by the voluntary relations of nations could be derived from the actual conditions in which nations find themselves – "from the natural liberty of Nations, from considerations of their common welfare, from the nature of their mutual intercourse," and from a proper understanding of the spheres of conscience and public life.[85] Vattel's next claim is surely the most telling of all:

> Now since Nations must mutually recognize these exceptions and modifications in the strict application of the *necessary* law, whether we deduce them from the idea of a great republic . . . or from the sources from which I propose to draw, there is no reason why the law which results therefrom should not be called the *voluntary* law of Nations, in contradistinction to the *necessary* law of Nations, which is the inner law of conscience.[86]

83 Linklater, *Men and Citizens in the Theory of International Relations*, pp. 85–9.
84 Vattel, *Law of Nations*, Preface, p. 10a.
85 Ibid.
86 Ibid., p. 11a; emphases in translation.

No matter how persuasively a commentator like Wolff or Vattel himself renders the content of the voluntary law, rule by rule, authority for each rule derives from its recognition by states through their practices, including affirmation of particular renditions, and not, at least in the first instance, from the commentator's position or stature. Vattel intimated that his version of the voluntary law would be found persuasive because he drew from the *sources* of recognized practices and not from nature authoritatively represented as the one and only *source* of all law. Vattel was right. States' leaders and their advisers and other commentators treated particular formulations of his, far more often than Wolff's (despite their marked similarity), as authoritative renditions of state practices – as a source of law. Vattel earned a measure of the authority Wolff failed to legislate for himself. Indeed, for the remainder of the century, no one's authority exceeded Vattel's, especially in the newly independent US.[87]

Nature as the source or fount (*fons*) of law is a recurring image from Cicero to Grotius.[88] Wolff had noticed a change: "The perverse idea has taken possession of the minds of nearly everybody that the mainspring [*fons*] of the law of nations is personal advantage."[89] Once and in passing, Wolff referred to sources in the plural.[90] Nature is the direct source of the necessary law and, thanks to the *civitas maxima* and its *rector*, indirect source of the voluntary law. As quoted above, Vattel's one use of the plural is a significant shift, because it refers exclusively to the voluntary law. In a world of states struggling for advantage, practical considerations yield several sources of common rules.

Vattel dispatched Wolff's great republic, not because the voluntary law of nations has a multiplicity of sources, but to maintain a "careful distinction" between voluntary and necessary law, "so that we may never confuse what is just and good in itself with what is merely tolerated through necessity."[91] As we saw, Wolff himself blurred the differences between the natural society of nations and his *civitas maxima*, thus compromising the distinction between voluntary and necessary law. Vattel's insistence on the integrity of this distinction demanded a repudiation of Wolff's untenable construction

87 C.G. Fenwick, "The Authority of Vattel," *American Political Science Review*, vol. 7, 1913, pp. 395–410; D.G. Lang, *Foreign Policy in the Early Republic: The Law of Nations and the Balance of Power*, Baton Rouge: Louisiana State University Press, 1985.

88 Cicero, "Laws," I v–vi, para. 49, in *De re publica, de legibus, Laws*, pp. 314–19; H. Grotius, *De jure belli ac pacis libris tres* (1646 edn), vol. 1, Washington: Carnegie Institution, 1913, Prolegomena, paras. 8, 12, n. p.; ibid., vol. 2, trans. by F.W. Kelsey *et al.*, pp. 12, 14.

89 Wolff, *Jus gentium* para. 162 Commentary.

90 "Therefore in the present work we have so presented the Law of Nations, that . . . those things may be distinguished that come from different sources." Those "things" are the necessary law, the voluntary law, and particular obligations, which nations accept, but Wolff excluded from consideration. Ibid., Preface.

91 Vattel, *Law of Nations*, Preface, p. 11a.

and supported a sharp discrimination, reminiscent of Machiavelli, between private and public spheres of life.

Vattel had finished with the *civitas maxima* at this point in his prefatory remarks. Ever faithful to the plan and content of Wolff's treatise, he then noted "another species of the Law of Nations," which he called "special law," applicable only to those Nations consenting to it, whether expressly or tacitly, by treaty or custom.[92] When he began his substantive exposition, Vattel changed this scheme. Voluntary law, conventional law and customary law became "three divisions" (not two species, one divided) that "form together the *positive Law of Nations*, for they all proceed from the agreement of Nations; the *voluntary* law from their presumed consent; the *conventional* law from their express consent; and the *customary* law from their tacit consent."[93]

By dividing the positive law into three categories, Vattel clearly anticipated the doctrinal development of a single law of nations with three discrete sources: the writings of commentators, like Wolff and Vattel himself, as the best available evidence of consent that might reasonably be presumed, treaties as evidence of express consent, and custom as evidence of tacit consent. Vattel still felt compelled to establish "what the necessary law prescribes" so as to "explain how or why these precepts must be modified by the *voluntary* law."[94] Thus preoccupied, Vattel failed to provide a systematic account of sources *as* sources in his exposition of the positive law of nations.

For the next half century, it seems no one went beyond Vattel in developing sources doctrine as we know it today. Given Vattel's immense prestige, we should not find this surprising. Pushed by circumstances, Madison finally did so, as Secretary of State, in his remarkable though little known legal brief, *An Examination of the British Doctrine, Which Subjects to Capture a Neutral Trade, Not Open in Time of Peace* (1805).[95] The British had claimed that in time of war a belligerent power has a legal right to interfere with commerce between its enemies and a neutral power when that commerce had not previously been permitted. Against this claim, Madison systematically marshaled a great deal of evidence, including "the evidence of treaties." On review, Madison concluded that never was the evidence of treaties "more uniform, more extensive, or more satisfactory." Shifting conceptual ground, he went on: "it may be affirmed that the treaties applicable to this case may fairly be considered in their relation to the law of nations last noted as *constituting* a law of themselves."[96]

92 Ibid.

93 *Ibid.*, Introduction, para. 27, p. 9; emphases in translation.

94 Ibid.

95 G. Hunt (ed.), *The Writings of James Madison*, vol. 7, New York: Putnam, 1908, pp. 204–375. See, further, Onuf and Onuf, *Federal Union, Modern World*, pp. 197–211.

96 Hunt, *The Writings of James Madison*, pp. 208, 238.

To assert that treaties are law in their own right is more than a shift; it is a significant conceptual innovation. If treaties function like law, then saying that they are "law" is more persuasive than saying that they are merely "evidence" of law. Furthermore, if treaties are the same as other legal rules in the obligations they create, then the law of nations is a conceptual whole, a "great code," subject to definition as such.[97] Its rules are constituted through the very categories of activities, like the conclusion of treaties, which are presented as evidence for these rules. In passing, Madison called these categories "sources" of law.[98] First came "the writings most generally received as the depositaries and oracles of the law of nations," followed by treaties, the conduct of nations, and finally "reasoning" as interpretation and not reason as such.[99] Without acknowledging Madison, Henry Wheaton adopted a similar list of sources, expressly so-called, for his influential treatise, *Elements of International Law* (1836), and sources doctrine took a recognizably modern form.[100]

Had Vattel developed a coherent position on the several sources of a single law, that law would have had a foundation in the state practice it regulates. Instead, by rejecting the great republic as a philosopher's conceit and a threat to the distinction between necessary and voluntary law, Vattel created a problem for himself. Natural society remains as a foundation for the necessary law. The voluntary law has nothing comparable. There is no evidence that Vattel recognized this problem as such. Nevertheless, he provided a solution in a famous discussion of the balance of power.

Vattel devoted himself to the balance of power in a chapter on "The Just Causes of War."[101] Wolff had earlier discussed "equilibrium" in this same context.[102] In Wolff's case, equilibrium was a matter of interest only in relation to its effects on a nation's rights. Indeed, their vindication entitled a nation to the use of force "even if the equilibrium among nations is destroyed."[103] By contrast, Vattel associated the balance of power – "an arrangement of affairs so that no State will be in a position to have absolute

97 Ibid., p. 240. See, also, pp. 238, 332.

98 Ibid., pp. 239n, 240 and especially 332:

> In testing the British claim, then, by the law of nations, recurrence must be had to other sources than the abstract dictates of reason; to those very sources from which it has been shown that her claim is an unauthorized innovation on the law of nations.

99 Ibid., p. 208. The term *source* appears only later in the text.

100 H. Wheaton, *Elements of International Law with a Sketch of the History of the Science*, Philadelphia: Carey, Lea & Blanchard, 1836, I, i, para. 15, pp. 48–50. Wheaton later acknowledged Madison with quotation marks and citation. *Elements of International Law*, 8th edn, p. 21.

101 Vattel, *The Law of Nations*, III, iii, at 243–53.

102 Wolff, *Jus gentium*, paras. 642–4, 646–51.

103 Ibid., para. 647.

mastery and dominate over the others" – with stability of the system and not just the rights of its members.[104] Because of the balance, Europe was "no longer, as in former times, a confused heap of detached parts."[105] Instead, it was another sort of republic, though hardly the sort that Wolff had had in mind.

The idea that Europe constituted some sort of republic was an Enlightenment commonplace, as widely accepted as it was unexamined.[106] At least Vattel identified the republic's implicit foundation – the source of its stability – in the balance of power. Ever shifting, the balance arises from the "constant attention of sovereigns to all that goes on, the custom of resident ministers, the continual negotiations that take place."[107] The positive law to which Vattel had given only glancing acknowledgment in his conceptual discussion also arises from these activities. The difference, of course, is that activities conducive to a self-correcting balance of power, and thus a stable system, had never produced a legal requirement to support the balance. The system was supposed to take care of itself. If the balance worked (or, on the evidence of the system's relative stability, *seemed* to work) in Vattel's time, a generation later it failed catastrophically.

Beyond a foundation in the balance of power, what Vattel had in mind for his republic is not at all clear. We could say that he failed to honor the separate senses of the term "republic": *polis, civitas*, body politic, on the one hand; *politeia, status*, form of rule, on the other. Madison's conception of a single law of nations with many sources has precisely this effect. The *polis* exists in nature, as Aristotle said, its character evident in principles of natural law to which Vattel and Madison subscribed. It also exists in the nature of Europe, though a Europe capable of extension by inclusion of new members like the US. All of the nations associated in Vattel's sort of republic participate through customary practices and the conclusion of treaties in its political arrangements, or *politeia*. Standing between the *polis*, or states associated by nature for common good, and the great bulk of international law and associated practices, are the sources of international law.

In Vattel's work the relation of natural society to the practice of states, of *polis* to *politeia*, is ambiguous and confusing. As Andrew Linklater has

104 Vattel, *The Law of Nations*, III, iii, para. 47, p. 251. See, also, A. Vagts and D.F. Vagts, "The Balance of Power in International Law: A History of an Idea," *American Journal of International Law*, vol. 73, 1979, p. 562; Linklater, *Men and Citizens in the Theory of International Relations*, pp. 90–2.

105 Vattel, *The Law of Nations*, III, iii, para. 47, p. 251.

106 Hinsley, *Power and the Pursuit of Peace*, pp. 161–4; T. Nardin, *Law, Morality, and the Relations of States*, Princeton: Princeton University Press, 1983, pp. 62–3. Enlightenment writers also thought of themselves as constituting a "republic of letters." Vattel remarked that "*la République des Lettres a perdu l'illustre M. Wolf*" while he was preparing his commentary on Wolff's system of natural law. *Questions de droit naturel*, p. xi.

107 Vattel, *The Law of Nations*, III, iii, para. 47, p. 251.

argued, Vattel's " 'subjectivising' of natural law" results in a "radical state-libertarianism."[108] Vattel surely did not see a Hobbesian potential in this result. Had he done so, he might have imputed to state practice a more substantial foundation for international society than the balance of power could ever provide. Whether Vattel's influence would then have been so great is another question.

The politics of the founding period in the US reflects a similar tension between republican and liberal tendencies, perhaps in part because of Vattel's influence.[109] The difference is that the founders deliberately sought to clarify the relation of *polis* to *politeia* by creating a federal union and developing republican institutions within the framework of the union. Only then were life, liberty and liberal pursuits possible. In temper an optimist, Vattel thought the republic of Europe could have peace and prosperity with no more help than he had provided. He was wrong.

After Revolutionary France shattered any possible conception of Europe as a republic in its own right, state libertarianism prevailed. Acknowledgment that international law has specific sources – sanctioned methods for states to constitute the arrangements under which they conduct their relations – effectively divorced an evanescent natural order from the practice of states and supported "a balance of rights" among them.[110] The extraordinary growth of trade and prosperity made such a balance attractive, at least for several decades into the 19th century. Vattel's contingent, exiguous republic gave way to the conceptually self-contained international sphere which, for all its vicissitudes, remains with us today.

108 Linklater, *Men and Citizens in the Theory of International Relations*, pp. 86–9, quoting p. 87.

109 So A.-M. Burley [Slaughter] seems to suggest. "The Alien Tort Statute and the Judiciary Act of 1789: A Badge of Honor," *American Journal of International Law*, vol. 77, 1983, pp. 484–6.

110 P.W. Schroeder, "Did the Vienna Settlement Rest on a Balance of Power?" *American Historical Review*, vol. 97, 1992, p. 698.

21 Review: *A Normative Approach to War: Peace, War, and Justice in Hugo Grotius*, edited by Onuma Yasuaki, 1993 (1994)

Working with my brother Peter Onuf on federalism as a passing feature of the modern world, and thus on the historic relation between republicanism and liberalism, had prompted me to explore republican political theory. Instead of a single, coherent republican tradition, I discovered diverse roads, all leading back to Aristotle and the Stoics. I took advantage of a sabbatical early in the 1990s to immerse myself in Aristotle's wide-ranging works (and not just the *Nicomachean Ethics* and the *Politics*). When I turned my attention to federal theory in the new Constitution of the United States, I saw Aristotle's tracks everywhere I looked (as any reader of the book Peter and I wrote, *Federal Union, Modern World*, will quickly discern). I also turned my attention to early modern writers for whom natural law was a subject of great interest: Hugo Grotius, Thomas Hobbes, Samuel Pufenforf, John Locke, G.W. Leibniz, Christian Wolff (recall Chapter 20, above) and Immanuel Kant. Their works I now read as milestones in republican thinking and, even more, engagements with Aristotle's legacy.

An epochal shift in ways of thinking ended the Enlightenment, Aristotle's often unspoken presence and, indeed, the republican moment. One result is the contemporary tendency to read early modern texts anachronistically, as if they anticipated the modern state, liberalism, or sovereignty as an organizing principle for the relations of states. Most interpretations of Grotius's *On the Law of War and Peace* and Immanuel Kant's *Perpetual Peace* offer flagrant examples; talk about Grotian and Kantian traditions find liberal premises where there are none. An invitation to review the Onuma volume on Grotius for the *American Political Science Review* proved to be unexpectedly rewarding. The authors' careful reading confirmed Aristotle's pervasive presence in a work as alien to the modern mind as it is important.

Once the honorific "father of international law," Hugo Grotius remains a figure of considerable interest, not only to legal scholars, but to students of international relations and the history of political thought. Grotius published the first edition of his great treatise, *De jure belli ac pacis libri tres* (hereafter, as in the book under review, *JBP*) in 1625, during the last and greatest of Europe's religious wars. His aim was to identify all legal rules (laws are rules of moral action imposing obligation, *JBP*, I, ix, para. 1) that might limit both the occasions for and the effects of organized violence, whether public or private, just or self-serving, and present those rules in "a comprehensive and systematic manner" (Prolegomena, para. 1). If his ambitions transcended the particulars of sectarian conflict, so too did the Thirty Years War and the peace that followed. Grotius inevitably came to be identified with the advent of the Westphalian system of international relations and a secular, rationalist worldview.

Was Grotius an early modern thinker? His stature in Western thought for the century and a half after his death would seem to suggest as much. So do frequent contemporary allusions to a "Grotian tradition." Many of those who have examined his work are less sure. The more carefully scholars read *JBP*, the more cautious become their claims on the author's behalf.

A Normative Approach to War is the most careful, sustained reading of *JBP* in English. Its authors are six Japanese scholars, all members of a research group that began studying Grotius in 1976. A Japanese version of the book appeared in 1987. The English version is updated and abridged; the translation, by Sakamoto Mikio with assistance from James Crawford, is clear and as graceful as the subject permits. The book's authors follow the complete text of *JBP* as Grotius presented it, for convenience dividing the material into nine chapters bracketed by the editor's introduction and conclusion. Clearly a team effort, the book exhibits an exceptionally coherent perspective.

The team's members see Grotius as less modern than the many scholars writing in English who find Grotius a rights theorist (Tanaka Tadashi, pp. 36, 51).

> Unlike Hobbes, Locke and Rousseau, Grotius constructed his theory of law without seeking to dismantle the household and the various intermediate corporate bodies. He adhered to the traditional view of man (as *zoon politikon*) that had prevailed in Europe since Aristotle, assuming the existence of multi-layered independent powers. His concept of natural law tended to justify existing political institutions rather than criticize them from the point of view of justice (Onuma Yasuaki, p. 9).

Although Grotius took issue with Aristotle's conception of justice and distanced himself from the Scholastics, he was "uncritical" of the Aristotelian tradition in general (Tanaka, pp. 20–2, 26). This interpretation finds support in an extensively cited literature from continental Europe and Japan.

In one respect, Grotius seems modern – not early modern, but fully modern. Despite some principled equivocation (*JBP*, Prolegomena, paras. 16, 57; cf. Onuma, p. 72), "considerations of utility and practicality underlie the whole structure of *JBP*" (Onuma, p. 347). As the Japanese team shows, Grotius's pragmatism stems from his desire to limit the horrors of war by whatever means possible – law in every conceivable manifestation, appeals to conscience, authority and tradition, considerations of prudence. Grotius made his system as comprehensive as he could, indiscriminately adding categories, spinning distinctions and invoking authorities. By the Cartesian standards of the early modern era, he also made his system a shambles.

Viewing Grotius as practical but not very modern, the Japanese team translates key terms from Grotius's Latin with due caution. They find that Grotius seems to have construed *summum imperium* "as a matter of relative priority in a hierarchy of bearers of *imperium* on various levels" (Tanaka, p. 137). Their Grotius is no Bodin. Thus, unlike the standard English translation of *JBP*, they refrain from using Bodin's term, *sovereignty*, except to show that Grotius's resistance to "popular sovereignty" makes him even less an Althusius (p. 138). By translating the term *civitas* as *state*, the team does yield to anachronism, despite a sensible discussion of Grotius's corporate conception of "civil society," a term he used interchangeably with *civitas* (pp. 125–7).

For many scholars, the proof of Grotius's modernity is his conviction that there would be a law of nature by which to govern human affairs, "even if we should concede that which cannot be conceded without the utmost wickedness, that there is no God" (*JBP*, Prolegomena, para. 11; cf. Tanaka, pp. 26–9, 74–7). If by this remark Grotius began the process of secularizing natural law, which Hobbes and Pufendorf soon completed, this was hardly his intent. Rather, it was to support a proposition with an ancient pedigree: human beings have "an impelling desire for society," what "the Stoics called 'sociableness' " (*JBP*, Prolegomena, para. 6). Sociableness necessitates society, and this makes human nature "the mother of the law of nature." From this position (which *is* radical in its implications), Grotius could conclude that all law, including law that human beings voluntarily create for themselves, "derives its force from the law of nature" (*JBP*, Prolegomena, para.16).

According to the Japanese team, volitional law and natural law "often overlap and penetrate each other" (Tanaka, p. 53). Many writers take Grotius at his word (*JBP*, Prolegomena, para. 1) and separate natural law from volitional law (divine and human), as if Grotius were eclectically naturalist and positivist. Insofar as all law derives its force from human nature, it hardly seems "a methodological weakness" (Tanaka, p. 43) for Grotius to have used the same inductive method to determine the content of natural law and volitional law. On the evidence, human nature is exceedingly plastic.

Starting with the necessity of self-preservation, an otherwise plastic human nature yields a "hierarchy," though hardly a system, of law (Tanaka, pp. 51–5). First is mandatory natural law, then a permissive domain of natural law, itself possessing four levels of flexibility (pp. 39–41) that make it effectively indistinguishable from volitional law. The latter includes municipal law, some rules of which are common to many peoples (*jus gentium*), and law "that in the strict sense concerns the mutual society among nations (*mutua gentium inter se societas*)" (p. 54). Finally there is what today we might call "soft law" in the form of precepts advising humanity and moderation. Although none of the team's members says so clearly, Grotius had no independent, "Grotian" conception of "international society." Given human nature, if there is law among nations, then there is a nominal society among them as well. Grotius canvassed not just the law of nations, but law in all its variety, for one purpose. Where there is law, there are limited just causes for war and unlimited opportunities for its mitigation.

22 Review: *International Law and Political Reality: Collected Papers*, Volume One, by Anthony D'Amato, 1995 (1995)

In my review of Anthony D'Amato's contributions to jurisprudence (Chapter 15), I portrayed him as continuously shifting ground on basic questions about law: what makes legal rules distinctive, how do rules relate to social processes and human purposes, do we have control over law or does it have control over us? D'Amato's valiant effort to address these uncertainties makes him an important thinker, even if conclusions he drew on different occasions and from different perspectives are impossible to reconcile. D'Amato must have thought my review constructive, and not merely critical, for he had, as an advisory editor for the *Journal of International Legal Studies*, suggested to the student editors of this new journal that I review the first volume of his collected essays in international law. I welcomed another opportunity to engage D'Amato's always timely and often arresting contributions to international legal scholarship – contributions that reach well beyond the way we think about the sources of international law (Chapter 4, above).

I had been absorbed for some time in both the way we all use language to effectuate our intentions – words constitute deeds on their own and in conjunction with whatever else we do – and by extension in the ways that scholars abuse language, especially when they claim to speak about *reality*. And I was increasingly aware of the perils of reading the factual record, and even more the history of concepts, from the present backwards (see Chapter 21). As a result I had some harsh things to say in my review, but I was perhaps unduly generous when I pointed out the parallel between his work and that of Hugo Grotius, once the latter is freed from anachronism. D'Amato seems to have liked the review well enough, for it is prominently cited on his internet home page.

Anthony D'Amato, Leighton Professor of Law, Northwestern University, is one of the most distinguished international legal scholars in the US. In a brief foreword to the volume under review, L.C. Green puts D'Amato in the "younger school of writers" (p. v). Himself retired, Green does D'Amato and his generation an injustice. The term "younger" belies the intellectual maturity of scholars whose careers, like D'Amato's, now exceed three decades, just as this term belies their stature and influence among scholars of all ages. It is a mark of D'Amato's productivity, stature and influence that his collected papers should now be appearing. The first volume consists of 29 papers (including excerpts from a coauthored book, Congressional testimony, letters to the *New York Times* and privately published consultant's reports) organized into 20 chapters. Three additional volumes are planned.

Perhaps Green means to suggest with the word "younger" a shift in substantive orientation from his own generation to D'Amato's (and mine). As D'Amato's early papers (Part I, The Vietnam War) so eloquently testify, the experiences of the US in Vietnam had a formative impact. For D'Amato, as for many others, Vietnam's legacy is a recurring concern with the responsibilities of the US as a world leader. Many of D'Amato's shorter essays (Part II, Other Wars and Interventions) manifest this concern in reference to permissible uses of force. Other papers reveal a concern for technological hazards (Part III, Nuclear Weapons and Technology) largely ignored by the preceding generation. While a few papers (Part IV, Minority Rights) return to one of the great concerns of the interwar period, D'Amato's enduring preoccupations remind us how much the world had changed in his youth.

D'Amato invests all of his topical essays with an energy born of conviction. For an earlier generation, D'Amato's sense of urgency and sometimes combative tendencies hardly comport with the measured, magisterial tone favored by its leading figures. Evidently, style as much as substantive orientation separates D'Amato from his predecessors. D'Amato's style is quite his own. Brash and learned at the same time, he has become even brasher over the years as he has learned the complexities of the law and the power of partisanship. Only in D'Amato's latest work (chs. 7 and 17) do we hear a teacher's voice – patient and perhaps a little patronizing. Working through the fundamentals yet another time, D'Amato reaches for the magisterial register, but does not quite achieve it.

If D'Amato's style sets him apart, it hardly serves to unite his enduring yet disparate concerns. Pulling together materials written over many years on diverse subjects and for diverse reasons requires an organizing principle. Order of appearance is an obvious possibility. It has the advantage of allowing readers to follow the evolution of the author's thinking. D'Amato rejects this principle, perhaps, on the evidence of these papers, because the underlying pattern of his thought has changed so little through the years.

Any other organizing principle requires the retrospective discovery of a unifying theme. According to D'Amato, the theme unifying *this* collection is an awareness of "political reality": "I have a hard-headed view of international law" (p. ix). D'Amato's very brief Preface says little more. Nor do we learn what D'Amato thinks political reality is from the new material prefacing most chapters. Nevertheless, a number of papers offer assistance.

Despite the claim of hard-headedness, D'Amato does not wish us to think him a political realist.

> My starting picture of international relations, therefore, is the opposite of that painted in the past by "realist" political scientists such as Hans

> Morgenthau. I do not agree with them that states exist in a jungle-type environment, a Hobbesian war of all against all. I do not agree with them that international law pops up, from time to time, to deal with specific problems, but that it is fragile and easily trumped by nations that decide to resort to force. Instead, my view of international relations is more Lockean – that it is basically a system in peace, and that it strives with great ingenuity to avoid war. (p.143)

D'Amato wrote these words for an essay on sanctions due for publication in 1995. Five years earlier, he charged Robert Tucker with "*realpolitik*" for defending a possible attack on a Libyan plant evidently manufacturing chemical weapons. After calling Tucker the political realist he avowedly is, thereby clarifying what D'Amato himself is not, D'Amato turns querulous. Tucker "may be conveying to the reader a view that legal considerations are a dispensable form of rhetoric" (p. 160). Readers may also conclude that, in Tucker's view, "legal considerations" – meaning the operative rules of law – permit the use of force in some instances, including this one. Not only do I think this was what Tucker wanted readers to conclude (I should note here that while Tucker was my first teacher of international law and relations, I do not presume to speak for him on this or any other matter), it is a view that D'Amato himself seems to support in another context (the US invasion of Panama, pp. 185–9).

In D'Amato's opinion, a political realist would simply dispense with legal considerations. Since Tucker is a political realist, he cannot take law seriously. The problem with this syllogism is that Tucker is not just a political realist, and he does take law seriously. Devising a caricature of Tucker and then assailing it, instead of complimenting Tucker for a hard-headed appreciation of law and disagreeing with him on particulars, is itself a rhetorical strategy. It may also be a rhetorical blunder, unlikely to win D'Amato very many hard-headed supporters.

A knowing political realist might devise loose rhetoric about international law to discredit its rules, but it seems unlikely anyone would bother. More plausibly, enthusiastic but undiscriminating rhetoric from international law's supporters invites political realists to ignore legal considerations. This may be what D'Amato has in mind when, in his preface, he claims that "much of what passes for 'international law' is little more than international rhetoric" (p. ix). Rendered vacuous by the twinned terms "much" and "little," any such claim can only be rhetorical. Moreover, it is a risky claim to make, for it creates the distinct impression that D'Amato has joined with political realists against international law in order to save it from its admirers. Compounding the confusion, D'Amato tells us, in his discussion of the Panama invasion and its critics that "Professor [Tom] Farer has been carried away by the rhetoric of statism" (p. 183). "Hegelian" (p. 287) as well as "tautological" (p. 190), statism is a sin that political realists and international lawyers jointly commit in their service to the status quo.

If anyone has gotten carried away by rhetoric, it must be D'Amato, who shows no signs of recognizing this tendency in himself. Instead, D'Amato seems to believe that the mark of his realism is close attention to the facts. D'Amato's discussion of Panama is a good illustration.

> We are better off with rules of international law that at least point us to important factual and contextual considerations than we are with rules that point us only to an endless series of subrules, explanatory rules and learned commentary regarding the interpretation of all those rules – commentary that then itself must be interpreted. . . . The factual situation of the people of Panama cannot be found by consulting textbooks on the legality and exceptions regarding the use of force in international law (p. 187).

Rules *always* point to factual considerations by virtue of their propositional content. Obviously some rules refer to other rules and the way rules are related, but those other rules and relations among rules are facts that any given rule may point to as warranting consideration. Rules must be interpreted with respect to status and function. Are they legal? What are they for? In performing these tasks, scholars must examine the propositional content of the rules in question, not to mention the content of other rules and any number of other statements about these rules and their relations.

Furthermore, the propositional content of rules must also be interpreted with respect to a larger world of facts – factual claims not confined to rules and their relations. Are the facts proposed by the rule contestable? Are they relevant to factual conditions claimed for the world? Are the latter claims contestable? If D'Amato means to say that scholars ("academic apologists," p. 181) spend too much time and energy on the first set of interpretive tasks, and not enough on the second set, one can see the force of his position and the source of his frustration without necessarily having to agree with him in every instance. If, however, D'Amato wants us to believe that there are facts about Panama, for example, that need no interpretation, he can be right only in the most trivial sense. Any fact that bears significantly on the invasion (notice the interpretive freedom that the term "significant" affords) is subject to contestation on grounds of accuracy, relevance and weight.

Obviously facts are not equal in weight. D'Amato insists on a metafactual criterion for assigning weight to facts. What people do counts more than what they say (pp. 176–7). D'Amato is not alone in making this claim, and I have addressed its conceptual inadequacies elsewhere.[1] I turn here to the

1 Nicholas Onuf, Review, *Custom in Present International Law* (2nd edn) by Karol Wolfke, *American Journal of International Law*, vol. 88, 1994, p. 556. See, generally, *World of Our Making: Rules and Rule in Social Theory and International Relations*, Columbia: University of South Carolina Press, 1989, ch. 1.

practical difficulties that arise from insisting on such a criterion. According to D'Amato, "what I am suggesting requires research into the *history* of governmental interactions, the *facts* that occurred, the *settlements* that were reached, the *agreements* that were entered into" (p. 177, his emphases). History is a matter of words and thus a matter of choices about which words to use, which events to render into words, and so on. Settlements and agreements are typically events that cannot be extricated from the words used to record their occurrence. We are left with no criterion: facts are the facts we should give weight to.

D'Amato goes on to say that "the researcher should be highly skeptical about the negotiating positions taken by the governments involved, their unilateral proclamations, the briefs they file in a court or arbitral tribunal, the opinions of their attorneys general or their foreign offices" (p. 177). This is of course good advice. Some words count more than others. The point, however, is that weighing words involves judgemental, metafactual criteria. Words count more when more people use them. Words count more when people repeat them exactly. Words count more when people mark the occasions for their use. The work of lawyers is substantially to specify many such criteria, assign them weights and apply them to factual claims. Throughout these papers, D'Amato does this kind of work routinely and effectively. One might wish him to value it more.

Instead, D'Amato constantly urges us to accept reality as he sees it. On the very page I have just been quoting from, he speaks of "what goes on in the *real* world." "The *truly* operative rules," he also asserts, "are the rules that *in reality* accommodate the most deeply felt interests of the community of states" (my emphases). D'Amato's real world (also see pp. 51, 62) is one that scholars in general cannot see, in part because they are prisoners of their "paradigms" (p. 189). More damningly, scholars are members of, or beholden to, ruling elites who "invent" rules – "quasi-rules" as opposed to "real rules" – "for their own self-interest" (p. 188). Real rules should reflect "real values" – values that D'Amato confidently attributes to ordinary people whose world presumably *is* real, values that get lost in "academic, abstract and formalistic linguistic exercises" (p. 185).

D'Amato's rhetorical appeals to reality undermine his professions of fidelity to the facts. Whether he admires the values and rules for which elites may indeed be responsible, it does him little good as scholar or advocate to deny that these values and rules function as *facts* in the world we all find ourselves. It does him, and us, an even greater disservice when he loads his picture of reality with insupportable factual claims and inferences. D'Amato's letter to the *New York Times* (1983, pp. 190–1), defending the legality of the US intervention in Grenada is an egregious instance.

The occasion for intervention was the murder of Prime Minister Maurice Bishop by "leftist thugs" (D'Amato quoting President Reagan, p. 190). By omission, D'Amato implies that Bishop himself was a worthy man. In fact (this is my factual claim, for which there exists a great deal of support),

Bishop was himself a leftist thug, and his murder the result of a falling out among thugs. Yet even this account does not do justice to the facts.

Presidents Carter and Reagan, and their advisers had viewed the Grenadian revolution of 1979 with growing suspicion because, at least in its early stages, of the popular fervor it had unleashed. Revolutionary leaders turned against the people and toward Cuba, in part because they styled themselves a Leninist vanguard, in part because US officials had already reacted with hostility. With Cuba and the Cold War ever in mind, these officials tended to believe that popular revolutions are contagious and unpredictable, that revolutionary leaders almost always sell out the people, and that these "facts" have dire implications for the stability of the region. As the revolutionary leadership slid into thuggery, US officials found their suspicions vindicated. They authorized intervention, not to bring the revolution back on course, but to roll it back entirely.

A number of years later, D'Amato held that "the episode can safely be cited as an instance of humanitarian intervention on behalf of the citizens of Grenada," thereby contributing to "the current global revolution of popular sovereignty" (1990, pp. 189–90). Given "the facts" as I have presented them and the "real values" that D'Amato espouses, I see the episode as an instance of intervention against the expression of popular sovereignty. For the usual "statist" reasons, the US government misinterpreted this expression of popular sovereignty, thereby substantially fulfilling its own, factually misguided prophecy. I cannot imagine why D'Amato thought he could "safely" conclude otherwise, unless he had not bothered to review the mountains of evidence that had accumulated in the several years after the intervention. I see no basis at all for relating events in the Caribbean to the "global revolution" to which he refers, and I fail to see the use of depicting this revolution as a triumph of popular sovereignty over statism. Indeed, I believe that the doctrine of popular sovereignty has consistently worked to strengthen states and support the state system from the end of the 18th century onward.

Writing for *The Times* soon after the intervention, D'Amato may be forgiven for undue reliance on President Reagan's factual claims. Nevertheless, those "facts" induced D'Amato to propose an argument in favor of the intervention's legality that is certainly more sophistic, even "unreal," than anything other scholars have ever produced in defense of "statist" interventions. D'Amato noted that international law permits any government in power to invite foreign military assistance. If Bishop had not lost his life, "he might well have invited the United States into Grenada to protect him" (p. 190). D'Amato then asks, does Bishop's death "erase an invitation that otherwise would surely have been extended? Is there not a constructive invitation to the US to preserve the legitimate government?" (ibid.).

The problem with D'Amato's doctrine of constructive invitation is that it invites a meretricious and self-serving construction of the *facts* by any government already disposed to intervene. Given my account of the facts, Bishop might well have invited Cuba into Grenada (Cuba already had official advisers on the scene), but never the US. If he had done so, and if Cuba had responded with a substantial infusion of military personnel, US officials would surely have interpreted these deeds in the worst possible light. If Cuba had intervened after Bishop's death and not the US, and if Cuba had offered D'Amato's doctrine of constructive intervention as its rationale, I doubt that D'Amato would have defended the claim. I doubt that anyone but an "apologist" for the Cuban government would do so.

As a "linguistic exercise," the doctrine of constructive invitation is transparently oriented to the interests of particular governments and their construction of the facts. Any defense of a government's actions is apologetic, I suppose, but factual credibility and apparent disinterestedness make some defenses more persuasive than others. An utterly unpersuasive defense calls for the scorn that D'Amato is so accustomed to heaping on others. D'Amato reprinted his letter to *The Times* without the slightest indication that he has changed his mind either about the facts or the doctrine of constructive invitation. He has passed up an important opportunity to review a precipitate intervention of his own in the "real world" of public affairs. More than a decade later, we might have expected a more fastidious regard for the facts – or, more properly, for the selection and arrangement of factual claims – and then, just possibly, an admission that some ideas do not stand up to the test of time.

D'Amato is also careless with the facts when he feels compelled to impress us with his learning. In a long treatment of "State Responsibility for Exporting Nuclear Power Technology," D'Amato and his coauthor, Kirsten Engel, date Vattel's great treatise on the law of nations from 1785 (p. 278), not 1758 (a fact beyond dispute).[2] A few pages later, D'Amato and Engel call Wolff a statist and put him after Vattel (p. 287). In fact, Wolff concluded the publication of his grand system of natural law in 1750, which Vattel then sought to adapt for diplomatic use; in the process Vattel expressly rejected Wolff's last-ditch stand against statism. Although Pufendorf was indeed a naturalist who preceded both Wolff and Vattel, his conception of sovereignty came not from Grotius, as D'Amato and Engel seem to believe (ibid.), but from Hobbes, against Grotius. One by one, D'Amato's factual misrepresentations of 17th and 18th century thinkers mean very little. Added together, they undermine my willingness to believe that he understands the naturalist tradition to which he so frequently proclaims his allegiance.

D'Amato also has an oft-expressed fondness for contemporary scholarship that brings the assumptions and analytical power of modern economic theory to the study of law. Again in the paper on nuclear power, what he and Engel claim for fact casts doubt on their depth of understanding. They note "the fact that a reasonable person would prefer to avoid a serious physical injury than to receive monetary damages as compensation" (p. 302 n.).

2 This mistake survives from the original version. *Virginia Law Review*, vol. 74, 1988, p. 1035.

Rational choice theory states, not as a fact, but as a theorem, that a reasonable person would be completely indifferent as to receiving a *fully* compensated injury and not being injured at all. We could hypothesize that a reasonable person might guess that the chances of better-than-full compensation outweigh the risk of worse-than-expected injury, but we would also expect that any given person's tolerance of risk, assessment of life prospects, information about compensation in similar cases, and so on, would significantly affect that person's decision calculus. Research might uncover a statistical pattern with respect to such choices, but such a pattern constitutes a "fact" only in the most provisional sense. If D'Amato fails to grasp simple concepts that are nonetheless indispensable to rational choice theory, then I begin to wonder if he understands the difficulty in reconciling the uncompromisingly positivist character of that theory with his own naturalist inclinations.

I cannot say whether D'Amato is always cavalier with the facts – I have focused only on matters that I have recently given some attention to myself – but I do not think it likely. I certainly do not want to leave the impression that D'Amato's considerable reputation as a scholar is undeserved. To this end, I conclude with a comment on one of the essays that I think shows D'Amato at his very best. Indeed D'Amato's essay on preparations for a war crimes tribunal dealing with atrocities in Bosnia (written in April, 1994) reveals him to be a striking contemporary version, not of Locke (even if he sees himself a Lockean), but of Grotius.

Just as it was for Grotius, D'Amato's overriding concern is the human cost of war. Quite plausibly, D'Amato reasons that pushing for the tribunal, as justice requires, "has the practical effect of prolonging the war" (p. 214), because alleged criminals can expect to be prosecuted once they have made peace. D'Amato deftly performs an "economic" (i. e., rational choice) analysis of the situation to support this conclusion, and he suggests that we think of the tribunal as a "bargaining chip" (pp. 211–14). If the tribunal were made credible, then an offer to shut it down might induce the war's beneficiaries to make peace. War criminals would be rewarded for ending a war sooner than later; punishing them for damage already done is not worth the additional costs of war, including more atrocities.

D'Amato acknowledges that this solution is "distasteful" (p. 212) – so distasteful that no one in a responsible position could face down adverse public opinion in striking the bargain. In the absence of a properly instrumental analysis, D'Amato worries that some officials "may be proceeding on the assumption that the tribunal cannot be negotiated away, while others may be in the process of giving it away without getting anything in return" (p. 214). Either way, "the lack of institutional clarity could result in an unnecessary prolongation of the brutal war in Bosnia" (ibid.). Responses to D'Amato's essay were marked, as he notes "by the temperature of their rhetoric" (p. 215). In condemning war and not its perpetrators or, for that matter, his critics, D'Amato puts the rhetorical emphasis where it belongs.

As recent scholarship makes clear, Grotius also combined a fierce hostility toward war and a coolly instrumental orientation toward its mitigation.[3] Whatever might prove useful is worthy of consideration: justice is justice done. Grotius was brash (what for the time could be brasher than his hypothesis that natural law would hold even if there were no God), immensely learned, but not systematic: nature is complexity, not harmony. Grotius immersed himself in the affairs of his time: natural justice meets its test in what people do to each other and what we all do about it.

What matters to us about Grotius is the thrust of his work and not its particulars. My sketch of Grotius fits D'Amato better than any other international legal scholar writing in English today. If this judgement is even close to the mark, then I am disposed to overlook D'Amato's flaws and foibles, just as we all forgive the same ones in Grotius. Instead, it is the cumulative effect of D'Amato's great body of work – paper after paper, volume upon volume – that warrants attention, now and far into the future.

3 Onuma Yasuaki, *A Normative Approach to War: Peace, War and Justice in Hugo Grotius*, Oxford: Clarendon, 1993, reviewed above, Chapter 21.

23 "Tainted by Contingency": Retelling the story of international law (1995)

In 1994, Jarat Chopra organized a symposium series at Brown University's Watson Institute for International Studies on "The Evolution of International Society: Historical Origins and Legal Perspectives," and invited me to present a paper. I argued in my paper that the standard account of international legal history was both too simple and too little connected to the many other stories devoted to the rise of the modern world. As an alternative, I folded the story of international law into the story of republicanism – the story of its Aristotelian origins, its early modern revival and Enlightenment apotheosis, its relation to natural law thinking, its eclipse as liberalism converged with positivism in law and science. Making that story a key to the "big story" of modernity's rise provided an overview of work that I had begun collaboratively with my brother and then pursued on my own. (Chapter 20, above, examines a decisive episode in the recast story of international law.) I revised "Tainted" for publication in a symposium volume, which Chopra, as editor, had titled *Elements of International Society* in recognition of Henry Wheaton, a Brown University alumnus, and his treatise *Elements of International Law*.

Chopra's *Elements* never materialized. I adapted a few paragraphs from "Tainted" for a book woven from the many strands of my work on republicanism (*The Republican Legacy in International Thought*, 1998). Thereafter, the paper languished in a file drawer until 2000, when Richard Falk asked me if I had anything at hand for a volume he was editing, with Lester Ruiz and Rob Walker, to be called *Reframing the International: Law, Culture, Politics*. I was happy to send him "Tainted," which I had carefully polished and always liked, and which seemed germane on the face of it.

> Kant's idea of a *perpetual peace* guaranteed by a federation of states . . . presupposes an *agreement* between states. But this agreement . . . would always be dependent on particular sovereign wills, and would therefore continue to be tainted by contingency.
>
> (G.W.F. Hegel, 1821)[1]

1 G.W.F. Hegel, *Elements of the Philosophy of Right*, trans. by H.B. Nisbet, Cambridge: Cambridge University Press, 1991, para. 333R, p. 368.

Most international legal scholars repeat a simple story about their field – how it came about and how it came to be what it is today. With Hugo Grotius (and the new European order brought on by the Peace of Westphalia) came naturalism. With Emmerich de Vattel, naturalism was spent. Soon thereafter came positivism, which remains dominant in international legal scholarship.[2]

None of this is wrong. It is not the full story, but no story, no history, ever is. Nevertheless, *this* story is too simple, too sketchy, even as a *story*. I propose to tell the story more broadly by connecting its simple elements to republicanism, which (hardly coincidentally) dominated European social and political thought at the same time naturalism was ascendant. As positivism displaced naturalism, republicanism faded into liberalism, and the modern world took form as we know it today.

Why do I bother? There are three reasons. First, I wish to offset the impression that the story of international law is a story unto itself. Thus told, the story is clearly related to modernity's triumph, yet somehow unrelated to the many other movements and tendencies identified with modernity. However useful this story is for the field's own identity, its telling convicts its tellers of a provincialism very much at odds with the field's premises. Second, telling the story of international law more broadly will help to explain the dramatic shift from naturalism to positivism that the usual story merely stipulates. Rapidly changing material conditions associated with modernity engendered an increasing concern for contingency and fostered a new way of dealing with it. Third, I believe a new and broader telling of the story will help in assessing claims that modernity's moment has passed and that all such stories can no longer validate a field's premises and possibilities.

In keeping with these three objectives, I divide this paper into three sections. The first shows why scholars tell stories about their fields and recapitulates the usual story about the field of international law. Historians of political thought assemble the elements of this story into something quite different: the story of natural rights in relation to emergent liberalism. The second section introduces republicanism as a broader frame of reference within which to place both stories. From Grotius to Vattel, the naturalist founders of the law of nations were all republicans. Yet as such they were hardly alike. I identify two systems of republican ideas that intersect with naturalism and foretell the coming of positivism in altogether different ways. The last section more briefly considers the current condition of modernity and its relation to positivism – both philosophical and legal.

2 The terms *naturalism* and *positivism*, as used here, are conventional shorthand for natural law and positive law doctrine, respectively. Philosophers often use *naturalism* to refer to the ontological claim that nature and society are sufficiently alike to be studied alike. As will be seen, this was indeed the position of natural lawyers; today it is at the core of the philosophical program I call positivism, including legal positivism.

An oft-told tale

Every field of scholarship has a story about the field's origins and the large contours of its development. For the most part, historians are not responsible for these stories. Historians tell stories; I do not wish to suggest otherwise. Giving any chronicle, or temporal ordering of events, a beginning, transitions and an end makes it a story.[3]

Stories about fields emerge from within fields; they take on weight but not density. Without them scholars would be less certain of their field's distinctive character and its place in the world of learning. This is the reason we hear simple stories, easy to learn and marked by a relatively high degree of consensus. We might even expect such stories to take on mythic proportions.

The story of international law bears out these propositions. In the 19th century, when Romantically inclined scholars and intellectuals constructed myths of national origin and identity, international legal scholars wholeheartedly adopted a myth of origins centered on Grotius as the "father" of international law. In due course, international legal scholars exhumed a number of early modern writers to share the glory with Grotius and ensconced them in a suitable mausoleum: the monumental Carnegie "Classics of International Law" series (1911–1950). By reproducing and translating any work of any conceivable relevance to the field's origins (22 in all), the series provides the field with a canon that is uncontested because it is substantially unread.

International legal scholars know that these foundational texts are in the stacks of their research libraries, always available and ever undisturbed. Meanwhile, they recite an exceedingly simple story about the field – the same tale they heard as students or encountered in the field's general surveys.[4] First they mark a transitional period, from the medieval to the modern world, during which Francisco Vitoria and Francisco Suárez brought Catholic theology face to face with Spanish practices in the new world. Then Alberico Gentili led Grotius to the center stage, and the naturalist era began.

Notwithstanding the fumbling efforts of some early positivists (Cornelius van Bynkershoek comes off best), naturalists like Samuel Pufendorf and Christian Wolff dominated the scene until the end of the 18th century. If Thomas Hobbes is mentioned, it is as a "denier of international law," his denial ascertained by inference.[5] Pufendorf's contemporary, John Locke,

3 H. White, *Metahistory: The Historical Imagination in Nineteenth-Century Europe*, Johns Hopkins University Press, 1973, pp. 5–7.

4 The most influential telling of this story in English is A. Nussbaum's *A Concise History of the Law of Nations*, rev. edn, New York: Macmillan, 1954.

5 Ibid., pp. 144–6; C. De Visscher, *Theory and Reality in Public International Law*, rev. ed. trans. by P.E. Corbett, Princeton: Princeton University Press, 1968, pp. 14–15. But see L. Oppenheim, *International Law: A Treatise*, 8th edn by H. Lauterpacht, vol. 1, New York: David McKay, 1955 p. 95, where naturalists are called "Deniers of the Law of Nations" because their conception of natural law leaves no place for positive law.

figures not at all: "he was not concerned with international law as such."[6] Nor does G.W. Leibniz figure in this story, despite his many writings on the law of nature and of nations, and despite the resemblance between his philosophical system and Wolff's. A heroic era closes with Vattel, who, as Wolff's self-styled and very successful popularizer, is deemed facile, imprecise and unoriginal.[7]

As the time of heroes ends, where is Immanuel Kant? While Kant advanced his critical philosophy to save naturalism from the "dogmatic" embrace of Leibniz and Wolff (*dogmatic* is Kant's term), only his late, minor essay on *Perpetual Peace* gets him noticed, and only then in a peripheral story of peace plans and the utopian thinking that lies behind them.[8] This is a cautionary tale, reminding scholars of premises upon which fields cannot be founded.

In the story of international law, Vattel, not Kant, comes at the end of the chapter on natural law precisely because Vattel wrote a systematic treatise devoted to the law of nations, and Kant did not. Unencumbered by philosophical speculation and any but the barest outline of a social theory, Vattel's treatise went through innumerable editions and translations. It was the model for Henry Wheaton's *Elements of International Law* (1836). This treatise and others like it dominated the next century. They, and not their authors, organize the next, long chapter in the story of international law.

Positivism identifies law in, and for, state practice. Starting with Wheaton, treatises reprise the heroic genealogy, but their main business is to make the positive law coherent and accessible. Vattel is thus the decisive transitional figure – last naturalist (however anemic) and first author (even if an amateur) to treat international law as a vocation. With Vattel there to move the plot along, what further need is there to explain this remarkable transition?

The history of political thought is a considerable enterprise, a field of scholarship in its own right. The field is chronologically organized as the story of individual thinkers who appear one after the other. Their ideas are held up as keys to understanding the great issues and themes animating the history of Western civilization. There are as many stories within this master narrative as there are political thinkers and interpretive keys. One important story makes natural rights its theme. This story involves a number of international law's heroes: Vitoria, Suárez, Grotius, Pufendorf, Kant. It adds

6 Nussbaum, *A Concise History of the Law of Nations*, p. 164.

7 Ibid., p. 161.

8 See, for example, S. Hemleben, *Plans for World Peace through Six Centuries*, Chicago: University of Chicago Press, 1943, pp. 87–95, and F.H. Hinsley, *Power and the Pursuit of Peace: Theory and Practice in the History of Relations between States*, Cambridge: Cambridge University Press, 1963, pp. 62–80. Joining Kant are such 17th and 18th century figures as Emeric Crucé, William Penn, John Bellers, Charles Francois Irénée Castel de Saint-Pierre, Jean-Jacques Rousseau and Jeremy Bentham.

other characters no less heroic: Hobbes, Locke, Jean-Jacques Rousseau, American and French revolutionaries.

In this story a coherent theory of natural rights – rights individuals possess in nature – emerges from the prevailing view that nature imposes duties on individuals through necessary social arrangements. Grotius is as important to this story as he is to the story of international law; according to Richard Tuck, he was the point of departure for all who followed in the next century and a half.[9] Nevertheless, after Grotius the two stories diverge markedly. In the rights story, Hobbes and Locke are the main figures.[10] Though secondary, Pufendorf has a place, just as in the story of international law.

Rousseau and Kant complicate the rights story. They contribute to its grandeur perhaps, but less to the main story line – the development of liberalism – than political economy does.[11] Some versions of the rights story focus on Kant's moral philosophy, making him a liberal rights theorist.[12] Yet Kant was concerned with duties imposed by nature, and not duties entailed by others' rights.

An unlikely pair, Jeremy Bentham and G.W.F. Hegel escort nature into the background. Constitutional law and civil society take its place in securing individual rights in the liberal state. The rights story has no counterpart to Vattel. Rights make the transition from nature to society with so much help, including Vattel's, that they seem to be doing it on their own. Rights themselves make up the last important character in the rights story; they do battle with the appalling wrongs committed against humanity in the 20th century.

Both the story of international law and the rights story entwine with yet other stories. All such stories together constitute the story of modernity. This is the big story for a peculiarly reflexive culture – the story of how we denied the world any purpose than our own and purposely made ourselves over at the same time. Its master teller, Max Weber, found modernity in what is lost (rationalization as disenchantment), sought (universal reason manifest in natural law), and duly achieved (instrumental rationality and professionalization associated with state, market and positive law). On Weber's telling, universal reason gave way to instrumental rationality, and natural law to positive

9 R. Tuck, *Natural Rights Theories: Their Origin and Development*, Cambridge: Cambridge University Press, 1979, pp. 175–6. Contemporary scholarship divides over Grotius. Against Tuck's view, pp. 58–81, that rights theory as such begins with Grotius is N. Bobbio's view that this theory "is born with Hobbes. There is no trace of it in Grotius." *Thomas Hobbes and the Natural Law Tradition*, trans. by D. Gobetti, Chicago: University of Chicago Press, 1993, pp. 149–71, quoting p. 154.

10 For a useful overview, see I. Shapiro, *The Evolution of Rights in Liberal Theory*, Cambridge: Cambridge University Press, 1986, pp. 23–149.

11 Ibid., pp. 151–271.

12 F.R. Téson provides an especially earnest, elaborate and misconceived example. "The Kantian Theory of International Law," *Columbia Law Review*, vol. 92, 1992, pp. 53–102.

law, at the end of the 18th century.[13] This is modernity's greatest transition: it marks two great phases in the making of the modern world.

If everyone tells the story of international law as a story about modernity, not everyone tells the story in Weberian terms. Let me offer two examples. One is Myres S. McDougal and associates' well-known discussion of "trends in theories about international law," which they organized by reference to six "frames": the non-law, natural law, historical, analytical, sociologistic and limited factor frames.[14] These frames identify theories of two sorts – theories of process and structural theories – that follow each other more or less dialectically through time.

This version of the story is not Weberian for two reasons. First, it inserts the historical school, with its emphasis on process, between naturalism and positivism (epitomized as the analytical school), both of which emphasize structure. Yet early "analyticalists" like Bentham and John Austin thought naturalists, not "historicalists", were the problem, while the historical school set itself in opposition to Bentham and Austin. Putting the historical school where it does not belong effectively eliminates the transition from naturalism to positivism by eliminating any direct and immediate relationship between them.

Second, sociologistic and limited factor theories (both frames are process-oriented) cannot be said to supersede analytical theories. Both sorts of theories have had their partisans over the last century. Furthermore, many sociologistic and limited factor theories are positivist in the general sense noted above. In effect, McDougal and associates have made too much of some theorists' dissatisfaction with positivism's theoretical limitations and too little of its positive relation to instrumental rationality and law as vocation. In this telling, modernity gets lost in the many scholarly squabbles conducted under its auspices.

David Kennedy has provided a second example of the story of international law told in terms that are not Weberian. According to Kennedy, there have been three chapters in the story, the time (before 1648) of "primitive legal scholarship," followed by the "traditional" and "modern" periods (1648–1900 and 1900–1980 respectively). Nineteen-eighty starts a new chapter, a self-consciously postmodern period exemplified by Kennedy

13 M. Weber, *Economy and Society: An Outline of Interpretive Society*, many translators, Berkeley: University of California Press, 1978, is his most comprehensive statement on modernity, buttressed by an astounding range of comparative material. Note, however, that Weber made little use of the term *modern* and its cognates.

14 M.S. McDougal, *et al.*, "Theories about International Law: Prologue to a Configurative Jurisprudence," in McDougal and W.M. Reisman (eds), *International Law Essays: A Supplement to International Law in Contemporary Perspective*, Mineola, NY: Foundation, 1981, pp. 43–141. Also, see Chapter 19, above.

himself.[15] Kennedy's concern is not what legal scholars say, but how they say it. More particularly, his concern is the way authors relate to their own and other texts to advance their views. Primitive texts invoke authority; traditional authors use their texts to substantiate authority; modern texts seem authoritative because their authors have disappeared from view.

Kennedy's story has Grotius the last of the primitives. Given the way Grotius indiscriminately dropped names, and his successors' comparative circumspection, this judgement has much to commend it. Clearly Wolff was the consummate traditional author. His texts are remarkable for the absence of any authority but himself. His method, like that of geometry, and the system it produces, like that of Euclid, *are* authoritative; author and authority are one.

From this point of view, Vattel was considerably more modest, even self-effacing. His treatise marks the retreat of the author. Yet this tendency, which Kennedy thought to be distinctively modern, starts a century and a half before Kennedy dated it, and dominates the 19th century. Positivism necessarily puts authors outside of their texts, for it is they who find the positive law in state practice and place it within those texts.[16] Authority is something authors merely translate from practice to the text; it is inherent neither in author as reasoning agent nor in the text as nature's writ.

Kennedy's postmodern method of textual interrogation ought to have prompted him to confirm the usual, Weberian story about modernity: first naturalism (to 1800), then positivism (from 1800). By dating the modern period from 1900, I suspect Kennedy has confused *modern* and *modernist*, the latter being a movement in literature, art and architecture, beginning late in the 19th century, to get behind or beneath the superficial appearance of things to their deeper, unsuspected organization. Functionalism is typically modernist. It is merely modern to let a text, picture or building speak for itself (so to speak) – on its own authority, as if its creator (author, artist, architect) did not matter (this being the creator's presumptive intention).

Republicanism

In general terms I am persuaded by the Weberian story of modernity. Its two great parts accord with the transition from the law of nature and of nations to positive international law. At the same time there is another great transition, no less world-embracing (I speak of course of the Western world): the transition from republicanism as a cosmopolitan ideology to liberalism as a

15 Kennedy has told some parts of the story in great detail. The plan for the whole story is briefly sketched in "Primitive Legal Scholarship," *Harvard International Law Journal*, vol. 27, 1986, pp. 1–13. Also, see Chapter 16, above.

16 See my *Republican Legacy in International Thought*, pp. 202–5, and Chapter 28, below, on this property of positivism in general (and not just legal positivism).

way of life. The transition from 18th century republicanism to 19th century liberalism is obviously also related to the transition from natural to positive law. Nevertheless, scholars have shown little interest in how these two incidents in the big story of modernity might fit together.

The reason for this is, I think, the modern practice of organizing the world – the world of human activities – into three levels. The basic level consists of autonomous, rights-bearing individuals; the second consists of whole societies organized as states; the third is the system of states, itself organized more or less as a society. This particular scheme (or at least its second and third levels) is a product of modernity's second Weberian phase. It fosters a division of labor among scholars who anachronistically project it back to modernity's first phase and the transition between the two phases. Yet social thought and practice before modernity's second phase had no clear conception of the state as such and made no clear distinction between social relations within and among states.

In other words, the transition from natural law to positive law is part of an *international* story because it took place among and within societies more or less at the same time. Nothing points to it more sharply than the shift from the law of nations to international law. In contrast, the transition from republicanism to liberalism is only *national*, because it took place more or less separately, even serially, in major societies. Republics became liberal (and remain republics) while cosmopolitan republicanism folded into liberalism as a way of life. At what came to be the international level, the practical manifestations of liberalism showed themselves to be relatively tenuous, and the persistence of major coercion among states still keeps the advocates of liberal internationalism on the defensive.

If this division between the international story and a whole series of national stories has become plausible over time, it is not plausible before its time. The movement from natural to positive law has much to tell scholars whose first concern is one or another of the national stories. The shift from republicanism to liberalism has just as much, or more, to tell those of us whose story is international. The first of these claims is well-illustrated by the recent, quite extraordinary revival of interest in republicanism in the US, initially among historians of the founding period and then among political and legal theorists.[17] Symptomatically, none of these scholars give even passing attention to the law of nature and of nations.

In the 1970s a number of historians began to challenge the prevailing view of the American founding as the consolidation of a liberal society built on

17 See P.S. Onuf, "Reflections on the Founding: Constitutional Historiography in Bicentennial Perspective," *William and Mary Quarterly*, 3rd Series, vol. 46, 1989, pp. 350–6; D. Rodgers, "Republicanism: The Career of a Concept," *Journal of American History*, vol. 79, 1992, pp. 12–19, for useful summaries.

the natural rights of its members. The challengers noticed a pervasive concern with social decay and civic duty at the time of the founding, which they interpreted as characteristically republican. Liberalism came, but later, once the republic had a proper constitution to secure itself and the rights of individuals. To offset the premature emphasis on liberalism, there was need for another story no less sweeping than the natural rights story.

This, J.G.A. Pocock more than anyone else provided: the story of Atlantic republicanism.[18] Historian and political theorist, Pocock made this story long and complex, giving it a density that stories about fields rarely have. The story begins with Aristotle, to whom we must turn for an interpretive key.[19] That key is virtue, the commitment of any citizen to the public, or common, good. No less important a character is Polybius, for the story is about virtue's vicissitudes. Even good societies founded on virtue face decline. The virtuous must renew them, only to have the cycle repeat itself.[20]

In telling this story, Pocock had an exemplary predecessor, Machiavelli – the Machiavelli of both *The Prince* and *The Discourses*. In *The Prince* Machiavelli pitted the virtuous prince against *fortuna*, "the symbol of contingency."[21] In *The Discourses*, Machiavelli drew more systematically on the republicanism of antiquity, to which Aristotle gave an overarching theme – the public good in relation to rule by one, few or many – and Polybius a motivating force – the tendency for any form of rule (*politeia*), including the best of republics, to decay with time and give way to rule in some other form.

> In the theory of the polis and the polity [*politeia*, here meaning rule by the many for public good], it was possible to recognize the republic as a universal, because a comprehensive and therefore stable, harmonization of particular values; and such a harmonization should in principle . . . remain stable and unchanging in time. Yet against this there was a presumption that the republic, being a work of men's hands, must come to an end in time; there was the unmistakable historical fact that Athens, Sparta, and Rome had all declined and ceased to be; and there were, inherent in the Aristotelian analysis, excellent theoretical reasons why this should be so.[22]

18 J.G.A. Pocock, *The Machiavellian Moment: Florentine Political Thought and the Atlantic Political Tradition*, Princeton: Princeton University Press, 1975.

19 Ibid., pp. 66–73.

20 Ibid., pp. 77–80.

21 Ibid., p. 157. See generally, pp. 156–82.

22 Ibid., pp. 76–7. Aristotle used the term *politeia* in two senses, one generic (form of rule), and one specifically a good form of rule (rule by the many for common good). The latter Pocock interpreted as the one form "in which power is shared among all the groups or categories" oriented to particular ends. Ibid., p. 72, following Aristotle's *Politics*, Book III., trans. by B. Jowett, in Jonathan Barnes (ed.), *The Complete Works of Aristotle*, vol. 2, Princeton: Princeton University Press, 1984, p. 2030.

With time, contingencies accumulate. Failures compound; success corrupts. Change is inevitable, although for Polybius, change in the form of rule follows a regular cycle. For his "Renaissance readers," however, "the point must be that each simple virtue must degenerate precisely because it was simple and particular. The problem of the particular was its finitude, its mortality, its instability in time, and once a virtue (itself universal) was embodied in a particular form of government it partook of this general instability."[23]

Forms of rule matter because character matters. The virtuous are few, and those few should rule. As is well-known, Machiavelli saw virtue as a masculine trait. Virtue resides less in what one says than in what one does. The model citizen is a man of action, a warrior, for whom contingency, personified as woman, is ever present, a danger and an opportunity.[24]

Pocock traced the republicanism of Aristotle, Polybius and Machiavelli to the shores of the Atlantic – first England, where James Harrington espoused it and opposition politics reflected its tenets, and finally British North America, where it governed the constitution of a durable republic. Yet the preoccupation with time and contingency cut a broader swath than this in republican thought. Montesquieu found that climate and geography function the way history did for Machiavelli. They give shape to virtue as it plays out in law and institutions. Vattel found much the same in diplomacy as the play of contingency on the plane of states. With time's passing, diplomacy and its adjunct, law, account for the stability that makes Europe a republic.

Pocock gave 18th century Europe scant attention. Montesquieu, David Hume and Adam Ferguson figure in his story, as do Adam Smith, John Millar and Rousseau, though barely.[25] Vattel does not, despite the fact that he was well known to the founders. This should be no surprise: Vattel belongs in the story of international law. There are a number of other republican thinkers who also fall outside the story Pocock tells, and not because they are necessarily part of an international story.

Here I have in mind Johannes Althusius, Grotius, Leibniz and Wolff. Moving from the low countries to Germany, their republicanism was continental (as opposed to Pocock's Atlantic republicanism). It was inextricably associated with natural law (as its Atlantic counterpart was not), in opposition to which natural rights thinking emerged (and with which Atlantic

23 Ibid., p. 78. Not everyone shares this judgement. Thus, according to Hannah Arendt, "Machiavelli's chief interest in the innumerable *mutazioni*, *variazioni* and *alterazioni*, of which his work is so full that interpreters could mistake his teachings for a 'theory of political change,' was precisely the immutable, the invariable, and the unalterable, in short, the permanent and the enduring." *On Revolution*, New York: Viking, 1963, p. 29.

24 Pocock, *The Machiavellian Moment*, pp. 168–9. Also, see H.F. Pitkin, *Fortune Is a Woman: Gender and Politics in the Thought of Niccolo Machiavelli*, Berkeley: University of California Press, 1984.

25 Pocock, *The Machiavellian Moment*, pp. 486–505.

republicanism became affiliated).[26] Continental republicanism had no noticeable influence on the American founding, which of course is the final chapter of the Atlantic story and the reason for telling it at all. The continental story has only one character in its final chapter. This is Kant, who turns up in any number of other stories. In closing the door on natural law, Hegel closed the book on continental republicanism.[27]

There are two stories about republicanism (and not just two versions of one story), even if they have a common origin in antiquity. Both trace back to Aristotle. While there is a great deal more to ancient republicanism than Aristotle, later republicans used Aristotle to make sense of antiquity. He was their interpretive key.[28]

Aristotle's view of society is bound up in the whole of nature (*physis*), which is purposive in its whole and all its parts. The *polis* is one such part, necessary to the purpose of the greater whole. Whatever else people may associate it for, the *polis* is the whole within which their social being finds purpose and to which all their associations contribute.[29] Political society in this encompassing sense is a republic, a public thing, whose nature – to secure the public good – nature has fixed. A republic's form of rule (*politeia*) is a matter of convention (*nomos*). Contingent features of a republic, such as its size, affect such conventional features as its form of rule, but only within nature's limits, ascertainable as nature's law.

As Pocock himself conceded, Aristotle's teleology is spatially, not temporally, oriented.[30] The *polis* is a "public space," the boundaries of which reflect its purpose.[31] Within the *polis*, its constituent associations have boundaries suiting their more limited purposes.[32] Outside the *polis* is nature's space,

26 Labels are confusing here. Many writers use the terms *natural law* and *natural rights* interchangeably and often exclusively for the natural rights story. Bobbio, *Thomas Hobbes and the Natural Law Tradition*, pp. 1, 5, is an instructive example.

27 See M. Riedel's masterful account, *Between Tradition and Revolution: The Hegelian Transformation of Political Philosophy*, trans. by W. Wright, Cambridge: Cambridge University Press, 1984, especially Parts II, IV.

28 P. Rahe, *Republics Ancient and Modern: Classical Republicanism and the American Revolution*, Chapel Hill: University of North Carolina Press, 1992, amply demonstrates how much more there was to ancient republicanism but underestimates Aristotle's importance for later interpretations.

29 Aristotle, *Politics*, trans. by B. Jowett, in J. Barnes (ed), *The Complete Works of Aristotle*, vol. 2, Princeton: Princeton University Press, 1984, I, ii (1253a19–28), p. 1988.

30 Pocock, *The Machiavellian Moment*, pp. 76–7.

31 "Public space" is Arendt's expression, applied to 18th century republics. *On Revolution*, pp. 122, 258.

32 On the *polis* as bounded space, its law "quite literally a wall," see H. Arendt, *The Human Condition*, Chicago: University of Chicago Press, 1958, pp. 63–4. Arendt sharply walled the private space of the household (*oikos*) from the *polis* as public space – too sharply in my opinion, for the latter's purpose, which is the public good, necessarily regulates the household's or, more generally, the economy's relation to political society.

suiting purposes unrelated to human association. This way of thinking invaded Stoic thought to yield the striking spatial metaphor of the very universe as a republic.[33]

Stoicism also affirmed a central tenet of Aristotle's: people are sociable by nature.[34] Furthermore, people are sociable in a way that merely gregarious animals are not. "Nature, as we often say, makes nothing in vain, and man is the only animal who has the gift of speech." According to Aristotle, speech lets us "set forth the expedient and the inexpedient, . . . the just and the unjust."[35] Speech links reason, judgement and sociability in making us human. As Cicero had it, everyone "is a sharer in reason."[36]

Continental republicans made sociability and rationality the two axes enabling humanity to find its place in nature. Hobbes and his successors substituted equality and liberty for sociability on the first axis. This enables human beings to make societies according to their natures.[37] Sociability pops up in the natural rights story, but only as a desirable character trait in a society that free and rational individuals would create for themselves.[38]

Sociability accounts for human association. Human associations all differ with the diverse needs of their members. Aristotle memorably asserted this at the beginning of the *Politics*. He further asserted that nature orders all such associations in an ascending series (that is, in space), capped by the *polis*.[39] With Aristotle's medieval recovery, this way of thinking reasserted itself in Western political thought, where it persisted for centuries.[40]

Jean Bodin framed his conception of sovereignty in an ascending series of associations without fully understanding the effect of the former on the latter (it remained for Pufendorf to make this clear). Althusius spelled this frame-

33 See Onuf, *The Republican Legacy in International Thought*, pp. 90–2.

34 "A social instinct is implanted in all men by nature." Aristotle, *Politics*, I, ii (1253a30), p. 1988. "[A]s the Stoics believe," and Cicero affirmed, "everything produced on earth is created for the use of mankind, and men are born for the sake of men, so that they may be able to assist one another." *On Duties*, trans. by M. Atkins, Cambridge: Cambridge University Press, 1991, I, para. 22, p. 10.

35 Aristotle, *Politics*, I, ii (1253a7–18), p. 1988.

36 Cicero, *On Duties*, I, para. 11, p. 6.

37 See A. Rapaczynski, *Nature and Politics: Liberalism in the Philosophies of Hobbes, Locke, and Rousseau*, Ithaca: Cornell University Press, 1987, on "the crucial postulate of the natural priority of human individuality to social interaction," quoting p. 8.

38 This at least is Neal Wood's interpretation of Locke's preference for sociable and tolerant individuals. *The Politics of Locke's Philosophy: A Social Study of "An Essay Concerning Human Understanding"*, Berkeley: University of California Press, 1983, pp. 135–42.

39 Aristotle, *Politics*, I, i (1252a1–6), p. 1986. In Cicero's words, "[t]here are indeed several degrees of fellowship [*societas*] among men." Cicero, *On Duties*, para. 53, p. 22. Cicero's formula orders associations in a descending series, starting (in good Stoic fashion) with "the fellowship of the entire human race." paras. 50–51, pp. 21–2.

40 Bobbio, *Thomas Hobbes and the Natural Law Tradition*, pp. 6–8; P. Onuf and N. Onuf, *Federal Union, Modern World: The Law of Nations in an Age of Revolutions, 1776–1814*, Madison, WI: Madison House, 1993, pp. 57–69.

work out in striking detail to support what we now call popular sovereignty. Grotius expressly affirmed a Stoic conception of sociability and argued on Aristotle's authority that associations ranging from brigands to the human race itself are maintained by their own law.[41] That he took a multiplicity of associations for granted makes *The Law of War and Peace* almost unintelligible as an international legal treatise, for sovereignty in Bodin's sense is nowhere to be found, and muddies any claim on his behalf as a rights theorist.[42] Pufendorf effectively split the difference between Grotius and Hobbes by claiming that human frailty makes "sociality" (*socialitas*) a general law of nature.[43] This move left little room for associations between the individual and the sovereign republic.

Hobbes and Pufendorf simplified social reality to a radical and, for the time, unwarranted degree. At the other extreme stood Leibniz. He generalized the Aristotelian series of ascending associations into a cosmological principle ordering all of nature.[44] Wolff's claim that the law of nature mandates a virtual republic above all known republics – a *civitas maxima* – is nothing more than a logical extrapolation of his general, Leibnizian position (see Chapter 20, above, for details).

Like Pufendorf, Kant sought to negotiate between the poles of Hobbesian alienation and Stoic sociability. Imputing to individuals an asocial sociability as part of nature's design, he saw the realization of nature's design a long, painful, highly contingent and very social process to which republican principles duly contribute. Kant's self-styled "Copernican Revolution" allowed him to posit a design for nature without making it a feature of the world outside the mind – his critique of Leibniz and Wolff hinges on just this point. Instead, every mind constructs its world to conform to nature's design by use of the same few a priori principles. From this follows the central moral law: act as if the maxim of our action is a law of nature. Acting as if the world is a republic will make it so. With Kant, the continental republicanism reached an apotheosis of sorts: within each of us is a republican template, awaiting projection upon the raw materiality, and utter contingency, of the world outside.[45]

41 H. Grotius, *De jure belli ac pacis libri tres*, trans. by F.W. Kelsey, Washington: Carnegie Institution, 1925, Prolegomena, paras. 6, 23, pp. 11, 17, on sociability and association, respectively.

42 See Onuma Y. (ed.), *A Normative Approach to War: Peace, War, and Justice in Hugo Grotius*, Oxford: Clarendon, 1993, and Chapter 21, above.

43 S. Pufendorf, *On the Duty of Man and Citizen*, trans. by M. Silverthorne, Cambridge: Cambridge University Press, 1991, I, iii, pp. 33–8. Also, see J. Tully's Introduction, pp. xxiv–xxix.

44 A.O. Lovejoy, *The Great Chain of Being: A Study of the History of an Idea*, Cambridge, MA: Harvard University Press, 1936, pp. 144–82. Also, see C.R. Rossi, *Broken Chain of Being: James Brown Scott and the Origins of Modern International Law*, The Hague: Kluwer Law International, 1998. Rossi's highly original retelling of the story of international law hinges on the figure of the great chain and its Aristotelian resonances.

45 I elaborate this interpretation of Kant in *The Republican Legacy in International Thought*, pp. 104–6.

As I pointed out earlier, Kant's moral philosophy puts the emphasis on duties, not rights. It is nature's design that rational individuals learn to act like dutiful republicans, however hesitantly, in order to achieve nature's design. The emphasis on duties and their source in natural law makes Kant a faithful adherent of continental republicanism. This way of thinking descends from Aristotle and the Stoics to Cicero, whose Aristotelian conception of natural law and emphasis on rhetoric – on words as deeds – and thus on persuasion and learning, more deeply influenced the 17th and 18th centuries than did Aristotle himself.

Nothing Cicero wrote exceeded the influence of his handbook *On Duties*, which he composed for his son's benefit. Pufendorf, who wrote *On the Duty of Man and Citizen* to fulfill an "obligation to the young," was but one of many latter-day imitators.[46] The great treatises on the law of nature and of nations, like Pufendorf's *De jure naturae*, differ only in scale and systematization. They are nothing but catalogues of duties proclaimed on behalf of nature.

Being sociable by nature does not makes us equal socially. Aristotle infamously said so: "some men are by nature free, and others slaves."[47] Being sociable does not make us unequal either. The claim of inequality would not seem to follow necessarily from Aristotle's system of thought. More to the point, human associations are unequal in purpose and importance.

Individuals owe duties to those associations to which nature has assigned them. As Cicero taught, "there are degrees of duties within social life itself"; associations at a higher level take precedence over those at a lower.[48] By implication, the ordering of all possible associations results in duties for individuals that are differentiated by reference to the place of their associations among all others. Duties owed to parents who are slaves, for example, differ from duties owed to free parents. Even if individuals can change their place in society (because, as Cicero seemed to believe, the contingent circumstances of birth had misplaced them), they always have duties appropriate to their place.

According to Cicero, "those who are equipped by nature to administer affairs must abandon any hesitation over winning public office and engage in public life. For only in this way can the city be ruled or greatness of spirit be displayed." Those few who are fit have a duty to rule for public good. All others have other duties, including that of being ruled for their own good. A society based on the performance of duties is a society ordered by statuses. Every station has its duties; the station itself is nothing more than the ensemble of duties relevant to it.

46 Pufendorf, *On the Duty of Man and Citizen*, Preface, p. 6.

47 Aristotle, *Politics*, I, v (1255a1), p. 1991. Nor can the family as an association consist of equals: "the male is fitter by nature for command than the female, just as the elder and full-grown is superior to the younger and more immature." I, xi (1259b3–4), p. 1998.

48 Cicero, *On Duties*, I, para. 160, p. 62. Note, however, that Cicero put duties to "the immortal gods" first, and not duties to humanity, as "his degrees of fellowship" would seem to require.

Whether Kant's autonomous, willing individual would indeed will a society in which most duties are common (because people and their associations are equal) depends on how those individuals understand nature. Kant's own view ought not to be confused with the rights-flavored liberal construction of nature that self-proclaimed Kantians favor in our own day. At best, the claim – Kant's as much as Aristotle's – that cognitive capacities exemplified by speech and reason make us human yields a minimal universal duty not to treat people like animals. While this may preclude slavery as unnatural, Aristotle notwithstanding, it hardly requires the equal treatment of people in other respects.

Obviously the natural rights position does present a striking contrast to the Ciceronian conception of differentiated duties under natural law. Rights universally held by individuals imply correlative, equally universal duties. Additional rights and duties must be voluntarily assumed, including those of association and rule. Society is the result.

Natural rights free individuals from the (metaphorically spatial) constraints of natural law. Late in the 18th century individuals asserting their rights turned to Atlantic republicanism in a moment of need and opportunity. This alliance took the form of a social contract among the free and equal – a constitution fixing the alliance for the foreseeable future. The American founders used the occasion to solve a chronic problem for Atlantic republicanism: small republics cannot provide security; large republics undercut republican rule.

Rejecting the spatial logic of comprehensively differentiated duties, the founders nevertheless went back to Aristotle for a scheme of ascending political associations to solve the size problem. This is the federal principle, which they extricated from natural law and differentiated duties by insisting that citizens are free, among other things, to choose their representatives at every level of association. The federal republic must consist of republican states, as the Constitution specifies (Section IV, 4), and those states must be equal in the sense that individuals are. States in turn consist of "county republics," as Thomas Jefferson called them. At least potentially, counties consist of "ward republics."[49] The founders acknowledged Aristotle's teleology but refused its implications; they brought space back into the picture without its encumbrances. Instead they created a framework, a spatial grid, for liberalism and democracy.[50]

Positivism deploys a generalized version of the same grid even as it suppresses any intimation of teleology. All things have their place within its coordinates,

49 Jefferson set the entire scheme out in a letter from 1816, as quoted in P.S. Onuf, *Jefferson's Empire: The Language of American Nationhood*, Charlottesville: University Press of Virginia, 2000, p. 120. See pp. 117–21 on the importance of equality at every level.

50 See Onuf and Onuf, *Federal Union, Modern World*, Part I, for the full story.

but no purpose in relation to the whole. Everywhere on this spatial grid, procedure harnesses contingency. Things go on, more or less predictably.

Natural law points in the opposite direction. That everything has its purpose gives natural law its content. In an 18th century context, that content was almost certain to be seen as comporting with continental republicanism and the European status quo. In other words, a society ordered by statuses, legitimated by reference to natural law and supported by differentiated duties reduces social contingency to a bare minimum. Little is left to chance.

Any such society works best when it is isolated from other societies and changing material conditions. Eighteenth-century Europe and North America faced changing conditions and a rising tide of contingency, leaving the old order in disarray. Events of the 19th century swept its last remnants away. The Aristotelian vision of purposeful nature lost relevance to all but a beleaguered few.

We see the burden of contingency in the categories natural lawyers devised. Grotius introduced a distinction between volitional and necessary law, and Wolff affirmed it: nature requires human assistance when it comes to matters of will; otherwise law needs no human intercession. This strategy for insulating nature's law from human sociability depends on a distinction with no practical meaning. There is no necessary law to speak of, and voluntary law is hard to separate from positive law on any but the most formal of grounds. In deference to tradition, Vattel made a last, unconvincing effort to maintain this distinction, even as his treatise brought state practice and positive law into the foreground.[51]

As we saw, Kant used the premise of asocial sociability to account for social contingency. Indeed, contingency is the key to nature's plan. That plan is not available through rational inspection, because there is no lawful nature as such. It can be achieved only through a slow, contingent process of social learning. Hegel's claim that Kant's republic of republican states would be "tainted by contingency" is undeniable, although for Kant, contingency is no taint because its cumulative effect is not the decay that Polybius and Machiavelli so feared.

With natural law's passing, Hegel had more than a passing interest in contingency: "arbitrariness is *contingency* in the shape of will."[52] Despite "provisions" against contingency of this sort, civil society is its particular realm (just as civil society is the realm of republican character and conduct).[53] The family is "exposed" to contingency, as indeed is the state in its relations with other states.[54] Clearly for Hegel, the state is the only answer to

51 For more on this, see J.L. Brierly, *The Law of Nations: An Introduction to the International Law of Peace*, 6th edn by H. Waldock (1963), pp. 37–9, and Chapter 20, above.

52 Hegel, *Philosophy of Right*, para. 15, p. 48, emphasis in translation.

53 Ibid., para. 188, p. 226; also see paras. 231–232, p. 260.

54 On the family: ibid., para. 171, p. 209; also, see para. 238, p. 263. On the state: para. 340, p. 371.

contingency, and even this is an imperfect or, we might say, contingent answer. "The state is not a work of art; it exists in the world, and hence in the sphere of arbitrariness, contingency, and error, and behaviour may disfigure it in many respects."[55] Nevertheless, for Hegel and his followers the state very much does resemble a work of art, less of this world, closer to nature, and less buffeted by contingency, than any other social creation.

Contingency and irony

In modernity's second phase, contingency is the source of much ambivalence. The liberal attitude is to welcome contingency as opportunity and to interfere with it only as needed to assure individuals the opportunity to take advantage of their opportunities. Success in this respect encourages a belief that humanity can master nature, both by exploiting its possibilities and thwarting its harmful contingencies. Science and its philosophical rationale, positivism, enable liberalism to pay off by increasing favorable contingencies and limiting harmful ones.

As a philosophical program, positivism takes the knowing, willing subject for granted. Enlightenment epistemology grants positivism its fixed point of reference from which to take full measure of the world. The observing I/eye stands apart from and looks into the world – a world that includes the observer as an object. Ontology guides positivism; methodology governs it. There is an objective, lawful world "out there" (Kant notwithstanding), the contingent properties of which we can measure and the behavior of which we can predict.

What is true for nature must also be true for society. Ontologically speaking, all sciences, natural and social, are unified. They all occupy positions on the same spatial grid. Nevertheless, they are methodologically differentiated, because the diverse objects, or positivities, of the world differ in properties and relations. Reliable knowledge of the world forms a hierarchy of sciences.[56]

Legal positivism is fully compatible with positivism as a philosophical program. As epistemological subjects, individual observers stand apart from law and, observing its properties and relation to other *social facts* (Emile Durkheim's term), make the state their primary ontological subject. The state is a legal fact. Sovereignty is a summary statement of the causal relation of that legal fact to many others.

Law is a method for controlling contingency (just as the scientific method is); sovereignty grants the state control over the control of contingency. The

55 Ibid., para. 258, p. 279.

56 This last claim is specifically a Comtean contribution to the positivist program. See *The Positive Philosophy of Auguste Comte*, trans. by H. Martineau (1853), Introduction, ch. 2, reprinted in G. Lender (ed.), *Auguste Comte and Positivism: The Essential Writings*, Chicago: University of Chicago Press, 1983, pp. 87–101.

state cannot eliminate contingency and, in any event, civil society depends on it. Nevertheless, in an age of instrumental rationality, the benefits of controlling contingency are easy to see, and people want more of them. Law and the state increase in importance, though not always at the expense of civil society.

In the relations of states, sovereignty is a summary description of reciprocal as opposed to causal relations. Control over contingency is the more difficult, and, as Hegel implied, states inflict its disfiguring effects on other states by attempting to control its effects on themselves. Yet the relations of states are subject to positive law – law that states make in order to dampen untoward contingencies. Like all law, international law works better to the extent that the law itself is removed from the domain of contingency. This, I think, has been the dominating concern for international legal scholarship over the 20th century.

The project of freeing international law from contingency, of clarifying its status as positive law, has proceeded by reference to the sources and subjects of that law and to the sanctions backing it up. Many scholars have sought to buttress these three pillars of positivist doctrine, as I have called them elsewhere.[57] Other scholars have been skeptical – for McDougal and associates, their theories belong in the non-law frame – and still others have thought these efforts misdirected. Members of this last group are to be found throughout modernity's second, positivist phase. McDougal and associates identified them as process theorists, first historicalist and then sociologistic (but not "sociological" because they fail to meet the methodological standards of positivist sociology[58]).

Positivism has always met with resistance. In 19th century arts and letters, the Romantic movement repudiated positivism down to its premises. In the context of law and society, Romantically inclined scholars have been the ones to tell stories, name epochs and their heroes, pass judgement. They are critics – of positivists, each other, even themselves – but not just for the sake of criticism. They would rather see the world fully than clearly.

I would put the matter somewhat differently. As Atlantic republicanism yielded to positivist liberalism, positivism's critics made time their central concern. In the beginning they did so with a vengeance, rejecting the formal, universal conception of natural law central to spatially oriented continental republicanism (here McDougal and associates were right). In due course positivism lost all connection with Atlantic republicanism and its temporal affinities; critics of positivism gradually found their temporal flourishes subject to criticism from rigorous positivists. By making time a precise and universal metric, positivism took time for itself.

57 "Global Law-Making and Legal Thought," in N.G. Onuf (ed.), *Law-Making in the Global Community*, Durham, NC: Carolina Academic Press, 1982, pp. 6–8. These pages postdate the material printed in Chapter 6, above.

58 McDougal *et al.*, "Theories about International Law," p. 260.

For two centuries positivism faced attenuating criticism. Material success is hard to argue with. Toward the end of the last century, however, things seem to have gotten out of hand. Material success imperils the positivist drive to control contingency – or so a new and substantial wave of critics assert with increasing fervor. Some of these critics go further. They say that modernity itself has come to an end.

I want to conclude with a few observations about recent claims that modernity, or at least modernity's positivist, liberal phase, has ended. The strongest, most direct attack on modernity starts with the radical separation of subject and object. Enlightenment epistemology is based on this "opposition," as its critics call it, and modernity's second phase depends on its efficacy. The postmodern attack on epistemology makes the self completely contingent in a world of contingency. Such radical relativism effectively denies modernity any conceivable future; no subject is available to superintend a transition of any kind.

The attack on modernity through its Enlightenment epistemology elicits the charge of nihilism and easy dismissal. Much harder to dismiss is an attack on the positivist ontology of modernity's second phase. Positivists presume that the social world differs from the natural world in complexity but not in kind, and that the same methodological rules govern the acquisition of reliable knowledge about both worlds. It is just this position that positivism's critics have spent the last two centuries challenging. To call them postpositivist, as I and many other scholars are wont, hardly does their challenge justice.

Instead, following Richard Rorty, we might call them *ironists*:

> I use the term "ironist" to name the sort of person who faces up to the contingencies of his or her most central beliefs and desires – someone sufficiently historicist and nominalist to have abandoned the idea that those central beliefs and desires refer back to something beyond the reach of time and chance.[59]

As long as there have been literal-minded positivists, there have been ironically minded doubters – Romantics and historicists, most poets and some philosophers, and now postpositivist social theorists. Hegel was an historicist. Was he also an ironist? Rorty thought "the young Hegel," "the Hegel of the *Phenomenology*," was.[60] By implication, the older Hegel of the *Philosophy of Right* may have lost his sense of irony. Yet terms like *tainted* and *exposed* suggest an ironic attitude toward social contingency, and not just dismay.

59 R. Rorty, *Contingency, Irony, and Solidarity*, Cambridge: Cambridge University Press, 1989, pp. xv.
60 Ibid., pp. 101–4.

For Rorty, the positivist preoccupation with reliable knowledge, with the *truth* about ourselves and the world, is a quest not just to control contingency, but to eliminate it. I have told the story of positivism somewhat differently than I think Rorty would have. Positivists have only gradually come to see contingency as the enemy (just as natural lawyers did in their time), to be extirpated wherever it materializes, in the name of instrumental rationality and the truth. With time has come positivist intrusion into every corner of human experience; success has engendered an impatience with time itself.

Rorty's story is the ongoing resistance to positivism's success, which takes the form of an ironic, almost subversive acceptance of contingency – the contingency of language, self and community. While there may indeed be subversive epistemological implications to the story, its subject is not the self as subject. Indeed the self creates its world with language, and "truth is a property of linguistic entities, of sentences."[61] What remains of the self beyond contingent beliefs and desires is the small truth of their marginal redescription. What remains of community is the willingness to live with commitments that must be contingent.

What do these three claims about contingency tell us about international law as a field of study so long dominated by the project of making the law among states more like law within states? Acknowledgment that language creates truth – that language is performative – dramatically enhances our understanding of the way law works to control contingency. More modest claims about the self offset the righteous fervor of the rights movement without giving up our concern for human suffering and humiliation.[62] More modest claims about community demystify the state, loosen sovereignty's grip and perhaps signal a revival of republicanism without pretensions.

An acceptance of contingency in general would become the study of international law. We would be less dogmatic about our categories (it must either be law or not) and less casual about creating new categories (if neither, it must be "soft" law). What is law, after all, but some transient ensemble of contingent events? We might overcome the positivist habit of seeing the world in the space of the present. We might learn from the field's rich past, its long history of confronting contingency.

Whether the positivist phase of modernity has come to an end remains to be seen. Any transition on the scale of the transition from naturalism to positivism will be clearer in retrospect than in the moment. My prescriptions for modesty in response to positivist excesses, along with the efforts of post-positivists in general, could help in saving positivism from itself. If this

61 Ibid., p. 7, footnote deleted.

62 "Liberal ironists are people who include among [their] ungroundable desires their own hope that suffering will be diminished, and that the humiliation of human beings by other human beings may cease." Ibid., p. xv.

happens, there is no transition, at least in our time; a chastened, healthier positivism would enable modernity to continue on its way. This, after all, has been the general if diminishing effect of criticism over two centuries. Alternatively, postpositivist challenges may have the cumulative effect of dismantling the edifice of positivism itself, thus to effect a transition to a world we can hardly imagine.

24 How to think about "The Golden Age of International Law" (1999)

In 1994, my brother Peter and I sketched out the second volume of *Federal Union, Modern World*, which we subtitled *Law, Diplomacy and the Crisis of the Union, 1815–1865*, and for which we recruited a diplomatic historian as collaborator. We continued to think that Henry Wheaton, as a US diplomat and author of a landmark treatise on international law, would serve as an exemplary figure in marking the rise of the liberal world. Wheaton was my responsibility, and I immersed myself in his writings (even to the extent of examining the small proportion of Wheaton's papers housed at Brown University). I soon realized Wheaton's highly stylized history of international legal thought revealed a shift in premises needed for the emergence of an international society that could fairly be described in liberal and not republican terms. Eventually I concluded that a liberal international society actually preceded and thus helped to precipitate the development of liberal societies in Britain and the US. I developed and substantiated this controversial claim in a paper that I worked on intermittently and twice presented to scholarly audiences. In both cases the response was tepid and perhaps skeptical; I wondered if I had failed to make my claim sufficiently clear.

When friends in Brazil asked if I might contribute a paper to *Contexto International*, I sent them the version printed below, which they translated into Portuguese. Folded into additional work for the book project, I reiterated the argument publicly several more times and was rewarded with a more enthusiastic reception. Meanwhile, our diplomatic historian dropped out of the project, and the organization and content of the book changed markedly. Renamed *Nations, Markets, and War: Modern History and the American Civil War* (2006), the book as published contains a good deal of the material appearing here.

Several decades ago, Arthur Nussbaum spoke for many scholars when he declared the 19th century to be "the golden age of international law."[1] Yet

1 Arthur Nussbaum, *A Concise History of the Law of Nations*, rev. edn, New York: Macmillan, 1954, p. 232.

this commonplace had little enough support, as measured by the attention that Nussbaum and his peers actually gave to doctrinal developments in this golden age. Nussbaum, for example, devoted five times more space to doctrinal developments in the years between 1648 and 1815 than to such developments in the following century. To be fair, he was inclined to view the 19th century as a golden age, precisely because international law had substantially completed its doctrinal development by the end of the 18th century. Thereafter, it was the rapid expansion of positive law and the professionalization of legal practice that warranted retrospective appreciation. In this story, doctrinal refinements are beside the point.

More to the point, Nussbaum and his generation began their scholarly careers early in the 20th century. The golden age was hardly a remote time for them. It is rather more likely that they saw themselves an integral part of it. In their eyes, the golden age of international law had not yet come to a close. After the regrettable interruptions of two world wars and the fascist assault on the rule of law, they saw themselves as principals in a great project of restoring the golden age of international law to its former glory

One of the most conspicuous features of 19th century international law was its role in turning large regions of the world into colonial dependencies. During the very years in which so many scholars took the golden age for granted, this gigantic system of subordination came under sustained attack. Yet, decolonization had the paradoxical effect of strengthening international law (indeed decolonization had the same effect when it took place in the Americas much earlier). By reversing gears and making colonies into states, 19th century international law confirmed itself as the only available machinery for regularized relations among states, old or new, in the second half of the 20th century.

Nevertheless, decolonization in the 1960s and 1970s also eventuated in a postcolonial sensibility, increasingly prominent in the 1980s and 1990s and deeply antagonistic to the idea that international law could ever have enjoyed a golden age. Postmodern tendencies in Western scholarship have reinforced this sensibility. It is in this context that doctrinal developments in the 19th century have finally begun to receive some attention. It is serious attention, long overdue, but hardly flattering.

The postcolonial critique identifies international law as one of several instruments that Europeans used in the 19th century to gain control over other peoples, to exploit them and their resources systematically, and to justify having done so. Europeans made the best of their tangled political arrangements by erecting them into a formal, universal standard of sovereign equality that other, ostensibly less civilized peoples were unlikely to meet. Such peoples were fit only to be colonized and, as colonies, would receive the benefits of civilization indirectly. Only because Europeans had failed to prevent an earlier wave of decolonization, the states of the Americas could claim to be the sovereign equals of European states. Elsewhere the alleged absence of sovereignty gave Europeans all that they needed to institutionalize inequalities and exploitation. Nineteenth-century doctrine confirmed the propriety of these activities, even if it made a mockery of the universalistic pretensions of its authors.[2]

Rising civilizations are prone to arrogance. In the European case, extraordinary material success in the 19th century coincided with civilizational decline elsewhere. Nevertheless, European arrogance dramatically increased after mid-century. Expressed as a romanticized concoction of violence and racism, and dignified as social Darwinism, it fueled the imperial rampage of those decades. In due course bringing general war to Europe and beyond, arrogance in this degree set the last decades of the 19th century apart from all others.

However convenient it is to mark time with the turn of the centuries, it is misleading to consider the 19th century as an unbroken stretch (even we shift its dates from 1815 to 1914). There are several decades (roughly 1815–1865) that are too easily dismissed as precursors of the more egregious decades to follow. Even if earlier decades in the century were hardly free of arrogance, or of imperial adventures for that matter, they invite a view of international law rather different from the one that postcolonial critics offer for later decades.

The large claim of this paper is that doctrinal developments in the early decades of the 19th century should be considered together, because together they constitute a distinctive, substantial and enduring contribution to the makeup of the Western world. To be more specific, we can see in these developments the defining features of the liberal world before it took on global proportions. The term *liberal* in this instance refers to society whose members – be they individuals or corporate entities such as states – are free to put their interests before society's.

This paper is a sketch. I make no claim to having surveyed relevant materials in anything even remotely resembling an exhaustive fashion. Instead, I focus most of my attention on a single treatise, Henry Wheaton's *Elements of International Law*. Its appearance in 1836 conveniently dates the world of liberal international relations as a conceptually coherent project, though hardly a complete one. If not a golden age, then this was at least a compelling moment in the history of European international law.

There are two reasons for treating Wheaton in particular as an exemplary figure. First, no writer exceeded him in influence for at least three decades. His book went through several editions, including a French edition in 1848 – the year of his death – and a Chinese edition in 1864. The latter is famous for being the first translation of any international legal treatise into a non-European language. The eighth edition, which Richard Henry Dana,

2 See, for example, S.N. Grovogui, *Sovereigns, Quasi Sovereigns and Africans: Race and Self-Determination in International Law*, Minneapolis: University of Minnesota Press, 1996; A. Anghie, "Finding the Peripheries: Sovereignty and Colonialism in Nineteenth-Century International Law," *Harvard International Law Journal*, vol. 40, 1999, pp. 1–80.

Jr. edited for publication in 1866, assured a continuing wide influence for Wheaton's *Elements* during the later decades of the century. Perhaps not too surprisingly, postcolonial critics draw on this edition – selectively, I might add – in their making the case that international law gave colonialism its practical and moral foundations.

Wheaton's enduring fame and influence draw attention away from the second, decisive reason for treating him as an exemplary figure. Wheaton's *Elements* provided his contemporaries with a cogent and all but complete exposition, not just of the elements of international law, but of the several elements which, taken together, make liberal internationalism a coherent representation of a world that took form in the decades following the Peace of Vienna. The key to this achievement is Wheaton's doctrinal genealogy. Definitively recapitulating the long, messy and uncertain process by which writers came to separate legal relations among states from legal relations within states, he did a great deal to make the liberal world conceptually independent from developments within societies.

While Wheaton's doctrinal genealogy demanded a show of respect for natural law, he gave practical primacy to positive law. At the same time, he disarmed the positivist deniers of international law. In so doing, he made it clear that states together constitute a society, but not, at least on a priori grounds, a universal society. On the contrary, he took international law to be grounded in legal practices specific to Europe. Finally, he rendered the entire body of international law – natural and positive – in the language of rights and thus the only language that makes liberal ideas intelligible in practice.

The language of rights is no doubt one that Wheaton found especially congenial, born as he was in the US and seasoned in constitutional law as well as diplomacy. Yet he was not the only, or even the first, writer in his time to use this language in making international law uniformly available for liberal needs and uses. Who said what first is perhaps incidental to the point. In step with the times, Wheaton earned his influence because of what people could thereafter take for granted.

We often think that liberal ideas due to Thomas Hobbes and John Locke represent a sharp break with the past. Transparently liberal, Wheaton nevertheless emphasized doctrinal continuity. He held that states are "independent moral beings" – moral, because their corporate character implicates them in human society; independent, only by virtue of rights that confer duties on other, equally independent states.[3] Obviously, the society that states constitute among themselves is a legal order, and thus a moral condition. Within

3 H. Wheaton, *Elements of International Law with a Sketch of the History of the Science*, Philadelphia: Carey, Lea & Blanchard, 1836, p. 95. The notion that corporate beings constitute socially situated moral personalities has classical antecedents and a great deal of early modern support. See Chapter 26, below.

that society, states are no less obviously free to pursue their interests individually and collectively.

Indeed the world became liberal, in just these terms, before Britain and the US did. As Alfred Rubin has forcefully argued, practice among states and its construction into positive law preceded any recognition of a legal order unique to states in their relations.[4] Such a world was not liberal; it needed an appropriate doctrinal accommodation to become liberal. The same must be said for those societies that we most closely associate with liberalism.

Petty commercial activity, rights in common law and social contract theorizing had not turned Britain and its North American colonies into liberal societies during the 18th century, and perhaps could never have done so. Republican ideas and practices pulled in a different direction, and so did the vestiges of feudal life. Once states found themselves relating to each other in liberal terms, those societies where conditions were most propitious changed rapidly and reaped material advantages by doing so. The liberal world fostered liberal societies, and not the other way around. If states moved to institute or rationalize internal markets, for example, they did so in response to pressures from beyond, so to speak, more than from within.

The key element in Wheaton's construction of the liberal world is a doctrinal genealogy codifying the separation of international and domestic law. It is to Hugo Grotius that Wheaton gave credit for the "new science of natural jurisprudence" – "a mixed science of the law of nature and nations."[5] In the great succession of "scientific writers," Christian Wolff, following on Samuel Pufendorf, "entitled himself to the credit of first separating the law which prevails or ought to prevail, between nations, from that part of the science which teaches the duties of individuals; and of reducing the law of nations to a full and systematic form."[6] These claims on Wolff's behalf are at least nominally true, since Wolff's systematic, multivolume treatise on natural law concludes with a separate volume devoted to the law of nations – the first such to appear. Yet a close inspection of that volume yields little evidence that Wolff entertained any such separation on conceptual grounds.[7]

Wheaton gave the genealogy of doctrine far more attention in his *History of the Law of Nations*, which appeared nine years after *Elements* had. There he repeated his claim that Wolff was the first to consider the law of nations on its own, but with a significant difference: "To Wolf [sic] belongs, according to his elegant abridger [Emmerich de] Vattel, the credit of separating the law of nations from that part of natural jurisprudence which treats the duties of

4 A.P. Rubin, *Ethics and Authority in International Law*, Cambridge: Cambridge University Press, 1997, pp. 19, 64.

5 Wheaton, *Elements of International Law*, p. 30.

6 Ibid., p. 31.

7 See N.G. Onuf, *The Republican Legacy in International Thought*, Cambridge: Cambridge University Press, 1998, chs. 3–4 (and Chapter 20, above).

individuals."[8] To substantiate this new, more subtle claim, Wheaton reviewed Wolff's system and Vattel's reaction to it. As Martti Koskenniemi has argued, Vattel "is logically led to making a boundary between international and municipal law."[9] Wolff resisted the logic in question – the logic of territorial sovereignty – and drew no such conclusion.

While Wheaton's discussion of Vattel shows how inescapable this conclusion is, nowhere did Wheaton quote Vattel as having come to it in such straightforward terms. Indeed, in paraphrasing Vattel (very closely, it should be noted), he made it clear that Vattel never really came to it at all. Here it pays to quote Wheaton at some length:

> According to Vattel, that law of nations, in its origin, is nothing but *the law of nature applied to nations*.
>
> Having laid down this axiom, he qualifies it in the same manner, and almost in the identical terms of Wolf, by stating that the nature of the subject to which it is applied being different, the law which regulates the conduct of individuals must necessarily be modified in its application to the collective societies of men called nations or states. A state is a very different subject from a human individual, from which result, in many cases, obligations and rights very different.[10]

For Vattel to have acknowledged the logical implications of territorial sovereignty, he would have had to reconsider the "axiom" that the law of nations derives from natural law.

The same logic drives Pufendorf's incisive critique of irregular political systems.[11] Nevertheless, as Wheaton remarked, Pufendorf was content to lay down "the general principles of natural law, leaving it to the reader to apply it as he might find it necessary to private individuals or to independent societies."[12] Later writers, up to and including Vattel, were no less content to compile the rules applicable to states, leaving the reader to decide whether nature made these rules necessary, presumably within states as well as among them. In short, all of these writers lacked a clear understanding that legal rules must have sources specific to, and valid for, the legal orders within which they are to be found.[13]

8 H. Wheaton, *History of the Law of Nations in Europe and America; From the Earliest Times to the Treaty of Washington, 1842*, New York: Gould, Banks, 1845, p. 177. Also, see p. 183.

9 M. Koskenniemi, *From Apology to Utopia: The Structure of International Legal Argument*, Helsinki: Finnish Lawyers' Publishing, 1989, p. 92; also, see Onuf, *The Republican Legacy in International Thought*, p. 163.

10 Wheaton, *History of the Law of Nations in Europe and America*, p.186; his emphasis.

11 Here, see P. Onuf and N. Onuf, *Federal Union, Modern World: The Law of Nations in an Age of Revolutions, 1776–1814*, Madison, WI: Madison House, 1993, pp. 65–8.

12 Wheaton, *Elements of International Law*, p. 38.

13 Onuf, *The Republican Legacy in International Thought*, pp. 81–2.

Wheaton possessed just such an understanding, largely due to James Madison, which he fully articulated in *Elements*.[14] As a consequence, he viewed the separation of international and domestic orders as obvious, and not only to himself. On logical grounds, he thought it had to be obvious to Wolff and Vattel when, in their time, it was not. His error in this respect led to an anachronistic reading of his predecessors and an imaginative genealogy specific to the liberal world. Notice that the line of descent leading to himself (Grotius → Pufendorf → Wolff and Vattel) parallels the line of descent for liberal thought in a domestic context (Hobbes → Locke → Montesquieu, Hume, Smith, Rousseau *et al.*). Fully separate from the standard domestic genealogy, Wheaton's genealogy leads the other by a few years at every interval. Moreover, due at least in part to Wheaton, his genealogy moves toward conceptual coherence while its domestic counterpart moves in the other direction.

The second element in Wheaton's construction of the liberal world was substantiation of an international society grounded in law and specific to Europe. He was hardly alone in working out the properties of such a society. It might better be said that he completed a conceptual development that Wolff had initiated and Vattel advanced. In the process, he helped to eliminate a long history of confusion over natural law and how it relates to positive law.

For Wolff, natural law came in two forms – necessary law and voluntary law – the latter inferred from the former to suit particular circumstances. Not only did Vattel defend this distinction. Making the former "the inner law of conscience," and the latter truly voluntary, he reinforced it. At the same time and somewhat contradictorily, he gave the voluntary law, now indistinguishable from positive law, the ascendant position in the practical affairs of states, even as he continued to profess his belief in natural law principles.

Consistent with natural law in two forms, Wolff held there to exist a "natural society" ordained by the necessary law and, beyond that, a *civitas maxima*, or great republic, comporting with voluntary law. Vattel famously repudiated the latter but not the former. Andrew Carty has argued that this act was tantamount to repudiating the possibility of an actual international society, because the natural society that remains consists solely of individuals, human or corporate, free to do as they wish.[15] With natural law confined to conscience, it is hard to fault the conclusion that Vattel's natural society is strictly notional. Carty is wrong, however, to think it applies equally to Vattel's successors.

This conclusion *does* apply to British writers such as Jeremy Bentham and John Austin, whose unqualified positivism has had such doctrinal importance, though less in Wheaton's time than in retrospect. For them, the concept

14 For details, see Onuf and Onuf, *Federal Union, Modern World*, pp. 197–211.

15 A. Carty, *The Decay of International Law? A Reappraisal of the Limits of Legal Imagination in International Affairs*, Manchester: Manchester University Press, 1986, pp. 16–17, 68.

of any society among states, natural or otherwise, was entirely vacuous. Wheaton's reaction to Bentham and Austin helps to make it clear why Carty is mistaken about writers who kept a place, no matter how limited, for natural law. True to Vattel, Wheaton honored natural law as one "branch" of international law, and he limited it by making the positive law a separate branch.[16]

Vattel had no doubt that an actual international society existed in his time, and that this society had existed for some time. Curiously, he never troubled to provide a basis for it in positive law, perhaps because most Enlightenment thinkers took its existence for granted. Instead, he evoked the time-honored practices of Europe's many sovereigns and their agents, which, by fostering a balance of power among the chief of these sovereigns, brought stability and prosperity to the "Republic of Europe." (For more on this, see Chapter 20, above.) Notwithstanding the convulsions that France had brought upon Europe in the intervening years, Wheaton adopted Vattel's position that Europe constituted an actual international society.[17] He also took a step that neither Vattel nor, as far as I have been able to determine, anyone else before him had taken. In his Preface to the third edition of *Elements* (the first revised edition, 1846), he identified a specifically juridical basis for a distinctively European international law.

On Wheaton's account, the law of nations had its origins in the Middle Ages, thanks to two developments.[18] First, the "Christian states of Europe" were drawn together by the moral authority of the Latin Church. Codified in the 13th century, canon law enhanced that authority by guiding "decisions of the Church in public as well as private controversies." The second development was the "revival of the study of Roman law, and the adoption of this system of jurisprudence by nearly all the nations of Christendom, either as the basis of their municipal codes, or as subsidiary to the local legislation in each country." Wheaton could not have made his point more clearly: "The origin of the law of nations may thus be traced to these two principal sources, – the canon law and the Roman civil law."

After the Reformation "undermined one of the bases of this universal jurisprudence," namely, canon law, jurists "continued to appeal to the Roman civil law, as constituting the general code of civilized nations."[19] The idea of "universal jurisprudence" has less significance than it might seem in this

16 Wheaton, *Elements of International Law*, p. 47.

17 Nor was he alone. As Onuma Yasuaki has pointed out, many writers in the late 18th and 19th centuries took Europe as the frame of reference for their treatments of international law. "When Was the Law of International Society Born? – An Inquiry of the History of International Law as Seen from an Intercivilizational Perspective," *Journal of the History of International Law*, vol. 2, 2000, pp. 38–9.

18 Preface to the Third Edition (1846), reprinted in H. Wheaton, *Elements of International Law*, Oxford: Clarendon, 1936, photo-reproducing 8th edn (1866), p. xiv. All quotations to follow in this paragraph are from ibid.

19 Ibid.

context. For Wheaton, European international law is universal only to the extent that its "sources" reflect an ancient tradition of universalizing discourse. Roman civil law did not supply universally valid rules so much as it supplied analogies which, by informing practice among European nations, contributed to the emergence of customary rules of European international law.

Wheaton's use of such terms as *Christian* and *civilized* is also less important than it seems. Their presence in the Preface to the third edition is an incidental effect of the way that Wheaton corroborated the specifically European ancestry and reach of international law. In that text, Wheaton's main concern was eminently secular and practically oriented. He wanted to provide European international society with a solid foundation in law, not as a substitute for the balance of power to which Vattel had granted such importance, but as a complement to the balance as a source of stability. These terms are also found in the original edition of *Elements*, for example, where Wheaton specifically argued against the universality of international law: "The public law, with slight exceptions, has always been, and still is, limited to the civilized and Christian people in Europe or to those of European origin."[20] With the Preface to the third edition as a guide, it should be clear that Wheaton used these terms without the lofty pretensions of superiority which, later in the century, their use all too typically conveyed.

It cannot be said that Wheaton was entirely free of these pretensions. Consider the following:

> If the international discourse of Europe, and the nations of European descent, has been since [Grotius] marked by superior humanity, justice and liberality, in comparison with the usage of the other branches of the human family, this glorious superiority must be mainly attributed to these private teachers of justice [such as Grotius], to whose authority Sovereigns and States are often compelled to bow, and whom they acknowledge as the ultimate arbiters of their controversies in peace.[21]

Yet even here, the claim of superiority is incidental to the claim that the jurists whose genealogy Wheaton was so careful to document, and who drew so resourcefully on Roman law and ancient authority, had made European international law into the effective system of order that it had become over the preceding two centuries.

Practically speaking, Wheaton considered natural law less a repository of specific, universally valid rules than a conditioning presence, shared by canon, Roman and international law and shaping successive generations of

20 Wheaton, *Elements of International Law*, 1st edn, p. 18. Also, see G.W. Gong, *The Standard of "Civilization" in International Society*, Oxford: Clarendon Press, 1984, p. 27, who also quoted this passage on the way to showing that the term *civilization* acquired practical and legal significance only much later.

21 Wheaton, Preface to the Third Edition, pp. xv–xvi.

juridical craft. Thus his definition of international law seems almost to make a virtue of ambiguity:

> The law of nations, or international law, as understood among civilized, Christian nations, may be defined as consisting of those rules of conduct which reason deduces, as consonant to justice, from the nature of the society existing among independent nations; with such definitions and modifications as may be established by general consent.[22]

Once defining international law in such process-oriented terms, Wheaton introduced Bentham's and Austin's famously rule-oriented objection that international law, backed as it is by "moral sanctions," is law only "by an analogical extension of the term."[23] Equipped with an opportunity to reject this claim, Wheaton proceeded to ignore it.[24]

He did so undoubtedly because he agreed with Bentham and Austin about the kind of sanctions that both branches of international law depend on to work.[25] Conceived as an integral development over many centuries, the rules of international law and the sanctions backing them up are specific to European international society. Moreover, Wheaton failed to see why anyone should be bothered by the claim that international law qualifies as law only by analogy. In itemizing the sources of international law, he observed that treaties embody rules that "are familiarly called *laws* by analogy to the proper use of the term."[26] One of Wheaton's contemporaries, J.L. Klüber, went so far as to list analogies as a source of international law.[27] Clearly these writers saw the use of analogy, not as a threat to the integrity of international law, but a mark of its distinctive status. Reciting the sources of international law, as I suggested above, has the same effect.

State recognition is yet another mechanism for insuring the independence, and perhaps the primacy, of international society as a legal order. Neither Klüber nor, at least initially, Wheaton conceived of it as such.[28] Citing Klüber, Wheaton observed in 1836 that a state acquires sovereignty when "it separates itself lawfully from the community of which it previously formed a part, and on which it was dependent."[29] Begged is the question,

22 Wheaton, *Elements of International Law*, 1st edn, p. 46. Wheaton took this definition, almost word for word, from James Madison, who penned it while US Secretary of State.

23 Ibid., p. 47, quoting Austin.

24 For a striking contrast much later in the century, see T.A. Walker, *A History of the Law of Nations*, vol. 1, Cambridge: Cambridge University Press, 1899, pp. 2–19.

25 Also, see Wheaton, *Elements of International Law*, 1st edn, p. 44, where he affirmed "amicable or vindictive retaliation" in support of international law.

26 Wheaton, *Elements of International Law*, 1st edn, p. 49, his emphasis.

27 J.L. Klüber, *Droit des gens moderne de l'Europe*, Stuttgart: J.G. Cotta, 1819, pp. 17–18.

28 See C.H. Alexandrowicz, "The Theory of Recognition *in Fieri*," *British Year Book of International Law*, vol. 34, 1958, p. 176, on the early history of recognition, with particular attention to Klüber (pp. 187–9) and Wheaton (pp. 192–5).

29 Wheaton, *Elements of International Law*, 1st edn, p. 70.

whose law? – nature's, international society's, the aforesaid community's? Wheaton meant the community's law, as his discussion of Latin America confirms: "where a revolted province or colony has declared, and shown its ability to maintain its independence, the recognition of its sovereignty by other foreign states is a question of policy and prudence only."[30] For Wheaton, as a US citizen, this is a surprisingly conservative position.[31] A decade later he developed a new position on recognition better suited to the liberal world on conceptual as well as policy grounds.

The revised edition of *Elements* (1846) invokes the now familiar distinction between internal and external sovereignty before turning to recognition.[32] Internal sovereignty is a matter of constitutional law, and external sovereignty of international law. "The internal sovereignty of a State does not, in any degree, depend on its recognition by other States."[33] Wheaton then concluded that the US obtained internal sovereignty by declaring independence in 1776.

"The external sovereignty of any State, on the other hand, may require recognition by other States to render it perfect and complete." It is through recognition that a new state enters the "great society of nations," which has now clearly become Wheaton's frame of reference. Nevertheless, other states are "at liberty to grant, or refuse, this recognition" as they see fit, and recognition is not perfect until it has become "universal."[34] Wheaton's concise exposition definitively captures the tension between recognition's declaratory and constitutive properties. In a fully liberal world, no membership rule could be otherwise.[35]

A final element in Wheaton's construction of the liberal world is the systematic rendition of its rules in the language of rights. Here we find no doctrine

30 Ibid., p. 74. For Klüber, state practice led him to view recognition as a "declaratory act dictated by the requirements of political expediency." Quoting Alexandowicz, "The Theory of Recognition *in Fieri*," p. 188.

31 Alexandrowicz called it a "legitimist" position, consistent with old world practice. Ibid., p. 194. On the political complexities of recognizing new republics in the Americas, see J.E. Lewis, Jr., *The American Union and the Problem of Neighborhood: The United States and the Collapse of the Spanish Empire, 1783–1829*, Chapel Hill: University of North Carolina Press, 1998, chs. 4–6.

32 Wolff had no clear conception of external sovereignty. While Vattel possessed just such a conception, he did not specifically distinguish between internal and external sovereignty. Onuf, *The Republican Legacy in International Thought*, pp. 75–6, 164–6. Klüber drew no such distinction. G.W.F. Hegel did so in 1821 but with little elaboration. *Elements of the Philosophy of Right*, trans. H.B. Nisbet, Cambridge: Cambridge University Press, 1991, paras. 278, 315, pp. 321, 359.

33 H. Wheaton, *Elements of International Law*, 3rd edn, Philadelphia: Lea & Blanchard, 1846, p. 56; *Elements of International Law*, 8th edn, p. 28.

34 Wheaton, *Elements of International Law*, 3rd edn, p. 57; *Elements of International Law*, 8th edn, p. 28.

35 Alexandowicz, "The Theory of Recognition *in Fieri*," pp. 195–6, suggested that Hegel may have influenced the development of Wheaton's position on recognition. While Wheaton was steeped in German intellectual developments, any influence specifically due to Hegel seems

as such. Furthermore, the expository format of his treatise strikingly resembles the format that Klüber had used in his treatise some years earlier. Gone from both is the language of perfect and imperfect rights, with its Aristotelian resonance and long history from Grotius to Vattel.

Instead we have absolute and conditional rights.[36] Klüber and Wheaton agreed that self-preservation, independence and equality are absolute rights, and presented them in just this order. Klüber thought that property is a conditional right, but Wheaton classified it as absolute. For both writers, the rights and duties of states that constitute the bulk of the positive law are conditional. As Wheaton put it, states are entitled to these rights "under particular circumstances"; they "arise from international relations existing either in peace or war."[37]

After careful analysis of Klüber's treatment of absolute and conditional rights, Koskenniemi concluded that, in the end, Klüber made natural law secondary to positive law.[38] Koskenniemi's best evidence for this judgement is to be found, however, in Klüber's discussion of the sources of international law. There he considered natural law a source only when positive law did not suffice.[39] Wheaton's discussion of sources listed natural law first and without qualification. Nevertheless, for reasons already discussed, he did not want to make natural law primary except in a formal, notional sense.

The way that Wheaton defined international law, presented its sources, and then ordered rights from absolute to conditional creates a firm structure of two levels. In recognition of Wheaton's vocation as a constitutional lawyer, we might call it higher law in the sense that a constitution is.[40] In effect, natural law grants international society a liberal constitution. Within the broad reach and permissive terms of that constitution, states' agents are free to conduct themselves as they see fit except insofar as they collectively agree to limit their conduct. They interpret those limits subjectively as rights, and

unlikely. The latter said in his brief remarks on international law that the "state has an absolute and primary entitlement to be a sovereign *in the eyes of others*, i.e., *to be recognized* by them." Hegel conceded that this entitlement is "purely formal" and "abstract"; actual recognition "depends on the perception and will of the other state." Hegel granted recognition a declaratory role but not the constitutive one that Wheaton also provided for. As "the absolute power on *earth*," Hegel's state makes itself. Nothing could be further from Wheaton's assumptions about the society of states. Hegel, *Elements of the Philosophy of Right*, para. 331, p. 366, emphasis in translation.

36 But see Wheaton, *Elements of International Law*, 1st edn, p. 151. Positive law can modify an absolute right in respect to the "mode of its exercise"; on the authority of Grotius, Pufendorf and Vattel, such a right is imperfect.

37 Ibid., p. 81.

38 Koskenniemi, *From Apology to Utopia*, pp. 108–111.

39 Klüber, *Droit des gens moderne de l'Europe*, p. 18; Koskenniemi, *From Apology to Utopia*, p. 110.

40 See, further, Onuf, *The Republican Legacy in International Thought*, ch. 7. On levels, see ibid., ch. 8.

regard them objectively as binding rules, for which the term *law* seems entirely appropriate.[41]

Wheaton's firm structure of law in two levels makes international society analogous to the US as a legal order. The contents of the top level make international society liberal in a more thorough-going way than the Constitution makes the US a liberal state. The timeliness and simplicity of Wheaton's conception help to account for its quick ascendancy, and the advantages that it conferred on liberal societies organized as independent states help to account for its remarkable staying power.

This sketch hardly includes all the elements that the liberal world needed to achieve conceptual coherence. Rubin is surely right to insist that the development of private international law at just this time is highly significant.[42] That Joseph Story – US Supreme Court Justice and Wheaton's patron – wrote the first great treatise on conflict of laws in 1834 is telling. I close, however, on a speculative note.

Why has this simple conceptual scheme to lock the liberal world in place, retrospectively so obvious, garnered so little attention? I suggest that British intellectual tastes are responsible. Clearly British positivism fails to capture the distinctively liberal character of international society because it leaves no place for international society of any kind. The so-called Grotian tradition hopelessly muddles the relation of natural law to positive law and, in so doing, it loses all sight of the relation between law of any kind and the liberal world.[43] Behind these intellectual failures is the misguided assumption that British liberalism provided the template for the liberal world in the 19th century. Thanks in large measure to Wheaton, the template for a liberal legal order among states came from across the Atlantic, where liberalism found its greatest support in constitutional practice.

41 Wheaton, *Elements of International Law*, 3rd edn, p. 57; *Elements of International Law*, 8th edn, p. 28.

42 Rubin, *Ethics and Authority in International Law*, pp. 130–5.

43 For a comprehensive review and critique, see B. Kingsbury and A. Roberts, "Introduction: Grotian Thought in International Relations," in H. Bull *et al.* (eds), *Hugo Grotius and International Relations*, Oxford: Clarendon, 1990.

25 A virtual interview conducted by Professor Onuma's students in Tokyo (2002)

After my favorable review of Onuma Yasuaki's edited volume on Grotius (Chapter 21), I made Onuma's acquaintance at annual meetings of the American Society of International Law. In 1999, I spent an academic year teaching in Kyoto. While I was in Japan, Onuma and I spent quite a bit of time together traveling in the country, and he invited me to present my work to his colleagues and graduate students in the Tokyo University's Faculty of Law. I was pleased to learn that he routinely assigned my long essay on "Global-Law-Making and Legal Thought" (of which Chapter 6, above, is an early, incomplete draft) in his international law seminar. Three years later, he encouraged his students to contact me in preparation for their discussion of this essay, and they sent me a list of questions for my clarification or elaboration. In the circumstance I would have responded seriously even if the questions had been silly. But they were not. They reflected a careful reading of the assigned text – which is difficult enough – and of my 1989 book, *World of Our Making*, which my English-speaking associates tell me is also difficult reading. Furthermore, the Tokyo students had read a recent article in the *Columbia Journal of Transnational Law* in which my work figures, but which I had not seen.

In responding to the students' questions and, in the process, to the way my work had been characterized in the article, I took the opportunity to restate my position on several of the most central issues for international legal theory and to consider how my views might have changed over the years. Onuma reported that the seminar discussion went very well. Here I have edited the students' questions for style and made a few small changes in my responses.

Two species of law

Question: In the article Professor Onuma asked us to read, you say:

> We have derived from the sociologies of Durkheim and Weber two characterizations of law as different from each other as they are from

> Austinian law. Neither characterization excludes the other. . . . They are characterizations of law typical of two different species of law.[1]

(1) Why do two characterizations of law – law as standard solutions (derived from Durkheim) and law as lawyer's artifacts (derived from Weber) – result in the *two* different species of law? Or, since "[n]either characterization excludes the other," do you mean that all laws have Durkheimian and Weberian properties in various proportions?

(2) Do these characterizations and species exhaust all possible characterizations, or species, of law? Aren't there any other possibilities, inspired perhaps by other sociologists?

Answer: I appropriated the term *species* from John Austin to emphasize that we should not treat international law as a systemic whole with homogeneous functional properties.[2] This is of course how Austin treated law and, in so doing, excluded international law from the "province of law." Austin's opponents always accepted this general orientation, with the result that they cast about for a set of distinctive properties that would make international law "truly" law and yet still separate it from law in general. Hans Kelsen solved the problem by proposing a general theory of law (more specifically, of legal rules), and Myres McDougal by denying that international law has distinctive properties when considered as process (and not as a body of rules).

While I sympathized with Kelsen's general theoretical aspirations and insistence that rules are existentially central to social reality, I also took to heart McDougal's claim, reflecting his own background in legal realism, that social process is a matter of agents acting on their goals in complex patterns of interaction. And finally, I accepted and developed Richard Falk's intuition that rules occupy different categories depending on the function that they perform for the agents putting them to use and thus for the system of relations among agents. Taking this view beyond anything Falk had proposed, I held that different functional categories meant that rules in each category have distinctive properties, allowing them to fulfill that function, but not others. Hence *species* – a term highly suggestive for someone working as extensively with anthropological materials, and as influenced by sociological functionalism (especially Durkheim), as I was then.

I was soon dissatisfied with these claims, and revised them substantially

1 "Global Law-Making and Legal Thought," in Onuf (ed.), *Law-Making in the Global Community*, Durham, NC: Carolina Academic Press, 1982, p. 39. In an earlier version of this passage, I had used the term *kind* instead of *species*. See Chapter 6, above.

2 J. Austin, *The Province of Jurisprudence Determined, and The Uses of the Study of Jurisprudence*, 1832, 1863 eds, ed. by H.L.A. Hart, London: Weidenfeld and Nicolson, 1954, Lecture I.

in my 1985 piece in the *Harvard International Law Journal* (Chapter 14, above). There I turned to ordinary language philosophy, and especially to speech act theory, to revise and extend my functional categories for rules, now conceptualized as instruction-rules (this category contains both the Durkheimian and Weberian species/categories); directive-rules (this is the Austinian–Kelsenian category of "command") and commitment-rules (rules inferred from the claimed existence of rights and duties). These categories follow from the existence of three primary categories of speech acts (assertives, directives, commissives), which I show to be functionally differentiated in the most basic ontological terms (word-to-world fit). I subsequently elaborated a philosophical and social theoretic framework to reflect this new configuration of categories (no longer described as species) and their existential consequences in my 1989 book, *World of Our Making* (with which I brought a fully articulated version of constructivist social theory to the field of international relations).

To reply directly to (1), insofar as a rule has a definite existence (as a Durkheimian social fact), it can be shown to have properties that place it squarely and fully in one category. Given the abundance of rules in all categories and in all degrees of formality and scope, no situation is ever to be characterized solely by reference to one category of rules. There are tendencies, however, in the mass of rules and related practices, about which we can generalize. For example, Japan has generally (typically) relied more on instruction-rules than on directive- and commitment-rules, such as we find so abundantly in the US. The system of international legal rules consists of a small set of very general and formal instruction-rules (summarily coded as sovereignty) ordering a panoply of commitment-rules (rights and duties of states), but no directive-rules to speak of.

As for (2), I do claim, fervently but no doubt tendentiously, that my threefold scheme does exhaust the possible categories for social rules. Note that I cast this discussion in the broadest possible terms; legal rules are a subset of social rules marked, or set apart, by their formality and generality; these are conventional if protean criteria. I do reject the standard positivist association of legal rule with sanction. All rules are intended to induce a behavioral response (agents are supposed to follow them, but may not do so for good and sufficient reasons). Yet rules do so in functionally different ways, depending on the category that they fall within (here see *World of Our Making*, ch. 4).

Positivism

Question: (1) In the article, are there two kinds of positivism – simple positivism and pure positivism – or just one positivism (positivist doctrine) pure and simple? Is positivism synonymous with positivist doctrine?

(2) If there is only positivist doctrine, are you trying to get rid of it altogether?

If there are two kinds of positivism, are you trying to get rid of both, or only pure positivism?

(3) Professors Brunnée and Toope speak of Onuf's "positivist bias in reading international law" in their article, "International Law and Constructivism."[3] Are they correct?

(4) Isn't your method positivistic because you identify laws using criteria external to those laws?

(5) The external approach toward the identification of law seems to have difficulty in explaining the validity of law. How can the two species of law be validated? Or, are they not to be validated at all?

Answer: (1) In the article you read, I distinguish between positivist doctrine and practice, the former largely deductive, the latter inductive.[4] Given my theoretical concerns in the article, I should guess that most of my unqualified remarks about positivism refer to positivist doctrine (I have not reread the article in many years). From a constructivist point of view, this distinction is undoubtedly artificial, and I would be disinclined to retain it except as an historical artifact already evident in Grotius and his methodological remarks about natural law.[5]

(2) I do not accept the severe limitations of positivist doctrine, whether Austin's, Kelsen's or H.L.A. Hart's, but I think analytical positivists are very helpful in getting us to think about stable patterns of rule-mediated social relations, or systems and their properties, even if they mistakenly concern themselves with systems that are defined exclusively by "legal" criteria.

(3) Now that I have had a chance to read the few pages that Brunnée and Toope have devoted to my work, I am not altogether certain what they mean by positivist. If they think that I am a positivist because I believe that rules have an ontological status as social facts, then they are right about my beliefs and perhaps also right to call me a positivist in philosophical terms. Nevertheless, this is a thorny, highly controversial matter beyond the scope of my remarks here, and I do believe that I have adequately defended my version of constructivism as postpositivist in *World of Our Making*, ch. 1 (and see Chapters 13 and 14, above, and Chapter 28, below).

3 J. Brunnée and S. J. Toope, "International Law and Constructivism," *Columbia Journal of Transnational Law*, vol. 39, 2000, p. 41.

4 "Global Law-Making and Legal Thought," pp. 1–6. This material postdates the draft essay, forming Chapter 6.

5 Tadashi T., "Grotius's Concept of Law," in Onuma Y. (ed.), *A Normative Approach to War: Peace, War, and Justice in Hugo Grotius*, Oxford: Clarendon, 1993, pp. 41–3.

If Brunnée and Toope mean that I am a positivist in a more mundane, legalistic sense, it is difficult for me to see how this is possible, since I am so clearly committed to the proposition that rules are "binding" in degree. One of the central tents of philosophical and legal positivism is that facts and values/norms constitute separate and readily distinguishable categories. While I agree that linguistic competence enables us to distinguish between *is* and *ought* with no difficulty, I also hold that we traffic between is and ought so routinely as to make the distinction meaningless *in practice*. Insofar as Brunnée and Toope espouse Lon Fuller's version of naturalism, conceptualized by reference to "internal morality," they are talking about processes of internalization and socialization that Talcott Parsons long ago brought to attention in social theory (by reference to Durkheim and Weber) and that constructivists in general have emphasized.

Fuller's tendency to find normativity "in the air" is just the sort of mushy imprecision that this kind of talk encourages, and that a good dose of analytical positivism corrects, without making anyone into an unacknowledged positivist. What Brunnée and Toope mean when they further define "legal legitimacy" by reference to "the specificity of legal rationality, a specificity generated in large measure by rhetorical practices," I did not read enough of the article to find out, but it sure sounds to me as if any such specificity brings positivism in *some* form back into the picture.[6] Even members of the Critical Legal Studies movement and postmodern scholars in other fields routinely slip into positivist or philosophical realist modes of expression to avoid total subjectivity or solipsism.

(4) I am not sure what difference it makes in theoretical/doctrinal terms that legal rules are identified as such by external vs. internal criteria. Agents must know how to characterize the positive items in their world (otherwise these items have no ontological status – they do not *exist*), and we as observers know how agents do this, mostly by virtue of what they say; when agents learn what observers have to say about what agents have to say, observers become agents for the system of relations in question; inside and outside are relative conditions for agents and observers.

(5) Again, I may be missing the point, but I fail to see why inside/outside should matter with respect to validity, which agents and observers are disposed to ascertain in order to reassure themselves that putative rules are the correct rules, that is, applicable to the circumstances that agents find themselves in (scope). I do concede that informal instruction-rules (both kinds – Durkheimian and Weberian) lack a clear relation to other rules that would validate them; this is precisely what informality means and why it is an incentive for agents to make rules more formal (more readily identifiable as legal).

6 Brunnée and Toope, "International Law and Constructivism," Abstract, p. 19.

Properties of law

Question: At one point in the same article you present law as a random sequence of events leading unexpectedly to order.[7] Can such a material, de facto order be equated with law? Doesn't law have its own properties, which cannot be reduced to the mere result of the aggregation of similar conduct?

Answer: A random sequence presumably permits no inference about purpose, intent or cause. As David Hume made clear, such a state of affairs lacks normative potential. Nevertheless, even the appearance of a pattern, however illusory or epiphenomenal, can induce an inference about causal consistency and normative implications. Hume described the process of inference from an apparently consistent pattern as the source of conventions. Many scholars, including me, hold that conventions are only weakly normative, but that they become more strongly normative as agents make inferences from other agents' ascription of normativity to these conventions, thereby making them into customary rules. Even then they may lack the formality and generality needed for us (agents, observers) to characterize them as legal rules (and by doing so we contribute to making them such).

Relations between law and human behavior

Question: Criticizing the prevailing methodologies of legal science, you argue that it is more important to know that legal artifacts reflect social realities than to reveal the influence of law on the course of behaviors.[8] What kind of relations are there between existing, recognized law and human conduct? Is the influence of already established law on subsequent practices negligible?

Answer: The point I was making here was in the context of a generally sympathetic rendition of behaviorist learning theory in relation to legal realism. While I heartily concur with the empirical proposition that agents normally respond to rules by following them, and that this empirical generalization underlies learning theory from John Locke and Jeremy Bentham down to 20th century behaviorism, I also wanted to make it clear that agents can always choose between following rules or not, and that the pattern of rule

7 What I did say is that "law *could be treated* as a random sequence of events leading unexpectedly to order." "Global Law-Making and Legal Thought," p. 57, emphasis added. See pp. 49–51 for such a treatment, albeit in highly qualified terms. Again, this material postdates the draft, forming Chapter 6, above.

8 Ibid., p. 73:

> To assume that legal artifacts conform to behavior might be the first step in developing systematic research on law-making; indeed it was the first step taken in these pages to develop a framework for the study of global law-making freed from positivist assumptions.

following affects the rules (here styled "legal artifacts"). I would suggest that the impact of subsequent practice is never negligible, although often invisible in the case of rule-affirming practice. In constructivist terms, rules are the recursive medium through which agents and structures constitute each other; rules define conditions of agency and give structure its institutional specificity; as such, rules change as agents and structures affect each other, even if the relevant change is to strengthen the rules in question.

The Notion of *Order*

Question: In *World of Our Making*, you explicitly condemn the notion of *order* as follows:

> [I]nvoking the problem of order is a rhetorical strategy which, by metaphorically associating order, nature, and social arrangements, serves to disguise another problem, no less "real" (once we understand the construction of reality) than the problem of order. This is the problem of privilege. (p. 128).

Was your view the same when you wrote "Global Law-Making and Legal Thought," or did you change your view?

Answer: This question quite correctly points up an inconsistency in my work or, I would prefer to say, points to a change in view. I had routinely used the phrase *international legal order* in my early work. (See, for example, "International Legal Order as an Idea," Chapter 9 above, written after "Global Law-Making and Legal Thought," but appearing in print three years earlier). In doing so, I had accepted rather unreflectively both my Kelsenian training and the world order concerns of my associates at Princeton. During the 1980s I had immersed myself in Western Marxist and postpositivist texts, which sensitized me to the buried normative assumptions in the term *order*. I chose the term *arrangements* as a substitute because it makes clear that agents are responsible for rules forming the conditions of rule, even if they hide behind the claim that orders are, or can be, spontaneous or natural states of affairs. It is quite correct to conclude that I am hostile to the unreflective use of the term *order*, even though I now occasionally use it in contexts where the pattern of agency and responsibility is entirely clear.

The actual identification of rules of international law

Question: (1) How can standard solutions actually be identified, especially in such areas as that of human rights law, where there are no universally accepted standard solutions?

And (2) how can lawyers' artifacts be rules of international law when such artifacts, as products of UN General Assembly resolutions, are not universally accepted?

Answer: (1) By and large I would say that human rights rules are not standard solutions whose normative impact arises from the consensus view of technicians (bureaucrats, staff lawyers) working in functionally differentiated environments. Instead, they are Weberian artifacts, or instruction-rules of high formality and generality, whose normative impact stems from their connection to other universalizing moral claims (the great ethical systems of the West). I develop this connection in an article called "Everyday Ethics in International Relations."[9]

(2) The legal status of Weberian artifacts is typically contested by the relevant functionaries. Human rights rules are a notable case in point. Notice that opponents will shift their ground because they have changed their minds (whether as a matter of principle or for instrumental reasons) or because they fail to see any normative significance in doing so (they believe that these artifacts are normatively irrelevant because they do not conform to the "command" model of law). Insofar as artifacts are contested, their normative impact is weakened. Here, recall my firm belief that normativity (binding power, obligation) is always relative – always a matter of degree. It is beside the point to ask whether something – some artifact, or social fact – is international law in the sense of assigning it to the correct category when the scheme of categories is itself problematic.

9 N. Onuf, "Everyday Ethics in International Relations," *Millennium: Journal of International Studies*, vol. 27, 1999, pp. 669–93.

26 Normative frameworks for humanitarian intervention (2002)

In 2000, Wayne Sandholtz asked me to participate in a Symposium series on "The Norms and Ethics of Humanitarian Intervention" at the University of California, Irvine. I was glad for the chance to consider a recently revived practice that I had given passing attention to years before (Chapter 7, above) – and especially to consider its origin at a time in the early 19th century when liberalism took hold. Thanks to a conversation with Onuma Yasuaki and Jörg Fisch about the abolition of *sati*, or widow-burning, in British India (a matter Fisch had recently studied), I realized that this striking episode in British imperial history coincided with two other closely related developments: the crystallization of nonintervention as an emblematically liberal principle of international law and claims on behalf of humanitarian invention as a warranted exception to this principle. Further investigation revealed a rising tide of humanitarian sentiment in liberal societies after 1815, most obviously manifest in the abolition movement. Yet this surge of liberal activism was not generally articulated in the language of human rights. I revised my paper, called "Humanitarian Intervention: The Early Years," for publication in a planned symposium volume. Neither the book nor my paper went anywhere until one of my former students saw to the latter's publication in the *Florida Journal of International Law* (2005).

Meanwhile Anthony Lang asked if I might contribute to a volume he was editing on *Just Intervention* (2003). I took the opportunity to adapt and combine some of the material from my paper on humanitarian intervention with work underway for a book my brother Peter and I were writing. While some of what appears below also appears in that book (*Nations, Markets, and War*, 2006), the discussion of modernity by reference to three normative frameworks appears nowhere else.

In recent years, millions of people have experienced great hardship, injury and loss – not least, loss of life – in circumstances that have been politically charged and well-publicized. War can cause suffering on this scale, and we can count the many wars that have done so. Indeed, we might wish to say that any great calamity that some people inflict on other people is war. Yet we only say this for a rhetorical flourish, because the term war refers generally to a situation where two parties knowingly choose courses of action that will cause great suffering on both sides. Few instances of massive human suffering in recent years fit this general description. People suffer on a scale that we associate with war but not as parties to war.

That war has the properties it does is an institutional fact of the modern world. Several centuries ago people in Western Europe began to put their traditional ways of life behind them. In doing so they saw themselves and their world as modern. Change is an institutional fact of the modern world, and the global reach of the modern world today is one of its consequences. Institutional facts always have normative implications. In the instance of war, at least some of these implications are so formal and extensive that we know them as the law of war – a body of rules said to be authored by and binding on states. These rules are predicated on the assumption that governments do not conduct war against their own people unless the latter have themselves organized for war. Yet governments and other organizations have made a mockery of this assumption. How then are we to think about one-party wars, bring our normative resources to bear on them, and prevent them from happening?

What can we do? When we see massive suffering, we can intervene on humanitarian grounds. Most of us would say that the victims have been denied their human rights. Whether we invoke the body of rules that tell us what these rights are and how they operate, or refashion the law of war to include these rights, we take advantage of one obvious normative resource, but not the only one or perhaps even the best one.

The burden of this essay is to show that we have other such resources available to us. We are only able to appreciate what these resources are by standing back and locating them within the largely implicit normative frameworks that we draw upon to make moral sense of the world that we have made for ourselves. On first look, we see two frameworks, which give liberalism and socialism their moral content. On second look, we can see the outlines of an older, more encompassing framework – one that is rich in history but recessive today. It has long given republicanism its moral content, and it presents us even now with normative resources that we may too easily overlook when we are confronted with massive human suffering.

Constructing frameworks

Who is this we? What do we mean by our *world*? After all, one can speak of the modern world, of the whole world, and of many worlds, in the same breath.[1] We know that these variant terms are imprecise and ambiguously

1 See R.B.J. Walker's important book, *One World, Many Worlds: Struggle for a Just World Peace*, Boulder, CO: Lynne Rienner, 1988.

related but evocative. It is these very properties that make such terms so suitable for our rhetorical needs. When we wish to be more precise, few terms come to mind. The term *civilization* is even more evocative than *world*, more laden with affective resonance. Samuel Huntington's alarm over the "clash of civilizations" offers a notorious example.[2] Joining these terms – *civilized world, world civilization* – compounds the rhetorical effect with no gain in precision, and perhaps some loss.

An alternative term is *paradigm*. Although hardly free of ambiguity, its use by scholars in many fields suggests a core meaning sufficiently precise to orient their goals and projects in some larger context. A paradigm provides a coherently articulated set of goals, standards and activities to anyone willing to accept them as a set. Adopting a paradigm supplies a firm but not completely fixed relation between one's goals and projects and those of anyone else who has adopted the same paradigm. The term implies a reasonable division of labor, a basis for evaluating one's own and others' activities, and a sense of belonging and achievement.

In the usual conception, observers take their paradigms to be about the world as an objective reality. This world has a discernibly coherent structure. Within paradigms, progress means an ever-closer fit between the world under study and the contents of the paradigm. When competing paradigms offer accounts of the world that are either incomplete or incompatible, a new, more inclusive paradigm better fit to the world, signifies a higher order of progress.

Missing from this standard conception is any sense that some paradigms fit the world as well as they do because they make the world what it is – they contribute at least some of the structure that they tell us to look for. Our world is a world of our making, but not entirely. There are as many worlds as there are paradigms of this sort, but none of these worlds is unrelated to any other.[3] To distinguish these paradigms from the ones that observers believe to be simply, or merely, about the world, we might follow Sheldon Wolin by calling them operative paradigms.[4]

Operative paradigms constitute worlds within worlds, ways of life within the form of life common to the human species. The modern world is distinctively a world of its own because it is an operative paradigm of remarkable power, coherence and durability – the very properties that we typically attribute to a civilization. Yet this world is hardly uniform across its structure because too many of us have had a hand, or a say, in its making. It is also less

2 S.P. Huntington, *The Clash of Civilizations and the Remaking of World Order*, New York: Simon & Schuster, 1996.

3 I advance this claim and address its many conceptual implications in *World of Our Making: Rules and Rule in Social Theory and International Relations*, Columbia: University of South Carolina Press, 1989.

4 S. Wolin, "Paradigms and Political Theories," in G. Gutting (ed.), *Paradigms and Revolutions: Appraisals and Applications of Thomas Kuhn's Philosophy of Science*, Notre Dame: University of Notre Dame Press, 1980, pp. 160–91; Onuf, *World of Our Making*, pp. 14–23.

coherent than we would like to believe.[5] We can identify its distinctive features only in the most general of terms.

According to Anthony Giddens, the distinguishing feature of the modern world is the degree to which we whose world it is think and talk about ourselves, our world and the ways in which we and our conceptions of the world relate to each other. "The reflexivity of modern life consists in the fact that social practices are constantly examined and reformed in light of the incoming information about those very practices, thus constitutively altering their character."[6] We might say that modern reflexivity is heightened paradigm awareness, which is systematically applied to the modern world as an operative paradigm. Correlative features of modernity are a sharp discrimination between subjective and objective states (my world, the world), an instrumental disposition toward the objects of the world, and a religiously freighted belief that the human species is uniquely favored in its ability to reflect on the world, to form goals and plans, and to change the world by carrying them out.

The modern world acquired its distinctive features over the course of two or three centuries: epochal thinking has made a world of an epoch.[7] In the story that we tell (about, to) ourselves, we (here meaning our forebears in northwestern Europe), put tradition behind us (by 1800, perhaps earlier), but only after two or three centuries of sustained effort.[8] Success has meant a dynamic, expanding modern world; the contest between traditional and modern ways continues into the present. Our world has become the whole world, and whatever happens in it is, at least in principle, our business. Of course this epochal story is conveniently simple, self-serving and morally complacent.

Normative complexity in the modern world

Because paradigms provide standards by which to form goals, develop plans and evaluate conduct, they are always normative frameworks. As a normative framework, modernity resists generalization along the lines just indicated. The struggle against tradition is not a simple story of universal truths, systematic thinking and beneficial consequences prevailing over ignorance,

5 On the modern belief that modernity forms, or should be made into, "a coherent and integrated whole," see B. Yack, *The Fetishism of Modernities: Epochal Self-Consciousness in Contemporary Social and Political Thought*, Notre Dame: University of Notre Dame Press, 1997, p. 4 and throughout.

6 A. Giddens, *The Consequences of Modernity*, Stanford: Stanford University Press, 1990, pp. 36–45, quoting p. 38.

7 Yack, *The Fetishism of Modernities*, pp. 17–25.

8 This is a broadly Weberian rendition of the story. See Giddens, *The Consequences of Modernity*, pp. 3–6, 17–21; Yack, *The Fetishism of Modernities*, pp. 30–36; and my *The Republican Legacy of International Thought*, Cambridge: Cambridge University Press, 1998, pp. 18–23.

superstition and benighted practices. Nor is it a simple story of hubris and greed running roughshod over nature and imposing an artificial, homogeneous culture of consumption on a gullible planet. The normative complexity of the modern world, with its discord, indignities, debilities, disasters and despoliation, suggests a selective appreciation of the past and its moral legacy, superabundant standards, mismatched means and ends, and the disjuncture of intentions and consequences. In such a situation, we have to surmise that several operative paradigms variously compete and converge to give modernity its distinctive character.[9]

The early modern world saw the advent of three paradigms operating on a scale sufficient to have the effects just indicated. For present purposes, we might call them normative frameworks, thereby limiting the task of describing their descent, distinctive features and current relevance. Here, given familiar labels – republican, liberal and socialist – they are rarely discussed in a way that makes them normative frameworks in the first instance.[10] Instead they are typically identified as socioeconomic and political theories, ideologies or institutional frameworks, in practice subject to the vicissitudes of history. While it may be fair to say that the republican framework is, politically speaking, recessive and the socialist framework in disarray, it is hardly appropriate to say that the liberal framework has come to define the modern world for all intents and purposes – and least of all for my purposes in this essay.[11]

Early modern thinkers focused on human nature and the human condition. These earnest discussions epitomized modern reflexivity. They also constituted a philosophical anthropology anchored in the art and literature of Classical civilization. Among early modern republican authors as different as Niccolò Machiavelli and Hugo Grotius, it is Grotius to whom we must turn to appreciate republicanism as a normative framework.[12]

"Man is, to be sure, an animal," Grotius observed in 1625:

> but an animal of a superior kind, much farther removed from all other animals than the different kind of animals are from one another; evidence

9 I have deliberately excluded consideration of paradigms operating to give other worlds their distinctive features, and thus the thorny question of whether, or to what extent, our modern paradigms might have drawn from them, or should do so. Nor do I consider whether any complex and lasting world will produce similar versions of the same few paradigms. But see *World of Our Making*, ch. 3, where I suggest that an affirmative answer to the latter question does not mean that cultures, as I call them there, will develop similar features.

10 In *World of Our Making*, pp. 17–22, I also identified three operative paradigms, there labeled *liberalism, Marxism*, and (again following Wolin) *political society*, but emphasized different features than I do here.

11 See F. Fukuyama, *The End of History and the Last Man*, New York: Free Press, 1991, for an egregious example of this practice.

12 See Onuf, *Republican Legacy*, ch. 2, on Machiavellian and Grotian versions of the republican paradigm, there styled Atlantic republicanism and Continental republicanism.

> may be found in the many traits peculiar to the human species. But among the many traits characteristic of man is an impelling desire for society, that is, for the social life.[13]

There is nothing novel in this claim. Grotius immediately signaled his Classical allegiances: "this social trend the Stoics called 'sociability' "; quoting Marcus Aurelius in a footnote, "we were born for fellowship."[14]

The Stoic emphasis on *societas*, or fellowship, set the tone for a republican normative framework for another century and a half. For Thomas Hobbes even to raise questions about the framework prompted Samuel Pufendorf's point-by-point refutation.[15] Society is the "natural state of man," Pufendorf wrote in 1672, "instituted and sanctioned by nature herself without any human intervention" – this is the law of nature, binding on everyone "endowed with reason," just as Grotius had said.[16] Fellowship entails fellow-feeling – "a phrase of this present time" Hobbes called it in Leviathan (1651) – and fellow-feeling, or sympathy, is a natural feature of the human experience.[17] A century later, Adam Smith put a natural disposition toward fellow-feeling at the center of his *Theory of Moral Sentiments* (1759).[18] Indebted no less than Pufendorf to Stoic thought, Smith relied less overtly on natural law for normative support.

We should be clear on what natural sociability entails. We need each other in order to flourish, and to flourish is to be able to act on our plans and achieve our goals individually. This is as much Hobbes's position as it is the position of Grotius, Pufendorf and Smith. A Stoic goes on to say that we should strive for self-sufficiency, even if we can never achieve it fully. An Aristotelian goes on to say that we should orient ourselves to the common good in order to achieve collective self-sufficiency. Both imply that our plans and goals can never be simply our own.

Aristotle's conception of the good life as a life lived not just in common with others, but in mutual support and assistance, is the normative foundation for republicanism in all its variety. If society – the *polis* – is our natural condition, then each of us owes the rest such aid as nature causes them to need and equips us to provide. Nevertheless, we cannot infer a condition of equality from this familiar equation of abilities and needs. Doing what nature

13 H. Grotius, *De jure belli ac pacis libris tres*, trans. by F.W. Kelsey, Washington: Carnegie Institution, 1925, Prolegomena, para. 6, p. 11.

14 Ibid. In the Kelsey translation, *affectus socialis* is rendered *sociableness; sociality* is also often used.

15 S. Pufendorf, *De jure naturae et gentium libri octo*, trans. by C.H. Oldfather and W.A. Oldfather, Oxford: Clarendon, 1934, I, ii, pp. 154–78.

16 Ibid., I, ii, para. 11, p. 175. Grotius, *De jure belli ac pacis*, Prolegomena, paras. 7–10, pp. 11–13.

17 T. Hobbes, *Leviathan*, Cambridge: Cambridge University Press, 1991, I, vi, p. 43.

18 A. Smith, *The Theory of Moral Sentiments*, Oxford: Clarendon, 1976, I, I, i, paras. 3–5, p. 10.

has equipped each of us to do best takes care of most needs collectively but unevenly. Extraordinary need calls for assistance directed specifically to that need.

We cannot find in Aristotle and his republican followers a general duty to come to the aid of others because need is not itself generalizable. Instead, we find them commending a disposition to respond to others' needs. To be thus disposed is a virtue and not a rule of conduct. Stoic thought simultaneously recommended that we individually strive for self-sufficiency and we collectively imagine our social arrangements on the largest scale.[19] The problem here is that universal duties, whether Stoic or Kantian, are too abstract to guide conduct in most situations. Aristotle at least offered two rules – so informal that they are never described as such – to help us know when to act on the disposition to give others our help, and most republicans took these two rules for granted.

First, our assistance to others should not disrupt the natural order of the household writ large; men rank over women, masters over slaves for good reasons. Second, the *polis* as an association of households is naturally self-sufficient; assistance beyond its confines defeats the point. Even Cicero, a Stoic of enormous importance to early modern writers, accepted these normative qualifications on virtuous conduct. "There are indeed several degrees of fellowship among men," running from familial to universal.[20] With each comes privileges and duties appropriate to social life on that scale.

The small size of early modern republics meant that each member knew everyone else's social position. Visitors could expect to benefit from the rule of hospitality. Beyond this, considerations of status and honor shaped everyone's response to anyone else's need. Always sensitive to these considerations, the Church made charity a duty and coordinated the niceties of giving and receiving. By definition, there were no unaccounted needs. As an institutional innovation, confederal arrangements could make small republics less vulnerable to imperial neighbors, but they did so without altering the conception of need as local and the response to it as paternal.

The liberal paradigm grew out of the republican one. Yet the family resemblance is deceptive. As normative frameworks, both start with moral persons. Nevertheless, liberalism stresses abilities and achievements over needs and differences. Objective individual rights prevail over subjective duties to one's

19 Here see M. Nussbaum's helpful discussion of Stoicism in relation to compassion. *Upheavals of Thought: The Intelligence of Emotions*, Cambridge: Cambridge University Press, 2001, pp. 356–86.

20 Cicero, *On Duties*, trans. M. Atkins, Cambridge: Cambridge University Press, 1991, I, para. 53, p. 22, and see Onuf, *Republican Legacy*, pp. 49–55. Recent discussions of communitarian and cosmopolitan values reflect the continuing relevance of contrary tendencies in republican thought: family, humanity; small world, big world. C. Brown, *International Relations Theory: New Normative Approaches*, New York: Columbia University Press, 1992.

fellows. Thus we find Grotius following his Stoic claim of natural sociability with an analysis of *jus* – the justness of an act or, more familiarly, right. *Jus* is a property of any moral person (*qualitas moralis personae*) forming aptitudes and faculties. He further divided aptitudes and faculties into powers, titles and contractual rights.[21]

The Grotian emphasis on natural rights is necessary but not sufficient for the development of the liberal paradigm. After all, natural law consists of rights and duties, each entailing the other. The moral person is a social being, perhaps an individual human being, perhaps a corporate being such as a guild. Only gradually did some early modern writers reconceive the person as a being whose right to autonomy took precedence over the encumbrances of society.

The key here is the Hobbesian claim that a corporate being is a moral person (in his terms, "civil person") only to the extent that the natural persons composing it have empowered some agent to act on their behalf.[22] Preeminently, nations meet this requirement because sovereign agents act for them. To say that these nations are sovereign is to claim for them rights and duties in their relations and thus to acknowledge that they are subject to a branch of the law of nature called the law of nations.[23] The natural society of nations formed a liberal world before there were liberal societies.

In theory, liberal society consists of natural persons – individual human beings – who have aptitudes and faculties – abilities – that come close to making them self-sufficient. In this respect they are substantially equal, even if particular abilities are normally, not equally distributed. Initially they need society to allow them to develop and employ their abilities to good effect, and society does this by protecting what is rightfully theirs by nature. Faculties translate into rights; holders of the same rights are formal equals.

In John Locke's definitive analysis (Chapter V, "Of Property," *Second Treatise of Government*, 1690), faculties translate into property whether considered on their own or applied to whatever else nature makes available for the satisfaction of human needs.

> Though the earth, and all inferior Creatures be common to all Men, yet every Man has a Property in his own Person. This no Body has any Right to but himself. The Labour of his Body, and the Work of his Hands, we may say, are properly *his*.[24]

21 Grotius, *De jure belli ac pacis*, I, iv–v, pp. 35–6.

22 Thomas Hobbes, *On the Citizen*, trans. by R. Tuck and M. Silverthorne, Cambridge: Cambridge University Press, 1998, V, para. 11, pp. 73–7; H.F. Pitkin, *The Concept of Representation*, Berkeley: University of California Press, 1967; D. Runciman, *Pluralism and the Personality of the State*, Cambridge: Cambridge University Press, 1997, chs. 2, 11.

23 I trace this development in Onuf, *The Republican Legacy in International Thought*, pp. 58–81.

24 J. Locke, The Second Treatise of Government, II, v, para. 27, in Locke, *Two Treatises of Government*, Cambridge: Cambridge University Press, 1988, pp. 287–8, his emphasis.

On Locke's account, we flourish in society because we, as "Proprietors" of our faculties and whatever we produce by using our faculties, are free to exchange and combine what we rightfully own as we see fit.[25]

Locke foreshadowed the liberal faith in the division of labor as the answer to human need. Smith made it the central tenet of *The Wealth of Nations* (1776). Smith postulated a natural human "propensity" to engage in exchange as the basis of specialized productive activity.[26] In a "well-governed society," the division of labor produces "universal opulence which extends to the lowest ranks of the people."[27] Clearly, Smith's well-governed society is one in which government interferes as little as possible in the natural operation of society.

For liberals, the division of labor takes care of most needs through its multiplicative productive powers and distributive dynamics. If people could count on minimal security for themselves and their property and institutional remedies to infringements on their rights, they would have few if any needs that doing what they do best would not fulfill. Insofar as this is not literally true, liberals could always fall back on the republican normative framework and its institutionalized response to human need in its many manifestations. Doing so routinely has blurred the boundaries of operative paradigms.

If the liberal paradigm emphasizes abilities over needs, the socialist paradigm reverses the equation. Needs become the primary normative focus, and the common good calls for a comprehensive assessment of what we need and how institutions should be designed to provide for these needs. Socialists believe that, intentions aside, the strong will victimize the weak if circumstances permit. Yet this is not their starting point. Liberal competition increases the neediness already implicit in the human condition. Some of us are weaker and thus needier than others, but all of us are weaker, and needier, than we realize.

Among early modern writers, Pufendorf most clearly articulated the starting point for the socialist paradigm of endemic neediness and comprehensive institutional design.[28] Consider Pufendorf's general sense of the human condition:

25 See Locke, First Treatise of Government, I, ix, para. 92, p. 209, and Second Treatise, II, v, para. 44, p. 298, for the term *proprietor*, and C.B. Macpherson's well-known discussion of its implications. *The Political Theory of Possessive Individualism: Hobbes to Locke*, Oxford: Clarendon, 1962.

26 A. Smith, *An Inquiry into the Nature and Causes of the Wealth of Nations* (1776), vol. 1, Oxford: Clarendon, 1976, I, ii, paras. 1–2, pp. 25–7.

27 Ibid., I, i, para. 10, p. 22.

28 While the term *socialist* seems highly anachronistic in an early modern context, some 18th century writers used it specifically to describe Pufendorf. I. Hont, "The Language of Sociability and Commerce: Samuel Pufendorf and the Theoretical Foundations of the 'Four Stages Theory'," in A. Pagden (ed.), *The Languages of Political Theory in Early-Modern Europe*, Cambridge: Cambridge University Press, 1987, p. 253.

> It is clear that man is an animal extremely desirous of his own preservation, in himself exposed to want, unable to exist without the help of his fellow-creatures, fitted in a remarkable way to contribute to the common good, and yet at all times malicious, petulant, and easily irritated, as well as quick and powerful to do injury.[29]

Our circumstances are even more miserable than Hobbes reckoned; they are so dire that we must assist each other simply to survive. Among these circumstances, none are more compelling than those of our birth. We are completely vulnerable and utterly dependent: "scarcely any other animal is attended from birth with such weakness [*imbecillitas*]."[30]

We enter the world helpless, and we never fully outgrow our dependence on others. Furthermore, the immediate source of help is the family into which we are born, and so it has always been. Pufendorf insisted that nature supplies paternal authority (*patria potesta*) in the degree necessary for parental support.[31] If the household organized around paternal power is the primary vehicle for meeting our needs, then the family writ large is the model for all other social arrangements whose purpose is to meet needs exceeding the family's capacities. Endemic neediness calls for rationalized authority; just as parents care for their children, watchful guardians of the common good care for their civil wards.

While the liberal paradigm has something of a British flavor, the socialist paradigm has a German one deriving from conditions in central Europe. Throughout the 18th century, German teachers and writers developed a science of administration – *Cameral-Wissenschaft* – for the promotion of public order and well-being. As Keith Tribe has pointed out, "concepts such as wealth, liberty, need, and happiness" were "linked in a chain of meaning which is founded on the economy as a constitutive moment." In linking them, one finds an imperative to regulate human conduct. Yet "this process of regulation cannot be conceived in terms of state intervention in the economy, for state and economy have no independent existence – or put another way, they are the same thing."[32]

The social context, whether household, agrarian estate or kingdom, provides rationalized paternal authority with a comprehensive response to every conceivable need and eliminates any possible threat to the statuses and privileges ordering society. This is modern thinking in defense of the old regime, or

29 Pufendorf, *De jure naturae et gentium*, II, iii, para. 15, pp. 207–8.

30 S. Pufendorf, *On the Duty of Man and Citizen* (1673), trans. by M. Silverstone, Cambridge: Cambridge University Press, 1991, I, iii, 3, p. 33. Also see II, i, para. 4, pp. 115–116.

31 Ibid., II, iii, paras. 1–2, p. 124.

32 K. Tribe, *Strategies of Economic Order: German Economic Discourse, 1750–1950*, Cambridge: Cambridge University Press, 1995, p. 12. See, generally, pp. 8–31 and, for more detail, Tribe, *Governing Economy: The Reformation of German Economic Discourse 1750–1840*, Cambridge: Cambridge University Press, 1988, pp. 19–118.

possibly in aid of its perfection. And this is G.W.F. Hegel when he linked civil society to the "system of needs" in *Philosophy of Right* (1821).[33] Some 19th century socialists saw planning and regulation as the answer to the many deficiencies of modernity, and some saw paternal authority as an artifact of the old regime. Either way, they suffered the charge of utopianism, whether from liberals or their own kind. In practice, a broad conception of need fostered the limitless extension of rationalized authority, and with it the collision of paradigms for which the 20th century would pay so dearly.

Framing humanitarian intervention

In 1758, Emmerich de Vattel presented his many readers with an elegant and accessible exposition of the republican normative framework. Supporting it are two general laws of nature. "The first general law, which is to be found in the very end of the society of nations, is that each Nation should contribute as far as it can to the happiness and advancement of other Nations." Vattel's first law makes mutual assistance a duty among nations limited only by the duties that any nation's leaders have to their own people. "Since Nations are free and independent of each other as men are by nature," Vattel went on to say, it is a "general law of their society that each Nation should be left to the Peaceful enjoyment of that liberty which belongs to it by nature."[34] The second law of nature establishes the principle of nonintervention in the relations of sovereign nations.

There are five things to notice about Vattel's formulation. First, it hews to the early modern standard in ascribing normative properties to nature. Second, it presumes that people are both free by nature and needy in many ways; as such, they choose to subject themselves to public authority and its normal operations for the common good; as a consequence they live in societies that are also nations. Third, it takes for granted the existence of a society of nations; by implication, the society of nations is a world that nature has set apart with a normative framework of its own. Fourth, it follows Stoic thought in holding that nations owe each other assistance in principle, as if need itself were a generalizable condition. Fifth, it nevertheless makes nonintervention a practical feature of the normative framework that nature grants

33 G.W.F. Hegel, *Elements of the Philosophy of Right*, trans. by H.B. Nisbet, Cambridge: Cambridge University Press, 1991, III, ii, paras. 182–256, pp. 220–74. Illustratively:

> For the *poor*, the universal authority [*Macht*] takes over the role of the family with regard not only to their immediate deficiencies, but also to the disposition of laziness, viciousness, and the other vices to which their predicament and sense of wrong give rise (para. 241, p. 265, emphasis in translation).

34 E. Vattel, *The Law of Nations or the Principles of Natural Law Applied to the Conduct and to the Affairs of Nations and of Sovereigns*, trans. by C.G. Fenwick, Washington: Carnegie Institution, 1916, Introduction, paras. 13, 15, p. 6.

to the society of free and independent nations, and this makes the society of nations a world unlike any other – a liberal world.

Vattel seems not to have been troubled by the apparent tension between the requirements of mutual aid and nonintervention. There is, of course, no problem if needy nations request assistance and other nations respond accordingly, or if nations offer assistance that other nations freely accept. The problem comes when nations refuse pleas for help, or when nations insist that other nations, or their societies, or some people or institutions in those societies, need help that those nations, represented by their public authorities, refuse to countenance. The principle of nonintervention enjoins nations – as public authorities and as societies – to refrain from unwanted assistance, and the absence of any generalizable conception of need prevents nations from invoking the principle of mutual aid to override the principle of nonintervention. If nations are to intervene, they must offer grounds for doing so that are at once situationally specific and normatively powerful.

Vattel's liberal way of thinking separates what goes on between nations – their intercourse is by choice and thus not interventionary – and within nations. Civil war and insurgency lead the list of concerns that nations may have about what goes on elsewhere. Public authorities are free to suppress civil disturbances within their nations. A prolonged civil war might threaten the peace and order of Europe, but even in this case intervention is not to be undertaken lightly. The liberal world that Vattel helped to create saw interventionary conduct, surely enough, but it also saw a concerted effort by intervening nations (we can now call them states without risking anachronism) to provide a plausible rationale for their conduct.

George Canning, who became Britain's foreign minister in 1822, offered just such a rationale in 1818 at the beginning of a new era in material prosperity, social reform and, for Britain, world leadership. In Canning's words, intervention is appropriate only "in great emergencies and then with commanding force."[35] Urgent need warrants a concentrated response, one that is immediate, focused and temporary. Even for liberals, a disastrous situation in another state justifies whatever means the intervening state's government deems necessary to overcome the resistance offered by the other state's government. A coercive response is unquestionably acceptable, and coordination with other governments is desirable.

While civil wars have humanitarian implications, foreign governments are reluctant to view these situations as emergencies until the actions of other governments prompt them to. At least in the first instance, Canning's emergencies were more likely to be framed as diplomatic crises than as humanitarian disasters. Conversely, humanitarian concerns are likely to well up from a

35 Quoted in C. Webster, *The Foreign Policy of Castlereagh 1812–1815: Britain and the Reconstruction of Europe*, 2nd edn, London: G. Bell, 1934, p. 147, and R.J. Vincent, *Non-intervention and International Order*, Princeton: Princeton University Press, 1974, p. 82.

society, without particular relation to a government's position on these matters or indeed to the normative framework of a world defined in liberal terms. We need only take a quick look at the best known instance of humanitarian intervention in Canning's era to see these dynamics at work. Here is a concise description from a leading 20th century international legal treatise: "Great Britain, France and Russia intervened in 1827 in the struggle between revolutionary Greece and Turkey when public opinion reacted with horror to the cruelties committed during the struggle."[36]

And here is a slightly fuller account.[37] Unruly Greeks rose up against the Ottoman Empire in 1821. Both sides committed atrocities: Greek Christians first when they massacred thousands of Moslem Turks in the Peloponnesus, and Turks most notoriously when they massacred perhaps 100,000 Greeks on and from the island of Chios. Governments could hardly ignore these events, which brought the Sultan and the Tsar almost to war in 1822. While great power diplomacy kept the peace, hundreds of progressive Europeans, many of them admirers of Hellas, went to fight in Greece but accomplished nothing; a frustrated Lord Byron died there in 1824. The war dragged on, outside support faded and the Empire held together. The Turks resisted diplomatic efforts to give Greece autonomy within the Empire until allied naval forces defeated them in 1827. Russia went to war against the Turks in 1828, and Greece became fully independent in 1830.

Even this spare account makes it clear that the Greek insurgency severely strained the public order of Europe. The diplomatic response was episodic and ineffectual; local peoples acted without restraint; shocked outsiders responded nobly but to no avail; forcible intervention by governments bore almost no connection to the incidence and magnitude of local violence. If we go by Canning's liberal formula, there was no humanitarian intervention, despite the later claims of international legal treatises.

The republican normative framework casts quite different light on the whole affair. Modern Europeans took pride in their civilization and nourishment from their faith. They knew their debt to the ancients. In a world of statuses, they believed that human beings possess a common status requiring them not to be treated like animals. Human dignity is a natural and thus universal state of affairs, and the common good is a civilizational responsibility, however attenuated. They knew that there are as many ways of acknowledging worth and doing good as there are occasions of need. Greece offered

36 L. Oppenheim, *International Law: A Treatise*, 8th edn by H. Lauterpacht, vol. 1, New York: David McKay, 1955, pp. 312–13. Canning died in 1827.

37 Among my sources are G. Finlay, *A History of Greece from Its Conquest by the Romans to the Present Time B.C. 146 to A.D.* (1877), vol. 6, New York: AMS Press, 1970, pp. 96–438; W. St. Clair, *That Greece Might Still Be Free: The Philhellenes in the War of Independence*, New York: Oxford University Press, 1972; Y. Stivachtis, *The Enlargement of International Society: Culture versus Anarchy and Greece's Entry into International Society*, New York: St. Martin's, 1998, pp. 112–86.

an instance of conspicuous need; conscientious Europeans responded by sending material assistance and freedom fighters, and by mobilizing public opinion and pressuring governments to redefine a diplomatic morass as a humanitarian disaster.

Years of carnage, war, failed initiatives, duplicity and stalemate in Greece point to the weaknesses and limitations of the republican paradigm as a normative framework. Yet there were also successes – humanitarian interventions that worked – primarily involving Britain during this time of transition to liberal societies in a liberal world. One striking success was the emancipation of slaves throughout the empire.[38] Less successful, though hardly futile, were the British government's persistent efforts to extirpate the international slave trade. Condoned by Aristotle, Grotius and Locke, slavery had become a principled issue for Enlightenment writers. In Britain, dissident religious groups agitated against slavery; courts freed Britain's few slaves in the 1770s. Thereafter, antislavery sentiments grew rapidly, with Caribbean slavery their focus.

In 1807, Parliament stopped slave trading in the empire, and on Britain's lead the Congress of Vienna condemned the international slave trade. Millions of people petitioned Parliament to end slavery in the empire, which it did in the 1830s. Ending the slave trade on the high seas took longer because some other states refused to become parties to relevant treaties. In a liberal international society, the slave trade was a matter of states' rights.

By contrast, no one saw the battle over slavery as a matter of human rights in the societies where it was practiced. Indeed, the historical treatment of slaves as property complicated the issue for liberals, and liberal predilections in the US did nothing to spare it from an agonizing sectional confrontation over slavery, constitutional crisis and civil war. For progressive intellectuals and evangelical Christians (often the same people), slavery was odious and intolerable. Its very existence translated into an urgent need, a humanitarian emergency, to which diverse moral and institutional resources could be directed. Governments constituted an arena for action, a target, and an institutional resource for use at home, across the empire, and against other governments.

We can see the same pattern with *sati*, which is the Hindu practice of widow burning. For the British public, this reprehensible practice was not a human rights issue, but a matter of honor and a mark against civilization. That *sati* took place within the empire made humanitarian intervention easier and all the more imperative. William Bentinck – utilitarian, evangelical

38 Here I draw on D.B. Davis, *The Problem of Slavery in Western Culture*, Ithaca: Cornell University Press, 1966, pp. 291–445; T. Bender (ed.), *The Antislavery Debate: Capitalism and Abolitionism as a Problem in Historical Interpretation*, Berkeley: University of California Press, 1992; A. Porter, "Trusteeship, Anti-Slavery and Humanitarianism," in Porter (ed.), *The Oxford History of the British Empire*, vol. 3, Oxford: Oxford University Press, 1999, pp. 198–221.

Christian and Governor General in Calcutta – abolished it by decree in 1828.[39]

The 1820s and 1830s stand as a high point in the modern response to distressing situations and odious practices in distant places. Thereafter, specifically liberal features of international society embodied in the principles of sovereignty, nonintervention and national self-determination rapidly undermined the relevance of the republican normative framework.[40] Uneven development in liberal societies pointed to unmet human needs and unrealized human capabilities. Meanwhile, utilitarian ideas, awesome feats of engineering and compounding material achievements served to dampen normative awareness, whether socialist or liberal, or subordinate it to grandiose claims about human possibilities. The last decades of the century witnessed the rise of two such claims that reverberate even today.

One was social Darwinism. On scientific authority, social Darwinists claimed for themselves and their bourgeois compatriots superior abilities in order to justify their inordinate privilege and the right to rule. They invoked a new, allegedly scientific conception of nature – of natural history – to free the liberal paradigm from anything that resembles normative constraints of any kind. Racist, sexist and culturally smug, they were at their best capable of republican style paternalism; such was "the white man's burden." At their worst, they despised human weakness.

In theory, social Darwinists could sound like republicans. In practice, they supported to an egregious extreme the liberal presumption that anything goes. Their new science of nature alienated large numbers of Christians for whom modern skepticism was deeply disturbing and enduring status arrangements a source of comfort. That utilitarians and evangelical Christians could come together in the popular reform movements of the 1820s and 1830s seems so odd today is but one indication of the Darwinist impact on the way that we in the modern world think about our world.

The second, no less grandiose claim about human possibilities focused on needs, not abilities. Needs are the great equalizer in the human condition; institutionalized inequalities exacerbate endemic neediness; the systematic elimination of such inequalities is the first stage in dealing with endemic neediness, and not just an eventual consequence of doing so. This is utopian socialism. Some early versions suggest a nostalgic longing for premodern

39 See V.N. Datta, *Sati: A Historical, Social and Philosophical Enquiry into the Hindu Rite of Widow Burning*, London: Sangam, 1988; J. Fisch, *Tödliche Rituale, Die indische Witwenverbrennung und andere Formen der Totenfolge*, Frankfurt: Campus, 1998, pp. 213–328; L. Mani, *Contentious Traditions: The Debate on Sati in Colonial India*, Berkeley: University of California Press, 1998. As for Bentinck: J. Rosselli, *Lord William Bentinck: The Making of a Liberal Imperialist 1744–1839*, Berkeley: University of California Press, 1974.

40 As John Stuart Mill's essay, "A Few Words on Non-Intervention" (1859), makes clear. In J.S. Mill, *Dissertations and Discussions: Political, Philosophical, and Historical*, vol. 3, Boston: Spencer, 1864, p. 238–63.

social arrangements. Invoking science in support of a systematic response to human need made later versions no less utopian and perhaps more so.

An abstractly humanitarian objective and reliance on the authority of science had the effect of freeing the socialist paradigm from normative constraints. Sworn enemies of other social arrangements and dedicated to the necessity of planning for all needs, utopian socialists insisted on their need to rule and inevitably succumbed to the corruptions of privilege. At their best, they construed religious conviction as ignorance, dismissed conventional ethics and treated spiritual needs with indifference; many people responded with the same hostility that believing Christians felt for Darwinist science. At their worst, socialists butchered and brutalized vast numbers of people for utopian ends.

Utopian socialists matched social Darwinists in taking the operative paradigms of liberalism and socialism to normatively disabling extremes. Mirroring each other in so many ways, they were jointly responsible for the institutional machinery and human catastrophes identified with Lenin, Stalin, Hitler and Mao. All four combined a Darwinist conception of struggle, fitness and desert with a utopian commitment to planning for every need in all possible detail. They shared a longing for "total revolution" (Friedrich Schiller's term, taken over by Karl Marx), a totalizing vision of modernity and an abiding faith in the instrumental powers of science.[41] Intervention is the standard, not the exception. If humanity is to fulfill its potential, then it must endure what amounts to a permanent state of emergency, complete with mass internment, concentration camps and extermination programs.

A common faith in mastery through science spans the modern experience from the utopian left to the Darwinist right. At both ends of the spectrum we find a ruthless disposition to act on principle with maximum efficiency and minimal emotional involvement. It is tempting to blame this disposition on the rapid rise of positivism in science, law and society after 1800. Early moderns held a normative view of nature. Positivists took a detached, instrumental stance toward nature, which they held to consist of discrete, measurable things and their causal relations. Yet faith in science and positivist predilections inspired a good many 19th and 20th century moderns to act on limited objectives and humane sentiments, and it helped them achieve remarkable successes from the organization of productive activity to the provision of public health and safety.

The instrumental methods and successes of positivist modernity nourished liberal and socialist paradigms in ways that have brought them closer together without making everyone into ruthless ideologues. In this collusion

41 "The longing for total revolution develops out of reflection on the obstacles to overcoming the dehumanizing spirit of modern society." B. Yack, *The Longing for Total Revolution: The Philosophic Sources of Social Discontent from Rousseau to Marx and Nietzsche*, Princeton: Princeton University Press, 1992, p. 9.

of paradigms, liberal-minded positivists have used their skills to organize activities on a large scale, thereby drawing on many people's diverse abilities and rewarding them accordingly. Welfare-oriented positivists have used theirs to find solutions to needs defined as problems – for example, health, nutrition, and sanitation problems – thereby enabling many more people to use their abilities productively. The extraordinary growth in organizational and problem-solving activities has occasioned their progressive differentiation along functional lines. Aristotle based his conception of social life on the differentiation of activities necessary to the functioning of the whole. The same conception informs the division of labor upon which the liberal paradigm is predicated. As positivism's necessary complement, functional differentiation is a striking feature of modernity – modern societies and modern international society.

In the modern world, unleashed abilities and undeniable needs stand in complementary opposition, as do paradigm preferences and practices. Functional differentiation mediates their complex relations. It also permits piecemeal intervention, not by institutions as such, but by so-called problem-solving technicians. Carefully calibrated, such intervention is said to comport with individual rights when it produces the desired results. Cumulatively, functionally rationalized intervention threatens the delicate balance between paradigms. This threat has become a leading source of tension in modern social life.

Early on, positivist premises, functional differentiation and the perception of need eventuated in a solution to a problem – an urgent humanitarian problem – for which the republican normative framework had no meaningful institutional response. The problem was that wounded soldiers needed to be removed from the battlefield in order to be helped, and the solution took form as the International Committee of the Red Cross.[42] This response constituted humanitarian intervention in functional garb – a specialized non-governmental activity, institutionally situated in international society by multilateral treaty. Over the decades its success has generated a functional domain populated by a host of public and private institutions designed to respond to humanitarian emergencies.

Typically, natural disasters are the proximate cause of these emergencies. Appalled by the human suffering, large numbers of people from distant places contribute resources to relief organizations, many of them religious, to help bring the situation under control. Normally, local populations welcome the assistance, even if their governments worry about compromised sovereignty and the inevitable criticism that they were ill-prepared. In the last decade, people have started to see governments as the direct cause of human suffering on a scale recalling utopian–Darwinist calamities of the recent past.

42 For an overview, see D.P. Forsythe, *Humanitarian Politics: The International Committee of the Red Cross*, Baltimore: Johns Hopkins University Press, 1977, pp. 1–56.

Since they are both humanitarian emergencies and sociopolitical crises, beleaguered functional specialists are calling them complex emergencies.[43] As emergencies that are out of control, they subject governments to a great deal of public attention and make some sort of unwelcome intervention inevitable.

Meanwhile the legal framework for Red Cross intervention continued its well-known path of development as a humanitarian counterpart to the more broadly regulative law of war. Only vaguely differentiated functionally, these two bodies of law have now merged into a single regime that the International Court of Justice has advised us to call "international humanitarian law."[44] As Theodor Meron has suggested, this development "reflects the influence of the human rights movement."[45] A movement of gathering momentum, gigantic proportions and global significance, human rights advocacy marks liberalism as the ascendant normative framework for the modern world.

By liberal standards, international humanitarian law is massively interventionary. The modern distinction between a world of states, and states as worlds in their own right, has lost some of its normative power, although how much is hard to say. States are no longer the sole proprietors of their own domains, and the legal order is no longer theirs except in name.[46] Under the new dispensation, governments are more likely to be objects than agents of intervention. Emergencies once overrode the presumption that governments would not intervene in each other's affairs except on rare occasions. Now, notorious human rights violations trigger intervention. Acting on behalf of those whose rights have been violated are any number of institutions equipped with legal expertise, a vast liberal literature on the link between human rights and humanitarian intervention, and even the support of important public officials.

Take for example this statement by the UN Secretary-General Javier Pérez de Cuellar in 1991:

43 [United Nations] Office for the Coordination of Humanitarian Affairs, *OCHA Orientation Handbook on Complex Emergencies*, August 1999, pp. 2–3. Online. Available HTTP: <http://www.reliefweb.int/library/documents/ocha_orientation_handbook_on_.htm> (accessed 18 October 2007); US Department of State, *Interagency Review of U.S. Government Civilian Humanitarian & Transition Programs*, January 2000, pp. 3, 6–8. Online. Available HTTP: <http://www.gwu.edu/~nsarchiv/NSAEBB/NSAEBB30/Sec1.pdf> (accessed 18 October 2007).

44 *Advisory Opinion on the Legality of the Threat or Use of Nuclear Weapons*, para. 75, reprinted in *International Legal Materials*, vol. 35, 1996, p. 827.

45 T. Meron, "The Humanization of Humanitarian Law," *American Journal of International Law*, vol. 94, 2000, p. 239.

46 See, for example, T.G. Weiss and J. Chopra's assessment. "Sovereignty under Siege: From Intervention to Humanitarian Space," in G.M. Lyons and M. Mastanduno (eds.), *Beyond Westphalia? State Sovereignty and International Intervention*, Baltimore: Johns Hopkins University Press, 1995, pp. 87–114.

> We need not impale ourselves on the horns of a dilemma between respect for sovereignty and the protection of human rights. . . . What is involved is not the right of intervention but the collective obligation of states to bring relief and redress in human rights emergencies.[47]

Pérez de Cuellar's statement shows that in today's world, liberal terms, such as human rights and the right of intervention, suffuse all discussion of responding to humanitarian disasters. At the same time, any observer can see that these disasters constitute emergencies. The problem is that emergencies compel immediate action. Yet the appropriate institutional response to the violation of rights is necessarily cumbersome and slow.

There are several reasons why the institutional machinery associated with human rights is so unresponsive in emergency situations. First and most obviously, the liberal world continues to give international society room to play out its own liberal dynamics. As a practical result, the institutional machinery that governments have authorized for the protection of human rights greatly favors states over their nationals; in effect, states' rights trump individual rights. Second, the available machinery tends to define the protection of human rights as a matter of anticipating and preventing their violation by persuading governments to change their practices, and not a matter of providing effective remedies to individuals whose rights have been violated. Third, liberal institutional machinery always provides for third-party adjudication whenever one party claims that another has violated its rights. The procedural rigor, evidentiary requirements and legal expertise necessary to insure fairness in these situations restricts institutional access and makes the process lengthy, combative and often inconclusive.

It would seem that "relief and redress" are substantially incompatible goals undermining the very possibility of an effective institutional response to so-called "human rights emergencies." Urgent need calls for an immediate response. Insofar as the normative framework for such a response is liberal, then it is imperative to see the situation as an emergency. As such, it is analogous to a natural disaster that demands a quick fix and not a fastidious concern for anyone's rights.

Urgent moral need – for example, widow burning or the genital mutilation of young women – represents a special case. In such situations, liberals are reluctant to intervene directly, and their governments resist doing so even indirectly, for there is no actual emergency. The republican framework, with its emphasis on the common good, may seem to be more relevant. Yet from Aristotle on, republicans tend to conceptualize the common good by reference to the small worlds of their immediate experience. Thus they are characteristically reluctant to intervene where the need is distant, physically

47 J. Pérez de Cuellar, *Report on the Work of the Organization*, UN doc. A/46/1, 6 September 1991, p. 10, quoted ibid., p. 111.

and socially. Only by making universal claims about civilizational values can we who live in a very big, modern world think about humanitarian intervention far from home.[48] While anyone who appreciates the rich normative resources of modernity can argue the case for intervention where there is urgent moral need, it was easier to do so in 1828 than it is today.

48 See, further, my discussion of small worlds and universal claims in "Everyday Ethics in International Relations," *Millennium: Journal of International Studies*, vol. 27, 1998, pp. 671–7.

27 Eurocentrism and civilization (2003)

When I presented my paper on Henry Wheaton and the rise of a liberal international society (Chapter 24) at Tokyo University, questions focused on what I meant by the term *liberalism.* My host, Onuma Yasuaki, later suggested that I had taken insufficient account of the global situation, in which liberal nations engaged in imperial and colonial practices hardly compatible with liberal premises. Readers of Chapter 24 may detect a rather modest effort on my part to acknowledge this concern, which I felt was somewhat misplaced in Wheaton's case. At that time Onuma was working on an important paper developing what he called an "intercivilizational perspective on international law" as a corrective to the cultural arrogance of cosmopolitan liberals and their universalizing claims. After the *Journal of the History of International Law* published Onuma's paper, he arranged for a number of interested scholars, including me, to write comments on it for a subsequent issue of the *Journal.* I was then tracing the conceptual history of the familiar trope "civilized nations" for the book I was writing with my brother Peter. The terms *civilized* and *civilization* are Enlightenment neologisms. While 18th century Europeans were happy to apply these terms to other times and regions, they distinguished between the vitality of their world and the decadence of other worlds. In the most general terms they attributed this difference to the fact that Europeans lived in a society of nations, while all other civilizations were formed as empires.

To broaden Onuma's intercivilizational perpective, I thought it would help to show how Europeans viewed other civilizations long before the imperial excesses of the late 19th century. To this end I used several pages of text that were later to appear in *Nations, Markets, and War*, suitably introduced for the purpose at hand.

The great virtue of Onuma Yasuaki's "intercivilizational perspective" on the history of international law is his insistence that every civilization produces a perspective on the normative ordering of its "world."[1] Onuma identifies three

1 Onuma Y., "When Was the Law of International Society Born? – An Inquiry of the History of International Law from a Civilizational Perspective," *Journal of the History of International Law*, vol. 2, 2000, pp. 8–11.

such worlds: the Sinocentric world of East Asia, the Muslim world, and the Eurocentric world of self-styled "civilized nations." He suggests that historically such worlds were regionally dominant and that they developed "an egocentric world image." His account of the civilizational perspective of the Sinocentric and Muslim worlds supports this general claim, as would a comparable account of the South Asian world of Hindu civilization. So do the many studies of European developments, which Onuma understandably chose not to recapitulate before exploring the 19th century "collision" of worlds.

Onuma's decision not to offer his own account of the Eurocentric perspective on what it means to be civilized leaves him dependent on the accounts of others. At least in the context of international legal history, these accounts focus on the late decades of the 19th century, when Europeans took for granted their material and moral superiority. Yet, Europeans developed an explicit and distinctive civilizational perspective fully a century before. They did so in a context quite unlike that in which other civilizational perspectives took form.

Eighteenth-century Europeans knew that "the world" into which they were so actively inserting themselves was a large and diverse place. It consisted not only of themselves, and of uncivilized or barbarous peoples, but of civilizations with ancient and distinguished pasts. To suggest, as I do, that the familiar binary of civilized and uncivilized nations does an injustice to the European perspective is not to imply that the Europeans were any less egocentric in their claims or self-serving in their conduct than their critics have made them out to be. I want to suggest instead that the reason Europeans thought that their civilization was morally superior to other civilizations had implications for conduct quite different from the way Europeans conducted themselves toward peoples whom they regarded as uncivilized – perhaps irredeemably so.

The terms *civilization* and *civilized nations* were indispensable inventions of "Enlightened" Europeans in their struggle against traditional practices and despotic regimes. In their opinion, Europe had experienced a remarkable trajectory of material and moral improvement after languishing for centuries. As J.G.A. Pocock has so extensively documented in the two volumes of *Barbarism and Religion* (1999), every attempt to explain what had happened in Europe took the fall of Rome and return of barbarism to be decisive events. Adam Smith's interpretation in *The Wealth of Nations* (1776) was more detailed, and darker, than most.

"The rapine and violence" of the barbarians "interrupted the commerce between the towns and the country," and left great tracts of uncultivated land in the hands of indifferent and irresponsible proprietors.[2] Europe was unable to recover until the Italian cities took up long-distance trade.

2 A. Smith, *An Inquiry into the Nature and Causes of the Wealth of Nations* (1776), vol. 1, Oxford: Clarendon, 1976, Book III, ch. ii, quoting para. 1, p. 380.

> The inhabitants of trading cities, by importing the improved manufactures and expensive luxuries of richer countries, afforded some food to the vanity of the great proprietors, who eagerly purchased them with great quantities of the rude produce of their own lands. The commerce of a great part of Europe in those times accordingly, consisted chiefly in the exchange of their own rude, for the manufactured produce of more civilized nations.[3]

As towns throughout Europe prospered, agriculture returned to the countryside, and with it commerce between town and country within the nations of Europe. According to Smith, this was an inversion of "the natural order of things," in which agriculture comes first, followed by manufactures, and finally by foreign commerce. The development of an "unnatural and retrograde order" in Europe was the result of "manners and customs" dating back to the barbarian disruptions and culminating in the court societies of early modern Europe.[4] In the natural order of things, Europe should have entered the age of commerce on its own, its prosperity and its manners more appropriately reflecting the dynamics of internal development.

Instead, the civilized nations of Europe were dependent on luxury goods imported from "richer countries" and "more civilized nations." As Smith pointed out, "China is a much richer country than any part of Europe."[5] Any such concession threatened the presumption that related developments in commerce, arts and sciences (including the art of war and the science of government) had enabled the civilized nations of Europe to advance beyond all others. China offered an explanatory challenge, and not just to Smith.

The challenge was to explain Chinese wealth and devalue Chinese civilization at the same time. Smith undertook both tasks by observing that China was rich, fertile, cultivated, industrious and populous, and yet in all respects it "seems . . . to have been long stationary."[6] This was a commonplace; David Hume had remarked on it in his *Essays* of 1740–1:

> In CHINA, there seems to be a pretty considerable stock of politeness and science, which, in the course of so many centuries, might naturally be expected to ripen into something more perfect and finished than what had yet arisen from them.

Hume provided an elegant explanation for this state of affairs. "CHINA is one vast empire, speaking one language, governed by one law, and sympathizing

3 Ibid., III, iii, quoting para. 15, pp. 407–8.
4 Ibid., III, i, para. 9; p. 380.
5 Ibid.
6 Ibid., I, viii, para. 24; p. 89.

in the same manners."[7] In *The Spirit of the Laws* (1748), Montesquieu held that "manners govern the Chinese"; "manners, mores, laws, and religion are but the same thing there, one cannot change all of that at once."[8] Smith joined the refrain. China had "acquired that full complement of riches which the nature of its laws and institutions had permitted it to acquire."[9] As a society of manners, there was no way for China to change.

Enlightenment observers condemned two constants in Chinese civilization. Despotic rule insured extraordinary luxury for an indolent few. Meanwhile the great multitudes of China lived in the meanest possible circumstances. According to Montesquieu, despotic rule is "corrupt by its nature."[10] A Romantic preoccupation of the rationalist Enlightenment, oriental despotism is not just a corruption of monarchy, to be expected in the natural rhythms in forms of rule. Oriental despotism reproduces itself.

In China, as Montesquieu observed, it had done so for dynasty after dynasty – 22 in succession.[11] In the process, despotic rule had permanently distorted life for everyone. It undermined the relation between labor and the benefits that normally accrue from labor, and it disrupted normal family arrangements. Poor men could not provide for their families, while wealthy men had many wives and concubines. The Chinese were civilized perhaps, but their mannered ways offended nature.

Oriental despotism produced slavery – household slavery – on a grand scale. In the "rich and voluptuous nations," as Montesquieu put it, polygamy meant that rich and powerful men were able to keep "a very great number of wives."[12] Eunuchs, concubines, even wives *were* slaves. Seventeenth-century travelers had returned from the East with reports of harems with hundreds, perhaps thousands of cloistered women, most of them slaves, entrusted to the care of equally large numbers of slaves who had been emasculated for the task. Paradoxically, the harem's inhabitants had preferential access to the rulers and other wealthy men who possessed them, and thus a corresponding influence on public life. Many eunuchs rose from slavery to high office and great wealth in their own right.

From the Topkapi Seraglio to the Forbidden City, Europeans could see the

7 D. Hume, "Of the Rise and Progress of the Arts and Sciences," in *Essays: Moral, Political and Literary* (1777 edn), Indianapolis: Liberty Fund, 1985, p. 122.

8 Montesquieu, *The Spirit of the Laws*, trans. by A.M. Cohler *et al.*, Cambridge: Cambridge University Press, 1989, Book 19, chs. 4, 17, pp. 310, 318.

9 Smith, *The Wealth of Nations*, I, viii, para. 24; p. 89.

10 Montesquieu, *The Spirit of the Laws*, Book 8, ch. 10, p. 119.

11 Ibid., Book 7, ch. 7, p. 103. Indicatively, Montesquieu consistently treated despotism as a fourth form of rule; Books 2, 3, 5, 7, 8, *passim*. For treatments of oriental despotism rather different than this one, see F. Venturi, "Oriental Despotism," *Journal of the History of Ideas*, vol. 35, 1963, pp. 133–42, and L. Krader, *The Asiatic Mode of Production: Sources, Development and Critiques in the Writings of Karl Marx*, Assen: Van Gorcum, 1975, pp. 19–43.

12 Montesquieu, *The Spirit of the Laws*, Book 16, ch. 8, p. 269.

same pattern of practices repeated across the great arc of the Orient.[13] The dire consequences of polygamy and household slavery were a constant refrain. "Those who pass the early part of life among slaves, are only qualified to be, themselves, slaves and tyrants," Hume remarked in an indictment of polygamy.[14] "Having multiple wives," according to Montesquieu, "leads to the love that nature disavows; this is because one sort of dissoluteness always entails another."[15] Smith told his no doubt impressionable students at Glasgow University that "all the countries where polygamy is received are under the most arbitrary and despotic government."[16]

Enlightenment writers were convinced that conditions in Europe made slavery unnatural. Emerging from the long shadow of Rome and the barbarian past, European nations had "abolished" slavery as they became civilized in their own distinctive way. "The chief difference between the *domestic* œconomy of the ancients and that of the moderns," according to Hume, "consists in the practice of slavery, which prevailed among the former, and which had been abolished for some centuries throughout the greater part of EUROPE."[17] When confronted with the horrifying spectacle of Africans being enslaved and then shipped to the new world, many Europeans held blacks to be inferior to whites, ill-suited to freedom, and morally incorrigible. Still hunters and gatherers, they were demonstrably incapable of becoming civilized. Or, on the evidence of settled agriculture, social organization on an impressive scale and effective participation in the slave trade, they were judged despotic in the oriental manner. Reports from travelers to West Africa confirmed as much; the King of Dahomey had two thousand wives.[18]

Either way, slavery was the way of life outside Europe. That European nations condoned slavery in its overseas colonies, that Europe as a whole benefited from a world economy based on slavery, that slavery might not be natural anywhere or as efficient as free labor – all this was beside the point. Very much to the point was a barely sublimated fear and loathing of Eastern licentiousness. There could be no better evidence of what happens to civilizations lacking the competitive spirit of the European nations and the moral code of the Christian world.

If intercivilizational trade had its advantages, the risk of moral contamination demanded legal arrangements that kept worlds apart. On this all three

13 See P.O. Scholz, *Eunuchs and Castrati: A Cultural History*, trans. by J.A. Broadwin and S.L. Frisch, Princeton: Markus Wiener, 2001, chs. 3–7, for some sense of the origins, features, scale and persistence of these practices.

14 D. Hume, "Of Polygamy and Divorces," *Essays*, p. 185.

15 Montesquieu, *The Spirit of the Laws*, Book 16, ch. 6, p. 268.

16 A. Smith, *Lectures on Jurisprudence*, ed. by R.L. Meek *et al.*, Oxford: Clarendon, 1978, Report of 1762–3, iii, 33–4, p. 154.

17 D. Hume, "Of the Populousness of Ancient Nations," *Essays*, p. 383, his emphasis.

18 See D.B. Davis, *The Problem of Slavery in Western Culture*, Ithaca: Cornell University Press, 1966, ch. 15, for a detailed discussion.

worlds could generally agree. India was a special case. Imperial Britain tolerated local practices, but only up to a point marked by the abolition of the morally reprehensible practice of widow-burning.[19] "Uncivilized," child-like peoples presented little risk of moral contamination. Europeans drew on the Roman legal heritage of tutelage and guardianship, not to mention Christian duty, and embraced a legal regime that justified intervention in the affairs of their colonies for every imaginable reason.

19 See J. Fisch, *Tödliche Rituale, Die indische Witwenverbrennung und andere Formen der Totenfolge*, Frankfurt: Campus, 1998, pp. 213–328; L. Mani, *Contentious Traditions: The Debate on Sati in Colonial India*, Berkeley: University of California Press, 1998.

28 Practicing theory (2006)

Over the course of 40 years, almost all of my work has dealt with theory. Arranged chronologically, this work bears witness to an early enthusiasm for theory specific to international law, even when I drew on anthropological and sociological materials. In time I devoted increasing energy to social theory in the hope of showing that international law and international relations jointly lend themselves to systematic treatment. Eventually I turned my attention to the specific historical experience I rather grandly call the rise of the modern world – an experience in which discussion of international law figures significantly and to which almost all social theory is oriented. My evolving interests resulted in a decreasing volume of material that might be usefully included in a volume intended for international legal scholars. Indeed the flow of relevant materials had dwindled to the point that any book assembling them would end, in the familiar words of T.S. Eliot, with a whimper, not a bang. As I assembled materials, I realized I needed a bang-up concluding essay.

I knew I had the makings of such an essay in a long paper I had prepared in 1997 for a conference on "International Norms" at the Hebrew University of Jerusalem. The paper, entitled "How Things Get Normative," remained unpublished. Salvaged and variously altered for use here is somewhat less than half of that material, now constituting somewhat less than half of the material appearing below. The rest reflects my interest in modernity's philosophical underpinnings. Scattered references to my other recent work speak to other loosely connected theoretical interests. If conclusions are meant to wrap things up, this one fails. Even if narratives demand endings, it seems to me, as a practicing theorist, that social reality – the social construction of reality – is a messy process, a cavalcade of loose ends.

Theory and practice is a familiar turn of phrase. It is also perplexing: an aporetic conjunction, an irreconcilable combination, an inescapable opposition, a warrant for taking sides and a plea for the missing middle term. In the *Organon* Aristotle held that opposites could be "contraries" (*enantia*) because an intermediate condition is possible. Or they could be "contradictories" (*apophaseis*), in which case intermediate degrees or conditions are logically excluded. Legal positivists treat normativity and its opposite as contradictories; *weak normativity* (a phrase I used in Chapter 14 and again, below) is a contradiction in terms. Whether some condition is normative or not, I would suggest, is a conventional and thus normalized contrary and, as such, a member of a series of conditions for which we adopt a paradoxical and sometimes ironic third term: shifting premises, receding limit, porous boundary, loose interpretation, thin justification, weak obligation, soft law. *Practicing theorist*, as an epithet I would claim for myself, is just such a term.

For the most part, modern social scientists have simply ignored theory and practice as a conventional opposition. More precisely, they are disinclined to use the term *practice*, which they tend to associate with the highly normative Marxian concept of a revolutionary *praxis*. Instead they oppose theory and method to make sense of their vocation as scientists. The tension between rationalism and empiricism has a long history in science, perennially reconfirming the importance of form and substance, ideas and matter, as scaffolding for Western metaphysics. For this we have the Greeks to thank, and especially Aristotle, who gave sustained attention to substance (what we say things are) in relation to form (which we see in and give to things and their relations) and matter (the stuff of the world to which we give form). Because Aristotle started with predication (what we say things are), substance and matter are not interchangeable terms, and form and substance not the binary opposition that most of us take it to be.[1] In this essay, however, I bow to convention and refer to form and substance (meaning formless stuff) as logically opposed terms.

Convention notwithstanding, Aristotle should also not be held responsible for the opposed contraries conveyed more specifically by the terms *theory* and *practice*, in this case because he gave *theōria*, or contemplation, relatively little attention. His more detailed treatment of *praxis*, or action, in *Nicomachean Ethics*, Book I, has inspired quite bit of discussion among critical and postmodern social theorists, for whom Karl Marx's legacy is a concern for the material conditions of everyday life. Aristotle's definition of action points in two directions. On the one hand, it seems to include everything that we do. On the other hand, it excludes what we do for any end beyond the action itself. When we eat to satisfy our hunger, this is *praxis* in a narrow sense. When we build a ship, this is *praxis* generally conceived, but also *energeia*, or an activity chosen with an end in mind.

Action narrowly conceived is routine, habitual and easily imitated; activity is episodic, deliberate and often opaque, even mysterious, to an observer. The former is mechanical, and the latter technical – Aristotle associated it with

1 See *Categories*, Book I, *Topics*, Book I, *Metaphysics*, Book VII. I have developed this and related themes in a paper entitled "Constructivism: A Philosophical Prologue," and presented at the Pontifícia Universidade Católica de Minas Gerais, Belo Horizonte, Brazil, in May 2006.

craft (*technē*), or the acquisition and use of skills, for shipbuilding, medicine, military leadership or household management (to use his examples). Habitual actions and technical activities are contraries. For Aristotle, contemplation is an activity, indeed the only activity giving us the kind of pleasure that should be everyone's goal (*Nicomachean Ethics*, Book X).

Every normal human being has the cognitive equipment necessary for such an activity; we all engage in theorizing, whether we know it or not. Nevertheless, proposing theories that others will find coherent, plausible and compatible with the existing stock of theories is hard work. Working with theory is a craft; it takes training and practice; it depends on specialized skills and well-formed routines; its challenges and its pleasures never cease. Practiced long, hard and well (so one hopes), theorizing becomes an end in its own right, a vocation.

Aristotle's treatment of practice is compressed and unclear. When Jürgen Habermas invoked the "Aristotelian distinction between *praxis* and *techne*," his misconstruction of Aristotle and the point of his formulation are clear enough.[2] For Habermas, *praxis* refers to critical practice, such as his own, directed against the dehumanizing effects of modernity's technical accomplishments, summarized as *techne*. Yet critical practice is an activity that involves a good deal of theorizing in turn dependent on training, skill and practice. In short, critical practice is a craft and, clearly for Habermas, a vocation. Not exactly Aristotle's opposed contraries to start with, *praxis* and *techne* form together a third term and epithet this time suiting Habermas himself: practicing theorist.

No doubt the most influential practicing theorist of practice has been Pierre Bourdieu, whose anthropological studies of everyday life in peasant communities and modern societies have a distinctly postmodern flavor. In his two major works on practice, Bourdieu did not draw on Aristotle directly. Yet both books quote the same passage from Aristotle's *Poetics* in chapter epigraphs. In this passage Aristotle claimed that our penchant for mimicry sets us apart from other animals.[3] Imitation is something we do without much reflection on ends. In this it resembles habits that form from repetitive behavior about which we think less and less. Both are typical of action in the narrow sense of *praxis*, and both would seem to be primary sources and integral features of "the systems of durable, transposable dispositions" that Bourdieu called *habitus*.[4] In Bourdieu's world, *habitus* is more important than strategic calculation, and the "orchestrated improvisations" that result from

2 J. Habermas, *Theory and Practice*, trans. J. Viertel, Boston: Beacon, 1973, p. 2.

3 P. Bourdieu, *Outline of a Theory of Practice*, trans. R. Nice, Cambridge: Cambridge University Press, 1977, p. 96; *The Logic of Practice*, trans. R. Nice, Stanford: Stanford University Press, 1990, p. 25.

4 See, generally, Bourdieu, *Outline of a Theory of Practice*, ch. 2; *The Logic of Practice*, chs. 3–6, quoting p. 53.

habitus do not depend on rules that agents offer as reasons for their choices or that observers infer from regularities of conduct.[5]

Bourdieu's conception of everyday *praxis* abolishes *theory and practice* as opposed contraries, discounts craft and paradoxically leaves no place for practicing theorists such as himself. While postmodern scholars might see a delicious irony in Bourdieu's position (all the more because theorizing is a vocation for many of them), it betrays Aristotle's perhaps too subtle understanding of action, activity and ends, and it fails to address the many practices that make the modern world (or any other civilization) a distinctive undertaking. Among those practices are the ones lawyers engage in – practices that take the presence of rules as a substantive point of departure. Legal practice is a craft for which there are many rules to be mastered, a vocation demanding an unflagging allegiance, and a profession constituting a world with its own rules. In such a world, there will be perennial questions about law: What is it really? Where does it come from? Why do people obey the law? Why should they? Even if most practicing lawyers find these questions distracting or the usual answers unhelpful, there will always be practicing theorists (not all of them lawyers) returning to them again and again.

If legal theory is necessarily linked to the practice of law, then each exerts an inexorable pull on the other and no less insistently pushes the other away. The philosopher's world of abstraction beckons whenever theory gives up too much to the immediacy of experience and the nuances of the lawyer's craft; the lawyer's world of experience beckons whenever theorists show signs of slipping into metaphysics. In every domain this pendulum swings. In recent decades the practice of international law has eclipsed international legal theory. Or so it seems to me, as a practicing theorist (and not a lawyer) taking the development of my own craft into consideration. (Compare these remarks with sentiments I expressed in 1993, Chapter 19, above.) Urgent policy considerations, an exponential growth in lawyering, more generally the professionalization of problem-solving, a concomitant proliferation of organizations, the sheer complexity of the late modern world: all of these related developments would seem to have contributed to theory's decline.

When I peruse law journals (especially those published at law schools in the US) and encounter the word *theory* – a theory of customary international law, a theory of compliance – what I see most of the time is mechanical, narrowly conceived and unoriginal. The same old ideas are perpetually, unimaginatively recycled and the same limits inevitably reached. Books that

5 Talk of rules, a euphemized form of legalism, is never more fallacious than when applied to the most homogeneous societies (or the least codified side of differentiated societies), where most practices, including those seemingly most ritualized, can be abandoned to the orchestrated improvisation of common dispositions.

Bourdieu, *Outline of a Theory of Practice*, p. 17.

two decades ago took international legal theory seriously and confronted philosophical challenges directly, have no successors. Here I am thinking of Terry Nardin's *Law, Morality, and the Relations of States* (1983), David Kennedy's *International Legal Structures* (1987) and Martti Koskenniemi's *From Apology to Utopia* (1989), all of which I discussed in previous chapters of this book. Thomas Franck's *The Power of Legitimacy among Nations* (1990) marks the end of an era, its coda the postcolonial critique of blinkered theory.[6]

I do not wish to suggest that these scholars have not continued to do important work. Nardin is a political theorist and not a lawyer; in recent years he has directed a good deal of his attention to international ethics, where many of the perennial questions of legal theory appear without the benefit (or perhaps the burden) of lawyers' language. Kennedy has written extensively on "international law as a series of professional performances rather than as an edifice of ideas, doctrines, and institutions"; questions about professional legal expertise take precedence over the perennial questions of legal theory and their relevance for international law.[7] Complementing Kennedy's interest in international law as a profession are his recent books on its relation to humanitarianism and warfare as professions (*The Dark Side of Virtue: Reassessing International Humanitarianism*, 2004; *Of War and Law*, 2006). Koskenniemi has written a major history of the international legal profession between 1870 and 1960, in which a parade of legal theorists are considered, not for contributions to theory, but "as actors in particular social dramas."[8] Prolific as ever, Franck has most notably sought to foster an "emerging right of democratic governance."[9]

The turn from legal theory to international law as a profession reflects a concern for the ethical issues raised by any disciplined, institutionalized practice that has consequences, some intended, some not, for the world at large. The revival of ethical concerns we see in Nardin, Kennedy and Koskenniemi's recent work is also to be found among many scholars in the field of International Relations (IR). These concerns are, however, less focused on professional practices than on the large, rapidly changing features of the

6 Onuma Y., "When Was the Law of International Society Born? – An Inquiry of the History of International Law from a Civilizational Perspective," *Journal of the History of International Law*, vol. 2, 2000, pp. 10–66; A. Anghie, *Imperialism, Sovereignty and the Making of International Law*, Cambridge: Cambridge University Press, 2005.

7 See, especially, D. Kennedy, "When Renewal Repeats: Thinking against the Box," *N. Y. U. Journal of International Law and Politics*, vol. 32, 1999–2000, pp. 335–500, quoting p. 337.

8 M. Koskenniemi, *The Gentle Civilizer of Nations: The Rise and Fall of International Law 1870–1960*, Cambridge: Cambridge University Press, 2002, p. 7. This passage continues: "International law is also a terrain of fear and ambition, fantasy and desire, conflict and utopia, and a host of other aspects of the phenomenonological lives of its practitioners."

9 T. Franck, "The Emerging Right of Democratic Governance," *American Journal of International Law*, vol. 86, 1992, pp. 46–91. This project is an exemplar of weak theory well practiced.

modern world. Scholars in the field take the big questions to be their special province but find themselves inadequately equipped to answer them. In response to a felt need, they have in recent decades become more theory-conscious.

One might think that factors contributing to theory's eclipse in international legal scholarship would have had the same effect in IR. There is, however, an important difference. In IR the rise of theory has coincided with, and responds to, a quest for disciplinary identity and academic respectability. Big questions never suffice in guiding inquiry. If IR is to be a social science, then it must instead exhibit the relevant properties of any science as theory-guided inquiry.

Social science is science on the model of the natural sciences, and theory is scientific when it conforms to a set of ontological claims for which philosophers often use the term *positivism*. In the next section of this essay, I try to give the reader some sense of my craft as a practicing theorist whose career reflects an uneasy relation to the claims of positivist science (see Chapters 13, 14 and 23, above). I also show that the term *positivism* has diverging senses in law and science, and this results in significant differences in the way legal positivists and scientists use the term *theory*. Legal theory relates the form things take to the functions they perform together, while scientific theory relates the changing properties of things to unseen causes.

After situating positivism in Western metaphysics and exploring its implications for theorizing, I take up a theoretical framework now much discussed in IR called *constructivism*. Constructivists have had much to say about positivism but fail to agree on important issues. They also have had a great deal to say about norms and rules. In every case, where they stand on the claims of positivist science affects what they say about normative phenomena. Most constructivists are positivists who prefer to use the term *norm*, yet they do so with complete disregard for normativity – the very property that distinguishes norms (or as I would prefer to say, rules) from other social phenomena.

I proceed next in this essay to examine this endemic disinterest in normativity. Then I investigate the relevance of normative considerations when agents act on their preferences. My strategy for doing so is to start with positivist claims about normative phenomena, press these claims to the point of incoherence, and then relax positivist assumptions to regain some measure of credibility for these claims. Finally, in the last section of the essay, I try to show how certain kinds of things – normal practices, preferred outcomes – become normative. Here I return to an important theme in my earlier work by specifying the normative consequences of using language to achieve social ends (see especially Chapters 14 and 19, above). From a constructivist perspective, everything – every *thing* – resolves into process; theory as practice and theory of practice converge.

Throughout I counter the positivist devotion to a world of things with variously articulated claims about a normatively informed social reality.

These claims center on three features of the world we have made for ourselves, and continuously remake, in the first instance by speaking to each other about our wants and our world. The first of these features is the "mysterious" relation between form (forms of speech, rules, law) and force (the illocutionary force of speech acts, the effectiveness of rules, the force of law).[10] Second is the relation between formalization (symbolically ratified in degrees or grades) and normativity (thanks to positivism, rarely seen as a matter of degree). Third is the relation between form (again, forms of speech, rules, law) and functions (the kinds of work that the several parts of any whole perform in order for the whole to work).

This is a deeply Aristotelian way of thinking: every part is a thing formed as a whole in itself, and every whole is a thing formed as a part in some larger whole. Because wholes depend on the performance of complementary functions (or they fail to remain whole), a great deal hinges on the formal articulation, or classification, of things (parts, forms) by reference to the work they do (function) and the way they do it (force). Not just here, but in earlier essays, I use functional criteria to classify rules (including the highly formalized rules we call law). Increasingly I have come to see that Aristotle provided the philosophical warrant for doing so.

Positivist theory

As practice, most science most of the time presupposes a world "out there." As sentient beings, we are indeed a part of this world, but its existence does not depend on our existence. Furthermore, this world makes sense. Its contents have stable properties to which our senses give us access, even if this access is limited and not always reliable. For most of us most of the time, these claims are hardly controversial. Taken together, they are the commonsense bedrock of our experience, and they constitute an ontological stance that philosophers call *realism*.

Over the last two centuries, science has sharpened realism by extending and refining these claims about the world and our relation to it. Holding that the world consists of discrete objects and events (things) with properties affecting other things and their properties, realists have systematically developed a version of realism that is often called *positivism*. Positivist science subjects the things of the world to observation, measurement, manipulation. Already implicit in realist ontology, these operations turn things and their relations into *facts*.

Since only facts matter, what counts as a fact is the only philosophical issue that matters. Precise measurement raises our confidence that asserted facts

10 J. Derrida's essay, "Force of Law: The 'Mysterious' Foundations of Authority," trans. M. Quaintance, inspires this choice of terms. See his *Acts of Religion*, New York: Routledge, 2002, pp. 230–98.

are, in fact, facts. So does independent corroboration. Well-established empirical generalizations are facts about facts. So-called laws of nature recapitulate actual patterns that are never observed to vary. Where the facts do vary, an observed regularity may still count as a fact, but only if it is properly rendered as a probability statement.

When the factual evidence prompts us to make general statements, or inferences, about the effect of some things on other things, positivists call these general statements *theories*. Applied to the factual record, theories are said to explain why sequences of things happen as they do; theories permit us to predict what will happen before it actually does. In short, theories map the manifold causal relations that make an ever-changing world what it is. Evaluated against the factual record, theories stand, fall or undergo revisions that limit their scope and clarify their relation to other theories. Ontology leads inexorably to methodology, and the scientific method informs the practice of science.

In positivist practice, theories always depend on an ensemble of facts that constitute an intelligible domain of inquiry. These domains consist of things with observable properties that are, as a matter of fact, roughly comparable in familiar respects: size, number, position, duration, composition. If these things did not have comparable properties in at least some respects, we could make no inferences about their relations because they are not, in fact, directly related. Standing back, we visualize an ensemble of things factually characterized by comparable size as occupying the same *level*; we think of their relations laterally in space and serially in time.

Since things at one level seem to be composed of smaller things at another level, positivist scientists typically proceed by reducing things to their constituent parts on the assumption that the parts are easier to investigate with scientific precision. We call this operation *analysis*. Even if each level constitutes a substantially self-contained factual domain, analysis also reveals that each level is linked causally to the next level down and presses the scientist to identify specific links. Thanks to the analytic disposition that positivism fosters, the cumulative effect of positivist science organized by level is to make sense of the world as a whole. A world of levels orders nature from the most basic physical reality to the most ephemeral social reality.[11]

A world of levels is implicit in realist ontology and rendered explicit in positivist science. We can stand back and see levels because we also visualize ourselves, as observers, apart from the world. Again, positivism makes a claim implicit in realism explicit and spells out the consequent necessity of separating the observer's values from the facts of the world. In principle, nature includes society, even if nature and society are divided by levels;

11 See, further, N. Onuf, "Levels," *European Journal of International Relations*, vol. 1, 1995, pp. 35–58; Colin Wight, *Agents, Structure and International Relations: Politics as Ontology*, Cambridge: Cambridge University Press, 2006, ch. 3.

positivist science aspires to establish the facts of the world at every level. Observers must choose to look at the facts of the world – and even the many facts relevant to their own situations – with the detachment that scrupulous adherence to the scientific method assures.

There are reasons why scholars may reject this choice: they believe that social facts are real only insofar as we say they are, that observers never succeed in detaching themselves from their factual claims, that the world does not consist of things in the first instance, that we can never know what is true about the world. Rejecting positivism may simply affirm the practical differences between the arts and sciences, express a thoroughgoing methodological skepticism, challenge the ontological preference for what things are over what they do, or imply a radical repudiation of the epistemology that has dominated Western philosophy even longer than positivism has dominated science. In a field of study with pretensions to science, scholars disowning positivism for any of these reasons are likely to be called *postpositivist, poststructuralist* or *postmodern*, rather indiscriminately, even by themselves.

I have described positivism as a philosophical movement that transformed the practice of science over the last two centuries. At the same time, positivist ontology transformed the way we think about law, but not always in the same way it changed science. Before positivism, social reality was seen as pervasively normative by its nature – as indeed was nature itself. Philosophy, natural science and legal science were effectively indistinguishable.

As positivist ontology took hold, natural science treated society as ultimately reducible to nature and generally subject to the same methods of investigation. By contrast, legal science separated nature and society. It decreed that normativity depends specifically on human choice and behavior and achieves a factual expression in rules conceptualized as things in themselves. Even nations are things with the properties of human agents; they make choices and behave as we do. When positivists asked what rules make nations into agents, where these rules come from, and why nations follow them, they also framed their answers by reference to things: the familiar categories of things we call subjects, sources, sanctions.

Legal positivists also devise theories, but they do not use the term *theory* the way that scientific positivists do (see Chapters 6 and 14 for a fuller assessment of legal positivism). Instead they use the term very much as realists have always used it. In science, theories are general explanations for the apparent fact that the properties of different sorts of things vary together; factual regularities point to causal relations. In legal positivism as in ordinary language, theories are general descriptions of the form things take when they work together as a whole. Theories of this sort identify mechanisms, or relatively stable sets of functional relations. Factual regularities beget classification; form points to function.

Thus a theory of custom as a source of international law considers the conditions under which agents engage in regular patterns of conduct. The theory might give priority to the dispositions and motivations of specified agents or the cumulative experience of many agents. The theory might emphasize the properties of normative phenomena or the overarching structure of social relations and material circumstances. All such theories start with the whole and order its parts in order then to explain how each part does its job for the whole. These are, of course, just the kind of theories that I have devoted so much attention to in this volume.

Scientific theories start with things as parts and make inferences about the whole as a set of related things. As I have said, the practice of science fosters an analytic disposition, which renders an intractably complex world into more and more, ever-smaller parts. Smaller, tighter theories displace bigger, looser ones. The practice of science also demands a strict adherence to the rules of the scientific method, including the rule that the facts of the world and the observer's values must always be kept apart. By contrast, positivist legal scholars respond to a complex world as a given. At best their theories impose conceptual order on a complex world of social relations, frame complicated situations and orient discussion. Legal positivists unabashedly ask questions about conduct in these situations. As lawyers, they are skilled at tacking between facts and values without confusion or contamination.

The rules constituting the scientific method and the rules orienting the lawyer's craft demand the same devotion. Both regimes enable adepts to muster factual evidence and use it persuasively. Yet these two regimes function differently. While scientists use evidence to substantiate claims about what happens in the world, lawyers bring evidence to bear on their claims as to which laws and what practices should and do matter to their clients, judges, the world.

We should not be surprised that theory-oriented scholars in IR and practice-oriented international legal scholars have had so little to say to each other. Not only do they do different kinds of work. Preoccupied with positivism (whether for or, less often, against), most IR scholars are happy to leave normative phenomena to lawyer-advocates and partisan-polemicists. Positivism has also imbued IR theory with a distinct emphasis on formless stuff and specific causes, on behavior as against system, on parts as against wholes.

This philosophical bias (as I have come to see it) now permeates most of the sciences. The large and striking exception is to be found in the biological sciences, but not in those branches, such as genetics and cell biology, where analysis reigns and reductionist tendencies lead to chemistry as the next level down. Instead, ecology, developmental biology and evolutionary biology consider the relations of form, function and context that makes organs and organisms into wholes. Classification takes precedence over analysis, and inquiry points to the next level up.

Thus evolutionary biology has inspired the recent development of evolutionary psychology as a field of study. Most psychologists subscribe to positivist methods of inquiry; their facts straddle the border that assigns nature and society adjacent levels (all levels are always easier to see at a distance), and their inquiries tend to push through that border to the level below. Evolutionary psychologists already start a level down with human evolution as an historical condition. They seek to explain general patterns of human conduct a level up, as evidenced in the kinds of social facts that lend themselves to positivist treatment. In other words, evolutionary psychologists propose theories using the language of form and function, and they test these theories with methods that warrant the making of causal inferences.

We should not be surprised that evolutionary psychologists make controversial theoretical claims in the name of science, which they have difficulty supporting.[12] These claims are controversial because they focus on the mind an ensemble of mechanisms, each with its own evolutionary history, over which human consciousness, intersubjective exchange and social arrangements have relatively little effect. In other words, they are thoroughgoing materialists – more so than Marxists ever were. The theoretical claims of evolutionary psychology go a level up in order to deny that such a level – the level of society considered in its own terms – even exists. Of course it exists insofar as we say it does, but we can say the same for any delusion. On inspection, all that is social melts into air.

Evolutionary psychologists are well aware of what is at stake. As they see it, the social sciences traffic in an unexamined, pervasive idealism.[13] Idealists hold that what we think (feel, want, believe) explains what we do; what remains for social science is to spell out the ways in which what we do works, or not, for us, others and society in general. In my opinion, materialists have a point. Social scientists unduly discount the material conditions under which we live, think and do what we do, but not because they have fallen under the influence of "social constructionists."[14] Oddly perhaps, the culprit here is the philosophical bias that favors substance over form.

International Relations provides an apt illustration. Scholars in the field quarrel over the relative importance of what they take to be the ideational and material constituents of social reality. Liberal institutionalists are said to favor ideational factors; political realists emphasize material factors. For both sides, the question is whether ideas have causal effects on their own.

Political realists may concede that power, for example, is an idea, not unrelated to the idea of cause, but that it gains its power from the material capabilities that this idea brings to bear on the world. Indeed the idea of power is itself a capability; conversely, capabilities exist in the first instance as an idea that someone has about things in the world. Shifting the explanatory burden from power to capability does not make political realism materialist. Social science turns ideas into formless stuff; science explains the effects that

12 See D.J. Buller, *Adapting Minds: Evolutionary Psychology and the Persistent Quest for Human Nature*, Cambridge, MA: MIT Press, 2005, for an exhaustive and compelling assessment.

13 See, especially, S. Pinker, *The Blank Slate: The Modern Denial of Human Nature*, New York: Viking, 2002, Part I.

14 Ibid., pp. 22–9.

the properties of stuff have on other stuff. Ideas matter for most positivist social scientists (if society matters, how could ideas not?), even if some of them happen to believe they are materialists. What they all have in common is an anemic, undiagnosed idealism that denies the stuff of the world its formal features.

Positivism fosters this featureless, inclusive idealism by discounting form in favor of substance. On the whole, so does the postpositivist movement in the social sciences.[15] Some postpositivists might claim otherwise because they have gone back to realism as a philosophical position. They are prompted to do so because positivism, strictly speaking, has no place for the stuff of the world that cannot be observed directly. As reformulated by philosophers of science, realism joins positivism in distancing the world from its observers, but acknowledges formless stuff detectable only in its effects.

If there is no such stuff after all (ether, for example), there are no effects not otherwise accounted for, and all that remains is a figure of speech, a rhetorical formality. For a materialist, positivism is methodologically sufficient. For most social scientists, ideas qualify as formless stuff with observable effects; they must be real. Positivism folds into realism to form a secure philosophical horizon, and all problems of inquiry, no matter how vexing, are merely methodological.

Over the last two decades, I have advanced a theoretical orientation that I labeled *constructivism*, with scholars in IR my chief audience (but see Chapter 19, above).[16] Other scholars soon began calling themselves constructivists, and a good deal of self-styled theoretical development ensued.[17] Leaving aside my own work (modest enough in impact) and that of Friedrich Kratochwil (whose impact, though greater than mine, is less than it should be), the result is a formless mass of textual material. Almost formless, I should say, because the bulk of constructivist scholarship today exhibits two features distinguishing it from the many decades of liberal institutionalist scholarship preceding its emergence.

The first is reliance on a few indicative terms: *culture*, *norm*, *identity* and of course *social construction*. If the constructivists who use these terms so

15 I want to say this carefully, because poststructuralists are obliged to take form (manifest in or as structure) into consideration if only to dissociate themselves from it; Gilles Deleuze's work offers a compelling example. In the social sciences only a few postpositivist scholars would say more specifically that they are poststructuralists.

16 See, especially, N.G. Onuf, *World of Our Making: Rules and Rule in Social Theory and International Relations*, Columbia: University of South Carolina Press, 1989.

17 See, further, E. Adler, "Constructivism in International Relations," in W. Carlnaes *et al.* (eds), *Handbook of International Relations*, London: Sage, 2002, pp. 95–118; M. Zehfuss, *Constructivism in International Relations: The Politics of Reality*, Cambridge University Press, 2002; and my "Worlds of Our Making: The Strange Career of Constructivism in International Relations," in D.J. Puchala (ed.), *Visions of International Relations: Assessing an Academic Field*, Columbia: University of South Carolina Press, 2002, pp. 119–41.

rampantly, indeed indiscriminately, were to define and relate them systematically, they might have developed a coherent conceptual formation, or theoretical framework, for exploring the social construction of cultures, norms and identities in institutional settings themselves transformed by these processes. Peter Katzenstein and his associates undertook to do so in *The Culture of National Security* (1996), in part by drawing on recent scholarship in sociology and social psychology.[18] Yet their efforts to relate key terms in a coherent framework fell short. Least of all have they done justice to normative matters (a defining concern of the liberal-institutionalist scholarship they see themselves superseding).

Constructivism's second feature stems from Alexander Wendt's strong claims on behalf of scientific realism to bolster the general idea that ideas, however ineffable, have demonstrable causal effects.[19] Even if all constructivists followed Wendt's lead (and not all do), scientific realism cannot by itself provide a coherent conceptual formation that makes social construction its primary concern. Causally efficacious ideas are not enough. What is needed, and what I and a few others have tried to provide, is a conception of language which, by virtue of its performative nature, does the work of social construction both in its own right and through the medium of rules (see Chapter 14, above).

Dominating constructivism today is a philosophical slurry of positivism, realism and idealism, which fills a space ill-formed by two overlapping sets of theoretical boundaries. The first I have already alluded to. It runs between political realism on one side, and constructivism and liberal institutionalism on the other. The second set developed when scholars began in recent decades to postulate a simplified social reality consisting entirely of rational agents with fixed preferences (or stable interests: see below) making choices in highly idealized settings (for example, self-regulating markets, two-person games).

This way of thinking is widely known as rational choice theory. The term *theory* is misleading; we might better speak of it as an abstract model, or class of models, which focus attention on the kinds of choices we make. Rationality does not explain these choices; a theory formulated in terms of rational choice would presume to do so. Conventionally associated with economics, rational choice theorists believe that they have reorganized the social sciences by introducing a new level of scientific inquiry – one that separates themselves from their less rigorous colleagues. Anyone not using these models cannot hope to propose theories appropriate to positivist science.

18 See R. Jepperson *et al.*, "Norms, Identity, and Culture in National Security," in P.J. Katzenstein (ed.), *The Culture of National Security: Norms and Identity in World Politics*, New York: Columbia University Press, 1996, pp. 33–75.

19 See, especially, A. Wendt, *Social Theory of International Politics*, Cambridge: Cambridge University Press, 1999, chs. 2–3. Also, see Wight, *Agents, Structures and International Relations*, ch. 1.

At least in the US, rational choice theory took IR by storm in the 1980s. The undeniable elegance of rational choice models and the prestige they gain by association with economics have resulted in the ascendancy of neorealist and neoliberal theorizing, at the expense of so-called classical realism (here meaning the kind of political realism exemplified by Hans Morgenthau) and the old-fashioned kind of liberal institutionalism that gives international law its due. In some measure, the fashion for rational choice models prompted the emergence of constructivism, and today the field is marked by a tendency to put scholars in two camps – rationalist and constructivist – the former prevailing in the US and the latter elsewhere.[20]

The law and economics movement brought rational choice models to the fore in legal scholarship at the very moment they rose to prominence in the social sciences. That lawyers tend to see social reality as a matter of making choices and law as a formal system of relations suggests why rational choice models might appeal to legal theorists. Yet these models have been particularly slow in coming to international legal scholarship. Thus the arrival of a book firmly dedicated to revitalizing international legal theory by putting rational choice models to use is an event of considerable importance.

Jack Goldsmith and Eric Posner's *The Limits of International Law* (2005) is important because it brings rational choice theory to international law, because it borrows from rational choice theory in IR, *and* because its authors evince a decided hostility to international legal theory as they find it. As firm positivists and political realists, they believe that existing theory reflects the normative predilections of progressive liberal institutionalists. Not only does rational choice theory reveal the deficiencies of existing theory. Even more it explains why international law has such a limited impact on the conduct of states. To think otherwise suggests that international legal scholars chronically suffer from self-deception.

In most respects the sociologically inclined constructivism that I have identified with Katzenstein and Wendt and the rational choice theory that Goldsmith and Posner advocate could not be more different. Drawing on a formless mass of ideas, constructivists tend to treat social reality as if it too were substantially formless. Ideas float, everything floats. Rational choice theorists take a few highly formalized, closely related models and substitute them for manifold reality of constantly shifting shapes. One form fits all choices. Yet both ways of thinking have one tendency in common. They honor the fact–value distinction to a fault; the normative disappears into the factual. Constructivists accomplish this odd feat by stripping norms of their

20 *International Organization*, vol. 52 (1998), pp. 645–1061 (special issue: *International Organization at Fifty: Exploration and Contention in the Study of World Politics*), is indicative. There is some resistance. See K.M. Fierke and M. Nicholson, "Divided by a Common Language: Formal and Constructivist Approaches to Games," *Global Society*, vol. 15, 2001, pp. 7–25; J. Fearon and A. Wendt, "Rationalism v. Constructivism: A Skeptical View," in Carlnaes, *Handbook of International Relations*, pp. 52–72.

normativity; rational choice theorists do so by denying any relation between choice and obligation.

The robust constructivism advocated here makes necessity a virtue by giving form and function its due. Aristotle's metaphysics informs this kind of work but hardly provides it with a sufficient philosophical rationale. Something more is needed to keep constructivism from slipping into the prevailing positivist-realist mire of formless stuff. Immanuel Kant's metaphysics provided this something before positivism gave science the unyielding form it has today.

Scholars often label Kant's metaphysics constructivist. The Copernican revolution announced in the *Critique of Pure Reason* (1781, 1787) postulates a world we cannot know. Whether formless or not, it is formless for us and therefore inaccessible. Instead, the mind gives form to a world of stuff; cognitive operations transform the flood of perceptions that our waking minds constantly process. Form *is* ideational, but not stuff. We use a limited, more or less standard repertory of forms to construct a world that for all purposes relevant to our day-by-day existence *is* real, whole, fully formed and intersubjectively accessible.[21] When we act on what we see, we furnish our world with things and their relations, parts in wholes, parts as wholes.

Normative expectations

Katzenstein and his collaborators expressly adopted "a sociological perspective" in *The Culture of National Security*. Prompting this stance are the perceived shortcomings of rational choice theory and the "economic styles of analysis" that it calls for.[22] From a sociological point of view, rational choice models leave too much out, including "the normative context that helps define the interests of actors."[23] Advocates of a sociological perspective often speak of norms in context, and even more of norms *as* context. Indeed, the way Katzenstein and his collaborators went about defining *norm* and linking it to "the sociological use" of such concepts as identity and culture make context an integral feature of their conceptual apparatus.[24]

21 Kant's idealism is entirely subjective, taking for granted that every normal human being has substantially the same cognitive powers. I smuggled the term *intersubjective* into my construction of Kant's metaphysics in order to make Kant's constructivism properly *social*, taking for granted that language makes it so. Also, see the concluding pages of Chapter 23, above.

22 P.J. Katzenstein, "Introduction: Alternative Perspectives on National Security," in *The Culture of National Security*, pp. 2, 5, 14.

23 P.J. Katzenstein, "Coping with Terrorism: Norms and Internal Security in Germany and Japan," in J. Goldstein and R.O. Keohane (eds), *Ideas and Foreign Policies: Beliefs, Institutions, and Political Change*, Ithaca: Cornell University Press, 1993, p. 294. Also, see Katzenstein, "Introduction," p. 15.

24 Katzenstein, "Introduction," p. 5.

Katzenstein and his collaborators "use the concept of *norm* to describe collective expectations for the proper behavior of actors with a given identity."[25] Other definitions closely resemble this one. For Martha Finnemore, norms are "shared expectations about appropriate behavior held by a community of actors." By way of clarification, she affirmed that "norms are shared and social," and then offered a second formulation: "One could say that they are collectively held ideas about behavior."[26]

Writing later with Kathryn Sikkink, Finnemore altered her definition somewhat: "There is general agreement on the definition of a norm as a standard of appropriate behavior for actors with a given identity."[27] Whether an explicit reference to standards adds anything of importance is a question that I consider below. A last variation in this suite of definitions appears late in *The Culture of National Security*. "This volume," according to Paul Kowert and Jeffrey Legro, "treats norms as collective beliefs regulating the behavior and identity of actors."[28] Here at least we see more clearly why these definitions allude to actors' identities, even if it is not at all clear why we should treat their identities as a "given."

Evidently, norms belong to a larger category of social phenomena bearing the labels *expectations*, *ideas* and *beliefs*. Among these terms, Katzenstein favored *expectations*, which Finnemore also adopted and Andrew Hurrell has more recently affirmed.[29] *To expect* is a transitive verb: one expects some state of affairs to transpire. In this case, agents belonging to some collectivity expect proper behavior from all such agents. These agents often also expect adverse consequences to befall any of their number not fulfilling expectations. At least they would like to be able to have these expectations in the instance of other agents' behavior, and may themselves behave in such a way that these expectations are more likely to be fulfilled. Or they may wish to circumvent these expectations when applied to themselves, and behave accordingly.

Clearly, expectations have behavioral implications: I expect dark clouds to bring heavy rain, and I adjust my behavior to account for this eventuality. There is, however, nothing normative in my expectation. We need therefore to distinguish, as Hurrell has, between factual and normative

25 Ibid.; Katzenstein's emphasis. Also: "Norms are collective expectations about proper behavior for a given identity." R.L. Jepperson *et al.*, "Norms, Identity and Culture in National Security," in Katzenstein, *The Culture of National Security*, p. 54.

26 M. Finnemore, *National Interests in International Society*, Ithaca: Cornell University Press, 1996, pp. 22–3, citing Goldstein and Keohane, *Ideas and Foreign Policies*.

27 M. Finnemore and K. Sikkink, "International Norm Dynamics and Political Change," *International Organization*, vol. 52, 1998, p. 891.

28 P. Kowert and J. Legro, "Norms, Identity, and Their Limits: A Theoretical Reprise," in Katzenstein, *The Culture of National Security*, p. 483.

29 A. Hurrell, "Norms and Ethics in International Relations," in Carlnaes, *Handbook of International Relations*, p. 143.

expectations.[30] Only when agents attach some value to an expected state of affairs does normativity ensue. As Harold Lasswell and Abraham Kaplan put it, agents "make demands for values (on themselves and others) on the basis of various expectations."[31]

When I take note of "proper behavior" as something I and/or other agents demand, and I additionally state my expectation that this demand will be met, my statement is, according to Lasswell and Kaplan, "normatively ambiguous." Any such statement "refers to norms, even though it is unclear whether the norm in question pertains exclusively to the speaker, whether it is shared by the speaker with others, or whether, though a norm of others, it is not a norm of the speaker at all."[32] The norm in question is conveyed in statements indicating that some category of behavior is proper. Statements *about* (the statement of) the norm convey additional, quite possibly ambiguous information about the norm's scope. They also convey an estimate, quite possibly unreliable, about the likelihood that the norm will be followed. While the statement in all its parts should not to be confused with (the statement of) the norm, the whole statement (including stated expectations) does constitute normative context within which behavior is to be understood.

Expectations figure centrally in social processes where designated agents deliberately concern themselves with proper behavior. Such agents have authority, which Lasswell and Kaplan defined as "the expected and legitimate possession of power."[33] Authorities must have the means, in accordance with expectations, to issue norms and have other agents to follow them. Yet something more is required.

Legitimacy involves the expectation that authorities will behave properly. More specifically, authorities are expected to behave in accordance with norms indicating the kind of behavior that authorities are expected to exhibit. Norms induce and fulfill expectations, and this is especially so for norms for making and using norms. Layered patterns of expectation induce in observers an expectation, not always warranted, that norms about norms cause these patterns. Intimately related, norms and expectations are neither interchangeable nor indistinguishable.

Norms and expectations both refer to future conditions. There is, however, nothing automatically normative about anticipating the future: expectations

30 Ibid. Also, note C. Bicchieri's distinction between empirical and normative expectations and thus between descriptive and social norms. *The Grammar of Society: The Nature and Dynamics of Social Norms*, New York: Cambridge University Press, 2006, ch. 1.

31 H.D. Lasswell and A. Kaplan, *Power and Society: A Framework for Political Inquiry*, New Haven: Yale University Press, 1950, p. 16. Also, see F.V. Kratochwil, *Rules, Norms, and Decisions: On the Conditions of Practical and Legal Reasoning in International Relations and Domestic Affairs*, Cambridge: Cambridge University Press, 1989, pp. 52–6.

32 Lasswell and Kaplan, *Power and Society*, p. 22.

33 Ibid., p. 133. For Bicchieri, legitimacy is the defining property of normative expectations in general. *The Grammar of Society*, pp. 21.

(predicated on conditions) and preferences (predicated on values) are not to be confused. Other terms associated with normativity, such as ideas, understandings and beliefs, do not even point to the future as a necessary frame of reference. If an explicit orientation to the future is necessary to an understanding of normativity, then we could hardly expect any of these other terms to suffice. Why then do they seem relevant – what feature do all these terms have in common? Just as norms must be oriented to the future, must they also possess this other feature?

The answer to the first question is not hard to find. Expectations are said to be "collective" or "shared," ideas are "collectively held," beliefs are "collective." *Expectations, ideas, beliefs*: all of these terms refer to the cognitive activity of individual human beings, for whom the activity in question may be singular and private. The situation is no different with preferences.

Nevertheless, acquiring expectations, ideas, understandings, beliefs or preferences is a social event (directly or indirectly), and so is acting on them insofar as others are affected. Given that we are social beings, we can expect to share expectations, etc., and, in so doing, make them social. As social beings, we make and use norms affecting ourselves and others. This is social activity, related to many other social activities (such as sharing expectations), in a variety of complicated ways. Norms are social, but sharing expectations does not, by itself, make them so.

As Lasswell and Kaplan observed, norms need not pertain to all agents in a given situation. This is so whatever their expectations may be. Indeed, norms may pertain to agents who share no expectations relevant to the state of affairs to which the norms are directed, or even explicitly reject those norms, not to mention expectations shared by other agents. Katzenstein and his collaborators made note of this general state of affairs. "Norms may be 'shared,' or commonly held, across some distribution of actors in a system. Alternatively, however, norms may *not* be widely held by actors, but may nevertheless be *collective* features of a system," for example, "by being institutionalized."

It is not clear why any systemic "feature" needs further description as "collective" – it is trivially true for all systems that its features are collective – when the salient consideration is, for example, the degree to which expectations are institutionalized. In such case, they might have said: "Norms are highly institutionalized expectations about proper behavior." For all that they have left unexplained, their conclusion is inescapable. "The now typical identification of norms as necessarily a 'shared' social property is thus inappropriate."[34]

One might wonder who is responsible for this "now typical definition" and its shortcomings. Sharing with any number of other scholars (perhaps

34 Jepperson *et al.*, "Norms, Identity and Culture in National Security," p. 54 n. 69, their emphases.

Katzenstein and company among them) an expectation that the *International Encyclopedia of the Social Sciences* would provide at least some guidance, I looked up the concept of norms in that source. Robin Williams' entry starts with a definition:

> A norm is a rule, standard, or pattern for action (from the Latin *norma*, a carpenter's square or rule). Social norms are rules for conduct. The norms are standards of conduct by reference to which behavior is judged and approved or disapproved.[35]

Obviously behavior is proper, or not, when measured against some standard for that behavior. "A standard specifies a criterion against which one can in principle judge or appraise our actions, states of our psychology, states of our character, social institutions, and so forth."[36] Williams' definition says nothing at all about expectations, beliefs or any other shared cognitive phenomena. Nevertheless, we soon read the following: "Norms are learned by individuals in social intercourse with others – that is, in the process of socialization. By definition, then, norms are shared by two or more individuals."[37]

This curiously disordered formulation starts with "consequences for behavior," which are attributed not to norms as such, but to their acceptance. The more fully accepted a norm, the more likely it is that agents to whom the norm is directed will behave properly. If acceptance is the point, and agents (not norms) the actual subject of discussion, then (but only then) does learning proper behavior become the central theoretical focus of the discussion: socialization explains acceptance. By definition, then, socialization is a process of sharing, and acceptance is a collective condition. What is shared? Not norms, as standards of conduct, but their propositional content. Whatever it is that norms are about – whatever it is that they say constitutes proper conduct – agents are capable of sharing.

Concluding Williams' formulation, as quoted, is a reference to Muzafer Sherif's *The Psychology of Social Norms* (1936). At no point did Sherif, to his credit, actually say that norms are shared. As a social psychologist, he devoted a great deal of attention to the processes whereby people "incorporate in themselves a set of norms or standards from their social surroundings," or, to similar effect, "the concrete means by which the established norms of the group become interiorized." For his purposes, norms are "cultural products" – the products of shared experiences and bearers in their propositional content of shared understandings of the world. As products, norms exist independently of the agents incorporating their content. "We shall

35 R.M. Williams, Jr., "Norms: The Concept of Norms," in D.L. Sills (ed.), *International Encyclopedia of the Social Sciences*, vol. 11, New York: Macmillan, 1968, p. 204.

36 D. Copp, *Morality, Normativity, and Society*, New York: Oxford University Press, 1995, p. 19.

37 Williams, "Norms," p. 205.

consider customs, traditions, standards, rules, values, fashions, and all other criteria of conduct which are standardized as a consequence of the contact of individuals, as specific cases of 'social norms.' "[38] Recall that Williams also started here – norms are standards and, as such, rules for conduct – but ended somewhere else entirely.

Particular norms exist as standardized criteria of conduct whether any given agent accepts them or not. When agents accept given norms, they individually reproduce the content of those norms *as* criteria for their conduct. They may additionally expect others to accept this norm, and this additional consideration could affect agents' willingness to act along lines they otherwise find acceptable. Sherif's balanced exposition never allows norms to disappear into people's minds, their existence solely dependent on observers making the appropriate inferences from "social pressures" to "shared expectations." Decades later, the sociological use of the term *norm* shows just this slippage.

This state of affairs is hardly Sherif's fault. Indeed, his work on the way individuals incorporate norms had far less impact on sociological thinking than did Talcott Parsons' work, dating from the same time and developed over many years, on the "internalization" of norms.[39] While Sherif stipulated a world full of normative materials, Parsons wanted to know how these materials eventuate in social order. By giving Emile Durkheim credit for seeing that internalized norms alleviate the need for external modalities of social control, Parsons gave sociology a powerful theoretical orientation, complete with an impeccable pedigree.

Initially, Parsons defined norm as "a verbal description of a concrete course of action, thus regarded as desirable, combined with an injunction to make certain courses of action conform to this course."[40] In later work, he sometimes viewed norms as spelling out "general values" in "specific, operative" terms – they remain verbal descriptions, available as such to affected agents.[41] At times, however, he appears to have abandoned any such view of norms. Instead they disappear into the individuals internalizing them, only to reappear as "patterns of expectation."[42] While Parsons treated such patterns as subject to specification and institutionalization, his notoriously abstruse prose makes it more than likely that readers remember the words *expectation* in conjunction with *internalization*, and nothing more.

Leaping from expectations to proper behavior means leaping over some sort

38 M. Sherif, *The Psychology of Social Norms*, New York: Octagon, 1965, pp. 25, 46, 21, 3.

39 T. Parsons, *The Structure of Social Action: A Study in Social Theory with Special Reference to a Group of Recent European Writers*, New York: McGraw Hill, 1937, pp. 378–90.

40 Ibid., p. 75.

41 T. Parsons, "An Approach to the Sociology of Knowledge" (1959), in *Sociological Theory and Modern Society*, New York: Free Press, 1967, p. 145.

42 T. Parsons, "Durkheim's Contribution to the Theory of Integration of Social Systems" (1960), in *Sociological Theory and Modern Society*, p. 9.

of relevant information about what makes behavior proper. Obviously behavior is proper, or not, when measured against some standard for that behavior. Some conceptual discussions of norms mention *standards*, as we saw with Finnemore and Sikkink. Yet these discussions rarely give the term any sustained attention.

Sherif's list of the sorts of cultural products that count as norms includes standards. More importantly, he made it clear that all such products have been "standardized." Williams began his encyclopedia essay by defining a "norm" as "a rule, standard or pattern for action," but soon lost sight of his definition. When Jack Gibbs compiled a list of 14 "illustrative definitions" of *norm* from the literature in sociology and social psychology, including Sherif's and Williams', only five of these definitions used the term *standard*.[43]

Including Williams', five definitions equate *norm* with *pattern*. The latter term suggests that norms have enduring and presumably identifiable forms but implies nothing about conduct. The adjective *normal* suggests that some class of properties or events conform to a common standard, or norm, again without implying that the standard in question represents proper conduct. A great deal of positivist social science depends on the measurement and statistical manipulation of behavior that, in quantity, distributes normally. Measuring conduct is neither to condone nor condemn it; probability statements imply no judgement about propriety. The carpenter's square, or *norma*, is a form-making instrument, and so is any standard. Yet giving things form does not by itself make them normative.

As I suggested earlier, the separation of fact and value is a truism of positivist science. Whether it applies to the use of the terms *normal* and *normative* in ordinary language is another matter. Untroubled by the fact–value distinction, most English speakers use the term *normal* for descriptive purposes precisely because it implies the existence of a standard to which they attach prescriptive significance. The same holds for the term *regular*. Nor is it any different when people use more specific terms to express their prescriptive concerns: the measure of success, the wages of sin, the scales of justice, standard English.

Standards only exist if someone has stated them. Such statements take the standard form: one ought to do such and so, where such and so is the standard against which one's performance is to be measured. By indicating some course of action that one ought to follow, any statement in this form both *describes* what that course of action is (as a standard) and *prescribes* what one ought to do about it (match one's conduct to the standard).[44] In making a prescriptive statement, the speaker intends to regulate someone else's behavior. We expect compliance, whether we get it or not. Prescriptions that

43 J.P. Gibbs, *Norms, Deviance, and Social Control: Conceptual Matters*, New York: Elsevier North Holland, 1981, pp. 7–9.

44 Also, see Copp, *Morality, Normativity, and Society*, pp. 3–4, 19–22.

fail to achieve at least some measure of compliance may be regarded as having failed as prescriptions. Yet the term *regulation* suggests something more than the incidental or temporary effect that direct commands, for example, have on behavior.

Regulative prescriptions are those that have persistent effects. As such, they are capable of being stated in general terms. We often call these statements *regulations*. The more generic term, *rule*, has the same root. The Latin root of both terms – *regula* – refers to a straight line or straight piece of wood and thus a ruler (standard by which to measure things), or a rule. The Latin verb that is the source of the term *rule* – *regō* – has "to keep (sheep, for example) in line" as its root meaning.

There is an ineradicable sense in which this sort of activity is prescriptive – by intention and not just by implication – and not just for the moment. According to Frederick Schauer, rules are "prescriptive generalizations."[45] Let me define the term more fully. Rules address some class of agents, describe some class of actions as appropriate conduct for those agents, and link agents and standards with ought-statements: agents ought to behave in accordance with standards.

When Kratochwil said, "all rules are norms," it must be clear that I agree with him emphatically. When he went on to say, "not all norms exhibit rule-like characteristics," I find myself perplexed.[46] If a norm is capable of being stated, it must exhibit rule-like characteristics. Any alleged norm not capable of being stated (in the form of a rule) disappears into the background of diverse expectations, ideas, understandings and beliefs that agents individually hold yet somehow suffuse social relations. So construed, norms are the kind of formless, utterly passive stuff whose only function is to provide a nominal context for social construction. And Katzenstein and his collaborators assumed just this when they took up the subject of norms.

Behavioral regularities

If norms are an integral and pervasive feature of the social context that agents find themselves in, then we should expect to find norms wherever we look for them. This is what Katzenstein and his collaborators discovered: "an embarrassment of norms," as Kowert and Legro described the situation. The

45 F. Schauer, *Playing by the Rules: A Philosophical Examination of Rule-Based Decision-Making in Law and in Life*, Oxford: Clarendon, 1991, pp. 25–7. And see the conceptual treatments of *rule* in Chapters 14 and 19 above.

46 Holding that "the prescriptive (or evaluative) quality of 'oughtness' " is what "sets norms apart from other kinds of rules," Finnemore and Sikkink seem to agree that all norms are rules, but not that all rules are norms. "Norm Dynamics and Political Change," p. 891. If indeed we can say that some kinds of rules are *not* social, then those rules need not and perhaps could not be normative. Laws of nature come to mind. We need to ask, however, if this is an appropriate use of the term *rule*.

"ubiquity" of norms, many of them incompatible in content, is a problem because "it is difficult to predict which norms will be most influential."[47] Of course, anthropologists are intimately acquainted with this problem, which Marvin Harris has formulated in predictably striking terms:

> Even if one has a perfect knowledge of all the rules that one must know to act like a native – that is, even if one has been brought up like a native, a privilege all human beings enjoy with respect to at least one culture – predictions based on a knowledge of those rules alone cannot predict the great bulk of behavior stream events. On the other hand, in principle, the great bulk of rules can be predicted from a sufficiently detailed knowledge of behavior stream events.[48]

Clearly the problem involves something more than the sheer abundance of norms. According to Harris, rules are ambiguous, and not just from an observer's point of view. I do not think this is quite the way to put the matter. Agents may mistake the status or content of a rule, misjudge its relevance to the situation at hand, or construe the rule in a self-serving way. Rules that are broad in scope and permissive in application are more likely to suffer these responses than the more specific and stringent sorts of rules that most observers hold as a model. The rule directing people to drive carefully is hardly ambiguous. All drivers know exactly what they need to know about this rule, namely, that it sets an exceedingly loose standard for their conduct on the road.

Drivers also know that there are innumerable other, more specific rules of the road relevant to their conduct. At least some of these rules form "complementary opposites."[49] As Harris put this claim in order to refute it, for every rule there is an alternative rule holding up a contrary standard of conduct.[50] Yet pairs of rules are never simply symmetrical; there is no rule of the road that directs people to drive carelessly. Instead, there are rules that specify alternative standards of conduct for exceptional circumstances. For example, ambulance drivers are granted a more permissive standard than other drivers are. Many other rules – we might call them complementary substitutes – fix the meaning of careful driving in frequently encountered circumstances, for example, by setting a speed limit or marking an intersection.

47 Kowert and Legro, "Norms, Identity, and Their Limits," section title, p. 486.

48 M. Harris, *Cultural Materialism: The Struggle for a Science of Culture*, New York: Random House, 1979, pp. 269–70.

49 "The world community's prescriptions about coercion, like other world prescriptions, march and must march in pairs of complementary opposites." M.S. McDougal and F.S. Feliciano, *Law and Minimum World Public Order*, New Haven: Yale University Press, 1961, p. 127.

50 Harris, *Cultural Materialism*, p. 273. To say that *every* rule has an alternative surely claims too much on behalf of "cognitive idealists" to whom he attributes this position. Also see R.B. Edgerton, *Rules, Exceptions, and Social Order*, Berkeley: University of California Press, 1985.

According to Harris, rules that operate as alternatives to other rules are nothing more than "rules for breaking rules."[51] This is a somewhat misleading way of saying that some rules affect the scope of other rules. There will be rules for choosing between overlapping rules, not to mention rules for getting rid of old rules by introducing new ones. None of this is to say, however, that agents never see themselves as breaking a rule because there is always a permissive alternative for them to follow instead.

That people actively choose to follow a rule means that they also always have the choice of breaking it (this is a working assumption for any scholar adopting rational choice models). All such choices involve a reckoning, however quick and ill-informed, about the consequences of either course of action. The possibility of finding some other rule to follow complicates calculation, for example, by offering another course of action that has its own consequences, including the cost of ignoring the first rule or claiming it to be irrelevant. Rules afford people choices, and people's choices have effects on material conditions, available rules, future choices.

If indeed "we intuitively know that there is a rule for everything" (coming from Harris, this is an ironic proposition that we need not accept as stated), it does not follow that "we are easily misled into believing that rules govern or cause behavior."[52] We might better say: there are a great many rules that people take into account in their conduct. Obviously, no one rule is ever the sole cause of anyone's behavior. It is hard to imagine *any* one cause for most instances of human behavior. Behavior follows from the exercise of choices, a significant proportion of which people make in a context of many relevant rules. "Rules facilitate, motivate, and organize our behavior," as Harris pointed out himself.[53] If these are not causal factors contributing to the choices that people make and thus to "behavior stream events," then what else could they be?

Harris backed himself into an untenable position because he framed the issue of causality in terms of prediction. Obviously, the presence of rules does not permit reliable prediction because people can choose not to follow them. Prediction is rarely a reasonable goal in positivist social science. Scholars pursue it anyway because they are convinced that prediction is an indispensable feature of theory testing. Rules are a permanent source of discomfort because, by their nature, not circumstance, they never determine behavior fully: no theory in principle can start with rules and end up with predictions. Holding everything else constant does not solve the problem; science is not the answer.

51 Harris, *Cultural Materialism*, pp. 273–75. Edgerton, *Rules, Exceptions, and Social Order*, pp. 5–6, traced this arresting phrase to anthropologist Paul Bohannan.

52 Harris, *Cultural Materialism*, p. 275.

53 Ibid.

Over a considerable period of time, positivists have devised two, rather obvious remedies to the problem of not being able to formulate a good theory of rules in relation to behavior (and I have already alluded to both). They make rigorous theorizing possible by shifting attention from rules as such to some other, determinate cause of behavior. The trick, of course, is to show that this other cause is a necessary feature of some socially significant set of rules. The first of these remedies shifts attention from rules to the sanctions supporting them. The second attends only to those rules that have been fully internalized.

When agents choose to follow a rule, or not, they evaluate the consequences of either choice. If breaking a rule incurs a penalty, or following it a reward, agents are likelier to follow that rule. In other words, sanctions are punishments or inducements that cause people to follow rules. The more effective the sanction, the more closely the rule will approximate a determinate cause of behavior. The presence of sanctions suggests some measure of institutionalization. Those rules that are most effectively backed up by sanctions are, in this line of thinking, legal rules.

There are two obvious flaws in this argument. First, sanctions are never fully efficacious. Agents assessing the consequences of breaking a rule backed by a penalty may nevertheless decide that breaking it is worth the potential cost. Increasing the penalty or the likelihood of its application raises the potential cost to the agent in question, but it also represents an additional cost in resources assessable to other agents. Sanctions sufficient to cause perfect compliance are not an achievable or even an approachable goal.[54] If legal orders are obliged to tolerate some degree of rule-breaking, then sanctions do not suffice for theoretical purposes. Not being able to rely on them to predict rule-breaking behavior, we have no assurance that they cause agents to follow rules.

There is a second flaw with the argument that sanctions make rules into determinate causes of behavior. Legal rules represent only a fraction of the rules populating most social settings. Even the legal rules of the road constitute a fraction – perhaps quite small – of the rules that drivers actually know and generally follow. Informal sanctions help make informal rules effective, but the operation of informal sanctions is more readily postulated than demonstrated. International relations constitute an especially odd case. This setting offers an abundance of rules that agents call legal and tend to follow even if formal sanctions are rarely applied.

Extending the concept of sanction to include everything that causes an agent to follow a rule undercuts the possibility of a rigorously formulated theory. Positivist legal theory has generally resisted the temptation to define sanction inclusively. As a result, it fails even to address the great bulk of

54 O.R. Young, *Compliance and Public Authority: A Theory with International Applications*, Baltimore: Johns Hopkins University Press, 1979, pp. 113–24.

behavior that appears to be in conformity with rules not backed by sanctions. Insofar as positivist legal theory predicts compliant behavior because rules are backed by sanctions, the failure of agents to break other rules routinely and, in the process, eliminate them as rules would seem to compromise the theory.

The obvious alternative to institutionalization in explaining why rules are followed is internalization. The implicit claim here is that agents have become so familiar with the rule's propositional content that it takes on the properties of a necessary condition. "Should" drops out of the equation, and normativity no longer carries causal freight. Agents do what the rule calls for because that is what there is to do. They follow the rule, not as an active choice, but in the more limited sense of following any habit or belief.

Just as with the argument that sanctions make rules determinate causes of behavior, there are two flaws in the argument that internalized rules determine behavior. First, internalization, as a process, is never so complete that agents cannot choose to break an internalized rule. Choosing to override conditioning may be a personally disruptive and costly experience, but people do it when they see sufficiently large advantages. For other agents to reinforce the taken-for-granted properties of an internalized norm represents an additional cost to them. Beyond some point, inculcation becomes more costly than imposing sanctions, and some combination of internalization and institutionalization may be expected. Not only does this combination complicate the picture theoretically, but it will never suffice to cause behavior that is in perfect compliance with the rules.

The second flaw in the internalization argument becomes clear when we ask who actually internalizes the propositional content of rules. The agents in question must be individual human beings. Automobile drivers offer a useful example of agents who have (more or less) internalized a large number of rules, the bulk of which, as I claimed above, are informal. Yet many agents are institutions, which cannot be said to internalize rules in any meaningful sense. Institutional memory is at best a weak metaphor.

Any such institution has rules that specify the conditions under which individual human beings act, as agents, on its behalf. Ultimately, people respond to rules for institutions. These people come and go. They bring different life experiences with them and they leave their successors records that vary in completeness and advice that varies in cogency. Clearly, they will not have internalized relevant rules uniformly – both the rules making them agents for the institution and the rules that the institution is supposed to follow.

Any attempt to account for these institutional features of rule-following significantly complicates a theory that uses internalization to explain behavior in compliance with rules. There is yet another complication. Individuals are personally detached from the consequences of following rules, or not, on behalf of institutions. The evidence of behavioral science suggests that detachment militates against internalization. While sanctions internal to the institution may offset this tendency, taking them into account further sacrifices theoretical rigor for inclusiveness.

No positivist in quest of predictive power can be satisfied with theories such as these. The short route through these theoretical thickets is to postulate an expectation of rule compliance. People expect other people to follow rules, and they feel obliged to count themselves within that set of people who should do so. We might even say that there is a general, highly internalized rule telling all of us to follow rules, and a correlative expectation that most people do follow this one rule most of the time.

I suspect that the frequent but unwarranted substitution of expectation for normativity (as documented above) stems from scholars taking just this short cut. If shifting theory from rules to the conditions that make rules work – their institutionalization, internalization or some combination of both – does not work from a positivist point of view, then why not a further shift? When rules do work for whatever reason, we, as observers, can expect to see patterns of behavior that agents also expect to see, although perhaps not quite so clearly. Taking this route, we end up with the sociological orientation that Katzenstein and his collaborators have adopted. Rules are everywhere, and everywhere unseen. Only their effects register.

An abundance of rules provide agents with an abundance of choices. Even if positivist science cannot tell us how agents manage to navigate these choices, it would seem better suited to the task of explaining why agents make the particular choices they do. According to rational choice theory, agents choose whatever outcome they prefer. To avoid the tautology implicit in the subjectivity of preference (we would never choose what we do not prefer), we might better say that rational agents weigh costs and benefits of courses of action, and choose that course of action that benefits them the most.

By definition, then, agents have enough information about a situation calling for a choice where they can evaluate available outcomes with sufficient precision and confidence to rank them. By implication agents rank outcomes by reference to some objective criterion – a condition that they can articulate or we can plausibly impute to them: I need water; she is looking for support; I want your esteem; we believe each other; I believe in the truth; wealth is good; safety comes first. These criteria make choices rational if the situation supplies the valued things in question – water, esteem, trust, truth, safety – and agents have the means, also conceptualized as things of measurable value, to achieve them. When we have means that seem more or less appropriate to the ends we seek, we can properly call those ends *interests*.[55] If we make choices as best we can to realize our interests, we have acted rationally. Acting on behalf of institutions or other people, agents advance the interests of those

55 See further *World of Our Making*, pp. 270–83.

whom they represent, not to mention their own interests, by making the best possible choices.

Rational choice theory does not tell us what our interests are, any more than it can tell us what we prefer. Thus Goldsmith and Posner took "state interests at any particular time to be an unexplained given."[56] This is not to say that scholars using rational choice models have no theories purporting to explain why we hold some interests in preference to others. These theories typically generalize about the circumstances we find ourselves in. In IR, neo-realists (political realists who favor rational choice models) claim that situations of scarcity and danger cause people, or states, to put safety first, and that doing so makes everyone feel even less safe, which encourages everyone to make choices that make everyone even less safe. Conversely, neoliberal theorists (also using rational choice models) identify situations where an interest in wealth causes people to make choices that benefit others at the same time they benefit themselves, again with cascading effects.[57]

Goldsmith and Posner did not purport to offer a theory of international relations, which would require them to explain why states have the interests they do and what consequences follow from pursuing their interests. They did claim that states would prefer security and economic growth to compliance with international law. Few scholars would claim otherwise. To say that states might choose to comply with international law because they believe that such a choice would increase the likelihood of achieving other major values would be a more serious proposition, but not one Goldsmith and Posner chose to consider. Instead they directed attention to the consequences for states when they pursue given interests such as security and prosperity.

These situations can and often do result in stable patterns of choice, or "behavioral regularities."[58] According to Goldsmith and Posner, we can use the term *rules* for these regularities as long as we do not claim that they affect agents' choices. Why would we bother? The only reason to call these

56 J.L. Goldsmith and E.A. Posner, *The Limits of International Law*, New York: Oxford University Press, p. 9.

57 See D.A. Baldwin (ed.), *Neorealism and Neoliberalism: The Contemporary Debate*, New York: Columbia University Press, 1993. Missing from the field are theories that assign a central place for esteem as a human need, status (or prestige or face) as a thing of measurable value, standing as an interest, or honor as a powerful idea that becomes an end in itself. R.N. Lebow is about to correct this deficiency in a forthcoming book called *Fear, Interest and Honor: A Theory of International Relations*. Also, see B. O'Neill's creative, if not always convincing, use of rational choice models in *Honor, Symbols, and War*, Ann Arbor: University of Michigan Press, 1999.

58 "In sum, our theory contemplates that behavioral regularities will arise at the international level as a result of states maximizing their interests." Goldsmith and Posner, *The Limits of International Law*, p. 42. Cf. Eric A. Posner, *Law and Social Norms*, Cambridge: Harvard University Press, 2000, p. 26: "What we call a social norm . . . is a term for behavioral regularities that emerge as people interact with each other in the pursuit of their everyday interests."

regularities rules is because agents put them to use. Indeed they may not constitute an interest as such, but we can readily imagine ways in which they help in the rational pursuit of interest.

In the first place, rules have the effect of simplifying complex situations. They do so by reducing those situations to a series of binary oppositions (contradictories) and inviting agents to use simple logic in making choices. An agent selects one rule from many and chooses to follow that rule or not. Either choice then presents the agents with a new menu of rules to select from and choose to follow, or not. In Ludwig Wittgenstein's famously apt simile, rules are like signposts at intersections; we might better say that rules are like posted intersections.[59] Travelers know that at an intersection they cannot go both ways at once and that the signs contain information helping them to choose which way to proceed.

Of course, an intersection of paths may have no signpost. Yet if we take the same path that we always have, we expect to arrive where we always have. Furthermore, we know that following an unmarked path is usually better than leaving it, since the very existence of the path means that others have gone before and presumably gotten somewhere they had wanted to. The path is evidence of a behavioral regularity, and in the absence of other information or a supervening interest (I'm in a hurry, so I'll take a shortcut), we take the path because it is the easy thing to do.

Finally, if we think of rules as posted intersections and marked paths, the more we engage in any kind of sustained activity, the more they proliferate. The more they proliferate, the better we become in selecting among them and using them to advantage. As we become skilled in any craft, we enjoy the mastery of its rules and the exercise of our skills. More generally, if we have choice, we will follow the rules we know well and use them to do what we are good at.

I suggest that we are disposed to follow rules because they have properties, independent of their propositional content, that help us realize our interests – just as we prefer some ends to others, and we have reasons to prefer some means to others. We prefer to make simple choices in complex situations, and rules assist us in doing so. Given a choice, we prefer to do things the way we always have, and rules allow us to do so. We prefer to do what we are good at, and the mastery of rules enables us to do so. These preferred means might be innate dispositions, or they might distill the experience of living in a world that we, as social beings, have filled with rules.

Engaging in binary logic, customary practices and skilled performances helps us realize our interests. Our deep attachment to these activities also suggests that they are ends in themselves. Indeed we might think of them as

59 "A rule stands there like a sign-post. – Does the sign-post leave no doubt open about the way I have to go?" Ludwig Wittgenstein, *Philosophical Investigations*, trans. G.E.M. Anscombe, New York: Macmillan, 1953, para. 85.

meta-interests. That they are less easily recognized than the interest we all have in standing, security and wealth, suggests that they are even worthier of theoretical consideration.

Pragmatic rules

Clearly it is possible to think of reasons why rules work – to explain why agents follow rules – without imputing to rules the property of normativity. Since normativity is a property that positivists dismiss because they cannot "see" it, a scientific theory that does not depend on such a property has a good deal to recommend it. And, if other properties of rules suffice to explain why rules work, then we would not have to rely on claims about internalization, as so many constructivists do, at significant cost to the possibility of testing claims methodically. To make the case for social rules that are not normative, the usual procedure is to stipulate a function these rules are said to perform. The easy case assigns them a communicative function (recall Chapter 14, above): rules serve as "social signaling devices," or, as I just suggested, sign-posts and path-markers.[60]

Instructions, guidelines, scripts, menus and recipes are just such devices. In many instances someone states them more or less formally (orally, in writing) to expedite a desired outcome, along with a warning, often implied, that agents failing to follow them can expect an undesirable outcome. Sometimes signaling devices arise and disappear spontaneously as some activity or artifact inspires imitators; people follow fads and fashions more or less faithfully and abandon them as they see fit. Some rules arise spontaneously because they solve obvious coordination problems; if everyone engages in an activity the same way, they will minimize failures to achieve jointly desired outcomes. When these signaling devices persist (because they work) and become more formal (making them work better), we call them conventions.

Rational choice theorists hold that a convention is one of at least two equilibrium points in a coordination game. Which of the possible equilibria becomes a convention depends on arbitrary precedent (driving on the left, driving on the right) or some notable feature of the environment (often called a focal point). Even if conventions establish *good* and *bad* choices, they are not *right* or *wrong* choices in any normative sense. For rational choice theory and positivist science, following conventions is a rational choice for all relevant agents. As a consequence, conventions do not need support, either by being normativized or by being enforced – they are *not* social rules.

In Chapter 14, I argued that conventions are weakly normative because agents have implicitly agreed to follow them; agreement depends on speech acts affirming the propositional content of whatever is spoken. Even if agents

60 Bicchieri, *The Grammar of Society*, p. 41. See, generally, pp. 34–42; Posner, *Law and Social Norms*, pp. 18–27.

follow conventions without speaking, their silence speaks for them. I grant that this may not be an entirely convincing claim, at least if we conceptualize normativity in binary terms. Yet claiming that conventions are *not* social rules is also unconvincing when so often they "become entrenched in the texture of our lives, so imbued with social meanings that we cannot ignore them with impunity."[61]

Is there a way out of this impasse? I quite agree that conventions, and indeed signaling devices in general, are social rules when "we cannot ignore them with impunity." Rather, in the spirit of positivist science, I suggest that "we" – meaning the way we respond to signaling devices – offer the best means for determining whether the device is normative. By definition, rational calculation controls rational choice. If we feel good about a choice we make, this response is a consequence of choosing well. Yet emotions such as feeling good are clearly more than effects of rational choice.

If we value good feelings, they constitute a preference or interest subject to rational calculation. Faced with a choice, we ask how we will feel about the outcomes we anticipate. In a wide range of settings, how we feel depends on how others respond to our choice, and what we choose depends on what we expect others to feel about that choice. When they feel good, they approve of our choice and we feel proud. When they feel bad, they disapprove and we feel shame.

We normally expect that following signals (that we know other people approve of) will gain approval. Furthermore, we think this is what we *ought* to do. We internalize the audience sitting in judgement, and we do what we should even if no one is looking (stop at a red light, for example), and feel good about it. In short, approbation and disapprobation have normative consequences. They give rise to many of the duties, or obligatory undertakings, that we take for granted in our social relations.[62] To use the terminology I introduced in Chapter 14, normatively freighted signaling devices are instruction-rules – rules that we *know* we are duty-bound to follow because we feel good when we follow them and bad when we do not.

The easy case for nonnormative rules is not so easy after all. Normativity creeps in even when their function is "merely" communicative; conventions

61 Bicchieri, *The Grammar of Society*, p. 41.

62 Adam Smith gave this argument its most powerful expression:

> Nature, when she formed man for society, . . . endowed him, not only with a desire of being approved of, but with a desire of being what ought to be approved of; or of being what he himself approves of in other men.

The Theory of Moral Sentiments (1759), Oxford: Clarendon, 1976, III, ii, paras. 6–7. In Smith's view, however, we follow rules by performing our duties not only to secure praise (or avoid blame), but because we have an additional "sense of duty" or regard for general rules of conduct "impressed by nature, and afterwards confirmed by reasoning and philosophy." Ibid., III, v, paras. 1–3.

end up communicating duties. When the function claimed for a rule is regulative, and the effect is not merely conformity but deterrence, it is still possible to imagine the rule to be nonnormative (or, more precisely, to imagine the rule's formal properties do not cause the substantively regular behavior that ensues). Following Hans Kelsen, we might say that every rule directing us to behave in a certain way is accompanied by a sanction, and the relevant *ought* is not the one stipulated formally by the rule but the one conveyed by the sanction. Also a rule, the sanction directs a designated agent to act in a certain way when the rule it accompanies is not followed.[63]

In other words, we do not follow directive-rules (as I call them) because we have a duty to do so, but because we fear the consequences of not doing so. A strong emotion, not obligation, rules our behavior. The result is the same even if the sanction is an inducement or reward instead of a punishment. The "we" in question includes the agent whose duty is to enforce the rule. Agents act on their fears and wishes all the way up the chain of command (and this, according to Kelsen, is what makes any rule effective), while the rules convey duties all the way down (and this is what makes all of them valid). Logically speaking, there is just one formal locus or source of obligation, at the apex of a pyramid of fear (or greed).

In Kelsen's treatment, the substantive source of formal obligation is the expectation that people will behave as they customarily have behaved, and thus more or less predictably.[64] By convention we attach normative significance to predictable behavior, and, as we have seen, conventions acquire normative significance. If predictability is a plausible expectation for the one agent at the apex of the pyramid, then it is at least as plausible for everyone else. Duty joins fear and greed in explaining why people follow rules; (formal) validity and (substantive) effectiveness are properties that reinforce each other to give rules their normative force and cause agents to follow them.

Kelsen's conception of what he called a "coercive order" is a variation on the solution Thomas Hobbes proposed for any situation where people have a rational interest in making other people insecure in order to enhance their own security. Hobbes's solution substitutes a pyramid of fear for a fearsome world of fearful people. At the apex is an agent whose directives subordinates must follow and who issue directives to their subordinates and so on. For Hobbes, however, the validity of all such directive-rules derives not from a normatively freighted convention but from a binding agreement between the agent at the apex, or "sovereign," who is thereupon responsible for collective security, and the "multitude" whose security is thereby provided for. This

63 H. Kelsen, *General Theory of Law and the State*, trans. A. Wedberg, Cambridge, MA: Harvard University Press, 1945, pp. 60–2.

64 Ibid., pp. xv, 120. Note that in this context *predictability* is a property of a rule that may not be followed, as opposed to *prediction* as a test of a theory's empirical relevance.

agreement is a voluntary act, taking the form of a contract, which Hobbes understood as an exchange of promises between two or more parties to act in accordance with the terms of their agreement.[65]

If accepted, a promise must be kept. In Hobbes's words, "a Promise is equivalent to a Covenant; and therefore obligatory." In the terms I introduced in Chapter 14, a formally acknowledged exchange of promises is a commitment-rule distributing rights and duties (expectations warranted by others' obligations). As Hobbes recognized, the point of accepting an obligation by making a promise is to elicit trust.[66]

While the source of obligation is a law of nature requiring that "*men performe their Covenants made*," people will find reasons to break their promises, avoid their contractual obligations and betray the trust of others.

> The force of words being . . . too weak to hold men to the performance of their Covenants; there are in mans nature, but two imaginable helps to strengthen it. And those are either a Feare of the consequence of breaking their word; or a Glory, or Pride in appearing not to need to break it.[67]

Hobbes denied the multitude the remedy of rebellion, and a sovereign breaking the people's trust had nothing to fear; only the sovereign's pride could help. Yet all other exchanges of promises create obligations and an additional expectation of performance – on Hobbes's account, an expectation born of an entirely justified fear. Perhaps pride contributes to the likelihood of performance, since in addition to the sovereign's directive-rules, there will be relevant instruction-rules. I would also suggest that the emotions of guilt and self-satisfaction will make themselves evident. We are disposed to keep our promises because we know they create an obligation by being accepted, and we feel bad when we break our promises. In short, guilt is one measure of the normative power of the rules that derive from making and accepting promises.

Making a promise is a speech act, as is accepting the promise that someone else makes; so is issuing an order or giving a command. Describing the way one sees things, affirming what someone else says about things, explaining how to achieve an end: all these are assertive speech acts. Promising is a commissive speech act and issuing an order is a directive speech act.

Speech acts are performative. They have what some philosophers have called an illocutionary force – they make things happen. As I explain in Chapters 14 and 19, these (and only these) three kinds of speech acts perform different functions in making social relations possible. Furthermore, speech

65 T. Hobbes, *Leviathan* (1651), Cambridge: Cambridge University Press, 1996, ch. 17.
66 Ibid., p. 95. See, generally, chs. 14–15.
67 Ibid., p.100, emphasis in original; 99.

acts give form to rules that perform these same functions in a general and continuous way, and rules give speech acts a normative force augmenting their illocutionary force.

Most assertive speech acts are only latently normative; their illocutionary force stems in part from the emotions they elicit (trust, respect, shame, pride); they give rise to conventions and other instruction-rules as, or when, they acquire normative force and focus emotions on conformity or compliance (en*force*ment by another name). Directive speech acts combine illocutionary and normative force because the implicit relation between speaker and hearer is already normatively ordered (as Hobbes and Kelsen showed); they acquire additional normative force, as directive-rules, by bringing emotions (trust, respect, fear, greed) to bear on the performance of duties. The illocutionary force specific to commissive speech acts is intrinsically normative (making a promising is an offer to be obligated); commitment-rules focus emotions (trust, respect, guilt, self-satisfaction) on the exercise of rights and the correlative performance of duties. I suggest that trust is an emotion that all rules call forth, and call upon, because their general function is to coordinate agents' expectations and render their choices predictable. Respect seems to be generally relevant in giving rules normative force because instruction-rules are always in the background, if only to assign agents their respective statuses as speakers and hearers. Other emotions are functionally specific in giving force to rules.[68]

Rules succeed in doing what they do because they always and necessarily take the form of performative speech. Speech acts indicate that speakers expect a response from hearers, even if it is not spoken – assent to that state of affairs, fulfillment of a demand, acceptance of a promise. Whether speech acts have the effects speakers intend for them hinges on what hearers do. Speakers can increase the likelihood of an affirmative response by casting their speech acts in deontic form – as an ought statement.[69]

An assertive speech act may, but need not, be formulated as an ought statement. If I were to say to you, "people are careless," you could assent to this general pronouncement with no immediate implications for your conduct. If I were to say that you should be more careful, you might choose to dissent (perhaps silently). If you assent, I would expect to see an effect on your conduct. A directive speech act is implicitly deontic even if this is not the speaker's intention; the hearer supplies the deontic element. A commissive speech act is always deontic. As we saw earlier, a promise conveys an intention to be obligated.

68 For more on shame, fear and guilt as the key emotions respectively implicated in the support of instruction-, directive-, and commitment-rules, see my *World of Our Making*, pp. 120–6.

69 On this general subject, see J.W. Forrester, *Why You Should: The Pragmatics of Deontic Speech*, Hanover, NH: University Press of New England, 1989.

Rules *are* speech acts with specific additional properties. As I said earlier, they set some standard for conduct, they must be formally rendered as an ought statement, they should be public and general, and they are likely to followed. To the extent they do not have these properties in full measure, their utility in presenting agents with binary choices is compromised; positivists will not call them rules but may call them norms. The one property of any rule that would seem not to be a matter of degree is its deontic form. And this *fact* is what gives rules their normative force and gives positivists their faith in the fact–value binary.

All rules set standards for conduct. They *cannot* do so in the absence of deontic formulation. How they do so is obvious when our intention is to make rules: we form a sentence with a subject (stated or implied) to whom the rule applies and a predicate consisting of a verb in deontic form and an object. Fully stated, the complete sentence sets out a standard and specifies its scope, makes that standard obligatory and attests to the validity of the undertaking. Of course there are many rules that no one has made; nowhere is there a complete sentence, in the form of a speech act, conveying everything we need to know about these rules.

The problem is all too familiar: too many speakers, too many sentences qualifying other sentences, too many incompatible ought statements, too many ambiguously related, substantively uncertain rules stipulating binaries that we know are contraries and not contradictions. In these circumstances, we look for patterns to which we might ascribe normative significance; any such pattern gives form to what we hear. Examples might be constantly repeated speech acts with similar content that always elicit the demanded response, highly ceremonious speech acts whose speakers have some special status among hearers, or claims by other speakers that patterns they have identified are normatively significant. By speaking about, or interpreting, these patterns in normative terms, we contribute both to the mass of normative material and to the patterns in that material that we claim to have discerned.

Two aspects of this process are themselves normatively significant. First, we render patterns in a standardized, commonly intelligible form; as I suggested in Chapter 19, we synopsize them. Second, the process of standardizing patterns is already standardized and therefore normative. Standards take standard form in standard ways. Speech acts formulated by reference to rules synopsize patterns of speech acts into rules.

Speech itself exemplifies this situation. All rules depend on speech, which always depends on speakers more or less following the rules of speech. Some of these rules – grammatical rules and rules of syntax – are formal, systematically related and reasonably strict. When speakers fail to follow them, whether by choice or ignorance, listeners find it difficult, if not impossible, to understand what they are hearing. Other, pragmatic rules expedite exchanges between speakers. These rules are informal, loosely related to very general rules and permissively construed. When speakers follow them, speech acts are more likely to have the consequences intended for them.

Rules of the first sort work to standardize speech, but not social conduct – at least directly. Rules of the second sort function as practical rules for social construction. Philosophers have only recently begun to enumerate them. Paul Grice identified nine rules supporting the principle that conversation should not be aimless.[70] With Grice's work in mind, James Forrester identified 18 pragmatic rules for getting people to do what you say they should.[71] The two lists overlap, and neither need be considered exhaustive. There are potentially as many lists of pragmatic rules as there are social settings in which people use speech to accomplish their ends.

Some few rules are likely to turn up on any such list as rules for synopsizing patterns of practice. In other words, I see a pattern and I think it is normatively significant. I have in mind rules of economy, knowledgeability, veracity, relevance, clarity, brevity and continuity (all of them Gricean rules). These rules are produced through social construction as an ongoing interaction among many speakers, yet they are a necessary precondition to social construction as a normative activity.

Obviously pragmatic rules are not randomly produced or completely contingent on the immediate circumstances of their production. They too exhibit a pattern. Better to say, I "see" a pattern in the way they relate to each other substantively, I give this pattern a form no doubt simplifying what I see, and I attach normative significance to that form. Forming what I see into a speech act, I suggest that all pragmatic rules derive their form and function from three master rules, or general principles, of social construction. Here I have in mind rules of consistency, proportionality and reciprocity.

Consistency in conduct gives rise to the patterns we see in social relations; as a rule, it gives form to the world and value to its contents. Proportionality calls on us to evaluate what we give to others, or take from them, in relation to other values (things or relations that we value). Reciprocity tells us to give back in value what others give us. (On reciprocity and proportionality, also see the discussion of "interaction rules" in Chapter 7 and "guidance criteria" in Chapter 8.) These rules are informal, often not followed, and readily interpreted in self-serving ways. Yet they have a cumulatively powerful effect in giving what we do with, to, and for, each other, a sense of being appropriate to the circumstances we have constructed for ourselves.

The reader may have noticed that I used forms of the verb *to give* several times in the preceding paragraph. This was no accident. When we speak, we make a gift of words. Judging us sincere, others can take these words, as we say, "at face value," or they can for any number of reasons give our words back to us (we are mimics after all), reject our gift or bestow one in return. Etymology dictionaries tell us that the Indo-European root for this verb is

70 H.P. Grice, *Studies in the Way of Words*, Cambridge, MA: Harvard University Press, 1989, pp. 26–37.

71 Forrester, *Why You Should*, pp. 49–59.

**ghab(h)*, which also means to take, hold or have; *habit* has the same root. For speakers of the family of languages that gave rise to legal theory and most other features of the modern world, the gift would seem to be an ancestral feature of their social relations, a deeply embedded institution, and a practice with potent effects, not just on special occasions of gift exchange, but in our daily affairs. It seems likely that this is the case for every language and every culture that human beings have talked into existence.

Insofar as we associate gifts with special occasions, we tend to think of gift-giving as a generalized duty and gift exchange as the source for reciprocity's normative force. Marcel Mauss's famous essay on *The Gift* identified three obligations: giving, receiving and repaying.[72] Perhaps the ancestral institution of the gift taught us the meaning of *ought* (in English a term deriving from the verb *to owe* and translating the Latin verb *debere*, to be in debt, to be obligated). Yet gifts as such do not create obligations. This is so even when you "give your word." Whether this speech act offers a promise or declares one's intentions, its normative impact derives from the circumstances of its utterance.[73] Different occasions have different rules telling when to give and what to do about the gifts that others proffer.

Bourdieu has suggested that challenges, gifts and insults are structurally identical. To be offered a challenge, gift or insult is to have one's honor called into question; to accept the challenge, offer a gift in return or retort with an insult is to salvage one's honor.[74] If indeed considerations of honor constitute a deep, and perhaps the deepest, concern that social beings have (and I am convinced they do), then challenges, gifts and insults leave us no choice but to act honorably or be shamed. We are bound; the occasion takes on normative properties; rules tell us what to do. No doubt the most important rule tells us that the obligation to respond to challenge, gift or insult holds only for people who hold the same rank. As Mauss observed, when nobles fail in their obligations, "rank is lost," and so is dignity.[75]

Lords suffer no loss of honor when their "inferiors" offer them gifts as signs of respect and the lords give nothing in return. More generally, only status equals can exchange gifts, make promises and conclude contracts. To be free and equal in the modern world means that people can exchange goods and gifts, insults and compliments under the same normative umbrella. As status equals, they know how to take turns and when to cue up. As friends, rivals or enemies, they are equals in amity, competition or enmity. As individuals, they know they can give and take without providing a reason or incurring an obligation, but only sometimes. "Much of our everyday morality

72 M. Mauss, *The Gift: Form and Functions of Exchange in Archaic Societies*, trans. by I. Cunnison, New York: Norton, 1967, pp. 37–41.

73 I say more about this in "Speaking of Policy," in V. Kubálková, (ed.), *Foreign Policy in a Constructed World*, Armonk, NY: Sharpe, 2001, pp. 87–90.

74 Bourdieu, *The Logic of Practice*, pp. 100–1.

75 Mauss, *The Gift*, pp. 38, 40.

is concerned with the question of obligation and spontaneity in the gift"; questions of honor are never far from mind.[76]

Occasions for gift exchange give reciprocity its normative force. Rules give these occasions their formal properties. When we exchange words, what we say has normative force, but only if we follow the many rules that tell us what sequence of words to use in which context. From a constructivist point of view, the rules we use to give form to the patterns we see do not have temporal or conceptual priority. Nor do the patterns we see. Practically speaking, what we experience is a single process. We talk; rules happen; our world and we continually remake each other.

76 Ibid., p. 63. And see my "Everyday Ethics in International Relations," *Millennium: Journal of International Studies*, vol. 27, 1998, pp. 669–93.

Author index

Subject index

Printed in the USA/Agawam, MA
October 28, 2011
562128.074